22 Lungotevere - Flaminia,
Rome — August 1950

5 W. 63rd St.
N.Y.C

Tennessee Williams
Mens Res. ane Club
36th Street
New York City

8¼ E. New Jersey
Hawthorne, California

Tenn. Williams
151 E. 37 - N.Y.C.
June 1940

(c) 14 Dumaine, New Orleans

When a sailor has crossed the equator
three times, he can wear gold ear rings.

# NOTEBOOKS

# NOTEBOOKS

## Tennessee Williams

Edited by Margaret Bradham Thornton

Yale University Press
New Haven and London

Printed in the United States of America.

Library of Congress Cataloging-in-Publication Data

Williams, Tennessee, 1911–1983.
[Journals]
Notebooks / edited by Margaret Bradham Thornton.
   p. cm.
Includes bibliographical references and index.
ISBN-13: 978-0-300-11682-3 (alk. paper)
ISBN-10: 0-300-11682-9 (alk. paper)
   1. Williams, Tennessee, 1911–1983—Notebooks, sketchbooks, etc.
I. Thornton, Margaret Bradham. II. Title.

PS3545.I5365A6 2006
818'.5403—dc22
[B]        2005056268

A catalogue record for this book is available from the British Library.

The paper in this book meets the guidelines for permanence and
durability of the Committee on Production Guidelines for Book
Longevity of the Council on Library Resources.

10 9 8 7 6 5 4 3 2 1

*Keeping a journal is a lonely man's habit, it betrays the vices of introspection and social withdrawal, even a kind of Narcissism, . . . it has certain things to recommend it, it keeps a recorded continuity between his past and present selves, it gives him the comforting reassurance that shocks, defeats, disappointments are all snowed under by the pages and pages of new experience that still keep flaking down over him as he continues through time, and promises that this comforting snowfall of obliteration will go right on as long as he himself keeps going.*

*I have a sort of vertical five-foot-shelf of these journals. . . . I keep them locked in a closet, and now and then I go to them for that comfort and reassurance I spoke of above, a sense of continuity as a person, and though they were certainly never written for publication and have no literary value, I suspect that some passages from them may bore you less than the sort of formal essay that I could produce in my immediate condition, which is fairly close to exhaustion.*

*And of course, as usual, I am doing only what I feel like doing.*

—TENNESSEE WILLIAMS

# CONTENTS

*Someday I want very much to get all these journals together
and publish them intact. I think they should be eventually
published that way with footnotes by their author, since they
may have some usefulness as a history of an individual's fight
for survival, emotional travail . . . — very few bits would have
literary value, I am afraid, as I wrote them purely the way that
Catholics talk through a black cloth to the priest in the next
cubicle. Except that I was both Father Confessor and
Son Confessor.*

THE NOTEBOOKS OF TENNESSEE WILLIAMS span the years 1936 to
1981, the period from a few weeks before Williams' twenty-fifth birthday to almost
two years before his death at age seventy-one in February 1983. The thirty known
journals are a collection of unremarkable-looking notebooks, in which Williams
recorded his daily thoughts and emotions. Much of his writing is casual, spontaneous, and at times confessional. The notebooks are, for the most part, one-half to
three-quarter sized, the type bought at drugstores with names such as WriteRight
Composition Book or Montag's Ironclad Series Composition Book. Most are
stitched or spiral bound, with paper covers of undistinguished browns, blues, and
blacks. Included are a few clothbound notebooks purchased in Europe. Most of
the journal entries were handwritten in pencil and range in length from a few sentences to several pages.

Unlike his letters, where he modulated his tone and style to suit the recipient,
the journals reveal Williams' authentic voice — genuine and unadorned. As
Williams noted in his story "Three Players of a Summer Game," "It is only the outside of one person's world that is visible to others, and all opinions are false ones,
especially public opinions of individual cases." Here in the journals, where Williams
talks "to myself about myself," we are allowed glimpses into his interior world. He
records his health, often colored with hypochondria. "The patient has been doing
very nicely," he writes, adding less optimistically, "as well as could be expected."
He reveals his fears, feelings of social inadequacy, anxieties, loneliness, constant
restlessness, and panicky feelings of extinction: "Never, never, in all my life will I
know the meaning of peace." He chastises himself for his "wretched whining." He
assesses his personality: "My virtues — I am kind, friendly, modest, sympathetic,
tolerant and sensitive. Faults — I am ego-centric, introspective, morbid, sensual,
irreligious, lazy, timid, cowardly." He comments on his work, "Gosh! What a lot
of nature-faking I have done in my stories."

The journal entries are relatively consistent in their continuity, but they do
include a twenty-one-year gap from 1958 to 1979, during which there is no record
of Williams keeping a journal.

THOMAS LANIER WILLIAMS was born on 26 March 1911 in Columbus, Mississippi, the first son and second child of Edwina and Cornelius Williams. His mother was the daughter of an Episcopalian minister whose family had moved south to Tennessee from Ohio when she was a girl. His father came from a distinguished family in Tennessee and worked as a traveling shoe salesman. Williams was born sixteen months after his sister, Rose, the sibling he was so close to and who would feature so prominently in his fiction. A few months after Williams' seventh birthday, the family moved to St. Louis, where their status changed dramatically, from being the prominent family of the minister in a small southern town to being an undistinguished middle-class family in an unfashionable St. Louis suburb. Despite spending so few of his formative years in the South, Williams would always cling to his identity as a southerner.

Williams' interest in writing appeared early. When he was nine he wrote "Rainbows Comic Paper" for his sister which contained a sketch of a suffragette, "Mrs. Jane h. Rothschild," who was "afraid Miss Rose Williams will paint up so much That she will get all The million men. WIDO R.L. Williams has her tenth husband. all The Rest commided suicid becauce she was so strict." The title page promised, "you'll be so happy after you read Rainbows COMIC PAPER THAT YOU WILL SHINE LIKE A Rainbow." Williams signed the piece with a self-portrait and gave himself the title "The great finder of The end of The Rainbow."

The Williams family remained in St. Louis and moved every several years to more acceptable neighborhoods. With each move Williams changed schools. Williams continued his writing and while still in high school, at age sixteen, won his first writing award, third place in a *Smart Set* contest for an essay which addressed the question "Can a Good Wife be a Good Sport?" In his essay he recounted his "own unhappy marital experiences" and concluded that a good wife could not be a good sport, that is, she could not "after marriage maintain the same attitude towards other men as she held before marriage." A year later he published "The Vengeance of Nitocris" in *Weird Tales*, a story about an Egyptian queen's revenge of her brother's murder. Williams was paid thirty-five dollars for his gothic tale, which began, "Hushed were the streets of many peopled Thebes."

In 1929 Williams entered the University of Missouri with the intention of majoring in journalism. While in college, Williams continued to enter play, short-story, and poetry contests with considerable degrees of success. After three years of mediocre grades and a failing grade for the Reserve Officers' Training Corps, Williams' father refused to pay his tuition for his final year and instead made his son take a job as a menial clerk at the shoe company where he worked.

Despite his father's view of his abilities, Williams' talent had been noticed. When he did not return to college the following year, a professor, whose course on modern drama Williams had audited and who had encouraged him to submit pieces to creative writing contests, wrote to Williams: "Your absence from the University this year has been a matter for real regret to all of us who knew the excellent work you did here the last few years, especially in the field of creative writing. I hope very much you will be able before long to return and finish your course." It would be more than three years before Williams could return to college.

Williams worked from the autumn of 1932 until the spring of 1935 as a clerk-typist at the International Shoe Company, typing out orders, dusting off shoes, and delivering cases of samples. Despite a full day at work, he persevered with his writing. "When I came home from work I would tank up on black coffee so I could remain awake most of the night, writing short stories which I could not sell." His mother remembered: "Every evening when he came home from the shoe company, Tom would go to his room with black coffee and cigarettes and I would hear the typewriter clicking away at night in the silent house. Some mornings when I walked in to wake him for work, I would find him sprawled fully dressed across the bed, too tired to remove his clothes."

In the spring of 1935 Williams collapsed from exhaustion and did not return to work. Instead he traveled south to Memphis where he spent the summer recuperating with his grandparents. He wrote a light comedy about two sailors, "Cairo, Shanghai, Bombay," which was performed by an amateur theatre group. In the autumn of 1935, he returned to St. Louis, where he enrolled as a student at Washington University, first as a night student and then as "a student not a candidate for a degree." During this period Williams became acquainted with a fellow student and poet, Clark Mills McBurney, who "warned" him "of the existence of people like Hart Crane and Rimbaud and Rilke." "My deep and sustained admiration for Clark's writing gently but firmly removed my attention from the more obvious to the purer voices in poetry."

The following spring, Williams began his journals with a voice that was innocent, earnest, and at times melodramatic. In the summer of 1936 Williams wrote, "My situation now seems so hopeless that this afternoon it seemed there were only two possible ways out — death or suicide — however that was a bit melodramatic and I shall probably go on living and if I saw death coming God knows I'd run the other way as fast as my two legs could carry me." Now back at college, Williams concentrated heavily on literature and creative writing courses. After one of his stories was harshly criticized in class, "only one girl liked it and she didn't get the point," Williams encouraged himself to write "something really fine," "something strong and undefeated."

In these early years of his journal, Williams commented on poets and writers he admired: Crane —"the biggest of them all"; Chekhov — "above all the prose writers"; Lawrence — "I read from his letters and conceived a strong impulse to write a play about him"; Strindberg — "his unfailing fire to strike out profiles of life"; Faulkner — "by distortion, by outrageous exaggeration he seems to get an effect closer to reality"; Wolfe — *You Can't Go Home Again* has the "stamp of genius on it"; and Dickinson — "love her." Later Williams commented on Joyce — "a lyric talent which is controlled by intellect, the rarest of happy accidents in the world of letters" — and, perhaps most surprisingly, Hemingway — whose "great quality, aside from his prose style, is this fearless expression of brute nature."

The early years of the journals are in many respects a record of his creative journey. Williams refers to manuscripts he is working on, stories about popular subjects such as gangsters, melodramatic tales with dying heroines, and sophomoric tales of sexual awakenings. He writes a story, "This Spring," similar in style and theme to Saroyan's remarkable "The Daring Young Man on the Flying Trapeze." Influenced by Crane's poetry he attempts a modernist poem, "Middle West." He looks at Grant Wood's painting *American Gothic* and writes a one-act play of the same name from the perspective of the expressionless couple whom he depicts as the parents of a bank-robbing son, a Clyde Barrow–type figure.

By the time the journals commence, Williams was already beginning to have success with his plays. "The Magic Tower," a play about the doomed love of a newly married artist and his actress wife, won a local playwriting contest and was performed in the fall of 1936. Willard Holland, the director of a highly regarded St. Louis theatre group, the Mummers, spotted Williams' talent and worked with Williams on two new plays — *Candles to the Sun*, a tragedy about oppressed miners in a camp in Alabama, and *Fugitive Kind*, a drama about a doomed love affair set in a flophouse. Holland directed the Mummers' performance of these two plays, which were well received by St. Louis audiences.

For his final year of college, Williams was accepted for fall 1937 enrollment at the University of Iowa, which had a new and nationally recognized theatre department. While at Iowa, Williams focused his studies on drama and wrote a number of sketches and two full-length plays, *Spring Storm* and *Not About Nightingales*. Despite his output, he failed to distinguish himself and graduated with a record of mediocre grades of B's and C's and an F in Technical Practice in the Theatre.

Several months after he graduated from Iowa, in the summer of 1938, Williams, aged twenty-seven, traveled to New Orleans and within two months headed to the West Coast. After he left home, his instinct for survival, his growing sphere of experience, and his sexual indoctrination into the gay bohemian world shaped his innocent voice into one that was harder and more worldly. At the end of 1938, he entered a contest sponsored by the Group Theatre for writers under twenty-five with a group of one-acts and three of his full-length plays. In order to disguise the fact that he was too old, Williams, who had previously published under the name Thomas Lanier Williams, submitted the plays under the name Tennessee Williams, lied about his age by three years, and gave his grandparents' home in Memphis as his return address. Williams received a special award for three of the one-acts, and forever after was Tennessee Williams, born not in 1911 but in 1914.

After receiving this special award Williams wrote in his journal: "My next play will be simple, direct and terrible — a picture of my own heart — there will be no artifice in it — I will speak truth as I see it — distort as I see distortion — be wild as I am wild — tender as I am tender — mad as I am mad — passionate as I am passionate — It will be myself without concealment or evasion and with a fearless unashamed frontal assault upon life that will leave no room for trepidation." Such confessional writing would demand a courage Williams would soon find. Along the way he offered advice to himself. "I believe that the way to write a good play is to convince yourself that it is <u>easy</u> to do — then go ahead and do it with <u>ease</u>. Don't maul, don't suffer, don't groan — till the first draft is finished. Then <u>Calvary</u> — but not till then. Doubt — and be lost — until the first draft is finished."

During the autumn of 1939, Williams began working on *Battle of Angels*, a play about "a wild-spirited boy who wanders into a conventional community of the South and creates the commotion of a fox in a chicken coop." A year later the play was produced in Boston by the Theatre Guild, but it was marred by technical difficulties and, more importantly, met with a disapproving Boston audience. It closed after only two weeks. After the disastrous reception of his play, Williams headed south to Florida and spent the next several years moving back and forth between New York and such places as Key West, St. Louis, Provincetown, New Orleans, Jacksonville, and Macon.

Williams left New York in the spring of 1943 for the West Coast where his agent, Audrey Wood, had secured a job for him as an MGM scriptwriter. He enjoyed his private office and generous paycheck and ignored what he considered to be an absurd request to write a script with all the B-movie cliches for Lana Turner. Instead, Williams devoted his efforts to his own work. Over the summer he would return to manuscripts he had written about his sister's tragic situation. In 1937 Rose, aged eighteen, had been diagnosed with dementia praecox, an early term for schizophrenia. About her condition Williams had written, "We have had no deaths in our family but slowly by degrees something was happening much uglier and more terrible than death." Thoughts about her appear randomly in his journals: "Rose, my dear little sister — I think of you, dear, and wish, oh so much that I could help!" Unable to save her, Williams turned to his writing. Three months after his sister underwent a prefrontal lobotomy in January 1943, Williams began the play "The Gentleman Caller." He drew on his short story "Portrait of a Girl in Glass," begun in February 1941, and borrowed parts of more recent works, "A Daughter of the American Revolution," "Blue Roses and the Polar Star," and, most important, "The Spinning Song." He wrote a number of endings, and returned to his short story for a brief period before going back to the play that would emerge as *The Glass Menagerie*. The process of shifting scenes, borrowing bits from one piece for another, and returning to the short story as the basis for a play was representative of the nonlinear way in which he created.

The "shadow of what happened to Rose" stayed with Williams; she would be the model for more than fifteen characters, and Williams would give her name to many others. While the most important, Rose was not the only person Williams appropriated from life for his work. For example, stopping in El Paso in 1939 on his way to the West Coast, Williams noted in his journal that he met an "odd rather dear person" named Trinket. Over two decades later, he would borrow her name for the pitiful, maimed woman in his play "The Mutilated." Other people who appear first in his journals and then later as characters or names in his works include Warren Hatcher, Marian Gallaway, Hazel Kramer, her grandfather Mr. Kramer, Carl Butts, Jim Connor, Harold Mitchell, and Emily Jelkes. In wondering if his lover Frank Merlo would leave him, Williams concludes, "If he left me, and perhaps he will, I would go on living and enduring and I suppose turn him into a poem as I've done with others." On another occasion Williams protested too loudly: "First draft of a story today about the place where I had lunch, 3 Easter egg villas between here and Amalfi but the hero is <u>not</u> Gordon [Sager] and the lady is sort of a composite of various vampires I have known but <u>not</u> Peggy [Guggenheim] & <u>not</u> Libby [Holman]."

The habit of choosing aspects from his life and fitting with twists and turns in his fiction continued throughout Williams' work. Echoes of situations and sentiments he experienced are found in his fiction. Sometimes the distance between an experience or contact and appropriation spanned decades. As a student at the University of Iowa, Williams had described feeling "alienated" from the theatre crowd when one of the girls had a pocketbook stolen. "I became quite embarrassed . . . — afraid they might think me guilty — for absolutely no reason." In his story "Two on a Party," begun in 1951, "Billy had the uncomfortable feeling that [Cora] suspected him of stealing the diamond ear-clip. Each time she glanced at him his face turned hot. He always had that guilty feeling when anything valuable was lost." After Williams was beaten up in New York in early 1943, he reflected, "There was something incredibly sad and tender in the experience. . . . Not that I like being struck, . . . but the keenness of the emotional situation, the material for art."


WITH *The Glass Menagerie* Williams had finally written a work that was "a picture of my own heart." It premiered in Chicago on 26 December 1944 and, despite strong critical approval, initial public response was muted and by the second week it wasn't clear whether the play would continue. The Chicago critics, feeling the fragility of the play's success, responded with additional praise, and by the end of the third week ticket sales had dramatically increased. Years later, Arthur Miller commented on what a revolution *The Glass Menagerie* meant to the New York theatre:

> *The Glass Menagerie* in one stroke lifted lyricism to its highest level in our theater's history, but it broke new ground in another way, by legitimizing sheer sensibility as a driving force of dramatic structure. What was new in Tennessee Williams was his rhapsodic insistence that form serve his utterance rather than dominating and cramping it. In him the American theater found, perhaps for the first time, an eloquence and an amplitude of feeling that had traditionally found no welcome on the stage. And driving on this newly-discovered lyrical line was a kind of emotional heroism that seemed to outflank values themselves; he wanted not to approve or disapprove but to touch the germ of life and to celebrate it with verbal beauty.

Shortly after the Broadway success of *The Glass Menagerie*, Williams traveled to Mexico where he devoted himself to working on the play, initially titled "The Poker Night," that he would develop into *A Streetcar Named Desire*. By the end of 1945, Williams had rented an apartment in New Orleans and for the next two years made New Orleans his primary base. He continued to work on a number of manuscripts, most importantly on *A Streetcar Named Desire*, which premiered three years after *The Glass Menagerie* and ran on Broadway for two years. *Streetcar* won the Pulitzer Prize, the New York Drama Critics' Circle Award, and the Donaldson Award. Brooks Atkinson, writing for the *New York Times*, called

Williams "a genuinely poetic playwright whose knowledge of people is honest and thorough and whose sympathy is profoundly human."

Williams now had financial freedom, and he traveled extensively in the late 1940s and the 1950s and often spent summers in Europe. He was rarely without a journal on these restless travels — New York, New Orleans, Key West, Rome, Barcelona, London, the list goes on. When his writing stalled, Williams changed location. "Only some radical change can divert the downward course of my spirit, some startling new place or people to arrest the drift, the drag." Williams believed that one of the mysteries of writing was its "extreme susceptibility . . . to the influence of places."

Over the following eleven-year period, Williams had seven major plays performed: *Summer and Smoke* (1948), *The Rose Tattoo* (1951), *Camino Real* (1953), *Cat on a Hot Tin Roof* (1955), *Orpheus Descending* (1957), *Garden District* (1958), and *Sweet Bird of Youth* (1959). By 1959 Williams' body of work had earned two Pulitzer Prizes, three New York Drama Critics' Circle Awards, three Donaldson Awards, and one Tony Award. The richness and abundance of this collection of work is partly explained by the fact that a number of these works had beginnings as short stories or plays Williams had written well before he would develop them into full-length plays. For example, *Summer and Smoke* is related to the short story "Bobo" begun in 1941, *Camino Real* is based on a shorter play finished in 1946, *Orpheus Descending* was a revision of *Battle of Angels* finished in 1940, *Cat on a Hot Tin Roof* was developed from the short story "Three Players of a Summer Game" begun in 1951, and *Sweet Bird of Youth* was developed from numerous play fragments begun as early as 1948.

This prodigious output took its toll on Williams, and while his plays were winning awards and being made into films with stars such as Vivien Leigh, Marlon Brando, Elizabeth Taylor, Paul Newman, Anna Magnani, Maureen Stapleton, Geraldine Page, and Burt Lancaster, Williams was losing his way. Despite having earlier declared, "The best way to have new days is to travel or be sexually promiscuous or work with intensity on a long creation," by 1952 Williams reflected, "A promiscuous man . . . is never really satisfied. . . . What he is looking for is completion of himself." Sex was a diversion, but it was work Williams needed in order to live. In 1953, anxious about his ability to create, Williams confessed, "What fearful admission do I have to make that after 'Streetcar' I haven't been able to write anymore except by a terrible wrenching of the brain and nerves?" He recognized that rest might restore his energies, but admitted: "I can't face a day without the few hours of escape into the intensities of work, no matter how futile it becomes. Emptiness. Nothingness of my world outside of work." In 1954 he still struggled with his dilemma. "I can't recover any nervous stability until I am able to work freely again, and I can't work freely until I recover a nervous stability. . . . Just not working doesn't solve the matter for the need to work, the blocked passion for it, continues to tear me inside. Working against exhaustion bit by bit wears me down even further. Then there is no way out? None except through some bit of luck — another name for God."

While Williams was battling with his demons, he managed to write one more great success, *Cat on a Hot Tin Roof*, which like *A Streetcar Named Desire* won three major theatre awards — the Pulitzer Prize, the New York Drama Critics' Circle Award, and the Donaldson Award. Despite his stature as a playwright, by the mid- to late 1950s, more and more journal entries are written in the early morning hours when Williams, alone and lonely, kept himself company by writing in his notebooks.

In many ways what Williams left out of his journal is just as revealing as what he included. Rarely does he mention glamorous people, his successes, awards, or accolades. About an obscure friend of Carson McCullers he remarked, "Lonely people always touch me and appeal to me." In interviews, Elia Kazan, Paul Bowles, and Gore Vidal identified a number of people in the journal, and all three confirmed that Williams, despite his professed fears that he might "end up like Rose," was one of the sanest people they knew. He had to be, Bowles pointed out, given his prolific body of work. Kazan added another note — that Williams was one of the most secretive people he had ever known. "Latch onto that word," he instructed.

The notebooks allow glimpses into Williams' secretive world. He recorded his dreams, and none are more vivid or strange than the ones involving Rose. In 1948 Williams dreamed about lying in his sister's ivory-colored bed. In 1952 he dreamed, "I had missed a bus. My sister was on it. I managed to stop the bus, but the case containing my Mss. wasn't on it." A few weeks later he wrote, "Dreams of loneliness and rejection, involving my sister, but in a curiously changed personality as though she was a disguise for someone else." A year later he dreamed of seeing his sister in a cream-colored lace dress, and "then I had it on and then I was struggling to sit down between two tables and was wedged so tightly between them I couldn't breathe." In 1954 his dreams and journals collided. "Dreamed that a wealthy old lady, entertaining me and grandfather, read my journal and had her colored maid put it in [the] incinerator whence I rescued it twice."

The journals also record Williams' progressive addiction to alcohol and drugs, which began as early as 1936 when he was drinking so much coffee that he experienced heart palpitations. In order to sleep he needed to take sleeping pills. By 1957 he recorded having consumed, in one day, six mixed drinks, including two scotches and one daiquiri, six glasses of wine, two seconals, and two other tranquilizers. The journals stop in September 1958, and in the second-to-last entry Williams wrote, "Felt like death when I woke up this morning but, surprisingly, after coffee, double martini and pinkie, I felt pretty good and took a sanguine view of my work."

Over the next two decades Williams suffered unrelenting negative responses from the critics, beginning with a condemnation of *Sweet Bird of Youth* in 1959 by *Time*:

Sweet Bird of Youth . . . is very close to parody, but the wonder is that Williams should be so inept at imitating himself. The sex violence, the perfumed decay, the hacking domestic quarrels, the dirge of fear and self-pity, the characters who dangle in neurotic limbo — all are present — but only like so many dramatic dead cats on a cold tin roof.

Williams kept working, and over the period 1959 to 1979 wrote fifteen new plays, revised and expanded three earlier plays, and published a novel, a volume of poetry, and a collection of short stories. Only one work from this period, *The Night of the Iguana*, a play loosely based on the 1946 short story of the same title, received positive reviews. Even then the response to this play, described by Williams as being about "how to live beyond despair and still live," was mixed. Williams followed *The Night of the Iguana* with *The Milk Train Doesn't Stop Here Anymore*, derived from the 1953 short story "Man Bring This Up Road." Williams' play was, for the most part, damned by the critics and closed after two months. From this point onward, it was rare that a play ran for more than a few months, and many closed after only a few weeks or even days. Perhaps Williams had run out of subject matter, or perhaps he was trying to adapt his work to suit a public he no longer understood.

In an interview published in 1962, Williams recognized the talent of new playwrights such as Harold Pinter and Edward Albee. "I think the one beautiful and great thing about the new wave of playwrights is that they approach their subject matter with this kind of allusiveness . . . the thing that I've always pushed in my writing — that I've always felt was needed to be said over and over — that human relations are terrifyingly ambiguous." He recognized that these young playwrights were "exploring subtleties of human relations that haven't been explored," and he admitted that the spareness and style of their work drove him "crazy with jealousy." He also acknowledged that his style of writing for the theatre was on its way out. "My great bête noir as a writer has been a tendency . . . to poeticize . . . and that's why I suppose I've written so many Southern heroines. They have the tendency to gild the lily, and they speak in a rather florid style which seems to suit me because I write out of emotion, and I get carried away by emotion." Williams responded by trying to express his new work "more in terms of action. Not in terms of physical action; I mean, in sort of a gun-fire dialogue instead of the long speeches that I've always relied on before. Let me say that I depended too much on language — on words."

No artist ever completely changes his nature, and Williams' attempts to alter his style were not successful. His celebrated lyricism deteriorated into a bitterness and darkness. His late plays were criticized for their confusion, grotesqueness, derivative quality, and lack of freshness and spontaneity. *Period of Adjustment* (1960) was deemed "a mediocre jest," and *Slapstick Tragedy* (1966) a play in which Williams "stole from himself and reworked old characters." The reviewer for *Life* of *In the Bar of a Tokyo Hotel* (1969) compared Williams to a "white dwarf": "We are still receiving his messages, but it is now obvious they come from a cinder." *Small Craft Warnings* (1972) was condemned for repeating "mood and mode of much earlier work." *Out Cry* (1973) was judged "a colossal bore," and a reviewer of *The Red Devil Battery Sign* (1975) suggested Williams change his name to Missouri. *Vieux Carré* (1977) was labeled a pastiche, not a play. By the late 1970s, comments such as "The kindest thing to assume is that Williams died shortly after completing *Sweet Bird of Youth*, and that his subsequent, ever more dismal plays are the work of a lover of his who has learned to impersonate him perfectly in daily life, but only very crudely in playwriting," routinely appeared.

Williams resumed his journal in late spring 1979 in a journal entitled "Mes Cahiers Noirs" written in a style that is part confessional and part evaluative. Whether journals for the twenty-one-year gap will eventually surface is unclear. In 1962 Williams wrote to a friend that he abandoned the practice of keeping a journal in the 1950s. A habit of more than twenty years, however, is a hard one to break, and during the 1960s and 1970s Williams did continue working on manuscripts and, although to a much lesser extent than before, writing letters.

In "Mes Cahiers Noirs," which is more of a reflective essay than a record of daily activity, Williams looked back over the past decades and wondered, "Did I die by my own hand or was I destroyed slowly and brutally by a conspiratorial group? . . . Perhaps I was never meant to exist at all, but if I hadn't, a number of my created beings would have been denied their passionate existence. . . . The best I can say for myself is that I worked like hell." By the end of the notebooks Williams, who had made "a positive religion of the simple act of endurance," was tired, discouraged, and morose. His last entry, written in an almost illegible scrawl, records a paranoid fear about an agent and a lost manuscript. Williams asks, "Where do I [go] from here?"

The notebooks were Williams' last refuge. They were companions on his solitary journey — both emotional and physical. Occasionally, he would make a comment next to a journal entry, as if connecting with himself across the divide of years that separated the two personalities. Williams understood that his notebooks captured an elusive quality of life. In writing about his journals he noted, "They talk to me from the past in a comforting way, make the links more real. The past gets lost so sadly."

—MARGARET BRADHAM THORNTON
Bedminster, New Jersey
May 2006

Williams' first home, St. Paul's Rectory, Columbus, Mississippi

1911       Thomas Lanier Williams born 26 March in Columbus, Mississippi.

1918       Williams family moves to St. Louis, Missouri.

1925–29    Attends several high schools in St. Louis area. In 1927 submits an
           essay, "Can a Good Wife Be a Good Sport?" to *Smart Set* contest and
           receives third prize of $5. The following year publishes a short story,
           "The Vengeance of Nitocris," in *Weird Tales* and receives $35.
           Graduates from University City High School. Enrolls as a student at
           the University of Missouri planning to major in journalism. Has
           considerable success with his work in various university-sponsored
           creative writing contests.

1932       Forced to leave school after third year by father due to mediocre
           grades, and a failing grade for the Reserve Officers' Training Corps.

1932–35    Takes a job as clerk for the International Shoe Company in St. Louis.
           Devotes the evenings and weekends to writing. In spring 1935
           collapses from exhaustion and recuperates with grandparents in
           Memphis. Writes light comedy "Cairo, Shanghai, Bombay," which is
           performed by a local theatre group.

1935    In September, returns to St. Louis and attends night classes at Washington University. Short story "Twenty-seven Wagons Full of Cotton" accepted by *Manuscript*.

1936    Enrolls at Washington University as "a student not a candidate for a degree." Spends time with fellow student and poet Clark Mills McBurney, who introduces him to Crane, Rilke, and Rimbaud. Wins a poetry contest with a group of sonnets and a play-writing contest with "The Magic Tower," which is performed locally.

1937    Has two plays, *Candles to the Sun* and *Fugitive Kind*, successfully performed in St. Louis by the Mummers. In September, enrolls at the University of Iowa.

1938    Receives bachelor's degree from Iowa in August. At the end of the year travels to New Orleans.

1939    After seven weeks in New Orleans, heads west with Jim Parrott. While in California, wins a special prize from the Group Theatre for a group of one-act plays submitted under name Tennessee Williams. Audrey Wood becomes agent. Travels to New York. In December wins $1,000 Rockefeller Fellowship.

1940    Takes classes at New School for Social Research. "The Long Goodbye" is performed at New School. Spends summer in Provincetown and has an affair with Kip Kiernan, whom he would memorialize in his play *Something Cloudy, Something Clear*. At year-end Theatre Guild produces *Battle of Angels*, which is badly received in Boston and closes after two weeks.

1941–42    Continues writing and, for the next several years, leads an itinerant existence, traveling between New York and St. Louis, Provincetown, Macon, New Orleans, and Mexico.

1943    On 13 January, Rose undergoes a bilateral prefrontal lobotomy. In May Williams travels to the West Coast to begin work as scriptwriter for MGM. Spends summer working on manuscripts that would evolve into *The Glass Menagerie*.
*You Touched Me!* play written with Donald Windham, is produced in Cleveland and Pasadena.

1944    Collection of poems published in *Five Young American Poets*. Spends summer in Provincetown and continues working on manuscript of *The Glass Menagerie*.
*The Glass Menagerie* is produced in Chicago.

1945    *The Glass Menagerie*, New York (Drama Critics' Circle Award and Donaldson Award).
*Stairs to the Roof*, Pasadena.
*You Touched Me!* New York.

1946    Williams sets up base in New Orleans, works on *Summer and Smoke* and *A Streetcar Named Desire*. Spends summer with Carson McCullers in Nantucket. Returns to New Orleans, finishes a first draft of *Summer and Smoke*, and continues working on *A Streetcar Named Desire*.

1947    During the summer returns to Provincetown and meets Frank Merlo.
*A Streetcar Named Desire*, New York (Pulitzer Prize, Drama Critics' Circle Award, Donaldson Award).

1948    Spends first summer in Europe. Returns to the United States in August for rehearsals of *Summer and Smoke*. In New York begins long-term relationship with Frank Merlo. In December, Williams and Merlo visit Paul and Jane Bowles in Tangier.
*Summer and Smoke*, New York.

1949    Williams and Merlo remain in Europe until September when they return to the United States. Williams rents house in Key West at 1431 Duncan Street, which he would buy the following year.
Short-story collection, *One Arm*.

1950–56 For the next seven years Williams continues the pattern of traveling to Europe each summer and returning to the United States in late August or September.

1950    Novel, *The Roman Spring of Mrs. Stone*.
Film, *The Glass Menagerie*.
*The Rose Tattoo*, New York (Tony Award).
Film, *A Streetcar Named Desire* (four Academy Awards).

1952    Elected to National Institute of Arts and Letters.

1953    *Camino Real*, New York.
Directs Windham's "The Starless Air," Houston.

1954    Short-story collection, *Hard Candy*.

1955    *Cat on a Hot Tin Roof*, New York (Pulitzer Prize, Drama Critics'
        Circle Award, Donaldson Award).
        Film, *The Rose Tattoo* (three Academy Awards).

1956    Poetry collection, *In the Winter of Cities*.
        Film, *Baby Doll*.

1957    *Orpheus Descending*, New York.
        Father dies on 27 March. Begins psychoanalysis in June with Dr.
        Lawrence Kubie.

1958    *Garden District*, New York.
        Ends psychoanalysis in June and resumes summer travels to Europe.
        Film, *Cat on a Hot Tin Roof*.

1959    *Sweet Bird of Youth*, New York.
        Film, *Suddenly Last Summer*.

1960    *Period of Adjustment*, New York.
        Film, *The Fugitive Kind*.

1961    *The Night of the Iguana*, New York (Drama Critics' Circle Award).
        Films, *Summer and Smoke* and *The Roman Spring of Mrs. Stone*.

1962    Williams appears on the cover of *Time* magazine.
        Films, *Sweet Bird of Youth* (one Academy Award) and *Period of
        Adjustment*.

1963    *The Milk Train Doesn't Stop Here Anymore*, New York.
        Frank Merlo dies on 21 September from lung cancer.

1964    Film, *The Night of the Iguana*.

1964–69    Williams' alcohol and drug abuse worsen.

1966    Short-story collection, *The Knightly Quest*.
        *Slapstick Tragedy*, New York.
        Film, *This Property Is Condemned*.

1967    *The Two-Character Play*, London.

1968    *The Seven Descents of Myrtle*, New York.
Film, *Boom!*

1969    *In the Bar of a Tokyo Hotel*, New York.
Receives Gold Medal for Drama, American Academy of Arts and
Letters.
Converts briefly to Roman Catholicism.
Committed by brother, Dakin Williams, to St. Louis psychiatric ward
for three months to undergo treatment for substance abuse.
Film, *Last of the Mobile Hot-Shots.*

1970–83  Williams never regains equilibrium. For the rest of his life he remains
addicted to alcohol and drugs. His paranoia worsens. He perseveres
with his writing and offers work that gets slaughtered by the critics.
He continues his habit of restless travel to Europe, New York, New
Orleans, and Key West with an assortment of traveling companions.

1971    "Confessional," Bar Harbor, Maine.
*Out Cry*, Chicago.
Breaks with Audrey Wood.
Bill Barnes becomes agent.

1972    *Small Craft Warnings*, New York (Williams' first professional
appearance on stage).

1973    *Out Cry*, New York.

1974    "The Latter Days of a Celebrated Soubrette," New York.
Short-story collection, *Eight Mortal Ladies Possessed.*

1975    *The Red Devil Battery Sign*, Boston.
*The Two-Character Play*, New York.
*Memoirs.*
Novel, *Moise and the World of Reason.*
Receives Medal of Honor for Literature, National Arts Club.

1976    "This Is (An Entertainment)," San Francisco.
Elected member of American Academy of Arts and Letters.

1977    *Vieux Carré*, New York.
Poetry collection, *Androgyne, Mon Amour.*

1978    *Tiger Tail*, Atlanta.
"Creve Coeur," Charleston, South Carolina.

1979    *A Lovely Sunday for Creve Coeur*, "Kirche, Kutchen und Kinder,"
        and "Lifeboat Drill," New York.
        Honored by Kennedy Center for contribution to the arts.

1980    "Will Mr. Merriwether Return from Memphis?" Key West.
        *Clothes for a Summer Hotel*, Washington, Chicago, New York.
        "Some Problems for the Moose Lodge," Chicago.
        Mother dies on 1 June.
        Awarded Presidential Medal of Freedom.

1981    "A House Not Meant to Stand," Chicago.
        *Something Cloudy, Something Clear*, New York.
        *The Notebook of Trigorin*, Vancouver.

1982    "A House Not Meant to Stand" (revised), Chicago.

1983    In February Williams travels alone to Taormina, Sicily, but returns
        after five days to New York. On the morning of 25 February he
        is found dead in his hotel room. Williams is buried on 5 March
        in St. Louis.

COLLECTIONS

| | |
|---|---|
| Boston | Howard Gotlieb Archival Research Center, Mugar Memorial Library, Boston University |
| Columbia | Rare Book and Manuscript Library, Columbia University |
| Delaware | Special Collections, Hugh H. Morris Library, University of Delaware |
| Duke | Special Collections Library, Duke University |
| HRC | Harry Ransom Humanities Research Center, University of Texas at Austin |
| HTC | Harvard Theatre Collection, Houghton Library, Harvard University |
| Houghton | Houghton Library, Harvard University |
| Maryland | McKeldin Library, University of Maryland at College Park |
| NYPL | Billy Rose Theatre Collection, New York Public Library |
| Princeton | Department of Rare Books and Special Collections, Princeton University |
| SMU | DeGolyer Library, Southern Methodist University, Dallas |
| SHSW | State Historical Society of Wisconsin, Madison |
| UNC | Southern Historical Collection, Library of the University of North Carolina at Chapel Hill |
| UVA | Alderman Library, University of Virginia |
| Wesleyan | Wesleyan University Cinema Archives, Middletown, Connecticut |
| WU | Washington University, St. Louis, Missouri |
| Yale | Beinecke Rare Book and Manuscript Library, Yale University |

B O O K S

CS            Tennessee Williams, *Collected Stories*, with an introduction by
              Gore Vidal (New York: New Directions, 1985)

DLB           *Dictionary of Literary Biography: Documentary Series*, vol. 4,
              *Tennessee Williams*, edited by Margaret Van Antwerp and Sally
              Johns (Detroit: Gale Research Company, 1984)

DWL           *Tennessee Williams' Letters to Donald Windham, 1940–1965*,
              edited and with comments by Donald Windham (New York: Holt,
              Rinehart and Winston, 1977)

FOA           *Five O'Clock Angel: Letters of Tennessee Williams to Maria St.
              Just, 1948–1982*, with commentary by Maria St. Just (London:
              André Deutsch, 1991)

Leverich      Lyle Leverich, *Tom: The Unknown Tennessee Williams*
              (New York: Crown, 1995)

*Memoirs*     Tennessee Williams, *Memoirs* (New York: Doubleday & Company,
              1975)

RMT           *Remember Me to Tom*, by Edwina Dakin Williams, as told to Lucy
              Freeman (New York: G. P. Putnam's Sons, 1963)

SL            *The Selected Letters of Tennessee Williams*, vol. 1, *1920–1945*,
              edited by Albert J. Devlin and Nancy M. Tischler (New York: New
              Directions, 2000)

Spoto         Donald Spoto, *The Kindness of Strangers: The Life of Tennessee
              Williams* (Boston: Little, Brown and Company, 1985)

*Notebooks* is a complete transcript of all known journals written by Tennessee Williams. In order to preserve the rhythm and pace of Williams' voice, the text has been transcribed as faithfully to the original manuscripts as possible, including Williams' spelling, capitalization, punctuation, and underlining of words and phrases. Any ellipses are Williams' own and function as a form of punctuation. Deletions have been preserved where they are decipherable and informative. For the sake of clarity, punctuation marks have occasionally been inserted, especially in places corresponding to Williams' right margin, where he often failed to use punctuation.

In a few places a missing word, or part of a word, has been inserted in square brackets. Square brackets also enclose notes, in italics, recording incomplete or fragmented journal entries.

Williams' choice of paragraph form was inconsistent. Sometimes he indented and other times he used the block form with extra spacing. For economy of space, paragraphs have been conformed, with indented first lines.

Very few journal entries were fully dated by Williams. Many are headed by the day of the week only, and some are not dated at all. Sometimes when Williams provides both the date and the day of the week they do not correctly correspond to the particular year. In these cases, it has usually been assumed that the day of the week is correct. In dating the entries, the editor first considered the internal evidence of the entry itself and then such items as concurrent correspondence, telegrams, journals of friends, even a visitors' book. In a few cases only an approximate date can be given for an entry.

Occasionally Williams wrote several entries in one day and through the early morning hours. Entries written on the same calendar day are grouped together under the heading for that day — and in some instances include entries that are dated the previous day's "night" but were written in the early hours of the next day.

The journal entries are presented in the order in which they were written. This has sometimes involved putting entries from one notebook among entries from another.

Occasionally Williams would reread his notebooks and write comments next to an entry. These subsequent annotations have been reproduced in facsimile form.

In the notes, the letters and manuscripts that are quoted have been transcribed following the same principles as for the journals, with ellipses indicating omission inserted as necessary. Capitalization of titles of poems, short stories, and plays follows that in published volumes, but for unpublished works, capitalization follows that of Williams. Titles of longer published plays cited in the notes are italicized; all other plays are in quotation marks, regardless of whether they are published or have been staged.

LEDGER

Dead Planet, The Moon

I Salute you!

(A Writer's Journal)

A B C D E F G H I J K L M N O P Q R S U V W Y Z

1936

March 6 - Friday - Saw first robin today - two in fact - pains in chest all morning but okay 'tonite - Went swimming - mailed verse to Liberty Amateur contest at Miss Flo's suggestion - Now have 4 manuscripts in the mail not counting plays & poems in St Louis contest - Returned case of empty bottles - collected $1.00 felt rather stupid all day but will write tomorrow -

March 7 - Sat. - Nice day - went swimming in a. m - Wrote story "Cut Out" - pretty cheap but well done - feel rather guilty writing such stuff - so far from what I really want to do - I am writing this Sunday morning - Pinkish green buds all over the elm outside my window - first buds I have seen -

March 9 - Monday - A pleasant day - drove about city - Saw H. C. and was inspired to write a poem by certain lines in her face - went swimming - Felt fine all day - Visited Jewel Box with H. C. & Mr. Pansies blooming outdoors in park - Wish I could spend a few days in the country - Mr. Kantes dead - Mr. Wells dying - Mr. Kramer afraid of dying - me? Damned glad to be alive!

March 10 - Tuesday - Life is various. Today I would like to leave off the record - I was sick tonight - attack of nervous heart in short. Story class - got worked up over Prof. reading my story aloud - Why

1.  *Liberty* was a weekly magazine of short stories, topical news articles, photographs, and illustrations. On 8 February 1936, *Liberty* asked its readers to submit to its forthcoming feature, "Liberty's Amateur Page," "short, short stories, not over 500 words, short poems or jingles, grave or gay jokes, epigrams, wisecracks, cartoons, caricatures, and comic drawings." There is no record of what poem Williams submitted.

2.  Miss Flo was the affectionate name for Florence Kramer (d. 1943), the mother of Williams' close childhood friend Hazel Kramer. Mrs. Kramer was an animated divorced woman who retained her maiden name, and Williams was close to her despite his mother's disapproval. In *Memoirs*, he wrote, "Miss Florence covered up her desperation at home by a great animation and gusto of manner when she was out" (p. 15).

    Williams used Florence Kramer's surname for the woman who accuses the librarian of lending her daughter a "sordid" book in the play *Spring Storm*, as well as for the woman who takes care of Mrs. Melrose in the untitled fragment of the play he considered calling "Death: Celebration," "The Legend of Jonathan," "A Stranger from Home," or "Death of a Legend."

3.  The three additional manuscripts in the mail were the poem "This Hour" (sent to *Poetry*) and the short stories "Gift of an Apple" (sent to *Story*) and "The Bottle of Brass" (sent to *American Prefaces*).

4.  Williams had entered both a poetry contest and a playwriting contest. The poetry contest was sponsored by the Wednesday Club, a socially prestigious local women's literary organization. Williams entered three sonnets under the title "Sonnets for the Spring." The play contest was sponsored by the Webster Groves Theatre Guild, an amateur group located in a fashionable suburb of St. Louis. The one-act play Williams submitted was "The Magic Tower."

5.  Written in the vernacular, "Cut Out" is told in the first person by a narrator who acts as an observer of the rivalry between two working-class guys, "the Kid" and Rags, over a girlfriend. When the Kid steals Rags' girlfriend, Rags gets his revenge by staging a scene in which the Kid thinks he is stealing yet another girlfriend of Rags', only this time the girl is a drug addict. Influenced by his new girlfriend, the Kid turns into an addict himself, and the irony of the Kid's comment to Rags, "I guess I cut you out again," is felt at the end of the story.

    Williams was experimenting with using gangsters as his subject matter. Earlier in the year he had written a one-act play about gangsters, "Curtains for the Gentleman." Over the next several years, he wrote other pieces about gangsters, including the short story "Dago Hill" and the plays "American Gothic" and *Fugitive Kind*.

CUT OUT

It was one of them early spring days, the sun out bright and pretty, and me being off duty at the yards, I come on across the street to Bud's place for a couple of drinks and maybe a little game of pinochle. The Kid was there. He had on his watermelon shirt. You know. A green one with lots of pink stripes. He was leaning against the bar and bragging as usual about all the dames he had crazy about him. Five or six guys was standing there, leading him on, when the door swings open and in comes Rags. Nobody gives the Kid a sign to put him wise. He was talking about Rags' girl. Her name was Emma and she'd been going with Rags a long time. We all known she was no good but Rags didn't. He was stuck on that

*Friday, 6 March 1936*

March 6 – Friday – Saw first robin today – two in fact – pains in chest all morning but okay tonite – Went swimming – mailed verse to liberty amateur contest[1] at Miss Flo's[2] suggestion – Now have 4 manuscripts in the mail[3] not counting plays & poems in St. Louis contest[4] – Returned case of empty bottles – collected $1.00 – felt rather stupid all day but will write tomorrow –

*Saturday, 7 March – Sunday, 8 March 1936*

March 7 – Sat. – Nice day – went swimming in a.m. – Wrote story "Cut Out"[5] – pretty cheap but well-done – feel rather guilty writing such stuff – so far from what I really want to do – I am writing this Sunday morning – pinkish green buds all over the elm outside my window – first buds I have seen –

Hazel Kramer

6.    "H.B." is presumably Hazel Elizabeth "Beth" Kramer (1912–51?). At ages eleven and nine, respectively, Williams and Hazel became friends, and they remained close during their teenage years. Williams' parents and Hazel's grandfather did not approve of their attachment. When Williams went to the University of Missouri at Columbia, Hazel's grandfather decided she should go to another college. In *Memoirs* Williams wrote: "I suppose that I can honestly say, despite the homosexual loves which began years later, that [Hazel] was the great extrafamilial love of my life" (p. 15). He stated that, as a freshman in 1929 at the University of Missouri, he wrote a letter to Hazel proposing marriage (p. 25). Williams may have been romanticizing his relationship with Hazel, for her best friend, Esmeralda Mayes Treen, has said she was not aware of any proposal of marriage and would have been very surprised if it were true. Williams did, however, write about a marriage proposal in a fragment of the play "Death: Celebration." Thelma, the daughter of Mrs. Kramer, comes to tell her mother that she and Phil Williams are going to be married.

After Hazel married in September 1935, she moved to Wisconsin but would come back to St. Louis to visit her mother. Williams may have chosen to refer to Hazel as "H.B." since he was disappointed by her marriage to another man and may not have wanted to refer to her by her married name. Two early poems make reference to a young girl's face, "Lyric" and "The Mystery of Your Smile."

| LYRIC | THE MYSTERY OF YOUR SMILE |
|---|---|
| You have that clarity of brow | If only I had power to know |
| that special innocense of eye | The secrets of your smile — |
| that all the young and lovely have | To tell how much is tenderness |
| whose hearts have never learned to cry. | And how much simply guile! |
| | |
| You have that brave delight in dancing | What reason has your sadness? |
| through a golden summer's day | What meaning has your mirth? |
| that Trojan Helen may have had | The mysteries of life and death |
| before she danced too far astray | Seem not of greater worth! |
| | |
| You have that glowing atmosphere | I'd rather know the subtle thought |
| your white skirts whirling in a waltz | That hides behind your smiling eyes |
| that once surrounded Guinevere | Than all the secret worlds which lie |
| before she played a lover false | Beyond the veiling skies. |
| | |
| So when the harvest of much wisdom | |
| makes a shadow on your brow | |
| it shall console me to remember | |
| light that needs no memory now. | |

In *Memoirs* Williams noted that he included an incident with Hazel in the short story "Three Players of a Summer Game" and that "the little girl in the story was based upon Hazel as a child — including the bit about the old car, the 'electric'" (p. 29). Williams' unrequited relationship with Hazel is generally believed to be the starting point for three early works, the stories "The Accent of a Coming Foot" and "The Field of Blue Children" and the play "April is the Cruellest Month" (revised as *Spring Storm*), as well as for the poems "Letter to an Old Love" and "Letter to an Old Friend."

7.    The Jewel Box, so called because the flower patterns were said to resemble a jewel box, is located in Forest Park, a large public park of 1,380 acres in St. Louis. Officially named the St. Louis Floral Conservatory, the Jewel Box is a steel and glass conservatory of modern design facing a series of reflecting ponds. In *The Glass Menagerie* (scene 2), when Laura's mother asks her where she went when she was supposed to be attending Rubicam's Business College, Laura replies: "Lately I've been spending most of my afternoons in the Jewel Box, that big glass house where they raise the tropical flowers."

8.    "M.F." is presumably Miss Florence, Hazel Kramer's mother. Williams often went to Forest Park with the Kramers.

9.    Mr. Kanter and Mr. Wells were presumably fathers or grandfathers of Williams' acquaintances. Roy Kanter was in Williams' class at University City High School. Dorothy Wells was a fellow member of the Missouri Chapter of the College Poetry Society. In the short story "Heavenly," Dorothy Wells Stanton is attacked by a former lover of her husband.

*Monday, 9 March 1936*

<u>March 9 – Monday</u>. A pleasant day – drove about city – Saw H.B. and was inspired to write a poem by certain lines in her face[6] – went swimming – Felt fine all day – Visited Jewel Box[7] with H.B. & M.F.[8] Pansies blooming outdoors in park – Wish I could spend a few days in the country – Mr. Kanter dead – Mr. Wells dying – Mr. Kramer afraid of dying[9] – Me? Damned glad to be alive!

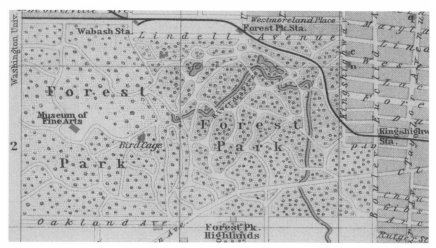

Map of Forest Park

The Jewel Box, Forest Park

Emil Kramer was the maternal grandfather of Hazel Kramer. He worked at the International Shoe Company with Williams' father. Williams wrote sympathetically about Hazel's grandparents in the short story "Sand." Williams used Mr. Kramer as a model for characters in three related short stories: Emiel Kroger in "The Mysteries of the Joy Rio" and "The Garden of Emiel Kroger" and Mr. Krupper in "Hard Candy." These characters, like Mr. Kramer, were overweight and of German descent. Williams also used the surname Kramer for male characters in several other works, including the short stories "Show Me the Way to Go Home" and "The Treadmill" and the play *Summer and Smoke*.

10.    Presumably "This Spring," a short story about a young woman with a terminal illness who travels to a southern seaport to spend her last spring. She seduces a traveling salesman but then instructs him to leave her so that she can be alone.

11.    After returning to St. Louis in summer 1935, Williams began taking night courses at Washington University College during the school year 1935–36 in order to accumulate enough credits to enter his senior year. Associate professor Frank Webster taught an evening class entitled "The Short Story" — a study of plot, character, and background in the short story and novel. The work was based entirely upon the student's own writing. Williams received a grade of A-.

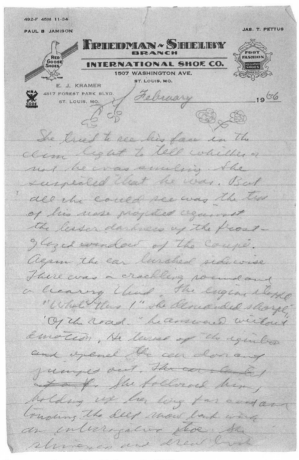

Fragment of an unidentified story by Williams

*Tuesday, 10 March 1936*

<u>March 10 – Tuesday</u> – Life is various – Today I would like to leave off the record – I was sick tonight – attack of nervous heart in short story class – got worked up over Prof. reading my story aloud – Why I don't know – I must learn to control my nerves – didn't last long – I took a pill – still it is always very depressing – Makes you feel cut off from the world – And just at a time when I am so eager to be a part – still – things like this prove one's spirit – ignore it I say – go on as if nothing happened – the only way – besides I'm no longer a coward about it – I was actually <u>not</u> afraid – just embarrassed because I felt my nervous agitation was so obvious – class criticized my story very harshly[10] – Only one girl liked it and she didn't get the point – Prof. Webster[11] seemed pleased with it however and told me to write more soon – But I was disappointed in story and feel discouraged about my whole prospect as a writer – what the hell – I'd better sleep it off like poor Old Sam –

THIS SPRING

As soon as she knew definitely that it had returned she drew all her savings from the bank and left at once for the large southern sea-port where she had gone the time before when there had seemed to be so little chance of escape. It was again spring as it had been the last time. This seemed, indeed, to be merely a continuation of that other time. How familiar the city was! The broad streets

He dressed in silence. Hurt. Or maybe just tired. When he left her he would probably return to the lobby and read his paper. No. Go to his room and sleep. Sleep until morning and then go on from **this city** **to** another city. Another hotel. From this adventure to other adventures. There would be no end for him. No end this spring nor for many other springs. Only for her was this spring final. An ending. The last of them all.

He went on out of the door and she heard his feet padding softly down the long carpeted hall, past all the dully gleaming numbered doors, the chambermaids and polished oval mirrors, and with him went the thing that they had made between them, the last perfect thing, complete and forever.

She closed her burning eyes. Sank back down upon the bed and the pain was with her again and she sobbed and clenched her hands and her teeth against blackness.

Thomas Lanier Williams

12.  In "Gift of an Apple," a nineteen-year-old hitchhiker meets an older woman living in a trailer alongside the road. The older woman gives the hungry boy an apple to eat and then attempts to seduce him. She stops when she learns he is the same age as her son.

13.  *Story* magazine was founded in 1931 by the husband-and-wife team of Whit Burnett (1899–1973) and Martha Foley (1897–1977). During the early years, a number of writers, including Norman Mailer, J. D. Salinger, Erskine Caldwell, John Cheever, Carson McCullers, and William Saroyan, had their work first published in *Story*. Williams began submitting stories to *Story* in 1933, and by 1936, according to an unmailed letter to *Story*'s publishers dated April 1936 (HRC), he had sent the magazine twenty-two stories, none of which was accepted for publication.

14.  "Dear," or "Dear Grand," was Williams' affectionate name for his maternal grandmother, Rosina Otte Dakin (1863–1944). She was a great source of support to him, both emotionally and financially, and in 1953 he wrote the story "Grand" as a tribute to her. He recalled the summers when

> she [w]ould take the long daycoach trip to St. Louis to visit her only child, my mother, and her three grandchildren. . . .
>
>      . . . Her coming meant nickels for ice cream, quarters for movies, picnics in Forest Park. It meant soft and gay laughter like the laughter of girls between our mother and her mother, voices that ran up and down like finger exercises on the piano. It meant a return of grace from exile in the South and it meant the propitiation of my desperate father's wrath at life and the world which he, unhappy man, could never help taking out upon his children — except when the presence, like music, of my grandmother in the furiously close little city apartment cast a curious unworldly spell of peace over all there confined. (*CS*, pp. 380–81)

In the story he also noted:

> I think the keenest regret of my life is one that doesn't concern myself, not even the failure of any work of mine nor the decline of creative energy that I am aware of lately. It is the fact that my grandmother died only a single year before the time when I could have given her some return for all she had given me, something material in partial recompense for that immeasurable gift of the spirit that she had so persistently and unsparingly of herself pressed into my hands when I came to her in need. (*CS*, p. 385)

Williams modeled the angel in the short story "The Angel in the Alcove" on his grandmother; in the related play *Vieux Carré*, the writer mentions seeing the ghost of Grand. Williams also wrote several poems about his grandmother, including "For Grand" (alternatively titled "Dear Silent Ghost") and one beginning "My grandmother died like this."

15.  One of the stories may have been "This Spring." In one version of the story, Williams wrote, "Near the seaward horizon a horned moon was brightening," and a few pages later, "The horned moon had attained its full brightness and was already sinking back into the ocean" — possibly Williams' rewritten reference to the moon.

*Wednesday, 11 March 1936*

<u>March 11 – Weds</u>. Evening closes down and I turn to my journal for lack of anything else to do. Felt remarkably well today – Even swam my usual 15 lengths – But how stupid! Looked thru some old stories and made half hearted effort to straighten out my desk. That's all – Feel as tho my writing is all a lot of trash – except the one story "Gift of an Apple –"[12] Maybe it will turn out to be the same when "Story" sends it back[13] – How I fool myself about my writing! In some way – if not all – I am a perfect idiot! But why worry about that? As Dear[14] says – All passes! Elm blossom all over tree in back yard – foamy red and white blossoms ruddy looking – a pussy willow blooming in our back yard – Moons do not have corners except in early evening – new moons do <u>not</u> rise – Gosh! What a lot of nature-faking I have done in my stories[15] – I am anxious to learn all I can about nature this spring.

Rosina Otte Dakin

16.   "This Spring" is one of Williams' first known attempts at writing in the stream-of-consciousness style. Williams was aware of the sensation William Saroyan's story "The Daring Young Man on the Flying Trapeze" had made when it was published in *Story* in 1934. In fact, Williams' stories "This Spring" and the similar story "The Red Part of a Flag" (started in 1937), published later as "Oriflamme," bear a strong resemblance to Saroyan's story. Like Saroyan, Williams uses the stream-of-consciousness style to detail one day in the life of a dying young person. In "The Daring Young Man on the Flying Trapeze," a young man starves to death. In "This Spring," a young woman is dying of an unnamed disease, and in "The Red Part of a Flag," a young woman is dying of tuberculosis.

      In "This Spring," Williams wrote, "Her loneliness swept about her like a black storm." Later, in *The Glass Menagerie* (scene 7), he wrote, "The cities swept about me like dead leaves, leaves that were brightly colored but torn away from the branches." Throughout his literary career, Williams used images, phrases, sentiments, and characters from earlier, lesser works in his major works.

17.   In the 1930s, sodium bromide could be purchased without a prescription and was frequently used for insomnia.

18.   Edwina Dakin Williams (1884–1980) was a strong and supportive force in her son's life. Born in Ohio but raised in the South, she was the model for Amanda Wingfield in *The Glass Menagerie*. She had an unhappy marriage which eventually ended in separation. Her closeness to her parents, who were also important influences in Williams' life, formed the family circle for her children. In her memoirs, *Remember Me to Tom* (1963), Edwina Williams quotes from the extensive memorabilia associated with her son's writing career which she had collected from the time he was a teenager. Williams' attachment to his mother, as evidenced in his correspondence to her, continued after he left home at the end of 1938. His letters and postcards to her in the several years following 1938 are filled with reports of his welfare, his travel plans, the progress of his writing, as well as requests for money.

19.   Edwina Williams was invited to join the Columbus chapter of the Daughters of the American Revolution (DAR) in 1905 since she had relatives who had either aided or fought for American independence. Williams would describe matrons as belonging to the DAR in a number of works, including *Spring Storm* and *The Glass Menagerie*.

      In a letter to his grandparents dated 12 March 1936 (HTC), Williams described the preparations for the tea:

      As you may have heard, Mother is having all the daughters over this Monday for an afternoon tea. It is going to be a big affair. We are having a caterer prepare the food — Dorr & Zeller. They will make the coffee and take care of everything. We are having cakes and ices and candies and over a hundred open face sandwiches.

20.   Three and a half years later, Williams would write to his friend Joseph Hazan (3 September 1940, HRC): Read the collected letters of D.H. Lawrence, the journals and letters of Katharine Mansfield, of Vincent Van Gogh. How bitterly and relentlessly they fought their way through! Sensitive beyond endurance and yet enduring! Of course Van Gogh went mad in the end and Mansfield and Lawrence both fought a losing battle with degenerative disease — T.B. — but their work is a pure shaft rising out of that physical defeat. A permanent, pure, incorruptible thing, far more real, more valid than their physical entities ever were. They cry aloud to you in their work – no, more vividly, intimately, personally than they could have cried out to you with their living tongues. They live, they aren't dead. That is the one ineluctable gift of the artist, to project himself beyond time and space through grasp and communion with eternal values. Even this may be a relative good, a makeshift. Canvas fades, languages are forgotten. But isn't there beauty in the fact of their passion, so much of which is replete with the purest compassion?

21.   George Bruner Parks was an associate professor of English at Washington University. He taught the night course at Washington University College on "Contemporary British and American Literature," for which Williams received a grade of B.

Later – Just finished re-writing "This Spring" – Had thought it was no good but reread it this evening and liked it. Rewrote it stream-of-consciousness style[16] – seemed very sucessfull – But tomorrow? Oh well. Tired out but happy. Yes. happy. drank four teaspoons sodium bromide.[17] Now I will rest from my labours and go downstairs.

Later I have read it over again. It seems very lovely. It seems my best. I have taken a sleeping pill as I was feeling terribly nervous. Now better. A cool and beautiful night. Wind. Or is it rain? I will turn out the light and see.

*Friday, 13 March 1936*

Friday – A.M. Bright day rather cool – preparations for Mother's[18] D.A.R. Tea[19] – Not feeling so well but nothing definitely wrong – Still working on "This Spring" – Gets better – almost final draft – Still no mail – suspense – Ah! Wednesday – Poetry announcements – will be a terrible strain or disappointment – Got "A" on Mansfield[20] paper last night – Parks is a pretty good guy[21] – It didn't deserve such a good grade – Swimming meet this P.M. – Will go over – car at home – May take a drive – now lunch.

Edwina Dakin Williams

22. Harriet Monroe (1860–1936) was the editor of *Poetry* magazine, which she founded at the age of fifty-one in 1912. A little-known poet herself, Monroe produced what was, at the time, the only magazine in America devoted solely to verse. She set forth the magazine's "Open Door" policy: "to print the best poetry written in whatever style, genre, or approach." In the decades that followed, *Poetry* has published, often for the first time, works by virtually every significant English-speaking poet of the twentieth century and today remains one of the premier journals of verse.

23. "This Hour" was published in *Poetry* in June 1937 under the heading "The Shuttle," together with "My Love Was Light," presumably one of the "others" Williams subsequently submitted. While Williams had at this point in his career published fifteen poems, the majority had appeared in student publications. Given the prestige of *Poetry* magazine, the acceptance of a poem by Monroe was a major event for Williams. He had been sending poems to *Poetry* for several years before Monroe accepted one. In a letter dated 11 March 1933 (HRC), Williams had asked Monroe, "Will you do a total stranger the kindness of reading his verse?" a question he would modify more than a decade later and give to Blanche as her final line in *A Streetcar Named Desire*: "I have always depended on the kindness of strangers."

   In a letter dated 27 March 1936 (HRC), Williams told Monroe he was "surprised and delighted" by the selection of "My Love Was Light." "It is the kind of poem which I write most naturally but am always afraid editors will find too much in the traditional style."

24. The *Atlantic*, now the *Atlantic Monthly*, was founded in 1857 as a general-interest magazine. Josephine W. Johnson (1910–90) was a poet and novelist who won the Pulitzer Prize in 1935 for her novel *Now in November*. Her poem in the March 1936 issue was entitled "You Who Fear Change."

> YOU WHO FEAR CHANGE
>
> You who fear change are like these sheep that turn
> Back from cold mountain creeks, and drink
> Only in small, familiar pools, or suck
> Green milk of these marshy ponds that lie
> Round and unmoving in a valley's palm.
>
> O slow and complacent muzzles, does it mean
> Nothing to you that dust and drouth
> Shrivel the little pools, and dung
> Stains the warm stagnant water where the steers
> Follow your little pathways to this pond?
>
> *Time fouls still water and slime lies*
> *Mucous and soft above all ponds.*
> *The lake by living springs unfed*
> *Shrinks to a caking slough.*
>
> Blind is that shepherd who would lead his sheep
> Back to these steer-trampled waters!

Williams was acquainted with Johnson as early as 1935, when she presented his first-place award in the St. Louis Writers' Guild contest for the short story "Stella for Star." He wrote to her on 2 February 1935 (WU), thanking her for his award and apologizing for not being gracious. He included lines by Li Po, an eighth-century Chinese poet, whom he had recently discovered: "I wanted to share them with someone who especially likes poetry. I tried reading them to my sister last week, she was knitting a sweater, and listened to them without missing a stitch, so I feel that was wasted effort."

> The Rabbit in the Moon pounds the medicine in vain,
> Fu-Sang, the tree of immortality, has crumbled to kindling wood,
> Man dies, his white bones are dumb without a word
> When the green pines feel the coming of the spring. . . .
> — From "After Ku-shih, No. 9"

*Saturday, 14 March 1936*

<u>Saturday Night</u> Woke up just now with very strange feeling – stomach I guess – went down and took Epsom Salts – now better – Last night letter from Harriett Monroe[22] accepting Poem "This Hour" and asking to see others[23] – Felt quite elated. But did not cure the "blues" – pretty awful all day – funny – must snap out of it – Rain tonight – Felt so much better walking home in rain – No sense in going on like this – Must forget it that's all – Read new poem by Josephine Johnson in Atlantic – disappointed in it – struck a sour note – about scummy pools, dung, Etc[24] – moon slightly more than half tonite – now a clear sky and wind – oak leaves almost gone – been going gradually last few weeks – wind like torrents of black water – trite. The air is delicious tonight. C'est Tout!

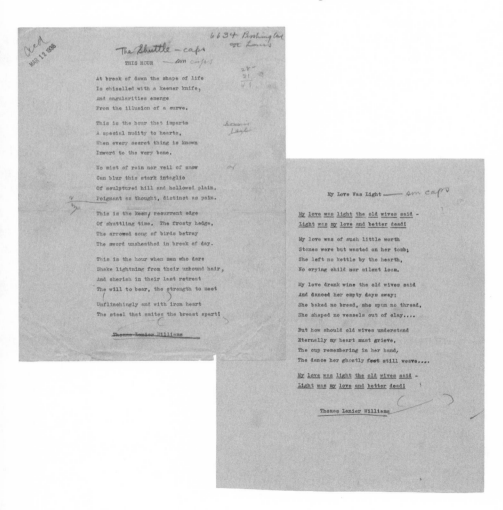

Little I prize gongs and drums and sweet meats,
I desire only the long ecstacy of wine, and desire not to awaken. . . .
— From "Song Before Drinking"

Tonight I stay at the Summit Temple,
Here I could pluck the stars with my hand,
I dare not speak aloud in the silence,
For fear of disturbing the dwellers of Heaven!
— "Lines on the Summit Temple"

Why do I live among the green mountains?
I laugh and answer not, my soul is serene:
It dwells in another heaven and earth belonging to no man.
The peach trees are in flower, the water flows on. . . . .
— "Question and Answer in the Mountain"

25.   The Little Theatre was a small semi-professional theatre in St. Louis. *Ode to Liberty* (1934) is a comedy adapted by Sidney Howard (1891–1939), an American Pulitzer Prize–winning playwright, from the French play *Liberté Provisoire* by Michel Duran. In *Ode to Liberty*, a young woman, Madeleine, leaves her husband and then falls in love with a Communist, who is in trouble with the police for having fired a shot at Hitler. Madeleine bargains with her husband and agrees to return to him if he helps the Communist escape.

26.   The event refers to an evening in March 1935 which Williams described in *Memoirs*, although he misdated it as March 1934:

One evening I was at work on a story titled "The Accent of a Coming Foot," perhaps the most mature short story that I undertook in that period. I had arrived at a climactic scene when I suddenly became aware that my heart was palpitating and skipping beats.

Having no means of sedation, not even a glass of wine, I did a crazy thing: I jumped up from the typewriter and rushed out onto the streets of University City. I walked faster and faster as though by this means I could outdistance the attack. I walked all the way from University City to Union Boulevard in St. Louis, expecting to drop dead at each step. It was an instinctual, an animalistic reaction, comparable to the crazed dash of a cat or dog struck by an automobile, racing round and round until it collapses, or to the awful wing-flopping run of a decapitated chicken.

This was in the middle of March. The trees along the streets were just beginning to bud, and somehow, looking up at those bits of springtime green as I dashed along, had a gradually calming effect — and I turned toward home again with the palpitations subsiding. (p. 38)

The episode Williams described could have been a rapid heart and extra heart beats caused by excessive caffeine consumption. In *Orpheus Descending*, Val says, "Once or twice lately I've woke up with a fast heart, shouting something, and had to pick up my guitar to calm myself down" (act 2, scene 3).

27.   In *Memoirs*, Williams referred to the onset of a phobia about the process of thought being "a terrifyingly complex mystery of human life" (p. 20). During the summer of 1928, when he was on a tour of Europe with his grandfather, Williams experienced three episodes of this phobia — in Paris, Cologne, and Amsterdam. In *Memoirs* he wrote that the third and last incident of this phobia was lifted away by the "composition of a little poem" (p. 22):

Strangers pass me on the street
in endless throngs: their marching feet,
sound with a sameness in my ears
that dulls my senses, soothes my fears,
I hear their laughter and their sighs,
I look into their myriad eyes:
then all at once my hot woe
cools like a cinder dropped on snow.

*Thursday, 19 March 1936*

Thursday Morn – March 19 – Let us not speak of it. This agony. Forget it. Find strength somehow to go on. Work to be done. Feel sometimes as though I could relinquish this life very easily. Last night I saw The Little Theater Play Ode To Liberty.[25] Very amusing. Between acts stood at an open window and saw the revolving electric cross over a Union Ave. church. Same one when I first became ill – that Sat. night last march[26] (an anniversary?) when I walked miles and miles with my heart nearly jumping out of my chest – That cross helped me that night. The cross and the money I gave the street beggar. And finally those new star-shaped leaves. A strange night. But I've had many since then.

<u>Thursday Night</u> Oh my, what blissful exhaustion! I haven't felt quite like this since that night in Cologne or Amsterdam – when the crowds on the street were like cool snow to the cinder of my individual "woe". Over seven years ago.[27] A state in which the damnedest seems to have happened and you can't be any more completely damned – and the tired brain and body has simply <u>got</u> to rest for a while. I am positively limp in every muscle. Feel deliciously warm and fuzzy – Tomorrow? There <u>is</u> no tomorrow! Ah, but there <u>is</u>! And I'll have to face it somehow – And I shall. Peace. Forever peace. No more fighting. I give up the struggle – I take what comes. I will try to be like a dumb cow in my patience. So help me God.

Williams' home, 6634 Pershing Avenue, St. Louis

28. *American Prefaces*, described as a Journal of Critical and Imaginative Writing, was founded in 1935 by a group that included Thomas Gaddis, David Ash, Robert Whitehand, and Wilbur Schramm. Based in Iowa City, the journal was first published monthly, under the sponsorship of the University of Iowa, and was edited by Wilbur Schramm. Despite rejecting several of Williams' short stories, Schramm offered great encouragement.

29. "The Bottle of Brass" is an expanded version of Williams' earlier short story "Big Black: A Mississippi Idyll," which had received an honorable mention for fifth place in the University of Missouri's 1932 Mahan Story Prize Contest. In "The Bottle of Brass," an unusually large itinerant black man, who works on a road gang, rapes a white woman in Mississippi. The man is described as looking as if "he had just escaped from a bottle of brass after being sealed up thousands of years for disobedience to Solomon. He was prodigiously huge and ugly and black." Williams no doubt was influenced by the 1931 Scottsboro case, in which nine black boys were wrongfully accused of raping two white women in a freight car passing through Alabama, as well as by various legends of John Henry and *The Arabian Nights' Entertainments*. Williams includes an excerpt from one of the tales, "The City of Brass," at the beginning of the story.

30. John Rood (1902–74) was an editor, artist, professor, and author. As co-editor of the bi-monthly magazine *Manuscript* (1934–36), Rood was particularly helpful to Williams. Rood was the first editor of a national literary magazine to publish one of Williams' short stories. On 22 September 1935 (HRC), he had written to Williams accepting "Twenty-seven Wagons Full of Cotton."

   In an unmailed response to a letter from Rood a year earlier, Williams expressed his gratitude for his "sympathetic letter and helpful criticism. Like most young writers, I lack the ability to criticize my own work and even my best friends can't tell me. Sympathetically critical letters are a courtesy I have received only from Martha Foley and the Little Magazine editors. Yours was particularly helpful. I am glad you rejected the stories, as I certainly don't want to publish inferior stuff" (circa March–April 1935, HRC).

31. In the short story "Twenty-seven Wagons Full of Cotton," an Arkansas woman, Mrs. Meighan, is seduced by the manager of a cotton plantation whose cotton gin has been burned down while her husband, Jake, gins the manager's twenty-seven wagons of cotton. This story would become the basis for the one-act play "27 Wagons Full of Cotton." Williams incorporated this play, along with the one-act "The Long Stay Cut Short, or The Unsatisfactory Supper," into the screenplay *Baby Doll*, which was made into a film in 1956. In the 1970s, Williams developed the screenplay into a full-length stage play, *Tiger Tail*.

32. "Gift of an Apple" was not accepted, but in a letter dated 6 May 1936 (HRC), the editor, Wilbur Schramm, wrote: "Some of these days you are going to burst out and write some fine stuff."

33. Most likely, "Moony's Kid Don't Cry," an expanded version of "Hot Milk at Three in the Morning," which had received thirteenth place in the University of Missouri's 1932 Dramatic Prize Contest. Williams, who often reworked earlier material, had in fact sent a version titled "Ride a Cock Horse" to the director of the St. Louis Little Theatre in October 1935. In "Moony's Kid Don't Cry," a working-class man, Moony, who feels like a caged animal, decides to walk out on his wife, Jane, whom he has known less than a year, and his one-month-old son, to return to the North Woods to work as a woodcutter. When his baby son cries, Moony changes his mind and stays.

   Williams studied Eugene O'Neill at the University of Missouri, and both Allean Hale and Lyle Leverich have noted the similarities between "Moony's Kid Don't Cry" and O'Neill's one-acts *Before Breakfast* and *The Dreamy Kid*. Williams' play also shared the image of the caged animal with O'Neill's play *The Hairy Ape*. In "Moony's Kid Don't Cry," Jane says to her husband, "Why didn't I marry an ape an' go live in the zoo?"

This afternoon Am. Prefaces[28] ret'd "bottle of Brass"[29] with letter saying story was "told" rather than "lived". I quite agree – in part. Also letter from John Rood,[30] long and very amusing – saying try to publish "27 Wagons"[31] in August issue. "Gift Of An Apple" gone to Amer. Pref.[32] Hope it will stick. Goodnight –

*Friday, 20 March 1936*

<u>Friday Morning</u> – Better – much better – a bright cool windy day – slept soundly – feel like a patient old cow – will finish dressing now and later try to finish my play[33] –

THE BOTTLE OF BRASS

("The fisherman broke the seal, and there came forth from the bottle a blue smoke that reached the clouds of Heaven and a terrible voice was heard crying: 'Repentance, repentance, O Prophet of Allah!' Then the smoke became a being of terrific aspect and of dreadful make whose head reached as high as a mountain, and he vanished before their eyes.")
<u>The City Of Brass, Arabian Nights' Entertainments.</u>

A gang of negros were excavating the sixteen-inch foundation for a waterbound macadam a few miles out of Clarksdale, Mississippi. It was an afternoon in August. On every side the flat fields of the delta were silently gathering the fierce yellow sunlight and translating it slowly into the soft, blind whiteness of cotton. Nature could not have intended the burning afternoon for any but that kind of effortless underground activity. The sun was pressed like a molten finger against the lips of the sky, bidding everything that moved beneath that blazing dome to be still and let the cotton do whatever necessary labor there was: let the green bolls bake in the sun till their inner whiteness, heat-swollen, bulges through the darkening cracks and spills itself into the light from which it has come, itself light but now tangible, golden sunlight turned into cotton.

The negros themselves would have gladly heeded the sun's admonition and stretched out comfortably in the shade while the cotton worked underground. But nature and the gang-boss were opposite forces. The gang-boss would give them no rest till the sixteen-inch foundation was dug. He was after them like a mad devil. Through the sweat streaming over their eyes they could no longer see him very clearly. He was just a great bulk of red and blue color, weaving unsteadily along the road-side with an automatic flow of curses and pointless commands, occasionally

34.  Dick Sharp lived in the neighborhood.

35.  Marian Collins attended University City High School and graduated a year earlier than Williams in 1928. He would use her last name for Lucretia Collins in the play "Portrait of a Madonna."

36.  Anna Jean O'Donnell was a fellow student at the University of Missouri at Columbia with whom Williams became friends during the 1931–32 school year. In *Memoirs*, he wrote that he had a "poignant and innocent little affair. . . . My feeling for her was romantic" (p. 35). He wrote at least four poems that were either about her or to her: "Not Without Knowledge," "To Anna Jean," "Madrigal," and "Can I forget" (and its variant "Fatal Moment"). Most likely the poems "To a Lost Friend" and "To Me Who Loved You Once" are also about her.

MADRIGAL
(to A.J.)

Today I am dull, I am dull!
The light has gone out of me:
My hungering soul is a gull
That circles an empty sea.

———

Hand in hand with the Spring you came —
Her's was your sweetness, her's your flame!
Your beauty with her's indivisibly blent,
Hand in hand with the Spring you went!

———

Today I am dull, I am dull!
The light has gone out of me:
My hungering soul is a gull
That circles an empty sea.

TO ANNA JEAN

You Damned Blockheaded Irishman —
You Blue-eyed, Darling little fool —
Your only use in life is making men your Tool —
You precious, lying, loving cheat
Your playing, praying, I repeat
is just a pose, a rouse, a Scene —
A well-staged play, with lights and screens,
Oh, well — At that you're mighty Damned Sweet!

Williams used the name Anna Jean in the short story "Crazy Night" for the senior who has been dating Phil, a freshman who has flunked out. On "crazy night," Anna Jean has a date with another student, a senior named Harry, but she returns that evening to see Phil. They make love, and Phil expects to marry Anna Jean — only to learn that she has married Harry earlier that night. Williams would borrow Anna Jean's surname for the Apparition of Father O'Donnell in the 1970s screenplay *Stopped Rocking*.

Marian Collins

*Sunday, 22 March 1936*

<u>Sunday</u> A swell day – Went to Holy Communion at St. Michael's Church at Christ Church Cathedral – enjoyed service at the latter – Saw Dick Sharp[34] on service car going down. In afternoon too[k] Marian Collins[35] out for ride. We went to Curtis Wright airport. Charming place. Windy and wide. Had soda in restaurant there. Then home to play cards and long walk. Felt perfectly well all evening. Encouraging – Marian is a rather lovely girl. Sweet and natural with a fund of homely wisdom. Some of that light Irish spirit that I admire so much – Anna Jean![36]

Williams and Anna Jean O'Donnell

37.    Williams was awarded first prize for "Sonnets for the Spring," a sequence of three sonnets: "Singer Of Darkness," "The Radiant Guest," and "A Branch For Birds." Winners were chosen from 420 poems submitted by 128 contestants. Frank Webster was one of the judges.

### SONNETS FOR THE SPRING

#### I. Singer Of Darkness

I feel the onward rush of spring
  once more
Breaking upon the unresistant land
And foaming up the dark hibernal
  shore
As turbulent waves unfurled on
  turbid sand!
The cataclysm of the uncurled leaf,
The soundless thunder of the
  bursting green
Stuns every field. The sudden war
  is brief,
And instantly the flag of truce is
  seen,
The still, white blossom raised
  upon the bough!
(Singer of darkness, Oh, be silent
  now!
Raise no defense, dare to erect no
  wall,
But let the living fire, the bright
  storm fall
With lyric paeans of victory once
  more
Against your own blindly surrendered shore!)

#### II. The Radiant Guest

These past few months my house
  has entertained
Guests of an oddly uncongenial
  kind:
With bitter words the atmosphere
  was strained
Among the cluttered chambers of
  my mind.
But now I hear them fluttering in
  mad flight
Down sun-invaded corridor and
  stair;
I hear them uttering shrill cries of
  fright
As they discover April on the air!

Now the regenerate heart
  renounces gloom,
The gospel of futility forswears,
Proclaims a holiday, decks every
  room
With laurel such as only April
  wears . . . .
The house is clean, the door is
  opened wide
Upon the radiant guest who waits
  outside!

#### III. A Branch For Birds

And when the spring returning in
  her time
Shall find my hand no longer at the
  door,
Nor any echo of the lyric rhyme
Which I had offered in her praise
  before,
She'll wear no mourning for my
  vanished sake
Nor breathe for me an unaccus-
  tomed sigh,
But over me her lovely hands will
  shake
A few white raindrops as she passes
  by . . . .

Then I, with fingers curled into
  the earth,
And passion gone as smoke from
  long dead fires,
Shall not endure the rapture of
  rebirth
That April of the living heart
  requires,
But shall myself, as any rooted
  thing,
Put forth a branch where summer
  birds may sing!

38.    The Williams family's Boston terrier.

39.    Williams' maternal grandparents, Rosina Otte Dakin and the Reverend Walter Edwin Dakin (1857–1955), a popular Episcopalian minister. In a tribute to his grandfather titled "My Grandfather's Letter" (circa 1937), Williams describes how one of his letters encouraged him: "You have talent and you should have time to develop it. . . . Write with strength!" In honor of his grandfather, Williams left his estate to the University of the South at Sewanee after the death of his sister, Rose. Williams loosely based the character Nonno in the play *The Night of the Iguana* on his grandfather. Williams dedicated his poetry collection *In the Winter of Cities* (1956) to the memory of the Reverend Walter E. Dakin.

*Tuesday, 24 March 1936*

<u>Tuesday</u> – Another piece of good luck yesterday – While I was out swimming lady from Wed. Club called up and told Mother I had been awarded the $25. prize for "Sonnets For The Spring."[37] Will get it at meeting tomorrow. Lovely bright day – Didn't sleep last night – the excitement and spring onions I suppose – but felt well all today – took long walk with Gypsy[38] and finished re-writing my "One Act" – "Moony's Kid Don't Cry" which I will submit to Prof. Webster tomorrow – A little too windy I'm afraid – but I think it would be effective on the stage – Wish I could have a play produced. – Dear Grand and Grandfather[39] sent me $5.00 for a birthday present – Bless them both! I wish I could see them this spring!

St. Louis Daily Globe-Democrat, Thursday Morning, Ma

## THREE POETRY CONTEST WINNERS

—Staff Photo.

WINNERS of first prizes awarded yesterday in the two poetry contests sponsored by the Wednesday Club and chairman of the poetics section of the club which supervises the contest. Left to right: Thomas L. Williams, 24, Washington University senior, who won the senior contest with a sequence of three sonnets; Mrs. Robert L. Latzer, chairman of the poetics section; and Miss Reka Neilson, 16, senior at Mary Institute, who won the junior contest with "Siesta Portraits," three poems of New Mexico. The prizes were awarded yesterday at a meeting at the club, 4506 Westminster place.

*St. Louis Daily Globe-Democrat*, 26 March 1936

40.    Clark Mills McBurney (1913–86), who published under the name Clark Mills, was a fellow poet whom
       Williams first met in 1933. In an unpublished "feature story" Williams wrote on Mills in 1938, "Return
       to Dust," Williams described their first meeting:

> It was at a literary meeting about five years ago. An electric victrola was playing a symphony by
> Brahms, the parlor was lighted by candles, twenty young writers were making a conscientious study
> of the ceiling and the chandelier. Somebody turned off the music.
> "Is everybody here?"
> "Everybody but Clark Mills."
> "Who is Clark Mills?" I asked.
> "Oh, don't you know?" said the young lady in black. "He's the boy that writes crazy modern
> verse nobody understands but God and himself!"

Mills and Williams became good friends while attending Washington University in 1935–37. In the summer of 1936, they met regularly in the basement of Mills' parents' house to work on their writing and to
discuss poetry. In "Preface to My Poems — Frivolous Version," in the third volume of *Five Young American
Poets* (New York: New Directions, 1944), Williams wrote: "It was Clark who warned me of the existence
of people like Hart Crane and Rimbaud and Rilke, and my deep and sustained admiration for Clark's writing gently but firmly removed my attention from the more obvious to the purer voices in poetry" (p. 123).
In the same essay, Williams noted: "Ideas from Clark's verse went into my plays, and ideas from my plays
went into Clark's verse" (p. 123).

Mills left St. Louis in 1937 to study at the Sorbonne, and in 1938 he became an instructor of French at
Cornell, where he also studied for a doctorate. In 1941, a group of Mills' poems, "Speech After Darkness,"
was included in the second volume of *Five Young American Poets*, and he published *The Migrants*, which he
dedicated to Williams. His translations include Stéphane Mallarmé's *Herodias* (1940), André Breton's *Fata
Morgana* (1941), and, with William Carlos Williams and others, Ivan Goll's *Jean Sans Terre* (1944).

After 1943, when Mills joined the Counter Intelligence Corps in World War II, he and Williams lost
touch with one another. After the war, Mills served as an intelligence officer in the CIA in Berlin, Bonn,
and Frankfurt, and in 1951 he returned to the United States where he took up teaching posts at Hunter
College, New York, and Fairleigh Dickinson University in New Jersey.

In the play *Not About Nightingales*, Williams named a guard McBurney, and in the short story "An
Out-of-town Date," Williams named the doctor Mills.

41.    Williams' father, Cornelius Coffin Williams (1880–1957), born in Knoxville, Tennessee, worked for the
       International Shoe Company. Williams failed to live up to his father's expectation and received very little,
       if any, support in his ambition to be a writer.

Despite their distant relationship, Williams drew on his father in his fiction. In the play "The Parade,"
written in 1940, the character Don, based on Williams, recalls an incident that had happened to Williams:

> When mother and me came north from Mississippi, Dad was already in St. Louis. he'd been so good
> a Mississippi drummer they'd made him salesmanager of their St. Louis branch. Well, he met us at
> Union Station in Saint Louis. And just around the corner from the station was an outdoor fruit-
> stand. I picked a grape as we passed it. Dad slapped my hand so hard it burned for a good while,
> and he said, "Don't ever let me catch you stealing again!" One goddamn grape was all! — And he
> taught me never to lie because he never lied. — Not lying, not stealing. . . .

Williams recounted this incident in *Memoirs* (p. 13).

The character of the absent father in *The Glass Menagerie* is loosely based on Williams' father, who
was working for the Cumberland Telephone and Telegraph Company at the time he met Edwina Dakin.
In scene 1 the narrator, Tom, says: "There is a fifth character in the play who doesn't appear except in this
larger-than-life-size photograph over the mantel. This is our father who left us a long time ago. He was a
telephone man who fell in love with long distances."

Williams modeled the main character, "C.C.," in the one-act play "The Last of My Solid Gold Watches"
on his father, as well as the traveling salesman in the short story "Grenada to West Plains." In addition, he
used his father's first name for Cornelius Rockley in the play *You Touched Me!* for Cornelius McCorkle
in the play "A House Not Meant to Stand," for the Apparition of Cornelius McCorkle in the play "Will
Mr. Merriwether Return from Memphis?" and for Cornelius Dunphy, Rosemary McCool's grandfather,
in the short story "Completed."

Williams wrote a short memoir about his father titled "The Man in the Overstuffed Chair."

*Sunday, 29 March 1936*

<u>Sunday</u> What a week is <u>behind</u> me! Wednesday received poetry prize. Not as gruelling as I expected. In fact it couldn't have been made any easier for me. No stage. No speech. Just a room full of tired, elegant old ladies, a couple of priests and some very young poets. Lovely sunny place. Nevertheless palpitations for about five minutes. Afterwards tea and talk – nervous but felt okay – A Mrs. Otis Turner talked to me a long time and wants to get me into Writers' Guild. Says Clark Mills[40] belongs. Probably won't be invited and am not sure I would want to belong. I'm hardly well enough for that sort of thing. Or am I? Feel horrible today. Sick yesterday at dentists. Extremely nervous. Didn't sleep hardly at all last night. Horrible now, but will try to pull myself together. Ghastly dinner. Snapped at everyone, even the old man,[41] but then he was particularly awful about the Kramers where I spent last night. Can I go on? Of course – and you will!

Clark Mills McBurney

Cornelius Coffin Williams

42. In "Sand," an elderly woman cares for her husband who has suffered a stroke. She fears her feeble husband's death, and she remembers the occasion when they were on the beach together and he trickled sand over her body.

43. Whit Burnett and his wife, Martha Foley, were the editors of *Story*. Williams used the last name of the main character of Sinclair Lewis' satirical novel *Babbitt* (1922) to refer to someone as unimaginative, self-important, and hopelessly middle-class. In an unmailed letter (April 1936, HRC), Williams gave further voice to his frustration: "There is just one thing that troubles me: what has become of your once-vaunted interest in the experimental short story?"

44. Bruno Richard Hauptmann (1900–36) was convicted of the kidnapping and murder of Colonel Charles Lindbergh's twenty-one-month-old son. Williams was assuming that Hauptmann would be executed as scheduled on 31 March, but at the last minute Hauptmann was granted a reprieve until 3 April. Hauptmann maintained his innocence until the end. Williams felt compassion for Hauptmann and wrote a poem beginning "Ask the man who died in the electric chair" and a prose elegy, "The Darkling Plain," the title of which he borrowed from Matthew Arnold's "Dover Beach."

> Ask the man who died in the electric chair
> what put him there?
> Ask the convicted criminal why he didn't go straight?
> Maybe he'll say it was fate.
> Maybe he'll say it must've been something he ate.
> Maybe he'll blame it on the crooked politicians
> that run the state.
> Maybe he'll break down and sob
> and tell you that his mother was dying of consumption
> and his old man was out of a job.
> and tell you that his mother, she had T.B.
> and the old man was out of a job . . . . .

THE DARKLING PLAIN
(For Bruno Hauptmann who Dies Tonight)

We do not die separately. We die together. There is no loneliness in death. In life there is loneliness. But none in death. The world is wide tonight beneath the spring moon. It is the last night of March. Tomorrow it will be April. On the limbs of the tree outside my window the small tight cluster of pink and green have expanded into the small perfect green of elm leaves. The willow branches that were like purple smoke a few weeks ago are now like tapering candles of green fire pointing down toward the earth. The sky pales. It is a delicate hyacinth shade filming over with grey. This is not a night for death or for thoughts of death. We should live tonight. We should exult in the power of breath. We should lie upon the bare earth with our seeing eyes lifted toward the wide dark question of the sky. It is not a night for death. But tonight we must die. Each of us must face death.

It is only a few steps from his cell to the death chamber and in half an hour he must walk them. Those few steps. I must walk them with him. I must prepare myself for this. We do not die separately in this world. We all die together. Even spring is not proof to our death.

Oliver Winemiller, the main character in Williams' short story "One Arm," is executed in an electric chair.

45. "Moony's Kid Don't Cry."

46. Mrs. Gardner was a housemother at Washington University. In the play fragment "Dragon Country," Williams named the matron, who is angry because her daughter has been given a copy of the poems of the English "Decadent" poet Ernest Dowson, Mrs. Gardner. A poem entitled "The Talk Went On" includes the line "'Do you believe in love, Mr. Gardner? I mean <u>real</u> love?'"

*Tuesday, 31 March 1936*

Tuesday. I've woke up feeling sick the last two mornings – Yesterday completed and mailed (to Story) my short story "Sand"[42] – feel rather pleased with it – about old Mr. & Mrs. Kramer – Don't know why I persist in sending things to Story – They probably quit reading them long ago – Sent letter to Harriet Monroe thanking for accept of "My Love Was Light" and enclosed 3.00 for subscription. Hurt to put out that much money but will be worth it. My last issue of "Story" arrived. That magazine has been deteriorating lately – I believe Foley and Burnett are becoming regular Babbitts[43] – prosperity doesn't agree with literary folk – Dreamed I saw Hauptmann being electrocuted last night – he was extraordinarily calm about it – The real execution is tonight – a horrible thing[44] – Tonight also my short story class – Will probably hear my play read.[45]

*Sunday, 5 April 1936*

Sunday. Been feeling fine since Tuesday night. Seeing that poor Mrs Gardner[46] such a wreck sort of pulled me together nervously – Forgot about my own misery feeling sorry for her – Went to picture show twice since then and felt no tension –

Bruno Hauptmann and his attorney, Edward Reilly

47. Presumably "The Little White Lady of Tsarko-Toye (a One-act Tragedy of the Russian Revolution)," the story of Princess Sonya who brings food to starving peasants. Only a fragment of the play exists.

Williams' choice of subject was influenced by Chekhov, whom he discovered in 1935. Williams wrote in *Memoirs*:

> That summer I fell in love with the writing of Anton Chekhov, at least with his many short stories. They introduced me to a literary sensibility to which I felt a very close affinity at that time. Now I find that he holds too much in reserve. I still am in love with the delicate poetry of his writing and *The Sea Gull* is still, I think, the greatest of modern plays, with the possible exception of Brecht's *Mother Courage*. (pp. 40–41)

48. *Voices* (published 1921–65) was a journal of verse edited by Harold Vinal in which two of Williams' poems had been published, "After a Visit" and "Cacti" (August–September 1934). "Variations" and "Trapped" appeared in the spring 1936 issue. In Mills' "Variations," a voice speaking for its generation speaks of the doom and death of war. The first eight lines follow:

> That afternoon while we came back from sleep
> the paper on the walls went gray, the silence grew enormous
> and sang from clock to chair across the room.
> We knew those charms our parents keep
> — to block the succour they believe will harm us —
> always before the mind, gone. We who had spelled out doom
> in headlines past our breakfast coffee, turned, with cold
> isolated posture of despair.

Josephine Johnson's poem "Trapped":

> This the last thing for which I pray:
> Strength to round out my day.
> A firm will for the closed lip,
> For the quiet hand,
> Watching in silence the delicate glass let slip
> Useless, the irrecoverable sand!

49. No manuscript of "The Golden Arch" is known to exist and was most likely an idea Williams never developed. Williams may have been inspired by Hart Crane's poem "To Brooklyn Bridge," in which the bridge is seen as a symbol of man's aspirations and achievements, or by D. H. Lawrence's novel *The Rainbow* (1915), which ends with a description of a magnificent rainbow arching over the ugly industrial landscape.

50. In "The Swan," an unexpected sexual encounter takes place between two people who meet late one night, a man unhappy with his wife, and a young woman whose love for her boss is unrequited. The story takes its title from a swan they see on a lake. When they make love, the man becomes aware that it was not the girl he was possessing but the "cool, white, unpossessable purity of the swan."

Williams would have been aware of Ferenc Molnár's play *The Swan* (1920), which was to be performed in St. Louis on 27 April 1936. By the 1930s Molnár had gained an international reputation as a playwright. In Molnár's play, Princess Alexandra, who was described by her late father as a "proud, white swan" who "conducts herself irreproachably," is reminded by her future mother-in-law what it means to be a swan "gliding proudly . . . majestically . . . where the moon gleams on the mirror of the water." Molnár uses the image of the swan at night as a complementary image to the virginity of Princess Alexandra, whereas Williams uses it as a contrasting image to the sexual promiscuity of the young woman.

Williams would add major parts of his story "The Swan" to the scene entitled "Every Girl Is Alice" in the play *Stairs to the Roof*.

51. Marie Louise Lange wrote Williams a letter dated 11 April 193[6] (Yale) in which she said, "Yes, I think April is a fine month to write poetry. All the little spear-points of green pricking up, all the little beginnings of new poetic thoughts, all the shafts of thoughts that will grow to future loveliness. . . ."

Williams had recently met Lange, a high-school student who won third honorable mention for a poem in the junior division of the Wednesday Club Contest. In a letter to his grandparents dated 6 August 1936,

This afternoon however began to get the jitters again – so I accepted Miss Flo's invitation to come over for the night – Done no work lately. Yesterday drank cup of coffee but could not write anything decent – Started a crazy something about Russian peasants[47] – wanted to write a pastoral story – but of course that is absurd because I know nothing about country life, farming, Etc. Feel hungry for that sort of thing – The quietness of earth –

Read new poems by Clark Mills in <u>Voices</u>, "Variations" – not so hot – also short poem by J. Johnson called "Trapped" – (1935) not very impressive as a poem but implications[48] –

*Tuesday, 7 April 1936*

Tuesday A.M. – If I could make of my spirit a golden arc to span this trouble!

Another bright windy morning rather cold – The branches are all lacy with young leaves – There are shimmering clouds of dust in the air – blackbirds are creaking – I am hungry for breakfast – I want to write something really fine this week – something strong and undefeated "The golden arch"?[49] – Perhaps –

*Wednesday, 15 April 1936*

<u>Wednes</u>. (April 15) Went over to go swimming and found pool was closed – perhaps for the season. How ghastly! I can't get along without swimming – at least I don't see how I could as it is my only physical "release". It's a horrible hot afternoon and I have that horrible oppressed feeling that hot weather gives me. This house frightens me again. I feel trapped – shut in. The radio is on – that awful ball-game – it will be going every afternoon now and hearing it makes me sick – I'm too tired to write – Can do nothing – I am disgusted with the story I wrote Saturday – "The Swan"[50] – It seems idiotic to me now – "Sand" was not much better. I wish I could write something decent – strong – but everything about me is weak – and silly – Terrible to feel like this – I have been so well the past two weeks – like a different person – now I guess it's all starting again. Well, I must learn to take things on the chin because nothing will be easy for me – nothing ever has been easy but I am always trying to make things easy, trying to dogde everything hard or disagreeable and the result is that I've just gotten deeper and deeper into this situation – this rather hopeless situation – I hardly dare to say hopeless but in my heart I know very well that it is – I would like to get away somewhere – Thank God I've got that money in the bank – Maybe I'll visit that little girl poet but her latest letter sounded a little trite and affectatious – "little spear points of green"[51] – It might be impossible – Oh, God I'm so miserable & lonely and so afraid of <u>people</u>! This reminds me of how I used to feel that first spring at College – afraid to go out on the street!

Williams wrote: "My little country girl friend came in last week and spent nearly the whole day with us. She is nice but terribly boring. Says when she starts to school (Washington) next Fall she will drop in all the time — but not if I can help it!" (RMT, p. 83).

Williams borrowed the name Mary Louise for the daughter in the short story "Three Players of a Summer Game" and the related story "Three against Grenada."

52.  "Nirvana" is the story of the doomed marriage between Caroline and Henry, an unemployed actor. On learning that his wife is pregnant, Henry lies to her and tells her that he has landed a job with a repertory company. After he has spent all their savings, he sends Caroline a telegram and tells her that he never got the repertory job and that all their money is gone.

53.  Washington University.

54.  Marie Louise Lange.

NIRVANA

She felt that she was leading a silly, useless sort of life. But she could not remember a time when she had been so happy and at peace with herself, not even in her early youth, for even as a girl she'd taken things very earnestly and had usually been in an anxious state over something or other. Now she seemed to be curiously detached from the usual current of her life. She seemed to have slipped off from the turbulent main channel into quiet, sunny waters where there was no perceptible motion.

The winter had been horrible, exhausting, with Henry, unable to find any new work now that the stock company had broken up, coming home every evening a shade more despondent than the evening before and she trying to hide her own desperate state of mind, putting on a bright face whenever he came dragging listlessly through the door after making another useless round of theatrical agencies. She could have told him what was the matter if she'd had the heart. He was still distinguished, still even handsome, but he didn't look like a juvenile anymore. That winter he was beginning to look like he ought to play character parts. When she married him nearly three years ago he could have easily passed for thirty-five. But now time had suddenly caught up with Henry and he looked every bit of his actual forty-six.

Things were bound to pick up in the spring. But they didn't. And then her own spirit collapsed. She no longer bothered to put up a brave front, not even for Henry's sake. She went into a mental and physical slump. Henry had to fix his own breakfasts. She lay on the bed all day, staring up at the ceiling - that horrible neutral grey surface, idiotically interspersed with a network of fine silver lines, affirming or denying nothing!

*Wednesday, 29 April 1936*

<u>Wednes – April 29</u>

There is a flaming barrier in front of me – what shall I do? Shall I quiver and quake on this side of it – not daring to make the leap? Or shall I charge straight ahead – accept the challenge – dash through the flames? Maybe they will burn. It is likewise possible that at my very approach, if I approach them bravely, they'll dwindle to ashes. And even if they burn high and hurt me, I may be able to leap high enough to get clear over – and into the sky!

I must remember that my ancestors fought the Indians! No, I must remember that I am a man – when all is said and done – and not a snivelling baby.

<u>Later</u> I have just finished writing "Nirvana"[52] which seemed very beautiful and fine to me during the writing. I have not yet read it over. Perhaps I had better not. Keep this good, satisfied feeling at least until tomorrow. If it is still as good, or nearly as good, as I think it is I will make one more assault on "Story" the invincible Fortress of Foley and Burnett –

Lovely music comes up from the radio – a symphony. Night insects are flying in my open window attracted by the light. The W.U.[53] machine shop hums softly across the car-tracks behind the block. I see people moving in lighted windows. The air is very still and warm.

*Friday, 8 May 1936*

<u>May 8</u> – It is a lovely fresh May morning – but I am tortured by thoughts. The last 3 days a steady crescendo – my head aches – I pound the bed with my fists and make horrible faces – Such a helpless, frustrated feeling – and all so silly! Like being scared of my own shadow and that's what it is – I must somehow overcome this idea of defeat – overcome it permanently – completely – or it will drive me mad –

This week-end I am going to see M.L.L.[54] at her country place. Maybe that will help – Something must – If only I could realize I am not 2 persons. I am only one. There is no sense in this division. An enemy inside myself! How absurd!

55. As a student at Christian College in Columbia, Missouri, Louise Bronaugh (1910–95) had become friendly with Williams as a result of their common interest in writing. At the end of 1933 Louise Bronaugh moved to Paris. In the 1950s and 1970s she and her husband, Charles Samuels, co-authored several books in the true-crime genre.

56. No verse drama based on "Moony's Kid Don't Cry" is known to exist.

57. Other one-act plays, besides "Moony's Kid Don't Cry," known to be dated 1936 are "Curtains for the Gentleman" and "The Magic Tower." In the spring of 1936, Williams was writing a number of poems in praise of beauty as well as some about unrequited love, including a group of sonnets titled "The Alien Heart."

58. Williams was greatly influenced by Hart Crane (1899–1932), one of the first poets to use the landscape of the modern industrialized city as his subject. Influenced by Rimbaud and T. S. Eliot, Crane wrote with a dramatic voice and complex, compact imagery. In 1926, he published his first collection of poems, *White Buildings*, and followed in 1930 with *The Bridge*, his long poem and most important work which is his celebration of the modern world centered on the Brooklyn Bridge. In 1932 Crane, returning by ship to the United States from Mexico, committed suicide by jumping overboard. *Collected Poems* was published in 1933.

Williams would go on to take titles from Crane's poetry. For example, "Spiritchel Gates," an early title of the short story "The Kingdom of Earth," is taken from Crane's poem "Emblems of Conduct," as is the title *Summer and Smoke*. *Steps Must Be Gentle* is from "My Grandmother's Love Letters," and *The Glass Menagerie* is possibly from "The Wine Menagerie." In 1979 Williams considered replacing the name of his play *The Red Devil Battery Sign* with "The City's Fiery Parcels All Undone," a line from the tenth stanza of "To Brooklyn Bridge."

Williams used epigraphs from Crane's poetry for some of his plays. For example, Williams chose the fifth stanza of "The Broken Tower" as the epigraph for *A Streetcar Named Desire*, the last two lines of "Legend" for *Sweet Bird of Youth*, the last stanza of "Chaplinesque" for "The Strangest Kind of Romance," the first three lines of the fourth stanza of "For the Marriage of Faustus and Helen" for a fragment of "Virgo," and the last line of the ninth stanza of "To Brooklyn Bridge" for "Will Mr. Merriwether Return from Memphis?"

A fragment of Williams' story "Driftwood" (a forerunner of "The Poet"), about a storyteller who enchants children with his tales, is dedicated to Hart Crane. One of Williams' last pieces published in his lifetime, *Steps Must Be Gentle* (1980), is an emotionally charged dialogue between Hart Crane and his mother, which begins with Grace Hart asking her son why he committed suicide.

Louise Bronaugh

*Tuesday, 26 May 1936*

<u>May 26</u> – And it did. That seems a long time ago. I should learn that nothing lasts because really nothing does. This book proves that if nothing else. Perhaps it would be better to forget, to leave the whole thing unrecorded but on the other hand this teaches a valuable lesson now and then – Of course I am not really so wretched as all this seems as it is usually when feeling worst that I feel the need to express it. Still – I am usually on the defensive and a mighty poor cowering defensive. Now it is my body again. Sickness. So weak and tired the past week and palpitations and what not. Feel completely run down – Been doing a lot though and felt really good before this – This week end Louise Bronaugh[55] came to town – I saw her twice – Rather dull – She is a swell person but the old attraction is just not there. I wish it were. Last night saw a show put on by the School for the blind. Very pathetic and appealing – the great, lightless building and the faltering bodies – feeling their way forward with strange, inward smiles –

Now I want to live very badly – I plan to write a verse drama for the Stanford University Contest possibly using "Moony's Kid Don't Cry".[56] Recently I have written two new one-act plays and rather decent verse[57] – but no stories – the stories just won't come. I feel plumb stupid tonight. I've been reading a lot of Hart Crane's poetry[58] – like it but hardly understand a single line – of course the individual lines aren't supposed to be intelligible. The message, if there actually is one, comes from the total effect – much of it has at least the atmosphere of great poetry – it is a lot of raw material, all significant and moving but not chiselled into any communicative shape.

*Sunday, 7 June 1936*

<u>June 7</u> This is what you might call the beginning of the "great offensive" – I am going to ~~deliberately~~ nail myself down to this job if it literally kills me – writing this verse-drama – I already have a vague but interesting plan in mind and a little already on paper. I <u>must</u> work on it every day. Clark Mills told me that he was able to <u>force</u> himself to work 3 hours a day on an outlined poem – if he can do this why shouldn't I? Of course I don't doubt that Clark is a stronger spirit than I. But I've got to buck up and be a man instead of such a damned whining sissy – I'm so lazy and easy going I'm not worth shooting at.

Must mention I saw Louise again before she left and this time we were very happy together and I've been feeling quite well after since – in really excellent condition compared to what I was – tho I miss not being able to swim now that the pool is closed – Summer school starts the 12th. I plan to take a ~~verse~~ course in the technique of drama for one –

59.  Both Williams and Mills were involved with the Union of St. Louis Artists and Writers. The writer and labor organizer Jack Conroy (1899–1990), author of *The Disinherited* (1933), a representative work of the Depression era, was a leading member of this group. Williams submitted the autobiographical story "Square Pegs," later retitled "This Can't Last Forever," to the magazine Conroy edited, *The Anvil: The Proletarian Fiction Magazine.* In his short story, Williams gave voice to the suspicion he believed these proletarian writers would harbor about him. Specifically, the narrator asks, "Do you believe in a bourgeois revolutionist?" His story was accepted but subsequently rejected by another editor.

W. W. Wharton (1908–85), known for his playful and caustic humor, published his first volume of poetry, *May Harvest*, in 1928. He served as business manager of *The Anvil* and later, in 1949, published *Graphiti from Elsinore*, a collection of satiric verse that parodies, among others, T. S. Eliot.

60.  In a fragment of the short story "All Kinds of Salvation," Williams' narrator, Tom Walker, gives voice to similar feelings:

recently i have joined . . . a gathering of revolutionary artists and writers all over the world we meet every other friday in the back room of a south side public library . . . and here i receive recognition and homage nobody suspecting in this citadel of all for all that my father is an executive in the worlds largest shoe company and that i the great revolutionary writer tom walker exist as a complacent parasite upon the toiling millions

61.  In a letter to Wilbur Schramm (circa 16 June 1936, HRC), Williams explained why the conference, which had been called to discuss the threat of fascism, was such a flop:

I've just returned from the Mid-West Writers' Conference in Chicago where I rather hoped I might find some representatives of American Prefaces. But Mr. and Mrs. Rood were about the only editors present. You were wise in staying away. As might be expected, the conference seemed more concerned with politics than literature and was so exhaustingly dull that I left immediately after the morning session and did not return. I found the Chicago lake front much more edifying. All this hullabaloo about Fascist repression seems like so much shadow-boxing to me at the present time. The fiercest of our revolutionary writers are now receiving monthly checks of well over a hundred dollars from the Government for activities which they themselves describe as mainly "boondoggling" — so I cannot feel that the Fascist peril is very imminent at this moment!

62.  Alice Drey Lippmann (1873–1971), according to Williams' good friend William Jay Smith, was "an early and ardent supporter of Tom's. The widow of a prominent St. Louis physician, she lived at first near the university in a large house. A published poet, a little woman with gray hair in a boyish bob, she carried around a reticule stuffed with unfinished poems, for which she constantly solicited visitors' help. She was passionate about poetry and was a passionate supporter of Clark, Tom and me. Even in her nineties when finally confined to a nursing home, she kept in touch with Tom and Edwina Williams" (letter to Margaret Bradham Thornton).

Her poem "Which?" was published in the May 1933 issue of *Poetry*:

WHICH?

Brown man, brown man, brown man brother —
Eyes of sunset, quenched of flame;
Faces etched of pain and glory;
Waifs of splendor now a name.

Brown man, white man, alien dreamers,
Which is ploughshare? No man knows.
Which is seed to plant the moonbeam,
Flower the field where daylight grows?

63.  Lionel Wiggam (1915–2005), born in Columbus, Indiana, was a poet who, by 1936, had had a number of poems published in national magazines such as *Vanity Fair*, the *New Yorker*, and the *Atlantic Monthly*, as well as most of the well-known poetry journals. He published two collections of poems, *Landscape with Figures* (1936) and *The Land of Unloving* (1961). Presumably Williams and Mills would have been very interested in a poet of their generation who had published a collection of poems by his twenty-first birthday.

~~Met~~ Saw Mills, Conroy and Wharton at a meeting of the "Discussion Group" last Thursday[59] – extremely interesting time. They were very suspicious of me at first – all of us on guard – but I think that I won them over fairly well[60] – as I was in good social form – Still – they think that I live in an "ivory tower" and perhaps I do! Only it isn't solid ivory. There's a great deal of plain disgusting <u>mud</u>.


*Tuesday, 16 June 1936*

<u>June 16</u>

I'm ashamed to report that the great offensive has hardly been started yet. The trip to Chicago to attend Mid West Writers Conference completely threw me off. The Conference was a flop for me.[61] The whole trip a ghastly fiasco. Went up on night bus with Clark Mills and Will Wharton. Sleepless night. Horrible humor. Sitting next to a negro on bus with Clark & Will across the aisle. Clark and I both very glum (though Clark was naturally excited over his trip) but Will in excellent spirits. Sleepless night. Arrived in Chicago feeling a wreck. In the morning Clark and I walked and rested along lake-front. Clark expressed an inordinate longing to own a yacht – I told him Hemingway had one but he would not believe he had earned it simply by writing.

On way back from lake we stopped in <u>Poetry</u> office but Harriet Monroe was not in. She was visiting Mrs. Lippmann[62] here in St. Louis.

We had a pleasant talk with Geraldine Uddell who is Harriet's business mgr. She had us sign visitor's book. Clark was quite rude. Introduced himself to the girl and left his name on card but <u>ignored</u> me – apparently did not wish to injure his prestige by having his exalted name associated with mine – At the close of the interview however I managed to introduce myself which probably displeased him. Considerably. Thereafter he was increasingly ill humored. We saw Lionel Wiggam's new book "Landscape with Figures".[63] Clark expressed his contempt

Williams on Grand Avenue, St. Louis

Williams would borrow aspects of Wiggam's poems in his work, including his title *Landscape with Figures* for a pair of short plays, "At Liberty" and "This Property Is Condemned." In 1941, they were published in *American Scenes* (edited by William Kozlenko) under the heading "Landscape with Figures (Two Mississippi Plays)." Williams also considered including under this heading the early one-act play "If You Breathe, It Breaks! or Portrait of a Girl in Glass," a forerunner to *The Glass Menagerie*.

64. Sidney Lanier (1842–81) was considered to be one of the most accomplished poets of the American South in the later half of the nineteenth century. His best-known poems include "The Symphony" and "The Marshes of Glynn." Williams, whose middle name was Lanier, was distantly related to Sidney Lanier, and before he adopted the name Tennessee in 1939, he often included his middle name when signing his work.

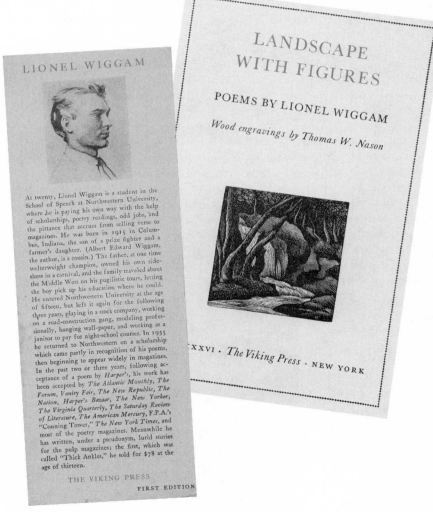

LIONEL WIGGAM

At twenty, Lionel Wiggam is a student in the School of Speech at Northwestern University, where he is paying his own way with the help of scholarships, poetry readings, odd jobs, and the pittance that accrues from selling verse to magazines. He was born in 1915 in Columbus, Indiana, the son of a prize fighter and a farmer's daughter. (Albert Edward Wiggam, the author, is a cousin.) The father, at one time welterweight champion, owned his own sideshow in a carnival, and the family traveled about the Middle West on his pugilistic tours, letting the boy pick up his education where he could. He entered Northwestern University at the age of fifteen, but left it again for the following three years, playing in a stock company, working on a road-construction gang, modeling professionally, hanging wall-paper, and working as a janitor to pay for night-school courses. In 1935 he returned to Northwestern on a scholarship which came partly in recognition of his poems, then beginning to appear widely in magazines. In the past two or three years, following acceptance of a poem by *Harper's*, his work has been accepted by *The Atlantic Monthly*, *The Forum*, *Vanity Fair*, *The New Republic*, *The Nation*, *Harper's Bazaar*, *The New Yorker*, *The Virginia Quarterly*, *The Saturday Review of Literature*, *The American Mercury*, F.P.A.'s "Conning Tower," *The New York Times*, and most of the poetry magazines. Meanwhile he has written, under a pseudonym, lurid stories for the pulp magazines; the first, which was called "Thick Ankles," he sold for $78 at the age of thirteen.

THE VIKING PRESS

FIRST EDITION

LANDSCAPE WITH FIGURES

POEMS BY LIONEL WIGGAM

*Wood engravings by Thomas W. Nason*

XXVI · *The Viking Press* · NEW YORK

Title page and dust jacket flap from
Lionel Wiggam's *Landscape with Figures*

for Wiggam – I said "Of course he's a typical romantic." And quoted two very lovely lines from one of his poems. Clark said "Yes, the only trouble with Romantic poets is that they've been dead and in the dust for about 100 years!"

We then talked of Sidney Lanier,[64] as he asked if I were related to him. Clark said he'd never read anything by the poet but remembered having heard that the "Marshes of Glynn" was rather good. I know he was probably lying about having read nothing by Lanier. Even illiterate people have read "The Marshes". It's almost inescapable – and Clark reads <u>everything</u> in verse. I admitted that Lanier was a poor poet but expressed admiration for him as a man.

We discussed Chicago architecture. I said tall buildings were hideous. Clark agreed that they were "in a way".

We went back to the meeting which was now fully assembled. It was dreadful. So long drawn out and tiresome that I was exhausted when finally we adjourned for lunch at about 3:00 P.M. I was actually sick. Shook hands with John Rood on the way out.

Clark and I went to a horribly cheap restaurant. I could eat nothing. Clark ate a hamburger and egg sandwich, black coffee and a piece of apple pie – I was so sick that I nearly passed out watching him eat. We were completely estranged by this time. At last when he had finished eating – with the greatest deliberation – he remarked "I bet you thought I would never get through." I said "It did seem rather drawn out." He seemed to relish my discomfiture.

I told him I could not stand to sit through the afternoon session but would see him at the evening's. He said he was leaving Chicago before evening. So we bade each other an exceedingly stiff farewell & parted.

I took the 6:00 bus for St. Louis.

Impression of Clark Mills, <u>Poet</u>: Very talented even <u>brilliant</u>. Clark Mills, <u>Person</u>: Very conceited, spoiled, bigoted, childish and painfully lacking in a sense of humor.

*Thomas Lanier Williams*

65.    Rose Isabel Williams (1909–96) was Williams' sister, older by sixteen months. As children, Rose and Williams were very close. Since her mid- to late teens, she had exhibited signs of severe depression and erratic behavior. Although Rose began seeing a psychiatrist in 1930, her behavior steadily declined. With the onset of her mental illness, her relationship with Williams deteriorated. Like Williams, Rose had difficulty getting along with her father. Diagnosed with dementia praecox (an early term for schizophrenia) in 1937, Rose underwent insulin shock treatment and a prefrontal lobotomy on 13 January 1943. She was institutionalized for the rest of her life, although Williams visited her often and made some attempt to have her under his care after his success. At his home in Key West were framed childlike pictures of houses she had painted.

In a number of his significant plays, Williams based characters on Rose. These include: Laura in *The Glass Menagerie*; Blanche in *A Streetcar Named Desire*; Alma in *Summer and Smoke*; Hannah in *The Night of the Iguana*; and Clare in *The Two-Character Play* (later rewritten as *Out Cry*). Lesser works in which a character is based on Rose include, in addition to forerunners (both plays and stories) of the plays mentioned above, the unnamed main character in the short story "Oriflamme" (or its earlier version, "The Red Part of a Flag"); the unnamed sister in the short story "The Resemblance between a Violin Case and a Coffin"; Ariadne in the short story "The Four-leaf Clover"; Rosemary McCool in the short story "Completed"; Miss Lucretia Collins in the one-act play "Portrait of a Madonna"; Rose Kramer, who goes to a Catholic rest home in the one-act play "Hello from Bertha"; Myra in the one-act play "The Long Goodbye"; Lily in the "short story in one act" "Why Do You Smoke So Much, Lily?"; Kyra in the play "The One Exception" (fragment); and Fisher Willow in the screenplay *The Loss of a Teardrop Diamond*.

Williams wrote many poems about and for his sister, including "Valediction" (beginning "She went with morning on her lips"), "The Beanstalk Country," "Lament for the Moths," "My sister was quicker at everything than I" ("The Paper Lantern," Part 3 of "Recuerdo") and the related "Talisman of Roses," "Elegy for Rose" (beginning "She is a metal forged by love," alternatively titled "Poem for Rose"), "My sister is discretion's self," and "Diver."

Williams wrote about or alluded to lobotomies and mental illness such as dementia praecox in such diverse plays as *Not About Nightingales*, *Spring Storm*, *Suddenly Last Summer*, *Stairs to the Roof*, *A Lovely Sunday for Creve Coeur*, the published version of "Moony's Kid Don't Cry," "Talisman Roses," "Alice at the Country Club" (fragment), and "The Paper Lantern" (fragment) and the closely related "The Spinning Song" (fragment), and also in the short stories "The Four-leaf Clover" and "Why Did Desdemona Love the Moor?" (fragment).

In addition to modeling characters on Rose, Williams often borrowed her name for characters in works, including the plays "Heavenly Grass or The Miracles at Granny's," four forerunners to *Sweet Bird of Youth* ("The Big Time Operators," "Brush Hangs Burning," "The Puppets of the Levantine," and "The Enemy: Time"), "The Long Stay Cut Short, or The Unsatisfactory Supper" (and the later *Baby Doll* and *Tiger Tail*), and "Kirche, Kutchen und Kinder," and the short stories "Miss Rose and the Grocery Clerk" (later rewritten as "Something about Him"), "Blue Roses," and "The Spinning Song," as well as a number of fragments.

66.    Walter Dakin Williams (1919– ) was Williams' younger brother and his father's favorite. After gaining a law degree from Washington University, he was sent to Harvard for officer training, where he also studied business administration. He served in World War II in the Pacific. From 1946 to 1949 he taught at St. Louis University and since 1965 he has practiced law in Collinsville, Illinois.

Dakin converted to Roman Catholicism in 1944 and is the author of *Nails of Protest: A Critical Comparison of Modern Protestant and Catholic Beliefs* (1955), with W. R. Stewart, and *The Bar Bizarre* (1980), as well as articles for Catholic publications. Dakin was instrumental in institutionalizing his brother for a short time in the psychiatric ward of Barnes Hospital in 1969 for his drug and alcohol abuse. Early that year, finding his brother in a very poor state, Dakin had proposed that he meet a local Jesuit priest, Father Joseph LeRoy. Within a few days, Williams was received into the Catholic Church, although he admitted later that he had not taken the conversion very seriously.

In 1983, Dakin published *Tennessee Williams: An Intimate Biography*, written with Shepherd Mead.

*Sunday, 5 July 1936*

July 5 (Sunday) I'm a swell one to accuse anybody of lacking a sense of humour. Apparently I've completely lost my own. Been brooding and whining to myself continually the last few days. Fancy myself being sick and refuse to do any work. Of course it is exhaustingly hot and this house – this domestic life – is quite fiendish. The old man like a dormant volcano, mother nagging a great deal, Rose[65] and Dakin[66] in continual stupid quarrels. Even I cannot keep my temper and act childishly. How stupid we all are! It is impossible to think of such fools as we are having immortal souls – we have plenty to eat but actually squabble over food sometimes as though we were starving. We say petty, annoying things to each other – today I feel as though I dislike them all and could feel no sorrow if they all were gone. Dreadful to hate everyone as I do sometimes. And yet I have such a profound capacity for love and even for happiness. I live in some kind of a cage – or enchantment – <u>nothing happens</u> – I seem unable to take any <u>action</u> – just drift along haphazardly from day to day – wondering what will turn up – I can't force myself to do anything – I've given up making myself write that verse drama – No use – If I don't want to write I <u>can't</u> write – I've written two

Rose Isabel Williams

67.    "Ten Minute Stop," about a young man, Luke, who travels to Chicago from Memphis to see a man about a job, echoes Williams' bus trip to Chicago for the Conference of Midwest Writers. When Luke arrives, he learns that the man is away and will not be back for some time. On the evening bus trip back to Memphis, Luke gets off during a ten-minute stop. He begins to think about existence and feels quietly detached from all that is around him. He decides not to get back on the bus.

The other story was very likely "Grenada to West Plains," completed by July 1936, about a traveling shoe salesman, on a train from Grenada to West Plains, who takes stock of his life and feels depressed and trapped by it.

68.    "Twenty-seven Wagons Full of Cotton."

69.    In "Las Palomas" (The Doves), a young sexually inexperienced sailor falls in love with a Mexican prostitute. After making love to her one evening, he returns the next day to find her, and his ship sets sail without him. Various drafts or fragments of the same story are titled "Las Muchachas" (The Girls) and "The Lost Girl."

Williams with his younger brother, Dakin

short stories lately – one pretty good I now think – "Ten Minute Stop" – sent to Story.[67] My story in Manuscript[68] will be printed this month says Rood. He wrote me a long letter explaining the Fascist peril which I express doubts concerning in my letter to him.

I've made peace with Will Wharton and sent Clark a letter of apology – no answer as yet – Doubt that I will get one – I'm sometimes ashamed of myself for being such a <u>worm</u>.

Dear Grand and Grandfather arrive this evening to be with us while the others are touring. Those are two persons I do love and always shall – more than anyone else in the world. My grandmother's got more of God in her than any thing or anybody else I've yet discovered on earth! When I think of God I think of her –

But it is hard to think of God these days except with a feeling of ~~dull~~ sorrowful perplexity.

<u>How strange this life is!!!!!</u>


*Thursday, 30 July 1936*

Today is Thursday, July 30. I shall write today all day in an effort to ~~obliterate~~ forget the nervousness which has come on me during the night. Perhaps it is a good thing because for days, even weeks, I've been horribly idle, doing practically nothing. Now I feel a new story working itself out. I will call it "Las Palomas"[69] just because I like the sounds of those words. I wonder if <u>Manuscript</u> will come out today. It is about 2 weeks late. I'm getting worried about it – my story is supposed to appear in this issue.

Looking back over the last entry, I'm reminded to say I did get a reply from Clark, a post card. Grand left Tuesday. Grandfather left over a week ago. Their visit was lovely. Like a dream now. The life here so quiet and perfect just like it was in Memphis when I was with them. Now that is over. The family has returned. We have a new dog. I feel them looking at me and wondering what I'm going to do with myself. I wish that I knew.

I woke at three o'clock. It is now light enough outside for me to write without the lamp. The world looks tired this morning. It needs rain. The wind sounds fretful and dry like a person squirming in a fever.

<u>Later</u>. The story came to practically nothing as I might have expected being based on nothing. My writing is really ghastly sometimes. It's because – mainly – I won't work. I am terribly lazy and childish.

I am furious with the whole family. ~~Dakin~~ I have to take insults from them all – can do nothing about it. How stupid we all are in this house and yet how full of pride and conceit! I suppose it is the same way in most other houses, and yet people are afraid to die. Especially myself. I hate the thought of ever dying – But what do I get out of this silly life?

70.    Tree Court was a public swimming pool near the Meramec River which Williams and his friends frequented in the summer.

Williams and Rose in the Ozarks, 1926

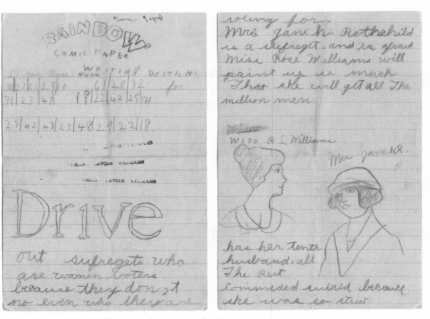

A "comic paper" that Williams, aged nine, wrote for Rose

I used to say it was a great show – if nothing else. I guess it is a great show – really – but it is like modern stories – without any meaning – No, it is like nothing else – it's incredible – that's all – And so dull – Oh, my God, so dull – And yet I say it's a great show. How can it be a great show and yet be so dull? The truth is that I am dreadfully dull – and not the show – of course I'm not always as dull as I have been lately – I must try to wake up and get more out of life!

Now the crickets are chirping outside, making little stabbing noises in the dark and a street car rattles along, a dog barks, water flows from the kitchen faucet – the bedsprings creak beneath me.

I feel as though I will go mad in this house tonight.


*Sunday, 2 August 1936*

Sunday Aug. 2 –

No, I did not go mad that night – because I had already gone mad years and years before. The next day I actually became rather sane. Manuscript arrived with my story and Marie Louise came over to see me – which was a sweet revenge – and the day passed almost pleasantly though the dear girl was pretty boring – and nobody liked my story but me!

"Next days" are funny things!!!

Saturday I went out swimming at Tree Court[70] – The water ice-cold – the sun warm – felt as fit as a fiddle but nervous again that evening. I keep telling myself that "it does not exist" – so why should I let it bother me? It is too absurd! I need above everything else to be master of myself – how marvelously that would solve all the problems of life – just being your own "boss" – having control of your thoughts & emotions! Is it a hopeless dream? or can I really do it? At any rate, I'm gonna try!

Maybe it is better not to try anything. To be like a patient cow taking what comes and for my comfort knowing only that all things pass.

I've spent the morning writing on that ugly & miserable and tiresome story "Las Muchachas". Worthless!! It frightens me to see how badly written it is! And I drank coffee that stirred up my nerves and made me go without dinner. Later I will go down and eat by myself. I am now feeling hungry – very hungry though still nervous – and eating is the only pleasant thing that I can think of at this present moment. Adios!

I wish I loved Somebody very dearly besides my self –


*Tuesday, 4 August 1936*

Tuesday A.M. Aug. 4. – I feel definitely stronger and more virile this morning. Do you know, I do believe I am acquiring a little masculinity as I go along. I feel a

71.    The publishing firm Little, Brown announced a prize of $2,500 for the most interesting unpublished work of fiction, between 15,000 and 35,000 words, submitted before 1 January 1937.

72.    No manuscript of "The Apocalypse" is known to exist. Williams may have taken the title from D. H. Lawrence's personal and peculiar interpretation of the Book of Revelation, *Apocalypse* (1931). The only manuscript known with this title is a poem, "Apocalypse." A shorter variant of the first section of the poem was published in the February 1938 issue of *The Eliot* as "Lyric."

Williams' idea for a story about a year in the lives of a number of young people could have been based on an earlier autobiographical short story, "Square Pegs," alternatively titled "This Can't Last Forever," about four graduating journalism students who discuss their future plans and the difficulty of finding jobs as writers. Williams went on to write a play entitled "April is the Cruellest Month," revised as *Spring Storm*, in the spring of 1937 which he described as "a study of the simultaneous crises in four contiguous lives against the background of a small Mississippi town where I once lived."

APOCALYPSE

I.

The glad morning coming
shall find us embraced with our longing
serene and uncaptured
devout as the sound of the bells

And the high steeples tingle
with rumour of birds in ascension
quick and enraptured
the shadow of birds in quick passage
like scarves in a wind
tossed over the summer-paved streets

And the orator's voice
proclaiming democracy's triumph
the army's return
the clanking of shields in the court-yard
the boast of the valiant
the spilling of wine in the gutters

The markets, the merchants
the morning-loud crying of wares
the smell of the fruit in the sunlight
that warmth and that sweetness ascending

the sound of the bells!

II.

And always the evening returning
the breast drawn bare
exposed to the lips of the lover
the fluctuant kiss
the ache of the flesh and its answer
like hands of the blind
that grope for a passage to freedom –

Suspension of time
ascension of fabulous towers
a bodiless climb
into a zenith of rapture
as carillons chime

The unreal laughter of children
blown up from the yards
and the wind and the violins singing
the myriad stars
the glittering arches of heaven

And afterwards sleep
sleep and a measured recession
back into the deep
gardens of opulent darkness –

the poppies of sleep!

good deal tougher and firmer in some ways than before – I don't let things completely disorganize me like I used to – I suffer as much but am now more patient of suffering – more – you might say – debonair in the face of unsmiling fortune –

Had a very exciting crazy dream last night. Dreamed I was mixed up in a bloody gang-war between lefts and rights. Josephine Johnson was slain. This was not a wish fulfillment I'm sure as I recall feeling definite sorrow – in the dream – on reading the newspaper accounts of her death. I was on the "left" side but shocked at their atrocities and spent most of my time in running away. I love to run away in dreams – down dark streets and crooked alleys. Only in this dream one of the streets was garishly lighted – it was old Westminster place with a park in the middle like Forest Park Ave. And I went down the middle of the park – brilliantly lighted by lamp posts – rather beautiful – in my dreams I often see very beautiful scenes.

*Friday, 7 August 1936*

Friday Aug. 7. I have just now thought of a subject for the short novel I want to write for The Little Brown Contest – about 35,000 words[71] – I think I shall [call] it "The Apocalypse" or something like that – and it shall be about a year in the lives of a number of young people – terminating in the apocalyptic experience of Spring – the Scene a University campus.[72]

I leave Monday for camp and am feeling <u>great</u>!!

Josephine Johnson

73.   Compare Williams' sentiment in his journal with an excerpt from a fragment of his early autobiographical story "Byron":

[Byron] plowed again through the bottom of his trunk. He dug up, in fact, everything that he had written since reaching what he considered his intellectual majority. He read poem after poem and story after story with a mounting horror, and a constantly tightening sensation, there in the back of his skull. So proud he had been of these manuscripts before! Every line of them had seemed to glitter and burn with a supernal creative fire! Now he recognized them as just a colossal pile of loose words. . . . . . .

In the end he gathered the whole bunch of them in his arms and rushed with them down to the cellar. There he tore open the door of the furnace and stuffed them all in. Seeing them greedily engulfed by the flames, he felt a momentary, passionate impulse to follow them with his body, into the holocaust. Why shouldn't he? There was really nothing left of him now; nothing but the worthless flesh! Had he not often reflected to himself, in moods of gentle self-abnegation: <u>My</u> <u>only</u> <u>real</u> <u>significance</u> <u>to</u> <u>this</u> <u>world</u> <u>is</u> <u>as</u> <u>an</u> <u>artist?</u>

It would have been a magnificent gesture. But the furnace was a trifle too warm for Byron's physical courage. So he crept brokenly up to his room. . . . .

74.   Williams' father, Cornelius.

75.   "Middle West" is comprised of stanzas of varying length in which the voices shift jarringly from describing contemporary scenes to gossiping about small-town matters to giving a weather and tidal report. Williams may have been inspired by Crane's poem "The River." In stanza eight, Williams models the character Luke Owens on himself:

Luke Owens he used to write po'try

when we was kids in highschool together

an' ev'rybody said that Luke was kinda queer in the head

though he was pretty smart at his books

an' so when he gets out of school his old man gets him a job

in a wholesale shoe company over at Alton

an' Luke he sticks at it a couple of years

an' then he gets sick or something an he comes on home

an' stays aroun' home a good while doin' nothin'

till the ole man Owens he gets sick an' tired

of seein' the boy roun' the house all the time

just scribblin' down stuff on paper that don't make sense

so he says 'When the hell

are you gonna git out and git yerself a new job

an' go back to work?

an' the boy says maybe tomorrow

an' he goes out that night, by God,

an' he hangs himself out in the orchard in back of the house –

It just goes to show how much some people hate work!

*Monday, 10 August 1936*

Monday. Aug. 10 – Well, this is Monday – and no camp! No, it all fizzled out and here I remain soaking in my own sour juices, sweltering heat – complete misery and dullness. My situation now seems so hopeless that this afternoon it seemed there were only two possible ways out – death or suicide – however that was a bit melodramatic and I shall probably go on living and if I saw death coming God knows I'd run the other way as fast as my two legs could carry me[73] – Still it is pretty much of a mess – I hate this house and today I hate everyone in it and they all look at me and wonder what the hell I'm doing here and despise me too – Yes, I heard ~~Dakin~~ D. saying last night that he (he) wanted to know when I was going back to work and it had better be pretty soon because soon I'd be too old (!!) and nobody would want me and D. said he didn't tell him[74] I was planning to go back to school this Fall and heaven knows what he'd say about that – That finished it. I felt sick and decided to stay at home – now if I could get my money out of the bank I think I would go off somewhere – anywhere – just to be out of this poisonous place – I can't write. I do nothing but lie around feeling sorry for myself – It is horrible.

*Tuesday, 11 August 1936*

Tuesday Aug. 11 – I'm an expert at graceful retreat but at vigorous assault I'm rather pathetically unskilled.

Today I want to start in on that novel I hope to write. I don't feel very fit for action of any kind. Had dreams last night rather pleasant but can't remember very plainly except that I was insulted and withdrew with a gentlemanly manner from the game – a tennis game of all things – another example of my skill at graceful retreat – a really positive young extravert would have dreamed about knocking the bastards out instead of saying "Now if you will excuse me gentlemen –"

After taking a walk yesterday afternoon I felt somewhat better about my disappointment and depressing situation – now life goes on in its usual fashion. I fly warily between the edges of my various neuroses and try to avoid getting cut on the brambles and despite this exciting pastime I feel pretty dull and out of sorts – Well, no complaints! This is the hour for action! First of all I shall brush my teeth as I have this A.M. a very bad taste in my mouth.

*Thursday, 13 August 1936*

Thursday Aug. 13 – Feel rather well for a change – no reason – just taken a shower – bodily freshness does a great deal for the spirit. Tried yesterday to write a modernistic poem called "Middle West"[75] – not much success – will try again

76.   Manuscripts of stories include "Ten Minute Stop," "Las Palomas," possibly "Grenada to West Plains," and possibly "Jonquils 10¢ a Dozen," the story of a young girl who, giddy with happiness over being in love, purchases a bunch of jonquils on her way home to meet her beau. "Jonquils 10¢ a Dozen" most likely is the "very innocent sort of love story with a sunny atmosphere" that Williams sent to *American Prefaces* in mid-June 1936 (letter to Wilbur Schramm, HRC).

77.   Williams and his brother went to a YMCA camp on Lake Taneycomo in Hollister, Missouri. On 30 August (HTC), Williams wrote to his grandparents:

> Dakin and I have just returned from a delightful two weeks at camp in the Ozarks. It was nicer this year than I have ever known it. We had everything, even a mild tornado, by way of diversion and escaped some of the worst heat, according to reports at home. Dakin gained some weight and we are both feeling fine. We produced three plays which I wrote and Dakin acted in. The last one was an old-fashioned melodrama and for the heroine we had a little Ozark girl that waited on the tables whose accent and manners were just perfect for the part. She pronounced villain as "vill-yun" and was so dumb she didn't realize the play was supposed to be funny, which made it all the funnier.

Fragments of the plays Williams refers to are "Der Trachedy uff Hamlut und Ahphelia in Vun Hact," a short Marx Brothers–style spoof; a skit with Romeo, Juliet, and Paris; and "Little Eva's Dilemma or Love Conquers All." Eva's dilemma is marriage to Percy Vile or financial ruin for her family because Percy, who holds the mortgage on Eva's father's farm, will evict them. Just in time, Eva's love, Dan Trueblood, returns and pays off the mortgage. Dakin played the role of Percy Vile.

78.   David Fuller Ash (1898–1980) was one of the founding members of *American Prefaces* and was on the editorial board from spring 1935 to October 1937. From 1929 to 1933 he was an instructor in English at the University of Missouri and taught Williams composition and rhetoric as well as narration. He was a judge for the University of Missouri's 1931 Mahan Story Prize Contest in which Williams received an honorable mention for "Something by Tolstoi."

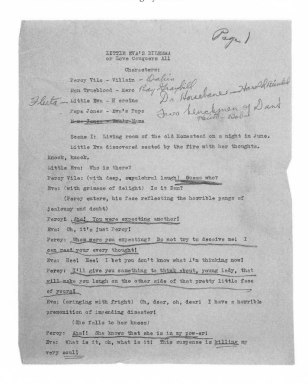

today – my novel has acquired a first chapter – but dreadfully cheap – I don't want to write that kind of stuff. So many cheap novels are being written. I want mine to be a good one – but I can't extend any of my present story ideas over that much space –

I haven't read a novel in almost a year – they all seem too dull – I can't get beyond the first few pages – I now have four stories and one poem "on the air"[76] – I ought to get at least one acceptance – don't you think? That would help so much!

*Friday, 14 August 1936*

Friday Aug. 14th How lovely!! I am going to camp after all.[77] I'm in the best of spirits about it. Leaving tomorrow morning. Also had a letter this afternoon from David Ash of American Prefaces[78] saying he was holding "Ten Minute Stop" and hoped the other editors would accept it – What a piece of good luck that would be! Ash is an old English teacher of mine. I had him at Mo. U. A swell fellow. So my hopes are high – It is extremely encouraging. Besides I just love that story & it would delight me to have it in <u>Amer. Pref</u>. It has been a hot day, full for me – went downtown shopping & library. Tonight there's a cool wind blowing and I feel like a kid again.

*Sunday, 30 August 1936*

Sunday Aug. 30 – Two glorious weeks of sun, water and starlight now gone. Like a jewel in the drab setting of my usual life. It was all pure light. Hardly a shadow except toward the end when I felt St. Louis creeping closer. I won't write about it in detail. It doesn't need writing about. It couldn't be forgotten ever.

Now I'm back "home". Which isn't quite true. The world is my home. That is what I've just found out. The whole world is really my home – not my single cramped unhappy place. But just the same I've got to stay here or so it seems and being here is very miserable. I hate brick and concrete and the hissing of garden hoses. I hate streets with demure or sedate little trees and the awful screech of trolley wheels and polite, constrained city voices. I want hills and valleys and lakes and forests around me! I want to lie dreaming and naked in the sun! I want to be free and have freedom all around me. I don't want anything tight or limiting or strained.

Here's the old life again with all its old problems. Maybe if I look hard enough into this fog I'll begin to see God's face and can manage to find my way out.

79. "Blue devils," Williams' expression for low spirits, was a term, dating back to the 1700s, popularized in the 1930s by blues singers. In a letter to his literary agent Audrey Wood, dated 27 February 1941 (HRC), Williams wrote: "The blue devils harrass me continually, however, so much has happened to discourage me about myself and my work. I feel sometimes like a piece of broken string."

Williams referred to the condition "blue devils" throughout his life and included it in his writings. For example, in the play *Not About Nightingales*, Butch describes "them little blue devils" to a fellow inmate: "They crawl in through the bars an' sit on the end of yuh bunk an' make faces at yuh" (act 1, episode 4). In *The Night of the Iguana* (act 3), Hannah Jelkes and the Reverend Lawrence Shannon discuss blue devils:

HANNAH: Yes. I can help you because I've been through what you are going through now. I had something like your spook — I just had a different name for him. I called him the blue devil, and . . . oh . . . we had quite a battle, quite a contest between us.

SHANNON: Which you obviously won.

HANNAH: I couldn't afford to lose.

SHANNON: How'd you beat your blue devil?

HANNAH: I showed him that I could endure him and I made him respect my endurance.

SHANNON: How?

HANNAH: Just by, just by . . . enduring. Endurance is something that spooks and blue devils respect.

80. *The Great Ziegfeld* (1936) is a film based on the life of the American theatrical producer Florenz Ziegfeld, best known for his elaborate revue *The Ziegfeld Follies* as well as musicals such as *Show Boat* (1927). *The Great Ziegfeld* received the Academy Award for best picture in 1936.

81. *Candles to the Sun*, set in a mining camp in the Red Hill section of Alabama, chronicles the plight of a family who tries to escape the poverty of the camp. When the workers strike against the oppression of the mine owner, the mother, who has been saving money for years to educate her son, is forced to donate the money to the strike, thereby destroying any chance her son has to escape to a better life.

Williams was obviously influenced by Jack Conroy's autobiographical novel, *The Disinherited* (1933), about the son of a coal miner who grows up in a company-owned town and who, as a young man, wanders in search of employment during the Great Depression. Williams was also very likely influenced by a one-act play, "The Lamp," written by Joseph Phelan Hollifield, a friend of his grandfather's. In a letter (circa 1935, HRC), Hollifield wrote that he hoped Williams could do something with "The Lamp" and said he would try to send Williams some material on mining people in Alabama.

On 18 and 20 March 1937, *Candles to the Sun* was performed by a nonprofessional acting company, the Mummers of St. Louis.

Y. M. C. A. CAMP ON LAKE TANEYCOMO, HOLLISTER, MO.

Postcard Williams sent to his mother

*Monday, 31 August 1936*

Monday Aug. 31. – A little crazy blue devil[79] has been with me all day. I wish I could shake him off and walk alone and free in the sunlight once more. There is one part of me that could always be very happy and brave and even <u>good</u> if the other part was not so damned "pixilated". I see so much beauty and feel so much that there is no reason why I should make myself miserable. I do believe in God. I know that I do. There are times like this when all doubt is forgotten – when reason is put away – and when I feel that God is sitting right at my side with one hand on my shoulder. Then I feel warm and safe and unafraid and the universe is not a cold mysterious immensity but a nice comfortable little house for me to live in. That is putting it a little too prettily but I do have such feelings once in a while and though cruel reason tells me that I am helplessly adrift on a shoreless sea full of hungry sharks there is a small, trusting little boy in me that won't believe it and still thinks there's a rudder on the boat and a good wind blowing –

*Wednesday, 16 September 1936*

Wed. Sept. 16 – Well I felt so much like writing in this journal for a change that I went all the way downstairs to get a pencil. A miserable pencil so I won't write much though I have <u>so</u> much to tell. Today has been as nearly perfect as any of my days in St. Louis ever are – Complete freedom from neurotic fears, pains, anxieties. Mother gave me a dollar and told me to go down and see "The Great Ziegfield"[80] which I did – and found it very entertaining – you really had the feeling for a man's whole life unfolding before you – a rare achievement on the screen –

A cool, rainy day – definitely Autumnal. It was pleasant to be out on the wet streets among the big impersonal crowds. Yesterday my sainted Grandparents sent me a check for $125. to pay my tuition at Washington University. So now it is definitely decided that I am to go there – I want to make every day of it <u>count</u> – since my lovely grandparents have sacrificed so much to send me. They are such dears. I want to go down there early this Fall to see them.

I have done shamefully little writing this week – just laziness. I am working on my long play[81] and it is improving but slowly. However I do feel the idea is worthwhile.

I want to have a party this week or go to one. I am lonely. I need people around me. That is because I am feeling good. I want to raise hell and make love and maybe get a little bit drunk.

82.  *The Sweet Cheat Gone* is a translation by C. K. Scott Moncrieff of *Albertine Disparue*, the sixth part of Proust's *A La Recherche du Temps Perdu*. The narrator seeks the return of Albertine, but after her death he observes the gradual disappearance of grief. Williams would borrow Proust's character Baron de Charlus for a character in the play "Ten Blocks on the Camino Real" and for the expanded version, *Camino Real*. In his essay "Prelude to a Comedy" (*New York Times*, 6 November 1960), Williams wrote:

>  No one ever used the material of his life so well as Marcel Proust, who made out of his life, recollected and continuing, what is possibly the greatest novel of our time, *The Remembrance of Things Past*, in which he made the passage of time (from past to present and to the future shadow) a controlled torrent of personal experience and sensibilities to it. It contains all the elements of a man's psychic history — his love, fear, loneliness, disgust, humor, and, most important of all, his forgiving perception of the reasons for the tragicomedy of human confusion.

83.  Norman Mattoon Thomas (1884–1968), originally a Presbyterian minister, became leader of the Socialist Party in 1926 and was its candidate for presidency six times between 1928 and 1948. In *Memoirs* Williams wrote: "My first year [at the University of Missouri] I came of age and I registered and I cast my first and last political vote. It was for Norman Thomas" (p. 37).

In "The Important Thing," a short story about two students, John and Flora, Williams wrote:

>  They saw a great deal of each other after that. They had many interests in common. They were both on the staff of the University's literary magazine and belonged to the Poetry and French Clubs. It was the year of the national election and John became twenty-one just in time to vote. Flora spent hours arguing with him about politics and finally convinced him that he must vote for Norman Thomas. Later they both joined the Young Communists' League. John became a very enthusiastic radical. He helped operate a secret printing press and distribute pamphlets about the campus attacking fraternities, political control of the University, academic conservatism, and so forth. He was once called before the Dean of Men and threatened with expulsion. Flora thought this was terribly thrilling.
>  "If you get expelled," she promised, "I'll quit school too!"
>  But it all blew over and they both remained in the University. (*CS*, p. 168)

84.  Friedrich Nietzsche, *Daybreak* (1881), para. 542 (book V). On the endpapers of a copy of E. A. Robinson's long poem *Tristram* (1927), part of the Williams family collection at Washington University, Williams quoted this line and attributed it to Nietzsche. In addition, Williams noted the following passages:

>  "How pleasant is the sound of even bad music and bad motives when we are setting out to march against an enemy." [*Daybreak*, para. 557 (book V)]
>  "The higher we soar the smaller we appear to those who cannot fly." [para. 574 (book V)]
>  "To accept a belief simply because it is customary implies that one is dishonest, cowardly, and lazy." [para. 101 (book II)]
>  "Then I get angry with all these people and afraid of them; and I must have the desert to become well disposed again." [para. 491 (book V)]
>  "The last argument of the brave man: But what do I matter?" [para. 494 (book V)]
>  "Your physical exhaustion will lend the things pale colors whilst your feverishness will turn them into monsters." [para. 539 (book V)]

Apart from the introductory course on philosophy that Williams was taking, he had only taken one other course in philosophy, an introduction to logic at the University of Missouri.

In two short stories Williams wrote during this period, he commented on Nietzsche. In "Season of Grapes" a seventeen-year-old boy who is at summer camp in the Ozarks reads a book by Nietzsche which he finds "especially disturbing. Was it possible," he asked himself, "that all things could be so useless and indefinite as Nietzsche made them look?" In "Ironweed" a young man about to go to college had been given a volume of Nietzsche to read. "He had read it and wholeheartedly embraced its doctrines. But late one August night . . . he had seized this volume and flung it out of his bedroom window."

85.  Willard Holland (1908–63) was the director of the Mummers of St. Louis. In his article "On the Art of Being a True Non-conformist" (*New York Star*, 7 November 1948), Williams wrote:

>  Holland always wore a blue suit which was not only baggy but shiny. He needed a hair-cut and he sometimes wore a scarf instead of a shirt. This was not what made him a great director, but a great

*Thursday, 17 September 1936*

Thursday Sept. 17. Another pleasant uneventful day. I continue to find life smooth and unannoying for the nonce though I feel an occasional twinge of conscience for accomplishing so little.

It's really not worth the trouble, agonizing over things. Why can't I remember that always – and refuse to torture myself?

I still feel the need of company – and no one calls! I wonder if I shall see anyone this week-end? I am reading "The Sweet Cheat Gone" by Proust[82] – nice but very slow. I admire his art above all others of the modern school.

*Tuesday, 22 September 1936*

Tuesday Sept. 22. It is good to be lying down – I'm exhausted – Registration at Washington the past two days – very strenuous. Today physical examination – what an experience! – It might have caused me acute embarrassment a few years ago but I'm getting delightfully casual about such things – examined the old carcass from A to Z omitting nothing. The lad in front of me flipped out while they were tuning in on his chest – fainted completely, suddenly slumped forward. They caught him and stretched him out on the floor – he lay there several minutes, cock-eyed – when he came to he asked what had happened to him – "What did I do?" – They told him he'd fainted – He said "I was feeling sort of dizzy a few minutes ago." "It's pretty hot in here" said the attendant and then asked him if he'd ever fainted before. The boy said "occasionally". They asked him to describe a previous "faint" and he said "once he was sitting on a counter and he fell off and hit his head on the counter."

Poor kid! I guess I'm not the only sensitive person in the world.

My blood pressure is 136 – high as ever. I've been feeling "off" the last few days – will have to take things easier – It is going to be a year full of problems I'm afraid – but perhaps I'll be too interested to worry. I heard Norman Thomas[83] speak last night – I was feeling badly but found it impressive nevertheless. My reaction to most things is determined by my own state of mind and body. I must always remember that in forming judgements. As Nietzche says "Do not let the evening be judge of the day."[84]

Tomorrow I want to turn in my play to Holland.[85]

director he was. Everything that he touched he charged with electricity. Was it my youth that made it seem that way? Possibly, but not probably. In fact not even possibly: you judge theater, really, by its effect on audiences, and Holland's work never failed to deliver, and when I say deliver I mean a sock!

In the fall of 1936 Holland first approached Williams about writing a short play against militarism as a curtain-raiser for his production of Irwin Shaw's *Bury the Dead* (1936). Williams' play was entitled "Headlines" and was the beginning of Williams' collaboration with Holland. Holland had great admiration and respect for Williams as a playwright and, early on, spotted his strength at characterization and dialogue. They worked together on several of Williams' longer plays, namely *Candles to the Sun*, *Fugitive Kind*, and *Spring Storm*. In 1937 Holland and the Mummers produced *Candles to the Sun* and *Fugitive Kind*.

Williams used Holland's surname for a character in the fragment of the play "The Chosen Virgin." In the play *Stairs to the Roof*, Bertha's girlfriend broods over a man called Willard.

86. By 1936 Williams was very familiar with the life and work of D. H. Lawrence (1885–1930). Williams may have been remembering a passage in Dorothy Brett's account of her friendship with Lawrence, *Lawrence and Brett* (Philadelphia: J. B. Lippincott, 1933), in which she recalls Lawrence counseling her: "'If you are nervous in the night . . . don't light a candle, but lie and look at the stars: the stars will take all your fear away'" (p. 90). Williams would use a variant of this line two months later in his one-act play "The Big Game."

In an interview in the *Paris Review* (fall 1981), Williams mentioned Lawrence as a writer who had influenced him as a young man and highlighted Lawrence's understanding of sexuality. Williams' attempt to include descriptions of nature in his short stories written during the mid-1930s may well have been due to Lawrence's vivid evocations.

Williams' play *Battle of Angels* was influenced by Lawrence's work, most significantly by *Lady Chatterley's Lover* (1928). In a letter to Audrey Wood about the play ([14 March 1941], HRC), Williams described a character as being a "symbol of . . . animal sexuality." On one manuscript of *Battle of Angels*, Williams wrote: "For D.H. Lawrence / Who was while he lived the brilliant adversary of so many dark angels and who never fell, except in the treacherous flesh, the rest being flame that fought and prevailed over darkness."

87. "The Magic Tower" had won first prize in the Webster Groves Theatre Guild Contest in April and, as a result, was one of three one-act plays presented by the guild on 13 October.

88. Manuscripts include "Ten Minute Stop" at *American Prefaces*, "In Spain There was Revolution," and possibly "Season of Grapes."

Willard Holland

Later: How lonely it is in this room! Tonight I feel sick and afraid. If I can beat this down and be strong again everything will be all right. I must be strong again. I must never turn back down that dark road. I've gone on from there into the high sunlit places. I must keep on going through light and through shade but with my face lifted always toward the open sky. D.H. Lawrence said that when you look at the stars you can't be afraid.[86] I must keep looking at stars. And at the sun. Death itself is nothing. But life is a precious possession and I want to keep life as long as I can.

Tonight I would like to be with warm, friendly people. Here I am – alone as usual. People could be so helpful. Some of them are. That kind young medical examiner for instance. He didn't want me to be alarmed. But of course I was and that is what's wrong with me now. The old enemy – Fear.

Tonight I will lock him out – of my house – I will set the dogs on him. I'll drive him a thousand miles away!


*Wednesday, 23 September 1936*

Wed. Sept. 23. Felt rotten all day – stomach burning with gas – general uneasiness – tomorrow classes begin – what foul luck starting out in such a shape! But I will pull myself together somehow – being busy may be my salvation – Right now I feel as though I had swallowed a hot coal – It is so demoralizing – I hope tomorrow will be bright and happy – It could be – There is always the equal possibility of things getting better – I am going to attend a rehearsal of my play[87] tomorrow evening at the home of the director, David Gibson – I haven't met him yet nor any of the cast – He sounds over the phone like a nice fellow. Hope I'll see someone at school tomorrow and get my mind off myself. It is sickening to be like this!

Think I'll take some Sodium Bromide and try to get some sleep. I have 3 manuscripts in the mail[88] – one at "Story" for about three weeks – what a heavenly surprise would be an acceptance from them! I am really a very lucky boy – I just don't know it!

There is still the night music of the insects – but that will soon be over – the nights will be clear and frosty and quiet – I hope not too quiet. Au Revoir.


*Friday, 25 September 1936*

Friday – Reading back through this journal I discover there were other times when I was feeling as bad as this so perhaps this will pass also. I am genuinely ill – mostly mental or nervous I suppose. Extremely disquieting.

89. Williams had sent "In Spain There was Revolution," a story about a boy and a girl who work at nearby camps in the Ozarks. They arrange times to meet each day, and one morning the boy, a lifeguard named Steve, seduces the girl. Later in the story, a man asks Steve:
    "What do you think of the trouble in Spain?"
    The life-guard shrugged his coffee-brown shoulders.
    "Trouble in Spain? Didn't know there was any."
    On occasion, Williams would use titles of earlier works as lines in later works. He would use the title of this story as a line in Tom's opening monologue in the first scene of *The Glass Menagerie*.

90. Wilbur L. Schramm (1907–87) was an educator, editor, journalist, and author. Early in his career he taught at the University of Iowa where he edited *American Prefaces*. He went on to become an authority on mass communication and wrote a number of books on the topic.

91. Meridel Le Sueur (1900–96), a well-regarded novelist and short-story writer, was the guiding spirit of the Conference of Midwest Writers in Chicago in June 1936, out of which grew the Midwest Federation of Arts and Professions. She was editor of the federation's magazine, *Midwest*, launched in October 1936, and was also associated with *The Anvil*. In the early 1950s her political views and activities were deemed "subversive" by Senator Joseph McCarthy, and she fell into obscurity.

92. Betty Chappell was a student at Washington University whom Williams had met in Frank Webster's short-story course. In *Memoirs* Williams remembered her incorrectly as Betty Chapin and described her as one of the "pretty girls" who were members of the Poetry Club and "who provided lovely refreshments and décor" (p. 123).

93. Otto Heller (1863–1941) was a distinguished professor of modern European literature at Washington University between 1914 and 1937. His publications included *Henrik Ibsen: Plays and Problems* (1912). In the fall of 1936, Williams took his course "Principles and Problems of Literature" and received a grade of A. Williams later changed his opinion of Heller when, at the end of the next semester, he gave him a D in the course "General Literature III." Williams had written a paper entitled "Birth of an Art (Anton Chekhov and the New Theater)," on which Heller commented: "This paper in no way fulfills the requirements of a term paper as indicated repeatedly. All of this, or nearly all, was written without reference or relation to literary standards and criteria as studied in the course."
    Harcourt Brown was head of the department of French at Washington University. Williams was enrolled in his course French 16, "Origins of the Philosophic Movement." In the fragment of the play "Alice at the Country Club," Williams used his name for two off-stage characters, Dr. Harcourt and a "man named Brown."

94. "A person who has withdrawn or secluded himself from the world; usually one who has done so for religious reasons, a recluse, a hermit" (*Oxford English Dictionary*).

95. William Jay Smith described Frances Van Meter: "a long-term girlfriend of Clark's, tall, willowy, beautiful, she accompanied us on our late-night drinking bouts" (letter to Margaret Bradham Thornton).

96. At the time of this journal entry, Rose was about to turn twenty-seven. By 1936 she was having periodic fits of hysteria, depression, and paranoia.

97. The party took place when Williams' parents were on vacation in the Ozarks. He had invited his friends, including William Jay Smith, Clark Mills, and Will Wharton, to come over. Their party turned quite wild with much drinking and, according to Smith, "a drunken Wharton [making] a series of loud telephone calls to people picked at random from the telephone book using very obscene language" (letter to Margaret Bradham Thornton). On returning home, Mrs. Williams found Rose in an agitated state, and Rose told her about the wild party and the obscene phone calls and the drinking. About this incident Williams would recall in *Memoirs*:
    After she had tattled on my wild party . . . when I was told I could no longer entertain my first group
    of friends in the house — I went down the stairs as Rose was coming up them. We passed each other
    on the landing and I turned upon her like a wildcat and I hissed at her:

The "Story" Ms. came back with nice letter from the great Burnett.[89] No news yet from Rood or Schramm[90] or Meridel Le Sueur.[91] Last night a marvelous time. Went out with Mills & Betty Chappell[92] to play rehearsal – got drunk and made love to Betty – and was in best of spirits – But had to pay the piper today – Almost a crisis of misery – physical and otherwise – I fear death – I must get over that – There are times when death doesn't frighten me much – I love school – Especially Heller & Brown[93] – Good night – I hope!

*Saturday, 26 September 1936*

Later – It certainly was not a good night – I have just now gotten up – the milkman having gone – and forsaken the hope of sleeping – not a wink – misery – If I can only pull myself together this week-end how fortunate I shall be. God help me!

*Thursday, 1 October 1936*

Oct 1. The first morning in October will have to go on record as one of the world's worst. I am disgraced at home and disgusted with the world – especially literary people. Sick at my stomach. Never spent such a nauseous night. I no longer have any trust in human nature. Honestly I had better live the life of an Anchorite[94] than go with such people – selfish, egotistical, vulgar, absurd. All that I said of McBurney following the Chicago trip was true – He is really an ass – Poor Wharton is simply nuts – And I am a damn fool to tolerate such a bunch. Pet aversions – girls like Frances van Meter![95]

*Wednesday, 7 October 1936*

*God forgive me for this: (5/20/39)*

Oct. 7. I have just turned up the new picture on my calendar – It is lovely – forest rangers, pine woods, bears, a clear mountain stream. that is where I would like to be! I am hungry for the great out doors – I guess I'm just an out-door boy in disguise – Today I signed up for the freshman swimming team – so that I could get out of that loathesome "gym" class – Swimming is lovely and I feel quite happy about it.

The house is wretched. Rose is on one of her neurotic sprees[96] – fancies herself an invalid – talks in a silly dying-off way – trails around the house in negligees. Disgusting. They are still hounding me for the party Tuesday night.[97] But I am

"I hate the sight of your ugly old face!"

Wordless, stricken, and crouching, she stood there motionless in a corner of the landing as I rushed on out of the house.

This is the cruelest thing I have done in my life, I suspect, and one for which I can never properly atone. (p. 122)

98.    In his letter to Williams dated 1 October 1936 (HRC), the editor of *American Prefaces*, Wilbur Schramm, wrote: "["Ten Minute Stop"] is possibly good enough to be published as it is. However, it has such fine possibilities and can be made such an excellent story that it seems a crime to publish it in its present form." Schramm's criticism was that Williams had not presented any clear reason why the main character should stop in Champaign. Schramm added: "I think this can be remodeled into a story . . . which will do more to make your reputation than a dozen rather foggy stories like this one in its present form." There is no record of Williams ever revising "Ten Minute Stop."

99.    "The Magic Tower" is about a young couple, Jim, a struggling artist, and Linda, a former vaudeville actress, who live in the attic room of a boardinghouse. The magic tower is the name Linda gives to their room, which is transformed into a magical place when she is there with her husband whom she loves so much. When Jim fails to interest a well-known art dealer in his paintings, Linda leaves him to return to the stage. She is persuaded by friends who come to visit her that giving Jim his freedom is the highest act of love and self-sacrifice, enabling him to pursue his career without the responsibilities of a wife or family.

"The Magic Tower" received very good reviews and was described by Anne H. Jennings in the *Webster News-Times* of 16 October 1936 as "a poignant little tragedy with a touch of a warm fantasy . . . Exquisitely written by its poet author."

100.    Ernest Christopher Dowson (1867–1900) was one of the most gifted of the English poets of the 1890s. He published two collections of poetry: *Verses* (1896), which contains his poem "Non sum qualis eram bonae sub regno Cynarae," well known by its refrain, "I have been faithful to thee, Cynara! in my fashion"; and *Decorations* (1899), which contains some of his experiments with prose poems. Dowson also published a one-act verse play, *The Pierrot of the Minute* (1897), which is one of the best-known plays on Pierrot.

In Williams' short story "Dolores Sleeps Under the Roses," two spinsters in the small southern town of Green Hill gossip about another inhabitant, Captain Sam Henderson, who is wild and reads the poetry of Ernest Dowson, which they regard as immoral because it is about drinking and loose women. At the funeral of his daughter Dolores, Captain Henderson recites his favorite lines of Dowson from the frontispiece of Dowson's *Verses*:

> They are not long, the weeping and the laughter,
>     Love and desire and hate:
> I think they have no portion in us after
>     We pass the gate.
>
> They are not long, the days of wine and roses:
>     Out of a misty dream
> Our path emerges for a while, then closes
>     Within a dream.

In the incomplete play manuscript "Dragon Country," an angry matron chastises Bernice, a librarian, for giving her daughter a copy of Ernest Dowson's poems and cites lines from "Cynara" as evidence of their unsuitability. Bernice quotes the above two stanzas as support for Dowson's beautiful poetry but fails to convince the matron.

In the related play fragment "The Chosen Virgin," a mother complains to the new minister, the Reverend Shannon, about the town librarian having given her daughter *The Collected Verse of Ernest Dowson*. The mother draws attention to the opening lines of "Cynara" to prove that his poetry is "horrible" and "disgusting."

getting tough – I can take it. The damned "American Prefaces" returned my story with suggestion I <u>revise</u> it completely – made some preposterous suggestions[98] – The story seems sort of rotten now that I read it over – but good enough for that bunch. Ash however seems a nice guy. I think he must be on my side.

Willard Holland just called up. Wants me to see him tomorrow. He has read my long play – Next Tuesday (a week from tonight) my one-act[99] will be presented. But I feel dull and disinterested in the literary line. Dr. Heller bores me with all his erudite discussion of literature. Writing is just <u>writing</u>! Why all the fuss about it?

I have a periodically painful tooth – that <u>worries</u> me. It is surprising that all of us don't go mad in this world. Problems, problems, problems – somebody must have lost the answer book. However I do not feel in a petulant mood tonight – I feel strangely light & free – perhaps the effect of a good physical workout.

*Friday, 9 October 1936*

<u>Friday Oct. 9</u> Last night Clark and I went to see rehearsal of my play. Pleasant evening. Met Gibson in café. A nice fellow – despite Clark's ill opinion of him. Drank a couple of beers and felt rather desperately gay – recited Ernest Dowson[100] on the way home. Wet streets and lamps. Disappointed in the play. Too sugary. But I don't feel like doing anything better. I am in one of my defeatist

Program for the Webster Groves Theatre Guild production of "The Magic Tower"

101. In *The Wind and the Rain*, by Merton Hodge (1903–58), a New Zealand playwright and doctor who emigrated to Britain, a medical student, Charles, leaves his fiancée, Jill, and mother in London to study in Edinburgh, where a young woman, Anne, takes their place. At the end of his five years of study, Charles realizes he cannot live without Anne and breaks his engagement to Jill. *The Wind and the Rain* was first performed in London in 1933, where it ran for three years, and in New York in 1934.

In a college paper on *The Wind and the Rain*, Williams noted: "It is not a very original story. The striking thing about the play is the complete naturalism of the dialogue. . . . I would say that situation in this play is secondary to character. Aristotle says that plot is the most important factor of a play but I'd rather have a bad plot with interesting characters than a good one with a bunch of stooges."

Williams would use Hodge's title in the poem "Soldier's Memoranda" (line 10):

> My personal trinity let me think of them,
> Whitman the brawler, the cosmic-voyager Crane,
> and soft-spoken Chekhov on evenings of wind and rain.

Edwina Williams reading to Rose and Tom

moods about writing. If only I could always love my work – then I would be a great artist. But I would never be vain. That is the one very decent thing about me. I have no inclination toward vanity. Another decent thing about me is my tolerance and my love of people and my gentleness toward them. I think I have acquired that through suffering and loneliness. But when I go a few good things will go with me – as well as some pretty bad ones.

Poor Rose is worse than ever today. We must pray. That is all there is to do. One very indecent thing about me is my indifference. I do not worry about her nearly as much as I should. But life is all so confused and mad – it is no wonder that I behave in a mad fashion. I am grateful tonight for a comfortable bed. I am so very deliciously <u>tired</u>.


*Monday, 12 October 1936*

<u>Monday</u> Oct. 12 –

Ought to be asleep by now. After midnight. Reading "The Wind & The Rain" – charming play[101] – feel miserable about my own work – the old defeatist attitude – I must cast it off. Spoils everything for me – Grand is here for an unexpected visit. Tomorrow night my play – feel absolutely no interest – Isn't that silly? Nothing to say tonight – Except I feel in excellent shape physically – no nerves – just depression.


*Wednesday, 21 October 1936*

Wednesday – Oct. 21 – This has been a long siege of worry. My brain feels like a million pin points tonight. I am, oh, so tired of this thing. I think it will <u>have</u> to stop now. It <u>can't</u> go any further. This ridiculous fear of defeat. I am too tired to do my Greek homework tonight – I will just let it go – and sleep! It is raining and I am <u>lonely</u>. Oh, God, help me to do what I should do – be brave and live a free life.


*Sunday, 8 November 1936*

<u>Sunday</u> – Nov. 8 – A good while since I've addressed this journal – a good sign as this is where I usually record my less exuberant moments. Today there is nothing really wrong with me. The patient has been doing very nicely – as well as could be expected. I am a bit alarmed about sudden, jolting pains that I have in the back of my head – 3 this evening – And a sore spot on top of my head when I press it – blood pressure I'm afraid – no wonder – I've been running like a pack of hounds ever since school opened – It's been marvelous for my nerves – but my body may find it too much – Last night the thought of death disturbed me greatly – Tonight I view it very objectively like a stone wall at the other end of the road –

102.  Intended as a curtain-raiser for the Mummers' production of Irwin Shaw's *Bury the Dead*, on 11, 13, and
      14 November, "Headlines" was comprised of four short scenes using headlines and statements made by
      people against the war.

103.  "[T]here was about [the Mummers] that kind of excessive romanticism which is youth and which is the
      best and purest part of life," Williams would write in the *New York Star*, 7 November 1948. He continued:
      Most of them worked at other jobs beside theater. They had to, because The Mummers were not a
      paying proposition. There were laborers. There were clerks. There were waitresses. There were stu-
      dents. There were whores and tramps and there was even a post-debutante who was a member of
      the Junior League of St. Louis. Many of them were fine actors. Many of them were not. Some of
      them could not act at all, but what they lacked in ability, Holland inspired them with in the way of
      enthusiasm. I guess it was all run by a kind of beautiful witchcraft! It was like a definition of what
      I think theater is. Something wild, something exciting, something that you are not used to. Offbeat
      is the word.
          They put on bad shows sometimes, but they never put on a show that didn't deliver a punch to
      the solar plexus, maybe not in the first act, maybe not in the second, but always at last a good hard
      punch was delivered, and it made a difference in the lives of the spectators that they had come to
      that place and seen that show.

104.  In "Return to Dust" Williams identified, along with the novelist Jack Conroy, "the short-story writer" J. S.
      Balch (1909–80) as being one of the star members of "The League of St. Louis Artists and Writers" (also
      known as the Union of St. Louis Artists and Writers). Aged twenty-two in 1931, Balch published a collec-
      tion of sonnets and rhymed lyrics, *Castle of Words and Other Poems*. From 1935 to 1940 Balch was assis-
      tant director of the WPA-sponsored Missouri Writers' Project. He wrote a novel, *Lamps at High Noon*
      (1941), about his participation in a strike by a group of writers employed in the St. Louis office of the
      Missouri Writers' Project.
          While working as a reporter and drama critic for St. Louis newspapers (1940–48), Balch began writ-
      ing plays. In 1948 he moved to New York, where he worked as a television director. In 1959 he became
      managing editor of *The Theatre*, for which he wrote "A Profile of Tennessee Williams" (April 1959).

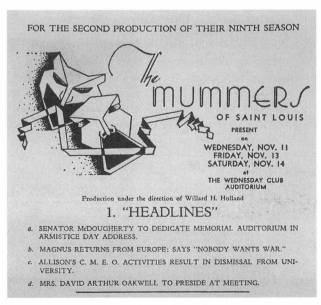

Program for the Mummers' production of "Headlines"

of course I'm in no hurry to reach it.

This afternoon I was thinking what a dull, sordid, despicable wretch I have become. I apologized to me and my maker for being the way that I am. I do sincerely wish that I were a more lovely sort of person than I am. Coming home tonight beneath that dark frosty sky I felt clean and perfect again. I seemed to sense a new kind of morality that has nothing to do with one's social relations but only with one's universal relations – one's relations with the <u>universe</u>!

But I guess that's a lot of rot – or is it?

Bon Soir!


*Wednesday, 11 November 1936*

<u>Wed</u>. <u>Nov. 11</u> It is after 5:00 A.M. and I've gotten not a wink of sleep. Might as well give it up. Think I may cut my French class. Ate too much before going to bed or am just too restless. My prologue "Headlines"[102] will be given this evening. Holland has made something very clever out of it. He's a genius I think – a real genius – though I can't say I like him especially as a person. He's too slippery. I enjoy working with "The Mummers". A delightful bunch of young people. Nothing snotty or St. Louis "Social" about them.[103]

Tonight I feel very separate from the rest of the world – very much alone – and yet I've been seeing more people and doing more things than ever before in my life. It's a dazzling show – dazzling and cruel – I am getting cold and hard like the rest of them. I don't care about anyone but myself – that's the horrible thing – despicable selfishness – I can't pity those that I ought to pity – Instead I feel revulsion – I want to be let alone by them – not touched – What's going to come of it all? – I don't know – I wish I could get away for awhile – Maybe I could recover my lost "soul" –

Still feel no drowsiness – street cars grind past – cars begin to mutter – it lightens very faintly – The city begins to stir – another day is starting – what for? – So people can live – go on living – I am not blue – I'm not even disgusted really – I too am ready to rise and continue my life – But I wish that I believed quite thoroughly in the efficacy of prayer. There are so many things that I would like to pray for.

Wed. Nov. 11 – 11:30 P.M. Just returned from "Bury The Dead" – Very forcefully done – My prologue however was rather botched – A stupid, pointless thing any way – a piece of hack work. Saw Jack Conroy and Balch[104] in lobby – They were not very civil. Conroy quite rude after performance when I asked him if he liked it. There's just a natural uncongeniality between me and that bunch. They are professional "againsters". I don't believe in that stuff. It's not necessary to be against everything else in order to be for Communism. They seem to think it is. I want to get my play done and produced. Will work on that now. Dead tired. Goodnight.

105.   No manuscript of a poem entitled "Gold Leaves" is known to have survived, but in a notebook for his course "The American System of Government," Williams wrote:

Some of these lines would appear in part X of a fragmented draft of a poem published as "Sacre de Printemps" in *College Verse* (May 1937). The published version, which omitted part X, begins: "The gold leaves / storms of February / freshets of spring."

106.   In the December 1936 issue of *College Verse*, the publication of the College Poetry Society, Thomas Lanier Williams, Marie Louise Lange, and Helen Longmire were listed as new members of the Washington University Chapter. Chapters of the College Poetry Society had been organized at a number of universities across the United States to encourage and nurture aspiring young poets.

107.   "The Big Game," a one-act play about three male patients, centers on a young man called Dave, who is suffering from a terminal heart condition. The second patient is Tony, a well-known quarterback for a football team, who is released later in the day so that he can watch the big football game that afternoon. Despite being strong and accomplished, Tony is fairly insensitive and is not able to give much comfort to Dave. The third patient, Walton, is a former soldier who is admitted that afternoon for brain surgery. Before he undergoes the surgery, from which he does not recover, Walton is able to share with Dave his philosophy of courage, which gives Dave comfort as he faces his death:

> When you're scared the best thing you can do's look up at the stars. . . . it makes you feel kind of small and unimportant they're so cold and far away — you look at them and say to yourself, well, what the hell do I matter? There's millions like me being born every day! D'you see? You look at those stars and you know they were there thousands of years before you ever came on this earth — and they'll be there thousands of years after you're gone! They kind of — represent — eternity or something!

Williams, who always believed he had a bad heart, often gave characters afflictions he either had or imagined himself to have. It was a practice he began in his early years and continued throughout his writing career. Other characters with heart conditions in early works include Jay in the short story "The Spinning Song," Miriam in the short story "Oak Leaves," Bud in the one-act play "Fate and the Fishpools," the Father in the play fragment "Family Pew," and David in the short story "The Preacher's Boy."

Characters with heart conditions in works from the 1940s and 1950s include Alma in the play *Summer and Smoke,* Kilroy in the play *Camino Real,* Sebastian in the play *Suddenly Last Summer,* the Lutheran minister in the short story "One Arm," the Reverend Guildford Melton in the play *You Touched Me!,* the husband of Mrs. Stone in the novel *The Roman Spring of Mrs. Stone,* Laura Jean in the short story "Blue Roses and the Polar Star," Donald in the short story "The Vine," and Candy in the play "And Tell Sad Stories of the Deaths of Queens."

Williams continued this characterization into the late 1970s with Jack Jones in the short story "Miss Coynte of Greene" and Dorothea in the play *A Lovely Sunday for Creve Coeur.*

*Sunday, 15 November 1936*

Sunday. Nov. 15 – My, how this Fall is going by. It's perhaps the happiest season I've had since the spring of '31 – or was that really as happy as it seems in retrospect? Nostalgia for an old love – it does strange things – what I need now is love – life is empty without it – I need a great love for someone beside myself – That would keep me from being morbid and silly – I would like to lose myself in some great love or great noble cause – I am not happy now. I am just busy and fairly comfortable – I have few grand moments of exaltation – but some – nature affects me a great deal lately – the clear beauty of Autumn mornings – smoke of burning leaves – Oh, but I want something real in my life – when will it happen? when will it come? Never? Yesterday I wrote a poem called "Gold Leaves"[105] which I think rather fine – for me. Me being me.

*Tuesday, 17 November 1936*

Tuesday. Felt horribly nervous this evening – took a shower and a sleeping pill to calm me – guess I've been going too hard – read over "gold leaves" hoping that would cheer me but it seemed quite messy – at times like these I realize what a difficult job life is – it is marvelous how one manages to go on and on and on in spite of all these adversative things – these fears and disappointments and all the other "slings and arrows of outrageous fortune" – I think Shakespeare must have been in a mood like mine when he wrote that soliloquy. I bet he was a guy that had plenty of guts. No damn sissy. It takes guts and plenty of them to be an artist in this unartistic world. Especially when you aren't even a very good artist. Just an artistic sap.

*Saturday, 21 November 1936*

Saturday – Nov. 21 – This Saturday just about sets a new "low". I have never – or have I? – felt so wretched before! Yes. Many times. But that's no consolation. The poetry Club[106] was horrible. I got lost in the country afterwards. Almost panic-stricken. Flunked a Greek test this morning. Wrote nearly all afternoon on a play – "The Big Game"[107] – which is so lousy it smells. My belief in my work is all smashed again. I'm afraid I won't stand up under much more. I ceasing to be I. Incredible! But still – it will happen some day. If only I could have more respect for myself. I am not a bad person. But neither am I a positively good person. I'm not a positive anything. That's just it. Everything I do is make-shift and sloppy. What are all the words about? Surely it is all just a dream. I will wake up and find I was only dreaming all these tiresome things happened – I want to get away. But where?
   Sur l'autre côté de la lune!

108.  Presumably "The Big Game."

109.  Mebaral, a barbiturate, contains mephobarbital and was prescribed for anxiety. Its side effects include sedation, dizziness, and mood changes.

In Williams' play *A Lovely Sunday for Creve Coeur* (scene 1), Helena Brookmire says: "My physician told me [Mebaral] tablets are only prescribed for persons with — extreme nervous tension and asthenia."

110.  Cornelius Williams was taken to Barnes Hospital in St. Louis. He had been playing poker late that night with one of the salesmen at the International Shoe Company. The salesman had been drinking heavily, the two men got into a fight over the game, and a piece of Cornelius Williams' ear was bitten off. The incident was one of great embarrassment to the Williams family. In a letter to her mother dated 12 December 1936 (HRC), Edwina Williams discussed the matter and added that Cornelius' boss, Paul Jamison, "has been so fine about it. He phoned me not to worry, that he was keeping it from being known, all the men concerned sworn to secrecy and it has been given out to the men that he is at home with an infected ear."

```
                      LOUDSPEAKER


         Ladies and gentlemen of the radio audience, this
   microphone through which I am addressing you is located
   directly beneath the flag-draped rostrum in the middle
   of this magnificent room which is the Assembly room
   of the gigantic new Memorial Auditorium which has been
   erected in memory of our war dead and which is being
   very appropriately opened for the first time on this
   sixteenth day of November, commemorating the signing of
   the Armistice that ended the World War.
         In just a few minutes you will hear the voice of
   Senator McDougherty who is making the dedicatory speech.
   H e is now mounting the steps to the Rostrum.  I wi sh you
   could see him - an imposing figure of a man!  Xé With his
   thick silvery white hair and bushy black brows and dark,
   gleaming eyes he is an inspiring sight.  He reminds you
   of one of the ░░░░░░░ prophets of the Old Testament.  Now
   the crowd is applauding.  Now the Senator is acknowledging
   the applause.  Now he is about to begin speaking - ladies
   and gentlemen - Senator McDougherty!
   Senator:  Thank you, my friends, thank you!  This is indeed
   a heart-warming reception.
         In this modern age we are too prone to see things objectively.
   We see only the material thing and overlook its spiritual or
   idealistic significance.  Hmmmm.  As I enter this magnific ent
   new building at first I noticed only its ░░░░░░░ architectural
```

Fragment of a manuscript containing Senator McDougherty's Armistice Day address, the subject of the first scene of "Headlines"

*Monday, 23 November 1936*

Monday – Nov. 23 – 10:20 P.M.

Just passed through dreadful nervous crisis. Can hardly write so shaken. Fear. Had been working on play all evening.[108] Got too tired I suppose. Miserable little fool, Tom. Will you never learn? Fear never helps. In fact fear is the only thing to be really afraid of. Now I feel very tired and weak. Much better. I took a mebral[109] and 5 teaspoon of sodium bromide elixir. Enough to tame a wild horse. I must get my mind off my body and onto other things. I must not worry anymore. I am praying tonight. After all prayer is quite a necessary thing. There are times when you simply can't help yourself. You can only hurt yourself. And that won't do.

*Tuesday, 24 November 1936*

Nov. 24. I have just risen after a sound sleep. I was afraid of the morning but now I find that the morning is as usual my friend and confederate against the forces of dark morning – I salute you! May we always rise so bravely together after dark nights!

*Friday, 11 December 1936*

Dec. 11. It is 3 A.M. Mother just received a call from Barnes' saying Dad had had an accident.[110] Didn't say what kind. Frightened. Can't sleep. A terribly still soundless night. I have taken a sleeping tablet and will read Ibsen. Hadn't enough things happened to us already? Apparently not. One thing and then another and another — It is important that we should be very strong.

*Sunday, 27 December 1936*

Dec. 27 – Oh, Lord, what a night and what a morning. My head is splitting. The next time I get lonely and want a party I'll remember last night and be grateful for solitude. Possibly each individual at the party was – taken individually a fairly decent person – but put together they become absolute asses and make me despise them. I was miserable and acted it. In one of my anti-social conditions. It is a wonder anyone ever likes me at all. Maybe no one does. And yet I'm not a bad guy at heart – am I? I just can't get along with "people"!

111. *Candles to the Sun.*

112. Helen Longmire was a student at Washington University and a member of the College Poetry Society. According to William Jay Smith, he and Williams frequently gathered at her house in Webster Groves to listen to music or read poetry. In "Return to Dust" Williams recounted an evening at Helen Longmire's house:

> [U]pon this occasion some thing like a riot occured with one male member chasing one female member round and round a fifty-dollar "vahse" which resulted finally in that ornament's complete demolition. Following this incident the girls went on strike — it was spring, anyway, and our meetings disintegrated into weekly picnics around the Meramec or Wild Horse Creek. . . .

113. *Letters to an Artist: From Vincent van Gogh to Anton Ridder van Rappard, 1881–1885,* translated by Rela van Messel, with an introduction by Walter Pach (New York: Viking Press, 1936).

Williams would go on to attempt a play about van Gogh. In a letter to Willard Holland ([9 October 1937], Harriett Holland Brandt collection), Williams wrote:

> I am still planning to write the "Van Gogh" for which I have chosen the title "The Holy Family" suggested by an anecdote from his life. He took a prostitute to live with him who soon gave birth to an illeg. child by another man. V.G.'s friend, Gauguin, tried to persuade him to leave the woman but V.G. remained devoted to her. In disgust, as he left, the friend exclaimed, "Ah! The Holy Family — maniac, prostitute and bastard!" — Does that sound too profane? I think the real story of the relationship is rather beautiful and would make good dramatic material.

In a fragment of an untitled play with the characters van Gogh, Margaret the Prostitute, and Gauguin, Williams used the lines quoted in the letter above.

In Williams' play "Will Mr. Merriwether Return from Memphis?" written "during a mental breakdown [and] typed up the month I was 'put away' [in Barnes Hospital in 1969]," van Gogh's apparition says, "Even in my last few days in a mad-house, I went on with my painting, on, on, on, till something possessed me to hang myself from a tree" (act 1, scene 1).

```
Sc. 2)  A short while later, the same night.  Vincent's rooms.
He enters with Magda who stands just across the threshold and
looks slowly around her in a dazed manner)

-This is the place. - You like it?
-Yes.
-It's very plain.
-I like it.
-This is my room.  This is Paul's.
-Paul's?
-He is an artist.  My friend.  We share these rooms.
-Oh.  He is the man who paid for the drinks tonight?
-Yes.
-Perhaps he won't like finding me here when he comes.
-


-She's going to stay here with me.

-Ah!  Beautiful - sublime!  The Holy Family - maniac, prostitute,

and bastard!

-Get out!

-Goodbye.

-Oh!

-What is it?

-The pain is beginning.

-You mean - ?

-Yes.

-I'll go for a doctor.

-No, don't.  I can take care of myself. - I've done it before.

            Curtain.
```

Fragment of Williams' play about van Gogh and Gauguin

*Sunday, 3 January 1937*

Sun. Jan. 3 – What negligence! But I have been oh so busy and having such a good time (comparatively) that recording myself seemed superfluous. School begins again tomorrow. Too bad. My play[111] is practically done and I have almost complete assurance that it will be produced this season. Willard Holland has such a swell sense of the incongruous. At our last meeting we discussed the play's ending and both agreed there should be mingled sadness and exaltation. Willard suggested that we have the triumphant singing of the workers interspersed with the screams of a woman in childbirth.

I have made up with everyone I got mad at the day after Xmas. Helen Longmire's[112] delightful dinner and theater party and the wet streets and hum of tires and the dark and the singing and the rabbit darting across the road and the frankness of speech and fresh ~~rai~~ wet air. At the end there was a little pain but even the pain was tinged with melancholy sweetness.


*Sunday, 10 January 1937*

Sun. Jan. 10. I have been pursued by the little blue devil of defeat all week but It is such a bright morning and I feel so clean and well after my shower perhaps he will abandon the chase.

I'm planning to deliver my play now complete (?) to Mr. Holland. Will he approve – or is it all just a – one of those things!

I want to hurry and get dressed so I shall have the privelege of buying the morning paper – it is good to be out in the sun on such a morning.


*Tuesday, 12 January 1937*

Tuesday – Jan – 12 – A sadness is rooted in me. Not violent but rather deep to bitter. I would rather have a violent outburst & get it over with instead of this slow cankerous ache. I long for the time when I will be free from it again. It will have to go finally. I could not live always under this shadow. It would kill me.

I am very quiet tonight and superficially peaceful. I am reading the letters of Van Gogh the ~~moder~~ artist to his friend (Amice) Rappard.[113] I know I would have liked him. We would have understood each other. He went mad & killed himself. Why? His letters are so full of rich, confident life.

114. Williams would include a variation of this line in the stage setting of "This Property Is Condemned": "The sky is a great milky whiteness: crows occasionally make a sound of roughly torn cloth."

115. Williams refers obliquely to the condition of his sister, Rose. During the autumn of 1936 Rose's mental condition had continued to decline. In December she had been admitted to Barnes Hospital in St. Louis where she stayed for nine days under observation. In a desperate attempt to help Rose through a change of scene, her parents sent her to spend the 1936 Christmas holiday with her Aunt Ella in Knoxville. Returning home on 20 January, Rose had to spend the night in the Louisville train station because of floods. She arrived home highly agitated, as Edwina reported in a letter to her parents ([25 January 1937], HRC):

> I'm facing my biggest problem again. What to do with Rose! She returned through this awful flood and is lucky to be here. . . . As soon as she crossed the threshold, I saw she was all off and no wonder for she had sat up all night in the station at Louisville with refugees. She began to rave as soon as she got inside. Cornelius is nervous at best and since this trouble with his ear, he is worse, so he lost his temper, told her she was crazy and that he was going to put her in the State Asylum. He will do this, too, if I don't do something else with her. I can't take her back to those doctors — I can't see that either Dr. Alexander or Dr. Saterfield helped her any. . . . The last time she went to Dr. Alexander he told her that what was the matter with her was "that she needed to get married". She has been raving on the subject of "sex" ever since and I was ashamed for Dakin and Tom to hear her the other night. It made them so nervous that I feared for the "finals" that both of them are taking. They each have five hard ones they are taking this week.
>
> Dr. Saterfield sent Cornelius a bill for ninety dollars and Cornelius said she couldn't go back there. Neither Ella nor Isabel seems able to do any thing for her. They don't want to believe the truth. I think they could have saved her. I suppose it is a good thing that I have this D.A.R. work that I've had to do. It has made me think of something else. Living in the house with Cornelius is bad enough. With the two of them it is terrible and there is liable to be a fatal tragedy. Now, father, is there not a Church home somewhere that I could take Rose to? Will you enquire around among the clergy? Things can't go on like this. I'm sorry to trouble you but there is no one else to whom I can turn for advise.

116. Elisabeth Bergner (1900–86), a Vienna-born refugee actress, was married to the film's director, Paul Czinner. She played the role of Rosalind and Olivier played Orlando.

At the time of this journal entry, Laurence Olivier (1907–89) had not gained his status as one of the great actors of the twentieth century and had achieved only limited success on stage and screen. Twelve years later he would direct his wife, Vivien Leigh, in the role of Blanche in the 1949 London production of *A Streetcar Named Desire*. Olivier played Big Daddy in the NBC-TV production of *Cat on a Hot Tin Roof* (6 December 1976).

117. *Winterset* was the film adaptation of Maxwell Anderson's play which won the New York Drama Critics' Circle Award for 1935. Told for the most part in verse, this tragedy set on the Lower East Side of Manhattan is the story of a young man out to restore the reputation of his father, who was executed for a crime he did not commit. The young man, Mio, falls in love with Miriamne, whose brother Garth could have proved the innocence of Mio's father but has withheld his testimony to save himself from being killed by the real murderer, the gangster Trock. The play ends with Miriamne having to choose between saving the life of Garth or Mio. She assists Garth in concealing a second murder by Trock, thereby allowing Trock to go unpunished, leaving Mio, who witnessed the murder, in danger. Mio is killed, and Miriamne, who loves Mio, dies with him.

Williams would have taken notice of Anderson's attempt to "make tragic poetry out of the stuff of [our] own times." The plot of *Winterset* has echoes in Williams' play *Battle of Angels*, where Myra tries to vindicate her father, falls in love, and is killed with her lover.

At the time of this journal entry, Burgess Meredith (1907–97), who played Mio, was enjoying the beginning of a long and successful career on stage, screen, and television. In the preface to his play *Stairs to the Roof*, Williams noted that the part of Benjamin D. Murphy was "created with Burgess Meredith in mind."

*The bare branches of the tree were full of black birds making sounds like the ripping of coarse cloth* [114]

*Wednesday, 13 January 1937*

Wed. Jan. 13 – Disgust! Drank coffee to write. Got the jitters so bad had to stop. Took a sleeping pill and then a mebral. Felt like I was blowing up. Read over plays. All seemed utter trash – why the hell do I take myself so seriously? Apparently I never had very much and show little if any improvement – madness this life is! Now more or less quiet inside. Will go out to the Varsity – see a good show may help my spirits. What's the good of facing the future? There is only tonight. There is always only tonight. That's right. Get lyrical about it, you damned fool.

After this perhaps I'll be more rational and end my obsessions. It is time I cultivated something like common sense. The world seems such a mad house tonight. It is not credible that such things could be.

*Monday, 25 January 1937*

Monday Jan. 25

Tragedy. I write that word knowing the full meaning of it. We have had no deaths in our family but slowly by degrees something was happening much uglier and more terrible than death.[115] Now we are forced to see it, know it. The thought is an aching numbness – a horror!

I am having final exams but can't study. Her presence in the house is a —
Now I must stop and study Greek. Oh, yes, Greek is so <u>important</u> just now.

*Saturday, 30 January 1937*

Sat. Jan. 30th – Though it is still mid-winter I feel this morning a presentiment of spring. Maybe because I saw a lovely blue jay perched in the fork of the elm right outside my window, trying to keep dry from the slow, soft spring-like rain.

Last night I saw two lovely pictures, Elisabeth Bergner in "As You Like It" with Laurence Olivier[116] and Maxwell Anderson's "Winterset" with Burgess Meredith, an exquisitely fine actor.[117] I have never been strongly impressed by Anderson's poetry but this cinema was certainly full of poetry. Magnificent poetry. There were some shots of Brooklyn Bridge that were fairly breath-taking. I can well understand Hart Crane's inspiration by this thing – probably the most exciting piece of architecture in America.

118.  Willard Holland played the character Birmingham Red in *Candles to the Sun*.

119.  The magazine *Forum and Century* (1891–1940) published articles on a variety of political and social issues, including women, war, money, and government, as well as short stories, poems, and other literary works. Clark Mills' "Proem" appeared in the February 1937 issue.

PROEM

In our time some deaths came
      sudden as clap of thunder
            across leaf-troubled night;
some histories, like flame
      from cloud, that we go under
            and use for source of light.

At bolt of death: at crash:
      their lives' way opens out
            vivid as midnight path
below green lightning flash
      — their fear and early doubt
            fading in aftermath.

Their lives cross ours among
      suburban pavements, trees;
            walking, we are aware
— past fluid phrase of tongue —
      of their deaths.  Mind's eye sees
            as clearly as through air

Lawrence, broken on wall;
      de Bosis, "lost at sea";
            those at Vienna, killed.
Even while these men fall
      they give off light; are free
            though coffined; loud though stilled.

120.  James Agee (1909–55), a novelist and film critic, is best known for *Let Us Now Praise Famous Men* (1941), a book on Alabama sharecroppers with photographs by Walker Evans. His second novel, *A Death in the Family*, was published posthumously in 1957 and won the Pulitzer Prize. The February 1937 issue of *Forum and Century* included his poems "Rapid Transit" and "Sun Our Father."

RAPID TRANSIT

Squealing under city stone
      The millions on the millions run,
Every one a life alone,
      Every one a soul undone:

There all the poisons of the heart
      Branch and abound like whirling brooks
And there through every useless art
      Like spoiled meats on a butcher's hooks

Pour forth upon their frightful kind
      The faces of each ruined child:
The wrecked demeanors of the mind
      That now is tamed, and once was wild.

SUN OUR FATHER

Sun our father while I slept
      You lifted like a field of corn
The smiling and the peaceful strength
      Of those that are the race new born.

The infant future waked in you
      Once more and at the world's rich breast
Drank the day's courage and lay down
      In fearless and refreshing rest.

And while the russian field you raised
      Dreams in the starflung shadow's keep
You wake these backward lands to work:
      Good work to do before we sleep.

Was with Holland all afternoon making some changes he wanted in my play. He is a <u>master</u>. Could get work out of an oyster. The play goes on Feb. 29, too soon I'm afraid. It shows promise of power but of course it may fall completely flat. I'm glad that Holland plans to play "Red"[118] – that's a break – Tonight I am going to the Phi Mu formal on the Congress tower. Anything in a tower ought to be interesting. Clark Mills' <u>Proem</u> came out in Forum[119] and I thought it exceptionally fine. The usual effect of restrained careful power. Some lovely things by James Agee in the same bunch.[120]

Washington University, St. Louis

*Red and Star*                                                          46

face against her breast)

Star:  (pushing him away)  Now <u>you're</u> going a little too fast.

Red:  Am I?  I thought you liked plenty of speed!

Star:  Well, I always slow down on the curves.  Go back over and sit in the chair.  (he doesn't move)  If you cain't act like a gentleman you'd better not stay.  (archly)  I like to CONVERSE with my gentleman visitors.  Let's see now, what was we talking about? Oh, yes.  You was telling me about your past life...

Red:  My past life?

Star:  Yeah, there's a lot of things about you I'd like to know. F'r instance what do they call you Red for?  Your hair ain't red.

Red:  No, but they say my neck is.

Star:  Red neck?  I know what that means.  That means a bolshevik!

Red:  XXXXXXXXX.  That's what they call any guy who's interested in saving somebody's skin beside his own.  I try to get the workers decent living conditions, try to keep 'em from being exploited by the operators for all they're worth - and they call me a Bolshevik!

Excerpt of a draft of *Candles to the Sun*

121.  Florence Biddle Ver Steeg (d. 1937) was a portrait painter and a friend of Rose Williams. Williams' character Vee Talbott, who paints a portrait of Christ in *Battle of Angels* and *Orpheus Descending*, may have been modeled on her. Williams' mother, in a letter to her parents dated 26 May 1937 (HRC), wrote: "Tom's lovely poem to Mrs. Ver Steeg was read at the memorial I conducted for the three members of our chapter [DAR] who have died this past year."

ELEGY FOR AN ARTIST
(For Florence Biddle Ver Steeg)

We keep you in all small and lovely things,
The scent of tea, the lilt of foreign strings,
A Chinese tapestry, a fragile cup —
These little things will never give you up!
But more than these, the flowers know you still,
Their momentary brilliance on some hill
Or vanished garden caught in constant spring
By your quick hand and eye. The dahlias cling
To your bright image. They'll not let you go
Though years inundate years in gradual snow!
These you have captured — these have captured you,
And kept you with us. The courageous blue,
The gallant Chinese red, the gracious gold —
These things will keep you, faithfully will hold
Your vagrant spirit. They will always bring
You back to us like lost, remembered spring!

In a fragment of an early draft of the short story "The Vine," Williams named a character Florence Biddle. He renamed her Florence Kerwin in the published version. A minor character in the play "Will Mr. Merriwether Return from Memphis?" is named Mrs. Biddle, and an off-stage character in a fragment of a late untitled play is named Baroness von Verstig.

122.  United Daughters of the Confederacy. In the play "Something Unspoken," Miss Cornelia Scott waits at home, anxious to learn whether she has been named Regent of her chapter of the Confederate Daughters in Meridian, Mississippi.

Painting of Rose Williams by Florence Ver Steeg

*Monday, 15 February 1937*

Mon. Feb. 15 – (1:30 A.M.) Just had a horrible surrealistic dream about the fear of death and taking pills to prevent it. Felt the need of a warm friendly light & someone to talk to. Probably too much delicious Sunday supper at Mrs. Ver Steeg's.[121] It was a swell evening. I won a picture by her in a shooting game.

In the afternoon was at Holland's for play rehearsal. Went nicely and I felt encouraged.

Date is now March 18 – better – I like the people playing in it. They seem to like me.

Last night went to U.D.C.[122] ball at Jefferson. Have seen stage (Little Theater) production of Winterset. Disappointing. Too much talk – It lacked the cinema's haunting atmospheric beauty.

So sleepy can hardly keep my eyes open. Guess I'd better submit myself again to the arms of Morpheus.

Set design by Jo Mielziner for the New York production of *Winterset* (1935)

123.    "The New Poet" appeared in the April 1937 issue of *American Prefaces*.

THE NEW POET

> I think of you as of rebellion's self,
> The flame-hoofed stallion that describes his ire
> In preternatural arcs of astral fire.
> I think of you as one who flings his wealth
> In riot down the cascades of the sky —
> I hear loud music as your pinions float
> Above the earthbound, note on deathless note
> Of one who dared to answer back the lie!
>
> No thing that creeps upon the earth by stealth
> Can bear the glitter of your stormy wing,
> The air is filled with bells that sudden ring
> And treble choirs transcendent anthems sing —
> There is no place to hide, no hole to shade
> The dungeon-creature from your fiery blade!

124.    In "The Treadmill" a married man, Anthony, is unjustly accused of having affairs by his neurotic wife. On his way home from work, he sees in a store window a "small furry grey animal" running round and round in a cylindrical cage. He identifies with the animal, and one day he is sickened to see that it is no longer in the cage and presumably has died. Ten years later, Williams expanded the story into "A System of Wheels." The image of the treadmill also appears in the later play "The Municipal Abattoir."

125.    *Candles to the Sun.*

126.    Williams played the part of the old father in a production of *Les Fourberies de Scapin* by Molière, organized by Mrs. Harcourt Brown, wife of the head of the French department at Washington University. In fact, the play was performed on Wednesday, 7 April. William Jay Smith related in his memoirs, *Army Brat* (New York: Persea, 1980), that Williams

> read his French lines with a kind of hound-dog ferocity and deliberation, as if he were chewing on a large section of the Mississippi delta. When he moved woodenly across the stage with absolute seriousness pounding the floor with his cane, small and square in his satin suit, an enormous blond wig flopping about on his shoulders, he gave a performance that a more sophisticated audience would have taken as deliberate high camp. (p. 193)

127.    *Mood Indigo* by Duke Ellington.

128.    In February Edwina wrote to her parents:

> I have Rose in the hospital again for observation and under a new psychiatrist suggested by Dr. Bunting to whom I took her this after-noon after she refused "to stay at home another night" and had packed her grip to go to the "Y." I'm quite worn out with it all. Dr. Bunting thinks she needs to go to a sanitarium and I went out and looked at it to-day. It is fifty dollars a week and I don't believe any better than the State one would be, so I don't know what to do. A pity the Church hasn't a place for girls like Rose. (Leverich, p. 201)

*Tuesday, 23 February 1937*

<u>Feb. 23</u> – Days pass quietly, pleasantly and with disturbing celerity. Sonnet accepted by <u>American Prefaces</u>,[123] story rejected with criticism "fairly undistinguished treatment of a common thing" – "The Treadmill"[124] – somewhat discouraging as I had liked the story. My new play[125] goes badly. I feel not especially bright these days – but peace is nothing to be valued lightly – I have accepted – of all things – a part in a French play – April 6 – Heaven knows how that will turn out![126] Still it is amusing. Hazel in town Monday and I spent the evening with her – Strange how completely dead all of that is now. Barely a flicker of interest. Just a friendly feeling. It could be revived however pretty easily as I still see in her all the old qualities that I once adored. ~~Tout change~~.

How things slip by – !! so quietly, so imperceptibly – Someday we will wake up and find that everything has gone. Youth like a bright distant dream – nearly forgotten.

It is nearly a year since I started this journal – such a strange, rapid year. The next? The pages are still unwritten. Their blankness is an exciting and rather intimidating challenge –

*Wednesday, 24 February 1937*

Feb. 24 – Downstairs the radio is playing "Mood Indigo".[127] That's just about how I feel – pretty low – tired of myself – nervous and sad – not for any particular reason and not to any crucial extent – so I should give myself a good kick in the pants and quit slobbering! Went over to gym to swim and watch a wrestling match. Not much energy for swimming. Dad leaving for week's trip tonight. Maybe the car will be available for party some evening. That's what I need. That and to write something worth while! Rose talks wildly again ~~just now~~.[128] I guess there'll be no end to that. It comes slowly. That's the way with most awful things. Perhaps a great mercy. We couldn't stand them all at once.

The Treadmill

Going to work one December morning Anthony noticed a black wire cage in the window of a cigar store. The cage contained a smaller cage of cylindrical shape in which was imprisoned a small furry grey animal of a species which Anthony could not exactly identify. Curiosity was his first response. He wondered mildly what kind of animal it was. Chipmonk, woodchuck, opossum were names without distinct connotation to Anthony's urban mind. Then he wondered also what purpose the creature served. There was no placard or label

129. Williams' interview with the *St. Louis Star-Times* is reported in "Mummers to Present Play by Washington U. Student" (9 March 1937). About *Candles to the Sun* he said:

> The candles in the play represent the individual lives of the people. The sun represents group consciousness. The play ends as a tragedy for the individuals, for in the end they realize they cannot achieve success and happiness apart from the group, but must sacrifice for the common good.

130. "Five for Jules Romains" was published in the March 1937 issue of *Poetry* and consisted of the poems "Proem," "Portrait," "Fragment," "The Hounds in Autumn," and "Crossing: Webster Groves."

131. Williams' poems "This Hour" and "My Love Was Light" had been accepted the previous March. Although he was warned he would have to wait a year, the poems were not published until the June 1937 issue.

132. Virginia Moore (1903–93) was a poet and writer whose poetry collections include *Not Poppy* (1926), *Sweet Water and Bitter* (1928), and *Homer's Golden Chain* (1936). She was married for a brief time in the 1920s to the poet and anthologist Louis Untermeyer. According to William Jay Smith:

> She was a strikingly beautiful woman, but, along with her beauty, we admired her connection with the literary world. She had met all the important people and was a breath of fresh air, from the great outer world. Mrs. Williams thought her impressive, and found reassurance in her approval of Tom's work. (*DLB*, p. 27)

The Moores lived across the street from the Williams family on Pershing Avenue.

133. This is the first time that Williams refers to Rose by her initial. When thoughts of her condition were particularly painful, Williams would often refer to her as "R."

134. Cornelius Williams.

135. Presumably Wayne Arnold (d. 1996), a student at Washington University. Although Arnold and Williams were both enrolled in Professor William Carson's playwriting course, it is plausible Williams may not have become acquainted with Arnold. According to another student of Carson's, A. E. Hotchner (who was a friend and biographer of Ernest Hemingway), Williams did not often come to class. It was Arnold's play that would win first prize in the 1937 school contest to which Williams submitted "Me, Vashya!" For almost thirty years Arnold taught speech, drama, and English at a St. Louis high school.

*St. Louis Star-Times*, 9 March 1937

*Tuesday, 2 March 1937*

March 2 – Tuesday – Nearly a year since I started this Journal. One of the strangest years in all my strange life – A feeling of intellectual impotence hangs over me and darkens my spirits. Physically I am marvelously well. I shall have to conquer the other. I can and I shall. Busy day, went to Holland – then to Star to be interviewed.[129] Very stupid. I felt like a fool talking so much about myself. Mills poems came out in "Poetry" – "Five for Jules Romains"[130] – Disgraceful the way they delay mine.[131] But I don't much care. I feel a great indifference toward all things tonight. Virginia Moore[132] will visit the Poetry Club friday night. A charming person.

*Wednesday, 3 March 1937*

March 3 – Wed. – The same only more so. A headache – Must not go on like this. After all one's sanity is worth something. R.[133] makes the house tragic, haunted. Must be put away I suppose. An incredible horror to face. "No one is to blame" mother admitted. How true! But why do such things happen? There is no answer. Lovely weather.

*Thursday, 4 March 1937*

March 4 – Buds all over the elm outside my window. An early spring. Practically no winter at all. Never known a year to pass like this, especially the last 6 months which have simply gone swimming by. I write like a garrulous old woman, about the weather and passage of time. Yes, I am very stupid. Ça Va sans dire. R. seems about normal tonite possibly because D.[134] is home. Even she has sense enough to keep fairly quiet around him – sometimes. A long tiring day. Head aching from cold. Now stinging with Vick's vaporub. Tonite I think of the future and wonder. My wonder is not altogether unmixed with apprehension. Only two or three short months – and then? But there have always been big question marks in my life. I should be getting used to them. W.A.[135] is coming to Poetry Club. Will like to meet him and record impressions later. Always a thrill to meet new people.

136.  About *Candles to the Sun*, which opened on 18 March, Colvin McPherson, the drama critic of the *St. Louis Post-Dispatch*, wrote in "Mummers Present Play by St. Louisan" (19 March 1937):

> Williams, 25-year-old Washington University senior, is revealed not only as a writer of unusual promise but one of considerable technical skill right now. . . . [H]is writing is rarely unsteady and his play has an emotional unity and robustness.

137.  Rose would remain in institutions for the rest of her life. Williams wrote two poems, "Valediction" and "Elegy for Rose," about her leaving home. They anticipate the scene in *A Streetcar Named Desire* when Blanche is led off to an institution.

| VALEDICTION | ELEGY FOR ROSE |
|---|---|
| She went with morning on her lips<br>down an inscrutable dark way<br>and we who witnessed her eclipse<br>have found no word to say. | She is a metal forged by love<br>too volatile, too fiery thin<br>so that her substance will be lost<br>as sudden lightning or as wind |
| I think our speechlessness is not<br>a thing she would approve,<br>she who was always light of wit<br>and quick to speak and move — | And yet the ghost of her remain<br>reflected with the metal gone,<br>a shadow as of shifting leaves<br>at moonrise or at early dawn |
| I think that she would say goodbye<br>can be no less a lyric word<br>than any song, than any cry<br>of greeting we have heard! | A kind of rapture never quite<br>possessed again, however long<br>the heart lays siege upon a ghost<br>recaptured in a web of song. |

138.  Presumably Williams had an engagement with someone at the Webster Groves Theatre Guild and had only written Groves in his diary and was confused.

139.  Marie Louise Lange.

140.  Rose was never sent to a sanatorium in Asheville, North Carolina. Instead, she was moved from the psychopathic ward at Missouri Baptist to St. Vincent's, a Catholic convalescent home in St. Louis. The Reverend Walter Dakin had written to Highland Hospital in Asheville about the possibility of Rose being admitted but had also expressed concern over expenses. A response from a doctor in the psychiatry department revealed that the hospital had only a four-month program for patients who had had nervous breakdowns.

In April, Williams wrote a poem about Rose entitled "Diver," which was published in the May 1937 issue of *The Eliot*.

DIVER

| Deep in distant waters,<br>menacing with frost,<br>I see your fluent image<br>glittering and lost . . . | Your circles are too silver,<br>too sudden and too fleet<br>for one who has a shadow<br>straggling at his feet . . . |
|---|---|
| Webbed with constellations<br>in a crystal well,<br>I see you move to music<br>fragile as a bell! | So must I be contented,<br>loveliest of girls,<br>to see you caught in jewels,<br>lost in many pearls! |

141.  In 1738 John and Mary Williams emigrated to America from Wales. Their grandson, Colonel Joseph Williams, Williams' great-great-great-grandfather, settled in Surrey County in western North Carolina. Some of John and Mary's children moved west and settled in Tennessee.

*Saturday, 27 March 1937*

March ~~28~~ 27! Twenty-four days passed since last entry. Feel very low tonite. Nervous lately and not well. Though I ought to be feeling good, the play such a success and the future so much brighter potentially than it seemed before. I'm certainly a damned pessimist or a nervous wreck or something. Colvin McPherson called and wants me to call him, I was out. That's interesting. I liked him when I met him at play and he gave me a swell review.[136] I feel as though I'll never do another thing tonight. So tired and weak.

    R. in psychopathic ward at Missouri-Baptist.[137] I belong in one myself. Tomorrow see Florence and Holland. Life will go on I suppose.

    I've gone through plenty in my time. I guess I ought to have a little smooth sailing for a change. How about it, kid?

*Sunday, 28 March 1937*

March 28 (Easter) Woke up feeling very wretched. Hot, gassy feeling inside and neurasthenic weakness. Not in a fighting humour but I shall certainly have to put up a fight if I'm going to pull myself together today. It is a cool, cloudy Easter. No church. Too tired to get up for it. I wish that I had. What will happen this week? Something to improve my condition, I hope.

*Sunday, 4 April 1937*

Sun. April 4 – Many times I've felt as though I'd reached the dead-end of misery. Each time I hadn't really. I suppose this is just another mile-post like the others.

    Very weak and tired this morning – Got drunk twice last week. Yes, I'm a social success but I don't like it especially – It means and matters so little. Love is the thing and that I haven't got. No wonder I find life tiresome now.

    Clark called last night and asked me to go to the show with him but I was too tired. Holland called also. Wants me to come over this afternoon but I doubt that I shall. Anyway I have an engagement with Groves – whoever that is – for 7:30.[138]

    I have done nothing for weeks. When will this miasma end? It must eventually! Why not now? Because I'm too tired to put up a fight.

    Wed. the French Play. How can I get through it – je ne sais pas!

    Was unkind last week to M.L.L.[139] and hate myself for it.

    This morning I had a fitful sleep with those weird neurasthenic dreams that reflect and magnify so cruelly the favorite fears of the mind. R. will probably go to Sanitorium in Asheville, N.C.[140] The Williams family originated in N.C.[141] So now the triumphal return!

142.    William Jay Smith (1918– ) was Consultant in Poetry to the Library of Congress (a position now called Poet Laureate) from 1968 to 1970. Professor emeritus of Hollins College in Virginia and a member of the American Academy of Arts and Letters since 1975, he has published more than fifty books of poetry, literary criticism, children's verse, and translations. His most recent collection is *The World Below the Window: Poems 1937–1997* (1998). In his memoirs, *Army Brat* (1980), Smith wrote of his close friendship with Williams at Washington University in St. Louis in the 1930s.

143.    George Marsh was a professor in the department of Spanish at Washington University and a friend of Clark Mills'.

144.    The Webster Groves Play Contest was the annual competition sponsored by the amateur theatre group which Williams had won with "The Magic Tower" the year before.

145.    No manuscript titled "Death of Pierrot" is known to exist. A fragment of an untitled play about Pierrot and Pierrette, however, exists and is the story of the clown Pierrot who fakes his death by falling from a high wire to determine if Pierrette loves him. Given Williams' familiarity with Ernest Dowson, Williams very likely was inspired by Dowson's dramatic fantasy *The Pierrot of the Minute* to write a play on the subject.

146.    This incident appears to be a milder form of the attack Williams suffered in the spring of 1935 on his way home from the movies. He would have been feeling particularly fragile at this time. Rose was confined in St. Vincent's sanatorium and would soon be diagnosed as having dementia praecox. Five days earlier Williams had been placed on academic probation due to poor grades.

147.    In "Escape," a one-act play, Donald Fenway, a boy "of about seventeen," is depressed by his inability to be accepted by his peers and is upset by his parents' recent separation. His and his mother's stay at a lakeside summer resort is cut short because of his parents' financial situation. Instead of returning to the home he hates in the city where he is unable to fit in, he goes swimming in the lake he loves so much and does not return, presumably having committed suicide. Alternative titles for "Escape" were "Quicksilver," "The Lake," and "Summer at the Lake."

 "Escape" is notable as one of Williams' first works to touch on the subject of homosexuality. Donald Fenway's mother says to him, "No wonder you don't make friends. People think you're queer when you look at them like that."

 Suicide was a romantic notion for Williams. Four of his favorite artists, namely Sara Teasdale, Vachel Lindsay, Hart Crane, and Vincent van Gogh, committed suicide. Williams was familiar with suicide as early as 1920, aged nine. He wrote his sister a short comic paper and drew a woman, "WIDO R.L. Williams" who "has her tenth husband. all The Rest commided suicid becauce she was so strict." He next took up the subject of suicide in 1928 in his short story "The Vengeance of Nitocris," in which Queen Nitocris burns herself to death.

 Throughout his life, Williams continued writing about suicide, with the last known example being his screenplay *The Loss of a Teardrop Diamond* (1980), in which Aunt Adie overdoses on opium. Over a fifty-year span, Williams would write about suicide or attempted suicide in more than twenty works. The methods of suicide chosen for his characters include burning to death ("Auto-Da-Fé"), running in front of a train ("Dragon Country" and "April is the Cruellest Month"), jumping off a building (*Stairs to the Roof*), slitting wrists ("His Father's House"), smoking opium ("The Poppy Paradise"), overdosing on pills ("The Long Goodbye"), drinking Lysol ("Suitable Entrances to Springfield or Heaven" and "The Day on Which a Man Dies"), poisoning by gas (*The Roman Spring of Mrs. Stone*), shooting oneself with a revolver ("Every Twenty Minutes" and *The Two-Character Play*), drowning in a river ("The Malediction" and "The Negative"), drowning in the ocean ("The Poet"), starving ("The Purification"), and hanging ("Will Mr. Merriwether Return from Memphis?").

148.    "April is the Cruellest Month," later revised as *Spring Storm*, is a three-act play about "the unconscious savage cruelty of the sexual struggle in youth." Helen Critchfield is in love with Richard Miles, a restless young man who is considered less than respectable by the community. Arthur Shannon, a wealthy young man educated in England, is in love with Helen, but she is not interested in him, despite her mother's desire for the two to marry. Hertha Neilson, a librarian from a simple background, is in love with Arthur, and

*Sunday, 18 April 1937*

Sun. April 18 – Just finished vomiting for about 5th time. Sick as a dog from last night's French play dinner, Etc. – Also sick of that crowd – Smith[142] and Marsh[143] are nice but the others are silly.

*Tuesday, 20 April 1937*

Tues. April 20. – What a hang-over that was! Okay Sunday night. Went over to Clark's and spent pleasant evening with him and Marsh so I must retract that unkind remark about my intellectual friends. I am never quite sure of what I think of anyone.

It looks like I got eliminated from the Webster Groves Play Contest.[144] Tonight they make the announcements and I haven't heard a word about it. Feel quite sore and depressed about it. I thought the play I submitted was pretty good – "Death of Pierrot",[145] a fantasy – was I as badly mistaken as this would seem to indicate? The thought is disturbing. I would like (almost) to put a stick of dynamite under their damned old play tonight. Yes, I'm still very touchy about such things. They hit me where it hurts most. Well, if there's been any dirty work I'll get back at the sons of bitches some way! With this tender little sentiment I may as well close – and procede to study for my Poli-Sci quiz tomorrow morning. On the whole a very delightful evening – eh, what?

*Sunday, 25 April 1937*

Sun. April 25 – Feel ill, exhausted. Thursday went down town and had nervous crisis after leaving theater[146] – Terribly shaken. Went to library till I regained some poise. Very weak and nervous since then. Last night sleeping pill again. This morning re-wrote first part of "Escape".[147] It pleases me somewhat better. The boy in it is <u>me</u>. More than any other character I've ever created except of course that he was capable of violent action and I am not – and of course at the bottom of my heart I really love <u>life</u> very dearly.

I have an engagement to see Holland at his study 2:30. Hope I'll feel better. He said he was feeling badly too so we can condole each other – I'm delivering ms. of my long play "April Is the Cruellest Month"[148] but feel very uncertain about it. Think I shall pull myself up by my bootstraps now and be strong again. It is necessary, you know.

the two of them, both lonely, enjoy a platonic relationship. When Richard Miles leaves Helen, she becomes interested in Arthur, who in turn rejects Hertha. Hertha commits suicide by throwing herself under a train.

149.   Williams' mother, Edwina.

150.   Roger Moore was the brother of the poet Virginia Moore. He was enormously talented, having won a Rhodes Scholarship and having gained a Ph.D. in political science at Yale. He ran for mayor of University City and lost. After his political defeat he was committed to St. Vincent's sanatorium.

151.   English 16 was a course on playwriting taught by William Carson. During the semester, students were required to write one-act plays. At the end of term, the plays were entered in a contest, the best play received an award of twenty-five dollars, and the best three were staged.

152.   In the film *Maytime* (1937) an opera star falls in love with a poor singer. Her impresario becomes jealous of their relationship and shoots the singer.

153.   Either "April is the Cruellest Month" or *Fugitive Kind*. A month earlier, Williams had delivered a copy of "April is the Cruellest Month" to Holland but wrote him that the play needed substantial work. Williams had just begun to work on *Fugitive Kind*.

Scene from the performance of *Les Fourberies de Scapin* (Williams is fourth from right)

*Wednesday, 28 April 1937*

Wed. April 28 – Just rising with difficulty to face another day – Felt horrible lately – Like I was about to blow up. Last nite sleeping pill at 8:00 P.M. to calm myself. After all if one is in good health there is little else to worry about.

*Monday, 17 May 1937*

Monday May 17 – Rising tide of neurasthenia all week – seems relieved tonight. Thank God. Very tired. Seems difficult to go on – and with exams coming – what hope? I've got to be a little easier on myself. Hope to have a good time for a change this week-end. So – <u>so</u> tired – good night. – How full of bitterness this little book is – and yet I still love life and have courage to go on facing it.

*Friday, 21 May 1937*

Friday – Yesterday the first relief. Today better but M.[149] driving me wild with nagging.
 Invited to dance. Had almost decided not to go – raining. Started to read. Then opened window and saw moon was coming out. So maybe I shall dance tonight after all – I'm a very odd person.

*Thursday, 27 May 1937*

Thursday – (Went. And had a delightful time).
 Roger Moore killed himself yesterday morning.[150] Jumped in front of a truck near sanatorium. Ghastly! I doubt that I shall ever do that. Having no self respect one doesn't have the pain of losing it. I am so used to being a worm that the condition seldom troubles me. Now I face the problem of the summer – what will I do? Heaven knows. Two exams today, Philosophy and Amer. Govt. – both easy – I may have passed. Genl. Lit. tomorrow Greek Monday. Play announcements[151] – when? Horrible if I were eliminated! Varsity tonite – Saw <u>Maytime</u>[152] – Hope to have another party this week-end with Clark, Etc. as I need relaxation badly. Feel swell – physically & nerves not so bad. Au revoir.

*Saturday, 29 May 1937*

Sat. May – 29 – Woke with the jitters – Will try to write on my play[153] – oppresively hot – yellow sunlight – problem of summer unsolved – My grades will be bad yes. I'm getting to be an awful ass –

154.  Blandford Jennings (1897–1980), a Webster Groves high-school teacher and drinking buddy of Clark
Mills', was married to Anne Jennings. In a letter to Wilbur Schramm, the editor of *American Prefaces*,
Williams wrote: "Mr. Blandford Jennings, English and Dramatics teacher at a local high school . . . told
me he thought I would be greatly benefited by study in Prof. Mabie's department at your University"
(unmailed letter dated 22 August 1937, UVA).

155.  The Williamses were members of Westborough Country Club. The two more exclusive country clubs were
Bellerive and the St. Louis Country Club. In a fragment of a poem titled "Belle Reve" Williams would use
the name of the more socially prestigious country club for the name of a plantation.

> We lived on Belle Reve plantation, eight miles from the town
> of Columbus, Mississippi.
> The slow Tombigbee divided our world from the world, and that
> would have been all right except for bridges.
>
> There were two bridges, one for trains to go over, and one for
> people and wagons and automobiles.
>
> One time our father, a traveling man, came home with a shiny
> new automobile and from that time our mother went traveling
> with him. We stayed on the plantation with Grandmother.
>
> My grandmother's name was Rosina Maria Francesca.
> My sister was Rose.

Williams also used the name Belle Reve for the plantation in the early play "The Spinning Song or The
Paper Lantern" and for the plantation lost by the DuBois family in the related *A Streetcar Named Desire*.

156.  "Me, Vashya!" is a one-act play about a wealthy munitions manufacturer of humble birth, Sir Vashya
Shontine, who marries a princess. Williams described a version of this play as being suggested by the career
of Sir Basil Zaharoff (1850–1936), who was married to a Spanish *duquesa*. When the princess becomes
infatuated with a young poet, Sir Vashya Shontine has the poet sent to the front line, where he is killed.
The princess becomes disturbed and begins to see men such as the poet at the foot of her bed and urges her
husband to go with them to the front line. She shoots her husband. Dying at her feet, he begs his princess
to remember him and pleads with her that he will be good to her. Other versions of this play are titled "The
Tears of Christ," "I, Vaslev," and "Death is the Drummer." "Me, Vashya!" was condensed by Willard
Holland as a radio play, "Men Who March."
     Williams was severely disappointed not to have "Me, Vashya!" included among the top three plays. In
an interview in the *New York Post* (28 April 1958), Williams would remember:
>      It was a terrible shock and humiliation to me. It was a crushing blow to me. I had always thought
>      I was shy, but I discarded all humility. I stormed into Carson's office. (He was a good professor.) I
>      screamed at him. I forgot what my parting shot was, but I remember it was quite a shot. I surprised
>      myself.
About the contest Carson wrote: "When the judges were considering the [top three] plays for production,
I assumed that *Me, Vashya* would be one of them." It was not chosen, however, "partly because the judges
feared it would be impossible to cast Lady Vashya adequately." Carson continued:
>      Williams was deeply offended, and refused to come to the Chapel to accept his Honorable
>      Mention. . . .
>           . . . While I perceived that [Williams] had much more than the usual ability, I did not foresee to
>      what heights he would rise. The trouble was that he chose a subject completely foreign to his gifts,
>      except that Lady Vashya is perhaps the first of his slightly deranged heroines.

*Sunday, 30 May 1937*

Sunday – Last night went out with Clark Mills and B.J.¹⁵⁴ – to Black Forest beer garden – met two other teachers – very dull – at least I was – in one of my horribly taciturn humors from drinking beer – must remember never to drink beer again when I want to have a good time. Clark saw a man tapping rhythm on ~~glasses~~ beer steins and remarked, "That is the same thing that we do with our poetry, only a more elemental form." He says some very clever things at times. I felt like an awful bore – positively tongue-tied. Blue devils all this morning – I'm going to live this thing down – not dodge it but charge straight through it. I know that I can beat it all right.

Tomorrow Greek final which I will undoubtedly flunk. Yesterday afternoon Roger Moore's funeral. Virginia made a speech and read one of her poems. Very beautiful and touching. She wears sorrow very becomingly.

Later Felt horrible this evening after return from swimming at Westborough.¹⁵⁵ That trapped feeling. But now calm – Greek final tomorrow afternoon but no studying done. Can hardly blame myself, my nerves are in such rotten shape. Au Revoir. So sleepy can hardly hold my eyes open.

*Monday, 31 May 1937*

Monday. Never woke in more misery in all my life. Intolerable. The brilliant earth mocks my fear. Children and birds sing. People speak in casual voices. The poplar leaves shine. Yet I up here in this narrow room endure torture God help me! Please! I've got to have help or I'll go mad. What is this a punishment for? What? Or is it all blind, blind without meaning!

*Friday, 4 June 1937*

Friday – June 4 – Never a more ignominious failure! My play for English 16 rejected for presentation – given fourth place – Went to Carson's office this morning and he gave me the news¹⁵⁶ – without any apparent compunction – But why should I expect sympathy from anyone – especially a Washington University Professor – the stronghold of the Reactionaries! Still it does hurt to get a direct kick in the face like that and if there is any guts left in me I'll make up for it some way. It looks like I'm on the way down – hitting the tobaggon – but maybe not – –

157. *Fugitive Kind* is set in a flophouse in a large Midwestern city during the Christmas holidays. The owner, Mr. Gwendlebaum, has two children: Glory, his adopted daughter, who falls in love with a bank robber, and Leo, his biological son, an idealistic college student who is expelled from college and leaves home only to return.

158. Buzz Bland was the younger brother of a good friend of Hazel Kramer's, Isabel Bland. Ivy Jennings was another close friend. In *Battle of Angels* Williams named two minor characters Dolly and Pee Wee Bland.

159. The Municipal ("Muny") Opera, located in Forest Park, was in the 1930s the largest outdoor theatre in the United States.

160. The Bell Trail, a hiking trail named after Nicholas M. Bell, a state legislator, ran diagonally across Forest Park and passed near the Muny Opera.

161. Jim Connor (d. 1978) was a classmate and Alpha Tau Omega fraternity brother of Williams' at the University of Missouri. In addition to using his name for the gentleman caller in *The Glass Menagerie*, Williams would use his name in a number of early plays. In "Moony's Kid Don't Cry," Jane's employer is Mr. O'Connor; in *Candles to the Sun*, there is a minor character called Sean O'Connor, described as a "hard-drinking Irishman"; in *Fugitive Kind*, there is a federal agent named O'Connor; and in the one-act play "Sacre de Printemps," there is a priest Father Conner. Williams would also use the name for the main character in the poem "The Dirty Louse," later titled "Jim Connor Went." The poem is about a character who, having led a wild and sinful life of gambling and drinking, dies a quiet, kind old man.

162. Rose's condition had a serious impact on Williams. A month earlier, after Williams and his mother had gone to visit Rose, Edwina wrote to her parents (11 May 1937, HRC):

Tom and I went out to see Rose Sunday. She sent word that she didn't want to see us but I insisted upon going in, as I wanted to see for myself just what condition she was in. Her face looked so yellow, and bloated and she was so full of delusions about people and things that I see she has not improved. . . . The visit made Tom ill so I can't take him to see her again. I can't have two of them there!

163. *Fugitive Kind*.

Jim Connor

*Saturday, 5 June 1937*

Sat. A.M. Slept after sedative but woke up with same old thoughts in my head. It's a fight now and I mustn't be my own enemy. I've got to shake off this defeat and go on. It looks like I've lost my sense of humor. I feel very tired of it all. Suppose I will try to write a little this morning – grey windy rainy morning and someone accross the alley is practicing the piano – the air has a fresh smell – usually after shocks of this kind something pleasant occurs to buoy me up – the law of compensation? – Buck up, kid – the worst is yet to come!

*Saturday, 12 June 1937*

Saturday P.M. That was a week ago and is all but forgotten – at least the sting is removed – I suppose the psychological shock still remains – among countless others – Do not feel very proud of myself. Dull lately. Have very little to say. Difficult to make conversation. Did some fair writing this afternoon but after reading new play – laid in a flophouse[157] – felt thoroughly disgusted – will I ever produce another full length play that's worth producing? Maybe. Going to Kramer's tonight – Buzz Bland and Ivy[158] –

*Sunday, 13 June 1937*

Sunday: Had a delightful evening with Miss Florence and Buzz. Walked up to the Muny Opera.[159] Laughed and acted like kids. The Bell Trail.[160] Miss Flo. is really a grand old trouper. Pretended to flirt with all men passing in cars – flaunting her tremendous pearl necklace. Buzz a sweet child.

One strange interlude – saw Jim Connor[161] at opera – He also saw me I'm sure but neither of us spoke. How silly! My shyness is a never-ending affliction. I know it was only shyness in Jim, too. He is not the type that would deliberately snub anyone. There is something mysterious and touching about him. He looks so wise and sad – as sad as I am and very much wiser. For that reason I should like to renew our acquaintance.

Today wanted to go swimming but the old women prevented because of my bruised nose. Angry and bored. Wonder if I shall end up like Rose?[162] God forbid! My play[163] goes badly – will I ever manage to write it? So long – I must take a long walk this evening, and try to regain my spiritual poise. At least no blue devils at present.

164.   *Fugitive Kind.*

Rose Williams

*Saturday, 19 June 1937*

~~Sunday~~ Saturday. Registered for summer school. Trying business. How I loathe procedures of that sort! My dizzy spells improved. None today – but nearly all last week – light-headed and very tired. Tomorrow will try to write third act – First Two fairly presentable – a <u>good</u> day Monday or Tuesday – Holland called and wants to see me – He's going to take a Paramount Screen test in Hollywood – I don't wish him any bad luck – but if he should get in the movies – what chance would I have of producing a play next season? Feel shy and remote now that school is out and I'm so much by myself. Quo Vadis?

Je ne sais pas!

Grandfather is here and I enjoy his Company – today we visited Rose – she seemed <u>better</u>.

It is a warm, moony summer evening, the cicadas in good voice – a faint cool breeze now and then – I am grateful for these intervals of peace!


*Sunday, 20 June 1937*

Sunday P.M. Skipped dinner to write. But not much go – got dizzy spell and quit. Took a shower and a mebral and feel somewhat better though not exactly pleased with myself. It is such a warm, dreamy summer afternoon – I would like to be lying in a pile of hay – mellow lotus! – way out in the country – I should have been a shepherd – I have such a taste for pastoral life – alas, the day of shepherds is past – Poets have got to live in cities and adjust themselves to a social system which was definitely not made for poets!

But maybe I am not a poet but just a blooming idiot.

Now I feel very quiet inside – may try to write some more – No use giving up – Giving up is not my cardinal sin.

Later – Wrote some good stuff – all but last scene of first draft finished.[164] Took a long walk, clear up to Clayton Pool and back composing dialogue – some of it quite good – Retired about midnight – Dad left on trip –


*Monday, 21 June 1937*

<u>Monday</u> – Spent afternoon at Westborough Pool – swimming and sun-bathing – Tonight lonely, restless and sun-burned – Do not feel like sleeping nor staying awake – What else can one do at midnight of a warm June? I dream of going to a Tropical part and spending the rest of my days in a state of delicious sensuous intoxication – Yes, I want to escape from this deadly middle-west. Now I am getting sloppy so I had better stop –

165. Williams' short story "The Four-leaf Clover" is told from the perspective of a boy whose parents are deeply troubled by their older daughter's erratic behavior and sexual promiscuity. In the later version of the story, the sister's condition is identified as dementia praecox, an early term for schizophrenia.

166. Williams would borrow the name of St. Vincent's for the hospital in the play *Vieux Carré* where the tubercular painter, Nightingale, is taken.

167. Insulin shock therapy is the injection of doses of insulin to depress the activity of the brain. Its purpose was to change the pattern of brain waves in an attempt to modify behavior. Insulin shock therapy was abandoned in the 1950s as it was not considered successful.

168. This was the seventh time that the Williams family had changed addresses in less than two decades. Each move brought them closer to more fashionable residential sections of St. Louis.

169. *Fugitive Kind.*

The downstairs was empty. From above he could hear the now familiar sound of his mother's weeping. This time it was wild and hysterical to a degree it had not been before. He climbed to the landing and stood there in helpless foreknowledge of some unbearable hurt.

The door came open.

"Margaret, Margaret, don't! Keep hold of yourself! It isn't hopeless, you know. He says that it isn't hopeless. They have such wonderful new treatments, marvelous sanitariums and – "

"Insulin!" said his father. "They say it does wonders!"

"No, no, no!" cried his Mother. "Didn't you hear what he called it? – Dementia Praecox!"

Arthur turned mechanically back down the wide staircase.

The central hall was flooded with misty brightness which seemed to emerge from the swinging pendulum in the grandfather clock. All of the afternoon's gently retreating gold was now concentrated in that small metal disk as it leisurely swung back and forth in the tall glass cabinet. Arthur watched it in merciful suspension of thought. In the back of his mind he knew that something inalterable had occured. The house had really fallen. That is, everything that it represented no longer existed. Its walls would not keep danger away any longer. They would stop contradicting the things that you read in the papers. The pure white lace window curtains would filter no more the various winds of chance, excluding the ones that had peril in them, admitting only what was light and benign as they had before. Deception was now apparent in the sprightly flowered wall-paper. The crystall glass

Page from a draft of "The Four-leaf Clover"

*Thursday, 24 June 1937*

Thursday A.M. Yesterday our worst ~~suspicions~~ fears about Rose were confirmed. Her trouble has been diagnosed as dementia Praecox.[165] The doctor at St. Vincent's[166] said Insulin shock[167] was about the only hope – it is not decided yet whether to give her that – A catastrophe worse than death – I slept fitfully last night – that thought woven through my dreams – a living nightmare – Grandfather says "She is God's child and he will do what is best for her" – Why must a child of God have dementia Praecox? His ways are indeed mysterious – I am driven more and more to the conclusion that individual lives do not matter much in the cosmic scheme of things –

If only I can keep my sanity I shall count myself a fortunate man –

D. has returned and gone to work – I guess it is about nine – another fiercely bright morning with hammering and piano practice across the alley – and chirping birds in the yard – the desultory sounds of the house – and a street-car passing – one wonders if and how one will manage to survive this summer – By the same old method of compromise and evasion?

Later – Lay cowering on my bed for a while and then got up with the reflection that nobody ever died of being strong.

*Remember that now, mr. williams.*
*1/6/40*

*Sunday, 4 July 1937*

Sunday – July 4 – Firecrackers popping all over town – So stupid! – Spent afternoon at Westborough – Swimming & diving show – rather dull – Felt lonely being all by myself – This morning had odd experience – wakened by a bird call – gave me a strange, delightful sensation – an atavistic emotion from my early childhood – So clear and pure – the delight of an early morning in childhood – pure, spiritual delight – made me realize what a muddy stream my adult life has become – If only I could regain that lost clarity and purity of spirit! – They have just about decided on house at 42 Aberdeen Place – I will go to Memphis while they move[168] – which is a pleasant prospect – Play[169] going better – Rewrote first Act – in pretty good shape – but am dreadfully lazy about my work – Saw Holland just before he left for Hollywood – He read play and seemed fairly pleased though much rewriting is necessary. I suppose I shall swim again tomorrow – It is the only thing I feel like doing. Yes, I am a very dull boy. ~~The days open and shut like the wings of a bird that flies in endless circles.~~ Eh bien! Nous verrons!

170.  J. Richard Compton was a fellow student at Washington University with an interest in drama.

171.  Esmeralda Mayes (1913– ) was the best friend of Hazel Kramer and also a close childhood friend of Williams' in St. Louis. Williams used her first name for Esmeralda Hawkins in the play "Something Unspoken," for the Gypsy's daughter in the play *Camino Real* and the related play fragment "Cabeza de Lobo," for Heavenly Critchfield's mother in the play *Spring Storm*, and for Esmeralda Bachelder in the screenplay *The Loss of a Teardrop Diamond.* He used her last name for Lucretia Mayes in the short story "The Spinning Song." Williams transferred an anecdote Mayes had told him about the wife of one of her father's patients misunderstanding her husband's ailment of pleurosis as "blue roses" to *The Glass Menagerie*. In scene 2, Jim is reminded that his nickname for Laura, "Blue Roses," came about because he misheard her when she said she had suffered from pleurosis.

Fred Hirsch attended University City High School with Williams and was the 1929 editor of the *Dial* yearbook there. He moved to New York to pursue an acting career.

Dorothea Brookmire lived in Williams' neighborhood. Williams used her name for two characters in the play *A Lovely Sunday for Creve Coeur*, Dorothea Gallaway and Helena Brookmire, as well as for Dorothea Bates in the play *Period of Adjustment*.

Scott Robertson was at the University of Missouri with Williams.

172.  Jane Blackmer worked for the *St. Louis Star-Times.*

173.  Gordon Carter was director of the Little Theatre in St. Louis. He later worked in Hollywood as a producer and set designer.

174.  Tallulah Bankhead (1902–68), daughter of an Alabama congressman, had by 1937 starred in twenty-nine plays, in both New York and London, and eleven films. She went to Hollywood in 1931 and was promoted by the studios as the next Marlene Dietrich. Bankhead was gossiped about for her wild sexual behavior with both men and women and her incessant party going. Before she left Hollywood in 1932 for New York, Louis B. Mayer purportedly lectured her on her immoral behavior, telling her he was upset about rumors of her "hibernating with [women]" (Brendan Gill, *Tallulah* [New York: Holt, Rinehart & Winston, 1972], p. 54).

Three years later Bankhead would be approached to star in Williams' play *Battle of Angels*. In a letter to Williams dated 31 July 1940 (Yale), Lawrence Langner, co-head of the Theatre Guild, mentioned having sent Bankhead a copy of *Battle of Angels* but said that she was "tied up until Christmas." In August 1949, Bankhead was screen-tested for the role of Amanda Wingfield in the film version of *The Glass Menagerie*, but she failed to get the part because Williams feared she "would not be sympathetic enough in the softer aspects of the character" (letter to Audrey Wood, [late March 1947], HRC).

Bankhead did, however, go on to act in two of Williams' plays. She played Blanche in the 1956 revival of *A Streetcar Named Desire*, which previewed on 16 January at the Coconut Grove Playhouse in Miami and moved to New York's City Center Theatre on 15 February. The play did not receive good reviews. About Bankhead's performance, Williams allegedly made the drunken remark, "That woman is ruining my play." The comment was included in a *Time* magazine report on the premiere (13 February 1956). Williams alluded to this incident in the autobiographical play *Something Cloudy, Something Clear* (part 2, scene 1):

ACTRESS: . . . What was it you said I did to your goddamn play?

AUGUST: I said that you pissed on my play.

Eight years later, Bankhead played the role of Mrs. Goforth in the revival of *The Milk Train Doesn't Stop Here Anymore*, which opened in New York on 1 January 1964. The play closed after five performances and was Bankhead's last appearance on Broadway.

In anticipation of the opening of *The Milk Train Doesn't Stop Here Anymore*, Williams wrote a tribute to Bankhead entitled "T. Williams's View of T. Bankhead." In this essay, which was published in the *New York Times* on 29 December 1963, Williams wrote that he had written four parts for her: Myra Torrance in *Battle of Angels*, Blanche in *A Streetcar Named Desire*, Princess Kosmonopolis in *Sweet Bird of Youth*, and Flora Goforth in *The Milk Train Doesn't Stop Here Anymore*. Williams was more likely promoting Tallulah Bankhead and his play than remembering the truth. Bankhead's influence on Williams' work was much weaker. He did, however, describe his play "Woman Key," about a woman who arrives home in the Florida Keys to discover that her alcoholic husband has killed the cook, as "A Melodrama for Tallullah Bankhead."

*Tuesday, 6 July 1937*

Tuesday – July 6 – Yesterday spent a swell afternoon at Tree Court – drove out
with Dick Compton[170] – Saw many old friends – Ezzie Mayes, Fred Hirsch,
Dorothea Brookmire, Scott Robertson[171] – Met Jane Blackmer[172] and Gordon
Carter[173] – Hirsch is also an enemy of Carson's – I felt rather gay for a change –
drank 3 beers and learned to swim back stroke and do a jack-knife dive – Ezzie is
a rather pathetic person – and quite admirable in a way – She makes such an
effort to please – such a brave, indiscourageable effort – She is so homely and so
maladroit – and yet one likes her because she is so much an <u>enfant terrible</u> – She
showered me with embarassing compliments – also Gordon Carter – and asked a
girl in the crowd if she were pregnant and who had she been sleeping with.
Discussed Tallullah Bankhead's[174] alleged perversion and promiscuity – "Gable is
good but Garbo is better" – an obvious lie – So much filth nowadays – No one is
left untouched – Or is it filth? Perhaps it is only robust, natural life boiling up to
the surface – It is all the way you look at it. But I want something clean –
Something that is pure without being false or squeamish – is there such a thing?

Williams and Esmeralda Mayes (center)
on a hayride. Inset: Esmeralda Mayes.

175. *Fugitive Kind.*

176. In the Spanish Civil War of 1936–39, Conservative forces in Spain, supported by the landed aristocracy, the Roman Catholic Church, military leaders, and the fascist Falange party, overthrew the second Spanish Republic. The Loyalists, consisting of liberals, anarchists, socialists, and Communists, defended the Spanish Republic and inspired democratic forces around the world. With few exceptions, poets and writers of Spain rallied to the cause of the Republic and, in the case of Federico García Lorca, Antonio Machado, and Miguel Hernandez, died for it. Writers such as Hemingway, Auden, and Spender went to Spain to serve in some capacity or to observe, and many wrote major works set during this conflict.

177. *The Pulitzer Prize Plays, 1918–1934*, edited by Kathryn Coe and William H. Cordell (New York: Random House, 1935), included *Beyond the Horizon, Anna Christie,* and *Strange Interlude* by Eugene O'Neill, *In Abraham's Bosom* by Paul Green, *Both Your Houses* by Maxwell Anderson, and *Men in White* by Sidney Kingsley.

178. Sidney Kingsley's play *Men in White* (1933), about a young doctor's attempt to balance his medical vocation against his romantic involvement with his fiancée, a spoiled rich woman, won the Pulitzer Prize in 1934. Frustrated by her inability to understand the demands of his profession, the doctor has a one-night affair with an adoring nurse, which leads to her death from a botched abortion. Upon discovery of the affair, the fiancée breaks off her engagement to the doctor.

179. Born in London, John van Druten (1901–57) was a popular playwright and novelist. *There's Always Juliet* (1932) is a comedy about an English girl, Leonora Perrycoste, who over the course of three days falls in love and decides to marry Dwight Houston, an American she has just met in London.

180. Tom Collins, a cocktail made with gin.

Rose and Williams

Tonight I feel a little jittery – swam at Westborough – My hair is falling out alarmingly due to so much sun and water – it gets dried out – Play[175] smooths out but does not develop – Tonight I may go to see Clark Mills.


*Wednesday, 7 July–Thursday, 8 July 1937*

<u>Weds</u>. Suffering torments of the damned with an awful burning skin eruption on face and arms – Also blue devils. No sleep tonight. Am I losing my mind? Recent entries sound so chaotic – like the product of a diseased mind. No delusions but certainly not a normal state of mind – feel trapped tonight – frightened – have taken a sleeping pill but little effect – If only I had something definite to do with myself I might save myself. Well, I am not going to give up the fight yet. I want to finish this new play – visit Memphis or the Ozarks – Have something in the way of a genuine experience – My life is entirely too internal – I need action on the outside – in the world! Tonight I would gladly enlist in the Loyalist Army in Spain[176] – and might even relish the sounds of an aerial bombardment – wish I were going somewhere new and exciting – I wish that something would happen – And something <u>will</u> – I can feel it coming! – Less nervous now – I will read Pulit. plays[177] and then try to sleep –

Later – Read Men In White[178] – Turned out light and tried to sleep – but nerve-wracking neurasthenia – No chance of sleep – Possible crisis coming – Feel horribly unstrung – The pill did no earthly good – How can I get through this day? Steady now – You can't go on like this – You're going to chuck it now – Right <u>now</u> – and no more foolishness –


*Friday, 9 July 1937*

Friday – after 3 A.M. No sleep – but about one hour – ~~Pois~~ Skin infection torturing me – Just took sleeping pill – nerves shot – If I can only get through this! – what bliss to have a cool, smooth skin again – rid of this infernal burning and itching – this sleepless torment – I am paying a good price for all my sins, whatever they are – ~~That is – if there is such a thing as sin~~ – God help me through this – Courage! – Au Revoir!


*Wednesday, 21 July or Thursday, 22 July 1937*

<u>Wed – or Thurs</u>. A.M. – July 21 – About two weeks since last entry – seems longer – Miserable day so I feel like confiding – Last night went to see horribly stupid play – "There's Always Juliet" by Van Druten[179] – silly parlor prattle – went to Dr. Marsh's apartment and for some reason drank furiously – 5 or 6 "Toms"[180] –

181.   Antoinette Louise Krause was referred to as Louise, but Williams preferred her first name, Antoinette. William Jay Smith wrote (in a letter to Margaret Bradham Thornton):

> Louise Krause lived in a big house in the suburb of Ladue and had attended Mills College in California. She had come back to St. Louis to take a master's degree in English. Her subject was John Donne. She wrote metaphysical poems that impressed Tom and me.

The wife of the man diagnosed with dementia praecox in the published version of Williams' play "Moony's Kid Don't Cry" is called Louise Krause and one of the inmates in *Not About Nightingales* is called Krause.

182.   John Middleton Murry (1889–1957) was an English essayist, journalist, and literary critic. He was married to Katherine Mansfield. In *Between Two Worlds* (1924), published a year after Mansfield's death, he describes not only his relationship with Mansfield but also their relationship with D. H. and Frieda Lawrence. Williams included Murry and Mansfield, along with the Lawrences, as characters in the play fragment "The Night of the Zeppelin."

42 Aberdeen Place, St. Louis

At last we've just about selected a house. The lease is not signed yet but the agent assured us it would be. It is on 42 Aberdeen Place, one block west of Skinker and about two blocks South of the Washington University Campus. It is a fine location. It is just one block from Forest Park and right on the City Limits carline. I have not been inside the house yet so cannot describe the interior. It is somewhat larger than this house, as it has a third story.

Excerpt of a letter Williams wrote to his grandparents (undated)

became quite gay – party broke up early – I made Antoinette[181] angry – came
home and got horribly innauseated – Rushed downstairs to vomit several times –
at last too weak to rush downstairs so vomited in bedroom – arousing mother –
Ill till about 2 P.M. – Then ate a little something and drove mother to sanitarium
to visit R. – waited about an hour – M. came out crying – R. has taken a dreadful
turn – become raving – won't eat – thinks she is being poisoned – can't sleep –
disturbed the whole ward so has been isolated – looks a wreck M. says – She
could not tell me about it till after we reached home – This of course made me feel
very wretched – Then ride with D. who was mean as the devil – cutting remarks
– felt so inadequate and helpless and hated him so – ~~One can~~ He is sick himself I
suppose – and one cannot blame him for being disgusted with me – I am such a
fool – Night and nervous tension – Read Murry's autobiography "Between Two
Worlds"[182] – Fascinating portraits – Will now try to sleep – Maybe will go to
Clark's in morning and write – Something! – If only I could leave here – go to
camp – Is there any possible chance of it? – The beastliness of life frightens me so
– R. – when such things can happen to people, how to believe in any good power
over us mortals? The fear – the helplessness – what can we do?

   At least I have recovered from my poison ivy!!


*Thursday, 22 July or Friday, 23 July 1937*

Thurs – (or Fri. A.M.) – Yes – and gotten a tooth-ache – May have to have it
pulled out – what next? – Otherwise somewhat better today – Spirits still low but
no crisis – Did no writing till late this evening when I did some pretty good
dialogue – R. reported better today – I swam at U. pool and chauffeured mother
between here and new house – Quite dull like most other days this summer – My
chance of getting away seems increasingly remote –

   Tomorrow may write at Clark's – if he wishes – and my tooth recovers – Now
try to sleep – Not much longer in this house – We move next Thursday – I will
have a room in the attic – D. complains because he will have to heat it for me in
winter – But maybe – when winter comes – I will not be living there – Maybe I
will be living a new, exciting life somewhere else.


*Friday, 23 July 1937*

Later – (about 4 A.M.) Nervous frenzy – no sleep – can't even lie still – no sleeping
pills left – Must keep hold of myself – don't want to go mad – or am I already?

Later – Slept about three hours after daybreak – wakened by the old man
pounding at my door and yelling at me that "I had to do something around
here" – He raved at me for some time in this vein – That on top of every thing
else – I am just about driven to the last ditch – I have a suspicion that something

183.   YMCA camp on Lake Taneycomo in Hollister, Missouri.

184.   Owing to her deteriorating condition, Rose was moved from St. Vincent's to the State Hospital in Farmington, Missouri.

185.   Williams presumably worked on the penultimate scene of *Fugitive Kind* in which Leo, the son of the flophouse owner, returns home defeated. He pours out his heart to Chuck, a menial laborer at the flophouse:

> What's wrong with me, Chuck? Why don't I belong out there with the rest of those people? I've tried to pretend like I did. I went in those places where they work and I tried to ask for a job. But I couldn't.
>
> The words got stuck in my mouth. It scared me to watch them doing those things they were doing, operating machines, writing figures, selling goods, bustling around with piles and piles of letters and orders and — business! . . . [I]t's a world that I don't belong to, full of strangers. The only thing that I'm any good for, Chuck, is putting words down on paper. . . . Do you know what's wrong with that city out there? . . .
>
> They built themselves a big trap to jump into. . . .
>
> . . . [T]hey're all caught in it except just a few like us, you an' me. . . . Us, we didn't build walls around us, we don't belong — No, we're outcasts, lunatics, criminals — the Fugitive Kind, that's what we are — the ones that don't wanta stay put.

186.   In the last scene (scene 8) of *Fugitive Kind*, Glory, the adopted daughter of the flophouse owner, and Terry, a charming gangster on the run, plan to run off together. While Glory delays their escape to tend to her brother, Leo, Terry is ambushed by the law, shot, and killed.

187.   Warren Hatcher was a friend of Cornelius Williams' who killed himself after alcoholism ruined his career at the International Shoe Company. In the play *Stairs to the Roof*, a lawyer who arranges a clandestine meeting with a lover is named Warren B. Thatcher, and in the play *Sweet Bird of Youth*, the assistant manager of the Royal Palms Hotel is named Dan Hatcher.

Edwina Dakin Williams

is going to start happening around here – If only I were not so completely
disorganized I could make a complete break – But I am more than half sick, body
and soul this morning and see no way to turn – Again – the curse of inaction!
And forever – I suppose.


*Sunday, 8 August 1937*

Sunday – (Aug. 7 or 8) – Returned from camp[183] after one short week – freedom!
Escape! It was so comparatively sublime – Now I have come back and almost wish
I had not gone – the time was so short and the return so desolate – heart-breaking –
I act like a spoiled baby but I guess I can't help it. It is a grey Sunday morning.
Not even the sun to console me – my friend the sun – and I have been harassed
by the blue devils since leaving camp. The whole terrible sky seems to be crashing
down on my poor skull. We all (Dakin, M. and I) went to Early Communion to
pray for R. who has been taken to Farmington for insulin treatments.[184] We
arrived at church too late to go in. I've got to pity M. and stop pitying myself.
If I can keep my head through the rest of this summer I will be very grateful.

Later – Went to neighborhood café for coffee – Came home and wrote scene
between Leo and Chuck – very fiery and perhaps good[185] – rewrote last scene[186]
– still too melodramatic. Hatcher[187] for dinner – I feel somewhat better but still
uneasy – Very hot up here – will take a shower and maybe go out to a show – the
usual anaesthesia – something may turn up this week to make life more tolerable.
I would like to call Clark this evening but I am a little too nervous for company.


*Monday, 9 August 1937*

Later (about 5 A.M.) woke at four after night sleeping on back porch.
Increasingly nervous and despondent. Just took some of D's. sedative in hope of
getting little more sleep. Have got to plan an intelligent campaign against this
neurasthenia – must not let go – Another week in ~~campaign~~ might have saved me
from all this – that's what makes me feel so bitter about it – can you blame me? It
isn't right that any human being should be tortured like this.
   I have been drinking too much coffee – about five times in week – will cut that
out and will try to keep myself so active physically during the day that I will sleep
from sheer exhaustion – Now I feel quieter – I hear the birds chirping and a
rooster – I would like to get a bicycle – maybe that would help – I guess I'd better
do everything I possibly can to snap out of it.

Later – Must have slept several hours. Woke with same old condition – fearfully
hot in attic. And D. shaving downstairs. Feel weak but will try to lose myself in
some kind of activity – Amen.

188.   *Fugitive Kind.*

189.   "American Gothic" portrays a Midwestern farmer and his wife whose only son and his flashy, ill-mannered wife come to stay with them. When the couple suspect their son is involved in illicit dealings, the mother orders her son and his wife to leave. She gives back all the money her son has sent her because she believes it has not been honestly gained. She soon learns that her son is a bank robber and is fleeing from a posse of lawmen.

      As Williams noted on the title page, "American Gothic" was "suggested by the Grant Woods' picture, American Gothic." Williams imagined that the farmer and his wife depicted in *American Gothic* were the parents of a bank robber. Williams very likely was inspired in his characterization of the son and his wife by Clyde Barrow and Bonnie Parker who, after nearly twenty-eight weeks on the run, were murdered on 23 May 1934 on a country road outside the small town of Mount Lebanon, Louisiana, where they had been hiding out in an abandoned farmhouse.

      Williams would probably have also read Wood's article "The Writer and the Painter," which appeared in the first issue of *American Prefaces* in October 1935. In this article, Wood (1892–1942) discussed the similarities between the techniques of painting and of writing. Interestingly, the summer 1937 issue of *American Prefaces* included several portraits and a mural of farm scenes by Wood, who was on the faculty of the University of Iowa.

      The influence of paintings on Williams' work would continue throughout his life. Other works or titles suggested by paintings include the plays "Lily and La Vie!" or "One of Picasso's Blues," and "This Is the Peaceable Kingdom," a reference to Edward Hicks' painting, and the poems "Roses," inspired by a Hovsep Pushman painting, and "Garden Scene," inspired by a Bonnard painting. "Hide and Seek," an early title for the film script *Baby Doll*, was suggested by the Tchelitchew painting.

      In addition Williams used references to paintings to convey settings for plays. These include "Hell," an early version of *Not About Nightingales* (van Gogh), "This Property Is Condemned" (Hopper), *Stairs to the Roof* (Dalí), "A Balcony in Ferrara" (Matisse), *The Glass Menagerie* (El Greco), *Summer and Smoke* (De Chirico), *A Streetcar Named Desire* and the one-act precursor "Interior: Panic" (van Gogh), *Sweet Bird of Youth* (O'Keeffe), *The Night of the Iguana* (Rubens), "The Gnädiges Fräulein" (Picasso), *Stopped Rocking* (van Gogh), and *A Lovely Sunday for Creve Coeur* (Shahn).

190.   Williams had applied to the University of Iowa for admission in the autumn of 1937.

191.   On 12 September, the *St. Louis Post-Dispatch* announced that *Fugitive Kind* would be performed on 30 November and 4 December.

192.   In the first scene, Glory, the manager of her father's flophouse, is attracted to Terry, a gangster on the run, who has appeared and asked for a room. It appears Williams accepted Holland's criticism and made the appropriate changes, as the published text contains no interrupted sequences between Glory and Terry and no references to Leo, Glory's brother.

193.   Lola Pergament (1913– ) was born in New York and attended Washington University in St. Louis. She was a poet, lyricist, and playwright who published extensively in *Poetry* (1935–38). In her poems, she used the image of the bird to describe the combination of frailty and courage and the image of the fugitive to describe a creative and emotional restlessness. "The Trackless Way," published in *Poetry* in November 1935, refers to a fugitive wind and a fugitive heart, "birds huddled and alone" and "a bird blown to flight upward and alone." She describes autumn as "blowing down like the exquisite and frail body of a bird untroubled by the thunder." In "Slow Invasion," published in *Poetry* in May 1937, the persona of the poem says, "I am your fugitive stumbling out of pain." Williams would use images of the fugitive and the frailty of birds in his own writings.

194.   Terrence McCabe married Hazel Kramer in September 1935. In the 1970s play *The Red Devil Battery Sign* Williams would give the married boyfriend of King Del Rey's daughter the name of Terrence McCabe. King, upset that his daughter is unmarried and pregnant, blames McCabe (act 3, scene 1):
      Such a nice Irish name. You run out of potatoes too fucking quick and you come here too many and you decided it wasn't potatoes you wanted but liquor and parades and wakes and political power. Bosses and corruption. Oh, back home you're into revolution but here you're into — ripoff. . . . Christ, you babyface mother!

*Monday, 30 August 1937*

Mon. Aug. 30 – Past three weeks fairly pleasant! Great deal of social activity – some good work on play[188] – I got terribly disgusted with it last week but now it seems much better. Wrote new one-act this P.M. – "American Gothic"[189] –

*Wednesday, 8 September 1937*

Wed. Sept. 8. – Holding my thumbs for Iowa.[190] It is almost definitely settled that I will get to go up there – play will be announced in Sunday's paper[191] – Good thing I got it practically finished because I'm having one of my difficult periods with writing – First scene between Glory and Terry will not come to suit Holland – I think it is O.K. but he objects to interrupted sequence and references to Leo[192] – Holland is wonderful to work with – In most things his instinct is amazingly sound but on some things we simply cannot see eye to eye – I don't think he likes my atmospheric touches –
Lola Pergament[193] in town – I am anxious to meet her –
Feel pretty badly tonight – over rotten writing.
Iowa is still a fabrication of dream – will it be reality? Oh, how I hope!

*Wednesday, 15 September 1937*

Wed – Sept. 15 – Still looks as though I will go to Iowa but now I begin to have doubts about advisability of it. of course I will go if I get the chance – but feel something will probably develop to impede.
Saw Miss Flo. tonight – she is displeased with Terry.[194] Still feel artistically defunct – impotent period – play finished – will be produced in Nov. accding. to present plans – Feel no excitement –
Saw R. at Farmington Sunday – where she is undergoing insulin treatment. ~~Not~~ Much better than I expected. A horrible business, though. She is unconscious half of every day – swollen and exhausted physically but in remarkably good spirits – laughed and joked about other patients. Chief worry is her hair which she thinks is falling out –
Wind in trees – sounds like a change of season – perhaps a complete change of life – I need one – Au Revoir –

195. Sigma Alpha Epsilon fraternity house.

196. In a letter to Willard Holland ([9 October 1937], Harriett Holland Brandt collection), Williams described his skit, "Quit Eating":

I am having a play presented in the "laboratory theater" next Thursday. It is a dramatization of the Hunger Strike among convicts at the Stateville Illinois prison — in protest against new Parole policies which have reduced number of paroles from over 1300 last year to about 240 for the nine months of this year. These dramatizations are written in competition by the playwriting class. The three best are selected each two weeks and produced in what is called "a living newspaper".

University of Iowa

Dear Clark: I am seated in a coach
bound for Iowa City - it is 11:45 P.M. -
and I feel such a prodigious
excitement - in spite of a double
sedative - that I must communicate my feelings to someone or
else blow up. I know you will
be disappointed not to hear from
me after I get to Iowa City
where I will really have
something to write about - perhaps I can continue the letter
from there or else write a new
one. But of course the important
thing is that I am actually
going - I never really believed
in its possibility until I got
on the train!

Excerpt of a letter to Clark Mills that Williams drafted in his journal

*Thursday, 16 September 1937*

Thurs. Sept. 16. Tonight is pleasant – A crisp, chilly autumn night that elates the spirit and makes life seem a more definite, positive quantity.

Dakin is at the S.A.E. House[195] for his first rush-date – I am waiting up – in my garret room – to let him in. This is a charming room. I almost hate to leave it. You see, I feel in my heart that I will never really return to this place. Whatever happens good or ill, this next year I think it will surely divorce me at last from the paternal roof – wish-fulfillment! –

But of course my life has been a series of returns – I do not seem to have much capacity for exploring new fields although I have no lack of desire.

I will see Clark and Holland tomorrow morning. I plan to leave Wed. night or Thurs. morning if nothing happens to prevent.

No, I haven't forgotten poor Rose – I beg whatever power there is to save her and spare her from suffering.

My play is all but finished and I feel pretty well satisfied with it. Now I yearn for work on a new one – will not be content till I have made a good start on it. The next play is always the important play. The past, however satisfactory, is only a challenge to the future.

I want to go on creating. I <u>will</u>!!!


*Wednesday, 22 September 1937*

Wed. Nite – The miracle has happened – I'm on the train for Iowa City – at least I will <u>get</u> there – Deo volente I will <u>remain</u> – Feel pretty good – less ~~se~~ nervous than I expected and rather jubilant – At last I am really doing something – Making a definite move – that is a satisfying thing – It is interesting to speculate upon the possibilities of this coming year – So much may or may not happen! Of course I am a little frightened – <u>ça va sans dire</u> – but I think I will carry it off okay –


*Saturday, 9 October 1937*

Sat. Oct. 9 – Been up here over two weeks – love the place but am disgustingly ill and nervous – have jolting sensations in heart and almost constant tension – disturbed and frighten[ed] – I intend to avoid getting panicky about it – I must keep my head on my shoulders – but it is not very pleasant – Do other people have lives like this? Yes – some do – and endure it.

Aside from wretched bodily condition – which may pass off – I am getting along nicely – Encouraging enthusiastic letter from Willard – Skit to be presented by living newspaper[196] – Nice associates up here – pleasant atmosphere – much to be interested in – if only I could be strong and free – ! Please, God, <u>let</u> me! I

197.  When Williams first arrived in Iowa City, his lodging was at a boardinghouse located at 225 North Linn
      Street. Shortly afterward he moved into a boardinghouse at 325 South Dubuque Street where Johnnie was
      presumably also a boarder. A month later, at the end of October, Williams moved into the Alpha Tau
      Omega fraternity house.

198.  From John Keats' letter to his friend Charles Brown ([30] September [1820], *The Letters of John Keats*,
      edited by Maurice Buxton Forman, vol. 2 [Oxford: Oxford University Press, 1931], pp. 564, 565). It was
      one of the last letters Keats wrote before his death on 23 February 1821.

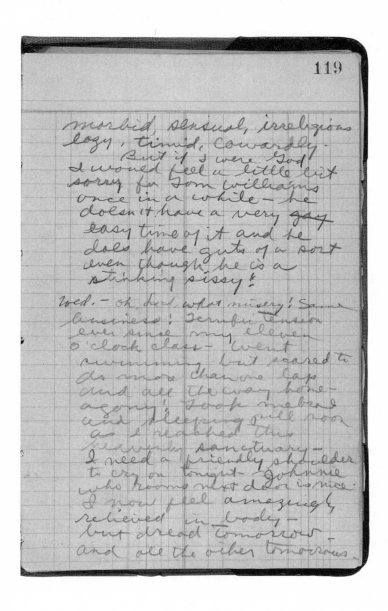

think of Rose and wonder and pity – but it is such a faraway feeling – how bound up we are in our own selves – our own miseries – Why can't we forget and think of others? It is the nature of the beast! I must admit that I have felt very beast-like lately and if things turn out well for me it will be better than I deserve.

My virtues – I am kind, friendly, modest, sympathetic, tolerant and sensitive –

Faults – I am ego-centric, introspective, morbid, sensual, irreligious, lazy, timid, cowardly –

But if I were God I would feel a little bit sorry for Tom Williams once in a while – he doesn't have a very ~~gay~~ easy time of it and he does have guts of a sort even though he is a stinking sissy!

*Wednesday, 13 October 1937*

Wed. – oh, Lord, what misery! Same business! Terrific tension ever since my eleven o'clock class – Went swimming but scared to do more than one lap and all the way home – agony! Took mebral and sleeping pill soon as I reached this heavenly sanctuary – I need a friendly shoulder to cry on tonight – Johnnie[197] who rooms next door is nice. I now feel amazingly relieved in body – but dread tomorrow – and all the other tomorrows – how can I ever find my way out of all this?

Je ne sais rien!

*Saturday, 16 October 1937*

Sat – Notes from John Keats letters – "Is there another life? Shall I awake and find all this a dream? There must be, we cannot be created for this sort of suffering."

(I wish that I shared this belief)

"I wish for death every day and night to deliver me from these pains and then I wish death away for death would destroy even those pains which are better than nothing"[198] –

Keats, did God pity and love you as much as I? You will be always remembered – I will be forgotten – if only we could stretch out our hands across these dark spaces of death and time – clasp hands and walk into the dark together – why must our ~~deaths~~ lives be so separate – so lonely? I am not one – now I am you and all the others – I have broken the walls of self – I have become a part of you all – lost myself in you – no, I am not afraid now! I do not ask for your pity – pity is a poor thing – give me your love – and go with me bravely dear companions – bravely together – the dark has no peril that love and courage cannot face when friends walk together!

199.  In "The Red Part of a Flag," a young woman, Anna Kimball, is dying of consumption and is no longer able to work in the dry-goods section of a department store. Awakening one morning feeling better than she had since quitting her job, she sees a red silk dress hanging in a store window and buys it and insists on wearing it out of the store. She considers the dress to be the red part of the flag formed by the blue sky and clouds. Her elation over feeling better is temporary; the story ends with her spitting blood. There are a number of manuscripts of this story, some with alternative titles, including "Fountain," "Etablissements de Saint Louis," and "Red Silk for the Street."

Williams most likely got the idea of a character dying of consumption from reading the letters of John Keats. In one of his last letters to his sister Fanny, Keats refers to a "spitting of blood."

200.  Williams was taking an English course from Schramm. Williams' "silly" paper, "Comments on the Nature of Artists with a few Specific References to the Case of Edgar Allan Poe," is excerpted below:

There are certain members of the human family cursed or blessed, as the case may be, with what I have seen defined more sharply in French than in English as "la volonté de puìssance". This means a fund of uncontrolled energy that exceeds the demands of ordinary living. . . . The artist's position strikes me as analogous to that of the prophet Daniel in the den of lions. I do not recall my Biblical folk-lore quite distinctly enough to know what was the exact outcome in Daniel's case. I believe he was saved by an act of God. It takes something nearly as unexpected to preserve the artist from dismemberment in the physical cell which he is forced to occupy with his savage beasts. If he succeeds in domesticating them, at least partially, he may train them to perform circus-acts that will startle and delight the whole world. He may lead his beautiful feline pets through graceful routines that will make the big tent resound with his acclaim. Nevertheless they are a constant peril: no matter how beautifully they are trained to perform they are still potential destroyers — that is, of their master!

The reasons for this vital excess is probably unknown: perhaps it is physiological or hereditary, the result of glandular disturbance or of marriage between hyper-sensitive types. At any rate, the man who possesses it finds himself completely unsatisfied with the usual acts of living. They leave a large portion of him still unused. This portion is his den of lions. Unless he puts them to creative use they will take out their vitality on him: they will make him sickly, neurotic or utterly mad. The red meat which they want is art — art is the "something else" of human life. It has been said by a philosopher (I believe James Branch Cabell) that laughter is the only distinctly human attribute: the only quality which man does not share with any of his animal cousins. But that is mistaken. I have seen dogs laugh: my Boston terrier is highly amused whenever I look for my socks in the morning and he knows that they are behind the water-boiler in the basement. Art is really the only thing that man does which none of the beasts can imitate. Some may mention religion as another: but religion is of course a form of art: it is another "something else": another exercise for the mysterious new perceptions which are beginning to slowly evolve from the human consciousness. . . .

The number of artists that survive out of the number of potential artists is probably comparable to the number of vitalized sperms in an act of sexual conjugation: millions are ejaculated: one out of that number achieves the fertilization which is its object. The artist is made out of an especially perishable substance: this is a fact which literary biography leaves beyond dispute. This may suggest that art is a compensatory gesture: something that the owner takes up to compensate for physiological or nervous weakness just as a blind man may develop acute auditory and tactile senses. I think it is rather a demonstration of the tremendous drain that the creative energy makes upon the physical being. Artists have always been particularly prone to degenerative diseases such as tuberculosis: the greatest of the moderns were afflicted with respiratory disorders: Chekhov, Mansfield died of tuberculosis: Marcel Proust of a similar disease: O'Neill has an arrested case of tuberculosis. It is rumored that he is now dying of it. Sidney Lanier struggled against that disease his whole creative life. John Keats died of it. Nervous maladies are so general among artists as to be almost universal. To offer a list of nervously afflicted artists would be an extravagant use of paper.

201.  Robert E. Whitehand (1910–45) was a graduate student in drama at the University of Iowa and associate editor of *American Prefaces*. On receiving his M.A., he went to teach drama at the University of Oklahoma and pursued his Ph.D. By the time he joined the air force in 1942, he had shown great promise as a writer, with published short stories, one-act plays, and radio dramas to his credit. He was killed in action at the end of World War II.

*Monday, 18 October 1937*

Monday – Oct. 20 – Started out bravely – thinking perhaps I would shake this thing off – by 11:00 I was again tense – could hardly sit through my class – worked in theater – carpentry! – felt fairly well – but palpitations on way over – swam a little but too nervous to enjoy it – Cannot seem to relax – Maybe this is the last mile! – I think of being trapped here – sick, unable to move – I wish that I had not left home – but that is cowardly – Nothing risked, nothing gained – Schramm has almost definitely accepted my ~~poem~~ story[199] – ~~(I gave him my silly paper on Poe and artists this morning~~[200] – He said he and Whitehand[201] liked it fine but the ending was not right – He seems to be a pleasant sort of person – I need to know someone sympathetic and intelligent up here – Oh, God, what a life this is!

"The Red Part of a Flag" – my best piece of writing – if only I could go on – and write more things like that! I could if only I — could go on!!!

This is morbid – I've got to get up and laugh some more. Laughter is my only escape these days. I have never laughed or jested so much in my life – and never been more miserable! Ah, well – there are other lives besides mine!

This all sounds very stupid – Maybe my brain is all shot –

solitude was shattered. It was like opening a door upon a raw, brutal wind. The whole body and spirit of Vandeventer's bargain basement swept around her again. She heard the vast, interminable shuffle of thousands of ~~thousands~~ of feet down the aisles. She heard the clang and clatter of the little change-boxes, swooping and darting about like vicious little predatory birds. Most of all she felt the knife-sharp eyes turned upon her and heard the shrill demands of the shoppers. She felt her bones turning to water again as they had that afternoon several weeks ago when the scissors had jagged right and left and when she had not been able to produce the suitable shade of blue ticking. Her fingers had

had come out on the delicate branches and — in the sun. The puddles of last night's rain had caught fire. Golden fire. The red silk flashed in the wind....

Once she felt something bitter come into her mouth and she spat on the sidewalk. She didn't look back to see what it was. Only the policeman standing upon the corner noticed that she had spit out a mouthful of blood.

Thomas Lanier Williams

Excerpts of "The Red Part of a Flag"

202. In "The Red Part of a Flag" Williams did heed Schramm's advice. In a later version, post-1939, he dropped the final paragraph. The story, however, was never published in *American Prefaces*. Williams continued reworking the story, and it was first published in 1974 in *Vogue*, under the title "The Red Part of a Flag or Oriflamme," and later reprinted as "Oriflamme" in *Eight Mortal Ladies Possessed* and *Collected Stories*. Williams restored the earliest ending, but in a much more delicate way. Instead of saying that the young woman spits blood, he wrote: "The foam of a scarlet ocean crossed her lips."

203. Williams may have sent Whitehand "Quit Eating" and "The Big Scene," the first two of the four plays he had written for the playwriting class he was taking with Professor E. C. Mabie, "Experimental Dramatic Production." In a letter to Willard Holland ([18 November 1937], Harriett Holland Brandt collection), Williams wrote:

> I'm having another short play "The Family Pew" produced this afternoon. The others were "Quit Eating" on the prison hunger strike, "The Big Scene" satire on Hollywood and a fourth one "So Glad!" which will be produced later.

204. The Williams family's Boston terrier.

205. In a letter to her parents postmarked 5 October 1937 (HRC), Edwina wrote:

> Yesterday, Dakin drove me over to see Rose and she seemed about the same in mind. The insulin is making her so fat that I'm distressed to see her. The doctor says it gives them a tremendous appetite. . . . He has now given her thirty of the forty treatments she is supposed to have. It will take two more months and then they will let her rest from them for a while. He didn't seem to think she was showing enough improvement though he said she was some better.

Despite Edwina's hope, Rose did not respond well to the insulin shock treatment. Her doctor, Dr. C. C. Ault, reported on 16 December 1937:

> There has been very little change in this patient. She received a course of insulin shock therapy and is now considered to have had a mere remission. She is not as bizarre and more cooperative, but still thinks she is filthy, remains to herself and frequently becomes overtalkative. Delusions are still very prominent. (Leverich, pp. 246–247)

*Tuesday, 19 October 1937*

Tuesday – Today have felt slightly better – very slightly – Managed to sit thru morning classes – Swimming no relief – attended rehearsal of skit – saw Schramm – wants to cut final paragraph of story about blood-spitting[202] – Perhaps he is right – anyway if he will print story I will let him have it his way – Whitehand returned plays[203] – through Schramm – will talk to me about them later – apparently did not like them – none of these things seem of any importance to me now – all I can think of or care about is my damned miserable body – Home-sick! Yes, I really am – Most of all I miss little "Jiggs"[204] – It is strange how deeply I love that little animal – Mother's last letter said Rose was "reasonable" on last visit[205] – I have been neglecting my school work and done not a lick of ~~good~~ new writing – all because of this awful sick, neurotic condition – This week I am going to gradually climb out of it – Thursday – day after tomorrow I may move in fraternity house – Perhaps that change will help – the piano will be nice, at any rate, and I like Mrs. Moore –

Iowa City is really a very unattractive place – no charm of atmosphere like Columbia, Mo., or southern towns – I am dull and weary tonight – but not so nervous – just consumed a candied apple – I am lonely and bored – among interesting people and in a pleasanter atmosphere I would soon forget my sickness and get well – why not be a man and throw it off anyway? <u>En Avant!!</u>


*Wednesday, 20 October 1937*

Weds. – Came home utterly exhausted after one class – which I could barely sit through – Could not eat lunch – Barely raise a fork to my mouth – Took sleeping pill – and now bed – at 1:00 P.M.! – How will this end? – Oh, God, I'm so tired and frightened – no mail – no money – I have exactly one dime – and that borrowed – Heaven knows I've been through the mill in my time! They've given me "the works".

University Theatre, University of Iowa

206. During the autumn, Williams had an affair with a student, Elizabeth Mary "Bette" Reitz (1914–88). According to *Memoirs*, it was his only consummated affair with a woman. "After she had irrevocably dismissed me in favor of the new stud, I tried to date other girls. Somehow I didn't manage" (pp. 42–45). According to another student, Dorothea Henderson Forsythe, Williams was distraught when Reitz ended their relationship after the Christmas holidays and he asked Dorothea to deliver a poem, "Remember me as One of your Lovers," to Bette.

In 1932–35, before coming to the University of Iowa, Reitz had attended Coe College in Cedar Rapids where she majored in economics and sociology and was a member of a number of organizations including the orchestra, the Writer's Club, and the College Players. Her brother, John Reitz, noted that she left the University of Iowa after one year to work as a vaudeville performer. She married twice and did not have any children (interview with Margaret Bradham Thornton).

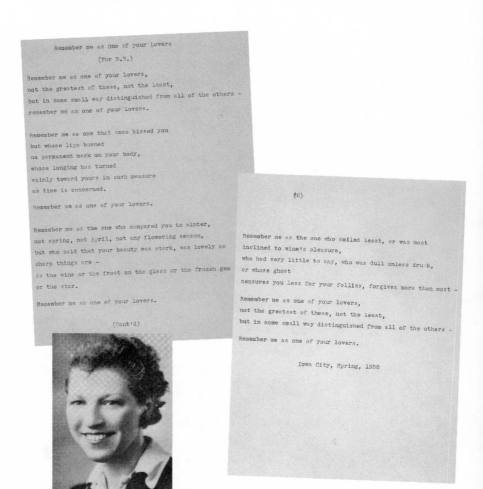

Elizabeth Mary "Bette" Reitz

*Sometime during this interval the course of my life subtly but definitely changed. I began to integrate more firmly – to grow more independant, detached, balanced, sophisticated, a deep physical love affair with a girl and freedom from home were important factors. 1940*

*Friday, 29 April 1938*

April 29 – Well, well! Dug this journal up out of trunk at fraternity house – read through it and was rather shocked to see what a conglomeration of wretched whining it contains – Was all that necessary? Surely not! One may as well shrug one shoulders and say this is the game we've got to play –

Now my situation is as bad or worse than it's ever been – my prospects aren't a bit brighter – but I'm not groaning and gnashing my teeth about it as I apparently was a while back – grown apathetic? Perhaps. On the other hand I may have acquired a little guts –

Was taking an inventory of year and decided it was virtually wasted – as far as any material or visible gain – except that I did have a passionate physical love affair for a few months – (last winter) – it ended very badly – I was thrown over by the beloved bitch – but the experience was valuable.[206]

Aside from that, ~~I'm back~~ I've gotten nothing out of Iowa City. Yes, I know more about the theater but I can't see that my plays are any better.

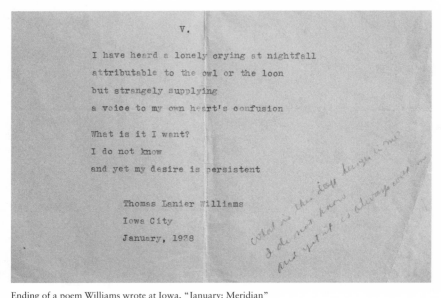

Ending of a poem Williams wrote at Iowa, "January: Meridian"

207. Ellsworth Prouty Conkle (1899–1994) was an assistant professor of speech and drama at the University of Iowa during the period 1936–39. He then moved to the University of Texas at Austin where he became a professor of drama. He was a recognized playwright, and his plays include two New York productions, *Two Hundred Were Chosen* (1936) and *Prologue to Glory* (1938), as well as a folk comedy, *Sparkin'* (1928). Conkle and Mabie taught the course "Experimental Dramatic Production" for which Williams obtained a grade of B.

208. In a letter to Willard Holland ([9 October 1937], Harriett Holland Brandt collection), Williams wrote, "I am going ahead with 'April Is The Cruellest Month' which stage facilities here would make possible." By spring 1938, Williams had rejected the opening lines of T. S. Eliot's *The Waste Land* in favor of the alternative title "Spring Storm," even though it was also the title of a recent novel (1936) by Alvin Johnson.

209. Joseph Safra (1916– ) was Williams' roommate for a short time when Williams moved for the fourth time, from the ATO fraternity house to a rooming house called Scott's at 409 North Dubuque Street. In two undated letters to his mother (HRC), Williams described his roommate as a graduate student in the dramatics department who was from Istanbul: "very cosmopolitan and refined, but he has Oriental fatalism in regard to such things as dusting and washing dishes."

210. Williams would use this experience in his short story "Two on a Party" begun in 1951:
Billy had the uncomfortable feeling that [Cora] suspected him of stealing the diamond ear-clip. Each time she glanced at him his face turned hot. He always had that guilty feeling when anything valuable was lost, and it made him angry; he thought of her as an irritating old bag. Actually she wasn't accusing anybody of stealing the diamond ear-clip; in fact she kept assuring the barman that the clasp on the ear-clip was loose and she was a goddam fool to put it on. (*CS*, p. 283)

Williams (second from left) as one of Falstaff's "Charge of Foot" in *Henry IV, Part I* at the University of Iowa, 5–8 April 1938. The production was directed by E. C. Mabie with costumes by Marian Gallaway and light control by Lemuel Ayers. The stage crew included Bette Reitz.

*Still no self-confidence. at the mercy of others' opinions, however conventional or bourgeois, where my work was concerned*

Badly deflated by Conkle[207] & class this week when ~~I read~~ they criticized my new play.[208] Hardly a favorable comment – Conkle hesitated when I asked if it was "worth working on" – and said, "well, if you've got nothing else –" Yes, I was horribly shocked, felt like going off the deep-end. Feared that I might lose my mind.

That was day before yesterday. It passed off quickly. I don't believe the play is really that bad – it's virtues are not apparent in a first reading but I think it would blossom out on the stage – but I see plainly now that I'm a distinctly second or third rate writer – and I wonder how I ever got into it so deep – now what? No degree – flunked 2 hours last term – have not yet broken the news to mother – dread doing that – She has been so marvelous, so lovely, so generous – I think of her and Grand and poor little Rose a great deal – I'm not really so hard & cynical after all – in fact I'm ~~da~~ still dangerously soft.

Taking a calm, cold estimate of myself – I think I will probably turn in my checks one way or another in the next 2 or 3 years (maybe less) unless some startling good luck comes along – my mind can't stand up forever under the neurotic burden it carries and I'm driving my weak heart too hard.

Drove out in country with Joe the Turk[209] – me driving – and it gave me a thrill – I still respond quickly and sensitively to the beauty of things –

A silly business has alienated me from the theater crowd. One of the girls had a pocket book stolen and I became quite embarrassed while they were talking about it – was afraid they might think me guilty – <u>for absolutely no reason</u>!!! – idiotic – have felt uncomfortable with them and avoided them ever since.[210] One of silliest things I've ever experienced. But it isn't insanity since I realize how ridiculous it is – but perhaps my queer actions have actually made them suspect me – Sounds like dementia praecox, doesn't it? But it's just the old guilt complex – the feeling ~~of inf~~ of social inadequacy in a new guise.

<u>So long</u> – we are going to see it through to the end of the road – wherever that may be – What do I want? I want love and creative power! – Eh bien! Get it!

211. Truman Slitor (1917–90) received a B.A. in philosophy at the University of Iowa in 1938 and lived in the same rooming house as Williams.

212. Most likely an early version of "She Walks in Beauty." In a letter dated 8 August 1938 (HRC) to Professor E. C. Mabie, regarding his application for National Youth Administration work, Williams mentioned enclosing a list of projected new plays, some "already in progress." On the verso of an incomplete draft of the 8 August letter (HRC), Williams listed three plays, including "She Walks in Beauty" or "Grammar of Love," a play based on "the only platonic love in Lord Byron's life":

> Situation: he comes to visit a titled friend. The ladies of the house are fascinated and terrified by his reputation as a rake. The stupid, boorish husband makes elaborate efforts to safeguard his wife's honor from possible injury by Lord Byron and she, insulted by her husband's concern, deliberately flirts with their guest. Husband's spinster Aunt or sister imagines that she is the object of Byron's subtle pursuit, which makes some comic complications. The poet and the sensitive wife fall really in love but recognizing her real goodness he for once sublimates his passion, writes her the immortal lyric, and goes into exile from England. The wife is a semi-invalid with consumption so there is a great deal of poignancy in her promise to meet him in Italy next winter if she is well enough to go. Rather light and romantic in treatment but with a poetic sadness in the close. First act written and final scene sketched.

This fragment was based on an actual incident. Byron wrote amusing letters to Lady Melbourne about the progress of his flirtation with Lady Frances Webster, the wife of James Wedderburn Webster, a friend whom Byron regarded as a buffoon (Leslie A. Marchand [ed.], *Lord Byron: Selected Letters and Journals* [London: John Murray, 1982]). About Lady Frances, whom Byron described as "a pretty pleasing woman . . . but in delicate health," Byron wrote to Lady Melbourne, "I have made love . . . & if I am to believe mere *words* . . . it is returned" (pp. 67, 72). The relationship did not go much further. In his diaries, however, the Irish poet Thomas Moore, Byron's good friend, noted that "[Byron's] head was full of her, when he wrote the Bride" (p. 113n).

213. On 13 May 1938, in an article in the *St. Louis Post-Dispatch* entitled "Mummers Wind Up Season with 'The Man on Stilts,'" *Spring Storm* was announced as a play to be performed by the Mummers in their upcoming season. The Mummers disbanded before the play could be performed.

Truman Slitor                          Joseph Safra

*Monday, 30 May 1938*

May 30 – Memorial day – Spent a delightful afternoon on the river – canoeing – with Truman Slitor[211] – we went to Coralville and got some beer and drifted back down to town – then drove out again with Joe the Turk in his car and drank with a bunch of journalism students. Now I'm broke – I've got 15¢ in my pocket and have to move tomorrow to my summer residence.

*Remember that afternoon very clearly – sunny water – bare skin – free, logy motion – youth. '40.*

Things have run fairly smooth of late – no climactic events – this is sort of an indeterminate stage of the game – like most others – God only knows how the summer will turn out –

I have enjoyed walking about town lately – the funny old houses and the rural streets are fascinating –

At the end of the year I have found very few persons that I can call friends – loads of acquaintances – Slitor is the best of the bunch and even he wouldn't lend me a buck when I'm down to my last dime – Ah, well –

"What is it about people?"
"There's an awful lot of them."

Dull! Very dull – too much beer – I guess I'd better go back out for a walk – nothing else to do – Why do women ignore me so consistently these days? Sometimes they look at me as though I weren't there – I believe it's mostly because I'm so damned short – and then I'm too lazy to be interesting when I'm out among people I don't know well. And when they ignore me it hurts my feelings – a vicious circle –

I've started a silly comedy[212] that may turn out fairly well if I get some impetus in the way of plot – shows my rather trivial state of mind.

"Spring Storm" announced in St. Louis[213] but Holland has not yet seen the script –

214.  In "The Four-leaf Clover," Helen returns home after being expelled from boarding school for an incident involving "something about a young married man and a New Orleans hotel and an attempted jump from a window." At home and unnaturally calm, she shows her sixteen-year-old brother a four-leaf clover and tells him it means good luck, but he responds angrily at her for disgracing the family. The brother does not understand that his sister is mentally ill.

"The Four-leaf Clover" bears a resemblance to the fourth poem in Lionel Wiggam's grouping "Heart-shaped Leaf" in his collection *Landscape with Figures*:

HEART-SHAPED LEAF

IV

The girl who has taken her first lover
Assumes at once a dignity and pride.
The haughty queen is no more proud than she,
The tyrant-empress no more dignified.

Her heart is a strange wing, stirring and subsiding;
She turns to mountains, then she wanders south.
Nothing remotely pacifies her anguish,
Save her lover's mouth.

Her friends will question her, but she is distant:
Careful to keep her fear unmanifest.
She coolly smiles, her piteous avid heart
A wild and fluttering thing inside her breast.

Only her lover silences that panic.
Only his touch, his smile, subdue the grief.
Running to meet him, she is a child who whispers:
"Look! I have brought you a curious heart-shaped leaf."

215.  Joe Safra.

216.  Bette Reitz.

217.  Only fragments of scenes from "Hello Moon" are known to exist. The play centers on Paul Ashland, the twenty-year-old son of a sharecropper, and the landowner's wife, Celeste Thorndike. Paul is seduced by Celeste, who likes to be whipped by her impotent husband. The sexual awakening of Paul by a much more experienced woman parallels Williams' relationship with Bette Reitz and has faint echoes of O'Neill's *Desire Under the Elms*. A small fragment of this play, a scene where a ghost named Laura blows out her candle, would find its way into *The Glass Menagerie*.

218.  "Hello Moon" and *Spring Storm*, formerly "April is the Cruellest Month."

219.  Heavenly Critchfield, the main character in *Spring Storm*. In earlier versions of the play she is called Helen.

Allons – the summer is just begun! – hope to do something worthwhile – have written a rather nice short story – "The 4-leaf Clover" – about a girl going mad[214] – memories of Rose – oh, God have pity on my poor little sister! – this I mean if nothing else – pity her and forgive us all – Goodnight

*Wednesday, 8 June 1938*

Wed. June 8 – Been working exactly a week at State Hospital waiting tables in restaurants – horribly exhausting, nerve-wracking work and it has made me nervous and ill – ~~palpitat~~ jolting heart and tension and gas – quite uneasy today – but not the old frantic fear that I used to have – Is this courage – ? Or what? Anyway it's a blessing. No doubt I could be scared out of my wits again – but at least I am <u>now</u> able to put up a fight.

Have done nothing but work and sleep – too tired for anything else – seen no one hardly – new house is pleasant – alone now but will have a room-mate soon. Enjoy this quiet and tranquillity after the noisy, disgusting Turk[215] that shared my apartment – one of most revolting persons I've ever known –

This work at hospital is good experience for me if I can survive it – Fortunately today I was given an easier job – due to my inefficiency in the first – I didn't break any dishes – not one! – but forgot orders and got terribly nervous & confused.

It is funny how the days slide along and you find yourself still living – living – <u>living</u>! – and wanting so badly to go on living – because you do love life and dread death – but have the guts now to take what they give you – that is, when you know it's got to be taken! –

Truman's left town – one fellow I really liked – I was to meet him for a final beer last nite but was too tired to go so wrote him a card this A.M. – Wish I could get things started again with Bette[216] – we are now friendly but <u>pas de plus</u>.

Started anew on my expressionistic drama Hello Moon[217] – it may be pretty good eventually. Hope I'll have strength & time to put in some good hard work on it this summer so I can go home with <u>two</u> plays[218] under my belt – Will go out now for a beer and a bit of social life if any is to be found at this dead in-between season – winter students gone – summer students not yet arrived – Poor Tommy is more or less by himself these days and is not quite the brilliant companion he would like to be! So long – Moon –

*Tuesday, 2 August 1938*

Aug. 2 – Well this is almost "le fin d'été" – mournful phrase! – Read final version of my second act and it was finally, quite, quite finally rejected by the class because of Heavenly's[219] weakness as a character. Of course it is very frightening & discouraging to work so hard on a thing and then have it fall flat. There is still a chance they may be wrong – all of them – I have to cling to that chance. Or do

220.  Edward Charles Mabie (1892–1956) was the formidable head of the department of speech and dramatic arts at the University of Iowa and is credited for transforming the department of public speaking into a theatre department of high national standing. He was recognized as a leader in educational theatre work and one of the foremost contributors to the community theatre movement in the United States. Mabie could be very emotive at times and, in both contemporaneous letters and *Memoirs* (pp. 48–49), Williams erroneously explained Mabie's emotional behavior as caused by an inoperable brain tumor.

Williams used Mabie's surname for a character in the play fragments "The Windows of the Blue Hotel" and "Death: Celebration."

221.  Both Milton Lomask (1909–91) and Hazel Teabeau (1898–1969) were graduate students at the University of Iowa. Lomask was born in Fairmont, West Virginia, and received a B.A. from the University of Iowa in 1930 and a M.A. from Northwestern University in 1941. Lomask became an educator and writer whose interests ranged from history and biography to children's literature. Hazel Teabeau went on to teach English and speech at Lincoln University in Jefferson City, Missouri, and in the 1940s she acted in and directed a number of plays at Lincoln. She became the first African American to gain a doctorate at the University of Missouri at Columbia.

222.  The Federal Writers' Project was established in 1935 by the Works Project Administration (WPA), one of the New Deal programs created by President Franklin Delano Roosevelt to alleviate widespread unemployment. The Federal Writers' Project employed writers, editors, and research workers to produce more than a thousand books and pamphlets which included state guides, ethnic studies, folklore collections, local histories, and nature studies.

223.  The National Youth Administration (NYA), also established by the WPA in 1935, obtained part-time work for unemployed youths so that they could continue their education. As unemployment decreased and war approached, emphasis was gradually shifted to training youths for war work until, early in 1942, all NYA activities not contributing to the war effort were withdrawn.

E. C. Mabie                    Milton Lomask

I? Why can't I be brave and admit this defeat? – Because it means the defeat of everything? Perhaps. I haven't the slightest notion what comes after this summer. Holland is about my last resource. If he likes it and will produce that would at least give me a spar to hang onto for a few months. I would do better to come back here but how? Mabie[220] won't get me a scholarship.

### Sunday, 16 October 1938

Sun. Oct. 15 (or 16th) I resume writing after another long lapse – The closing weeks of summer, from about time of last entry till about one week ago – were one of the best periods in recent years. I became quite well adjusted at Iowa City – met a boy named Milton Lomask and his mulatto mistress, Hazel Teabeau,[221] two intellectual radicals and they made excellent comrades for the rest of time. Got my degree and then spent 12 or 14 days in Chicago – which was very good for me – tried to get a job on Writers' Project[222] – but did not quite come through – Returned to St. Louis and tried for Radio work – at first encouraging prospects – Clark was here and we had a good time – much social activity and my health excellent as it had been nearly all summer – then Clark left – the radio prospects petered out – I found myself caught in St. Louis with nothing to do – I had turned down a chance of getting NYA[223] work at Iowa City – drank coffee almost daily to work on new

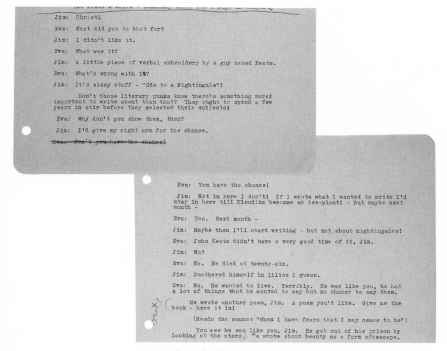

Excerpt of a draft of *Not About Nightingales*

224. Drawing on his earlier sketch "Quit Eating," Williams based *Not About Nightingales* on an incident which took place in a Pennsylvania prison ("Guard Admits Turning on Heat But Says Official Ordered It," *St. Louis Star-Times*, 1 September 1938). Convicts who had led a hunger strike were locked in a steam-heated cell, and four were killed. The play Williams wrote contained two main stories. The first focused on the struggle between the corrupt prison warden, Boss Whalen, and Butch O'Fallon, the tough leader of the prisoners. The second, which is intertwined with the first story, is the romance of Canary Jim, the literary prisoner who edits the prison's newspaper and whom Butch despises as a "songbird," and Eva Crane, the secretary to Boss Whalen. The prisoners, led by Butch, go on a hunger strike to protest the awful prison food. After a number of days, the leaders are locked up in a steam-heated cell, called the "Klondike," where the heat is turned on so high that they die of dehydration. Jim escapes from the prison, situated on an island, by jumping into the water. The play ends with the audience not knowing whether Jim survives the half-mile swim to shore.

    The title *Not About Nightingales* refers to a scene in which Jim, who has been reading Keats, rips out the poem "Ode to a Nightingale" and throws it onto the floor in disgust. Concerned about his fellow inmates who may soon be sent to the heated cell, Jim asks: "Don't those literary punks know there's something more to write about than that?" (act 2, episode 1). When Eva asks him what he would write about, he says, "Not about nightingales," suggesting that he would write about appalling social conditions and wrongs against humanity.

    *Not About Nightingales* includes of one of Williams' first overtly homosexual characters, the Queen, who feels he is persecuted because he is "refined." Over the next several years Williams would include effeminate characters such as the Designer in the play *Stairs to the Roof* and the Director in the play "Why Did Desdemona Love the Moor?" It would not be until *A Streetcar Named Desire*, *Cat on a Hot Tin Roof*, and, later, *Small Craft Warnings* that Williams would deal with the idea or hint of homosexuality in a serious manner.

225. Harold Mitchell roomed with Williams for one semester at the ATO fraternity house during the 1930–31 school year at the University of Missouri. Raised in a rural farming community, he had a great appreciation for Williams' talent as a writer. In *A Streetcar Named Desire* Williams named Blanche's suitor Harold Mitchell (Mitch).

Harold Mitchell

play "Not About Nightingales" – a prison melodrama based on the prison atrocity in Philadelphia County[224] – ~~gradually~~ soon my nerves began to pop – heart neurosis developed this week – a crisis last night – after several previous – This morning felt very weak and sickly – although I had gotten a fair sleep – Once again I feel dangerously cornered, cut-off – wonder how I am going to fight my way through – Some external stimulus must be applied to snap me out of <u>this</u>. But what? A trip somewhere would be the best – Naturally I feel uncomfortable in the house with Dad when I know he thinks I'm a hopeless loafer – Soon as I gather my forces (and I shall!) I must make a definite break – because this stagnation is debilitating my will – making me ~~thin~~ weak and timid again – Perhaps I can get hold of about $20. and just lam out for Florida – bum my way South – Sounds too improbable for words – but something desperate should be done to escape <u>this</u>.

Dear Grand is here – arrived sick with cold and had to spend first days in bed – now better thank God! – She is so utterly good – it helps to be near her – She gave me [*unfinished sentence*]

Now I feel my nerves relaxing a little – from their tight knots – tomorrow I can swim – start the climb back up and as soon as it is fairly achieved – Be this hereby <u>resolved</u> – I am going to do some one definite thing to escape the present situation which – if allowed to continue – would only make me a wreck –

I wonder about my old friends. Jim? Milton? Bette? Mitch?[225] Truman? Clark? I suppose we all make pretty shabby compromises with fate –

And then there is always the shadow of what happened to Rose!

What makes all this so stupid is that the fear is so much worse than the thing feared – the ~~slight~~ heart defect, however actual, would cause me little discomfort – no actual pain – if I were not afraid of it – it is the fear that makes all the concommittant distresses, the dreadful tension, the agora and claustro-phobia, the nervous indigestion, the hot gassy stomach – the heart might fail and end my life – but fearing that does not improve it and without the fear I would be immeasurably relieved – I would have few symptoms as long as I lived reasonably – and when I died it would be quickly perhaps and without much suffering –

So let's snap out of the whole silly business – once and for all!


*Monday, 17 October 1938*

Monday –

Felt much, much better all day – in fact felt that I had pulled out of the rut – till tonight when – on the way home from Hotel Roosevelt – I had pains in my chest accompanied by much tension. The pains really were alarming – of course they might have indicated nothing serious – but were ~~the most severe I can remember~~ more severe than gas-pains – scared me – but I did not lose my head & get panicky – I took mebral & hot chocolate and now feel better – writing this in bed – 1:A.M –

226.  Anne Jennings (1895–1977) was married to Blandford Jennings. She was interested in the theatre and often acted in plays at the Webster Groves Theatre. She had written a positive review of Williams' "The Magic Tower" for the *Webster News-Times*.

227.  The anti-fascist article Williams wrote for Anne Jennings was his program note for Sinclair Lewis' play *It Can't Happen Here*, which opened on 1 December 1938:

It is significant that the great thinkers and artists of Fascist countries have become voluntary exiles because they cannot exist and create in states where the science of government has become confused with that of penology. Thomas Mann, Einstein, Freud, Max Reinhardt, leaders in every field of science and art, have fled from the black-shirted countries. Without such men there would be no progress in civilization. Culture would become merely a product of the munitions factories.

Most of these great exiles came to America because they thought that America was free from Fascism. Is it possible that they were mistaken in that belief? Can Fascism come to this country?

You will find the answer in Sinclair Lewis' dramatization of his famous novel "It Can't Happen Here" which the Mummers of St. Louis have wisely chosen as their next production. It is a thrilling and powerful play and nobody who values his liberties can afford to miss it. (Leverich, p. 270)

228.  *Not About Nightingales.*

229.  No manuscript with this title is known to exist.

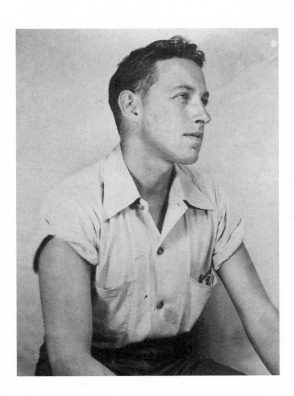

Anne Jennings[226] sent me a card asking me to write an article about "It Can't Happen Here" – I wrote a pretty ~~good~~ strong denunciation of Fascism.[227] I am at last becoming sincerely aroused in my social Consciousness – I begin to appreciate the very real danger of Fascism –

Swam 20 lengths – felt swell afterwards till about 8:00 – then the renewed illness began –

Oh, I hope I can throw it off <u>soon</u> – I want to live, live, <u>live</u>!!

The world is so strange and exciting and life is such an endlessly glamorous mystery –

I don't want to leave it all prematurely – unanswered. Oh, is there any answer? There must be –

God, who are you, where are you? What is the Truth of it all?

How many before me have asked and gotten no answer – but I want to know –

So God let me live out my due length of time and say my full say – glean all the knowledge possible and drain my last ounce of beauty into words before I go.


*Wednesday, 26 October 1938*

Wed. – Ten days since I started this new chapter – Physically I am about up to par – but still doing nothing to free myself from this stagnant condition – Perhaps the scene tonight will rouse me to action – Dad started griping about my lack of job, Etc. – Surely I won't stay on here when I'm regarded as such a parasite – Now is the time to make a break – get away, away – I have pinned pictures of wild birds on my lavatory screen – Significant – I'm desperately anxious to escape – But where & how? – No money – Grand & Mother the only possible source – What a terrible trap to be caught in! – But there must be some way out and I shall find it –

"N.A.N."[228] seems pretty cheap stuff – Holland had it since Saturday without a word – I'm pretty sure he wishes it had never been written.

Another one begun – promisingly – "All My Sins"[229] – but it may fizzle out – what I need is contact with the world – <u>vital</u> contact – which I'm too cowardly – so far – to make.


*Wednesday, 16 November or Thursday, 17 November 1938*

Nov. 16 or 17 – (I'm a bit vague about the calendar these days) –

I wish to report one happy circumstance – an almost definitely decided departure for New York – Seems almost too fabulous, doesn't it? – But no serious obstacles apparent now – My miraculous grandmother is going to finance the trip – Will it <u>happen</u>? <u>Can</u> it happen. Oh, I hope so! –

Finished 3rd draft of "N.A.N." – It may be very good or very bad – I don't know – haven't even read it yet – just writing, writing – drinking coffee nearly every day – and feeling well in spite of it – But it is only the prospect of leaving St. Louis that

230. Williams presumably returned to the play about Byron, "She Walks in Beauty," to which he alluded in his 8 August 1938 letter to Professor Mabie (HRC). Only fragments are known to exist. In the first scene we learn that Sir James Webster wishes to send Lady Frances, his virgin wife, away to protect her from the charm of Lord Byron, who is coming to stay. In other scenes, Lord Byron flatters Lady Frances for her beauty and charm; Lady Frances flirts with Lord Byron by telling him she has enjoyed reading the third canto of *Don Juan*; Sir James' sister, Lady Veronica, deludes herself that Lord Byron has proposed marriage to her; and Sir James, spurned by Lady Frances who refuses to sleep with him, confesses his attraction to Lady Melbourne.

   Williams apparently was not able to complete this play, but he would include aspects of it in later plays. For example, he would use the situation of the virgin wife seduced by an aquaintance of her husband's in the screenplay *Baby Doll*. Williams would use the description of Lady Frances as arriving with a house "mortgaged beyond all restitution and a trunk full of fanciful impractical clothes" for Blanche in *A Streetcar Named Desire*. When Williams expanded "Ten Blocks on the Camino Real" into *Camino Real* he included the character Lord Byron.

   Williams' identification with Byron is evidenced in an early fragment of a short story in which the main character, Paul Bagby, modeled on Williams, was known as "Byron, the Campus Poet."

   The play Williams did complete with reference to Byron is "Lord Byron's Love Letter" (1941), set in the French Quarter of New Orleans. In this one-act play, a spinster, Ariadne, charges admission for tourists to look at one of Lord Byron's love letters, which had been sent to her grandmother, Irénée Marguerite de Poitevent. Williams based this later play on a character he had only heard about from his grandfather, a Columbus, Mississippi, native named Julia Meek Geherty. Over ten years later, in a letter to his lover Frank Merlo dated 9 May 1952 (HTC), Williams would describe a trip to Columbus: "Met the lady who has Lord Byron's love-letter, she is mad as a hatter, was sitting crouched in a dark corner when we arrived."

Rose with Jiggs

keeps me up – Sometimes I fancy that I am happy – because I am eager for each new day's work – but that is restlessness & frustration – perhaps nothing more –

Will I <u>live</u> again in New York? Or will I finally & completely die? There is adventure in life – but a slow ~~methodic~~ plodding adventure that creeps around you like – like fog – (awful writing!) – I am dull & tired tonight – Had my eyes dilated at oculist – thought of beautiful theme for a painting – Four people – eyes closed – in ante-room of oculist office – forced to sit with eyes closed – awake – possibly for first times in their lives – Each thinking of what? – Trivial things? Yes, but – there is beauty and wonder in it if you look deep enough –

Visited Sanitarium & saw Rose – She is like a person half-asleep now – quiet, gentle and thank God – not in any way revolting like so many of the others – She sat with us in a bright sunny room full of flowers – said "yes" to all our questions – looked puzzled, searching for something – sometimes her eyes filled with tears – (So did mine) – Only the little dog stirred her – she was delighted with him – held him and gave him water – She said once "I can't believe he is!" – meaning 'alive' – I suppose, as she always feared so much for his health – Strange, sad –

It rains tonight, lightning, low thunder –

Tomorrow I go to the Poetry Club at Prof. Webster's – I have seen no one lately – a quiet somnabulistic life – perhaps I have a touch of my sister's disease?! – But let's not close with such a thought – Let us remark, rather, that New York will be exciting – or that our Grandmother is <u>the</u> <u>sweetest</u> <u>thing</u> <u>God</u> <u>ever</u> <u>made</u>!!

P.S. I notice that in Sept. of last year – before leaving for Iowa – I remarked that I felt I was leaving the paternal roof for good – Well, here I am back under it – yes, my life <u>is</u> a series of returns – I guess the damned old roof will fall down on my head someday!! The rain sings gently – I will go to bed.


*Sunday, 20 November 1938*

Nov 20 Sunday – Read "N.A.N." last nite – It seemed incredibly bad and I felt quite desperate about. Thought I couldn't look at it for another 6 Months – yet this A.M. I was writing on it as usual –

And writing badly –

Will try to salvage something from the wreck – but I think a production this year is almost out of the question –

Very disturbing to find myself So ineffectual after writing all these years – I ought to take a vacation – gather material – <u>live</u>! –


*Monday, 5 December 1938*

Dec. 5 or 6 – Monday – <u>Blue</u> Monday –

N.A.N. is tucked away in the desk with so many other derelict scripts – And I have started a new one – This, a romantic comedy about Lord Byron[230] & Lady

231. Knute Heldner (1896–1952) was a Swedish-born painter who emigrated to the United States in 1902. In the 1920s he began spending winters in New Orleans, where he painted Vieux Carré scenes and Louisiana landscapes. In 1926 he won highest honors at the Swedish-American Art Exhibition in Chicago. His work is in the permanent collections of the Smithsonian Institution, the White House, and the Luxembourg Museum in Paris. He was married to Colette Pope.

    In a letter to his mother (2 January [1939], HRC), Williams wrote: "Mr. & Mrs. Heldner (Alice Lippmann's friends) say that if I get desperate I can earn bread as a model — but I trust something better will turn up. The Heldners live in two rooms with a baby girl — he is brilliant and very good-hearted. Showed me his canvases which have won fine critical comment but during his whole sixteen years in New Orleans he has only sold four. They are very modernistic so are not popular as decoration for homes. He has a red beard and often forgets where he is going when he leaves the house — but not as bad as Mrs. Lippmann!"

232. Herbert Ashton Jr., director of the WPA theatre. The Works Project Administration (WPA), created in 1935 in a period of widespread unemployment as part of the New Deal program of President Franklin Delano Roosevelt, established four programs to employ artists, writers, musicians, and actors. One of the four programs, the Federal Theatre Project, employed theatre professionals in more than a thousand productions which included classical and modern drama, children's plays, musical comedies, and documentary theatre. The Federal Theatre Project also produced plays by young unknown playwrights and presented radio broadcasts of dramatic works. In 1939, appropriations were reduced due to charges of mismanagement, and by 1943 the WPA was eliminated.

Knute Heldner, *Self-portrait*, c. 1940

Frances Webster, should be a natural – if there is anything left in me. But I write very weakly – am dull & listless – Grand sent me $3.00 today – I wandered around town – spent a dollar on dinner, hi-ball and a stupid show – If only there were some forward motion in my life! – There isn't – It's all stagnation – I hope not <u>regression</u> –

New York or New Orleans seems the last or only hope – Maybe a new scene will revive me –


*Wednesday, 28 December 1938*

Dec. 28 – 1938 – <u>Wed</u> How strange!

Immediately after the above entry I find myself reporting that <u>here</u> I actually <u>am</u> in a completely new scene – New Orleans – the Vieux Carré. Preposterous? Well, rather! Somehow or other things do manage to happen in my life. It's a miracle, performed, of course, by my miraculous grandmother to whom I owe almost every good thing in my life and none of the bad.

I am delighted, in fact, enchanted with this glamorous, fabulous old town. I've been here about 3 hours but have already wandered about the Vieux Carré and noted many exciting possibilities. Here surely is the place that I was <u>made</u> for if any place on this funny old world.

I am lying (on the floor) in front of a gas grate at about 2 A.M. to make this entry – I feel very quiet & comfortable – but full of anticipation! If only it can be done – financially – if only <u>only</u>! Much will happen I am sure in the days, weeks or months to come –

Sufficient to say now that I am sleepy and happy or as nearly happy as old T.L.W. is able to be!

The bed looks clean – I hope it is! – Tomorrow I will go out first thing to locate a cheap furnished room in the artists' section – & meet Knute Heldner[231] to whom I have a letter of introduction from Mrs. Lippmann – <u>En Avant</u>!


*Friday, 30 December 1938*

Fri. Judas Priest! – It's no use denying the fact that I am very blue & lonesome – enough so to be really worried about the prospects – I've met nobody but the Heldners and seen them only once – being completely alone for 48 hours, even in the most enchanting of cities, has gotten on my nerves.

Something will have to happen to relieve my depression tomorrow <u>or</u> – perhaps all will be lost – Nothing constructive done so far except a brief meeting with Ashton, Director of the WPA Theater[232] who told me to see a young lady about submitting my scripts – think I'll do that tomorrow – I <u>must</u> do something.

Somebody has just moved in the room next door – even a stranger across a wall is comforting to me in this state.

233.  In a letter to his mother (2 January [1939], HRC), Williams gave a more detailed description of the events
of New Year's Eve:

> The Lippmann's friends [the Heldners] have been lovely to me. They invited me to a New Year's Eve
> party which lasted till day-break and traveled through about half-a-dozen different homes or stu-
> dios and I met most of the important artists and writers. They are all very friendly and gracious.
> Roark Bradford, famous author of negro literature, and Lyle Saxon, who wrote Fabulous New
> Orleans, both live in the Quarter and I am promised introductions to them. I met Mr. Ashton, direc-
> tor of the WPA theatre.

Williams would use this occasion in scene 2 of his play *Vieux Carré*:

> WRITER: . . . Well, New Year's Eve, I was entertained by a married couple I had a letter of introduc-
> tion to when I came down here, the . . . man's a painter, does popular bayou pictures displayed in
> shop windows in the Quarter, his name is . . .

234.  Williams rented a room at 722 Toulouse Street from Mrs. E. O. Anderson. He wrote to his mother
([9 January 1939], HRC) about his prospects:

> She has promised to let me serve tables for my meals and says if the business is successful she may
> also give me my room and a few dollars a week. However her capital is very small and she plans to
> do the whole work herself — cooking and taking care of rooms — so I don't know how it will turn
> out. She's an extremely practical, energetic woman — a widow who lost her money in Chicago. With
> her enthusiasm and business-sense she may make a go if it. She's having some cards printed which
> I'm going to distribute for her. . . . She said she would give Grand and Grandfather a beautiful front
> room on a balcony. . . . I wrote them about it.

235.  Frank David Bunce (1905–80) was a writer from Amberg, Wisconsin, who had previously worked as a
feature writer for newspapers. In addition to contributing articles and stories to various magazines, he went
on to publish two novels in the 1950s. In a letter to his mother ([18 January 1939], HTC), Williams reit-
erated what he wrote in his journal and added, "Since [Bunce] has a car and many attractive girl friends,
he has proved a very valuable friend to me."

236.  No manuscript of "Strange Companions" is known to exist.

237.  The Young Men's Christian Association (YMCA) provided housing, sports, and recreation to build character and supply a sense of community to young unmarried men who had left rural families and emigrated to
the cities. By World War I, a number of YMCAs had become centers of sex and social life for young gay men.

238.  Very likely "Vieux Carré" (dated January 1939, New Orleans).

YMCA, 936 St. Charles Avenue, New Orleans

*I haven't always been so pleased with myself*

*Sunday, 1 January 1939*

New Year's Day – 1939 – What a nite! – I was introduced to the artistic and Bohemian life of the Quarter with a bang! All very interesting, some utterly appalling. This morning I shall call for my hat which was left at one of the parties.[233]

*Saturday, 14 January 1939*

Saturday – Jan. 14. I have been here over 2 weeks now – a new epoch in my career is under weigh – I am about to resume my job as waiter – also cashier – working for my landlady – the widow – who is opening a restaurant – How it will turn out God knows! – A rather exciting prospect[234] – Life here has been rather even & pleasant – Nothing really dramatic since New Year's Eve – I've made a nice friend in Frank Bunce who gets about $500.00 a month writing for the Sat. Eve. Post.[235] Our view points in art & life are so dramatically divergent that it is amazing that we should be friends – It struck me today as an idea for a novel or play – "Strange Companions"[236] – in which a boy of my sort is contrasted to a fellow like Bunce, their reactions to each other, influence, Etc. – a psychological thing.

I swim every day at "Y"[237] – eat at cafeterias, go to movies – write rather badly – especially my verse which I made the error of sending off[238] – Things are impending in my life – of that I feel sure – & so I am reasonably content for the nonce – willing to wait & see what's up!

In the meantime – Au Revoir!

P.S. When I read through this book I'm appalled at myself – what a fool I am! – Quelle sottises! – Comment je suis bête! Parbleu!!! – It is valuable as a record of one man's incredible idiocy! – who is reputed to be at least partially sane – or is he? – probably not! – Once in a while – rarely – I show a glimmer of intelligence – most of the time an abominable dullness – what is there in me that remains above and beyond all this – level-eyed, serious, tender, brave, immaculately clean? Yes, there is something in me like that – something that remains apart & keeps the record – "engraves the reckoning" – when that dies then I will be finally & completely dead. Or is that an illusion? Am I all animal, all willfull, blind, stupid beast? Is there another part that is not an accomplice in this mad pilgrimage of the flesh – ?

Ah, well, you're getting rhetorical, old boy – good night.

VIEUX CARRE

Thy dark freight,
                slipping past these wharves,
becomes a myth,
                involved with fog that drifts across
                the Cathedral square.

                Iron Horseman, plunge!
                The white mist covers you –
                        Your hat, three-cornered in a brave salute,
                cannot resist
                this vaporous oblivion the river gives
                and kindly gives,
a long, quiet breath exhaled,
the first in sleep's
                cool answer to the fever in the skull .

                The tryst you keep,  ghostly receding hull,
that many waters take across one portal
becomes a legend of swinging yellow-lantened passageways,
                secret compartments,
betrayed by sailors to prostitutes hired as informers –

                Narcotics seized at Havana!

                And so no dreams
                tonight for the tired anhedonic,

Our Father of constant forgiveness
                has little stone hands pigeons rest on....

                        Iron horseman before the Cabildo,
                        your cocked bravado
        is lost in the river's slow breathing!

                Shuffling remotely
                    among the vastness of dreams,
                    drunk vagrants
stumble along Toulouse.

                The whispers of women
                    pursue them past shuttered doorways.

                Come in!
                Come in and I'll take you to heaven!

                        Is heaven no further
                        than your brass bed,is, mulatto?

                        You don't have to climb
                        a single flight of stairs even!

                Oh, God!
                My baby's a wonderful baby!
                What do you say?

                        Slow, slow
                        is the derelict motion about us,

                restless, unsleeping
whose enthusiasms waned at forty and were not revived.

                Watchman, what of the night?

                  Il pleut.
                Il pleut dans ma coeur comme il pleut
                dans la ville.

The low-peaked roofs
        now sleep, or simulate sleeping,
                at least no more laughter,
                      drunken or otherise,
        and the mist climbs higher,

                Is gentle,
                it preaches Christ's word,
                it advocates gentle behavior,

And even the gutter-sprawlers
                    have radiant, uplifted faces,
                an angelus ringing
                the hour of spirits unshrouded,
                  crypts vacant,
                a breathless ascension through vapors!

                The slow, slow fog.
                No, watchman, the time is not yet,
                the dead are still visibly sleeping.

Tamale vendors at midnight
                crying in narrow streets
                explicit of sorrow
                as poems or violins

                    And the broken lamplight
drawn along steep gutters....

                    Tennessee Williams
                    New Orleans
                    January, 1939

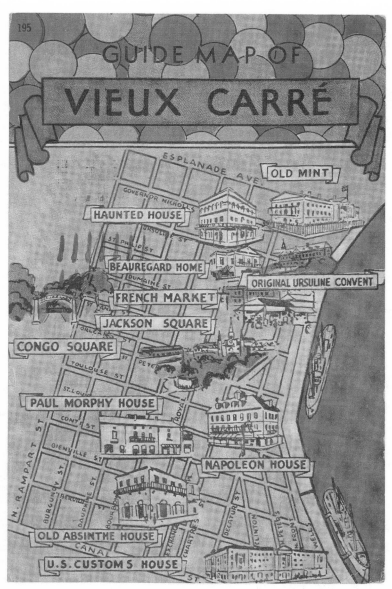

Postcard Williams sent to his grandmother

239. In a letter to his mother ([18 January 1939], HTC), Williams wrote: "I just have time for a few lines. Am enclosing one of our printed cards which I composed and have been distributing around town. The slogan [Meals in the Quarter for a quarter] is my own invention and seems to be effective. We opened yesterday. . . . I serve as waiter, cashier, publicity manager, host — in fact, every possible capacity, including, sometimes, dish-washer. When not busy in the dining-room I stand on the sidewalk and try to drag people upstairs!"

240. Verbeck may well have been the model for the man in the short story "The Malediction" and the one-act play "The Strangest Kind of Romance." In both works, a man who rents a room in a boardinghouse finds a cat which he adopts. The cat had belonged to the room's previous occupant, who had died of tuberculosis. The epigraph of "The Strangest Kind of Romance" is the last stanza of Hart Crane's poem "Chaplinesque": "The game enforces smirks; but we have seen / the moon in lonely alleys make / a grail of laughter of an empty ash can, / and through all sound of gaiety and quest / have heard a kitten in the wilderness."

241. Richard Orme owned a fashionable antiques shop in New Orleans and in 1946–47 rented Williams his apartment at 632½ St. Peter Street.

242. Richard Orme.

243. In "Preface to My Poems — Serious Version" in *Five Young American Poets* (New York: New Directions, 1944), Williams wrote: "I remember Joe Turner who wrote sea-stories more vivid and beautiful than Conrad's. He was a merchant sailor because there was nothing else for him to do when the W.P.A. Writers' Project ceased to exist, and now not only Joe but his mss. have disappeared altogether" (p. 125).

244. Lillian Romano lived in the French Quarter on Decatur Street.

431 Royal Street, the hotel in New Orleans where Williams first stayed

722 Toulouse Street, the rooming house where Williams moved in January 1939

*The last I heard of Ver Beck — he was coming to L.A. — I remember the peculiarly benign morning sunlight of N.O. — & those wheat cakes with corn syrup!  8/20/39*

*Monday, 16 January 1939*

<u>Monday</u> – Jan. 16 '39 – Tomorrow "The Quarter Eat Shop"[239] will be open for trade – let us hope there <u>is</u> some!

Today a funny little fellow named Verbeck[240] came running into the house in search of a lost black cat – turns out to be a poet who writes about "dragons & chrysanthemums" – very <u>precieuse</u> but very nice.

– Yesterday I went to The Orme's,[241] had a dull evening – there again this A.M. – S. took me to breakfast & D.[242] cashed my checque & they promise to attend our opening but I think they are a pretty foul lot and will probably be more reserved toward them in the future – clever, good-humored people but altogether lacking in anything of a lyrical nature – which I think is indispensable to a decent "human soul" – world apparently on the point of explosion – war, war, war! – And I write fanciful introspective little stories & precious verse!

*How rarely I seem to notice events in the outside world!  8/20/39*

Tom, Tom, what are we going to do with you? Throw you out on the front sidewalk where they put their garbage here in the <u>Vieux</u> <u>Carré</u>? – I deserve nothing better – well, nothing <u>much</u> better! Goodnight.

*Saturday, 28 January 1939*

Saturday Midnite – Jan. 28 – 1939 –

Well, the "Quarter Eat Shop" had a very brief existence – exactly one week – It is now past history – Little Man, what now? – I wish I knew – My life seems to be a pretty constant state of 'wishing I knew' – well, I've found out before – & shall again –

I have applied for work on the Fed. Writers Project – Joe Turner[243] & I both – Joe is a nice guy I met at the Eat Shop – I think I may count him on one of those 10 fingers that I reserve for O.K. people. Him & Frank Bunce. Also met a little girl, Lillian Romano,[244] who is sweet & appealing but no mental giant.

245.  In a letter to his mother (circa early February 1939, HRC), Williams described his "colorful experiences" that he was using "as the background for a new play ["Dead Planet, the Moon"] which is well under way":

It is just as well Grand and Grandfather decided to delay their visit, as we've had a very hectic time at 722 Rue Toulouse. As I've probably mentioned, the land-lady has had a hard time adjusting herself to the Bohemian spirit of the Vieux Carre. Things came to a climax this past week when a Jewish society photographer in the first floor studio gave a party and Mrs. Anderson expressed her indignation at their revelry by pouring a bucket of water through her kitchen floor which is directly over the studio and caused a near-riot among the guests. They called the patrol-wagon and Mrs. Anderson was driven to the Third Precinct on charges of Malicious Mischief and disturbing the peace. The following night we went to court — I was compelled to testify as one of the witnesses. Mrs. Anderson said she did not pour the water but I, being under oath, could not perjure myself — the best I could do was say I thought it was highly improbable that any lady would do such a thing!

An incomplete manuscript of "Dead Planet, the Moon," originally titled "Vieux Carré" (dated January 1939), exists. The first scene is set in a Bohemian restaurant and includes the incident related in the above letter. This manuscript also includes the characters Valentine, a poet, and Sky, a washed-up musician, both of whom were included in the much later play *Vieux Carré*. Williams borrowed the title "Dead Planet, the Moon" from a letter D. H. Lawrence had written to Dorothy Brett (8 March 1927):

Aldous and Maria [Huxley] and Mary Hutchinson came a week ago. . . . I feel myself in another world altogether. They seem to me like people from a dead planet, like the moon, where never will the grass grow or the clouds turn red.

The manuscript of "Dead Planet, the Moon" as well as the poem "Vieux Carré" were signed Tennessee Williams and represent a change in the way he signed manuscripts. In a letter to his mother (2 January [1939], HRC), Williams mentioned sending off plays from Memphis. He was referring to the Group Theatre Contest for writers under the age of twenty-five, which he had entered under the name Tennessee Williams. He changed his name and used his grandparents' mailing address to conceal the fact that he had lied about his age. At the time Williams was twenty-eight and had already published under the name Thomas Lanier Williams.

246.  Williams would use the image of the fugitive extensively in his stories, plays, poetry, and letters. As noted earlier, Williams was a fan of Lola Pergament's poetry, which included images of the fugitive. No doubt Williams was also influenced by Wordsworth's use of the image in the ninth stanza of "Ode: Intimations of Immortality from Recollections of Early Childhood": "That nature yet remembers / What was so fugitive!"

*a crucial time – might have ended easily have ended in some form of disaster. 8/20/39*

I write badly or not at all – Started a marvelously promising new play[245] last week – but can't seem to get going on it – Dull, dull! – I sit down to write & nothing happens. Washed up? – No! – I need a rest from my creative labors – I'm stale or I need a new stimulus.

The Eat Shop was ideal as it gave me something else to do – saved my eyes & my brain & my money – but like all lovely things it proved too fugitive[246] – ah, well –

Visited Ver Beck's studio tonite – Rather dismal – talented & yet completely uninteresting – I wonder about next week – running short of funds & I don't know what to do with my tiresome old self these days – hair falling out alarmingly, too – Many complaints tonight – What's <u>right</u> with me? – My health – I've been feeling damned good. But that doesn't seem to offer much consolation. What good's the old carcass when it's gotten nothing inside but a ~~very weak~~ 25 watt bulb that seems about burnt out. Shit. Don't gimme that stuff. G'nite all.

*lucky I was able to "smile bravely" at this time! 8/20/59*

*Sunday, 29 January 1939*

Sunday Nite – Well, here I am sailing bravely into another week – not-knowing what it may bring – wondering – but not too daunted by those speculations – A little tipsy tonite – out with Joe & Frank Bunce – felt inferior & stupid – but rather merry toward the end in spite of that – Why do people put up with silly old Tommy? I'll be damned if I know!

247.   Williams met Jim Parrott (1916–2001), formerly an English teacher, at the rooming house on Toulouse Street. Parrott, armed with his clarinet, was on his way to Los Angeles to pursue his interests in acting and directing. Williams, enticed by the idea of finding work at the film studios in Hollywood, decided to join him on his drive to the West Coast. Williams had written his mother a postcard, postmarked 18 February 1939, with a gilded description:

> A musician under contract in Hollywood has offered me free transportation to West Coast, no expense except meals on road, which seems too good to refuse, so I am leaving this A.M. We plan to take southern route along Mexican border, will stop several days at El Paso, Texas. You can write me there, General Delivery, enclose a small checque. Parrott, the musician, thinks he can get me work in studios. (Leverich, p. 284)

Williams would write about Parrott in his short story "In Memory of an Aristocrat":

> It was exactly one day after this that I lost my job at the Bohemian eating place which resulted in such a crisis in my personal affairs that nothing else seemed to matter. A fellow named Parrott had a jalopy that he was hoping to get to Hollywood in. Between us we had sixteen dollars: with that and a ten-inch section of rubber tube we managed to reach the West Coast about three weeks later. I was going to write pictures for Parrott to star in, but both of us were shortly employed as pin boys at a bowling alley in Laguna Beach. (CS, p. 91)

Later, in *Vieux Carré* (scene 8), Williams would model Sky, the young clarinet player, on Parrott:

> WRITER: — Were you serious about the West Coast offer?
> SKY: You're welcome to come along with me. I don't like to travel a long distance like that by myself.
> WRITER: How do you travel?
> SKY: I've got a beat-up old '32 Ford across the street with a little oil and about half a tank of gas in it. If you want to go, we could share the expense. Have you got any cash?
> WRITER: I guess I've accumulated a capital of about thirty-five dollars.
> SKY: We'll siphon gas on the way.
> WRITER: Siphon?
> SKY: I travel with a little rubber tube, and at night I unscrew the top of somebody's gas tank and suck the gas out through the tube and spit it into a bucket and empty it into my car. Is it a deal?

Williams in the El Paso desert

*What a strange time – Trinket – odd rather dear little person we me there – Jim wrote her just recently after we talked over this episode in El Paso. 8/20/39*

*Sunday, 26 February 1939*

Sunday in El Paso, Texas (God knows why!) – about the 25th of Feb. 1939 –
Well, here I am, Etc. Etc. Etc. – The Great west – Very bright & windy and dusty – We have completed about ¾ of our pilgrimage to the west coast but now appear to be at least temporarily "stymied" by lack of funds – I could choose a more desirable place in which to be stalled – the air is fairly choking with dust and the town quite dull – the mountain scenery sterile and uninspiring – Went on a picnic with some rather nice people who are not too exciting – Returned & tried to write – Pretty ineffectually – when will this dullness end? At what last barrier will you collapse, Mr. Williams?

I smile at myself these days, rather bitterly but with a marvelous acquiescence.

*I felt like I was going to cry – could scarcely control my voice – Jim left me at the Y.M.C.A. and I was completely lost! 8/20/39*

*Tuesday, 7 March 1939*

<u>Los Angeles</u> – <u>Tues.</u> March 6 (?) 1939
Arrived late this afternoon at this, the apparent end of our journey. I went to the "Y" – got a room – Jimmie[247] had supper with me & then drove on out to his uncle's – I feel terrified at finding myself alone in this huge foreign place – Quite appalled at my isolation! I have never felt lonelier in my life – or less enterprising – so the fate which now faces me is inscrutable to say the least. Oh, God, be a little bit sorry for Tom tonight and let him sleep and wake up stronger & able to go on.

The days on the Road were rich and bright and I felt more alive than in months or perhaps years. Yet not intelligent. The dullness continues and I can't help wondering if it is not an actual recession. But I have got to go on. However

Parrott recalled his experiences with Williams in "Tennessee Travels to Taos," published in the *Tennessee Williams Literary Journal*, spring 1989.

In a letter to Margaret Bradham Thornton, Jim Parrott remembered Trinket:

She was a leading lady who played opposite me in one of Lloyd Head's Coconut Grove (Fla.) Theater productions at the women's club in Coconut Grove in 1938. She left the Players in late fall and moved to her family's in El Paso, Texas. Before she left she gave me her family's El Paso address and said that if I ever got out there to look her up. When Tennessee and I left New Orleans in 1939 and started west . . . we left with limited funds. By the time we got to El Paso in a little old Ford, we were nearly broke. I suddenly remembered that I had Trinket's address in my wallet and that she lived in El Paso. On a wild thought we looked up Trinket who was staying with her mother in El Paso. We lived free for the next three days and Trinket and her mother toured us around El Paso. . . . After three days we left for the west.

Williams would use the name Trinket in a late play, "The Mutilated," set in the French Quarter of New Orleans, for one of the down-and-out prostitutes.

248.  Cornelius Williams had put his son in contact with Sam J. Webb, who worked for the International Shoe Company. Webb got Williams a job at Clark's Bootery in Culver City, but he was let go shortly afterward due to a slowdown in business.

249.  Williams would use this image in the play *The Night of the Iguana*, as well as in the short story of that name, changing the fox to an iguana.

Williams with Trinket and her mother in El Paso

*I shall never forget that lonely night in the y.m.c.a. room in the heart (?) of downtown Los angeles. 8/20/39*

foolish the choice I've made I have to see it through now – and keep my chin up – show some guts, Tommy old kid.

I miss Jim, of course – such a swell guy that at times he made me feel almost awed – my lost youth and clarity in that glass – Ah well – so long, Tom

*Wednesday, 8 March 1939*

<u>Next night</u> – Awful! Awful! – Such appalling loneliness – Jim didn't call, Sam Webb[248] was out – met no one and feel too miserable to live – but will have to just the same. Remember the little grey fox you saw chained to the wall in a little Texas town on the way here? He looked at you with frightened, miserable eyes – then shuddered and buried his little face in his fur – shutting out the sight of the world that made his little savage heart a captive – Tonight he is my brother – he is my <u>self</u> – The little fox and I are together in our great loneliness, our lostness

*These first days in L. a. were really appalling – I deserve my own pity for what I went through! 8/20/39*

and desperation[249] – Tomorrow? Tomorrow! Tomorrow?! – Oh, God, give me another chance!

Goodnight.

Later – Took a shower – relaxed a little – so many people around but nobody talks to me – that stuff about the little grey fox sounds like crap – but it <u>is</u> the way I feel – only I can't even bury my face in my fur – or is that what I will do when I go to sleep? – I hope I can and that the morning will not be as fiercely, intolerably bright as I fear it will be. Why did I come here? Why have I done <u>any</u> thing that I've done? – If only tomorrow I'll meet somebody who'll help me somehow! – at least be kind to me and relieve my loneliness.

250.  In a letter to Anne and Blandford Jennings ([16 March 1939], HRC), Williams wrote:

Well, here I am, of all places, on a pigeon ranch in Hawthorne, California — quite a jump from the
Vieux Carre! I was offered a free ride out here with a highschool English teacher from New York
State who was fed up with his profession and wanted to rough it a while. . . . I am boarding here
on the pigeon ranch with his Uncle and he with his first cousin — I'm working for my board, killed
and picked sixty squabs yesterday and drove them into the markets. We're about twenty miles out
of L.A. . . . The owner gets dead drunk every night and one of my principal duties is to take him
home and keep him out of communication with the local police. . . .

A very strange life for me to be living, even after the Vieux Carre! I seem to have a propensity
for getting into fantastic milieux nowadays — when I write about them people will say it's ridiculous, such people and things don't occur!

. . . I may start selling shoes Monday — one of Dad's salesmen in L.A. is getting me a job I don't
want in a retail shoe store — but I need the money to pay some debts — I skipped out of New
Orleans owing everyone.

Jim Parrott and I in front
of the "pigeon ranch" at
start of bicycle trip.
The yard, which you can't
see, is swarming with
roses of every kind.

*I should always be grateful to Fred and Adelaide Parrott for their real kindness when I came to their house that night in the rain – "like a wet dog"* 4/20/39

*Wednesday, 15 March 1939*

Wed –

   Feel quite calm now after a pretty bad spell – At first it was a sublime relief to
be out here in the country with Jim's Aunt Adelaide & Uncle Fred Parrott.[250]
Then I got lonesome again – isolated feeling returned – today I felt panicky –
Went out to see Jim – he'd gotten a job at the Airplane factory and was way
up in the clouds which made me feel lower than ever – Got him to drive me to a
bar where I drank a hi-ball & 2 beers – a good substitute for suicide! – but it didn't
last long – depression returned & I left before supper, feeling quite desperate – This
really does seem rather like "Custer's Last Stand" – but this journal is a succession
of such apparent finales which turn out to be continued in the next issue –

   Had supper here & took a long walk with Fred to see a sick man – he was
friendly and kind and the visit did me good – also the walk – this flat country

*It's a wonder I didn't crack up about this time – it looked like a dead-end,* 8/20/39

isn't so bad at night with the lighted derricks and the palms, the frogs singing and
the stars – it always helps me to walk out under the stars – Afterwards read a
story through Fred's magnifying glass (I lost my glasses just before I left N.O.) –
enjoyed it – Fred went out to get drunk – Adelaide nervously waits for him to get
back – we drink warm cocoa, paint a little and decide it's better to go to bed.

   Tomorrow I shall be quiet & patient as an old cow – and so on till this
difficult period is over & I can see a little more light on the road ahead.
Goodnight, old boy. Keep your shirt on –

251.   The Group Theatre, founded in 1931 when Cheryl Crawford, Lee Strasberg, and Harold Clurman left the
Theatre Guild, was one of the most influential theatre groups operating in the 1930s. The Group Theatre
had two major objectives: to produce plays that had a strong commitment to the social world by respond-
ing to human needs; and to advance the craft of acting through its attachment to the Stanislavsky method,
which stressed psychological and emotional realism in performance.

Emphasizing plays with a leftist proletariat slant, which showed that the plight of the human condition
could be improved, the Group Theatre had its greatest success with the plays of Clifford Odets. Unable to
achieve financial independence, however, the Group Theatre disbanded in 1940, and some of its members
went on to found America's two principal acting schools, Lee Strasberg's Actors Studio and Stella Adler's
Theatre Studio.

Ramon Naya won the Group Theatre Contest with his play "Mexican Mural." In a letter dated 20
March 1939 (HRC), the Group Theatre informed Williams that he had won a $100 special prize for the
first three sketches in "American Blues." Williams submitted four one-act plays, most likely "Moony's Kid
Don't Cry," "The Dark Room," "Hello from Bertha," and "The Long Goodbye" under the title "American
Blues," along with two full-length plays, *Not About Nightingales* and *Spring Storm*. Williams sent a third
full-length play, *Fugitive Kind*, but it arrived too late for consideration. They excluded the fourth one-act
play, possibly "The Long Goodbye," because it was "inferior in quality to the first three, both in the writing and in theatrical validity."

There is some uncertainty as to the exact identity of the four one-act plays. In a memorandum dated
20 February 1940 (Yale), John Gassner, of the Theatre Guild, evaluated four of Williams' one-act plays
under the title "American Blues," namely "Moony's Kid Don't Cry," "The Dark Room," "Hello from
Bertha," and "The Long Goodbye." Gassner wrote:

These short plays have the same quality and nearly the same distinction as O'Neill's S.S. Glencairn
one-acters. They possess the same bitter, uncompromising realism, atmospheric power, and feeling
for the proletariat and for bedevilled people in general. Since, moreover, poverty is the Antichrist in
at least two of them, and the picture also conveys the restlessness and anguish of common people,
the author rightly calls them a "social panorama."

Of the four plays, Gassner felt that "The Long Goodbye" was "not too well organized." "I doubt," he
wrote, "that it is a commercial possibility." A letter to Audrey Wood from Fleet Munson (14 February
1940, HRC), praising Williams' talent, helps to confirms the exclusion of "The Long Goodbye" from the
special prize: "I am told that The Long Goodbye is but one of Tennessee Williams' lesser works, not considered worthy of much attention by such prize awarding bodies as the Group Theatre."

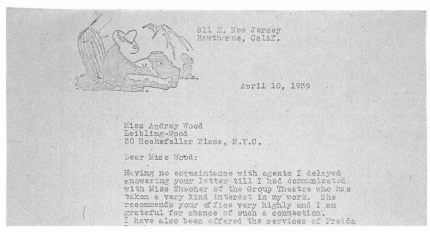

Excerpt of the first letter Williams wrote to Audrey Wood

*Shortly this before this entry I got the Group Theatre award which radically changed my state of mind – hence this manic elation about "a next play"* [251]

*8/20/39*

*Sunday, 9 April 1939*

April – Easter Sunday –

My next play will be simple, direct and terrible – a picture of my own heart – there will be no artifice in it – I will speak truth as I see it – distort as I see distortion – be wild as I am wild – tender as I am tender – mad as I am mad – passionate as I am passionate – It will be myself without concealment or evasion and with a fearless unashamed frontal assault upon life that will leave no room for trepidation –

God give me strength to write it even though it may not be an altogether Godly play – it will have in it at least a passionate denial of <u>sham</u> and a cry for beauty.

I remain at the pigeon ranch and life is static – smooth, uneventful – waiting, waiting – for what? the old, old question and still no answer to it. –

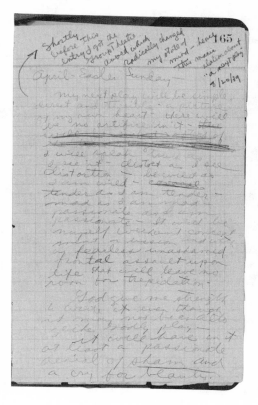

252.   In a letter to his grandmother ([10 May 1939], HTC), Williams gave an account of the new place to which he and Jim Parrott had moved:

I have moved again! This time only sixty miles down the coast to a little artist's colony known as Laguna Beach. . . .

Laguna is located on a bay surrounded by mountains — it is just opposite Catalina Island — you can see it plainly on clear days. The water is a marvelous blue and the hills thickly wooded and covered with gorgeous wild flowers. The coast along here is very rocky but we have a beautiful sandy beach for swimming. . . .

Jim Parrott and I are renting a little cabin about two miles out of town, in a beautiful canyon. . . . I have a nice out-door studio in which I do my writing and painting — Oh, yes, I'm quite an artist these days! Mrs. Parrott, who was a WPA art instructor, gave me a good start and I have completed about a dozen landscapes and portraits in oils — nearly everybody paints around here and there are a few really celebrated artists. They have a free art school and a large gallery and a fine little theatre and library.

A painting by Williams

*Thursday, 25 May 1939*

May – 26 (?) Thursday Evening –
    And still no answer!
    Life here at Laguna Beach[252] is like that haunting picture of my favorite painter, Gauguin – "Nave Nave Mahana" – The Careless Days – It is like a dream-life – Nothing of importance occurs but it is all so quiet and sun-drenched and serene – with just a little shadow of sadness in the knowledge that it will have to pass away. It has been <u>years</u> since I have felt so calm and relaxed. All my neuroses are smoothed out under the benign influence of this glorious sunlight, starlight and ocean.
    Mornings writing or lying around – afternoons at the beach – I am brown and firm-muscled – feel like a perfect young animal – and love it – only I wonder, with some uneasiness, if the old passion and unrest is gone and with it the rebellion that expressed itself in my lyrical writing – But that is foolish of me – this is just a little sunny interlude – The great storms will come back too soon and with them the old lightning that I put into my work.
    Today Jim mysteriously disappeared – left a cryptic note saying not to worry till I saw him again – He is just about as crazy as I am which makes us excellent companions. And has problems so similar to mine that it is almost like having a younger, clearer image of myself to study and work with. It is good for me to have somebody around that I can feel an unselfish affection for – I actually forget my own problems sometimes considering his – and feel quite fatherly – though God knows that Jim is probably better able to take care of himself than I am.
    It's night, almost, and I feel rather lonely – frogs singing, autos humming now and then along the canyon – the light fading on top of the big hills.
    What to do? ~~without~~ I feel a bit lost – by myself in a lonely cabin – I hope Jim comes back tomorrow.

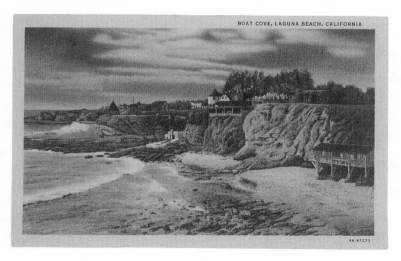

BOAT COVE, LAGUNA BEACH, CALIFORNIA

TENOR SAX TAKING THE BREAKS

1.

We have come down by the moon
    brilliantly
swinging on spangled trapeze
skeins of thin silk
the lunar moth's milky cocoon

Singing the latest jazz tunes
with trumpets, with trombones
the tenor sax taking the breaks!

    Ride out, boy!
    Send it solid!

Or at high noon
on beaches disporting our bodies
that imitate bronze

While the drums beat out a quick rhythm
    the tango, the rhumba
the blues-singer shouting the chorus!

        She's in the groove, that baby!
        She's tearing it down!

Jitterbugs
        snakes
            swing-addicts!

Boy in blue trunks
    surf-rider
girl with your breast half-naked.

Where is disaster?
Only in newspaper head-lines.

        Swing out!
        Give it the gun!

    2.

Our time is immortal
(approximately)

Calendars make white snow
whose flakes are a tempest our faces
laugh through,

    Shouting
See you on the beach tomorrow!
Meet you at Mona's!

Imperishable cry through sunlight
(our throats have arrows for tongues)
    the speed-boat leaping
the frantic tinsel of midnight —

    It makes a man dizzy,
feeling the planet's swing eastward beneath him

tilts the bottle too far
    and shakes out laughter,
blown backwards, shattered
against the stone walls of rock quarries —

    Bitch, he called her,
    blanket in culvert,
    teeth against her nipple

    Kiss, limbs locked, divided,
    breath gone
        Mona's, Tomorrow

(Makes a man feel dizzy,
the planet's swing eastward beneath him

Too far, too far!)

    Shouting

        Mona's!  Tomorrow!

    3.

Whose deaths are the deaths of heros
    sudden, distinct
as rockets exploding in starlight

(This is our myth
defiant of your contradiction!)

The coast of the moon
is where we are bound for at last
    on silken trapeze
        as acrobats in quick passage
with trumpets, with trombones
the tenor sax taking the breaks!

Will meet you tomorrow!

            Thomas Lanier Williams
            Laguna Beach, May, 1939

Self-portrait, 1939

253.   Given no prior mention of a homosexual experience it is likely that this is Williams' first homosexual encounter. Jim Parrott noted: "the identity of 'Doug' in Laguna Beach is an unknown factor to me. It must have been one of the guys on the volley ball court" (letter to Margaret Bradham Thornton).

Years later, in a television interview, Williams implied that his first homosexual encounter took place in New Orleans. It is quite possible Williams had reread his journal, as he sometimes did, and had erroneously interpreted his statement on 1 January 1939, "I was introduced to the artistic and Bohemian life of the Quarter with a bang!" as a veiled reference to a homosexual encounter.

A poem beginning "Your passion is arranged in decimals," dated August 1939 (Santa Fe, New Mexico), further suggests that Williams did have a sexual encounter with a man.

*Sunday, 11 June 1939*

Sun. June 11 – Getting a pack of neuroses on my heels – heigh ho! Off Again –
Rather horrible night with a picked up acquaintance Doug whose amorous advance
made me sick at the stomach[253] – Purity! – Oh God – It is dangerous to have ideals.

*Wednesday, 14 June 1939*

Wednesday – June 14 – The downward turn of the cycle continues – a week or so
ago I seemed to be living in a state of enchantment so marvelously calm and serene
I remarked that it was like Gauguin's "Nave Nave Mahana" – The Careless
days! – Then quite strangely everything went sour – I had the experience Sat.
night which confused and upset me and left me with a feeling of spiritual nausea.

Went to Hawthorne to escape – a fairly pleasant interlude – painted a good
picture – But nervousness returned and I hitchhiked back to Laguna. Felt better when
I reached the quiet little cabin in the Canyon – Jim & I drove in town – he then left
me in the bowling alley to go off with a bunch of new acquaintances. people of the
sort who bore me and I bore. I felt quite lonely and all at sea. I don't fit in with the
careless young extraverts of the world – people of my own kind are so difficult to find
and one is always being disillusioned & disappointed – Oh, hell! – I must learn to be
lonely and <u>like</u> it – at least there is something clean about being lonely – not cluttered
up and smeared over with cheap, filthy personalities who take everything out of you
that is decent and give you nothing but self-disgust! But oh, God, it's so hard, so hard
to be self-sufficient – Can I ever manage it? If not I'll probably end up very badly –

I'm going to try it the rest of this week – stick pretty.

*Sunday, 25 June 1939*

Sunday – June 25 – I seem to be my <u>normal</u> self again – full of neurotic fears, a
sense of doom, a dreadful lifeless weight on my heart and body. Oh, of course that
isn't <u>quite</u> my normal condition. But without periodic spasms of it (from which I
had been rather free the last few months) I would not be Mr. Thomas L. Williams.

Enough small-talk.

This Laguna Period seems to be at the point of disruption. Jim, grown restive,
and no wonder, plans to go to L.A. where & how I don't know but his departure
Mon. or Tues. is fairly decided. I may remain here a week or so by myself if I can
stick it out & then shove off again for home? God forbid! But <u>where then</u>? God
only knows! I formulate vague plans of writing home for bus-fare & then using it
to hitch-hike along the North Coast and ultimately across the continent but this
seems a bit fantastic, don't you think? At any rate the big job now is to shake off
this unmanly weakness and pull myself into shape for the great battle whose
sultry fumes and distant thunder are even now quite evident on the horizon! –

254. The correct version of this old Welsh proverb is "A fynno Duw a fydd" which, loosely translated, is "What God wills will be." The Williams family was descended from the old Welsh family of Langallen.

   Williams would carry this saying with him. Not long after he had been released from Barnes Hospital, Williams ended a letter to his brother Dakin (11 November 1970, HTC):

   Finally — you must get over the dangerous idea that any and all publicity is <u>good</u> publicity. I have had so much publicity that my notoriety has [been] almost entirely eclipsed by accomplishments as an artist. But I am a Williams, and I will continue to fight. Y Fynno Dwy Y Fyd.

255. The first two lines of the last stanza of Williams' poem "This Hour."

256. "Blow, winds, and crack your cheeks. Rage, blow!" (*King Lear*, act 3, scene 2).

257. J. M. Brecheen, who lived in Berkeley, California, was one of sixteen names Williams sent to Edith Austgarten at *Story* magazine (4 August 1939, Princeton) to receive a card announcing the publication of "The Field of Blue Children."

258. *The Letters of D. H. Lawrence*, edited by Aldous Huxley (New York: Viking Press, 1932). Williams would soon travel to Taos to meet Lawrence's widow, Frieda.

Beautiful langwidge, huh, kid?! – To arms! To arms! Y fyno dwy y fid[254] –

"This is the hour when men who dare – Shake lightning from their unbound hair"[255] Etc.

Funny, isn't it, how time sours a thing? Jim and I are like strangers and I am now quite alone in the face of the coming storm.

"Blow, blow" – (I ought to learn some suitable lines from King Lear!)[256]

*Thursday, 6 July 1939*

Thursday – July 6 – Went to Frisco on my thumb last week-end – on the whole a very profitable experience. Learned that I could survive on my own – take care of myself – and met a truly delightful personality who picked me up at Santa Monica & drove me all the way into Berkeley. One J. Brecheen,[257] a salesman, with an extraordinarily sensitive and philosophical mind – we talked quite beautifully for hours and it left a very nice taste in my mouth after the many hurts and loneliness of the recent period.

Strange experience to suddenly delve so deep into another lonely human heart just in the course of a few hours. I might have looked him up afterwards but somehow the experience was too perfect and complete as it was to risk a continuance that might have detracted from that perfection. Relationships shouldn't be carried beyond the point of complete revelation, perhaps – except in rare instances where a tranquil sharing of life is possible.

Today I read from D.H. Lawrence's letters[258] and conceived a strong impulse to write a play about him – his life in America – feel so much understanding & sympathy for him – though his brilliance makes me feel very humble & inadequate. Still – perhaps I can do it – Why not say I <u>shall</u>!!

Plans – Chaotic!

Mind – Chaotic!

Life – Chaotic! (Messy)

I want something straight and clean and perfect.

Why can't I make it with my art?

But I tire so easily – a lassitude comes over me while I'm working and it doesn't seem worth while to go on – nervous exhaustion perhaps – I wonder where I'll go next?

Questions! – <u>Questions</u>!!!

P.S. Jim plans to remain here after all – poor bastard doesn't know what he wants to do with himself – I can see him ten years from now – a fairly comfortable, slightly bewildered little bourgeois – still wondering sometimes but not enough to be seriously disturbed. I can see myself also – folded neatly away in the capacious garments of old mother earth or perhaps adding my peculiar note to the bedlam of a madhouse. Nice reflections ce soir – but I really don't feel too badly – Took a long cathartic ride up the canyon on my bicycle tonight – moon – hills – stars – the great wide cool embrace of solitude at night.

259.  No manuscript with this title, obviously borrowed from Wordsworth, is known to have survived. The play is very likely the one-act play referred to by Williams in a letter to Audrey Wood dated 30 July 1939 (HRC): I am rather steamed up about the possibility of making a solid three-act out of a one-act that I have been working on. . . .

   The play takes place during the course of July 4th in a cheap apartment at Long Beach, California. Mrs. Jonathan Melrose is dying of a lingering illness (cancer?), her husband has gone out to get drunk. They have no children, they live alone in a little 2 or 3 room flat. Both of them are fugitives from life. They live in the glorious expectations of the past. When Jonathan was young he was the golden-haired "glamor boy" of a small lake town in northern New York. He was the one person of whom great things were expected.

Williams considered several titles for this planned three-act play: "Death: Celebration," "The Legend of Jonathan," "A Stranger from Home," and "Death of a Legend." He never completed it.

260.  Pierre Bonnard's painting *Salle à manger à la campagne* (1913), one of two Bonnards on display at the Golden Gate International Exposition in San Francisco, was the inspiration for Williams' poem "Garden Scene."

GARDEN SCENE

(Recitation After a Painting by Pierre Bonnard)

1.

Because it was late afternoon
the fever subsided,
your gloves, the pale table-cloth
were white, were not white,
were blue spilled delicately over white.

Aida,
      the garden is hung
with lanterns like fabulous flowers,
like spring long delayed, arriving with late September -

When will you speak?

2.

The table is set for supper.

You lean, relaxed, both elbows on the window-sill,
waiting, dreaming -

(Your dress is the color
      of thin, thin sunlight reflected!)

The cat watches also
with eyes of exceedingly pale green crystal
   the antecedents of flowers, of leaves
in a premature season....

   Aida, when will you speak?

3.

I could not accept your understood invitation.

The garden with all its pale, thin tissues held me back.

Quite against my will I failed to arrive
at the appointed time for supper....

   Afterwards
I heard them - laughter, the slight, cold tinkling
of glass,
            the silverware's perfect decorum,
a jewel-like glimpse
            of wine poured under white candles!

      The delicate song of the vase
that was, oh, surely, your speech,
            transmuted,
your gracious acquiescence to strangers' plans!

         4.

Aida,
      your rings, your transparent necklace
      your jewels,
(a ghost of all lost, haunting colors)
      are sharp as my pain
who waited, crouched, at the further end of the garden
among the quiet stone lions
      who did not understand, who mocked
my cowardice -
      Aida!

*Monday, 10 July 1939*

Monday Night – Yesterday completed my new one act "Intimations of Mortality"[259] in a spurt of really good creative labor & seemed to be writing brilliantly – also re-wrote my poem on the Bonnard picture which entranced me so at the Frisco Fair art exhibit.[260] But today read them over in iconoclastic humor & found the work sadly lacking. Now have a more constructive attitude however & will resume work &, <u>Deo</u> <u>Volente</u>, straighten the mess out a little. I guess these bitterly dissatisfied periods are ~~my best friend~~ good for me.

Jim and I are getting along fine now that my nerves are better. It is hard to remember – but necessary – that I discolor the whole world and everybody in it, at times, by my own restless, acid humors.

Now I feel quiet and relatively strong. The D.H. Lawrence project grows strong and clear – like the beginning of a great new day – sunrise – It is like being dedicated to something big at long last! Hope I can find the strength for it. – I <u>must</u> – I <u>shall</u> – somehow –

Contemplate trip to Taos, N.M. to see the Lawrence ranch & possibly meet Frieda & other friends of his.

Alone in cabin as Jim has thumbed a ride into Santa Ana. Read – with Jim's glasses which I'm afraid are not very good for my eyes – why do I risk blindness? Must take trip to Hawthorne & get my own glasses back – Dead broke & rent due in couple of days! – Jeepers!

Pierre Bonnard, *Salle à manger à la campagne* (1913)

261. "The Field of Blue Children" was included in the September–October 1936 issue of *Story* and was Williams' first work to be published under the name Tennessee Williams. In the story, a college student, Myra, is attracted to a young poet because of the poignancy and power of his poetry. When he takes her to the field of blue flowers, "the field of blue children" he has described in a poem, they share an amorous evening. The next day Myra cuts off their relationship as she is already engaged to another boy. After several years, Myra, now married, drives out to the field of blue children and allows herself to surrender one last time to unexplainable emotions before she returns to her conventional life.

262. Benson & Hedges cigarettes.

263. Presumably "Intimations of Mortality."

264. Irwin Shaw (1913–84) was a prolific playwright, short-story writer and novelist. *The Gentle People: A Brooklyn Fable* (1939) starred Elia Kazan and was one of the notable Broadway plays of 1939. In this story, two fishermen are forced to pay protection money to a small-time racketeer, Harold Goff, who believes that it is a law of nature that superior people make inferior people work for them. When one of the fishermen's daughters, Stella, begins to date Goff, the two fishermen murder him and avoid being caught. The so-called "gentle people" remain undefeated.

Portrait of Jim Parrott by Williams, c. 1939

*9/16/39 — I seldom think of Rose anymore.*

Incidentally I had news of story accepted by Whit Burnett[261] just before I went to Frisco. A long time objective at last reached! – Wonder if it will actually get into print – or will the mag. go bust! – The <u>spirit</u> in me is healthy now – clean & straight – but I am still much, <u>much</u> too self-centered and thoughtless of others – though full of a general compassion and good will, of course – but not active enough – my love of others is always too passive, too intellectual – this is getting to smell like crap – Goodnight. – Rose, my dear little sister – I think of you, dear, and wish, oh, so much that I could help! – Be brave, dear little girl – God <u>must</u> remember and have pity some day on one who loved as much as her little heart could hold – & <u>more</u>! Why should you be <u>there</u>, little Rose? And <u>me</u>, <u>here</u>? – No reason – no reason – anywhere – why? – why? –

Also I think of Grand. And love her and miss her. And hate myself for staying away – selfishly – so long – But, oh, Grand, you know how hard it is at home – and here I am <u>free</u>! But I remember and love – And am sad. God bless you tonight – my dear "Two Roses".


*Saturday, 15 July or Sunday, 16 July 1939*

Sat. nite or Sun. morn.

Feel awfully nervous having had 2 cups of coffee with Hedges[262] – & wrote on play[263] – will relax now. – Yes, now I feel better – took hot shower but am shivering something orful!!! – Well! – That was a close one – nearly developed a very bad case of the old coffee jitters – intercepted by 2 hot showers, 2 cups of hot water, and much mental castigation.

However I got a new slant on my one-act which may justify the rigorous consequences. Oh hell – I ought to go to bed – I sound silly even to myself.

Jim has gone up to cabin in hills – for indefinite period – Paid all but $2.50 of our rent which was my shamefully small contribution – I'm really in financial hot water – not a red cent and no credit, no groceries but dried peas and a few potatoes. But I will survive somehow.


*Sunday, 16 July 1939*

Sunday – Today nothing but scraps too eat – Bread without butter – tea without lemon – a pithy old tomato – some stale coffee cake! – Tomorrow if I get no money I will have to hitchhike into Santa Ana or L.A. to hock my valise. Heigh-ho!

I write & write & still the one act doesn't quite come off.

Tired & dull today – feel like an old man – reading "The Gentle People" by Irwin Shaw[264] – well done but it doesn't interest me – the problem seems to be invented by the author.

265.  Williams would use a version of this line in the first section of his 1943 poem "The Dangerous Painters":
"I told him of how the painters had had to make / a religion out of endurance that had no patience in it /
but only will and only defiance of factors."

Dear Mother:  I hope you haven't been alarmed about
my bicycle tour.  We returned Saturday after nearly
two weeks on the road.  It was really a marvelous
experience.  We went clear down into Mexico, visiting
Tia Juana and Agua Caliente and going for some distance
into the rural section, until the roads became so bad
we had to turn back.  As you can see from the enclosed
snapshots, I am flourishing out here.  The exercise and
the wonderful climate have made me feel like a new person.  I am now completely sold on California.  After
spending a few months out here you find it hard to
imagine how people live in the middle-west!

Williams in Mexico

*Sunday, 30 July 1939*

Sunday July 30 – ~~Nearly~~ the End of another month. Oh, strange trance-like existence – The dreadful heavy slipping by of the days like oxen on a hot dusty road toward some possible spring – dreadfully athirst but not knowing where the water is hidden. The parched tongue, the drooping back, the little buzzing stinging flies of irritation all around them.

Oh strange and dreadful caravan of tired cattle – Quo Vadis? – where? why? – What!!

So you see my humor – not desperate perhaps – only a quiet desperation – that has grown deep inside, is not violent any more.

Soon this little encampment will break up is already fundamentally broken. we live a few sad, brief days on the verge of departure – a sort of fin de siécle is in the air about this place.

Jim has gone again into L.A. to see a semi-official at a studio.

We are not happy together as we were. He is very generous, even patient with me but I demand so much, I give so much in a relationship – So there is a desert between us. My loneliness makes me grow like a vine about people who are kind to me – then it is hard to loosen the vine when the time has come for separation. All my deep loves & friendships have hurt me finally. I mean have caused me pain, because I have felt so much more than the other person could feel.

Then I am so pursued by blue devils – No wonder I cling for salvation to whomsoever passes by!

Now I must make a positive religion of the simple act of endurance[265] – I must endure & endure & still endure.

For to break would mean, I'm afraid, to follow my sister – and one of us there is enough.

The heart forgets to feel even sorrow after a while – Everything is trampled under the feet of these slow, terrible oxen.

Just read this over – when experience has repeated itself – only more bitterly even – Still there is wisdom here! 8/21/40

266.  In a letter to Audrey Wood dated 16 July 1939 (HRC), Williams wrote: "I have shelved the [Vachel] Lindsay idea for a much more compelling impulse to dramatize D.H. Lawrence's life in New Mexico. I feel a far greater affinity for Lawrence than Lindsay and the elements of his life here in America are so essentially dramatic that they require little more than a re-arrangement to be transferred directly to the stage. . . . I intend to run down to Taos, New Mexico, on my thumb before long — I understand Frieda Lawrence still lives down there, also Mabel Dodge Luhan and possibly Dorothy Brett who were intimates of Lawrence during this period. I want to take some pictures and absorb the atmosphere of the place and then start right to work if circumstances permit."

Two weeks later (29 July 193[9], HRC), Williams wrote to Frieda Lawrence about himself: "Briefly, I am a young writer who has a profound admiration for your late husband['s] work and has conceived the idea, perhaps fantastic, of writing a play about him, dramatizing not so much his life as his ideas or philosophy which strike me as being the richest expressed in modern writing."

Williams attempted to write several plays about the Lawrences. Manuscripts include "Adam and Eve on a Ferry," "A Panic Renaissance in the Lobos Mountains," and "The Night of the Zeppelin" (fragment). In a letter to Audrey Wood received 18 October 1941 (HRC), Williams mentions working on a long play about the Lawrences, titled "The Long Affair." No manuscript of "The Long Affair," or any long play about D. H. Lawrence, is known to exist. Williams wrote a one-act play about D. H. Lawrence, "I Rise in Flame, Cried the Phoenix," which is set on the French Riviera and imagines the last day of Lawrence's life.

Williams also wrote two poems, one titled "Cried the Fox" written "for D.H.L." and the second titled "The Legend" written "for Frieda Lawrence."

With Donald Windham, Williams wrote You Touched Me! a romantic comedy "suggested by" Lawrence's short story of the same title.

267.  Frieda von Richthofen (1879–1956) was the aristocratic German wife of D. H. Lawrence. When she met Lawrence she was married to a former teacher of his, Professor Ernest Weekley, with whom she had three children. She eloped with Lawrence in 1912 and left her family behind. In 1922, at the invitation of arts patron Mabel Dodge Luhan, the Lawrences visited Taos, New Mexico, and moved there in 1924. Williams described her: "You should see her. Still magnificent. A Valkyrie. She runs and plunges about the ranch like a female bull — Thick yellow straw hair flying — piercing blue eyes — huge — She dresses madly — a hat & coat of bob-cat fur — Shouts — bangs — terrific! — Not a member of the female sex — but woman" (fragment, HRC). She wrote a memoir of D. H. Lawrence entitled "Not I, But the Wind" (1934).

Dorothy Brett (1883–1977), the daughter of the second Viscount Esher, was a painter who studied at the Slade School of Art in London. In 1924 she went to Taos with the Lawrences and lived there until her death. Brett inspired a number of literary portraits, including Jenny Mullion in Aldous Huxley's Crome Yellow (1921), Miss James in D. H. Lawrence's story "The Last Laugh" (1925), and Dollie Urquhart in D. H. Lawrence's story "The Princess" (1925). Williams modeled the character Bertha on Brett in the one-act play "I Rise in Flame, Cried the Phoenix," in which she and Lawrence discuss the unfavorable public reaction to his exhibition of paintings in London.

268.  Audrey Wood (1905–85) was a prominent literary agent who had been introduced to Williams by Elia Kazan's wife, Molly Day Thacher, a playreader at the Group Theatre. Audrey Wood and her firm, Liebling-Wood, represented Williams from 1939 until 1971, when she and Williams had a falling out. Wood was a devoted agent who managed not only Williams' literary interests but his personal affairs as well. Her affection for Williams and his reliance on her advice and encouragement are very evident in their extensive correspondence. Her memoirs, Represented by Audrey Wood, were published in 1981.

269.  Willard "Spud" Johnson (1897–1968) was a journalist who had written for publications ranging from the Denver Post to the New Yorker. He was the secretary and companion of Harold "Hal" Witter Bynner (1881–1968), a poet-memoirist who had moved to New Mexico.

270.  Frank Waters (1902–95), a friend of Frieda Lawrence's, was a well-known Southwestern writer whose fiction and nonfiction reflected his deep interest in the culture and religion of the American Indian. At the time of his death, Williams had a copy of Waters' best-known work, The Man Who Killed the Deer (1942).

In Williams' play "This Property Is Condemned," Tom tells Willie that Frank Waters said, "You took him inside and danced for him with your clothes off."

*Sunday, 20 August 1939*

<u>Sunday</u> – 8/20/39 – Here I am in Taos, N.M.[266] – of all improbable places – But then the improbable has been a fairly consistent occurence in my latter days –

Have met Frieda & Brett[267] – No mood for descriptions tonight – Only emotions – I am <u>bored</u> – <u>lonely</u> – I wish I were back at Laguna – <u>dread</u> going <u>home</u> – Down to my last buck & if Audrey[268] doesn't come thru with checque tomorrow, situation will be really acute. Spud[269] puzzles me, intrigues me a little. Frank[270] is charming –

Mabel Dodge Luhan, Frieda Lawrence, and Dorothy Brett on the Lawrence ranch near Taos, c. 1938 (photograph by Cady Wells)

271.  In the 1930s and 1940s, the Governor Bent House was owned by Ida Gee, who rented out rooms. Williams presumably was introduced to Mrs. Gee by the Gusdorfs, who employed Mrs. Gee's son. Alex Gusdorf was an acquaintance of Cornelius Williams' and a prominent merchant who carried Red Goose shoes. Today the house is a museum and gallery.

272.  Marian Gallaway (1903–80) was a graduate student and assistant to Professor Mabie at the University of Iowa, where she and Williams became friends. In the foreword to her book *Constructing a Play* (New York: Prentice-Hall, 1950), Williams wrote:

> Quite possibly I derived more from this friendship than I did from any of the actual courses that I undertook, for Marian Gallaway was one of those persons who lived and breathed theatre and somehow managed to infect her associates with her own religious excitement about it. (p. vii)

After receiving her doctorate from the University of Iowa in 1940, Gallaway held several teaching posts and eventually taught at the University of Alabama, from 1948 to 1973, where she created the theatre department.

Williams used Marian Gallaway's surname for several characters: the former girlfriend of the narrator in the short story "The Kingdom of Earth" who spreads rumors about the narrator "having a mother with part nigger blood"; the Landlady, Miss Gallaway, in the play "The Strangest Kind of Romance"; one of the main characters, the "marginally youthful but attractive" Dorothea Gallaway, in the play *A Lovely Sunday for Creve Coeur*; and Mrs. Gallaway, whose husband runs the Gallaway Cotton Mills, in the play "Heavenly Grass or The Miracles at Granny's (a Primitive Libretto)."

273.  Blandford Jennings.

```
                AMERICAN BLUES

                  (In Taos)

    Brett:  And then Lorenzo said, 'Mabel -'

    Tennessee:  (rises abruptly)

    Brett:  (focussing ear-trumpet)  What's
    the matter, where are you going?

    Tennessee:  (frenziedly)  I've got a lunch-
    eon engagement!

    Brett:  (focussing ear-trumpet)  Who with?

    Tennessee:  Nobody!  But I can't stand to
    sit here and listen to you when I'm half
    dead of starvation!

    Brett:  Starvation?  Incredible! - What do
    you mean young man?

    Tennessee:  My agent hasn't sent me my
    STORY checque yet and I'm living on my
    landlady's trust in human nature which
    was exhausted last night.

    Brett:  Sit down.  How do you like your eggs?

    Tennessee:  In large quantities. - Miss
    Brett, I'm not going to write a play about
    Lawrence, I'm going to write a play about
    YOU! - D.H. will enter in the last act and
    ask where the bathroom is....

              CURTAIN.

    (This play has a social message)

    OR MORE EXPLICITLY - if my receipts from

    STORY (I suppose it was published, I haven't
    found the magazine out here) are not yet
    mailed, please, oh, please send by return
    Air-mail.  This is an arid country and I
    haven't quite cultivated an appetite for
    cactus, though they do say it makes delic-
    ious candy!
```

Part of a letter Williams playfully wrote to
Audrey Wood, 24 August 1939

Good God – the end of the book – Is that an omen? – I miss Jim but I feel good about the way it closed – Nothing but good feeling on both sides and I think a solid, enduring friendship. Wish I could help the boy – Better leave the rest of this final page for later. Goodnight.

*I remember that big quiet clean cool room in the Gov. Bent House in Taos*
9/16/39 *N. M. and how lonely I was with those two big double beds!*

*Taos is nice to Remember – 9/16/39* [271]

*Sunday, 17 September 1939*

Sunday – 9/16/39 – End of the St. Louis period – leave tomorrow midnight for New York. Time here has passed in a flash. Nothing happened. <u>Nothing</u> at <u>all</u>. Written practically nothing & so I don't feel too good. Had hoped – <u>intended</u> – to go to N.Y. with new play script. But I go almost empty handed simply because I want to go somewhere – to get away – the old flight motive – May God be merciful to me and open some door, some avenue of escape.

Saw Marian Gallaway[272] & B.J.[273] tonight. Pleasant enough but I felt on the defensive. Rather despise myself for my lack of progress these days and my self-absorption. Neurotic period here in St. Louis. Defeatist attitude toward work and physical uneasiness. N.Y.C. will have to be very good to give me a new impulse & straighten my troubled self out. Anyhow it ought to bring me into contact with good new personalities. Then – Maybe the West Coast again if I can manage the money. So long, kid – keep your chin up! (Yes, it's mysterious and intriguing and rather colossal – I mean still being <u>alive</u>!) – what's <u>next</u> <u>?????</u>

*Monday, 25 September 1939*

<u>New York</u> – Sept (?) – Monday – Have a date to meet the Group Theatre – Feel rather desperate but am carrying on somehow. Something's got to break soon – Be with you later. So long.

*Tuesday, 3 October 1939*

<u>Tuesday</u> – Oct. 2 1939 – New York City – Down, down, down! – feel wuss 'n wuss! ~~Head-splitting~~ dull headache from continual worry and a lack of all enthusiasm for the present or the future – only the past, in comparison, seems rather lovely. See I can't even — think.

Met lots of people here but nobody does me much good. They're all so

274. Shortly after Williams won the Group Theatre award, he received a letter from his agent, Audrey Wood (13 April 1939, HRC), proposing that he apply for a Rockefeller Fellowship. Granted through the Dramatists' Guild of the Authors' League of America, these fellowships amounted to $1,000 each. Williams did apply, but he would not learn of their decision until 21 December.

275. Around this time, Williams wrote to Audrey Wood (circa early November 1939, HRC): "I'm sending you a very hasty, rough description of the play I'm working on. . . . You won't like the pathological characters or violent theme but I'm hoping my final treatment of it will please you somewhat better."

276. On 8 November 1939 (HRC), Wood had written to Williams:

> Not until this morning did I get a chance to read the synopsis of the new play entitled SHADOW OF MY PASSION which you sent to me some time last week.
>
> Don't ever think I don't like violent themes. Also, don't think I go for plays about hearts and flowers. If you can write a play with a violent theme well enough to make me think it is commercial, I will go screaming down the street like a mad woman and deliver you a sale as soon as I can get someone else to go mad with me.
>
> Contrary to your opinion, I am very interested in the material in the synopsis, SHADOW OF MY PASSION. If you could write this in dramatic form (which is unfortunately usually the three-act form), making this play come alive, I think it may well be exciting theatre.

Williams had taken the title "Shadow of My Passion" from a poem by Rabindranath Tagore (1861–1941), "The Gardener" (stanza 30). Williams considered other titles for this play, including "Opus V, Written on Subways" and "Figures in Flame," before he chose *Battle of Angels*.

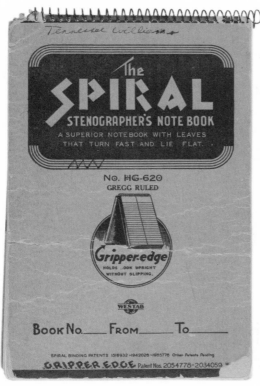

Notebook Williams began in November 1939

involved in their own lives. I need somebody to envelop me, embrace me, pull me by sheer force out of this neurotic shell of fear I've built around myself lately. Defeatist attitude toward work is the main difficulty. Loneliness next. Between the two of them I feel all but annihilated. Yes, something _does_ have to break and damn soon or I _will_. Think I may look up some people tonight. I _hate_ New York – long for the Taos desert or the ~~ocean~~ Pacific – or what? Anyhow I long for something that I haven't got. I hope I can end this journal on a more cheerful note so I'll leave a little blank space here for another final entry. So long.

_Thanksgiving Day – 1941 – Over two yrs. ago, that last frantic entry – Since then I have filled a couple of other notebooks with my private expostulations._

_Sunday, 5 November 1939_

Sunday – Nov. 1, 2 or 3 – 1939
  I wait! For the fates' decision. I mean the Rockefeller Fellowship Committee's.[274] It seems a last chance of escape. The waiting is almost unbearable and I dare not think what it will be if this last, wild hope is snatched away from me. I'm finishing up a new play[275] of highly uncertain quality. But I don't feel the strength in me to start something new without the relief, the escape that the award could give me. I must, however, steel myself for the shock of rejection. I can't let it break me. I must remember that my method of survival has always been a very oblique method. A kind of success through failure, program of dogged resistance to discouragement and constant bobbing up again after apparently final slap-downs and knock-outs.
  But no matter what happens there must be a way out of St. Louis for me. To stay on here – in this attic – especially without work to lose myself in – would be a very dangerous mistake.
  I must keep moving onward and outward to ward off the threat of regression!
  I am stronger than I used to be but my situation is alarmingly static.
  I keep making these humiliating, inglorious returns to a place I thought I was leaving forever on several past occasions.
  En Avant!


_Friday, 10 November 1939_

Friday – Feel in danger of a nervous and physical relapse as result of hard driving these past few weeks. Some encouragement today in letter from Audrey[276] but still a terrific amount of work on play to make it plausible. And I am nearing exhaustion.

277.  William Jay Smith and Louise Krause.

278.  William Faulkner's (1897–1962) work of the late 1920s and 1930s embodied what he declared in his Nobel Prize acceptance speech (1950) was the writer's imperative: "to create out of the materials of the human spirit something which did not exist before."

    *The Wild Palms* (1939) is composed of two narratives, alternating chapter by chapter. In the first narrative, titled "Wild Palms," a young intern falls in love and runs off with a married woman. The woman becomes pregnant but soon dies from an abortion performed by her lover who, as a result, is imprisoned for life. Williams would pick up the theme of abortion when he rewrote *Battle of Angels* as *Orpheus Descending*. In *Orpheus Descending*, Myra is renamed Lady and we learn that, as a girl, she had become pregnant by the wealthy David Cutrere: "I carried your child in my body the summer you quit me but I had it cut out of my body, and they cut my heart out with it!" (act 2, scene 1).

    In the second narrative of *The Wild Palms*, "Old Man," a convict is sent from prison to do rescue work during the great Mississippi flood of 1927. He finds a pregnant woman stranded by the rising water and rescues her, but the journey back home takes almost three months because of the flood. His efforts to return to prison are misunderstood and the authorities extend his prison sentence.

    In 1935 Williams had sent *Manuscript* a copy of his short story "His Father's House," which dealt with murder by crucifixion. The editor rejected the story (22 March 1935, HRC) as being "too psychopathic" and warned that studies in insanity took masters to handle them. He recommended Faulkner as one whose prose carried "that peculiar morbid, insane feeling."

279.  *Battle of Angels.*

280.  "Tomorrow is another day" is the famous last line spoken by Scarlett O'Hara in the 1939 Academy Award–winning film *Gone with the Wind*, adapted from Margaret Mitchell's 1937 Pulitzer Prize–winning novel of the same name.

    Williams was fond of this line and would use it several times in his work. Williams concludes "The Purification" with *"Mañana es otro día.* The play is done!" He also used the Spanish phrase in "The Lost Girl," a later version of the story he began in July 1936 entitled "Las Palomas" or "Las Muchachas." In the play fragment "Tomorrow is Another Day," set in a fashionable hotel in Monte Carlo, a young man in a white linen suit says to an "exquisite flower-like" girl of eighteen, "The Castilian peasants have a phrase that I'm awfully fond of using — Manana es otro dio."

281.  Jim Parrott.

A painting by Williams

Saw Bill and Louise[277] today. They were very nice – altogether too impressed by my apparent success.

Went to "Y" & swam – rode a bicycle tonight – read "Wild Palms" by Faulkner[278] – such a mad book – by distortion, by outrageous exagerration he seems to get an effect closer to reality (or my idea of it) than strict realists get in their exact representation. You say while reading 'This is delirium!' but the after effect is a close approximation of the actual –

I feel strangely remote from everything – insulated – cut off from the main stream. Home – the attic – the literary life – the creative trance – it makes you feel like you have practically stopped living for a while.

I want life and love again – and a swift flow of significant experiences.

The Rockefeller fellowship? Still no word!

I wait – J'attends! Goodnight – let us hope it <u>is</u> good.


*Thursday, 7 December 1939*

Thursday – Dec. 7 – Waiting, waiting that becomes daily more terrifying. Today my nerves broke – I felt almost insane with desperation – Mailed the new play[279] last week and still no word – The fellowship seems almost hopelessly remote from present probabilities. But without it? Oh, my God! what? what?

The walls here are closing in on me tighter and tighter. Humiliation, dependance, frustration – they're bearing down heavier all the time –

I've got to get <u>Out Out</u>.

How can I? I have 9¢ – And no guts.

G.N. – I mean N.G.


<u>A Moment Later</u> –

Well, have you quit?

Now. Not yet.

Manana es otro Dio.[280]


I feel deserted and helpless at the moment but past experience teaches me that dead ends are only apparent.

After all I'm not dead yet – in fact I'm pretty much alive or I wouldn't be kicking like this.

I'd like to see Jimmie[281] tonite. I'd like to ride my old bicycle up Canyon Road an' look at the stars and hear the ranch dogs barking.

I want to be free and I'm going to find a way to be soon as I can.

Hi-ho! Better days are coming.

282.  *Battle of Angels.*

283.  William Jay Smith.

284.  The one-act play was very likely "At Liberty," the story of Gloria La Greene, an unsuccessful actress who returns home to her mother in Blue Mountain, Mississippi. Gloria arrives, wanton and wasted by consumption, but clings to the illusion that her luck will change, and she will be cast for "a marvelous part in a Broadway production."

285.  Jane Garrett was an actress with the Mummers who played Star in *Candles to the Sun* as well as one of the girls of the Junior Welfare League in *Fugitive Kind*. She married Gordon Carter, the director of the St. Louis Little Theatre. Later they moved to Hollywood where Jane worked in the Actors' Lab and her husband was a producer and set designer.

286.  Molly Day Thacher (1906–63) was married to Elia Kazan and in 1939 was a playreader for the Group Theatre. She was one of the first people in New York theatre to appreciate Williams' talent. Along with Harold Clurman and Irwin Shaw, she was responsible for awarding Williams the special prize for his "American Blues" one-acts. She went on to write several plays that were performed in New York.

287.  Irene, an artist, is the main character in the short story "In Memory of an Aristocrat." In December, Williams sent Audrey Wood a copy of the short story along with a letter (undated, HRC) in which he wrote:

> The girl Irene in this story from my projected novel <u>Americans</u> will also be, most likely, the subject of my next full-length play, making a southern trilogy, Spring Storm, Battle of Angels, and this last one which I plan to call The Aristocrats. As you have observed by now, I have only one major theme for all my work which is the destructive impact of society on the sensitive, non-conformist individual. In this case it will be an extraordinarily gifted young woman artist who is forced into prostitution and finally the end described in the story. In "B. of A." it was a boy who hungered for something beyond reality and got death by torture at the hands of a mob — I hope that idea got across in the script. Your protracted silence has begun to disturb me, my dear!

The character Irene also appears in "A Letter to Irene":

> I haven't seen you in nearly two years. The last time I saw you was when you came to visit me at the House of Detention in New Orleans where I was briefly confined, and I think unjustly, because of a disturbance which occured at "the spring display". You remember what happened. We made red snowballs out of the raspberry sherbet and pelted a certain gentleman in a Prince Albert coat when he ordered your canvases removed from the walls because of "indecency" the afternoon that the spring display was opened. You got out on bail. I didn't. But you brought me cigarettes and mandarins and a pad of typewriter paper on which I wrote the first scene of my fifth long play. I asked you what you were going to do now that your New Orleans period seemed to be pretty thoroughly washed up. You said that you didn't know. But you smiled and I thought that you weren't very bothered about. When I was released a few days later, however, your little crib-like studio on Bourbon street was vacant and there was nothing to indicate you had ever been there except that charcoal inscription over the single burner. Remember? "There is only one true aristocracy — the aristocracy of passionate souls!"
>
> Who was that quoted from? You couldn't remember and I never could find out.
>
> None of the "Quarter Rats" knew where you had gone, Irene, or what had become of you. I asked everybody. They all had different ideas. Some of them thought you'd gone to New York, some said it was Mexico, some even suggested that you had been removed to the psychopathic ward or jumped in the river. I know that neither of those last two was correct. You were made for survival, Irene, just as surely as some artists are made for destruction. I'm not really worried about you. But I miss you terribly sometimes. You had a bigness and a strength about you which I know is unconquerable and I know that you are still living somewhere and still painting those coarse, brutal canvasses which had the impact of naked life in them.

Williams never wrote "The Aristocrats," or the novel "Americans," but there exists an untitled fragment of a play in which art dealers discuss the work of a deceased artist named Irene.

*Monday, 11 December 1939*

The year wanes –

Monday – Dec. 11 – A note arrived this A.M. from Audrey's Secty. saying play[282] had arrived – Nothing else – Ominous indeed! – I know in my heart the play is another failure but I scarcely dare to whisper it aloud. Otherwise the situation remains unchanged – although the last 2 days have been pretty comfortable in a dull sort of way. There is one titillating prospect – Friday evening at V's. We drank together Sat. nite and exchanged some interesting confidences. Ah, well – let us be prepared for any eventuality.

Went over to Bill's[283] room at W.U. Dorm. We wrote, I on a new one-act[284] which is rather feverishly, desperately flashy – Bill prepared his group for the Poetry Club. Some of his stuff is surprisingly good – he gets nice musical effects and good images – but comes down frightfully in some lines without realizing it at all – Still, Bill is a very nice kid and I hope will make some kind remarks over my grave.

Jane married[285] – Frances Van Metre getting married – lives are progressing rapidly all around me – Mine stands still – But maybe it is actually moving – imperceptibly – but faster and more directly than I dream.

Oh, Molly,[286] Oh, Audrey, Oh, ~~Group~~ Dramatists' Guild – ~~Oh God~~ Why don't you help me a little?

I'm stuck.

I have an idea for a new long play – rather, a <u>character</u> for a new long play – In New Orleans – Irene[287] –

Right now I can only watch the mail and check off the days till Friday – And hope, if all else fails, I'll get money enuf for Xmas to lam down to New Orleans the same as last year – to rot in peace! till the next Resurrection!

Hep! Hep!

William Jay Smith

Molly Day Thacher

288. Williams obviously changed his mind. In the short play "At Liberty," Gloria's mother uses this line to warn her daughter about the passage of time.

289. Possibly "At Liberty" and "This Property Is Condemned."

290. Douglas Fairbanks (1883–1939), who often played roles filled with romantic adventure and heroic exploits, was one of Hollywood's biggest stars in the 1910s and 1920s. With his wife Mary Pickford, D. W. Griffith, and Charlie Chaplin, he founded the United Artists Corporation. Fairbanks suffered a heart attack and died in his sleep aged fifty-six.

### Ballad of the Lost Girl

#### 1.

She was sprawled in wanton posture
by the storm-tormented bars
that divide the vaulting meadow
from the taller reach of stars

And I asked her for her name
but she was strangely reft of tongue
though her look was more explicit
than a language!

There among

The scattered winter grasses
on the moonward-slanting hill
we made a brief assay of passion
with no speech between us till

The veins within me faltered,
being flames that never stay,
and I heard no sound, no whisper
as she rose and crept away.

#### 2.

I remained there till the night air
toward the morning turning colder
like a sudden ghostly hand
was laid upon my naked shoulder.

Then I rose and sought about me
for the girl that I had lost,
for the longing was a jewel in me,
cruel as the frost!

But the landscape told no secret
for the meadows held their tongue
and the morning came up slowly
as a breath that torture wrung

And I tell you very truly
that her name, if it be known,
has been carved with knives of silver
on the moon's averted stone!

Thomas Lanier Williams
December, 1939
St. Louis

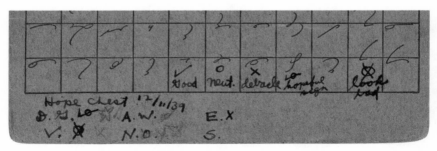

Portion of the inside back cover of Williams' notebook

P.S. Today I wrote one very good line – "The past keeps getting bigger and bigger at the future's expense." – Too good to be good in a play.[288] The tragedy of a poet writing drama is that when he writes well – from the dramaturgic, technical pt. of view he is often writing badly – one must learn – (that is the craft, I suppose) – to fuse lyricism and realism into a congruous unit – I guess my chief trouble is that I don't. I make the most frightful faux pas. I feared today that I may have taken a distinctly wrong turn in turning to drama – But, oh, I do <u>feel</u> drama so intensely sometimes! Again – Good night. I'm going to read some Lawrence or Joyce before sleep. Mailman – be good tomorrow!

*Tuesday, 12 December 1939*

<u>Tuesday</u> – I'm happy to report a real resurgence of hope through a letter received from Luise M. Sillcox, Exec. Secty. of the <u>Authors' League of America</u> – I am among 22 survivors of eliminations and she will try to facilitate things by making xtra copies of my stuff – Sounds very encouraging – Do I dare to <u>hope</u>? At least it gives me a new lease on life for the time being – relieves the depression and strain.

Wrote a little this A.M. – & answered letter – then went down town for a swim – the usual routine – took Jiggs for a long walk after supper – wait impatiently for Fri. – Funny how big something becomes when it offers relief from a rather dull routine of existence.

Tomorrow – probably go down town, mail 2 short plays,[289] letter to Marian, send present to Jane & Carter if I can rake up the money.

V. is the only thing worth thinking about – here is a new possibility that will be very exciting to explore – a whole new landscape appearing – will it prove a mirage? If so it will probably be my fault – my lack of finesse.

I feel like I ought to stop writing for a while now and renew my emotional reservoir with new experiences – to remember in tranquillity.

En avant!! – Mon Enfant Terrible! – with love to Grand – Good night. (Doug. Fairbanks died suddenly today – the way I will die.)[290]

*Friday, 15 December 1939*

<u>Friday</u> –

About the middle of the afternoon –

Went to Jim Connor's last night, drank too much beautiful whiskey – spent sleepless night and feel pretty unfit for any further adventures. Saw Alice Lippmann at hospital –

Jim has a lovely wife and a very attractive apartment, a beautiful car.

But he has gotten fat and I think is a little ashamed of his bourgeois position. Not unhappy – in fact I suppose much happier than in his wild, free days – but I

291.    Presumably "In Memory of an Aristocrat."

292.    By the late 1930s, Francis Lederer (1899–2000), born in Prague, was a well-known stage and screen actor. Williams had recently seen Lederer playing opposite Katharine Cornell in *No Time for Comedy*, S. N. Behrman's play about a playwright who wishes to deal with serious problems and the tragedies of his time but can write only light comedy. In a letter to Audrey Wood dated 30 November 1939 (HRC), Williams wrote:

> I saw Cornell and Lederer last night. I don't ordinarily use the word "exquisite" but I think I will on this occasion as it certainly describes the performances given and also Behrman's dramatic craftmanship.

No manuscripts for Francis Lederer are known to exist. At the beginning of his career Williams would occasionally dedicate his plays to well-known actors. For example, "The Last of My Solid Gold Watches" was "inscribed to Mr. Sidney Greenstreet, for whom the principal character was hopefully conceived." "Portrait of a Madonna" was "respectfully dedicated to the talent and charm of Miss Lillian Gish," while "Daughter of Revolution" was "inscribed to Miss Lillian and Miss Dorothy Gish for either of whom the part of Amanda Wingfield was hopefully intended." "The Case of the Crushed Petunias" was "respectfully dedicated to the charm and talent of Miss Helen Hayes." In "Auto-Da-Fé" the part of Eloi was "created for Mr. John Abbott."

The only light play Williams is known to have written around this time is "Once in a Life-time," a tourist comedy set in New Mexico. Only a fragment exists, but it does not appear to have a role for "the love pirate," as *Variety* had nicknamed Lederer. The main characters are a middle-aged couple "indulging a life-time ambition to make a big western tour."

293.    Williams was employed at his father's workplace, the International Shoe Company, from summer 1932 to spring 1935.

International Shoe Company, Washington Avenue, St. Louis

felt sorry for him somehow although he certainly has an abundant supply of good whiskey and the little wife looked like good stuff, too.

Alas, poor Yorick or something – I knew him well.

They'll do it every time, won't they?

Thank god I've gotten bitch-proof!

I don't feel as cocky as this sounds – got off the track on my story[291] and started writing a play – for Francis Lederer[292] – an easy, careless thing that I may actually go through with if nothing else intervenes.

Tonite? – I'll make a report before bed.

C'est Cela!

Later – no dice with Va.

*Monday, 18 December 1939*

Mon. Nite – Feel pretty rotten. Time drags – Nothing happens – the old complaint. I accuse others of wasting ~~my~~ their lives, preach inspired sermons on the supernal value of each passing second – then fritter my own fugitive youth away in worthless, ineffectual, idle, ~~wandering~~ shiftless "horsing around" without even getting much enjoyment out of it. In fact, damned little pleasure of any kind except the common, stupid little pleasures of food and movies and diverting myself with fairly commonplace people who have the courage, individuality and spiritual grandeur of field-mice! Of which I am one.

Yes, I must break away again – This hiatus has continued long enough. The fellowship situation appears more promising since Miss Sillcox letter but is by no means to be relied upon absolutely. I guess I will go on down to N.O. La. and try to stick it out "on the beach" till something delivers me from the horns of dilemma – or if nothing <u>does</u> – well? well? – well!!! (En Avant!)

*Today I am very dull – write something to console me if you can.*

*Tuesday, 19 December 1939*

<u>Tues. Nite</u> – Grouchy – tired – spiritless today – Did nothing but drive mother down to office to mail Xmas boxes – Loathed going in the old shoe – Co.[293] – always makes me feel so humiliated somehow. They regard me as a loafer of course and I feel like one. Went to "Y" for work-out – came home and ate – and <u>ate</u> – having nothing else to do. Sleep will round out another wildly exciting day in this St. Louis Period which will soon end – I hope! Let's try to make it a <u>real</u>

294. Rose's medical report, signed Kuhlman/Whitten and dated 14 August 1939, read:

> Does no work. Manifests delusion of persecution. Smiles and laughs when telling of person plotting to kill her. Talk free and irrelevant. Admits auditory hallucinations. Quiet on the ward. Masturbates frequently. Also expresses various somatic delusions, all of which she explains on a sexual basis. Memory for remote past is nil. Appetite good. Well nourished. (Leverich, p. 335n)

Williams wrote the poem below about his sister's condition.

### THE BEANSTALK COUNTRY

You know how the mad come into a room,
too boldly,
their eyes exploding on the air like roses,
their entrances from space we never entered.
They're always attended by someone small and friendly
who goes between their awful world and ours
as though explaining but really only smiling,
a snowy gull that dips above a wreck.

They see not us, nor any Sunday caller
among the geraniums and wicker chairs,
for they are Jacks who climb the beanstalk country,
a place of hammers and tremendous beams,
compared to which the glassed solarium
in which we rise to greet them has no light.

The news we bring them, common, reassuring,
drenched with the cheerful idiocy of noon,
cannot compete with what they have to tell
of what they saw through cracks in the ogre's oven.

And we draw back. The snowy someone says,
Don't mind their talk, they are disturbed today!

Williams and Rose

ending this time. No more vicious circles if possible. Look old and tired tonight – Sort of dried out and sapless – or sappy. Shit. Drive to Farmington tomorrow – I'm getting broken in gradually to the place. Can't feel any sincere sentiment for anyone tonight – I guess experience with Va. knocked a lot out of me. Felt sort of listless ever since.

Audrey still hasn't written. Plan to leave Sunday for Nola if I can make it.

Will see people every night for rest of week and will try to arrange one more evening with Va. before I put that definitely in the loss column. No coffee today, none tomorrow – good thing, rest my nerves – but makes me feel haggard. My eyes are a worry these days – Left gone out completely – right none too good. I'm a decimated individual but I still got hopes – oh, Boy!

*Mentally poverty-stricken – need a good shot of something 12/19/39*

*Wednesday, 20 December 1939*

Wednesday – Visited Rose at sanitarium – horrible, horrible! Her talk was so obscene – she laughed and spoke continual obscenities – Mother insisted I go in, though I dreaded it and wanted to ~~go out~~ stay outside. We talked to the Doctor afterwards – a cold, unsympathetic young man – he said her condition was hopeless that we could only expect a progressive deterioration.[294]

It was a horrible ordeal. Especially since I fear that end for myself. Life – life – how uncomprehendably brutal you can be – why? – That question is much too old – It does no good to repeat these old questions – except in art when we can give them, possibly, some kind of poetic expression. But everything seems ugly and useless now – hideously smirched – After all her naked subconscious is no uglier than the concealed thoughts of others – And is sex ugly? Not essentially – not from a cosmic viewpoint. But when it is divorced from reason – it looks like slime – it seems horrible you can't reason it away. Poor mad creature – if only it didn't make you so hideous you wouldn't dread it so much –

I am unnerved – The old man was nasty to me this evening about two trivial things – the lamp – the evening paper – any excuse is sufficient for him to be nasty. Oh, I feel so sick inside, having to endure it. What escape _is_ there? Can I even get to New Orleans? How can I _stay_ there?

Oh, but I've _got_ to because there's simply nothing else. Poetry Club tonight if Bill calls for me. Have dizzy attacks and feel an alarming dullness and lethargy – it scarcely seems worthwhile to move from one room to another. Catatonic? Jesus. No.

295.  William Jay Smith wrote: "Louise Krause was engaged at this time to Robert Haas, who was a protégé of Gertrude Stein's. At a Christmas party at her house in Ladue, which Tom & I attended, she announced her engagement with a little poem by Gertrude Stein which had been printed up with copies tied to the branches of the Christmas tree. It went something like this:

> They say How do you do?
> And we say How do you do too?
> One and one are two
> And that is you:
> Louise and Bob-o-link
> They are to be married.

After their marriage, they moved to California . . . and were divorced many years later" (letter to Margaret Bradham Thornton).

296.  Williams mistakes his age. In December 1939 he was twenty-eight.

297.  Jim Parrott.

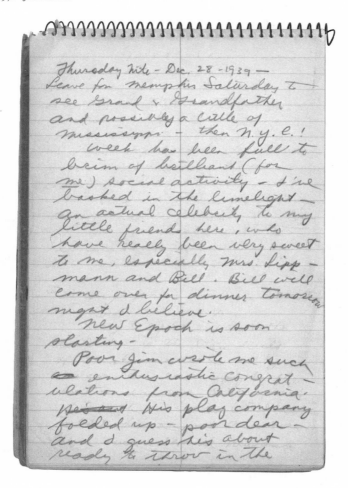

*Thursday, 21 December 1939*

Thursday – Wow! Received fellowship! – Was awakened this A.M. by arrival of congratulatory telegram from Audrey. Mother literally wept with joy – I felt numb – great merciful acts of this kind never give me a big immediate reaction – they sort of spread through me like a new, warm season – I have had to insulate my spirit against shocks in order to survive – result I'm dulled even to happiness (immediately).

Spent afternoon at newspapers giving them the tidings – Then went swimming.

Tonight Louise and her boy friend[295] and I visited Mrs. Lippmann – She is sweet and appealing in her odd way. Read us some poems and fed us pie so terrible that Bob stuffed his in his overcoat pocket. Pleasant evening though. Tomorrow maybe V. – we will see.

Happy? Yes, yes, yes!!! – It stills seems like a dream – trite statement but, oh, how true – Freedom – the one desire – now possible – for 10 months!

A miraculous amnesty for this weary battle-worn veteran of many wars – 26[296] – I feel like 76 – inside – but tonight young again – and oh, so grateful for it. It seems truly like an Act of God. If only I could share a little of this blessing with my little sister – beyond the reach of joy. Perhaps also beyond the reach of sorrow. Goodnight and God bless all the tortured world.


*Thursday, 28 December 1939*

Thursday Nite – Dec. 28 – 1939 – Leave for Memphis Saturday to see Grand & Grandfather and possibly a little of Mississippi – then N.Y.C.!

Week has been full to brim of brilliant (for <u>me</u>) social activity – I've basked in the limelight – An actual celebrity to my little friends here, who have really been very sweet to me, especially Mrs. Lippmann and Bill. Bill will come over for dinner tomorrow night I believe.

New Epoch is soon starting –

Poor Jim[297] wrote me such enthusiastic congratulations from California. His play company folded up – poor dear – and I guess he's about ready to throw in the sponge – wish there was something I could do – Marian also wrote very sweet letter – things apparently not going so well for her either. I don't appreciate how lucky I am – heaven knows I don't really deserve it.

Full of plum pudding and ready for bed – <u>G'nite.</u>

(And, Tom, please try to remember not to act like a regular sonovabitch!)

298. Anne Bretzfelder (1916– ) grew up in St. Louis, graduated from Bennington College in 1938, and studied in Europe. She recalled, "In St. Louis, Tom and I . . . didn't fit in. We were artists. I had always wanted to be a sculptor as much as he wanted to be a writer" (Leverich, p. 336). At the time of this entry she had an apartment where Williams would occasionally visit her. In a letter to Alice Lippmann ([21 February 1940], HRC), Williams wrote:

> I've only gotten to see her a few times but she has been extremely helpful in criticizing my new work and she's a person that I like immensely. I wish you would meet her, if you haven't already.

Bretzfelder went on to exhibit her work in galleries and museums in the United States, Israel, and Europe. After she married Joseph Post in 1942, she lost contact with Williams.

299. Richard Hinton Knight was an assistant in English at Washington University who also helped Professor Carson direct plays.

300. Roark Bradford's dramatization of his 1931 novel of the same title was based on a ballad of the black folk hero, a man of prodigious strength employed in the building of railroads.

301. Paul Robeson (1898–1976) was a great athlete, scholar, actor, and singer. After graduating from Columbia Law School, Robeson's stage debut was the lead role of Eugene O'Neill's *All God's Chillun Got Wings* in Greenwich Village in 1924. A year later Robeson, who had a remarkably deep, resonant voice, was launched to fame after he gave a concert of black spirituals in New York City. His concert and theatrical career continued to grow. In January 1940, he recorded "Ballad for Americans," a patriotic song which reached the top of the charts.

   Inspired by the evening, Williams may have written "Heavenly Grass or The Miracles at Granny's," a "Musical Fantasy for the Negro Theatre." One draft is "Dedicated to the American negro."

302. William Liebling (1894–1969) was married to Audrey Wood. In 1937 they had founded the firm Liebling-Wood. He managed performers and she managed writers.

303. Sidney Edison was the son of a senior executive of the International Shoe Company and had been introduced to Williams by Anne Bretzfelder. She described Edison as "an interesting, attractive, very amusing, imaginative, and spoiled young man from a very rich family" (Leverich, p. 350).

304. Harold Vinal was editor of the poetry magazine *Voices*. In the August–September 1934 issue Williams had had two poems published. Vinal had turned his family home on the island of Vinalhaven in Maine into a summer retreat for writers.

Audrey Wood

*Sunday, 7 January 1940*

Sunday – Jan 6 – on train about 1½ hours out of N.Y.

Sorry to report I feel rather dull due to the blue devils of defeatism which nearly always rear their ugly little faces in reaction to some period of triumph or elation. Will have to beat them out once more. They're such a damned nuisance – which is stronger, my will or these reasonless fears? I must ride them down like a nest of snakes, trample them under my heels!

Still I wonder and dream of what this coming period will hold. Adventure? Passion? Success? – or the opposites of all these! – one never knows – but as a usual thing (if not invariably) – you get one and miss the other – or have partialities and compromises in the End. Ah, well. Such is life for yours truly. My method is oblique – As I remarked at Anne Bretzfelder's[298] – I'm charistically oblique. That's quite true, huh. Success through failure, failure through success. East by way of west. The world is round, you know.

Everyone very good to me lately – everyone except myself. But even I am kinder to myself than I used to be – remember those old agonies! – Something has straightened out since then I believe.

Ann Bretzfelder, Dick Knight[299] two glamorous new personalities I've met lately – both not sufficiently explored yet.

Dream – A woman who was a giant jack rabbit, rather attractive in an esoteric, repugnant way – sitting with me in a bar and saying, "I've never tasted alcohol before <u>except in sewers</u>." – where did my subconscious get that from? – Page Mr. Freud!

Where will you be tonight, Tom? – I'll tell you later.

We are now in Schenactedy. So long. Good luck, old soldier, and keep your chin up!!!

(Nice folks – Bill, Anne, Louise, Dick, – and others)


*Friday, 12 January 1940*

Friday Nite in N.Y. – (been here 5 days now)

Been spending money like water for practically nothing – feeling pretty blue most of the time – the ole blue devils got my spirit still – Falling off a little though – Think I'll throw 'em tomorrow 'fore they throw me. I'm writin' like a nigguh cause ah jus' been to see "John Henry"[300] – with Paul Robeson[301] singin' it, boy! Audrey & Liebling[302] took me after dinner with them. I had lunch with interesting new personality Sid. Edison.[303] We got along swell together, his ideas falling in with mine quite remarkably. Then I spoiled things (I'm afraid) by upsetting a table and spilling whiskey and water all over the rug.

Too much smokin' an' drinkin' lately – ah don' feel good.

Tomorrow try some work, you no good boy!

Tomorrow night dinner with Vinal[304] – next report will take up that subject –

305. Williams begins to identify casual homosexual acquaintances only by initials. Williams uses "ashes hauled" as a euphemism for sex and most likely adopted the phrase from early blues singers. The use of metaphor has always been common in blues lyrics, especially in the early days of recording when graphic language was not permitted. Willie "Scarecrow" Owens sang "Want Your Ashes Hauled," and Sleepy John Estes in "Goin' to Brownsville" sang, "You may starch my jumper / Hang it upside your wall / You know by that, baby / I need my ashes hauled."

306. Williams' exaggerated romantic description of Donald Windham and Fred Melton, who had recently arrived in New York City from Atlanta. Donald Windham (1920– ), a writer, collaborated in 1942 with Williams on the play *You Touched Me!* suggested by the short story of the same name by D. H. Lawrence. His published work includes the novels *The Dog Star* (1950), *The Hero Continues* (1960), a roman à clef in which the protagonist is modeled on Williams, and *Two People* (1965); a short-story collection, *The Warm Country* (1960); and recollections of his childhood, *Emblems of Conduct* (1964).

   In addition, he published *Tennessee Williams' Letters to Donald Windham, 1940–1965* and wrote a memoir entitled *Lost Friendships: A Memoir of Truman Capote, Tennessee Williams and Others* (1987). Initially, Williams and Windham were very close, but their relationship was turbulent at times. In 1977, Williams and Windham had a falling out over the publication of the American edition of Williams' letters to Windham.

   Fred Melton (1918–92) was Windham's lover but left him in 1942 to marry Sara Marshall, a friend of Jordan Massee's from Macon, Georgia. In *You Touched Me!* Williams and Windham created a character named the Reverend Guildford Melton, "a rather mincing little man who lays great stress on refinement of voice and gesture" who hopes to find a woman "who shares [his] distaste for the carnal — physical — bodily side of —."

307. Odets' play *Night Music*.

308. Gordon Sager (1915–91) was an American writer. He grew up in St. Louis and attended Washington University. In September 1940 Williams came across him in Acapulco, where Williams first met Paul Bowles. Sager became a good friend of the Bowleses' and in 1950 published *Run, Sheep, Run*, a roman à clef set in the fictional West Indian village of San Pedro with characters based on Paul and Jane Bowles.

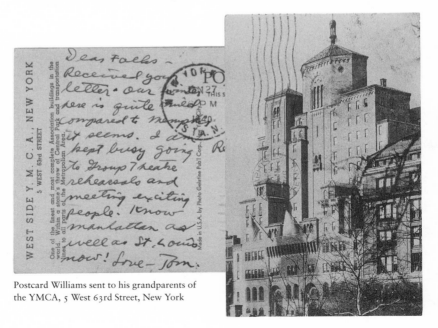

Postcard Williams sent to his grandparents of the YMCA, 5 West 63rd Street, New York

I presume. Gosh, something oughta start happenin' round here pretty soon cause Ise gittin' dees~~g~~usted!!

Saw B. my first night in N.Y. – ashes hauled but ~~somehow not much there~~ somehow pretty sick of it – you know.[305]


*Friday, 26 January 1940*

Friday – Jan. 26 – (2 weeks later) – Lotta water under the mill these last 2 weeks – Vinal introduced me to a new crowd – Starving artists from Georgia[306] – Became pretty absorbed in their problems – Various complications, Etc. – I live from day to day – attending Group Theatre rehearsals,[307] walking about town, eating, meeting people – falling into bed now and then with or without an accomplice – you see I'm rather drunk – Been over to Sid. Edison's – met Gordon Sager there[308] – We played records & drank apple jack brandy with beer chasers. Argued about Lawrence – Sager insisted (ridiculously) that he was anti-semitic –

Oh, Lord, I don't know what to make of this life I'm living. I suppose it's pretty good but it doesn't seem to get anywhere. Things happen but they don't add up to much. The big important love doesn't develop and there's no work of any importance and still some shadow of defeatism about my work. Still – It's not stagnant – It's active and has adventure aplenty.

I'm getting ugly though. My face looks so heavy and coarse these days. I feel that my youth is nearly gone. Now when I need it most! My figure is fine however – due to daily exercise. Oh, God, how idiotic this sounds – Excuse me I'm drunk – It's the truth, though – what I think about most is my "beauty" – my sexual preoccupations – and – ? and – ? – What! Nothing else? – I'm afraid not! That's the pity of it! – But I don't hate anybody. I have a tenderness for the world – G'night – You clown! – What about Monday? – Let me know.

Gordon Sager

309. Gilbert Maxwell (1910–79) was a poet and writer to whom Williams was introduced by Donald Windham and Fred Melton. They took Williams to Maxwell's rooms for one of his parties, at which invited guests were expected to provide the refreshments in exchange for Maxwell entertaining them with readings of his own poetry. By 1940, Maxwell had published two collections of poems, *Look to the Lightning* (1933), praised by such authorities as Harriet Monroe and Edna St. Vincent Millay, and *Stranger's Garment* (1936). His fourth and final collection, *Go Looking: Poems 1933–1953* (1954), included a foreword by Williams. Maxwell also published a novel, *The Sleeping Trees* (1949), and a memoir of Williams, *Tennessee Williams and Friends* (1965), in which he remembered Williams as being extraordinarily dedicated to his work.

   In the 1950s, Maxwell lived in Miami, where he taught a creative writing course at a vocational school. Williams would visit him when he traveled to Key West and Miami. "D." refers to Maxwell's lover, whose surname was Daly.

310. In a threesome, the person in the middle, socially and sexually.

311. Father Divine (1879–1965) was the controversial founder of a religious sect known as the Peace Mission Movement. In the 1930s and 1940s Father Divine was considered by many to be at best an eccentric, charismatic leader and at worst a dangerous, money-obsessed cult leader. More recently, however, Father Divine has begun to be appreciated as a powerful force for positive thinking, an influential advocate of racial equality, and one who helped desperately poor followers through the worst years of the Depression. Headquartered in Harlem at 152 West 126th Street, Father Divine presided over great banquets put on by the Peace Mission to feed its members. Interested outsiders were allowed to attend and were relegated to side tables. Williams and Maxwell may have attended one of these banquets, and they may have been asked to leave because of their less than sincere intentions.

312. Built in 1913 on 125th Street, the Apollo Theatre presented vaudeville and burlesque shows to white audiences. It launched the careers of scores of outstanding rhythm and blues, gospel, jazz, and Latin artists. Paul Robeson, Billie Holiday, Louis Armstrong, Duke Ellington, and Lionel Hampton all performed at the Apollo.

313. Sidney Edison.

Father Divine at a Holy Communion banquet

*Sunday, 28 January 1940*

Sunday Night – Another <u>mad</u> week-end with G.M. & D.[309] – who is sort of a current major theme. Went to D's last night – D. was Lucky Pierrette[310] which caused ~~two~~ a very dramatic scene. Rather disappointing outcome as G. was never quite mad enough to leave. Rather touching – though farcical – display of jealous devotion. G. and I went to Harlem – visited Father Divine's and were tossed out for invading the Sisters' quarters.[311] Then went to Appollo & saw good negro stage show.[312] Fooled around town. I wound up at the Group rehearsal. Very, very tired and the play seemed unusually weak.

Frittering my time away – Or am I? Maybe this period is really what I need to straighten me out.

D. is a distinct possibility. S.E.[313] is also – neither of them are bitches – that's what I like. Tomorrow – S.E. – denouement? – Probably just the Second act.

Sleep, baby, sleep – Manana Es otro dio! – I am as pure as I ever was – in fact purer – essentially – Ah, well. . . . .

Peace Mission grocery, Harlem

314. No manuscript of "The Earth is a Wheel in a Great Big Gambling Casino" is known to exist, although Audrey Wood sent a copy to *Story* on 4 March 1940 (Princeton). In Williams' play *Stairs to the Roof*, the main character, Benjamin D. Murphy, is fired from his job after a fragment of his writing, entitled "The Earth is a Wheel in a Great Big Gambling Casino," is discovered by his boss in a sales record book.

   Williams would use this title for an object in a later play. Chris Flanders, the wandering poet in *The Milk Train Doesn't Stop Here Anymore*, names the mobile he presents to Mrs. Goforth "The Earth is a Wheel in a Great Big Gambling Casino."

315. Harry Ellerbe (1901–92) was an actor who had several film credits by this time: *The Misleading Lady* (1932), *So Red the Rose* (1935), and *Murder on a Honeymoon* (1935). In 1936 Williams had seen him perform in St. Louis opposite the highly acclaimed Russian actress Alla Nazimova in Ibsen's *Ghosts*.

316. The film *Destry Rides Again* (1939) was a popular Western comedy spoof based on Max Brand's novel of the same name. James Stewart, in his first Western, starred as Destry, a tough law enforcement man who doesn't like guns, opposite Marlene Dietrich as Frenchy, a saloon singer. When the sheriff is killed by the town villain, Destry takes up arms. He kills the villain, but not before Frenchy takes a bullet defending him. She confesses her love for him and dies in his arms. According to Windham, Williams often listened to recordings of Dietrich singing "I've Been in Love Before" and "The Boys in the Backroom" while he wrote (interview with Margaret Bradham Thornton).

317. In "The Long Goodbye," after the death of his mother from cancer, a twenty-three-year-old writer, Joe, waits at his family's apartment for the moving company. By means of flashbacks, the play depicts the unhappiness of the young writer and his sister. "The Long Goodbye" was staged in the basement theatre of the New School for Social Research on 9, 10, and 14 February.

318. John O'Shaughnessy (1907–85) was associated with the Actors' Repertory Company. In an undated letter (circa 7 February 1940, HRC), Williams complained to Audrey Wood about O'Shaughnessy's tampering with his play: "Saw a <u>stinking</u> rehearsal of my one-act — Student actors at the School for the Feeble-minded! . . . Hope no one I know is there unless it improves vastly. John wrote a soap-box oration himself and inserted it in script to give it a social message."

319. Harry Ellerbe.

320. Donald Windham.

321. *Stairs to the Roof*.

Poem Williams wrote on the
back of an order form

*Wednesday, 31 January 1940*

Wed. – Jan. 30 (?) – Been working pretty hard on a good new story "The Earth is a wheel in a Great Big Gambling Casino"[314] – Seems good to be doing something constructive for a change. Saw H. Ellerbe[315] last night – had 3 Scotches and a pretty good time though nothing significant occured. H. decided that I was nicer than I seemed the first time. Anne called this A.M. I will see her tomorrow. Then I called D. – we'll drink together tomorrow evening. Eh bien! Looks like a pretty full day. They all are here in N.Y. – Saw Dietrich in "Destry Rides Again" – She was superb – especially when she sang "See what the Boys in the backroom will have"[316] – Dear old Grandfather wrote me a letter – he is suffering from eczema and probably won't get to Florida. God <u>bless</u> the old folks – and <u>keep</u> them. S.E. phoned and said Clark might be here this week-end. Indications with S.E. are not so favorable as they seemed. StiLL – !?

I feel like a rather vacuous, trivial, but ~~fortunate~~ happy young man. At least comparatively happy. No great source of joy in my life – like a real love-affair or big artistic triumph – but an interesting, stimulating flow of daily events – & comfortable living – <u>with</u> money!

So long – I'll report Friday on Thursday night. Hmm. Best wishes!!!


*Wednesday, 7 February 1940*

Wed. Feb. 6, 7, or 8 –

Good deal has happened in several ways. Thursday D. which was successful though nothing remarkable. Still better than anything previous. Painful however. Sunday night attended the last Group rehearsal and met P.M. – proceded straight to the point at the Hotel Laurelton for the night. Nothing remarkable but nice. So it goes. I ache with desires that never are quite satisfied. This promiscuity is appalling really. One night stands. Nobody seems to care particularly for an encore. I'm too pure I suppose. Wish D. would call again – Probably reconciled with G. Saw S.E. on street with something quite obviously trade. Encouraging. Well – !!!

Having a 1-act presented Fri. & Sat. by a student group. The Long Goodbye[317] – attended rehearsal this P.M. <u>Miserable</u> – made me quite disgusted. The play isn't bad but the acting & direction <u>deplorable</u>, which surprises me, as John O'Shaughnessy[318] impressed me as an intelligent fellow. Went to H.E's[319] the other night with Don.[320] Pleasant – uneventful. Still waiting for the big thing to come along – pretty busy, though, with my writing – well, relatively anyhow. About time I quit all this and started a new long play.[321] Because this is shit.

Goodnight.

322.   Presumably *Stairs to the Roof*.

323.   A casual acquaintance who lived at the YMCA.

324.   Donald Windham and Fred Melton.

325.   Nickname for Fred Melton.

326.   Audrey Wood had secured a scholarship for Williams to attend John Gassner and Theresa Helburn's Playwrights' Seminar at the Dramatic Workshop of the New School for Social Research. Gassner and Helburn were connected with the Theatre Guild, which Williams hoped would take an interest in *Battle of Angels*.

327.   Clifford Odets (1906–63) won acclaim in the 1930s as an outstanding proletarian dramatist with his plays *Waiting for Lefty* (1935) and *Awake and Sing!* (1935). Williams was particularly interested in Odets. In a letter to his grandparents ([2 October 1939], HRC) about his first trip to New York City, he wrote: "Everybody seems extremely interested in my work — they call me the 'Gentile Clifford Odets' which is quite a compliment in the New York theatre."
         In Odets' play *Night Music*, which opened at the Broadhurst Theatre on 22 February 1940, a messenger boy for a Hollywood studio is trapped over the weekend in New York with two monkeys required for a movie. He meets a girl from Philadelphia who is trying to be an actress. A benevolent police detective acts as an agent to keep them together and, after a weekend spent sleeping in Central Park, wandering around the World's Fair, and talking to everyone they meet, they become engaged in an airport. The play was reviewed in the *New York Times* of 23 February 1940 by Brooks Atkinson, who wrote: "'Night Music' is a foolish play by a man of great talent. It is time — high time — for him to awake and sing."

328.   According to Anne Bretzfelder, there were several attempts at "little love episodes" between herself and Williams. "He kept making advances that displeased me mightily. I felt pressured to the extreme by him — so much so that finally I would flee from him and hide from him. . . . And I didn't realize then . . . that he was probably profoundly being pulled in two directions" (Leverich, p. 351).

329.   Donald Windham, Fred Melton, Gilbert Maxwell, and B. Daly.

A session of the Playwrights' Seminar at the New School (Williams on far left, Arthur Miller on right with pipe)

*Monday, 12 February 1940*

Mon. Feb. 13 –
   Dull day, very dull. For the first time felt really a bit fed up with this New York period. Wrote a little this A.M. on a rather promising idea about white collar workers.³²² Nothing very good, though. Stuck around the "Y" nearly all day and for the first time went down to the tea. Silly business. Tonight no workout as gym was closed for Lincoln's birthday. Walked down to Times Sq. and back – found no show I wanted to see. Bought a detective mag. Read in my room till now – begin to feel a bit restless and lonely. It is not unlikely that I will drop in to see F!³²³ – Alas. This is a dreadful empty business and nobody knows it better than I. I was rather pleased with the play – stimulating to see how good my lines can sound when they're well-read. D. doesn't call but is nice when we meet at D. & F.'s.³²⁴ Still it offends my pride and my heart a little. The big thing hasn't come yet. Will it ever? – Let us be hopeful. To bed? I don't know. Probably wouldn't sleep. So long. (Take it easy, Butch)³²⁵

*Saturday, 24 February 1940*

Sat. Feb. 24 –
   Been jumpy lately, old neurosis back on me – anti-social, not comfortable around people – F. has moved right next door and is trying sometimes though very sweet.
   Play made great progress, nearly done but last few days pretty stale – nerves raw from too much strain – nothing of consequence going on – Except I won scholarship to playwriting seminar.³²⁶
   Odets play³²⁷ flopped as I expected. Met & talked to him in theatre lobby this P.M. when I took Anne to see play. He was nice and I liked him for the first time – sympathy for the defeated. He nervously fingered his watch and looked deeply hurt – almost completely deflated. Ought to do him good as an artist.
   Brief interlude with a stranger (young and attractive) who passed in the night – my only adventure of late and that one much too fleeting. B.V.L. the current dream figure. S.E. still a question mark. Anne leaves tomorrow. We had a little love ~~sequence~~ episode in her apt. one night but didn't mean much. Still I like her remarkably – for me.³²⁸
   I want to iron out my nerves and meet with some new and fascinating people. D. & F. are out – So are G. & B.D.³²⁹ I don't get along well with people lately. Nerves and general lack of social gifts. <u>Must</u> write letters. G'nite.

330. Gordon Sager.

331. In "Portrait of a Madonna," Lucretia Collins, a middle-aged spinster who is the daughter of an Episcopalian minister, becomes convinced she is pregnant by her fantasy male lover, and she is led off to an institution. The play was an important source for *A Streetcar Named Desire*.

332. Fleet Munson, a friend of Williams', wrote Audrey Wood on 14 February 1940 (HRC) to express his excitement about Williams' abilities after seeing the New School's production of "The Long Goodbye":

> Last Saturday night I had the good fortune to watch a group of not too fumbling student actors perform a piece called The Long Goodbye. . . . I have been profoundly moved by the playwriting talent of one whose ability is as clearly recognizable. . . .
>
> I'm sure you know how good Mr. Williams is but even so, I am impelled to add my small word. Gentle him, for pete's sake. . . . Don't let the drones get him.

333. John Gassner (1903–67) was a teacher, critic, and author. From 1931 to 1944 Gassner was play editor and then chairman of the play department at the Theatre Guild. In 1940 he was the head of the drama department at the New School for Social Research and was the chairman of the playwriting seminar Williams was attending. He went on to become the Sterling Professor of Playwriting and Dramatic Literature at Yale.
   In assessing Williams' status as a playwright of the twentieth century, Gassner wrote:

> Williams brought to his treatment of personal tensions and social backgrounds a rare poetic imagination and sensitive dialogue combined, as a rule, with an uncommon amount of naturalistic detail. (*The World of Contemporary Drama* [New York: American Library Association, 1965], p. 25)

On comparing Williams and Arthur Miller, Gassner wrote:

> Williams . . . has been concerned with the dream-mechanisms of unfortunate characters who try to create and preserve ideal images of themselves. Like Miller, he regards their delusions with compassionate interest as pathetic defenses against the frustrations or shipwreck of their lives. In fact, he is able to create a tracery of fantasy for them with much greater subtlety and grace than Miller, although he is vulnerable to the temptations of bohemian preciosity, as Miller is not. His portraits of women who cannot face reality are masterful. Unlike Miller, however, Williams gives primacy to the psychologically rather than socially relevant facts of each situation. (*The Theatre in Our Times* [New York: Crown, 1954], pp. 348–49)

334. *Battle of Angels.*

Gilbert Maxwell

*Monday, 11 March 1940*

Mon. March 12 – The Period drags along pretty slowly – or dully these days. One new one-night adventure with G.S.[330] in the Village mainly the result of my own initiative for a change. Not important enough (though worth while) to definitely break the tedium. was all set to leave for Mex. the 22 but that resolve is now shaken by disturbing reports about the summer climate. Will probably go somewhere as I feel myself going stale here. Where? – Don't know. Still it's nice to feel I can pack up and go. Don't appreciate it as much as I ought to –

No big news in my problematical career. Current possibility is news that Group is thinking of doing a one-act program – Maybe some of mine – maybe – You know, I feel old and unattractive lately. I don't seem to cut much ice these days with people I want to impress. I look kinda dreary. Sallow, heavy. Need a good, intense affair to bring me back to life and restore my spirits. Yeah. The big emotional business is still on the other side of tomorrow. That's why I'm restless. Maybe tropical sunlight – or moonlight – would stir something up that I'm in need of. Shit. – Wrote a one-act "Portrait of a Madonna"[331] which may be kinda good. Fleet[332] is gone – to Philly – should have got back Sat. Miss him more than I thought I would. Prospects? – Unusually vague. Can't see beyond breakfast. Got nothing much to kick about though – Knock wood. Will be broke if unexpected funds don't drop in to see me this week. S'long.

*Friday, 29 March 1940*

Thursday or early Fri. A.M. – March 29 –
Something has happened to the fellow that's been writing in here lately. He doesn't sound like the guy that I used to know in the days gone by. Sounds listless and coarse. Needs a good emotional shot in the arm. Something exhilerating. Some spiritual champagne. – Maybe it's the end of youth, my dear . . . . hope not – it mustn't be!

Plan to sail for Mexico after all, the fifth of April. Maybe that will work the necessary charm although I'm not too ~~opt~~ expectant of that. Probably be lonely and unhappy down there, too. Anyhow I'm going – this dullness can't go on – even the fire is better than the cold grease in this frying pan. Bad image, I know. John Gassner[333] at the Theatre Guild has taken an interest in "B of A."[334] but I'm not banking on that little development. The only excitement right now is S.E. – that business may come to some conclusion in the next few days – which promise to contain some changes. And after all, change itself is a definite good I think. Stagnation is unbearable. So am I. Good night. If this journal goes on like this, I had better destroy it.

*It certainly did. 4/1/40 – on April Fool's Day! — I shall always beware.*

335.   On 4 March 1940, Audrey Wood had sent Whit Burnett of *Story* copies of two short stories, "The Swan" and "The Earth is a Wheel in a Great Big Gambling Casino," neither of which would be accepted for publication. As mentioned previously in the journals, Williams had written a version of "The Swan" in April 1936.

336.   The New School for Social Research was founded in 1919 as a progressive academic institution. The New School's Dramatic Workshop provided training for the professional theatre and served as a link between academic education and a professional career. Although it was primarily designed as a complete two-year course in various major subjects, students who had previous training could enroll for individual courses. Williams was enrolled for the spring 1940 term.

337.   Felicia Sorel (1904–72) was an American concert dancer and theatrical choreographer. In a list of unpublished work prepared for Audrey Wood (May 1943), Williams mentioned Sorel as having his copy of "The Earth is a Wheel in a Great Big Gambling Casino."

338.   *Reunion in New York* was the follow-up revue to a show performed the previous summer by the Kleinkunstbuehne, a group of young refugee performers from Vienna. Reviewers were sympathetic to the plight of the refugees and most described the evening's entertainment as pleasant and informal, if light and sentimental. In a set designed like an old-time Viennese wine garden, the performance included Viennese waltzes, songs, light comedy sketches, and, perhaps notably for Williams, a satire on William Saroyan.

339.   Childs was a chain of restaurants in New York City. One was on Columbus Circle, near the YMCA where Williams stayed.

340.   Theresa Helburn (1887–1959), who headed the Theatre Guild with Lawrence Langner, offered Williams $100 for an option on *Battle of Angels*, which Williams understood to be the first step toward a complete sale. Williams would eventually be advised by Wood to return the check until a proper contract could be negotiated.

341.   *Battle of Angels*.

342.   Diamond Jim's, a bar with food on 42nd Street at Broadway, was popular with sailors.

343.   In *One Million B.C.* (1940) two young people from warring prehistoric factions, the Rock Tribe and the Shell People, fall in love. This fanciful tale placed Stone Age man among dinosaurs which were created by filming lizards, crocodiles, and iguanas, with various fins attached, and then enlarging the images.

344.   The Theatre Guild and the Dramatists' Guild.

345.   Bertha Case (1909–84) was an assistant to Audrey Wood who went on to become a literary agent on the West Coast.

Lawrence Langner and Theresa Helburn

*Monday, 1 April 1940*

4/1/40 – (P.M.) – For the first time since coming to Manhattan, I spent an evening in the "Y.M.C.A." lobby – alone with my thoughts, as it were. I don't recommend it as anything better than "fair entertainment". Another vaguely dull sort of day, jogging listlessly about town on a number of unimportant errands, such as calling for rejected mss. at Story335 and waiting, <u>waiting</u>, <u>waiting</u> for a 3-minute chat with Miss Foley, as unrewarding an interview as I have ever had, which is enuf said. Tomorrow Gassner at the New School336 – nervous. Rather momentous. Wish it were all over and done and I were dying of a <u>new</u> kind of ennui in Mexico. I – the boy who often boasts that he is <u>never</u> bored – that life is <u>always</u> exciting. Quêlle drollêrie! I need to write an important new play – it's all I'm good for – if I am good for that. So long, Mon Amour!

*Monday, 8 April or Tuesday, 9 April 1940*

Mon. or Tuesday A.M. April 8 or 9
    Tonight Germany seized Denmark and war was declared by Norway – but infinitely more important is the fact that my play will be discussed and perhaps a decision rendered by the Theatre Guild.
    Today was nice for a change – went to tea at new school, cocktails with Felicia Sorel337 whom I like, and to a charming revue called Reunion in N.Y."338 with Austrian refugee actors who were delightful – especially <u>one</u>. Sat in 3rd Row so I missed <u>nothing</u>. Then Fleet and I took a walk around park – it was an enchantingly beautiful night – misty, cool, sparkling – ate at Child's,339 came home and heard the war news – Disasters abroad merely add an edge of excitement to our evenings in America. <u>C'est la vie, c'est la guêrre, c'est l'amour</u>!

*Monday, 29 April 1940*

    During this interval I left New York – with a reading option checque for $100.00 from the Theatre Guild340 – went to St. L. – Memphis – Clarksdale, Miss. & returned –
    So beginneth the <u>3rd</u> N.Y period – I was called back for further consultation with the Guild – <u>So</u> Mexico is at least temporarily postponed. May <u>sell play</u>.341
    First night here – uneventful enough – Got a new room on a new floor – ate deviled crabs at Diamond Jim's342 – saw a silly picture called "1,000,000 yrs. B.C."343 C'est ça – Tomorrow will tackle the play in the A.M. & the T.G. afterwards – also the D.G.344 And B.C.345 – Enough of the alphabet at present. So long. (No – it hasn't occured.) (Still waiting for it)

346. After much wrangling and negotiation, Williams sent a wire home on 8 May saying that the Theatre Guild had finally signed the regular contract (*RMT*, p. 116).

347. Lawrence Langner (1890–1962), patent attorney of international standing, author, and playwright, headed the Theatre Guild with Theresa Helburn. Williams wrote a short satirical play set in the Theatre Guild office entitled "The Taj Mahal with Ink-Wells," which features Helburn, Langner, and Gassner. In the one-act play "The Last of My Solid Gold Watches," Charlie Colton tells Harper about the death of "Marblehead" Langner.

Williams celebrating the signing of the Theatre Guild contract with Anne Bretzfelder,
Fred Melton, and Donald Windham at the Village Barn, 52 West 8th Street, New York

*Sunday, 26 May 1940*

May – 25 or 6 – Sunday Midnight.

<u>And</u> still waiting for it! –

Though I've had considerable success in my work – play bought by Theatre Guild346 and apparently headed for Fall production – my emotional life has been a series of rather spectacular failures – so much so that I am becoming pretty thoroughly despondent about it. Last night was the grand anti-climax – Ah, l'amour, la guerre et la vie!! When will it happen – and how? I am losing my looks alarmingly.

Haggard, tired, jittery, fretful, bored – that is what lack of a reciprocal love object does to a man. Let us hope it spurs his creative impulse – there should be <u>some</u> compensation for this hell of loneliness. Makes me act, think, <u>be</u> like an idiot – whining, trivial, tiresome – I can only say in my defense that I do find myself a pretty despicable object, decent only in comparison to things like Hitler.

Yet I feel it <u>will</u> come. Perhaps when I move into the apt. or when the play gets under way. The new draft has gone to Langner347 and there is a disturbing possibility he may find it unsuitable after all. I am not yet satisfied. Although a new scene I wrote today might make a great improvement.

<u>You</u> coming toward me – <u>please</u> make <u>haste</u>!

J'ai soif! Je meurs de soif!

(You – you – is <u>this</u> you? – "Coming toward me?")

*Thursday, 30 May 1940*

Thursday – Memorial Day –

A delightful though not important episode assuaged my thirst in some measure. And I feel a bit more sane. It is unfortunate that I have to endure this feverish libido, distorting the mirror of the mind even more than it is by nature – this statement does not seem to make much sense. Skip it.

Holocaust in Europe – it really does sicken me, I am glad to say. Of course my reactions are primarily selfish. I fear that it may kill the theatre. But I dare hope that there is a considerable degree of altruistic sentiment also involved. I know myself to be a dog but – animal nature no longer appears embarrassing in one's self it has become so universally apparent in others and at least I am not a victim of hydrophobia, I do not attack, snarl, etc. I only grab my own little bone and begrudge you any large share of it – although if you were starving I might let you gnaw one end. If I were not starving, too. Or would I? Or wouldn't I? This too is becoming foolish & confused.

"<u>Me</u>" – that should be an adequate one-word-two-letter entry for every day!

I love people when they please me. When they don't please me, I dislike them. Is everyone like that? I hope not. Of course some strangers please me because they are pitiable. But pity is pleasure and so is selfish. I have ideals – I want peace,

348.  Alfred Lunt (1892–1977) and Lynne Fontanne (1887–1983) were a famous acting couple. At this time, they were starring in the Theatre Guild's production of Robert E. Sherwood's new play, *There Shall Be No Night,* which went on to win the 1941 Pulitzer Prize.

349.  Windham, Melton, and Williams sublet the apartment of the painter Stokely Webster at 151 East 37th Street, between Park Avenue and Lexington Avenue, for several months in the summer.

Williams in the East 37th Street apartment

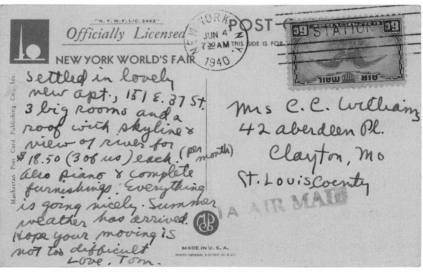

Postcard Williams sent to his mother

freedom, universal kindness, tolerance, understanding, good will. But doesn't everyone think he wants the same things? This is not only foolish but tiresome.

It is a clear night, cool. I went to see Lunt Fontanne.[348] Day after tomorrow move into the apt.[349] – So will begin a new Period, happier I hope, containing what I desire most – perhaps – a ~~deep~~ satisfactory love-relationship.

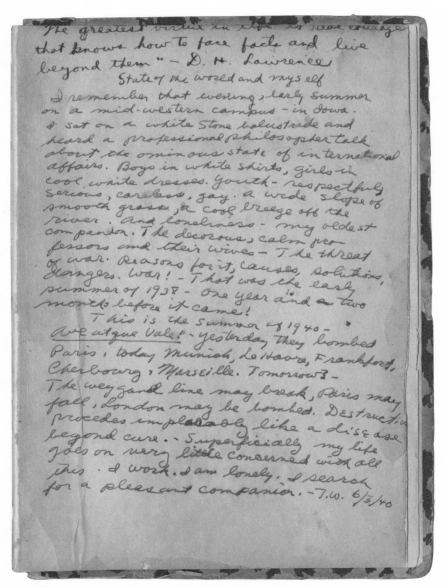

Williams' annotations on his copy of *The Collected Poems of Hart Crane*

350. The John B. Stetson Company produced a number of styles of hats including the Panama model. In *Something Cloudy, Something Clear*, Williams' play about the summer of 1940, August, the writer modeled on Williams, says: "when I came [to New York] on that sudden dispensation from the family Rockefeller, their foundation — gave me a grant. The silver victrola and the records I bought were reckless extravagance, cost almost half the monthly check but — I can't write without music — Bavarian blood in me. I'm one-quarter Hun. And the second thing I bought was a ten-dollar Panama hat, genuine, with a narrow black band."

351. "La Golondrina" (The Swallow) is a Latin American folk song by Narciso Serradell that was sung in the 1930s. "La Golondrina" is heard in the plays "The Purification," "Dragon Country," *The Glass Menagerie*, *Summer and Smoke,* and *Camino Real*. According to Windham, Williams had a recording of "La Golondrina" that he played over and over while he wrote (interview with Margaret Bradham Thornton).

352. Williams had traveled to New York City to check on the Theatre Guild's production plans for *Battle of Angels* but expected to return to Provincetown.

Donald Windham and Williams wearing his Stetson

*Wednesday, 12 June 1940*

Wednesday – June – abt. middle. Bought a $10.00 Stetson[350] today. No further remarks as I think that is sufficient to recall all the curious and sad procession of events which make this day more conspicuously empty than many others – even in my life.

Remind me to congratulate myself on being dead some day.

No – this is not nice.

Goodnight.

*Thursday, 4 July 1940*

"Fourth of July" – what a long time afterwards.

*Friday, 19 July 1940*

July – 16 – 17 or 18 – Friday –

Yes – a long time.

It is a rather pale bright summer morning – weak lemony sunlight on the brownstone fronts.

I am playing "La Golondrina".[351]

And feeling rather weary of it all.

Yes – in spite of the fact that the great anticipated thing occured – not once but apparently twice. Or maybe this wasn't what I meant. Love to be love has got to be love.

Do you get what I mean? Do I get what I mean?

I suppose tomorrow I will return to P.town.[352] Will it be all gone or will it still be there?

Why am I always restless, searching, unsatisfied?

My work lags – production plans uncertain. Writing this journal doesn't interest me much anymore. I will probably forget it entirely after a while. I have been taking too much nicotine, coffee, alcohol – try to ~~cut it out~~ reduce it. Have got to save myself for my work – Such as it is –

Unbearably stupid today – gbye.

*Friday, 26 July 1940*

Fri. – July 27 – Back at the Cape. Should be sublimely happy. Instead rather miserable due to one of my very oldest neuroses coming back on me. Plagues me viciously, makes it hard for me to bear the strain of people. I wear dark glasses almost continually – even this does not seem an adequate protection. It is worst

353.    Kip Kiernan, alias Bernard Dubowsky (1918–44), was an illegal alien from Canada who had studied ballet with Joseph Hazan in New York City. While rooming with Hazan and Kiernan on Captain Jack's Wharf in Provincetown, Williams was very attracted to Kiernan and had an affair described in a letter to Donald Windham ([29 and 30 July 1940], Yale):

> Your letter came at a very opportune moment as I was feeling blue. My life is now full of emotional complications which make me write good verse — at least a lot of it — but make my mental chart a series of dizzy leaps up and down, ecstacy one moment — O dapple faun! — and consummate despair the next. Never thought I could go through something like this again. But never do you know!
>
> Depression this morning occasioned by fact the ballet dancer stayed out all night. So far no explanation, though I suspect a nymph at the other end of the wharf and am moving to a single bed downstairs till suspicions confirmed or dispelled. . . .
>
> Later: Everything is okay again and I didn't have to move downstairs after all. He slept alone on the beach because he needed some sleep. Doesn't get much with me. But that's his own fault for being so incredibly beautiful. We wake up two or three times in the night and start all over again like a pair of goats. The ceiling is very high like the loft of a barn and the tide is lapping under the wharf. The sky amazingly brilliant with stars. The wind blows the door wide open, the gulls are crying. Oh, Christ. I call him baby like you call Butch though when I lie on top of him I feel like I was polishing the statue of liberty or something. He is so enormous. A great bronze statue of antique Greece come to life. But with a little boy's face. A funny up-turned nose, slanting eyes, an under-lip that sticks out and hair that comes to a point in the middle of his forehead. I lean over him in the night and memorize the geography of his body with my hands — he arches his throat and makes a soft, purring sound. His skin is steaming hot like the hide of a horse that's been galloping. It has a warm, rich odor. The odor of life. He lies very still for a while, then his breath comes fast and his body begins to lunge. Great rhythmic plunging motion with panting breath and his hands working over my body. Then sudden release — and he moans like a little baby. I rest with my head on his

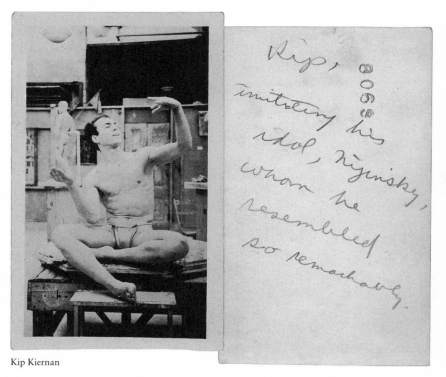

Kip Kiernan

Kip, imitating his idol, Nijinsky, whom he resembled so remarkably.

in the early mornings such as now – when I face another whole day of this tortured evasion. I feel however that it has just about run its course – its imaginative appeal must be nearly satiated. It has gone on with very slight intermission for about 3 weeks – the usual length.

Stupid – doing no decent work.

But love which I have been needing – only somewhat thwarted by this damnable tension.

Nerves feel raw this A.M. – will go off by myself for a while to ease them.

No news from N.Y. in some time. Worries me a little. Suppose the bottom fell out of the whole world tomorrow?

Work, my lad. Feel your power. Reject your fear, your weakness.

<u>En Avant!</u>

*Monday, 29 July 1940*

Sun. Night – Went to chamber music recital. K.353 moody – rushed off by himself. Moves me to find someone afflicted as I am with mental conflicts. Think I understand a little – Still it troubles me – this is so much what I need, what I want, what I have been looking for the past few months so feverishly. Seems miraculous. It is too good to be true – I can't feel sure of it. Can't believe it will go on. So K's moods worry me – I fear his being lost to me already. If that happened I suppose I would go on outwardly very much as usual – but, oh, what an ache of emptiness I would have to endure – for now, for the first time in my life, I feel I am near to the great <u>real</u> thing that can make my life complete.

Oh, K. – don't stay away very long. – I'm lonely tonight. – So long. It's after midnight – I am here alone.

Postcard Williams sent to his grandparents (postmarked 30 July 1940)

stomach. Sometimes fall asleep that way. We doze for a while. And then I whisper "Turn over". He does. We use brilliantine. The first time I come in three seconds, as soon as I get inside. The next time is better, slower, the bed seems to be enormous. Pacific, Atlantic, the North American continent. — A wind has blown the door open, the sky's full of stars. High tide is in and water laps under the wharf. And now we're so tired we can't move. After a long while he whispers, "I like you, Tenny." — hoarse — embarrassed — ashamed of such intimate speech! — And I laugh for I know that he loves me! — That nobody ever loved me before so completely. I feel the truth in his body. I call him baby — and tell him to go to sleep. After a while he does, his breathing is deep and even, and his great deep chest is like a continent moving slowly, warmly beneath me. The world grows dim, the world grows warm and tremendous. Then everything's gone and when I wake up it is daylight, the bed is empty. — Kip is gone out. — He is dancing. — Or posing naked for artists. Nobody knows our secret but him and me. And now <u>you</u>, Donnie. — because you can understand.

Please keep this letter and be very careful with it. It's only for people like us who have gone beyond shame!

Williams may have been exaggerating the extent of his relationship with Kiernan, for Joe Hazan remembers that Williams and Kiernan slept together only one night. In any event, according to Hazan, Kiernan was troubled by his affair with Williams and broke it off. Williams wrote several love poems to Kip Kiernan.

For K.

Sometimes the substance that is I,
as thin as light if not so pure ,
returns into the running sky
in search of something more secure.

Then I, without my shadow to
assure me of solidity,
am lost within a vault of blue
and perilous fluidity.

When in this insubstantial state,
my panic must direct me where
your lips can touch me and so take
me back from intercourse with air.

For only you have power to
collect those molecules which I,
through loneliness or lack of love,
surrendered to the empty sky

1940.

Poem for K.

If you be wanton in my arms
blame not yourself but only me
who long ago resolved upon
a newer kind of purity

For purity and passion are
things that differ but in name
and as one metal must emerge
when melted in a single flame

If you be wanton in my arms
then let the penitence be mine
who drink of passion as a priest
of ~~sacramental wine~~. of God's blood turned to wine.

Tennessee Williams

Kip married and joined the Hanya Holm Dance Company, but in 1944, at the age of twenty-six, he died from a brain tumor. Williams visited him in hospital just before his death and later dedicated his collection *One Arm and Other Stories* to his memory.

Besides using Kip as a character in several fragments, Williams wrote about him in his late play *Something Cloudy, Something Clear* (1980), which was based on a much earlier play, "The Parade or Approaching the End of a Summer," written in 1940. Williams made small changes between Kip and the character based on him. In the play, Kip's sister describes him to August, the character modeled on Williams:

Kip's a Canadian in the States illegally. He sneaked into the country to escape the draft because he has this passion for dancing, and he knew if he was drafted into the Canadian Army it would be too late, when he got out, if he got out alive, to learn to be a great dancer, which Kip is going to be, I mean he's going to be as great as Nijinsky. Well. He's in the States illegally. He could be stopped on the streets any time and asked for his draft card. That's why we stay off the streets nearly always. Oh, somebody gave him their draft card, but any time he might be stopped and not get by with that card and be sent back to Canada and not be drafted but thrown in jail for God knows how long, longer than he would even have to stay in the army if he hadn't skipped out of Canada before he was drafted. Are you following this? You're still staring at Kip.

*Tuesday, 13 August 1940*

August 12 or 13
Tuesday – <u>C'est fini</u> —

I can't save myself.
Somebody has got to save me,

I shall have to go through the world giving myself to people until somebody will take me.

We are moving into a new studio at the front of the wharf –
I am a little drunk –
the pain is dulled a little.

There is nothing. T.W.

The Hanya Holm Dance Company performing *Dance of Introduction* in 1941
(rear center, Kip Kiernan, and front right, Louise Kloepper), and (inset) Louise Kloepper
as the Raven-Phoenix and Kip Kiernan as Saturn in *The Golden Fleece*, also in 1941

354. The "stupid little girl" was Shirley Brimberg (1919–97), who was in Provincetown with a dance troupe. In *Memoirs* Williams explained why Shirley was the object of his anger:

> Toward the end of August, a girl entered the scene. I did not regard her as a threat. And then one day I was on the dunes with the group that included the yet-unknown, or uncelebrated abstract painter, Jackson Pollock. . . .
>
> Well, one afternoon late that summer I was on the dunes with the group, when Kip appeared, looking very solemn.
>
> "Tenn, I have to talk to you."
>
> He rode me into P-town on the handle-bars of a bike, and on the way in, with great care and gentleness, he told me that the girl who had intruded upon the scene had warned him that I was in the process of turning him homosexual and that he had seen enough of that world to know that he had to resist it, that it violated his being in a way that was unacceptable to him.
>
> It was no longer tenable, the two-story shack — now that Kip wouldn't share the loft with me. So we moved into a larger two-story habitation which was not furnished except with three cots and a table and a few chairs. (p. 56)

Shirley Brimberg Clarke went on to become an Academy Award–winning documentary filmmaker and leading figure in the American avant-garde cinema of the 1950s and 1960s.

355. Joe Hazan (1916– ), born Joseph Hassan, was a dancer who shared the two-story house in Provincetown with Kip Kiernan. He became a good friend and counsellor to Williams through the emotional trauma of Kip's rejection. Hazan went on to pursue a career in design. He is married to the artist Jane Freilicher.

356. In 1940, Donald Windham had a job selling Coca-Cola at the World's Fair in Flushing, New York. Blondie was a co-worker of Windham's.

Williams in Provincetown

Joe Hazan

*Thursday, 15 August 1940*

Thursday –
    Made a horrible ass of myself this A.M. – insulting a stupid little girl because she had been instrumental in my unhappiness.354
    Felt quite unnerved, almost hysterical –
    silly! – The whole mess has got to end <u>now</u> –
    C'est finit.

Later – Leave for New York tomorrow unless sudden change of some kind prevents. My neurotic loneliness – shattered love – broken-heart or what have you? – threatens to wreck me completely. It <u>mustn't</u>. Still got to go on somehow. It can't be much worse the next few weeks than I expect it to be, since I really expect it to be next to unbearable – and I am pretty badly frightened. Well – to <u>hell</u> with it. I am going to see it through. No bug-house for me, baby.
    Joe355 has been swell – a grand guy – kind, understanding – the kind of friend I would like to take through life with me, but know that I can't because I can never stand still – I'm always the fugitive – will be till I make my last escape – out of life altogether.
    Kip – I must not write about him now because I couldn't do it fairly. I feel that I have never given my love more uselessly in any whore house. No, that's not true. It's my hurt pride crying out again –
    This has got to stop – pass away – it can't continue.
    How will it be on the boat tomorrow? How will it be in New York?
    Oh, Christ, how will it be!
    You whoever you are – who takes care of those beyond caring for themselves – please make some little charitable provision for the next few days of Tennessee. So long.

*Sunday, 18 August 1940*

Sunday in Manhattan – August 18.
    A grey sultry heavy-lidded day –
    felt quite weighed down with fatigue when I awoke to face it.
    bad cold on chest, uneasy feeling which probably means the blood pressure is up.
    To hell with that, though. <u>Il n'importe rien.</u>
    Blondie356 was here last night and what was once so desirable – though still I rather wanted it as an hour's diversion – seemed pretty empty and sordid. Still it helped me over a bad night and cost nothing.
    I have just read an article about travel in Mexico. Perhaps this proposed trip will revive me.
    But, oh, K. – if only – only – <u>only</u> –

357.  Sonnet XLIII from Elizabeth Barrett Browning's well-known sonnet cycle begins "How do I love thee? Let me count the ways" and ends "I shall but love thee better after death." In *A Streetcar Named Desire*, Blanche discovers the latter line inscribed on Mitch's cigarette case, which had been given to him by a girl who was dying.

The *Rubáiyát of Omar Khayyám*, translated by Edward FitzGerald in 1859 and published as an anonymous pamphlet, was a free adaptation and selection from the twelfth-century Persian poet's verses. Williams selected the *Rubáiyát* for Joe Hazan because he was interested in East Indian dance and philosophy.

In a post-1939 revision of the short story "Square Pegs," titled "This Can't Last Forever," one of the four main characters, Kate, a romanticist, recites a verse from the *Rubáiyát* to her boyfriend:

> Ah, Love! Could you and I with Him conspire
> To grasp this sorry Scheme of Things entire,
> Would we not shatter it to bits — and then
> Re-mould it nearer to the Hearts' Desire!

Tom, one of the other main characters (based on Williams), says:
> "You know, if us kids had the chance that old Omar Khayyam wanted, re-moulding the world a little nearer to our Heart's Desire, don't you suppose we could fix things so that every talent could be used, that every man could find his own, natural place in the world. Get what I mean? No mis-fits! No square pegs in round holes!"
>
> "What we need is a little less Omar Khayyam," said Dick, "and a little more Karl Marx!"

358.  Paul Sweeney, a ballet dancer with the Metropolitan Opera. In an undated letter to Williams (HRC), Joe Hazan spoke highly of Sweeney and told Williams that Sweeney understood his feelings:
> I spoke to Paul for a long while, & discovered he was quite a deep intelligent person in many respects. . . . Paul has depth in the sense that he sees the stupidity of this mad race for pleasure — & feels quite complete with beauty — he has had quite a struggle — been very unhappy with other people always — tragic with love & has managed pretty well to make a profound & pleasant pattern of life. . . . Paul, by the way, perceived all aspects of your affair with Kip, saying he'd gone through the same thing — that it was a purely physical love & that you wouldn't suffer for long — out of sight — out of mind.

Commercial Street, Provincetown

What is the use of such thoughts? I have loved once in my life – and now it's over.

Now is the time for waiting for the heart to close in on itself, for rest, for recuperation.

Somewhere there is another rare and beautiful stranger waiting for me. And this one, perhaps, is the one who will <u>take</u> what I give. And I will stop being <u>lonely</u>.

Byebye.


*Monday, 19 August 1940*

Monday – Today was definitely better than it has been. Due mainly to Don's pleasant company, a couple of pleasant but unimportant meetings at Theatre Guild and Audrey's. Won't know anything till Wednesday when Langner gets back.

Took a long walk in the rain along Broadway and enjoyed it. Felt quiet and relaxed – only a little bit blue – for first time in days – and days –

Bought "Sonnets from Portuguese" for K. and "Rubaiyat" for Joe. Cheap gifts but my heart goes with them. I mark Sonnet XLIII for K's attention.357 Silly of me! – He'll probably think so, too.

Swam about 20 lengths and 10 widths at the "Y". Intent on preserving my figure, anyhow. – When I got out the sky was clearing and it was cool. It seemed, for the first time in too long, that I might derive some pleasure again from my natural environment.

A drunk wobbled up to me and caught my arm and called me "darling". Strangers still look at me with sexual interest in spite of the fact that I begin to feel old and jaded.

I think ~~eo~~ almost continually of K. – Memories – dreams – longings – little hopes and great desolations – Will he ever come back? Can there – will there be someone else? Or will I always be walking around streets at night all alone? Standing wearily in front of bright windows? Wondering where to go, what to do, when only someone I loved could give me a real direction in which to move. K., if you ever come back, I'll never let you go. I'll bind you to me with every chain that the ingenuity of mortal love can devise! Hmm. Getting rhetorical again. No letters today, no word from Paul358 who's supposed to be in town. Tomorrow? – Thursday I may leave for Mexico. Pray some encouraging word may come from Provincetown before then – Some little ray of hope for this love-lorn creature.

Feel tired tonight, and relaxed – the air is cool – I believe I am going to do some important new work before long – if I take a rest and clear the decks for action.

K. – dear K. – I love you with all my heart. Goodnight.

(I think I will start a new Journal with the Mexican Period and make it more complete.)

359. Clark Mills was in New York prior to the start of the school year at Cornell. Williams did see Mills, and he wrote Joe Hazan ([23 August 1940], HRC) about his visit:

> You remember Clark Mills mentioned in my journal? He came over last night and told me quite seriously that he had decided to kill himself within the next year. He is tied to an academic job at Cornell which smothers his creative life and he sees no possible escape as his poetry, very fine but completely non-commercial, could never support him. I reasoned with him for a long time about the infinite value of life, of the miracle of simply being alive, and through this I think I convinced myself of it. More, I'm afraid, than him. I saw very clearly the central fact of life and all the rest as being little motes in the sun, circulating around it. I wrote this line yesterday at the beginning of a long poem — "I want to infect you with the tremendous excitement of living, because I believe that you have the strength to bear it!"

The first few lines of a fragment of the poem to which Williams refers:

> I would like to infect you with the excitement of
> living because you are strong enough to bear it.
>
> There is a hollowness in you like a preface to
> spring, the hollow cup of the year before the
> storms begin breaking.
>
> There is white sky and nothing yet in it, not even
> the little red tissue-paper kites of enquiring passion.
>
> You sit here quiescent, waiting, and I would like
> to infect you suddenly with the great, intense
> excitement that comes of self-recognition, of knowing
> the fact of your being, your rising at morning and
> being yourself again after night, after dreams, after
> temporary cessation.

360. According to Joe Hazan, Doug was a very camp gay man with bleached blond hair. In a letter to Donald Windham ([28 June 1940], Yale), Williams described him: "The 'crowd' here is dominated by a platinum blond Hollywood belle named Doug."

361. Shirley Brimberg, later Clarke.

362. In a letter to Hazan two days later ([23 August 1940], HRC), Williams wrote: "Funny — in my wanderings about I have met a great many people, nearly all friendly, many of whom I was fairly intimate with in one way or another, but nobody has seemed as close to me in spirit as you are. That was why I thought only of you at those times when my life seemed in danger of falling to pieces."

363. In *Memoirs* Williams would recall the trip and credit a scene from it as perhaps being the germ for the play *Kingdom of Earth*, which began as a story in 1942 entitled "Spiritchel Gates" (later retitled "The Kingdom of Earth"):

> I determined upon a course of action, flight to Mexico. In those days there was an advertised service by which someone desiring transportation by car to some other city — in this case, another country — could contact a driver going that way and arrange to share the expenses of the journey. I applied to that service, when I'd returned to Manhattan in my state of shock, and was quite speedily introduced to a young Mexican who had come to New York by car to see the 1940 World's Fair and who had married a prostitute in Manhattan and now was taking her home to meet his wealthy family in Mexico City. There was a total language barrier between this young lady and her Mexican bridegroom. She was a voluptuous piece and he was voluptuous, too, and when you say a man, a bridegroom, is voluptuous it's not a compliment to him.
>
> We had a fantastic ride south. There were three other male Mexicans in the party and they took turns at the wheel. Sometimes a road map was produced but they couldn't follow it. We kept making involuntary detours from our route, some that took us hundreds of miles out of the way. . . .
>
> As we gradually approached the Texas border, the prostitute-bride became increasingly nervous

*Tuesday, 20 August 1940*

Tuesday –

Blues returned with a vengeance tonight.

Paul came over and we talked about K~~ip~~. I thought this might relieve me but it had the opposite effect, expecially since Paul, ~~I believe~~, intends to live with K. in the Fall and I believe wants ~~him~~ K. either consciously or unconsciously himself. Oh, God, how desolate and lost I feel – how utterly <u>alone</u> – <u>alone</u>.

It no longer seems likely that we will ever really come together again. Of course the play production means a tremendous amount. Audrey does not want me to count on it – and I don't. But what else can save me now? I can think of nothing tonight. – Tomorrow may open another door – Oh – K. – what have you done to me? Sounds like the wail of a blues-singer but it isn't funny at all. I give you my word it <u>isn't</u>.

frightened tonight – It all looks very black – I'm scared. but Buck up and go to sleep. Morning can't be worse than tonight. You're going to call Clark359 – maybe he'll help some. I think he will. I [*entry unfinished*]

*Wednesday, 21 August 1940*

Wednesday – Another one of the great, dusty oxen passed overhead, in their strange, ceaseless pilgrimage – toward what?

Today pretty bad – especially about 6 when I got home and found a letter from Doug360 that deliberately blasted my waning hopes for K. with further account of the affair with S.361 and K's indifference to any mention of me. Of course Blondie isn't an altogether perfect witness. But the news made me frantic. Little buzz-saws started in my brain – I felt dizzy. The roof of the world seemed to be coming down on my head. I sat on the sofa and whimpered like a sick dog. Then what Doug said of Joe's affection turned the tide, and the storm of desolation receded – I sat down and wrote Joe – seriously considered sending for him as it seemed his friendship could make me bear up.362 I still hold that as my chief solace but feel now I can go ahead with my ~~geographic~~ trip to Mexico. Met the car-owners and they seem to be a comfortable sort of couple. It may be bearable after all.363

at the prospect of entering her husband's household and I soon got the impression that things were not working out very propitiously between the pair in the sack. She looked gloomier and more separate from her new spouse and his bachelor friends each day and she began to give me nervous glances and whisper to me hints of apprehension. . . .

. . . We had checked into a motel in Monterrey. I had settled down in a small, hot bedroom with a book on a bed enclosed by mosquito netting when there came a rap at the door: it was the bride.

She was near hysteria. "Honey, I don't know what I've got myself into. You know what I mean?" I told her that I could imagine.

She then admitted that the marriage had yet to be consummated and other admissions and wails of trepidation continued for an hour. She had perched herself in an attitude of more and more permanency on my bed and at last I thought it best to inform her that I was quite ineligible as a surrogate for her bridegroom. And I told her why. She nodded sadly and there was a little respite of silence, during which perhaps the germ for *Kingdom of Earth* was first fecundated in my dramatic storehouse. At last she sighed and got up. (pp. 56–58)

364. Kurt Seligmann (1900–62) and his wife, Arlette Paraf. Seligmann was a highly regarded Surrealist artist who emigrated from Switzerland in 1939. He provided an etching for Clark Mills' translation of Stéphane Mallarmé's poem *Herodias* (1940).

Frontispiece by Kurt Seligmann in *Herodias*

See what Doug thinks – or does for me – he arrives tomorrow. Another small blessing that may help to turn the tide.

Clark was pleasant tonight – impressed by my poems – and really gracious about them – which helped some.

We went to the Seligman's.[364] I was dull, of course, but they liked me well enough.

What will take the place of this love? What will fill me up again? Give me legs to stand on?

The future is still a bit unimaginable, since I haven't even heard anything encouraging from the theatre.

We shall see – We shall be patient as an old cow – we shall <u>endure</u> – But also we shall try very hard to work out some permanent design for living that will hereafter sustain us in things like this. We must have a backbone, a central thing – in life. aside from work – which is impossible at times.

Bye bye, baby – be <u>brave</u>!


*Thursday, 22 August 1940*

~~Th~~ <u>Wednesday</u> – Another day has commenced – I think I can face it. Feel weak and dull but relatively quiet. Almost dead, in fact.

Bright, misty morning – so <u>sick</u> of Manhattan. See you later –

Sketch at the end of a letter Williams wrote to Audrey Wood's assistant ([14 August 1940]) anticipating his trip to Mexico

Notebook Williams began in September 1940

CASA VERDE III

I.

It is clear morning

O woman return
to the village across the dark mountains
I give you back to the sky
I have your complaints
your ecstacy in my body
your loneliness also

Gather the night in your shawl
and take it away

For my voice is exhausted
And words are nothing to give you

Speeches are lies
and nets flung into the wind
that is thinner than water

Gather the night in your body
and take it away

I give you back to the sky.

II.

It is clear morning

I stubbornly turn my face from you

because you must learn

that walls are better than faces
that faces have tongues
and tongues have a passion for language

And language is dull
and likely to be deceptive.

Gather the night in your body
and take it away

The pains, the arms
the little feathers of longing

are lost in the sky
I give them back to the sky

O woman return
to the village across the dark mountains
I give you back to the sky

Tennessee Williams
Mexico City, Sept. 1940.

Postcard Williams sent to his mother from Mexico City

365.    *Stairs to the Roof* is a fantasy about a young office worker, Benjamin Murphy, drawn from Williams' experience as a clerk. In "Random Observations," Williams' preface to the play, he wrote:

> It was written involuntarily as a katharsis of eighteen months that I once spent as a clerk in a large wholesale corporation in the Middle West. This eighteen months' interlude, my season in hell, came at a time when I was just out of high school and the world appeared to be a place of infinite and exciting possibilities. I discovered how badly mistaken it is possible for a young man to be.

Married and expecting a child, Benjamin Murphy is about to lose his job for escaping to the roof and writing lines of poetry on sales ledgers. One night he meets a girl and they steal the keys from a zookeeper, let all the foxes out of their cage, and go to a carnival to watch a performance of *Beauty and the Beast*. Murphy then goes back to the roof of the corporation where he works. The girl finds him there, and Mr. E., a god-like figure who has been watching Murphy through all his adventures, impressed by Murphy's courage and individualism, sends Murphy and the girl to colonize a new star in heaven.

In an earlier short story (pre-1939) entitled "Stair to the Roof," the main character, Edward Schiller, a sensitive young office worker, escapes to the roof to dream and write poetry. When his boss discovers his absence, he fires Edward, who commits suicide by leaping from the roof of the twenty-five-story office building.

As was a frequent habit, Williams went on to dramatize his earlier fiction. The play *Stairs to the Roof* not only develops further his short story but also incorporates parts of earlier works, such as "The Swan," "An Allergy to Pink," "The Pink Bedroom," and possibly "The Earth is a Wheel in a Great Big Gambling Casino."

366.    Kip Kiernan.

367.    "Mais où sont les neiges d'antan?" (But where are the snows of yesteryear?) is a refrain in "Ballade des Dames du Temps Jadis" by François Villon (1431–c. 1465). Williams had borrowed the phrase for the title of a sonnet he wrote in 1933. He would also include the line as a screen legend in scene 1 of *The Glass Menagerie*.

368.    *Cantina*, a bar or canteen.

369.    Paul Bowles (1910–99), an American writer, poet, composer, and translator. His most well-known novel, partly autobiographical, is *The Sheltering Sky* (1949), for which Williams singled him out among American

Jane and Paul Bowles outside Tangier, 1949
(photograph by Cecil Beaton)

*Sunday, 8 September 1940*

Sunday – Sept. 7 or 8, 1940.

So I begin a new journal. Not on a very auspicious day – not in a very auspicious time.

This is the period after heart-break and it is full of the dullness and tedium of a mind that no longer particularly cares for existence. Yet is desperate to continue, to survive, to fight the way through a mind that fears breaking because of its constant neuroses. But must & will <u>not</u>.

I have come to Mexico – running away.

I have settled down (?) for a while at Acapulco.

My brain is curiously dead. I find it difficult to carry on conversations – need companionship dreadfully but can't talk, can think of nothing to say. Well – nothing but stupidities. I have always disliked conversation but now it is all but impossible for me.

I am lonely, therefor, and wretched.

Life is merely endurance. Cannot relax. Cannot sit still. But no activity diverts me very much, not even swimming – thank God there is plenty of that. The best swimming I have ever had.

Tried writing yesterday. Did some work on Stair to the Roof.365 Not much energy but accomplished something. Even coffee doesn't wake up my torpid brain cells. Such heaviness, such dullness. Appalling.

Well, it is bound to get better. It couldn't get worse. The cause – heartbreak over K.366 – is all but forgotten. The effect will run its course also.

Never, never, in all my life will I know the meaning of peace. But there is such a thing as <u>relative</u> peace even for me, and that will return after while.

The old machine will not quit. It will keep plugging on somehow.

Tout se passe –

eventually! ou sont les neiges d'Antan.367

After lunch – feel much better – snapped out of my stupor a little, which was partly the result of a binge in the Cantenas.368 Had run into Gordon Sager and Paul Bowles.369 Later got very drunk, rum, beer, tequila. Carried on with a blond boy here – on the beach and in bed – and shocked a bunch of nice young American College boys – fraternity brothers, incidentally – with my drunken candor about homosexuality.

One was very nice – Jerry. Tried to put me to bed. To save my honor! or the fraternity's. The affair was no fun but it relieved the monotony.

writers as "a talent of true maturity and sophistication," in the *New York Times Book Review* (4 December 1949). In *Memoirs*, Williams remembered first meeting the Bowleses:

> It was there in Acapulco that summer that I first met Jane and Paul Bowles. They were staying at a pension in town and Paul was, as ever, upset about the diet and his stomach. The one evening that we spent together that summer was given over almost entirely to the question of what he could eat in Acapulco that he could digest, and poor little Janie kept saying, "Oh, Bubbles, if you'd just stick to cornflakes and fresh fruit!" and so on and so on. None of her suggestions relieved his dyspeptic humor.
>
> I thought them a very odd and charming couple. (p. 59)

Williams and the Bowleses became friends for the rest of their lives. Williams visited Paul Bowles in Tangier on numerous occasions. Bowles wrote the musical score for *The Glass Menagerie*, *Summer and Smoke*, *Sweet Bird of Youth*, and *The Milk Train Doesn't Stop Here Anymore*, and Williams dedicated his novel *The Roman Spring of Mrs. Stone* to him.

Paul Bowles was married to Jane Auer (1917–73). In the introduction to her collection of miscellaneous work *Feminine Wiles* (1976), Williams described her as one of the most important writers of prose fiction in America. A fragment of a dialogue exists between two characters whom Williams named Paul and Jane (presumably Bowles). In the dialogue Paul mourns the loss of his poetic powers: "The mysterious bird . . . has flown away from me." Jane attempts to console Paul and the dialogue ends with their making love.

370.  On the same day (20 September 1940, Yale), Williams wrote to the Theatre Guild about his royalty check:

> Jesus Christ! Your monthly remittance is alarmingly delayed, I've been broke ten days . . . and there's nothing to eat on the place but cocoanuts and a pot of cold <u>frijoles</u>! If you decide to give up the "battle of Angels" I hope you will give me thirty days warning at least, so I can arrange to move the body some place where it can spill its hard luck stories in English. . . .
>
> I am doing a great deal of writing here now. Something extraordinary is happening to the long play. It is like one of those Chinese poems that are hard, round pellets of paper until you drop them into a cup of warm tea, when they open and blossom out like flowers so you can read the verso on them. Apparently Acapulco or Todd's place was the cup of warm tea that my drama needed, because it is now unfolding at a surprising rate. I am packing into it practically all I have felt about life. It will probably take a good while after it's finished for weeding it out. But I feel it is going to be far and away my best piece of dramatic writing. At least from the literary point of view.

Williams in Acapulco                    Back cover of Williams' Pegaso notebook

*Friday, 20 September 1940*

Friday – Sept. 20

Well, I get up to face a new day which will probably be fairly tolerable – as the others here.

Usually in the mornings I glance at myself and say –

"Well, here you still are, you old bitch!"

This is the period to be remembered as "waiting for the royalty checque"[370] – several days late and I wonder now if it's coming –

If it doesn't – will I be able to take it?

Well ——

Let's eat.

---

*In October, Williams returned to St. Louis from Mexico, where he had finished a draft of* Stairs to the Roof. *By the third week he traveled to New York to work on the production of* Battle of Angels *planned for the end of the year.*

*Battle of Angels opened in Boston on 30 December. The audience was offended by the explicit sexuality and irritated by the final scene in which smoke billowed out into the theatre. The reactions of critics were harsh, with the* Boston Globe *accusing Williams of giving "the audience the sensation of having been dunked in mire" (31 December 1940). About his dismal failure, Williams wrote to Joe Hazan (circa 2 January 1941, HRC):*

> *I'm too exhausted to write much of a letter. The bright angels were pretty badly beaten in Boston — we are closing after the two weeks engagement for re-casting, re-writing and re-everything. Holiday crowds would not listen to poetic tragedy and the sexuality shocked the pants off the first-nighters.*

*Williams left Boston for New York where he underwent a cataract operation on his left eye. He then traveled to Miami and met Jim Parrott, who was staying in his parents' winter home. The two then drove down to Key West, from where Williams wrote his parents ([12 February 1941], HRC):*

> *I am stopping in the 125-year-old house [Trade Winds] you see on the envelope. It belongs to an Episcopal clergyman's widow, Mrs. Black. . . . I am to complete my re-write of "Angels".*

371.  Parrott wrote an article about this trip: "The Flop of *Battle of Angels* and the Flight to Florida," *Tennessee Williams Literary Journal*, fall 1995.

372.  In a letter to Lawrence Langner ([26] February 1941, Yale), Williams wrote:

> I am occupying the slave-quarters in back of this 125 year-old mansion which is made entirely of mahogany and surrounded by palm trees which rustle and whisper constantly night and day like a Boston audience at a scandalous play. It is owned by a clergyman's widow who gives me lodging at a ridiculously low price because I remind her of her son who was an aviator recently killed in a crash. I lead an exciting double life here, writing all morning, spending my afternoon's in an English widow's cabana on the beach where I associate with people like John Dewey, James Farrell and Elizabeth Bishop and in the evening consorting, in dungarees, with B-girls, transients and sailors at Sloppy Joe's or the Starlight Gambling Casino.

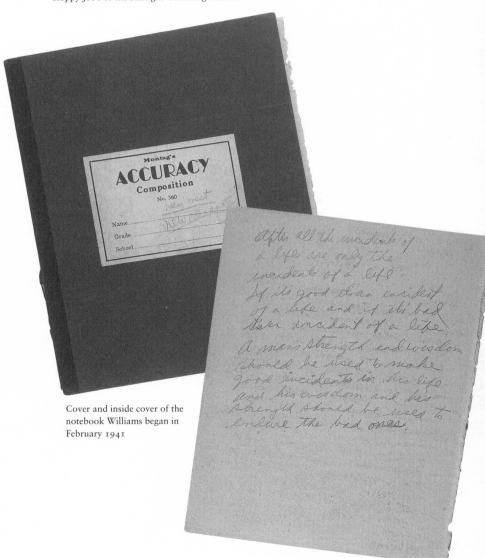

Cover and inside cover of the notebook Williams began in February 1941

*Period after Boston.*
*(The Final?)*
*no.* *'9/12/41.* KEY WEST

*Sunday, 16 February 1941*

Sunday Feb. ? – Been here about 8 days. By myself since Jimmie[371] left. No friends except a young transient "Chuck" who calls himself "My Pardner" and has sort of moved in on me. Definitely a problem but better than being altogether alone – I am not in a sociable state and making friends would be difficult even if I tried. Oh, yes, I have one other – an elegant old lady from England who allows me to sit on the porch of her cabana at "Rest Beach".[372]

What the hell am I chattering about? – Shit!

This is the most crucial period of my life ~~and I talk like~~

The Trade Winds, Key West

373.  Williams admired Walt Whitman (1819–92), Ernest Hemingway (1899–1961), and Thomas Wolfe (1900–38). The previous year Williams had written to Kip Kiernan ([22 or 23 August 1940], HRC), "I love you (with robust manly love, as Whitman would call it) as much as I love anybody." And years later Williams would also echo Whitman. In an interview with Studs Terkel in 1961, Williams said, "The world is incomplete, it's like an unfinished poem" (Albert J. Devlin [ed.], *Conversations with Tennessee Williams* [Jackson and London: University of Mississippi Press, 1986], p. 90). In his preface to *Leaves of Grass* (1855), Whitman had written, "The United States themselves are essentially the greatest poem."

In an unmailed draft letter to Lawrence Langner ([February 1941], HRC), Williams wrote: "I have written about seven different endings in search of the right one. I hate to spend so much time on one play — but after all Hemingway spent three years on 'For Whom the Bell Tolls'."

On 22 September 1941 (HRC), Audrey Wood wrote to Williams enclosing a letter from John Tebbel, the managing editor of the *American Mercury*, "which I think you should have framed and look at every night before you go to bed." Tebbel had written:

> Williams is sort of D. H. Lawrence and Hemingway and Thomas Wolfe rolled into one and leavened by a style which is not at all eclectic. I have a feeling that he'd be a better novelist than a short story writer. He has something to say and knows how to say it, which is more than can be said for nine-tenths of the American writers currently practicing. (*RMT*, p. 130)

In an undated letter (HRC) from Provincetown to Margaret Mayorga, editor of *The Best One-act Plays*, Williams wrote:

> Have you ever, incidentally, thought of adapting some of Thomas Wolfe's stuff for the one-act theatre? I recall passages I have read — cannot identify them specifically at the moment — which would make brilliant stage sketches and have the real quality of Wolfe. Some day I would like to adapt one.

374.  This is the first time in his journals that Williams uses the number 10 to denote his name. The first example of this signature is on a letter ([16 March 1939], HRC) written to Anne and Blandford Jennings.

375.  Presumably "The Case of the Crushed Petunias," which is a lyrical fantasy about Dorothy Simple, a twenty-six-year-old maiden of Primanproper (an area which was within the cultural bounds of Boston) who has barricaded her house and heart behind a double row of petunias. When a young man crushes her petunias, she reports his violation to the police, but when she meets the young man, she is overwhelmed by his charm and sex appeal and decides to follow him and leave Primanproper behind. The play was obviously Williams' response to the negative reaction of the prudish Boston audience to *Battle of Angels*.

The "few" poems most likely include "Moon Song: Key West" and "Heavenly Grass," both dated "Key West, March 1941." Other poems that Williams wrote in March 1941 include "The Minstrel Jack" and an untitled one beginning "The hawk that high in heaven wheels."

### MOON SONG: KEY WEST

Anything that you do by the moon is lovely:
maybe you die by the moon, that's lovely, too:
any kind of a shiny moon is lovely:
even the light of a crooked moon will do.

Maybe you take a walk on the esplanade:
maybe the wind is wild and the air is blue:
maybe the palm trees shake: that may be lovely;
maybe the bay is still; that's lovely, too.

Maybe you meet the rarest of all rare strangers
who smiles and offers a cigarette to you:
maybe the wind sweeps over the esplanade
and maybe the palm trees shake and the air is
     blue.

Maybe you take a walk on the broken pier
and maybe you pause for a while to admire the
     view:
maybe you make sweet love by the moon: that's
     lovely:
anyone that you love is lovely, too

Anything that you do by the moon is lovely,
maybe you die by the moon, that's lovely, too,
any kind of a shiny moon is lovely
even the light of a crooked moon will do.

(Key West, March, 1941)

God know what will become of me if I don't meet the ~~needs of the~~ demands
of the situation. And I am tired – dangerously tired – and not well – an almost
continual earache which plagues me – letting up a little. Ennui – don't know
what to do with myself – wander around in a sort of a daze – Really I seem more
mentally <u>dead</u> right now than almost anytime I can think of. Right when I need
the most vitality.

Not desperate, though, no – in fact rather placid.

Bad symptom?

Probably.

Well – these are the days A.B – "After Boston" –

So I am lucky to be conscious at all –

That is, if being conscious is lucky.

Better leave this till I feel more articulate.

Nothing to do till "Chuck" gets here – probably late.

I sit by my little fire – electric heater – with my typewriter and my books –
"Leaves of Grass" – "For Whom The Bells Toll" – "Look Homeward, Angel!"373

Anybody could tell that I was the quiet, literary type – I am determined to see
it all through – Somehow. As I always have before – And will till the last hour
strikes. So long. – 10.374

Later – I am ready to sleep.

It is rather nice in here. Pale green wood with lemon yellow curtain at the
windows – a wide comfortable bed with fairly fresh covers. – a lamp beside it
and a heater – my body naked and warm and still young – capable of passion
and tenderness – my mind – vague, dreamy, but sincere and thoughtful and
with a wealth of experience – my heart still with a purity, after all this time –
(sentimentality! about myself) – but there is only me right now – and one
unimportant other – who will arrive and seem important – and possibly <u>is</u>. –

The past – the future – a continuing stream – Something in me will save me
from utter ruin no matter what comes – Even if that thing which is my salvation
is only the final courage of necessity.

To you – whoever you are – when I am gone – ~~Goodnight~~. Remember to be
kind tonight to some lonely person – For me. – 10.


*Tuesday, 4 March 1941*

Tuesday – It is a week since Chuck left and I have been completely alone all that
time. It was better than I expected – rather beautiful – relatively – but now it is
gone – I am afraid this town is bad for me – Water, water everywhere – And I am
not a voyeur – any more. Bars alone – beaches alone – movies alone – I feel quite
unable to speak to anybody – I wrote a 1-act and a few poems375 but do little on
"Battle".

THE MINSTREL JACK

O witless Jack,

that lamplit knob, thy skull,

that pumpkin on a stick, much ventilated,

through which the world as smoke passed restlessly,

has now out-lived its frivolous halloween function.

Dunked in nothingness, a muddy bucket,

or into an old, abandoned cistern tossed,

those perforations twain which were thine eyes

peer dully upwards at no visible stars... -

The children's cries,

downhillward sledding in the frosty dark,

catch briefly at time's broken edge - are lost!

O minstrel Jack,

thy songs, those sudden larks,

miraculous progeny of pumpkin seeds,

alone survive the season of eclipse....

Blown from the top,

out of the twain triangular stars,

out of that penknife-sculptured grin, thy scalloped lips,

the reason instinct, blind desire the wing,

as bees that spiral toward a crystal hive

these fugitives toward light still rise and rise

into the vault of night - And rising, sing!

> Tennessee Williams
> Matecumbe Key, Florida
> March, 1941

---

376. *The March of Time*, produced by Time Inc., was first a radio and then a newsreel program that ran from 1931 to 1951. A narrator dramatized news events based on articles that appeared in the current issue of *Time*. In 1941 Orson Welles satirized it in "News on the March" in *Citizen Kane*.

377. While Williams had previously used the image of the nightingale in his play *Not About Nightingales* as a reference to Keats, this is the first time Williams uses the term nightingales to refer to sex.

I do not know how actually dangerous this – probably less so than I imagine when most frightened – we will see – God help us –

Met a young German Jew Wolfe – works for March of Time[376] – relieved the isolation somewhat today – we swam together – I feel difficulty in making conversation – always do when lonely – one consolation – earache better – recurs for a little while every night – tonight I went in a crowded movie – dull show – Tomorrow – probably drink 2 cups Cuban coffee and try to work –

*Wednesday, 5 March 1941*

Later – Terrible night!

Sleepless – now six – raging ear-ache – Plagued by the nightingale,[377] Etc. – Don't see how I can stick it out here – Even dread the beach tomorrow.

Roof drips slowly with moisture all night – crickets.

*Friday, 7 March 1941*

Friday – March 7 (?)

Resolution – Never drink Cuban coffee again at night. Never take more than 2 drinks without a damn good reason.

I was so bored last night that I committed both of these indiscretions. I have not yet learned to be completely Spartan against the vicious little fox teeth of ennui, which is my nearly constant companion. To escape it I fling myself into worse things without ever really doing anything strikingly aggresive.

I am quite limp this A.M.

Must absolutely determine to be ruled by prudent action, the voice of experience – and do nothing more to invite disaster which probably doesn't need a very cordial invitation anyway – walk softly – even if I don't go far in the right direction, I won't go quite so far perhaps in the wrong.

C'est tout pour maintenant – (Will breakfast help? Will there be mail? Dentist? – Escape?)

*Sunday, 16 March 1941*

Sunday –

An adventure last night provided some relief.

Meant to hitchhike to Miami but I am still here.

Did some pretty good writing on B.A. yesterday.

Now very, very tired.

How will this interlude end?

Oh, I hope not too badly – for an old friend's sake.

378.  Williams had returned to stay with Jim Parrott at his parents' winter home in Coral Gables on the corner of 7th Street and SW 55th Avenue.

379.  On 2 April 1941, Williams received a wire from the Dramatists' Guild (HRC) announcing that he had been granted an additional Rockefeller fellowship. Payments were to be made in monthly installments of $100 to commence when he wanted to begin the work.

380.  No manuscript with this title is known to exist. However, Williams did write a short one-act play entitled "Woman Key (A Melodrama for Tallullah Bankhead)." In this play Mary comes home to find that her alcoholic husband, who tries to kill her every time he drinks, has gone on a binge and killed their cook. Because she loves her husband, Mary tries, once again, to cover up for him and shoots a servant who tries to kill him.

381.  Marion Vaccaro (1906–70) was the daughter of Clara Atwood Black, the widow of an Episcopal clergyman. Her mother owned the antebellum home the Trade Winds where Williams rented the slave quarters. Marion was married to Regis Vaccaro, an alcoholic whose family founded the Standard Fruit and Steamship Company of New Orleans. Williams modeled the hard-drinking, hard-living Cora in the short story "Two on a Party" on her, and he borrowed her maiden name for Flora Goforth's secretary, Blackie, in *The Milk Train Doesn't Stop Here Anymore*. In the play "27 Wagons Full of Cotton," Williams named the superintendent of the Syndicate Plantation Silva Vicarro, which he changed to Vacarro in *Baby Doll*. In the play "Thank You, Kind Spirit," Williams named one of the people attending the spiritualist meeting, a liquor store owner, Regis Vicarro.

Marion Vaccaro went on to become a very close friend of Williams' and traveled with him in the late 1950s and 1960s. Williams dedicated his play *Orpheus Descending* to her.

382.  Williams described the situation in a letter to Audrey Wood dated 11 April 1941 (HRC):
Barely time for a note! Very, very happy and relieved about new funds.

Back on keys but leaving in a few minutes for Brunswick, Ga. Landlady's son-in-law, habitual drunkard, has run up gambling debts far in excess of his ability to pay — I have to smuggle him off the keys at once his life being threatened — to Georgia where I have instructions to keep him sober till his wife gets there in about ten days. What a job! But they have been so wonderful to me I can't refuse. — Driving his car up — leaving right away. — This done, I will probably come back north. . . .

PS. ONLY GOT TO MIAMI WITH CHARGE WHO IS NOW IN SANITARIUM. SEND ME ONE MORE CHECQUE OF THEATRE GUILD — TO GET HOME ON. Will leave here soon as it comes and return East in a week or two after visiting folks.

383.  From *Time* (14 April 1941) on the "Balkan Theater":
The campaign of 1941, the awful convulsion, began last week. . . .

. . . The steel teeth of the German Army struck into Yugoslavia and Greece from many directions with many techniques — with dive-bombing, parachute troops, tanks, mobile artillery, mechanized infantry. One group of attacks was concentrated on the relatively flat plains of northern Yugoslavia.

But the heaviest and by far the more important drives were farther south. Through the mountains from Sofia to Nish and Skoplje went drives intended to cut the vital Vardar Valley and divide the Yugoslavs from the Greeks. And down the Struma River valley towards Salonika went another drive to break the Greeks' back and roll the British into the sea.

The defenders . . . stressed they were "fighting against forces ten times superior and against mechanical implements one hundred times greater." (p. 25)

384.  A reference to the popular wartime song "A Nightingale Sang in Berkeley Square."

*Tuesday, 18 March 1941*

Tuesday – Approaching the end of my present funds – Checque overdue – Owe for rent, owe for bike. Capital = $5.00.

*Wednesday, 9 April 1941*

Wed. April 8 (?)

Coral Gables[378] –

Worn out completely.

Situation improved.

$500.00 from Rockefeller "to write new play"[379] – I think I have the basic situation for it. A Woman's Love for a Drunkard.[380]

Regis and Marion.[381]

Strange, melodramatic little interlude that was! – Too tired to write about it or anything.[382]

The nightingale sang sweetly once last week –

Brain excessively dull and body "just about out" –

Must start long uphill climb to refresh myself and revitalize my system for work on a new play, only thing worth doing – I am selfish – small – impose on my friends and neglect them – my kindness and sympathy are much too passive – All is overshadow by my own selfish needs, hungers, longings.

Germany is striking in Balkans – apparently with brilliant success[383] –

Will there be any decency, any peace, any reason, any sanity in our time? – In Mine?

I would forget all this to hear the nightingales – and not in Berkeley Square![384]

*Thursday, 10 April 1941*

Thurs. – So weary, so lifeless, so bored! – A letdown from the steady pounding of my nerves these past few months.

Still I must get away from here, and directly. Coral Gables is the worst place I've ever tried to live in – even worse I believe than Clayton, Mo.

*Friday, 9 May 1941*

Friday Night – May – Clayton, Mo. –

Leaving tomorrow for New York.

Feel better – jittery – one of my anti social neuroses – will make short shift of it however – with luck –

Been fairly pleasant here – sort of ill at first but that passed off –

385. This journal covering the spring and summer in New York has not been found.

386. Williams refers to the Pegaso notebook which he started on 8 September 1940 and last used on 20 September 1940.

387. Williams refers to success as the "bitch goddess." William James, in a letter to H. G. Wells of 11 September 1906, wrote: "a symptom of the moral flabbiness born of the exclusive worship of the bitch-goddess SUC-CESS" (Henry James [ed.], *The Letters of William James*, vol. 2 [Boston: Atlantic Monthly, 1920]). Williams would also come across D. H. Lawrence's frequent use of "bitch-goddess" in *Lady Chatterley's Lover*, for example: "The bitch-goddess, as she is called, of Success, roamed, snarling and protective, round the half-humble, half-defiant Michaelis' heels" (ch. 3).

   In an essay Williams wrote on the eve of the opening of *A Streetcar Named Desire* titled "On a Streetcar Named Success" (*New York Times*, 30 November 1947), he returned to the idea of Success as a bitch-goddess:

   You know, then, that the public Somebody you are when you "have a name" is a fiction created with mirrors and that the only somebody worth being is the solitary and unseen you that existed from your first breath and which is the sum of your actions and so is constantly in a state of becoming under your own volition — and knowing these things, you can even survive the catastrophe of Success!

   It is never altogether too late, unless you embrace the Bitch Goddess, as William James called her, with both arms and find in her smothering caresses exactly what the homesick little boy in you always wanted, absolute protection and utter effortlessness. Security is a kind of death, I think, and it can come to you in a storm of royalty checks beside a kidney-shaped pool in Beverly Hills or anywhere at all that is removed from the conditions that made you an artist, if that's what you are or were or intended to be.

388. *Battle of Angels.*

Marion and Regis Vaccaro

Accomplished some good work on Battle – hopeful about it.
Prayer.

Dear Grand isn't well. Suffers. Quietly. Is a miracle of gentleness. A faded golden rose in fading sunlight. The finest thing in my life. Goodbye?

I hitchhiked from Miami to Darien, Ga. Interesting. Some of it fun – especially Savanna. No nightingales. New York? – So beginneth and endeth another lesson – what is the next? <u>En Avant!</u>

(I'm still in there fighting — for <u>me</u>!)

(For life!)

(For life is me!)

*Note – The account of spring and early summer in N. Y. is in another journal. It was a rich, exciting period sexually – the most* ~~intense~~ *active of my life. But I wasn't happy. – neither was I unhappy.* [385]


*Friday, 27 June 1941*

June 27, 1941 – Friday

9 mos. later I resume this journal.[386]

How full the past months have been! I did not even faintly surmise what a dramatic period in my history was just around the corner when I made the last entry! –

It ended rather disastrously – in failure – but it gave me a taste of glory – it brought me within sight of the "bitch goddess"[387] – then whisked me rudely back to the near-oblivion I came from.

I survived it all fairly well.

Now I am entering another phase –

Seems more dangerous, perhaps, than anything yet.

Revised script rejected.[388]

$280.00 = total funds.

No new scripts.

Two months to find some solution.

Then destitution.

Then what?

So endeth the lesson.

I am fatigued, I am dull, I am bitter at heart.

But I do not suffer much. I have diverted myself with the most extraordinary amount of sexual license I have ever indulged in.

New lover every night, barely missing one, for a month or more.

I love no one.

389. Paul Bigelow (1905–88) was the constant companion of Jordan Massee (1914–2002). Williams met Bigelow and Massee through Donald Windham and Fred Melton in New York. Not much is known about Bigelow's background, but Massee confirmed that what their mutual friend Gilbert Maxwell wrote in *Tennessee Williams and Friends* (Cleveland: World Publishing, 1965) was "surprisingly accurate."

> Paul could tell marvelous stories about the world of arts and letters in which he apparently knew almost everyone — but somehow there was about him, personally, an air of reticence, even of mystery, which I found fascinating. I knew that he had been educated in England, had lived in Greenwich Village in the twenties, in Hollywood (where he'd been a newspaper reporter), as well as in Mexico, in the thirties, that he had a sister and stepmother in California, that he'd been married — and that was all. His stories, I thought, sometimes bordered upon the incredible, but I was to learn that when Bigelow told me a story that seemed most incredible, that one — of all his stories — was likely to prove most factual. (p. 39)

Bigelow and Williams enjoyed each other's humor and formed a close friendship which lasted well into the 1950s. Later in the summer Williams wrote a poem to Bigelow.

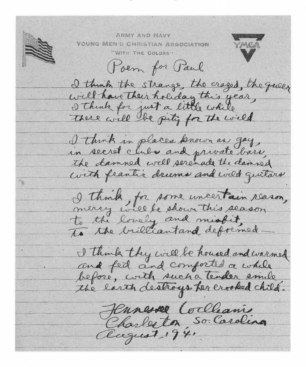

390. A fishing port to the north of Boston, Gloucester had a small artists' colony and would have had a similar appeal to Williams as Provincetown and was much closer to Boston.

> Bigelow wrote to Jordan Massee on 9 July 1941 (Massee collection):
> He had a horrid carbuncle on his shoulder blade which I tended as carefully as I might a rose garden . . . the combination of the carbuncle, the heat, and Tennessee was too much for me, and when he began to be restive in New York, I packed all his things firmly, picked out Gloucester as a respectable, cool place, and sent him to it. (Leverich, p. 413)

Williams wrote to his parents on 4 July 1941 (HTC):

> I have gone up here for a short visit to escape the terrific heat in N.Y. I was in a room on the top floor in N.Y. and it got so I couldn't sleep.
>
> There is a summer theater colony here at this hotel [The Moorland] and I have been given

I am loved by one whom I do not care for.

Paul B.[389] and I are together every day.

He is a charming companion – one of the "truly civilized" – one of the "genuine sophisticates".

~~Probably~~ The most stimulating, entertaining even brilliant companion I have ever had.

Without him I must confess my life would be as empty as a broken egg shell.

Nothing romantic of course – but a love of the spirit.

My main trouble is I cannot create. I am mentally torpid. And I do not even seem to care very much.

Perhaps it is the excessive sexual activity.

Perhaps I have really burned my daemon out.

I don't think so. I think he is still a phoenix and not a cooked goose.

But I must find purity again.

A whole, undivided heart.

Something simple and straight.

A passionate calm.

Where?

If only I could get out to N. Mex. I might find it there?

Am I still looking for God?

No – just for myself.

I will probably try Gloucester, lacking more rope.[390]

So long – 10.

Paul Bigelow

Jordan Massee

theatrical rates which is just half the usual price. A very elegant old hotel, on a cliff directly over the ocean. Extremely quiet, nearly all old ladies except for the actors. . . .

I will only stay here about a week, then probably spend some time in Provincetown. I get more work done out of New York, especially when the heat there is so intense. I never felt anything quite so bad in St. Louis — that I can remember. Also I developed a carbuncle on my left shoulder. . . . It is practically well now and I am taking vitamin tablets as the doctor recommended.

You would probably like these New England matrons — but they are a little too formidable for me. They look aghast at the "theatrical crowd" — we are not even permitted to go on the beach in shirtless trunks.

391. Williams traveled south to Sea Island, Georgia, to visit Jordon Massee for a few days and then moved to an adjacent island, St. Simons Island, and stayed at the Golden Isles Beach Hotel. The fiasco most likely refers to Williams' lack of money. While at St. Simons Island, Williams wired Audrey Wood for money but did not wait for a response. Instead, as he wrote to Paul Bigelow, he traveled back to New York via Charleston and Washington. When the train made a long stop in Washington, he got off to do some sightseeing but failed to return on time. The train departed with his belongings and the little money he had left.

"This" refers to the apartment on East 73rd Street that Bigelow, Massee, Windham, and Melton had shared. In a letter to Bigelow postmarked 27 August 1941 (Columbia), Williams wrote: "Baby, this place looks awful. The kids left everything in a terrible state. . . . There are scraps of paper and trash all over the floors and dust and complete disorder."

392. In November 1939, after Williams returned to St. Louis from Taos, he wrote the poem "Fable." The poem appeared under the title "Cried the Fox — For D.H.L." in *Five Young American Poets* (1944).

```
          FABLE

I run, cried the fox, in circles
narrower, narrower still
across the desperate hollow,
skirting the frantic hill

And shall, till my brush hangs burning
flame by the hunter's door,
continue this fatal returning
to places that failed me before!

Then, with his heart breaking nearly,
the lonely, passionate bark
of the fugitive fox rang out clearly
as bells in the frosty dark

Across the desperate hollow,
skirting the frantic hill,
calling the pack to follow
a prey that escaped them still!

     Thomas Lanier Williams
     November, 1939
     St. Louis.
```

*Sunday, 27 July 1941*

Provincetown – July 27 –
    Well – I sit in a lonely woods, beside a still lily pond – among the dunes of
Cape Cod. I am too tired to write.
    I am too tired.
    I am too.
    I am.
    I.

After this Returned to New York) – Then to
St. Simon's Island, Ga. – one
week. Lured there by Paul's
Considerably exagerative telegram
commending its charms. Found
it disappointing but tolerable
Returned to New York. This short
period there, about 2 weeks, was
better than the one just preceding
and contained some satisfactory
adventures. Money ran low and I left
        on New Orleans – to be poor.

*Friday, 8 August 1941*

Aug. 8 – Friday –
    Summer on the downgrade – feel pretty low –
    Will leave in a day or two for Georgia or Mexico.

*Sunday, 31 August 1941*

August 31
    Downgrade? Whew!!!
    I've really hit the bottom.
    Went to Georgia – a fiasco – but this, now that I have returned, is still worse.[391]
    I seem to be chasing [*unfinished*]

*Friday, 12 September 1941*

New Orleans – Sept 11, 1941
        (Friday)

    The Second New Orleans Period here commences.
    The much-bedeviled pilgrim – the fox who runs in circles[392] – has returned to

393.  New Orleans-born Fritz Bultman (1919–85) was a painter and sculptor who, between 1938 and 1942, lived in New York and Provincetown where he was studying under the Abstract Expressionist Hans Hofmann. Williams had met Bultman earlier in the summer in Provincetown. Bultman went on to become a notable Abstract Expressionist with work in the Metropolitan Museum of Art, the Guggenheim, and the Whitney Museum of American Art.

The Bultman family lived at 1525 Louisiana Avenue, around the corner from the funeral home they owned. "B." refers presumably to Fritz Bultman's father, Fred Bultman, as Fritz was in New York City at the time. In a letter postmarked 25 September 1941 (Columbia), Williams wrote Paul Bigelow:

> The Bultman's, it seems, could do me more <u>harm</u> than good — they are <u>not</u> accepted. It seems the grandfather used to ride as a <u>footman</u> behind a <u>hearse</u>.

In the winter of 1942, Williams would spend time at Bultman's New York apartment, though Bultman eventually tired of his slovenly habits and asked him to leave.

394.  Williams took a room at Mrs. Oglesby's rooming house at 1124 St. Charles Avenue.

395.  Williams met Oliver Evans (1915–81), a poet and writer, in Provincetown earlier in the summer. A native of New Orleans, Evans had just received his master's degree from the University of Tennessee and would go on to teach at various universities. Williams remained in touch with Evans and saw him when he stayed in New Orleans. In the summer of 1970, he and Williams took a three-month cruise to Asia where they met with Mishima, the famed Japanese writer who committed hara-kiri. Evans wrote an article that appeared in *Esquire*: "A Pleasant Evening with Yukio Mishima" (May 1972).

Evans' published work includes a book of poems, *Young Man with a Screwdriver* (1950), with a foreword by Williams; a biography, *Carson McCullers: Her Life and Work* (1965); and a guidebook, *New Orleans* (1959). Williams based the character Billy in the short story "Two on a Party" on Evans and used the name Oliver for the main character in the short story "One Arm," as well as for the main character in early drafts of *Camino Real* and the related play fragment "Cabeza de Lobo." The poem "The Eyes" in Williams' collection *In the Winter of Cities* is inscribed "For Oliver."

396.  Mack's was a bar on Canal Street. A scene in Williams' short story "Blue Roses and the Polar Star" is set in Mack's bar. The James bar (sometimes referred to as the St. James) was on the corner of Toulouse Street and Royal Street. In a letter to Paul Bigelow, postmarked 25 September 1941 (Columbia), Williams wrote: "'Cher,' I have a room [at 538] Royal, right opposite <u>the</u> gay bar — The St. James, so I can hover like a bright angel over the troubled waters of homosociety."

Fritz Bultman

one of those places that failed him (?) before.

He still looks for sanctuary.

Still hopes some new move will appease his unrest.

But he grows skeptical and sometimes thinks to <u>sleep</u> is the best thing. merely to sleep.

Tonight was dull and painful. I met the Bultmans', Fritzi's family. I could not make talk and I felt, oh, so stupid. B.[393] was attractive but all of them <u>not</u> interesting mentally.

We sat <u>interminably</u> in the Hotel Roosevelt bar and I drank to forget how stupid I was and they were.

I am supposed to call them tomorrow but I will probably excuse myself from society for the next few days till I feel more settled.

I am to be very, <u>very judicious</u> – from now on.

Yes – we want to be <u>saved</u>.


*Saturday, 13 September 1941*

Saturday – I have bought a used bike for ten dollars.

Paid a week's rent – $3.50.[394]

Seem to be settled for whatever is in store – One never knows, does one?

Tonight I have heartburn.

I am going to dress up and cruise about the Old French Quarter.

Maybe something will happen.

I will let you know later.

Wish me luck!


*Sunday, 14 September 1941*

Later – Sunday A.M.

Oliver Evans[395] – a sad but poignant episode. Mack's and the St. James bar.[396]

"We ought to be exterminated" said Oliver. "for the good of society." I argued that if we were society would lose some of its most sensitive, humanitarian members. A healthy society does not need artists, said Oliver. What is healthy about a society with no spiritual values? – Then you think spiritual values are identical with <u>us</u>? said Oliver. No, I admitted sadly, but we have made some unique contributions because of our unique position and I do not believe that we are detrimental to anyone but ourselves. "We are the rotten apple in the barrel," said Oliver. "We ought to be exterminated at the age of 25." "But Shakespeare had written no great plays at that age." – "He had written Romeo and Juliet," said Oliver. – "Yes, but he had not written Hamlet." And so on – "If you think we are dangerous, why do you act as you do? Why do you not isolate yourself?" "Because I am rotten." – How many of us feel that way, I

397. Presumably the Starlite Lounge, on the corner of Chartres Street and St. Philip Street, where hustlers congregated. In *Orpheus Descending* (act 2, scene 1), Val says to Carol:

     I'm thirty years old and I'm done with the crowd you run with and the places you run to. The Club Rendezvous, the Starlite Lounge, the Music Bar, and all the night places.

398. Gluck's was a German restaurant on Royal Street which burned in the 1950s.

399. In *Blossoms in the Dust* (1941), Greer Garson played a strong-willed woman who loses her child and husband but goes on with her life and founds an orphanage.

The Starlite Lounge, New Orleans

Postcard of Canal Street that Williams sent to Donald Windham

wonder? Bear this intolerable burden of guilt? To feel some humiliation and a great deal of sorrow at times is inevitable. But feeling guilty is foolish. I am a deeper and warmer and kinder man for my devigation. More conscious of need in others, and what power I have to express the human heart must be in large part due to this circumstance. Some day society will take perhaps the suitable action – but I do not believe that it will or should be extermination. – Oh, well. –

I go now for a long ride on my bicycle, probably out to Lake Pontchartrain for a swim and something more clarifying than last night. So long.

Later – My bicycle trip was cancelled by rain and I was stranded for over an hour in the door of a warehouse in the colored section across from the "Star ☆ Club"397 where I watched the careless, infantile play of negros, a spider, an ant with partly crushed body struggling to crawl across a concrete space with no companions and no apparent objective. I thought about the "hostilities of chance" that can foil an innocent outing and crush a harmless body. Not very novel reflections. Finally I braved the rain and came home. Now the rain still continues and I lie on my bed, smoke, and enter these banalities. I have such an ordinary type of mind, only a little more sensitive than most others, only my longings and my critical faculty, my sense of my own unfitness, has any dignity I feel stunted. I should have grown bigger than this. Certainly as an artist I should have grown much bigger and stronger and more durable. I am like, in my work, that half crushed ant dragging itself wretchedly and almost pointlessly forward. And, yes, I grow older and my physical self is on the wane, undoubtedly. That is, I am not the fresh young thing that I was at 20 when I could just be ornamental and nothing more. Nor have I acquired that practised glibness which compensates in our kind for the wane of youth. Oh, yes, I am much less timid, but still I usually sit and wait for others to initiate an acquaintance.

Well, this is a dreary story. But I continue to be interested in the course of events. I still hope to fulfill myself in creation and in love, at least partially and occasionally and for a while.

The rain seems to be petering out. Presumbably I will go out again – eat, see a show, possibly even go to the St. James bar.

I am not the one to lie and brood all day. – The rain has stopped. So shall I.

Later –

Went to Gluck's398 and had a 30¢ Turkey dinner – good.

Then along Canal St. and dropped into see a sentimental slush film about an orphanage399 – pretty bad.

Morbid shyness has developed, probably from being so much alone. And the crowds frightened me. I had a beer, bought a paper and a magazine (Time) and went home.

Read till my head felt stuffy – Quit.

400. No manuscript titled "Hawk's Daughter" is known to exist.

401. Williams began the short story "Portrait of a Girl in Glass" in February 1941. He would use it as the basis for *The Glass Menagerie*. In "Portrait of a Girl in Glass," a poet with "a job in a warehouse" remembers the evening he invited a friend from work to dinner with his mother and terribly shy sister, Laura. The friend, Jim Delaney, is kind to Laura, but the evening is shattered when Jim reveals he is engaged to be married. The story ends with Laura retreating to her room with her collection of delicate glass objects. Soon after, Laura's brother leaves St. Louis when he is fired for writing a poem on the lid of a shoe box.

402. Almost ten years later, Williams would describe his plans to include this nightclub in the film script of *A Streetcar Named Desire*. Williams wrote Elia Kazan (24 February 1950, Wesleyan):

> I am going to do my version of the night-out with both the startling ideas that I had for it, the WONDER CLUB on Lake Pontchartrain with the boy singing in drag and the playing of the Varsouvianna but I will write it so that the first item can be easily eliminated from the script if you still dislike it. It appeals to me as a fresh and bold piece of screen material and a legitimate motive for Blanche's beginning to break: the dancing of the Varsouvianna — the music penetrating the powder-room where she has fled after the removal of the boy's wig — seems a marvelous springboard to the intensity of her monologue about Allan. Mitch: You mean he was like that boy in the female outfit? Blanche: No, no, no! He wasn't at all like that, there was nothing the least bit — effeminate about him — but there was — Etc.

708 Toulouse Street, New Orleans, where Williams stayed before moving to 538 Royal Street

Tonight in the show I thought of possible new play, Hawk's Daughter.⁴⁰⁰ A man like my father. Sensitive, terrified children. Same two as in <u>Portrait of a Girl in Glass</u>.⁴⁰¹ Begins drunken father's entrance early morning. The girl in her bedroom and all the little colored glass.

Yes, my head feels funny. I must be careful – pull myself back together. Tomorrow I will ride out to Pontchartrain on bike if weather permits. Spend the day and go to the Wonder Club⁴⁰² out there in the evening. I hear it is "gay". <u>Try</u> to sleep now.


*Tuesday, 16 September 1941*

Tuesday Night

I am waiting for a friend who has just stepped down the gallery for a minute which seems like an eternity to me. I will tell you later how it was.

Still waiting. Footsteps!

I had another friend last night.


Later –

The cold and beautiful bodies of the young! They spread themselves out like a banquet table, you dine voraciously and afterwards it is like you had eaten nothing but air.


*Wednesday, 17 September 1941*

<u>Wednesday</u>

Started to work but found no energy in me in spite of the week's rest.

I suppose the reason that I am living as I am is because I have spiritually surrendered life. This is just the last greedy grabbing of the worn out flesh. It is like the reckless vandalism in a doomed city, the retreating beaten army breaking the shop windows and pillaging everything before the conqueror's arrival.

At five I meet Oliver and we keep an appointment with one of his friends.

The day is half bright, half cloudy, fretful, windy.

There is a wire stretched between the faded grey galleries of the house – a delicate green and lavender vine grows along it.

Sometimes living matter assumes such charming forms and then ~~equally~~ such hideous forms without apparent choice.

Damnation is not as painful as you might believe. Lack of much hope left creates a dullness, a partial anaesthesia. Almost you wished that your suffering might be more intense so that you might be driven to try to fight damnation off. But you have become, through practise, so horribly expert in the administration of palliative drugs – amusements, indulgences, little temporary evasions and

403.  Williams had studied August Strindberg (1849–1912) at the University of Missouri and here refers to Strindberg's early struggles and failures. Williams used a quote from Strindberg's letter to Paul Gauguin (circa February 1895), "I, too, am beginning to feel an immense need to become a savage and create a new world," as an epigraph to a draft (November 1939) of *Battle of Angels* and then later for the playbill for *Orpheus Descending*. Interestingly, in one of his late plays, *Something Cloudy, Something Clear* (started in 1940 but not finished until 1980), Williams would eventually name the struggling writer, modeled on himself, August. In an undated letter (HRC) to Bill Glavin, his companion from 1965 to 1970, Williams named *The Dance of Death* (1900) as one of his three favorite modern plays.

Williams was particularly drawn to Strindberg's later works, his symbolic dramas marked by a sense of suffering and a longing for salvation. "Ten Blocks on the Camino Real" would bear some resemblance to Strindberg's *A Dream Play* (1901), and Williams described one version of his play "A House Not Meant to Stand" (circa 1981) as "my Spook Sonata."

404.  Muriel Bultman Francis represented singers, musicians, and other types of performing artists.

Sketch Williams made of himself with his bicycle in the French Quarter

escapes – you use them instead of warfare with the final, inner antagonist –
maybe because you are not quite sure <u>what</u> he is.

I play my portable victrola and think of Strindberg and great artists who had
an unfailing fire in them to strike out profiles of life.[403] I – with my little embers,
my tiny broken forge!

How impotent, how <u>little</u> I feel! With so much I would say, I would <u>shout</u> if I
had the force –

No – this is a dream – I will surely wake up.

But I will certainly not.

Then I will go to sleep, then. Without any dreams. But not for a while.

And while I am waiting I will keep snatching at the nearly bare branches of
pleasure, this alone being left me.

I should have had a brain.

Oh, God, why didn't you give me a brain. And strength.

Or why did you give me longings?


*Wednesday, 17 September or Thursday, 18 September 1941*

<u>Late night</u>

I am so sleepy I can hardly hold my eyes open.

For 3rd night straight I had a new bed partner, this one shared with Oliver.

Sweet but not exciting. I am sexually exhausted anyhow, only the incessant
little itch of desire keeps on –

I left Oliver and the other at Mack's – early – and wandered about – "the
quarter" – lonely as a cloud, but did not discover any daffodils. Ran into Fritzi's
sister[404] and her crew – banalities. Bought the pocket book of verse and home to
read it.

Cardiac neurosis –

Verse soothed me as it always does.

Crane is so much bigger than them all, as Chekhov is above all the prose-writers.

Hart Crane and Anton Chekhov – breathe into me a little of thy life!

I leave here soon for Florida, though what arrangements I can make remain to
be seen.

This life is all disintegration here in N.O.

All the old bad habits and more.


*Thursday, 18 September 1941*

Thursday Morning

Cardiac neurosis very bad last night. Lay sleepless for quite a while. Feel
"drugged out" this morning. Must take some positive action at once – Move –
get out on the sea. Live for a while like a turtle – like one of those marvelous,

405. Williams refers to D. H. Lawrence's poems about tortoises, first published as *Tortoises* (1921) and then included two years later in the collection *Birds, Beasts, and Flowers* (1923).

406. Presumably "A Daughter of the American Revolution." Williams wrote to Audrey Wood (circa 7 October 1941, HRC): "Completed first drafts (practically) of <u>two</u> new plays, one, mentioned previously, is now called 'A Daughter of the American Revolution' is predominantly humorous now, a sort of 'life with <u>Mother</u>'."

"A Daughter of the American Revolution" had started out as "The Voices in My Sleep," but Williams was concerned that it was a "little too sad." In a letter to Wood received 25 September 1941 (HRC), he wrote:

> You will be glad to hear that I am working on what promises to be a <u>long</u>, or at least a medium long, play which is straight realism, heavily emotional but not "out of bounds" so far. It is the sudden out-growth of several short-pieces. It is the nostalgic home-memories of a boy sleeping in a flop-house (for which I am using some of the material in "Fugitive Kind") on Xmas Eve, and scenes alternate dramatically between the home and the flop-house. I call it "<u>The Voices In My Sleep</u>" — Its present tendancy is to be a little too sad, though there is some wry humor in most of the scenes.

Interestingly, "The voices in our sleep" is the first line of the prologue poem of *The Migrants* (1941), the long published poem written by Clark Mills and dedicated to Williams.

407. "The Men from the Polar Star" is the fantastic story of the widow Isabel Holly who runs a boardinghouse filled with three difficult and undesirable tenants. Mrs. Holly learns from a metaphysician that she is the first of her sex to be transplanted from another star. After a violent battle among her tenants she is left a note by Christopher D. Cosmos, Captain of the Polar Star, who has stopped the disturbances. As a result of his visit, Mrs. Holly's life becomes much more tranquil and her tenants depart.

Some time later Mrs. Holly finds Christopher D. Cosmos asleep in her bed. When he awakens he tells her that the earth is a terrible mess and that he is on earth to set it right. He pulls out a curious object, a "subtle mechanical ear to attach to the womb," which listens at night to the heart of the embryo to determine its moral character. If deemed in deficit, the womb aborts it.

The story ends with the Widow Holly pregnant and in a state of joyful bliss, having been made love to by Christopher D. Cosmos, as well as by his sailors from the Polar Star.

Williams would later rewrite the story as "The Coming of Something to the Widow Holly," modifying it to exclude any mention of the Polar Star or the sailors and to end it just as Christopher D. Cosmos awakens from his sleep, thereby excluding the description of the unusual object and any sexual encounters.

408. "I Rise in Flame, Cried the Phoenix."

409. Williams wrote about Bill Richards to his mother (undated, HTC): "I know you will be interested in hearing that the son of Dr. Richards of Columbus is living a few doors from me and I used his typewriter this morning as mine needed a new ribbon. He is an awfully nice boy — a painter — I cannot say whether his work is good or not as it is very modern and hard to judge. He said his parents remember you and Grand and Grandfather very well and spoke very highly of you. They are now living on the Gulf coast at Ocean Springs, Miss."

Williams explained more about Richards in a letter to Paul Bigelow postmarked 11 October 1941 (Columbia):

> I spent a night and day with the object of this pilgrimage, a youth named Bill who is the son of the Doctor who brought me into this world and apparently is trying to compensate for this injustice by providing me with such a congenial fellow-sufferer. Bill is an artist and a good one and the 24 hours at Ocean Springs were a nice change from the turbulent Quarter.

410. Eloi Bordelon (1919–85), from a French Creole family, was a friend of Williams'. In *Memoirs* Williams disguised him with the name Antoine:

> There was . . . one whom I'll call Antoine who walked about the streets of the French Quarter with a tiny cut-glass bottle of smelling salts in liquid form and at the approach of a woman or girl, would stop and lean against a wall with the stricken whisper of "*Poisson*" — and sniff his counteractive vial until the lady had passed; and even then he would affect a somewhat shattered condition . . .

slow tortoises of D.H. Lawrence, who crawl so slowly beneath the tremendous weight of their subconscious wisdom.405

Yes – wisdom is necessary right now and some integrated effort.

So pick up the pieces and off we go!


*Sunday, 28 September 1941*

Sunday – Aug. 28 –

Still in N.O. after all – and pretty well satisfied.

Almost amazingly so when you consider how unfavorably the period started –

Been writing like mad. Practically finished the first draft of a fairly long comedy.406 Interest has waned but it is still a promising undertaking. Also short story – The Men from the Polar Star407 – and a 1-act about D.H. Lawrence408 which is probably mostly shit. But I will keep at it another day or so.

Last night the nightingales sang very sweetly indeed – The rarest of all rare strangers, both beautiful and gay – and 19!

Dew from heaven!

I mean from Baton Rouge.

Spent the day with Bill Richards409 who is 27 and never had a real consummated affair – he says. Loves with his spirit – yet lusts with the flesh – he says. ??? – !!! – I told him pleasure was too important to be left out. But he believes in Plato. We read – I read aloud – Milton, Keats, Crane, Chinese verse – Nice. Swam at Athletic club – Then dinner & movies – the 3 of us (Eloi,410 Bill) – Home and to bed sans cruising. E.C. was the name –

Love? could be mighty easy. – A person named V. wanted to go home with me, too, and was quite annoyed. I am rather surprisingly successful down here – in a way.

Indian summer – I guess – Season of mellow fruitfulness.

I appear to be a little on the vain & trivial side tonight. So I will say goodbye. T.W.


*Thursday, 2 October 1941*

Thursday – The pleasant state continues. Work on the Lawrence 1-act every day and it is becoming worth-while though my creative spurt is beginning to recede. Will have to quit for a while.

Pawned my typewriter today – broke! –

Affair with beautiful hustler – satisfactory yesterday afternoon and a curious rather abortive affair with another that night.

Too sleepy – Goodnight –

I found him hilarious, but Antoine had a serious and gifted side to him, like most of our kind. He was not a brilliant painter but he had a distinctive and highly effective flair which later made him a successful designer in New York.

I remember an evening when Antoine, who had a charmingly decorated apartment on Toulouse, presented his production of *Four Saints in Three Acts* — the cast all homosexuals — and they did not camp it but presented it with true style and it was the best evening of Stein I've yet experienced. (p. 50)

The one-act play "Auto-Da-Fé" has a character Eloi, "a frail man in his late thirties, a gaunt, ascetic type with feverish dark eyes." Williams would borrow his friend's last name for another character, Father Bordelon in the play "Thank You, Kind Spirit."

411. During October, Williams worked on both a long play about Lawrence, "The Long Affair," as well as his one-act "I Rise in Flame, Cried the Phoenix." It is not clear from the journal entry to which play he refers.

412. Williams' reference to the place of Christ's crucifixion is another example of his tendency toward melodrama.

Eloi Bordelon

*Saturday, 4 October 1941*

<u>Saturday</u> Night –

I cruised with 3 flaming belles for a while on Canal Street and around the quarter. They bored and disgusted me so I quit and left Saturday night to its own vulgar, noisy devices and went upstairs to my big wide comfortable bed, and my book of Lawrence's letters – always so rich and friendly.

Tennessee is ill – diarrhoea for several days – weak and a little feverish.

Bill, the decent one of the crowd, left for Ocean Springs – I think I may follow on my bicycle soon as this condition permits.

Got disgusted with the Lawrence play⁴¹¹ – it suddenly seemed to be shit. But this A.M. I wrote a new scene for it that revived my hope. I am a rather bad artist most of the time – alas!

Such drunken confusion on the street – the night in full flower. bottles breaking, soldiers bawling, singing, traffic.

The sea would be pleasant. Also good, solid work. – I am disappointed in Bigelow – he has not sent my laundry – or mentioned it. Afraid he is not such a true friend after all. – ~~Though little negligences~~ I rather idealized him in N.Y. – Right now I am not terribly concerned about anybody – vaguely friendly toward all – of good will. It is so long since I have seen or heard of Clark – There is a personality with some solid foundations. –

Sunday stares me in the face not too pleasantly – Well, let's sleep. <u>Bon soir</u>.


*Sunday, 5 October 1941*

Sunday –

I believe that the way to write a good play is to convince yourself that it is <u>easy</u> to do – then go ahead and do it with <u>ease</u>.

Don't maul, don't suffer, don't groan – till the first draft is finished.

Then <u>Calvary</u>⁴¹² – but not till then.

Doubt – and be lost – until the first draft is finished.

A Play is a Phoenix – it dies a thousand deaths.

Usually at night – In the morning it springs up again from its ashes and crows like a happy rooster.

It is never as bad as you think.

It is never as good as you think.

It is somewhere in between and success or failure depends on which end of your emotional gamut concerning its value it actually approaches more closely.

But it is much more likely to be good if you <u>think</u> it is <u>wonderful</u> while you are writing the first draft.

An artist must believe in himself – Possibly not so passionately as Lawrence – but passionately. Your belief is contagious. Others say – He is vain – but they are affected.

413.  Williams wrote to Audrey Wood (circa 7 October 1941, HRC): "I enclose a little ballad, primarily for <u>your</u> amusement. Do you suppose 'Esquire' would like it? Or is it too risqué."

Cinder Hill.

1.

Half way up the cinder-hill
back of Jamison's stave-mill

was the cottage of Mathilda
who collected pocket silver

from field-hands and stave-mill workers,
grocers' clerks, and soda-jerkers,

anyone with half a dollar
and no brighter star to follow.

2.

She was neither young nor old,
her hair was red, six teeth were gold

Her frame was large, her bosom very
nearly shamed the local dairy —

Though no beauty, it is true,
Mathilda knew a trick or two

That could give a new sensation
to our oldest recreation.

3.

She maintained her social station
for a half a generation,

waxed in glory and in wealth
without apparent loss of health.

Then all at once, and God knows why,
Mathilda kissed the boys goodbye,

Drew the curtains, latched the door
and gave up practise as a whore.

4.

For a while the town was rife
with rumors of her cloistered life.

Was she crippled, was she blind,
had Mathilda lost her mind?

For six years nobody saw her,
the ice man was her only caller

and even he was quite unable
to distinguish fact from fable.

5.

So for six years she remained
in retirement unexplained —

Then, for no apparent reason
but that it was budding season,

old Mathilda reappeared,
like the sun when clouds have cleared,

She descended into town
and bought the boys drinks all around.

6.

She was lively, she was loud
as a brass band in a crowd —

Taught a beau a new stand of cotton
things their daddies had forgotten —

Seemed just like the old Mathilda —
but the effort must have killed her.

Ice man found her one day later
Cold as the refrigerator.

7.

Soon Mathilda's former "trade"
came with shovel, came with spade

Came with pick and came with hoe *
in the half moon's tender glow —

Dug the earth up all around,
Turned up every inch of ground,

It being rumored that Mathilda
had interred her shameful silver

Somewhere in the cinder hill
back of Jamison's stave-mill.

T. Wms.
New Orleans
Oct. 1941.

* This couplet can be eliminated
if you want an even no. in all verses.

I have never had much of that faith – I have been a little too honest with myself and people.

Let us make up some brilliant lies! – No – let's don't – Let's fight it out the old way –

There probably isn't much more to go before things settle one way or another –

Today I have been writing well. I look in the mirror. My face is fresh and glowing. I look young again. And <u>pretty</u>! – Tonight this glow will wear off, probably, and I will feel old and depressed and seek the meagre comfort of dull company and the possible excitement in bed. – Well – in a day or two I will hop off on my bicycle for the Gulf Coast. So long.


### Tuesday, 7 October 1941

Tuesday – Oct. 7 –

The blue devils are massed for attack! – Well, let them – I'm ready for any assault the devils can conceive! –

I'm going to give up this room, leave all my junk with the Bordelon, and hit the road on my bike.

Audrey sent a check with the barely stated suggestion it might be the <u>last</u>. In that contingency – Little man, what <u>then</u>?

Alas, I can think of <u>no</u> <u>answer</u>.

<u>En Avant</u>! – <u>En Avant</u>! <u>En Avant</u>!

What is Lear shouted into the Storm? What tortured, fearless cry? — Well, that's what I've got in my heart.

No, the Lawrence doesn't seem very possible, nothing seems very possible – But getting moving again –

Must cash my check, get the borrowed typewriter out of hock – and <u>away!</u>

Tuesday Night (About midnight)

O how sleepy I am, how <u>weary</u> – barely able to rise from the bed where I read and drag myself over to the wash-basin for a drink and a pee –

Presume I shall start on my bike trip tomorrow – Package came from home. Shoes, shirts, candy – Very sweet of them. Guess I'll keep this room after all. Better have some place I'm attached to. – Home. – No love life lately – Not for about a week – but one sorry, messy episode that was less than nothing. – Mainly lack of energy or initiative on my part. Feel so tired at night! – Sort of old-feeling. Well, I'm no chicken, am I? – Wrote "Cinder Hill" – rather nice – May send to Audrey[413] – Street noises – always – What's all this leading up to anyway? – I mean this stubborn existence of mine? So long.

414.   A bar in the French Quarter.

415.   Presumably "The Long Affair." In a letter to Audrey Wood received 18 October 1941 (HRC), Williams
wrote:
> The Lawrence is going along more rapidly than I expected, I guess I just about have the first draft
> completed and if I can get it typed I may mail it to you before I do it over — say in about ten days.
> — You may be disgusted with me for writing on something presumably so non-commercial, but I
> am not so sure it isn't commercial. I call it "The Long Affair" — it starts at D.H.'s first meeting with
> Frieda and ends with his death but the total effect is more tender than tragic and there is a good deal
> of humor in it. It might be something to interest the Lunts.

*Saturday, 11 October 1941*

Saturday – Oct. 11 – one of those queer, lost mornings. Love life resumed with a vengeance last night – 2 in the night, 1 in morning. Enjoyed it the first couple. Then a bit sordid. Ah, well, I guess it comes under the heading of fair entertainment. The blue devils have sort of squatted dumbly at the foot of the stairs as it were.

Practically no sleep which gives the day that sort of unnatural quality. Not sleepy or even nervous but – empty. Not desperate but disparate. Been on the Gulf Coast since Wed – Lovely – I mean nice. Left bike at Bay St. Louis and did the rest on my thumb. – Would like to run off again now. Pershaps will. Why not? – In the Cajun country.

Love is what makes it still seem nice after the orgasm. Then is when sex becomes art – after the orgasm – one must be an artist to keep it from falling to pieces uglily – Up till then it is simply craftmanship and of a pretty crude and simple kind. – It is also art, of course, when you first meet the person – selecting the attitude and sticking to it.

*Sunday, 12 October 1941*

Sunday A.M. It all went out, it's all gone, there is nothing left anymore. Chalk up one for defeat.

*Friday, 17 October 1941*

Friday Midnight
    Difficulties – financial. Blue devils dispersed. I am flat broke – stony – literally not one cent. Bummed a couple of cigarettes off a queen at Jean's.⁴¹⁴ Guess I'll have to sell a suit tomorrow. Hate to. But I do love to eat and one must have beer money on Sat. Night in the Quarter – Rent over due 3 or 4 days. The Lawrence play goes nicely – I think.⁴¹⁵ Well – let's hope a gift arrives in the mail. En Avant! – 10.

*Saturday, 18 October 1941*

Sat. A.M.
    I wake up with no money for breakfast and the landlady right outside my door.

Midnight – Bill loaned me $5.00 – God bless him! – I still have my good suit.
    Had a pretty satisfactory "roll in the hay" this evening – then a long, dull round of the gay places to kill time. I have nothing to say to these people after I've been to bed with one of them – Then it all seems utterly vacuous. I prefer to

416. The Cabildo, located on Jackson Square adjacent to St. Louis Cathedral, is the old Spanish council house. It was rebuilt in 1795–99.

417. Williams used the last name of Herbert Duclos, an acquaintance who lived in the French Quarter, for the spiritualist, Mother DuClos, in the play "Thank You, Kind Spirit."

418. Fleet Munson.

419. By 15 November a second German offensive against Moscow was under way. The Germans, hindered by the severe winter, made less than expected progress against the Russians, who held out as best they could. A few days later, on 18 November, the Russians, reinforced with fresh troops from Siberia, halted the German advance on Moscow.

The Cabildo, New Orleans

just sit and look at Bill & say nothing. Goodbye – Maybe a long, lonely bike trip tomorrow. <u>En Avant!</u>

*Sunday, 19 October 1941*

Sunday Midnight – Hot, sticky night – no air stirring – moved about the quarter pretty disconsolately, meeting no one – coffee at French Market and muscat grapes – Saw cops pick up an apparently lifeless body – a bum – near the cabildo.[416] Rapped the soles of his feet with a stick – one said "Harder! You ain't hitting him hard." – "He's dead to the world" – "Maybe he <u>is</u> dead." "He won't know when he <u>gets</u> there." So into the wagon and away. "Wait'll I get his hat." said one of the cops – Yes, they picked up his hat. – A man. a life. – Dead to the world – wait'll I pick up his hat – He was awfully thin, still fairly young and when they picked him up and dragged him very untenderly across the gutter his shirt parted from his belt and his bare belly was pure white – so clean and helpless looking, bare flesh – There is so much of it in the world, as thick as weeds, and so much wasted, thrown away.

I spent the afternoon riding bike with Herbert Duclos,[417] a nice boy. His lover V. came over – a screaming young bitch. Attractive as hell – so young and errant, such an <u>enfant terrible</u>. We sat entranced at the child's outrageous chatter. Herbert gave me some pictures of Lawrence & Frieda and showed me his scrapbooks – a simple, good person. Things will hurt him and hurt him until he gets old and hard. He incidentally informed me that my old lover F.M.[418] was in penitentiary for forgery. – Those nights in the West Side "Y" – F. was the most accomplished lover I ever had – what a linguist! He made a ritual of it. – A life that seemed headed for ruin – and <u>was</u>. – A great liar – a forger – a brilliant lover – Will I make any effort to help him? – I hope so. – The one who informed Herbert, who was also F's lover, was a priest. – I have "crabs" again and can't even afford to buy "The Personal Insecticide". – Literally a lousey writer, that's me. – A lousey guy. Want excitement! – Move? Florida? – No. Taos? – Wish I could. – New York? – Maybe soon. but I am probably better off here. – Relatively speaking, I am satisfied & the life is (relatively) pleasant. – And there is Bill, good, clean, quiet antiseptic Bill. – Maybe the nicest guy I've ever known. – Moscow is being seiged[419] – A footnote to all this trivial chatter. Typical bitch Tennessee. – Almost. 10.

*Monday, 20 October 1941*

Monday – Very, very blue!

A charming little incident climaxed an already miserable evening. The lover of Saturday night stopped me and said, "Say, do you know you have crabs? You gave them to me."

420.  The short story is very likely "Bobo" (dated October 1941, New Orleans), a forerunner to "The Yellow Bird." In this fantastic story, Alma, the wayward daughter of a Presbyterian minister, rebels and bleaches her hair blond and becomes a prostitute in New Orleans. She gives birth to a magical child who brings her gold and jewels. As Alma lays dying, her deceased favorite lover returns like Neptune out of the sea, bringing "a great conch-shell full of riches from sunk Spanish galleons," and she goes off with him.

421.  Charles Criswell (1910–60) was born and educated in West Virginia and came to New York to study painting with Arshile Gorky, John Sloan, and Kenneth Hayes Miller. Williams met Criswell in New York. He married a close friend of Jordan Massee's, Henrietta Callaway. After serving in World War II, Criswell wrote a collection of short stories, *Nobody Knows What the Stork Will Bring* (1958). According to Massee, Criswell was best known for his savage wit, which delighted both Bigelow and Williams.

Eight months later Williams' account of the typewriter would dramatically differ. In a letter to Criswell (circa 21 June 1942, HTC), he wrote:

Henrietta and Jordan both write that you want the typewriter back which you sent me in New Orleans. I may as well tell you the complete history of the machine which is about as dramatic as my own. Not having a place of my own for about a year now, I have been continually exposed to the whims and caprices of various bitches among whom was one Creole character I lived with in New Orleans. We shared an apt. and one night during her absence a plaster blackamoor which she claimed to be of great value and several other articles were smashed in a little difficulty which arose among visitors and myself. The Creole lady held me responsible for it and locked the door on me and my possessions (on opposite sides of it). Among these articles was the typewriter which, with my victrola and riding-boots, she refused to relinquish until I had paid for the blackamoor. Of course I could not pay for the Blackamoor. About this time my Grandmother took seriously ill and I was called to St. Louis. I trusted by the time I came back to New Orleans the situation would have cleared up. It so happened I did not return to New Orleans but to New York. . . . I wrote a number of letters asking for the typewriter to be forwarded, first to the lady and then to a friend I hoped might act as intercessor. I finally heard that the typewriter and boots were being shipped to St. Louis. This was late in the spring. I have not yet heard of their arrival there.

In a fragment of his play "The One Exception" (dated January 1983), Williams would borrow his name for Agatha Criswell, the nearest relative of the mentally ill Kyra.

422.  According to Jeanne Bultman, most likely George Mercer, an artist who had studied with Hans Hofmann.

423.  In "Thank You, Kind Spirit," the spiritualist Mother DuClos is exposed during one of her sessions as a fraud and alcoholic by a woman and a priest, Father Bordelon. In a letter to Audrey Wood dated 21 October 1941 (HRC), Williams wrote: "In response to the request for another one-act I have hastily banged out this little sketch of a spiritualist meeting I attended here in the quarter a few nights ago. — It did not end so dramatically as here represented but the characters are from life."

THANK YOU, KIND SPIRIT

SCENE:  A little crib-like room on the far end of Chartres street in the Vieux Carre of New Orleans has been converted into the chapel of a spiritualist.  There is an improvised altar with multitudes of prayer-candles in little pearly white, pink, and green glasses.  One whole wall is covered with religious pictures in rich colors.  Innumerable little crosses and plaster saints are stuck about the room.  There are bunches of artificial roses and lilies.  The room swims with richly soft religious light and color.

THE SPIRITUALIST is Mother DuClos, a small grizzled woman with a hunched back, robed in white like an angel.  A little white, frilled cap is on her head.  She is an octoroon and speaks with a Creole accent in a soft, emotional tone.

It is raining outside, a slow Autumn rain, and the wind is complaining a little.  On the five crude benches are seated perhaps a dozen people, ranging in age from a little girl of eight to an old man of eighty.

Enough of that! Tomorrow I sell every suit I own, if necessary, to buy an insecticide and be purified at least of my parasitic companions, a nasty, humiliating business – And I think Bill overheard it. He was standing nearby.

He had been cold all evening anyway and that must have been all that was needed – I am probably a social pariah from now on. And I suppose I should be. Oh, God!

Visited a chapel – Spiritualist – earlier in the evening. In the A.M. wrote a new scene in play and a short story.[420] at Bill's. Can't do that anymore. But no typewriter of my own. The one I borrowed from Cris in hock.[421] I must be <u>mad</u>. Still. It doesn't seem like I can help myself. What else could I do but go home – my father's house? <u>Impossible!</u> – <u>What else?</u> – I must work out something. Owe three dollars on rent and five dollars to Bill. Even if I sell my clothes – unless check comes I'll still be broke. Christ. It's all a little too much, too much. – Such <u>sordid</u> troubles. – I appear to be a vile creature, do I not? Unclean and vicious.

<u>Later</u>

Drank half a pitcher of water to relieve my hunger. Found a few grapes left in bottom of sack – <u>two</u> were eatable.

When hunger drives a man to a crime it should not be considered a crime – except against the man who committed it.

<u>Later</u> – Can't sleep. Empty stomach & "crabs".

Remember the New York days – the <u>plush</u> days when I had a room at the Woodrow – that pleasant little penthouse room that looked over Central Park. The portable victrola by my bed and always money enough to eat or smoke or fuck or almost anything else that I desired to do. George.[422] Charles. The little deaf and dumb belle picked up on 57th. And Bigelow coming over for lunch and the sunroof. And cruising the park at night. And eating, eating, eating! – I wasn't so happy. But I was well-off, huh? – O I want to have <u>money</u> again. I love the pleasures, the sensual pleasures so much. And how I loathe the squalor, the awkwardness, the indignity of being broke. I suppose I am too much body, not enough soul. – But how can one maintain a soul with so little for it to feed on? Meditation? Is that what the soul feeds on? I meditate and arrive at <u>nothing</u> – <u>nothing</u>. My thoughts, such as they are – and they are pretty impulsive – go into my work. Oh, I have <u>thoughts</u> – yes. But they don't seem to get anywhere. Only the body seems to get anywhere. In bed. At the table. In swimming. The soul makes its little private noises. But where does it get? – Let's smoke & try to <u>sleep</u>.

*Tuesday, 21 October 1941*

<u>Tuesday Midnight</u> –

Good humor returned with the sale of a suit, good food, the writing and dispatching of a 1-act about the Spiritualist,[423] and a kind letter from Audrey –

424. In *The Flame of New Orleans* (1941), Dietrich plays the role of the glamorous but impoverished Countess Ledoux, who has just arrived in mid-eighteenth-century New Orleans. She is forced to choose between a wealthy suitor and the adventurous but poor sea captain she loves. Despite her plans to marry for money, she runs off with the poor sea captain.

425. Williams refers to the "charming incident" in which he was accused of having passed crab lice to a lover.

426. Williams used the penultimate line from the Emily Dickinson poem "Elysium is as far as to" as the title of the short story "The Accent of a Coming Foot" and as a screen legend in *The Glass Menagerie* (scene 6). He also used the last four lines from Dickinson's "I died for beauty" for the epigraph of the play *The Night of the Iguana*:

> And so, as kinsman met at night,
> We talked between the rooms,
> Until the moss had reached our lips,
> And covered up our names.

427. In "The Lady of Larkspur Lotion," two characters, Mrs. Hardwicke-Moore and the Writer, rent rooms in a boardinghouse run by Mrs. Wire. Williams drew strongly on his experience at 722 Toulouse Street and named the owner of the boardinghouse after the successor to Mrs. Anderson. Mrs. Hardwicke-Moore uses larkspur lotion, a common treatment for body vermin, and also complains to Mrs. Wire about the cockroaches in her room.

Charles Criswell

Sketch of Charles Criswell

*The mulatto-looking youth in next room is beautiful. We merely exchange shy greetings. – He has a lover. – And I have crabs.*

*Roaches pig jam in my noise – a victim of the insect kingdom*

mailed before she got my request for a check for it contained none.

Bad humor and hunger will return tomorrow if the check doesn't come.

Saw Marlene Dietrich, a charming woman she is, in "The Flame of Old New Orleans"[424] – Second time.

Saw and talked to nobody, a pleasantly lonely time. Guess I still have "crabs" but they are not so evident. Wrote Bill a letter about incident[425] & apologies for my various impositions. – Read Hart Crane. Now feel hungry – May go out again & spend part of my last 50¢. ($2.00 to landlady – Spent $1.50 today – how? – Don't know. Well – let's see – Cigs. – 17¢ – Breakfast (2 – owed for one) 45¢ – Envelope & Stamps = 13¢ – Supper at Gluck's = 30¢ – coke 5¢ – got in show for nothing, usher not looking = 0, Sandwich = 10¢

*Could live O.K. on $1.00 a day.*

$$
\begin{array}{r}
17 \\
45 \\
13 \\
30 \\
05 \\
10 \\
\hline
120
\end{array}
$$

*Time has never flown so fast before. Fancy! Been here about 2 months! Work makes the days fly. They're all so much alike. Read Dickinson. Love her!*[426]

$120 = 30^d$ *unaccounted for*

5¢ to porter at N.O.A.C. – 20¢ – 5¢ typewriter paper – 15¢ – 2 orange juices – 5¢ – penny taxes on various things probably leave about 3¢ – ought to have 53¢ – first time I ever figured money out like this – getting bourgeois – Stuffy – No kidding, I'm getting too Rotarian lately.

Yep – goin' out now an' eat. Love to.

James' bar – music all the time. Horns tooting. I guess I like N.O. – It will always seem kind of home-like to me after this. No word from home lately but I am too hard to worry. Love Grand but don't think of her except casually – say, for a moment or two once a day. – I'm sorry I'm so selfish. Good night.

(Maybe won't go out. Feel sleepy. Stay in. Smoke cig. Sleep.)

*Monday, 27 October 1941*

Monday Midnight –

I have moved out of that pleasant, comforting room to a horrible windowless brown cubicle with a lumpy bed and a musty odor and big roaches crawling about the walls. Sad to return to at night. And Eloi is angry at me – for "perfidious bitchery" in confiscating a piece of trade last night that he wanted. Still, I wrote a new 1-act today – "The Lady of Larkspur Lotion"[427] & feel not too badly. Bill and I went to the Spiritualist meeting again. It seems St. Roch has

428. St. Roch is the patron saint of the plague-stricken who, having caught the plague himself, was fed in the woods by a dog. St. Roch reputedly miraculously cured sufferers from the plague. He is sometimes depicted as a pilgrim with a sore on his leg, accompanied by a dog with a loaf of bread in its mouth. Williams included aspects of St. Roch in the play "Thank You, Kind Spirit."

> MOTHER: I want you to go to St. Roch's cemetary on Saturday afternoon. I want you to go alone with your beads and I want you to make the journey around the stations, I want you to make all the stations and say your prayers and your beads. When you come to the third station you'll feel an icy cold chill, as cold as a winter's day, and the crooked limbs will be made straight again!
>
> Praise the Lord, be praised! Yes, thank you, thank you, Kind Spirit!

429. St. Anthony's devotion to the poor is remembered in the charity of St. Anthony Bread, which is devoted to the relief of the starving and the needy.

430. St. Raymond of Pennafort was a humble servant who helped the poor and was considered a perfect model for the clergy. He is remembered as having sailed across the sea on his cloak when King James of Aragon prevented him from taking passage on a ship. He is known as the patron saint of lawyers.

The mention of St. Raymond is echoed in Williams' play "Thank You, Kind Spirit." In his letter to Audrey Wood dated 21 October 1941 (HRC), he wrote: "Incidentally the Spiritualist told me she saw a middle-aged lawyer passing out lots of money." In the play, the woman who comes to expose the spiritualist says to her: "I won't even mention all the lies you sprung on me one time. . . . Told another good friend she seen a middle-aged lawyer and lots of money was gonna be passed around."

Café du Monde in the French Market, 813 Decatur Street, New Orleans

a dog he "sends out to lick sores and cure them".[428] deaf pronounced deef.
Choosen. Sacred heart of Jesus. St. Anthony.[429] St. Raymond.[430] Thin case of ice.

After this we stared and stared at a certain lovely Polynesian in the Phillipine
bar way up on Royal. How yearningly! – When we returned Eloi's parlor was
full of the most deplorable bitches. Bill dispersed them and I went my solitary
way on my bike, through the pleasant, lonely night streets – bought the Times
and ate at the Old French Market. Now bed – Money a most pressing concern –
May go home while Dad is away – and get teeth repaired & see Grand who has
been ill.

*feel little or no warmth for anyone right now – bad.*

*Wednesday, 29 October 1941*

Wednesday – We draw near the end of this particular journal – near the end of
this New Orleans period? – I rather hope so, though it has been nicer than I
really & truly expected. I have been writing a great deal and not badly I believe.
– Not too badly. – But the best is probably over. It begins to be a bit "warmed
over" – "Second day". – I mean the life here. – None of my essential personality
problems are solved. I have not found the sustained desirable lover. No new
convictions – no new lamp-post on the dark road I am stumbling crazily along. –
I think I grow steadily a little bit harder & emotionally tougher – Not what I
want. I don't need to be more cynical. – I have not become a confirmed amoralist
(?) but that seems to be the end of the present road. – Come! Let's turn onto
another!

Tonight ran into some "dirt" at the Polynesian bar – for the first time in my
life I was struck – not hard enough to hurt anything but my spirit. Close shave.
Returned to the safety of "James' Bar" where I met the companion of last night
and we resumed our cruising – again fruitless for me. – So I return home feeling a
bit disgusted with myself & things – "It's the same difference". – Oh, yes, sent
telegram home – for bus-fare to St. Louis – would I use it for that – or would
I – ? – I can suspect myself of almost anything these days. – yes. – I suddenly
remember myself a kid of 9 drawing pictures in Red Goose sample books,
waiting in Dad's office – Why? – Stupid! All this is the drivel of a sickly ego. –
Should expose myself for a long time to the sun – Florida? – Sounds good. – 10.

*Friday, 31 October 1941*

Friday –

Yes, it seems a change is imminent – Mother has sent me $25.00 to come
home on – will I? – I am completely in the dark about this. Of course I would
much prefer to elope to Florida – and devil take the consequences – Sun! Beach!

431.   Among the poems Williams was writing around this time were "Blood on the Snow," "Ice and Roses," "Warning," "The Stonecutter's Angels," and "Which Is He?"

```
                        BLOOD ON THE SNOW


        I cannot deny that I have lost in crossing

        all that impeded my flight or begged me to stay,

        that the hedge, that the bough with the stricken bird, in calling

        got no answer from me, though I passed that way.


        I passed that way and observed the fugitive's track,

        I guessed where the crippled and breathless victim lay,

        but also guessed that the killer was still in the branches

        and so I delayed but a moment and crossed away.


        It might be well to recount the tales of my valor

        to say that I kept the ravenous killer at bay,

        but what are lies to avail with the crippled singer's

        blood on the snow at the blood-red close of day?


        And what are lies to accomplish now that the killer,

        glutted and fanged and breathing a poisonous steam,

        stands in the branches, burning the ice in the branches,

        thawing the crimson edge of the ice-covered stream?




                        Tennessee Williams
                        Oct. 1941
                        New Orleans.
```

432.   While Williams was still working on *Stairs to the Roof*, the long play he refers to is most likely "The Long Affair." In a letter to Paul Bigelow postmarked 3 November 1941 (Columbia), Williams wrote: "I am taking the Lawrence script with me, hope to finish the first draft in Clayton." One of the poems Williams wrote in St. Louis was "Intimations," beginning "I do not think that I ought to appear in public / below the shoulders."

Bicycle! – No more bitches! – But will I? – It would be such a dirty trick on poor Mother – I don't want to.

Today – I worked on verse[431] and am finally going to send some off – an important step <u>maybe</u>.

I have censored myself sharply of late. And deserve it. – I will try to be stronger, now, and less obviously selfish.

<u>Midnight</u> – (or later) –

A nasty scene out at the Wonder Bar – Lost my temper with Eloi, and raged at him like a fish-wife. First time I've done such a thing since that occasion when I broke up with K. in Provincetown. Such idiotic, childish behavior, Tennessee! – But Eloi had been so abominably rude and exasperating I should have "knocked his block off" – So endeth the New Orleans period, on a very sour note – Bill stood by me, which I truly appreciate.

Well – dilemma! – Home or Florida or <u>what</u>? – Horrid dilemma! – Goodnight you bitch!

*Thursday, 20 November 1941*

I am now back in St. Louis from my 2nd New Orleans period. Been here 2 weeks and crazy to leave. Waiting for checque from Audrey. Hatred of my father & <u>fear</u> – yes, fear – make it about as impossible as usual to live at home. Also poor Mother's gross lack of sensitivity. Grand has been ill and I returned partly to see her, partly because my finances got horribly muddled. Well, we leave in a couple days <u>irregardless</u>. Dream of Fla. – beach – sun – bicycle trips. How I shall ever manage I don't know but on I shall go. <u>En Avant</u>! – Not well physically. Heart neurosis bad today. No sex here. None ever. And sex, alas, is necessary. Writing – a bad play, a good 1-act, two poems.[432] Shame.

*as an artist I seem weak & muddled Today. Sorry. Back again! new year's 1942*

*A few days later Williams returned to New Orleans. By the end of November he was hitchhiking from New Orleans to St. Petersburg, Florida, and he recorded aspects of his journey in a small flip-top notepad.*

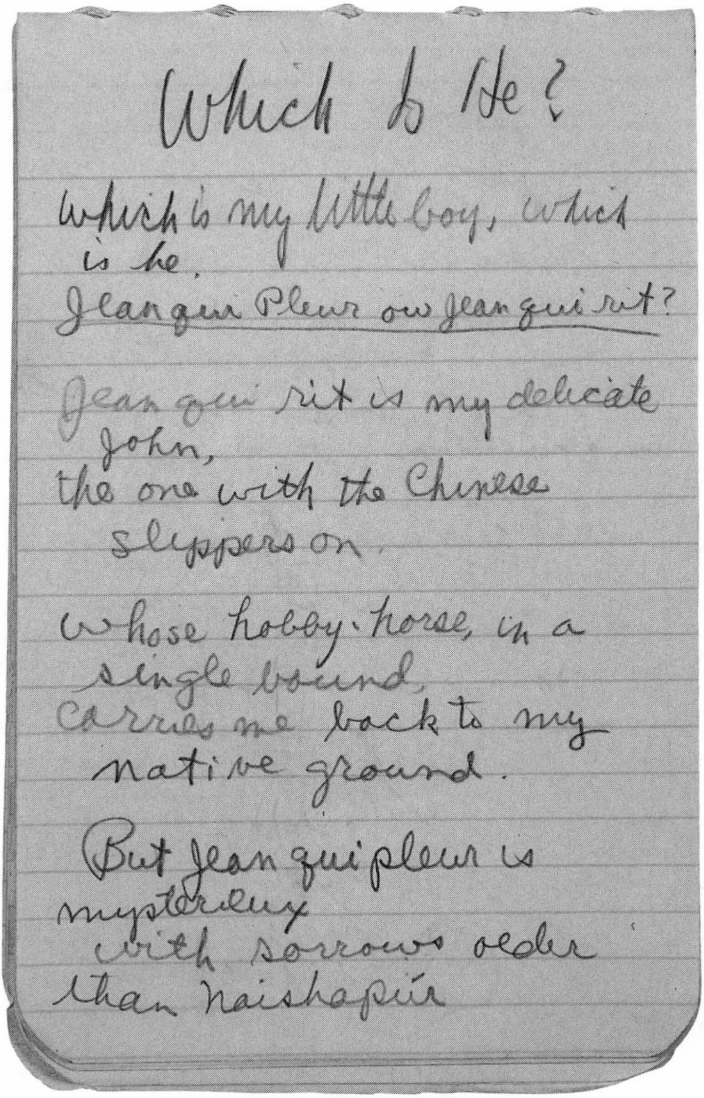

# Which Is He?

Which is my little boy, which
is he,
Jean qui Pleur ou Jean qui rit?

Jean qui rit is my delicate
John,
the one with the Chinese
slippers on,

Whose hobby-horse, in a
single bound,
carries me back to my
native ground.

But Jean qui pleur is
mysterieux
with sorrows older
than Naishapur

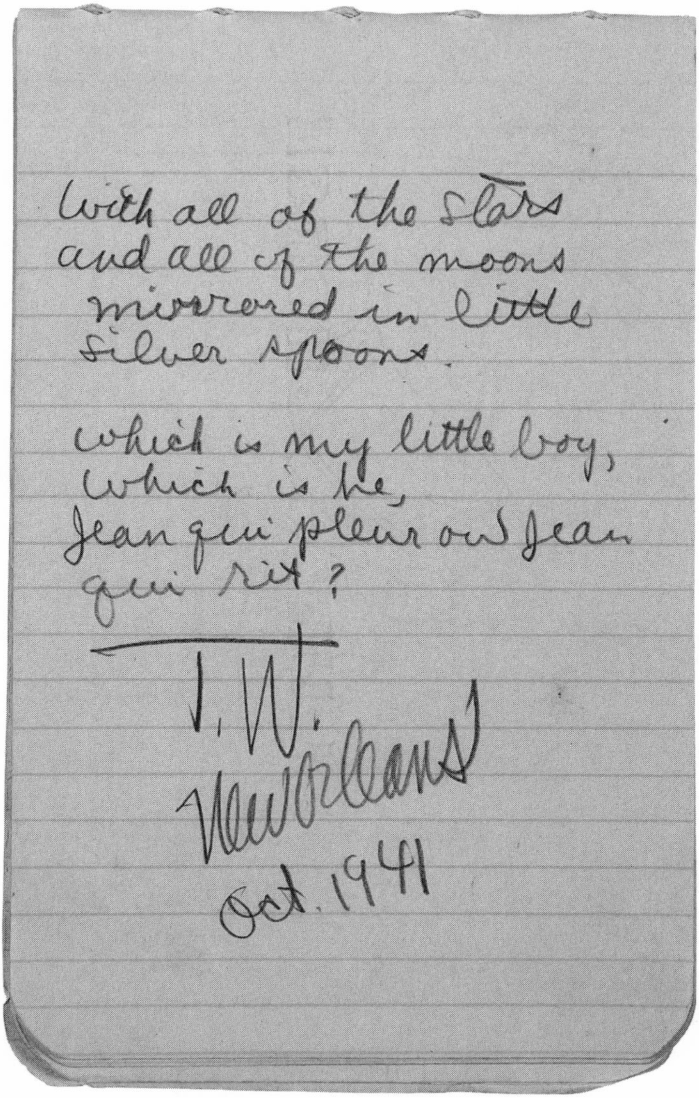

With all of the stars
and all of the moons
mirrored in little
silver spoons.

which is my little boy,
which is he,
Jean qui pleur ou Jean
qui rit?

T.W.
New Orleans
Oct. 1941

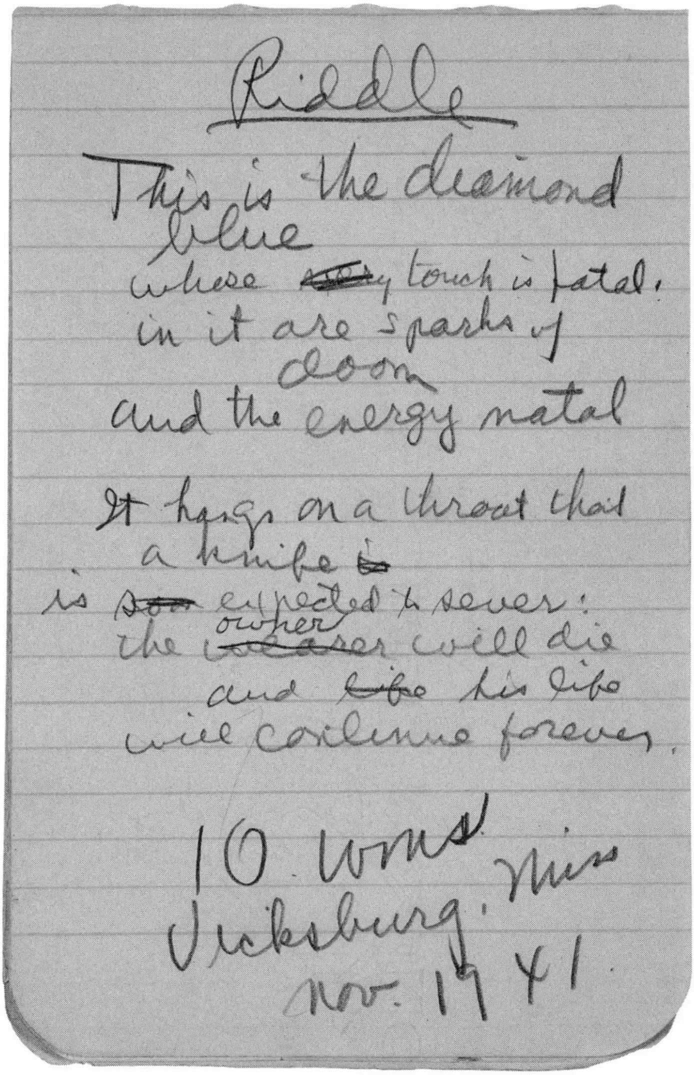

# Riddle

This is the diamond
blue
whose ~~ray~~ touch is fatal.
in it are sparks of
            doom
and the energy natal

It hangs on a throat that
a knife ~~is~~
is ~~too~~ expected to sever:
the ~~~~ owner will die
        and ~~life~~ his life
will continue forever.

10. wms.
Vicksburg. Miss
        Nov. 1941.

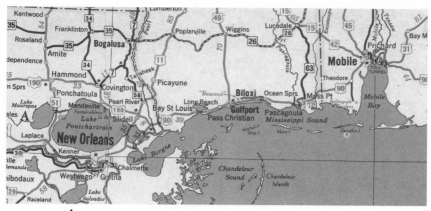

*The II Florida trip –*

*Sunday, 30 November 1941*

Sun. Nov. 30 –
Panic in Mobile. Arrived here to find all the street lights extinguished. Tired, disheartened. Became more and more nervous, walking about the streets. Sort of a panic of shyness developed. I got a 50¢ room in a ghastly flophouse. bought a copy of <u>Life</u> and went up to bed about 9:30.

Felt the trip would become a fiasco – regretted undertaking it.
I would have turned back had I not shipped my bike ahead to St. Petersburg.
So shy I could barely enter drugstore and ask for stamp! –
Am I crazy?
So it would seem – well – En Avant!


*Monday, 1 December 1941*

Monday A.M.
Well, it is better. I feel more contained. I rise after a restful sleep in Mobile And find the sun bright, the sky cloudless. – I will procede upon my vague journey
Yesterday morning Ed said to me "You are just a <u>gauche</u> little boy." – about it. In everything but years.
I got from N.O. to Mobile in one hitch with a "contact man" for a cigar co. – one of those cordial, personality men. Talked me to pieces. My main objection to hitchhiking is the necessity of keeping up a conversation with drivers who give you a lift because they want someone to talk with.

433. In Williams' play *The Red Devil Battery Sign*, the Woman Downtown's final rendezvous with King Del Rey takes place at the Crestview Pharmacy.

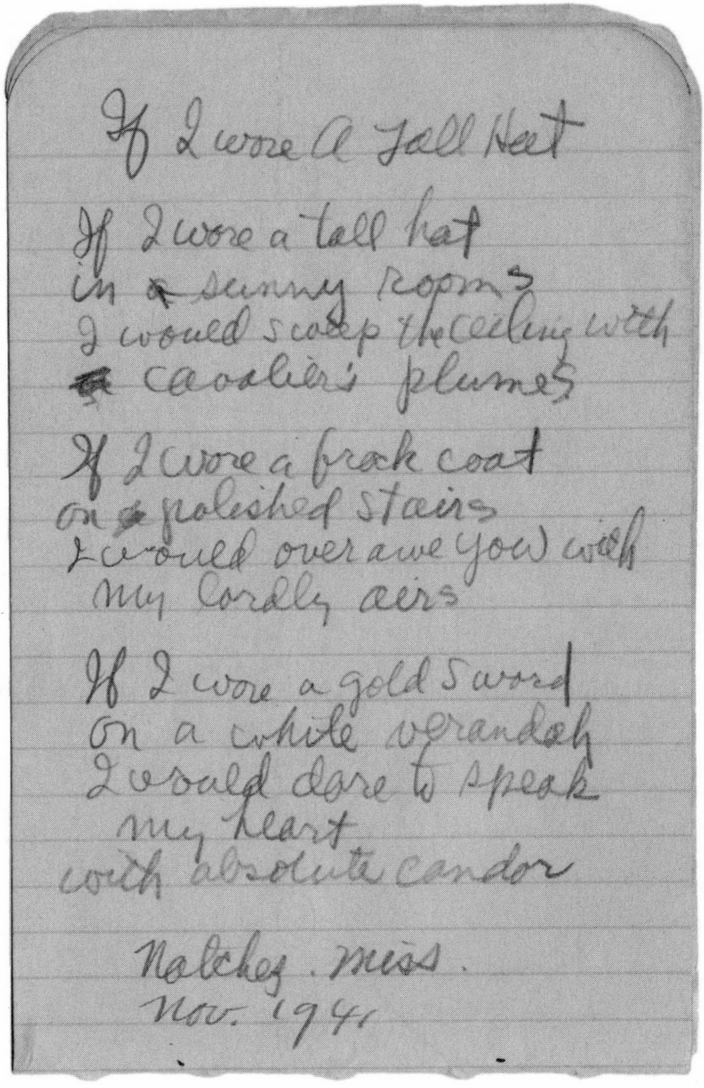

If I wore A Tall Hat

If I wore a tall hat
in a sunny room
I would scoop the ceiling with
a cavalier's plumes

If I wore a frock coat
on a polished stair
I would over awe you with
my lordly airs

If I wore a gold sword
on a white verandah
I would dare to speak
my heart
with absolute candor

Natchez. Miss.
Nov. 1941

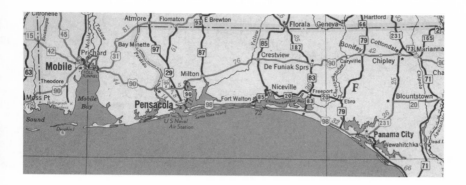

Later – Somewhere beyond Pensacola about noon –

Bad highway – Cars pass at 5 min. intervals at 70 or 80. Stalled about 15 min. now in front of a wilderness gas station run by a bearded ex-wrestler called Daniel Boone Savage. Nice warm sun – but looks like a tough stretch ahead of me. Had 2 rides – (another car just streaked past me) <u>Damn!</u> – Here comes a truck. No dice – 2 more duds. my good luck is failing – Just had a little chat with the wrestler. Says I'll get out of here in 2 days – good –

Most of the cars are headed west. well, here comes another – Look bright, son! – Nope. Looks like a trailer coming now. I'm going to get a nice sun kissed complexion. – yep, trailer. – nope. Gas on the stomach. – Another one way up yonder at the bend. Average about 4 min. I oughta get one out of 6. This baby stops for gas but he has a full seat. Here comes next one already. – fast. waves. goes by. The road is empty. Empty as my head. Hitchhiking should induce reflection but when it goes badly I get dull and mindless. Been here about ½ hour or more. Longest wait since Memphis. Here comes. Fast. Ought to be my baby. <u>2</u> of 'em – Get one – Not this one – Fucking tourists, woman <u>2</u> still coming. <u>Did.</u> A truck to Crestview.433

Short hop but grateful to move from Boone's. Lunch Crestview – 1st car down road picked me up. – a 30 mi. ride. Here I am at De Funiak Springs still on #90 and about 130 out of Tallahassee. Must be about 2:15 P.M. Lot more cars.

My life is very unsatisfactory but surprisingly endurable. Through my skill at evading pain and cultivated detachment. Traffic getting as thin as Boone's. But rain is holding off. Up. By. I have been passed up by about 12 cars. About 6 live ones. Live means single occupant. I ought to average at least 1 out of 10 live ones. Truck by. Truck up. Off – Well, this is better than last night in Mobile Bad, bad. Another by. up. Live by, <u>2</u>. Slipping, baby.

May not make Tallahassee tonight. Okay good luck. let's have it up. looks <u>live</u>. aw – off. up jalopy. Crawls by. Big lovely rooster strutting in yard. Ruddy orange and gleaming blue-black. An old tire swing. Nice for stage. Here comes a soldier hitchhiking damn – I'm sunk. already got a ride. Good! Pretend to be writing. I guess my military disguise is only moderately convincing. Getting tired. Been here ½ hour I reckon – up. Dead.

3 quick by. Terrible!

434. Williams passed through Vero Beach when he hitchhiked from Miami to Darien during the second half of April 1941. While in Vero Beach, he wrote a poem, "Towns Become Jewels," in which he transforms his displeasure into a lyrical question: "Oh, why are they not / as once we believed they were, / incorruptible gems, / true diamonds dropped in water?"

435. On 28 November, unable to advance further without fresh troops or supplies, the Germans suffered heavy losses as they withdrew from Rostov. On 24 November, Rommel had begun a drive toward the western Egyptian border from Libya. By the 26th he had ended his attacks near the Libyan-Egyptian border and had tracked back toward Tobruk, Libya.

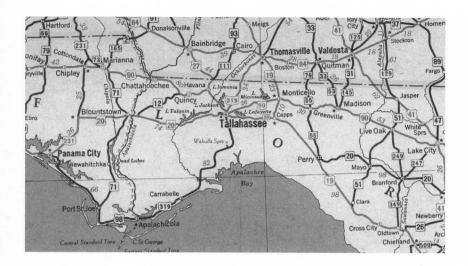

Old negro advised me to walk up here to filling station – I have done. See what happens. But this is very bad going. Negro community called Happy Hill. Well, this is a blank all right. Kids in truck, "Hi, soljer!" – fooling somebody. Couple at top of hill walking on. Live one goes by grinning. Been her 1½ hours. I believe. Awful.

Something must be wrong.

Man walking.

"Not stopping, ay?" short a instead of eh. This is nearly as bad as Vero Beach last spring.434

Sky less threatening clearing up in the west. May have a bright sunset. I may see it from here. Traffic is almost stopped. Florida people are yankees & dirty red necks. will pray for a ride now. Got one – 1 mile. Man told me a hitchhiker – got a ride just then – to Marianna – The power of prayer.

Just now bought this pencil off an old man with no legs – walking on stumps. He complained he couldn't get a room in this town for less than a dollar. – Town = Quincy, 26 miles from Tallahassee. It is about 8:20 and I am still hitting them on #90 – I stand in the red glare of a neon by a filling station – cool – pleasant enough – much better than last night in Mobile in that awful flophouse. A live one just gave me the go-by. Not likely to get out of here tonight – about 2-1 improbability. World news improved with Germans pushed back at Rostov and Libya.435 Gay music from radio in station.

Crickets – Remember Champaign, Ill., the "Ten Minute Stop"? Oh, my heavens, what a long, long, long ways back on this twisting highway!!!

The sky has completely cleared up and there's a big moon. (Got out)

436.  Presumably "I Saw Hell Break Loose at Alcatraz" in *Inside Detective* (November 1941), a narrative account of the background and trial of Henri Young for killing a fellow inmate at Alcatraz. In the trial twenty-two prisoners testified about the brutality, death of convicts unattended in damp, barren cells, and suicides intentionally disguised as attempted escapes. The jury found Young guilty of involuntary manslaughter and found additionally that the treatment of prisoners at Alcatraz was "unbelievably brutal and inhuman" and urged an investigation of the conditions.

437.  The Williamses had lived next door to the Wrights on Pershing Avenue in St. Louis. Presumably May Wright was a relative. In a letter to Paul Bigelow written on Golden Isles Beach Hotel, St. Simons Island, stationery (postmarked New York, 27 August 1941, Columbia), Williams wrote at the top: "I <u>saw</u> Miss Wright — What a <u>fluff</u>!"

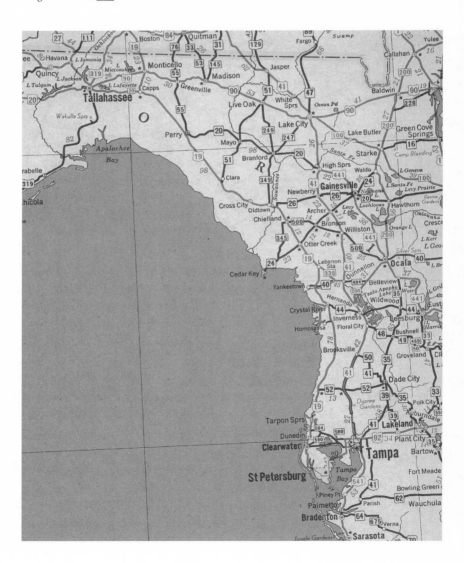

*Wednesday, 3 December 1941*

Wednesday Night.

Very blue. Very down hearted. Thoughts of despair in my feverish head. Very sick last night. Raging fever and pounding heart. The grippe I suppose. Tormented till daybreak. Then fell asleep and woke much improved, fever gone, but weak. Spent the day walking idly about Tampa – wound up at a movie, the usual anesthesia. Visited a bar with plump child-like B-girls & soldiers – called "The Broken Mirror".

Home & read a detective story account of the bestial treatment of prisoners in Alcatraz[436] – which made me feel even worse. I feel helpless, unprotected. This little moratorium seems to have stretched its limit and I have written no long play nor do I have a reliable idea for one – and my eye looks worse and I am unbearably shy and had no luck at sex for several weeks.

So I feel wretched & frightened. more than usual.

Tomorrow I will pack off to St. Pete and the beach – God be merciful. Truly. – En Avant.

*Thursday, 4 December 1941*

Thursday. A.M.

Just now coughed and spit up a bloodstained phlegm – first time since Mexico. Wasn't even interested really.

Okay. Now we pack up and invade St. Pete and brave the terrors of the general delivery. My agent's letters are frightening to me cause I never know when they will pronounce my doom.

Later –

Well, I have arrived in St. Pete and I have a dollar room for the night. Got here in the rain. Fever, headache. Very weak and aching. Lie in my room with a copy of Time.

Audrey's letter contained a checque without comment. She is bored & irritated no doubt.

A sweet letter from Mother enclosing $5.00 check & May Wright[437] address. I think I will be all right when the sun comes out and this fever passes. A fever is optimistic and imaginative and poetic. The poet's best friend is three degrees of fever.

I have cut out coffee & cigarettes last 2 days. will try to keep it up. So long.

438.  "O, for a draught of vintage! That hath been / Cooled a long age in the deep-delvéd earth" ("Ode to a Nightingale," stanza 2).

439.  Whitman's poem is included in his collection *Leaves of Grass*.

ME IMPERTURBE

Me imperturbe, standing at ease in Nature,
Master of all or mistress of all, aplomb in the midst of
    irrational things,
Imbued as they, passive, receptive, silent as they,
Finding my occupation, poverty, notoriety, foibles, crimes,
    less important than I thought,
Me toward the Mexican sea, or in the Mannahatta or the
    Tennessee, or far north or inland,
A river man, or a man of the woods or of any farm-life of
    these States or of the coast, or the lakes of Kanada,
Me wherever my life is lived, O to be self-balanced for
    contingencies,
To confront night, storms, hunger, ridicule, accidents,
    rebuffs, as the trees and animals do.

440.  Williams greatly admired *The Sea Gull*. In a paper Williams wrote at Washington University, "Birth of an Art (Anton Chekhov and the New Theatre)," Williams began his discussion of *The Sea Gull* with humor, but ended with insight.

This like the other major plays of Chekhov is a tragedy of inaction. I will not attempt to give the Russian names of the characters as they are both difficult to spell and pronounce and I have returned the plays to the library. . . .

The essential idea behind this play is the aimless frustration of certain lives: they are like sea-gulls shot down by chance. What happens to them is mainly outside of their own control. Circumstances make them captives. Nina is captured by her hopeless love for Trigorin, who loves the superficial older actress. Masha is captured by her love for Constantine, Constantine by his love for Nina. It is a tangle in which all are helpless victims: no one is really to blame.

The charm of the play is in its haunting atmosphere and the emotional poignance built up by each scene. It has an exquisite unity of color: a sort of nostalgic twilight pervades it from beginning. There is always the atmosphere of late summer evening with fire-flies and the droning music of locusts. What happens has a dream-like quality: yet it is as real as though we ourselves were the tragic protagonists.

Williams would soon attempt to emulate what he admired in Chekhov's play in his own writing, most notably in *The Glass Menagerie*.

Williams' fascination with *The Sea Gull* remained throughout his life. In 1980 the University of British Columbia commissioned him to write an adaptation of *The Sea Gull*. Williams' response was to write *The Notebook of Trigorin*. In his adaptation he made major changes and shifted the focus from Constantine to Trigorin, who in Williams' version is bisexual. Williams linked Trigorin's attachment to Arkadina to Arkadina's threat to blackmail him over his hidden bisexuality.

441.  Williams wrote Paul Bigelow (18 December 1941, Columbia) of his frustration with his work and gave an account of the end of his hitchhiking journey:

Oh how tired I am! I feel a perfect wreck and what is worse, I <u>look</u> it. I put a work-schedule on my wall and stuck to it heroically but with all but fatal results. Play almost ready to mail to Audrey — "Stairs to the Roof" — I put the Lawrence in abeyance as it seemed less likely to interest producers.

Such a business! I took a trip to St. Petersburg on my thumb. Caught the flu or pneumonia or something on the way — arrived there with fever 104° and a racking cough. Check was waiting for me at P.O. but it had not occured to this dashing adventuress that she knew nobody in St. Petersburg who would cash it. Result I was stranded desperately ill on the beach and would doubtless have gone to my reward but for a providential meeting with Wm. Eastman of Cleveland (Kodak people) a wealthy Auntie whom I had met in Taos, who gave me refuge, and got me out of my worst difficulties.

Later.

Williams is lying up in bed wondering whether he is going to die or get better. Head very hot and aching. <u>Mucho calor!</u>

There seems to be a good deal of genial banter about this place a great improvement on The Men's Hotel in Tampa, with its smell.

"O for a vintage cooled a long time in the deep delvéd earth" – Keats wrote that in a fever.438

Sometime late Thursday Night –

Pretty awful! Cardiac neurosis. Splitting head – insomnia even after mebaral. No better tomorrow – Doctor. I am a little relieved now. Oh, how I long for an ice pack, someone to feel my forehead and lift my head to drink a warm, bitter sleeping potion – oblivion can be sweet. O I must change after – be steady & strong – Me Imperturbe! Old Walt439 – Look out for me, will you? It's no use asking Hart Crane or Chekhov – They were too sick themselves. Well, maybe Chekhov. He'd be tender, but Crane – Heaven what nonsense!

I'm raving.

Why can't I write like Chekhov?

I could gouge my good eye out because I can't do something lovely and haunting like "The Sea Gull".440

Yes – raving.

*Monday, 8 December 1941*

Monday A.M.

America entered the war yesterday, against Japan. Dirty business. I knew some boys on the S.S. Oklahoma reported afire in Pearl Harbor.

*Thursday, 18 December 1941*

Thursday –

Been back in Nola. about a week.

Crisis is Approaching in my life.

Completing re-write of "Stairs to the Roof" by forced marches. wearing out my nerves – physical wreck – nearly explode every evening.441

Restless search for sex – fruitless, and tortured.

I look awful – Clothes shabby, eyes bleared.

Too nervous for any social composure. Feel little hope of production for a play. A commendable effort – no more I'm afraid. A frantic little caged beast – <u>Me!</u>

En Avant!

442. Possibly Frank Ford, about whom Williams wrote to Oliver Evans on 13 July 1950 (HRC):
Eloi Bordelon and William Richards, of New Orleans, were in Rome when I left. I think Eloi looks
better than I have ever seen him, he has had some really miraculous skin-treatments or a marvelous
new make-up for the pitted complexion was quite smooth. He told me that Frank Ford — do you
remember him? — has brought out a book of poems. Frank was my best friend in New Orleans.

December 18, 1941

Dear Tom,

Your letter came as a good surprise this morning! I had finally
concluded you had disappeared into anonymity forever so far as I was concerned. And now I think so much time has passed since we exchanged news
and ideas, it's impossible to catch up in one letter or even several. So,
first, if you plan to come east after the holidays, why don't you plan to
stop off here for a long week-end? I have a study now, with an ancient
studio couch in it, that would support your weight. Then we could have a
real visit, and perhaps resurrect our old "literature factory" for a day
or so. Let me know if this would be possible.

Also, can you let me have your exact address in St. Louis — or
wherever you may be — so that I can send on a couple of books? Did you
know I dedicated one to you? That was The Migrants, which I sent to you
c/o the Theatre Guild, asking them to forward it. As I did not hear from
you later, I presume it did not arrive.

Yes also, I'm married, and both Betty and I are flourishing as
well as one might expect, considering the vacuum one must live in here in
Ithaca. (A visit from you would be a considerable event!)

Otherwise, there must be all kinds of news, but I'm unable to
put my finger on it at the moment. Try to get here during or after our
holidays. I shall be free from classes from now until January 5; could you
get here during that period? And send me your address now — not three years
from day after tomorrow.

And Merry Christmas to yourself and anyone else in St. Louis who
deserves one.

As ever,

Clark

Why don't you give my parents a ring? My mother would be immensely cheered
if you'd drop in and say hello, and she'd love a chance to give you a huge

meal "in the old style". She was here late this fall, and kept asking
about you and wishing you had come out when you were there before.

Excerpts of a letter to Williams from Clark Mills

*Friday, 19 December 1941*

Friday –

A lover tonight. Picked up in Mack's bar. Nice not very goodlooking but pleasant exercise. Gay.

It is about 3:30 A.M. Heart pounding so I can't sleep. The old ticker has been taking a beating lately. Too much coffee. I suppose I am digging myself a grave. But what else would I do? – Today very bitter – play seemed bad. Only the athletic club pulls me thru these days – the hot shower the swim – the quiet, sedative reading room. What will it come to? Yes, the crisis is surely approaching I could probably go on skidding downhill quite a ways – but I am more likely to improve my fortune or crack up.

O how sleepy – Just taken a mebaral – peace except for heart. O how sweet peace is. I am not afraid of death anymore. I am clean and white like an old bone. There is nothing left. Yes. I am purified in a way.


*Saturday, 20 December 1941*

Saturday –

Morning again – Bright warm. Singing Sam The Coca-cola Man sings Home Sweet Home & Miss Mamie argues loudly with her handyman – My heart is quiet again but I dress and go out to drink more coffee because I am too tired to work without it. The one-legged man passes along the gallery on his crutches. All he has in his life is his radio. He swings along with energy. He is ~~happier~~ less miserable than I am.


*Sunday, 21 December 1941*

Sunday Night

Oh last night I was drunk and I kissed Otto and Jerry – the lovely, the young – I charmed them with my rare gaiety and wit – so seldom it flowers but when it does it is fine.

They gave me their lips freely, warmly – and we left them alone with each other to make love. Till 6 A.M. I tagged along with an attractive soldier but finally gave him up as he fell into the clutches of a female whore. Returned home and found Frank[442] had collected an attractive blond youth. He slept between us and the nightingales chirped a little. But I was judicious & respected F's priority tonight.

hungry – broke.

Heart <u>bad</u> – I think we draw near the close. So? – Byebye.

I talk about extinction. But do I believe it? Am I not rather inclined to think some startling good fortune is coming?

10 –

443.   "The day."

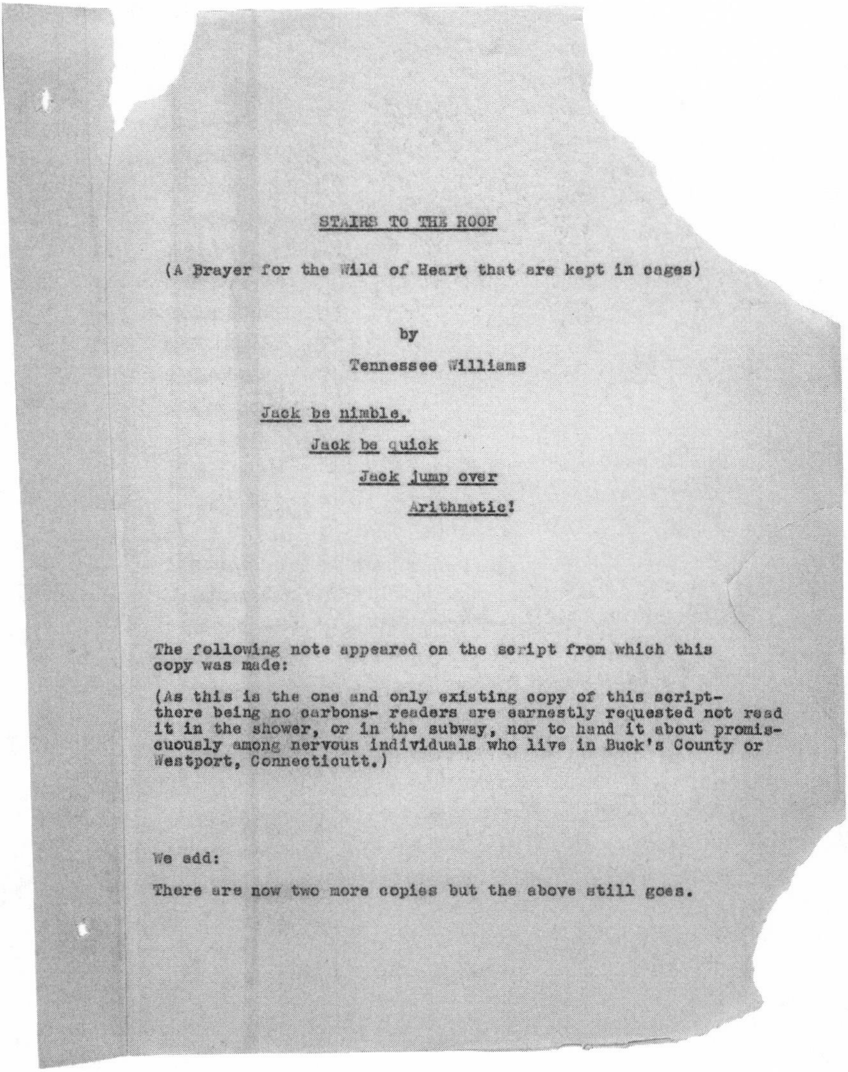

STAIRS TO THE ROOF

(A Prayer for the Wild of Heart that are kept in cages)

by

Tennessee Williams

Jack be nimble,

Jack be quick

Jack jump over

Arithmetic!

The following note appeared on the script from which this
copy was made:

(As this is the one and only existing copy of this script—
there being no carbons— readers are earnestly requested not read
it in the shower, or in the subway, nor to hand it about promis-
cuously among nervous individuals who live in Buck's County or
Westport, Connecticutt.)

We add:

There are now two more copies but the above still goes.

*Monday, 22 December 1941*

Monday – Xmas week

  Well, no letter from Audrey to answer my wire for check. Is this "<u>der tag</u>"?443
Pawned a rented typewriter for which indiscretion I could undoubtedly land in
the clinker. Read over "Stairs". Not so bad after all. Shines very brightly in
places. It is all I really have to say. Said about as well as I am able to say it right
now. In play form. Still I doubt that it would succeed on stage. I have on my
boots & red flannel shirt and prepare to face the antagonist whomsoever he be.

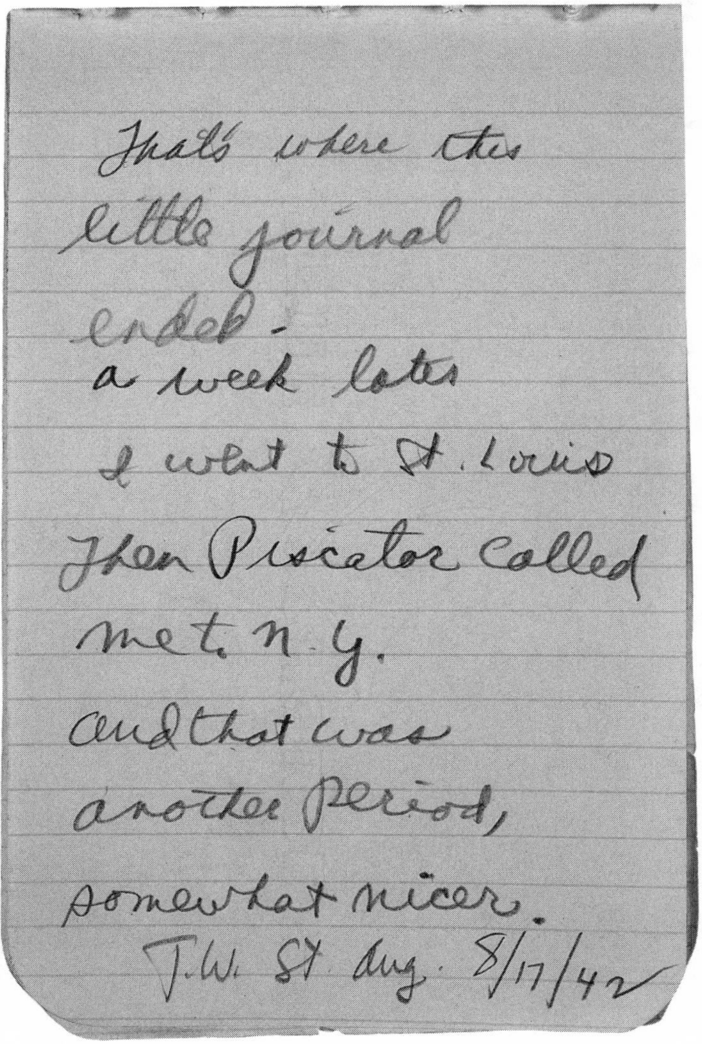

That's where this
little journal
ended.
a week later
I went to St. Louis
Then Piscator called
me to n. y.
and that was
another period,
somewhat nicer.
T.W. St Aug. 8/17/42

444. Williams wrote to Paul Bigelow (postmarked 5 January 1942, Columbia): "I think my next project will be a group of about seven more or less associated stories of Bohemian life in the <u>Vieux</u> <u>Carre</u> ending on December 7, 1941. Our <u>fin</u> <u>du</u> <u>monde</u>, as everyone feels too distinctly." Poems that Williams wrote during this period include "I Have Concluded Latterly," "Polly's Inn," and "Iron is the Winter."

Notebook Williams began in January 1942

*New York Period: The Fifth.*
*(Desperate circumstances*
*well-sustained)*
*8/17/42*

*Monday, 5 January 1942*

Monday – Jan. 5, 1942

So I begin a new journal – appropriately in the house of my parents, always a place to start from. and commence a new phase.

I am not well – a bad chest cold. A few days ago I surprised myself by spitting out a good quantity of blood.

Weakness. occasional vertigo. sometimes an overactive heart my complaints. I do not pay any more attention than is necessary. I write nearly every day. I have completed "Stairs to the roof" – I now wish to do a complete set of new stories and new poems.444

Hiccoughs! Gracious!

I am too tired to continue at present.


*Tuesday, 6 January 1942*

Tuesday – I have just acquired this new eversharp pencil.

It is 11:15 P.M. I am reading the opening pages of Proust in a book I inadvertently confiscated from the library of the University of Iowa. It is one of 3 books I own. My collected letters of D.H. Lawrence was acquired in the same way, but deliberately from the public library in New Orleans. Hart Crane was given me to prevent me from stealing it "from an idiot".

Why this discussion of my library?

I am frightened thinking of the changes or rather the increased vicissitudes the war may create in my life. I suppose if it did not affect me personally my feelings about it would be only abstractly regretful. Things have to impinge on my own life to matter to me very much. Is it that way with most people? Yes. I am sure that it is.

Well, I have been here about a week – no swimming, just sitting around, writing, eating, going to movies, relaxing in the effortless matrix of "home" created by Grand and Mother and grandfather. Bad for my figure, not much good for my soul. When have I ever done anything for the benefit of my soul? Horse shit.

Well, I must get moving. Where? Undecided as never before. A letter from Audrey will probably precipitate a decision. Macon? New York? Back to New Orleans? Or even, Florida – Mexico? Mexico City would be lovely, wish it were possible.

No, I feel no desire to participate in war work.

445.  First line of *Swann's Way*.

446.  After the deaths of his parents in 1903 and 1905, Marcel Proust withdrew increasingly from life and spent much of his time in his room, which he had soundproofed with cork, on the Boulevard Haussmann.

447.  Erwin Piscator (1893–1966) was a German theatrical director and producer who, with Bertolt Brecht, was the foremost exponent of the epic theatre, a genre that emphasized the sociopolitical aspect over the emotional or aesthetic. Piscator was noted for rearranging and altering texts of plays to suit his own theories. In his early work, he made use of expressionist techniques and employed film and animated cartoons to emphasize aspects of the play. In 1933 Piscator moved to New York to become director of the Dramatic Workshop of the New School for Social Research.
      On 19 November 1941 (HRC), Audrey Wood wrote to Williams:
      You will be amused to know I have the Dramatic Workshop at the New School interested in producing "THE BATTLE OF ANGELS". Piscator is going to have a talk with me and when he does I'll let you know more about this.
      A few days later Williams responded that he was mailing the latest changes in *Battle of Angels* to Wood for Piscator. Williams added ([24] November 1941, HRC): "I have heard that Piscator intends to put his actors on flying trapezes in his next production. (Joke)."
      Two months later, on 25 January, the *New York Herald Tribune* noted:
      Tennessee Williams, author of "Battle of Angels," has arrived from St. Louis to work on script revisions with Erwin Piscator. . . . Mr. Piscator is considering a Studio Theatre production of the revised version.
      Williams' revisions did not suit Piscator and the production was cancelled. Williams described the stalemate in letters to his mother and Audrey Wood. To his mother he wrote (circa mid-February 1942, HTC):
      Mr. Piscator is a terribly dictatorial German, completely impractical, and is trying to force me to turn the play into a dry, didactic sermon on social injustice, representing the South as a fascist state. To comply with his demands will destroy the poetic quality of the play. Right now we are deadlocked. . . . Either he will give in or the production will have to be called off. I am going out to his country place again tonight for another "battle".
      Williams later recalled the visit to Audrey Wood in a letter received 30 July 1942 (HRC):
      I arrived at this palatial estate on the Hudson, admitted by a Prussian butler. After waiting half an hour I was conducted to his bedroom. He was slightly indisposed with a cold. He was lying up in bed with his dinner tray. Over the bed was a fur robe — I believe it was mink — and he was wearing peach-colored silk pyjamas. He looked at me mournfully and said, "Mr. Williams, you have written a Fascist play — all of your characters are selfishly pursuing their little personal ends and aims in life with a ruthless disregard for the wrongs and sufferings of the world about them."

448.  Williams had undergone an operation on his left eye on 22 January 1941 for the removal of a cataract. In the 1940s the standard procedure for treating cataracts was to insert a needle in the eye to puncture the lens and break it up. A hollow needle with a syringe was inserted to withdraw the broken pieces of the lens. The procedure was inexact and often had to be performed multiple times. The second operation took place on 9 February.

449.  No manuscript by this title is known to exist, but in the one-act play "27 Wagons Full of Cotton" Jake describes his wife, Flora, as "A woman not large but tremendous" (scene 2). If Williams was beginning to work on the dramatization of the short story, he would not mention it again until 23 March 1943.

O, I ~~might~~ would be glad to be a Florence Nightingale if I could but —
incompetent and lazy me. Thank <u>god</u> I don't have to go to camp or fight.

Proust writes: "For a long time I used to go to bed early."[445]

Dear selfish, shameless, heroic, honest sissy – Proust.

We would have understood each other, my dear. How we might have
"dished" the world in that cork-lined room of yours.[446] ~~I wonder if you turned
over and would I—! heavens!~~

<u>C'est assez!</u> Good night.

<u>Later</u>

Proust bores me tonight – I find myself, "No, it isn't quite that involved,
dear boy, at least not quite that involuted. The involvement is not so subject to
analysis as you make it. A little more impressionism, please!"

*Monday, 12 January 1942*

Monday – Jan. 12 –

Again – Providence!

A telegram from Erwin Piscator[447] – summons to N.Y. – the day before I
was to have my second eye operation.[448] O let us be hopeful! What is it? A play
production? Too lovely to believe – almost. After this hiatus.

But I am a jerk. I write a great deal of drivel which I think is good – till
afterwards. I refer to "A Woman Not Large but Tremendous"[449] – and the
preceding filth in this journal. I do not want to keep <u>that</u> kind of a journal.

Yes. Happiness. Hope. Good night. (Love? The night after tomorrow night?)

I'm betting on it, baby!

Erwin Piscator

450. In *Memoirs* Williams recalled the disillusionment:

> During that period I was very briefly employed at a bistro called The Beggar's Bar, owned by a fantastic refugee from Nazi Germany named Valesca Gert.
>
> She was a dance-mime, and that is by no means all. I was working only for tips. She was licensed to serve just beer but she stretched the license a bit to include setups. There was food in the nature of knackwurst and sauerkraut. There was a singer who was either a male or female transvestite, I've never known which, and there was always and forever the incomparable Valesca.
>
> At times I supplemented my tips as a waiter by giving recitals of my light verse.
>
> The verse was pretty raw for those days and I became something of a draw. And tips were sizable.
>
> One night the Madam called the waiters together and announced a change of policy.
>
> She said that the waiters (there were three of us) had to pool their tips and then split them with the management, meaning herself.
>
> On this particular evening I had a number of close friends and acquaintances in the bar, among them the abstract painter. He was present when Valesca announced her new policy, just after closing time, in the kitchen of The Beggar's Bar.
>
> I told the lady that I had absolutely no intention whatsoever of pooling my tips with the other waiters and having it split with the management. The abstract painter was attracted to the kitchen by this noisy confrontation. Near the kitchen entrance there was a crate of quart soda bottles and as soon as he entered he began to hurl these bottles at the celebrated dance-mime. At least a dozen bottles were hurled at the lady before one of them struck her. The paddy wagon and an ambulance were summoned, the lady received several stitches in her scalp, and, needless to say, I was out of a job at that particular night spot. (p. 71)

451. On 15 February 1942 more than 130,000 troops in Singapore under British command surrendered to the Japanese. American newspapers called this defeat the darkest moment of the war to date and saw it as a decisive blow in the southwest Pacific.

452. Williams' generalization meaning people in Greenwich Village and homosexuals.

453. Williams was staying with Fritz Bultman in his apartment in Greenwich Village at 319 West 11th Street.

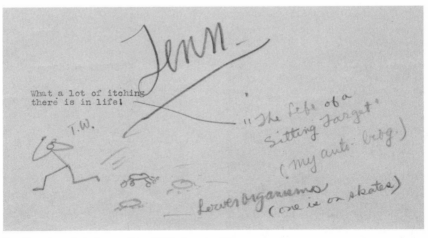

Doodle at the end of a letter to Donald Windham (24 February 1942)

*Sunday, 15 February 1942*

Feb. 15 or ?

New York – Greenwich Village –

What disillusionment waited for me here![450] – But we won't go into that.

Well, I bore up bravely and acted fairly sensibly I believe. So now we live for a while on our last remittance which will melt like snow in the coming spring.

Then? – Ah, <u>then</u> – – – –

I try to write today but I am suddenly quite dead and disgusted – so I go back to bed.

Singapore has fallen.[451]

Everyone in our little group[452] is cynical and hopeless and without an ounce of patriotic feeling.

We expect an air raid soon. We expect social disaster.

We go on with our little lives. We are kind to each other mostly. Sometimes we are hurt and cruel.

I do not write home – weariness, negligence.

Only once in a while I feel very desperate but even then I know how to soothe myself.

Who will be the strong ones? In this time?

The ruthless fighters?

No, I mean intellectually. Can't write – too tired. Excuse please,

I am not dead yet. I am not yet finished. My will is to live, to survive. To go on gathering the nights and the days –

I am temporarily "drugged out", battered, exhausted.

But I have the will to continue creation; the need to say more and clearer and more intensely. If only they would let me do it my way. No body loves another one's powers of creation enough to leave it alone.

When I made love to the young transient "with eyes like fjords" I seemed to be possessing distance and flight – space – freedom.

Now that I have gone swimming my body is quiet and cool and clean. I can sit still – my blood is not disturbing.

Oh it is good.

Fritzi[453] is tortured with waiting for a lover. I am not waiting for anyone and that may be better. Or worse.

F. reads two beautiful passages from Eliot and Crane –

I will soon go out –

454. No complete manuscript of "The Spinning Song" is known to have survived. A number of fragments of different drafts, some with the alternative title "The Paper Lantern," however, exist. The fragments appear to be of two types, one more closely linked to *The Glass Menagerie*, the other to *A Streetcar Named Desire*. The fragments relating to *The Glass Menagerie* include one in which a woman named Blanche lives with her two children on a plantation named Belle-reve. She is not compatible with her husband, who lives in New Orleans. In another fragment, titled "The Paper Lantern, A Dance Play for Martha Graham," direct references to Rose are found. A young girl, Ariadne, is diagnosed with dementia praecox, and her mother discusses with the doctor whether or not the young girl can stay at their plantation, Belle Reve.

455. In the early 1940s Eric Kocher (1912–99) was studying at the Yale School of Drama and the New School for Social Research. After serving in World War II, he made his career in the Foreign Service but continued his interest in drama and won several awards in the late 1950s for his plays.

Fritz Bultman, *New York Post*, 1939. Oil and paper on paper, 22 x 16 in.

*Wednesday, 25 February 1942*

Feb. 25 –

I have just finished writing "The Spinning Song"[454] a play suggested by my sister's tragedy –

The end is good. It is something to work on. Hard.

Now I relax and smoke and listen to the radio –

war bulletins and Cuban rhumbas.

Later – go swimming – rest and purify the body and soothe the nerves.

Then – cruising? – Nearly always seems the only thing to do.

Eric[455] and I discussed it last night and agreed it was the result of ennui. Nothing else to do.

Evening is the normal adult's time for home – the family.

For us it is the time to search for something to satisfy that empty space that home fills in the normal adult's life.

It isn't so bad, really.

Usually we go home with nothing.

Now and then we succeed.

Night before last a ~~love affair~~ in the shower ~~quick animal rutting~~ – over – off – goodbye. Sleep.

I am spending my last ten dollars.

What then?

Money from home?

Orders to return home?

No – won't do it.

Oh – Just remembered that boy in the neighborhood.

Shall I go see him? Why not. We used to chi-chi – last winter before the Boston debacle.

I wanted him badly but he played cagey.

I begin to see a little out of my left eye. – Amusing.

The world reappearing slowly before a blind eye.

What a world!

Why see it, darling?

Yeah, but I <u>want</u> to, though.

I must be able to be a post-war artist.

Keep awake – alive – New.

Perform the paradox of being hard and yet soft.

Survive without calcification of the tender membranes.

Be a poet. Be alive.

So long. – 10.

456. Eddie Dowling (1894–1976) was an American producer, playwright, songwriter, director, and actor. Williams would have been keenly aware of Dowling's success. He co-produced with the Theatre Guild and played the lead opposite Julie Haydon in Saroyan's *The Time of Your Life* (1939), which won both a Pulitzer Prize and a New York Drama Critics' Circle Award. Dowling would go on to co-produce and co-direct the Chicago and New York premieres of *The Glass Menagerie*.

457. "There'll be Bluebirds over the White Cliffs of Dover" was the popular song written by Nat Burton and Walter Kent. Connie Boswell (1907–76), a New Orleans native, rose to fame with her sisters in a group well known for singing rhythmic dance songs and jazz pieces.

   Interestingly Williams had used the image of the white cliffs of Dover in his one-act play "The Lady of Larkspur Lotion" written in October 1941. After the Writer and Mrs. Hardwicke-Moore have been told by their landlady that they must leave the next day, the Writer asks Mrs. Hardwicke-Moore about her imaginary Brazilian rubber plantation:

   WRITER: And the windows — I suppose they commanded a very lovely view!
   MRS. HARDWICKE-MOORE: Indescribably lovely!
   WRITER: How far was it from the Mediterranean?
   MRS. HARDWICKE-MOORE: (*dimly*) The Mediterranean? Only a mile or two!
   WRITER: On a very clear morning I daresay it was possible to distinguish the white chalk cliffs of Dover? . . . Across the channel?
   MRS. HARDWICKE-MOORE: Yes — in very clear weather it *was*. (*The* WRITER *silently passes her a pint bottle of whisky.*) Thank you, Mr. — ?
   WRITER: Chekhov! Anton Pavlovitch Chekhov!

458. "Dos Ranchos, or The Purification," as Williams titled the play in its first published form, is the story of the trial of a Rancher who had murdered his wife, Elena, for having an incestuous relationship with her brother, Rosalio. During the trial Rosalio stabs himself, and the play ends with the Rancher walking out into the rain to take his own life with the silver knife he is wearing. Williams later simplified the title to "The Purification."

459. Ramon Naya, pseudonym for Enrique Gasque-Molina (1912–?), won the $500 first prize for "Mexican Mural" in the Group Theatre Contest of 1939 in which Williams won a $100 special award for three of his "American Blues." "Mexican Mural" is comprised of four scenes ("panels") about people in the town of Vera Cruz who are oppressed by a despot. The first panel portrays two young lovers, Didi and Lalo; the second, a poor peasant woman, Celestina, whose young daughter dies; the third, the murder of Lalo by the despot's "Gold Shirts"; and the fourth, the daughter of the despot, who breaks away from her evil father and is confronted by Didi and Celestina. Interestingly, Williams titled a draft of a long poem "New Mexican Mural: Dos Ranchos" (dated July 1940), which he developed into the play "Dos Ranchos, or The Purification."

   On 24 April 1943 (SMU), Williams would write Horton Foote:
   [Naya] is like a box of roses in the luminous dark and ought to be reclaimed from that munitions plant. I cannot believe that he is through with the theatre. At any rate, I don't think the theatre is through with him. There is a primitive power in his writing that immediate criticism cannot destroy. He may be the Rimbaud of American drama.

*Monday, 2 March 1942*

March 2 –
    Night. rain.
    Fall and half a winter in New Orleans.
    Half a winter and probably a spring in New York.
    Was flat busted when a little money from Mother arrived today.
    I wrote an appeal to Dramatist Guild for a loan.
    Letter to Eddie Dowling[456] pleading for one-act prod.
    Saw Piscator.
    Eric, Fritz and I – all in good spirits at supper.
    Swam.
    A day disappears.
    "Spinning Song" about ready to start 2nd draft.
    I would like to get away and freshen myself for that job.
    If money comes I will – the beach! – <u>Bon</u> <u>nuit</u>

*Monday, 16 March 1942*

March 16 –
    Connie Boswell singing about the blue birds over the white Cliffs of Dover.[457]
    I with a capital of six pennies have just taken a hot shower to quiet my nerves,
agitated by coffee on an empty stomach.
    There is something in the mailbox but Fritz has the key.
    I do not feel like recapitulating the situation which remains about the same.
    I have written a verse play <u>Dos Ranchos</u>.[458]
    Outcome of this period is embarrassingly obscure but I do not seem to worry
except when I'm actually penniless and hungry.
    ~~Anti-so~~ Old neurosis which makes company a strain reappeared last week.
    I want to leave New York and rest in a strange place & prepare for new good
work.
    Broke the right lens of my glasses a few days ago.
    To somewhat balance the ledger, a black crevice has appeared in my cataract,
and the vision is definitely clearing –
    a third operation will probably be needed.
    Oh, how I hope I can manage [*page missing*]

produced. I wrote Ramon Naya[459] a gushy letter of felicitations which he has so
far ignored. He is in personality a shallow queen – that is, on first acquaintance.
Must actually be a great deal more. And of course he is a genuine artist of
unusual quality.
    Oh, I am troubled about this stupid neurosis. How to combat these fears?
Always they wear themselves out sooner or later – but they can return again at

460. Donald Windham had begun a dramatization of the D. H. Lawrence short story "You Touched Me." He had shared his idea with Williams, who had volunteered to collaborate. During the spring of 1942, Williams and Windham worked "furiously," first in Windham's apartment on Leroy Street and then, after he had moved, in his room at the West 63rd Street YMCA. By mid-May they had delivered a draft to Audrey Wood.

461. After leaving Fritz Bultman's apartment, Williams was invited to stay with the songwriter Carley Mills (1897–1962), fourteen years Williams' senior, in his penthouse apartment at 43 East 50th Street. For Williams it did not turn out to be a suitable arrangement, as he intimated in a letter to Paul Bigelow (postmarked 15 May 1942, Columbia): "There are too many restrictions in my present situation and I was never one to brook very many restrictions."

According to Windham, Carley Mills wrote the songs "So Nobody Cares" and "If I Cared a Little Bit Less" for Williams.

462. *You Touched Me!* is a romantic comedy in three acts suggested by D. H. Lawrence's short story in which an elderly captain lives at home with his two unmarried daughters. When the captain's adopted son returns home, the captain forces his elder daughter to choose between marrying her stepbrother or losing her inheritance. After much resistance, she agrees to the marriage.

While Williams and Windham kept much of the basic structure of Lawrence's story, they omitted the second daughter and gave the captain a sister, Emmie. As can be inferred from the "Story of the Play," they changed the tone significantly and gave prominence to the captain's sister:

"You Touched Me" is . . . about the final triumph of a bibulous old former sea captain [Rockley] over the domination of himself, his daughter [Matilda], and his adopted son [Hadrian], by a self-righteous and mentally sadistic spinster sister [Emmie]. Although the home in which she lived and ruled and the income on which she thrived in piety and pretension were her brother's, the unwed female had got the hearty buckeroo under her thumb after he had gone on a binge in the Caribbean, foundered his ship, and suffered the dishonor of losing his skipper's certificate. Thereafter, of course, he was hers to pity, suffer martyrdom for, take care of and — keep drunk, by constantly telling him what a disgraceful sot he was.

The return, on a brief furlough, of the waif the skipper had brought up, revives in the old boy a will to fight for his own survival as a free individual. His chance comes when he senses that a deep love has sprung up between his foster-son and his daughter — a love thwarted, for pecuniary as well as more obscure reasons, by the girl's spinster aunt, who has made an introvert out of the girl. The skipper's greatest difficulty lies in overcoming the fears and reticences that have been instilled in the boy and the girl by his sister.

In addition to the above mentioned changes Williams and Windham added personalized elements such as including the chaste character of the Reverend Guildford Melton, named after Windham's former lover, and having Matilda show Hadrian a poem she had written with the same opening lines as one Williams had written in 1941: "How like a caravan my heart / across the desert moved toward yours."

Sketches of Kip Kiernan, Fritz Bultman, and Joe Hazan in Williams' notebook

any time, and usually they choose the least convenient. I lie in bed – unable to sleep. It is only about 12:30. and I got up at 1:00 P.M.

Tomorrow? Work with Donnie.460 But my nervousness discolors the prospect of leaving the apartment for any purpose.

I am a child of adversity but <u>no</u> – I have adverse circumstances to contend with. However my inexhaustible endurance, my tenacity my certain sort of courage – my gift for evasion – are not all these, as well as my surprising turns of fortune at the last ditch, plenty to oppose adversities with?

Always the outlook appears to be finally tragic – but clears. Clears as we go. – Or darkens. Well – at any rate it changes.

En Avant! <u>Manana es otro dio! Hasta Manana!</u>

Q: who are you, man? A: I am man.


*Sunday, 29 March 1942*

Sunday – March 29 –

An inner equanimity of spirit sees me through and the neurosis thins out dissipates itself.

Today – I am dull but relatively at ease. Could not do any good writing.

Last night the apt. was filled with merchant marines – this a.m. F.'s electric razor was missing, which is <u>not</u> a <u>non sequiter.</u>


*Monday, 30 March 1942*

Monday March 30

F. asked me to get out of the apt. last night, on account of "constantly disregarding his wishes" – precipitated, no doubt, by the loss of the razor. Holds me responsible for it.

Don't know where I shall go. Very tired. I have $2.00.

End of March.

April??? – <u>En Avant</u>!!


*Sunday, 26 April 1942*

~~Tuesd~~ Sunday 1 A.M. April 26 –

Yes – <u>En Avant</u>, and always <u>En Avant</u> and so we come to the end of another journal. The situation above resolved itself with my installation in a penthouse with Carley461 who is kinder to me than most anyone before. I work on the comedy462 with Don and I eat well and regularly, I swim and live selfishly and cynically as a wise old alley cat. Integrity – I wonder. I keep a sort of it still: my own brand. I am not a snob and I can feel things deeply. – En Avant.

463.    Williams had traveled to Macon, Georgia, to spend the summer with Paul Bigelow. Prior to coming he had written Bigelow (postmarked 5 June 1942, Columbia):

> Is there any swimming in Macon — a bicycle available? I have already been born, christened, married and divorced informally too many times so prefer not to be caught up in that cycle of events which occupy the Macon calender, as you say — but only want peace and quiet and a single bed for a while. (I said for a <u>while</u>.)

464.    Andrew Lyndon (1918–89) grew up in Macon and became a friend and lover of Williams' during the summer of 1942. Williams described him in a letter to Windham ([14 June 1942], Yale) as "a charming little creature — breast of milkfed chicken!" In another letter to Windham ([24 June 1942], Yale), Williams wrote: "Andrew still has a crew hair-cut and I regard him as being extraordinarily beautiful and after a long string of purely objective relations, it's good for me to excercise a capacity for tender feelings."

After the summer of 1942, Lyndon went into service and after the war went to New York and enrolled in the New School with ambitions of becoming a writer. Later he was the companion of the photographer Harold Halma and a close friend of Truman Capote's. Williams and Lyndon remained friends. Their correspondence continued well into the 1970s, and Williams wrote several letters to Lyndon when he was committed by his brother to Barnes Hospital. Lyndon and Williams traveled to Tangier together in 1975–76. Later in his life Lyndon returned to Macon, where he died.

465.    Holt Gewinner (1917–96) was a friend from Macon. Jordan Massee described him as having very white freckled skin and bright red hair (interview with Margaret Bradham Thornton). During the summer of 1942, he worked as a news announcer for a radio station. In a letter to Windham ([24 June 1942], Yale), Williams wrote:

> Then there is Holt Gewinner — I wonder if you know him? He is my connection with the gay-mad world. He has the most fantastic house, decorated by himself. It is the maddest Victorian decoration with yellow silk parasols for lamps and gilt and scarlet framed mirrors for tables — that sort of thing — he calls it "Club Rococco".

Gewinner married Billie Fowler, "the brightest girl in our Macon circle." He went on to work in theatre, radio, and television in Macon and Atlanta. Williams would set his novella "The Knightly Quest" in the town of Gewinner and name the main character Gewinner Pearce.

Ramon Naya in his Santa Fe studio

*Monday, 27 April 1942*

Monday – April 27 –

Tortured by an episode involving 3, including me – I the one who went alone because of a friend's lack of feeling. How curiously intense such hurts can be! I usually will give up something before I will inflict that kind of thing on a friend. Well – <u>En Avant.</u>

*The Macon Period*

*Sunday, 14 June 1942*

Sunday.

Been here a week and one day. I guess it's what I wanted.[463]

Quiet. Easy.

A new problem came up where I should have found pleasure.

As for work – I've done some good scenes (comedy) in "You Touched Me!"

As for people – the pleasure – problem is A.L.[464]

Then there is H.G.[465]

but it is all shadowed now by the new neurosis.

the old conflict.

desire Vs. fear.

Tonight I went to Holt's –

white skin. Tantalizing.

A strange evening

ended with a feeling of emptiness.

I never had quite this before.

Andrew Lyndon

466.  The lines would be amended and included in "The Marvelous Children" published in *Five Young American Poets* (1944).

In his foreword to the play *Sweet Bird of Youth* (first published in the *New York Times*, 8 March 1959), Williams explained that these lines from "The Marvelous Children" were a description of writer's block:

I think no more than a week after I started writing I ran into the first block. It's hard to describe it in a way that will be understandable to anyone who is not a neurotic. I will try. All my life I have been haunted by the obsession that to desire a thing or to love a thing intensely is to place yourself in a vulnerable position, to be a possible, if not a probable, loser of what you most want. Let's leave it like that. That block has always been there and always will be, and my chance of getting, or achieving, anything that I long for will always be gravely reduced by the interminable existence of that block.

467.  Ruth Grace was a friend of Jordan Massee's and an excellent pianist. During the summer of 1942 they would occasionally go to her parents' house to listen to dance and classical music.

468.  Jack (John Griffith) London (1876–1916), the prolific novelist whose early life included adventures as a sailor, hobo, seal hunter, political activist, and Klondike gold hunter. *The Call of the Wild* (1903) established his reputation, and he went on to publish a number of successful and popular novels. Suffering from uremia by the age of forty, London hastened his death with an overdose of morphine.

469.  *Burning Daylight* (1910), a best-selling novel by London, is the saga of an entrepreneur nicknamed Burning Daylight who becomes enormously rich in the Alaskan gold rush. He loses his fortune on Wall Street, becomes a scoundrel, and then falls in love with a good woman who turns his life around.

Notebook Williams began in June 1942

*Monday, 15 June 1942*

Monday

I demand of life some violence even when I run to peace. Is it the need of violence that I am the fugitive of? Then there is the block: the invented phantom adversary always where desire is.

"He, the demon,
sought to block their progress,
set up barricades
of gold and purple tinfoil
labelled Fear
which they leapt over lightly
tossing backwards everlasting
marbles"[466]

The day is hot and bright – I wake up cross and plagued. I receive a letter from Carley with a check for ten dollars. Kindness. Also Mother's letter. She is thankful that my brother will be out of the army for 18 mos. attending an officer's training school at Harvard. My heart is bumpy so I do not work. Paul is sharp and irritable, probably because, out of ennui, I went to Holt's house last night. The sexual neurosis continues to occupy the center of my emotional stage and I wonder if this recent invention will not be a fairly perennial one. – It blocks the one violence open. – No, I must meet it and be the master, it challenges the manhood in me.

An empty day – I go to the library and swim. I come home to find Andrew – cool and remote and gossipy. Paul still cross. I write in this journal and wait for supper.

Tomorrow will be better. We swim with "Texas" and in the evening go with Andrew to hear music at Ruth's.[467]

This is all what I wanted (barring the neurosis – but then there is always the blue devils in one form or another – because I suppose I am more or less a divided being – one who lives at #1 ~~Hell Road, in~~ Brimstone Drive in Perdition – Shit! I am being silly.

Let us not complain of the bed we prepared for ourselves. They say if you smile it improves your disposition.

Later – I lie on a couch in the hall and the great trees throw the wind through the windows like rushes of cool water. I read about Jack London.[468] A hot and violent man, beautiful in his youth and his power, who wrote the brawling objective life of a young America. Not my kind but I like him. Paul says there are still those who knew him, in the Biblical sense, living on the West Coast – that he was "trade" for "everybody". I've read very little of his – Burning Daylight[469] I read while [*page missing*]

470.  Williams began drafting the poem at the back of his journal.

Recreation Park, Macon

*Wednesday, 17 June 1942*

Wed –

    I wake at 9:30 – bright.

    the peculiar blue devils occupy my waking fancy – Paul is up – suggests we go have coffee – against my prudent judgement, I will.

Later – I wrote a little today. It was good enough but no true liberation. All of my actions these past few days – since coming to Macon – have been cramped and conscious – why? – I see a terrifying, narrow vista of time like this – no real escape anywhere; effort and endurance – thirst of the body and of the heart that I cannot slake any longer. Am I beginning to walk across a long desert under a merciless sun? – If I am become my enemy at last – my own relentless antagonist – what is the use? – No. I know that finally death will seem the only complete, undivided thing left. And I will take it. It will be forced on me. Oh, no, I can't make peace. I can't accept a little or nothing. I will struggle and lunge which may only tighten the bonds. I won't ever make a good captive. No, I won't make a good end of it, either. I guess what I will do is drive beyond safety – till I smash. – Cleanly and completely the only hope.

*Thursday, 18 June 1942*

Thursday Eve. –

    Wrote a new poem of no special importance – "Speech"[470] – Went swimming – Bought & read "Time". The narrow vista remains, I must be cautious. Exercise my gift for evasion.

Lakeside Park, Macon

471.    Andrew Lyndon.

472.    Lyle Talbot (1902–96) was a veteran character actor who had a long career in film and television. Handsome, with a stolid manner, he appeared in more than 150 films, ranging from romantic comedies to westerns and gangster movies. In 1942, he starred in the film *They Raid by Night*, a story of a trio of highly trained World War II soldiers who are sent to rescue an officer being held prisoner in Nazi-occupied Norway.

473.    During this period Williams was working on several humorous scenes in *You Touched Me!*, two involving the insertion of a fox incident, borrowed from the D. H. Lawrence story "The Fox," and the third involving the addition of the Reverend Guildford Melton's description of his preference for a marriage of only "spiritual companionship." In a letter to Windham a week before this entry ([14 June 1942], Yale), Williams identified the genesis for his idea:

> I wish you would read a story called "The Fox" in a D.H. Lawrence volume of short novels called "The Captain's Doll". It is basically the same story as ours, the two women and man triangle — only these two women are not sisters but out and out "Lesbos" and the boy kills the rival one by chopping a tree down to fall on her. And the symbol of a fox is used very effectively — the boy is like a fox raiding a hen-coop. Bigelow says it is like me assaulting these little southern chickens — but that is beside the point. At any rate, it has some stuff in it we can use in the play, notably the fox — I don't know just how to use it yet but I think we can.

Ten days later Williams wrote Windham ([24 June 1942], Yale):

> I have written the fox into the play. His first attack comes the night of the touching and it is Emmie's wild shots that bring Mathilda downstairs, in negligee — after that she enters the study and touches Hadrian. Emmie always misses the fox and kills a rooster. The second attack comes while they are waiting for the police in the parlor. While Emmie's out to shoot the fox, Hadrian wins over Mathilda with an embrace — once again Emmie misses the fox and at the close of the scene the father ends with the dead rooster, the pride of the hen-yard and announces that all the hens are now widows. — I read Paul the first few scenes and he thought the play "excellent" and we laughed our heads off at the tea-scene which now contains a passage in which the Minister obliquely suggests a purely sexless marriage to Emmie, just before the Father bursts out.

474.    Holt Gewinner.

Ruth Grace                                          Holt Gewinner

<u>Tonight</u> I may call Holt. Called everybody I knew – out. Walked a good ways with Paul feel fairly quiet – a storm is coming up to cool things off. Tomorrow I swim at the lake with A.[471] – Mailed letter to Carley – To bed – will try sleeping in hall.

<u>Later</u> – Just now woke up with nightmares – the vampire dream, this time about Paul – a frightful thing – also sex and Lyle Talbot,[472] of all things – the scene was the exact hall in which I was sleeping.

*Sunday, 21 June 1942*

<u>Sunday</u> –
  hot – furiously –
  I try to work on the play.
  One little 2-page fragment of pretty obvious humor about the only result.[473]
  Ennui and no vitality.
  I quit –
  Had better lay off for several days.
  What shall I do? Call A? I'm afraid A's lost.
  The swim Saturday did nothing to help.
  I'm definitely not in one of my successful periods right now.
  Looks like the allied position.

*Friday, 26 June 1942*

<u>Friday</u>
  Okay again.
  Writing really good scenes.
  Sex o.k.

*Sunday, 28 June 1942*

Sunday
  Ennui – all encompassing and bleak.
  Yes, I want to get moving again.
  A. has lost interest or at least appears to, and there is nothing else to give me any intensity which I need in experience to pull me out of my desperate mental clinches.
  The last few days it was difficult to talk.
  Last night such an odious party at H's[474] that I resolved never to go back there. What tedium! Normal and abnormal people thrashing uselessly against each other around a table of tasteless sandwiches.
  The women appeared to entertain a false impression.

475. Holt Gewinner did not have a sister. Williams refers to Holt's unmarried aunt, Hazel Gewinner, who was a schoolteacher.

476. According to Jordan Massee, Ben Willingham looked rather like Andrew Lyndon.

477. In a letter to Windham ([14 June 1942], Yale), Williams explained his interest in Wesleyan College: "Incidentally there is a woman here, director of the Wesleyan drama Dept., who wants to open their Fall season with [*You Touched Me!*] and that might also be a good trial for us."

478. Robert Lewis (1909–97) was a founding member of the Group Theatre of the 1930s. The Group Theatre disbanded in 1941, and in April 1942 Lewis directed Ramon Naya's play "Mexican Mural." After World War II, Lewis co-founded the Actors Studio with Elia Kazan. Lewis went on to be a successful director of Broadway plays and musicals as well as films. In the years following, Lewis taught acting at the Yale School of Drama, the Lincoln Center Repertory Company, and his own Robert Lewis Theatre Workshop. In a letter to Windham ([24 June 1942], Yale), Williams wrote:

> I also got a letter from Robert Lewis the director confirming his determination to produce the one-acts. He is talking to financiers and may try them out first in Hollywood where he is going to spend the summer. — No money from him, though.

In his memoirs, *Slings and Arrows* (New York: Stein and Day, 1984), Lewis would recall:

> It was, oddly enough, a letter from Tennessee that I received in June 1942, two months after the opening of *Mexican Mural*, that helped me make up my mind to leave the East for awhile. He had borrowed thirty dollars for bus fare in order to get out of New York, he said, and was now stranded in Macon, Georgia, without a cent. Having wanted me to direct his early short plays, he now promised to include in the deal some new one-acters he was writing if only I could get up some option money. With the wipe out of *Mexican Mural*, I just couldn't. No prospective backers I went to had yet heard of Williams, and an evening of one-act plays was too tough for me to sell. (pp. 134–35)

479. David Merrick (1911–2000), born David Margulois in St. Louis, trained as a lawyer and in the 1940s began working for Herman Shumlin, a theatre producer, in New York. Merrick had written Williams on 14 June 1942 (HRC):

> Audrey Wood sent over your play Stairway to the Roof. I found it interesting and beautifully written. However, I think it is unlikely that you can get a Broadway production. I don't think a producer would be likely to risk a more than average amount of production money on a fantasy or semi-fantasy at this time. Not unless it had a chorus of pretty girls and a part for Gertrude Lawrence. Certainly not for one with some meaning to it. You told me that you were aware of the fact that your work was uncommercial, so I don't suppose this opinion will come as a disappointment.
>
> I don't think I should advise you to write about more commercial subjects because I feel that you write so well and with so much genuine feeling in your present form. Let's just hope that soon they'll get around to wanting something better.

On 24 June (HRC), Merrick wrote again:

> From what I have seen I think there is no question but that you are a fine playwright. I know you're going to stick with it but I want to add my word of encouragement to help you feel that you're right in sticking with it.

Merrick went on to produce such hits as *Gypsy* (1959), *Hello, Dolly!* (1964), and *42nd Street* (1981). Merrick produced four of Williams' plays: *The Milk Train Doesn't Stop Here Anymore* (1964), *The Seven Descents of Myrtle* (1968), *Out Cry* (1973), and *The Red Devil Battery Sign* (1975).

480. A young widow of the tobacco heir Smith Reynolds, Libby Holman (1904–71) was a dark-haired beauty who was known as a torch singer in the 1920s and 1930s. She acted with Montgomery Clift, under Robert Lewis's direction, in the April 1942 production of Ramon Naya's "Mexican Mural." In a letter to Jane and Gordon Carter (circa 20 July 1942, *SL*, vol. 1), Williams would refer to the work he was doing for Libby Holman (presumably "The Beetle of the Sun"):

> I had a one-act ["This Property Is Condemned"] produced early this summer in New York. Libby Holman and Bobbie Lewis saw it and are planning, tentatively, to produce a series of them in the Fall with Libby singing. I have had to write her a singing play — She still has a wonderful voice.

Poor Holt laughs nervously at everything said – his old maid sister[475] paints her face and puts on a long white dress and tries to be gay in the most helpless, bewildered fashion. There is a full moon.

I wake up feeling sickly and trapped by the current neurosis. It wears off. I meet Ben Willingham, A's friend, who strikes me as being perhaps the most attractive person in Macon.[476]

Dinner at Wesleyan.[477]

A. refused to come over – I feel that is reaching Nothing. Oh, well, I don't blame A. – I'm not Prince Charming or anything similar even.

Yesterday – nice letters from Robert Lewis[478] and David Merrick.[479]

Libby Holman likes plays and good prospect production. I wrote a sketch for her. Pretty good.[480]

Later –

I have rested – I feel quieter.

I observe the violence and untruth in my statements.

Last night was only foolish and pathetic – as I myself am foolish & pathetic time and again – hunger beneath it all – deep and beyond help.

And as for me, perhaps my life is a burden with its long drawn tension so mostly meaningless. But God knows I have nothing else and must cling to that.

It seems I might do so with a better grace.

And check my tongue more often when I am inclined to amuse by saying the obvious cruel thing – such as "The goddam Gewinner" about poor Holt. or "how stupid". Etc. – Am I not maybe a little tiresome myself? En Avant!


*Monday, 29 June 1942*

Monday – Whew! \ Quite devastating the condition of my nerves.

Wrote in morning.

Noon found me literally staggering.

A swim at the Y helped some – had a hair cut and I am now back and determined to let everything go at all costs –

Knots in my head loosening up a bit and I will not allow them to tighten – Not if I have to lock my door on the world and live alone for the rest of my life.

Later –

A. dropped by.

friendly.

I made no effort.

I spent the evening rooting among my papers – journals. What a struggle these past few periods have been! What a long-drawn fever!

I will go out now to get cigarettes and return to bed. I'd better make some money so I can move again.

481.    Lawrence's short story ends with Matilda agreeing to marry Hadrian on the deathbed of Mr. Rockley. In the last scene of Williams and Windham's play *You Touched Me!* Matilda agrees to run away with Hadrian, and Emmie (changed from a sister of Matilda's to an aunt) learns that her brother, Captain Rockley, has given her hand in marriage to the confirmed celibate the Reverend Guildford Melton. Fred Melton was Donald Windham's lover and had recently left Windham to marry Sara Marshall from Georgia.

482.    In earlier times southern ladies, following the examples of heroines in Victorian novels, frequently had "the vapors" or fainting spells and required smelling salts. This was considered a sign of breeding and delicacy. Paul Bigelow nicknamed Andrew Lyndon "Lady Abdy." Massee says Andrew modeled himself on Martina Burke, one of two sisters who lived together in Macon, which explains why Williams says he understands that Andrew would have "the vapors."

Libby Holman in "Mexican Mural"

*Wednesday, 1 July 1942*

Tuesday – 2 A.M. (or rather, Wed.)

God! – God!

A. – failure.

the sex neurosis again.

There seems to be no comfort anywhere.

Sex used to be the consolation prize – now it suddenly becomes another one of the psychological problems. Well, there is nothing to do but go on working.

I have to consider my family and their love – and be brave and enduring as long as it is humanly possible.

We mustn't think about disaster. I'm afraid it could only be messy and prolonged – what happened to my sister.

That way – No – I don't want it. And so tonight I turn back to the little boy who said "Now I lay me down to sleep."

I appeal to the darkness above me to stir and give help.

I am sleepy – I will probably sleep.

Tomorrow – coffee – <u>write</u>.

Can it be that I <u>love</u> A. – and that's what does it? – Creates the block of fear? – And is it hopeless?

I'm a silly ass – goodnight.

Wed. Eve. –

Better in spite of last night's amatory debâcle.

Read play to Paul and he liked it and made helpful suggestions. We hit on a solution for the last scene.[481]

Swam and worked with bars. Came home in tolerably good humor.

Paul says A. has the "vapors" – I understand why, of course[482] – Too bad – Tant pire!

I am a problem to anybody who cares anything about me – Most of all to myself who am, of course, my only ardent lover. (Though a spiteful and a cruel one!)

Paul and I will go to the pictures I guess.

A period that is rich in neuroses is also rich in invention.

I will probably get a good deal of work done this summer before the culminating disaster or the ~~resurrecti~~ regeneration takes place – which will it be, I wonder?

Little A. – I'm sorry! – And that is putting it mildly.

Mother writes that Grand is frail and thin and that she hopes I'll come home before I go back North.

Oh, God – there is too much to hurt, you can't think of it all – you have to evade and evade. You have to skip rope lightly! handyman – so long.

483.  Paul Bigelow's play, initially titled "A Woman Who Came from a Boat" and later "A Theme for Reason," is about Erna Eddington, an aging refugee dancer (based on Isadora Duncan, according to Massee), who awaits death at a remote Pacific port. Later in the summer ([28 August 1942], HRC), Williams would write Audrey Wood his opinion of the play:

> Entre nous, I also felt that something [was] wrong and I think it was that woman, Erna, the dancer. Too much of the grande dame and not enough simplicity about her. The intellectual content, the basic situation, the highly topical and poetic background of the play made it intriguing to me and I hope that Bigelow can create a more appealing character and put it in more dramatic terms. There is the material there for a very unusual and intensely beautiful play, I think.

484.  Williams and Bigelow were taken to jail. Jordan Massee was with his family in Sea Island, Georgia, so a cousin of Massee's in Macon got them out of jail. In a letter to Windham ([20 July 1942], Yale), Williams elaborated: "I was recently picked up on Cherry Street . . . as a suspicious character because of my dark glasses and cigarette holder and detained at the Chief of Detectives office for some time because I did not have my draft card with me." Due to his poor eyesight, Williams had been classified as 4-F, which indicated that he was physically unfit for military service.

485.  Mrs. Jelkes was a musician who taught at Wesleyan College in Macon. Williams' notes in parentheses relate to a story fragment, "Miss Jelke's Recital," which also includes a character named after another Macon resident, Henrietta Callaway. Miss Jelkes, who is slightly crippled, as is Laura in *The Glass Menagerie*, goes on a date with a young man. They swim in Recreation and he tries to make love to her and fails. She "did the thing she knew could best arouse him," and after they make love she says to him: "A woman is not what you're used to." She realizes she will love him and it will turn out badly for her.

  Williams would also borrow the name for Emily Jelkes in the story "The Night of the Iguana" and would modify the name to Hannah Jelkes in the play *The Night of the Iguana*. Williams also wrote a bawdy poem titled "Miss Jelkes Recital" about Edith Jelkes who is required by the faculty to give a recital. Unable to sing, she makes a vulgar mockery of the recital.

486.  George Elijah Rosser (1875–1945) was a biblical scholar who taught at Wesleyan College. He lived at 507 Georgia Avenue and rented attic rooms to Paul Bigelow and Williams during the summer of 1942.

George Elijah Rosser

*Friday, 3 July 1942*

Friday – I thought it was Sunday – because I had been writing a Sunday scene.
Went well –

Paul and I battled a couple of hours over my criticism of his 3rd Act – I found it too rhetorical and stuffy.[483] I hope he will pull it in shape. It could be beautiful.

No "A." in view or hearing since Tues. night and I feel disinclined to call – it seems too much an impasse to fight over.

The nerves much better – feel tired but well.

Picked up by police last night and questioned at Station because Paul and I were reported as "suspicious characters" and I did not have my draft card.[484] Surrounded by crowd on street –

Shows the change of our world – personal freedom is gone, even the illusion of it.

I have the material for a short novel in my mind. Maybe I'll write it this summer —

(Emily Jelkes[485] – armoire – a psychological <u>impotent lover</u> – soldier and wife in next room – <u>a song recital</u> = center – Dr. Rosser's[486] – heat – sleeplessness – <u>neuroses</u> – racial trouble in South – a feeling of impasse – <u>helplessness</u> – closing in – <u>lostness</u> – the effort at <u>"keeping face" with a set of uncomprehending people</u> – one who seems to know – the <u>struggle for contact</u> – the water out of reach – the ~~cold~~ frigidity and the ennui – final surrender – <u>the armoire closed</u>.) good material.

Macon swell background.

Well – I must go swim. Maybe see Holt.

Massee home at 619 College Street, Macon

487.  By 1942 Katherine Anne Porter (1890–1980) had published *Flowering Judas and Other Stories* (1930), *Pale Horse, Pale Rider* (1939), and *No Safe Return* (1941). "María Concepción," the first story in *Flowering Judas and Other Stories*, is the haunting account of a newly married and pregnant Guadalajaran peasant woman who takes pride in the fact that she was married in a church. She secretly discovers that her husband, Juan, is having an affair with María Rosa, the beekeeper and the love of his life. He and María Rosa leave the village that night and go to war. María Concepción's baby is born and dies shortly thereafter. Juan eventually returns with a pregnant María Rosa and is immediately imprisoned. He is released through the intervention of an English archaeologist for whom he had previously worked. María Concepción murders María Rosa. Juan, realizing what has happened, protects his wife from imprisonment, and he returns to live with her, though with a defeated sense that his life and love are over. María Concepción adopts María Rosa's baby, and the story ends with her sitting with the baby in her lap, feeling that justice has been done.

Many of Porter's stories were set in the South, Southwest, and Mexico and had themes of guilt, isolation, and spiritual denial. It is not surprising that Williams, who had been working on "Dos Ranchos," would be drawn to her writings.

488.  Williams and Bigelow never collaborated on a play. Jordan Massee commented: "10 and Paul Bigelow were attracted by Holt Gewinner's personality and he was very amusing. His house was a house for lost souls. The idea of a play was surely a passing fancy. He does not even appear in any of 10's plays. He and Bigelow eventually fell out and ceased seeing each other" (letter to Margaret Bradham Thornton).

489.  "The Malediction" is a short story, written in summer 1941, about a "panicky little man [who] looks for a place to stay in an unknown town." He finds a rooming house, befriends a cat, and gets a job in a factory. He loses his cat and then they are reunited. In the short story the man is mistakenly locked up for a week for drunken behavior. When he returns, his cat is badly injured and unlikely to recover. He walks into the river and kills both himself and the cat.

On 29 July 1941 (HRC), Williams had written Wood about the possible dramatization of "The Malediction": "I think the Chaplinesque character of the little man and the universal theme of loneliness might be poignant enough to be worked into a short expressionistic play using music and projected settings." Williams made several starts at a dramatization of the story, which would eventually become "The Strangest Kind of Romance."

490.  Williams had been offered a job in September "doing publicity work for Erwin Piscator at the New School for Social Research" (letter to Jane and Gordon Carter, circa 20 July 1942, *SL*, vol. 1). Presumably Williams wished to write Piscator about this job. It appears Williams never wrote him, for later that summer Piscator withdrew the job offer when he had not heard from Williams.

491.  The first paragraph of the "World Battlefronts" section of the 13 July edition of *Time*, which featured Rommel on the cover, stated:

Hitler is winning in Russia. If his armies continue to do as well as they did last week, and the Red Army does no better:
- Russia will be defeated.
- Germany will win the present phase of World War II in Europe.
- The best and the only present chance to destroy the main German armies will be gone; the Allies will then have lost their best chance to defeat Germany and win World War II. (p. 8)

In the report on the Battle of Egypt, *Time* wrote:

Germany's Rommel had chased the broken, retreating British 325 miles in eleven days, had rammed his armored spearheads down the coastal desert from Matrûh, taking the flyspeck towns on the railroad to Alexandria like peas ripped from a pod. (p. 9)

*Wednesday, 8 July 1942*

Wed – July 8 – Midnight

I have just read <u>Maria Concepcion</u> by Katharine Anne Porter[487] – A truly great story. Elemental and rich.

I did much writing today – my heart is not good – I should rest more.

Reminiscent. I looked back through my life – starting with the summer of 1938 that I graduated from Iowa. – Chicago – New Orleans – California – and all the shuttling times since – the travels, the people – the anxieties, hardships, affairs, events, disappointments, fevers, kaleidoscopic shifts and changes – What a four years it has been! A lifetime in itself – not one moment of rest, hardly a bit of real peace in it all. But good! And terrible – a liberation. a fight. Well, here I am, still living – and going on. Not young anymore. If one dared to face it, what a thing he would see! – this life.

It is a hot black night. I am not so much plagued by the nightingale these days. Is the nightingale embarassed? – Shy little Phoenix, he will sing again and recover his poise.

What exact rhythm these days and that is good. Write. Swim. Eat.

Paul and I plotted out a play we may write together – last night. H.G. the subject.[488]

I am writing a dramatization of "The Malediction"[489] – goes well. Will finish tomorrow – though I ought to rest.

I would like to spend August in another place – Will I be able to? How? – Not back to N.Y. or St. Louis. Yet. Must write Piscator a note.[490]


*Thursday, 9 July 1942*

Thurs.

My last day of work for a while.

feel too shakey to add more.

How will I fill the days?

Later –

Read "Time" – News appalling[491] –

What a world, what times confront us! Russia, Egypt crumbling – I cannot see

492. Set in a small town in the deep South, "Dragon Country" is the story of Miss Bertha Shapiro, a young Jewish librarian who shows tenderness to the governor's troubled son, Walter Lindenwood. "Dragon Country" refers to the hate, greed, fear, and anti-Semitism of the small southern town that does not accept Miss Shapiro, who represents the true nobility because of her compassion.

   Miss Shapiro has an uncomfortable relationship with the senior librarian, Miss Evans, a tall, slender woman in her late thirties who Williams describes as "seared and tortured by some inner intensity of a withering nature." Miss Evans treats Miss Shapiro as an outsider and does not approve of Miss Shapiro's friendship with Lindenwood.

   Although only an incomplete draft of "Dragon Country" is known to exist, it appears that Williams intended Miss Shapiro to tell the children gathered at the library a story, the tale of the Heaven Tree, a parable of how to live — how the dragon can be slayed by the fruit of the Heaven Tree. Williams also experimented with two endings, one in which it is Miss Evans who commits suicide by running in front of a train, the other in which it is Miss Shapiro.

493. According to Jordon Massee, Andrew Lyndon wrote in a small house in the backyard of his parents' home in Macon.

ahead nor can anyone. But I suspect it will be especially hard for us who are not made to be warriors. Our little works may be lost.

Here in Macon the crickets make the only noise at this time of night.

A new phase for me – tomorrow no coffee, no work. I will try to sleep late and read.

Of course I will be weak and depressed. – More depressed. 3 day since I have seen A. – it seems behind me. I do not think there will be anything but endurance this season. Survival is enough. – at least may have to be enough. I do not think of love – only a few primary needs – and work – and the various little tricks of evasion. Goodnight.

### Saturday, 11 July 1942

Saturday Midnight.

I only laid off work 1 day – Today wrote "Dragon Country".492

I wistfully hope that tomorrow unless I feel better I'll lay off again. Tonight I am aching all over – half my bones cracking – felt about to collapse after supper.

But days without work here are utterly void.

Saw A. last night and we had a lively, intimate evening of just talk in the little house.493 It is curious how I have so little urge for the bed – of roses – flying creatures – bugs – in the room – hate them – Just made a savage and successful attack on one – The sum of living organisms in the universe was reduced by one. – I will go to bed now. drinking a glass of milk and maintaining some equanimity for the morrow. So long – 10.

### Sunday, 12 July 1942

Sunday Night

Well, I never did like Sunday. So I shouldn't complain now. I'd like to live a simple life – with epic fornications.

I think I will stop writing poetry.

Looking through the collection.

It appears to be mostly crap with just enough quality to make it more distasteful.

Sometimes I delude myself horribly.

I glance at that big black book of verse and think that I must be an important poet. Well, I'm not – so there.

Maybe my plays are a little bit better – I hope.

Well, I ache and my joints crack and my head aches, too.

I try to make a long play out of "Dragon Country" – Maybe I can.

494. According to Massee, Bill Hope, who was not from Macon, was a friend of Andrew Lyndon's. He taught English literature in a school in Paris.

495. Eugene O'Neill's *Desire Under the Elms* (1924) is a tragedy set in New England. Abbie Cabot, the new young wife of Ephraim Cabot, seduces Eben, the youngest of her husband's sons. Abbie hopes to bear a son she can claim is Ephraim's. When Eben learns that Abbie has used him, he threatens to expose her infidelity. She smothers the child to prove her love for Eben. By 1942, O'Neill had won three Pulitzer Prizes and the Nobel Prize for literature (1936).

496. In a letter to Windham ([20 July 1942], Yale), Williams wrote:
> The play is finished. I will send it to New York as soon as I can get it typed. We have tried two typists, business school students, one typed two pages in three hours, and the other did the same number in the course of an afternoon. Another applicant will be tried tomorrow. . . . Naturally I have no money to pay for the typing and I have written to enquire of Audrey if there is not some fund that will advance five dollars for it.

497. "Pale Horse, Pale Rider" by Katherine Anne Porter is the story of a short-lived love affair between a young southern newspaper reporter and a soldier during the influenza epidemic of World War I. In the novella the young woman, Miranda, falls in love with Adam, a soldier about to be sent off to war. She collapses with influenza and when she recovers she learns that Adam, who told her that he loved her when she was ill, has died of influenza in an army camp. The final paragraphs confirm Williams' observations:
> At once he was there beside her, invisible but urgently present, a ghost but more alive than she was, the last intolerable cheat of her heart; for knowing it was false she still clung to the lie, the unpardonable lie of her bitter desire. . . . "Oh, let me see you once more." The room was silent, empty, the shade was gone from it, struck away by the sudden violence of her rising and speaking aloud. She came to herself as if out of sleep. Oh, no, that is not the way, I must never do that, she warned herself. . . .
>
> No more war, no more plague, only the dazed silence that follows the ceasing of the heavy guns; noiseless houses with the shades drawn, empty streets, the dead cold light of tomorrow. Now there would be time for everything. (*Pale Horse, Pale Rider* [New York: Harcourt, Brace and Company, 1939], p. 264)

Lyndon home, 2540 Vineville Avenue, Macon

*Tuesday, 14 July 1942*

Tuesday –

Yesterday was nice.

Bill Hope494 drove A. and I out to the lake.

We had a nice evening of it and at the end Bill and I talked for a long time about our mental difficulties and drank beer.

He has the same problem I have though it is different, too.

We called it the "mental double exposure" – the intrusion of self-consciousness into experience. Apparently he has suffered a good deal, though perhaps he is still an amateur beside me.

Today the writing slowed a bit.

I begin to feel qualms about "Dragon Country". It is too heavy and lacks grace and charm. Too macabre.

A sombre play has to be very spare and angular. When you fill it out it seems blotchy, pestilential. You must keep the lines sharp and clean – tragedy is austere. You get the effect with fewer lines than you are inclined to use.

A sad letter from Mother – The old man is being devilish. Paul has headache and is rude.

I read "Desire Under the Elms".495 Incredibly bad writing it seems to me. I go to bed early – desire to work in morning.

Play "You touched Me" remains untyped.496 No word from Audrey.

Horrid cold – head full of mucous. foul. – Well – I am a dull boy tonight. Bon nuit.


*Wednesday, 15 July 1942*

Wed. Midnight

Just closed the book on "Pale Horse, Pale Rider" a fine story. Pretty close to the way it might be. The reality of loss was caught perfectly. The mockery of going on afterwards.497

Today wrote not long but well. The invariable day. I will need to dip myself in something cool after this period in Macon. I will be nearly reduced to powder. Yes, it's like being a piece of toast forgotten in the toaster.

But after all I am my own incinerator mostly. And the work goes well. If I grow old and dry and all my hair falls out, it is no exceptional thing.

Tomorrow – a picnic in the country. I will eat and go off by myself. I don't want to be nice to a bunch of more or less nasty people. Endurance is what I ask for, that's about all.

498. Williams wrote to Donald Windham ([11 August 1942], Yale):

I finally went to Atlanta, to see Sally [Sara Marshall] off on the train. The only thing I liked there was the view across those open spaces to the sun on the distant buildings. . . . I am now heartily in accord with your decision to spend your "Return to Atlanta" fund on more or less riotous living in New York.

499. After Audrey Wood had sent five dollars, Williams had engaged Paul Bigelow to type the play.

500. The Pig'n Whistle was a famous sandwich shop, a block away from where Williams was living on 507 Georgia Avenue. Mrs. Griffin served meals at her house next door to Dr. Rosser. In a letter to Windham ([20 July 1942], Yale), Williams wrote:

Yes, money is a dull problem. Maybe dull isn't exactly the word, but problem is. I am about two weeks back on my board-bill and every time I slip unobtrusively up to the dining-room table the land-lady looks at me with a perceptibly reduced cordiality and of course I imagine that everybody at the table knows exactly what I owe her and I am afraid to lift my eyes from the plate or to ask for anything that isn't in my immediate reach — I have the arms of an Octopus, however! — Paul eats there, too. He is less bashful than I am and when he enters he heartily announces, "My dear Mrs. Griffin, I haven't the slightest intention of paying you for my dinner!" and laughs as though he had made some brilliant witticism. The poor woman is rather dull-witted but I think she is slowly evolving some plan of action that will probably take care of us both.

501. In 1938, Sergei Eisenstein and Sergei Prokofiev collaborated on a nationalistic film about the thirteenth-century prince of Novgorod, Alexander Nevsky (1220–63). Reputed as a fair, God-fearing, and brave statesman, Nevsky led Russian forces to victory over the invading Catholic Teutonic Knights. Williams did not write a play about Grigory Rasputin, but the idea of a play inspired by Eisenstein's film stayed with him. In September 1943 he wrote about the influence Alexander Nevsky had on "The Spinning Song":

The conception of this play began on my return one evening from seeing Sergei Eisenstein's film, Alexander Nevsky. Its pictorial drama and poetry of atmosphere, a curiously powerful blend of passion and restraint, an almost sculptural quality, had excited me very deeply and made me wonder if it were not possible to achieve something analagous to this in a poetic drama for the stage. The film of Eisenstein was immeasurably enhanced by a complete musical score by Prokofief, which combined with picture and action so perfectly that the effects were of blood-chilling intensity. The influence of modern music and surreal art, both present in this film masterpiece, could be used as powerfully in a poetic stage play. The passionate restraint, the sculptural effect noted in the film, became the artistic tone of this play as I began to conceive it.

In my dramatic writing prior to this I have always leaned too heavily on speech, nearly everything I have written for the stage has been overburdened with dialogue. In working on this new project I determined to think in more plastic or visual terms. To write sparingly but with complete lyricism, and build the play in a series of dramatic pictures. No play written in such creative terms could be naturalistic nor could it be comedy. It would have to be an epic story, as Eisenstein's film was, or a poetic tragedy. Written in verse, with a surrealist influence and a background of modern music, it would have to be independent of nearly all dramatic conventions.

. . . And it seemed to me that after sitting on my ass . . . in Hollywood, the noblest and most cavalier act that I could perform by way of atonement was to put all popular ambitions aside and devote whatever I had in the way of energy and emotion to this extremely challenging idea, a synthesis for the stage of those artistic terms that informed the film of Eisenstein — a classic theme with broad and familiar outlines, a tragedy purified by poetry and music of modern feeling, a vividly pictorial presentation that would offer the utmost visual excitement and be informed by the rich and disturbing beauty of surrealist painting. Win, lose, or draw, the following play, the story of the disintegration of a land-owning southern family, emerges from a desire to synthesize these elements I have noted, and anything in it of value is humbly inscribed to the Russian work that inspired it.

Williams most likely was reading *Rasputin: The Holy Devil*, by René Fülöp-Miller (Garden City, N.Y.: Garden City Publishing, 1928). One of the final chapters is titled "The Murderer with the Guitar."

*Sunday, 19 July 1942*

Sunday noon – Some nice times lately.
   The picnic – swell food & beautiful scenery [*page missing*]

Me". Thank God <u>that</u> much is completed. Really done. A. just left. Interests me so little mentally but stirs up so much desire.

*Monday, 27 July 1942*

Monday –
   Returned from a week-end trip to Atlanta.[498] Paul not back from Sea Island – play untyped.[499] The Atlanta trip contained an evening with Eros but otherwise was sorrowful. Dull. And dull.
   I return feeling weak, very weak, and ill. The cold has gone on my chest and this morning I observe traces of blood in the sputum. My knees shake on stairs. I go with out coffee which adds to my depression.
   A letter from Donnie he seems to be contented.

Later – I go out for a bite to eat at the Pig'n Whistle as lunches are discontinued at the house next door.[500] I have iced coffee and I feel somewhat better. The sky is overcast, it will likely rain. I return to the gable to read and smoke and let time drift away. I do not feel that I shall ever give battle to anything hereafter but such feelings are evanescent, have always been so before.
   I read <u>Rasputin,</u> life at the tragic court of Russia. Material for drama. A non-realistic play. Stylized. Something like Eisenstein's film <u>Alexander Nevsky</u>. Gypsies, dancing, an atmosphere of the Gothic and of the weird quality of Russia. Short scenes. Prince Yusupov, a murderer with a guitar – Rasputin's death speech.[501] the mystic and the voluptuary.

Pig'n Whistle, Macon

502.  The Washington Memorial Library was only two blocks from Rosser's house.

503.  William Saroyan (1908–81), short-story writer, novelist, and playwright, whose work is marked by an impressionistic style and an exaltation of personal freedom. Williams was impressed by Saroyan, whom he praised in an unmailed letter to the publishers of *Story* (April 1936, HRC): "Successful writers (with the brilliant exception of Saroyan and one or two others) are AFRAID of writing experimental stories."

   In 1939 Saroyan debuted as a playwright with two plays, *My Heart's in the Highlands* and *The Time of Your Life*. After *The Time of Your Life* won the New York Drama Critics' Circle Award and the Pulitzer Prize, Saroyan became established as the leading avant-garde playwright of his generation and one in whom Williams was keenly interested. In 1939, when Williams was in California, he traveled to San Francisco in the hope of meeting Saroyan. Williams failed to meet Saroyan and would try again in 1940 when both he and Saroyan were in New York. No record of a meeting is known, but they did exchange several letters and commiserated about the popularity of "the ordinary, commercial and shabby" productions on Broadway. After having read Saroyan's *Jim Dandy* in script form, Williams wrote to Saroyan (circa mid-November 1941, Historic New Orleans Collection):

   > Like your character Jim Crow, I make a series of profound obeisances before your chair-on-a-table, having just finished reading your play <u>Jim Dandy</u> which rings in my head and my heart like the multitude of soft and musical bells that bring down the curtain. It is a beautiful little mystery of a play: I read it twice: first time I was too confused to enjoy it: the second time it began to glow and vibrate, coming out like a star in "first dark". — Well, I loved it.

   The symbolism, madness, and "occasional speeches [that] ring the bell of pure poetry" of Saroyan's drama impressed Williams and influenced his writing, perhaps most directly *Stairs to the Roof*, on which Williams was working at the time.

   In a note on his short story "Blue Roses and the Polar Star," Williams quoted Saroyan: "Some things are put in merely for the charm of their strangeness and because as Saroyan has said 'When you go deep enough into reality you find that the core of it is fantasy.' In other words fairy-tales aren't nearly as odd as life."

Washington Memorial Library, Macon

The afternoon passes – and I am growing stronger. Soon I will go out to the library[502] and the swim.

*Tuesday, 28 July 1942*

Tuesday

I get up and drink 3 cups of coffee with Paul.

What suicidal folly!

I come home to write. And the story is wooden, the writing is awkward, only the idea is good, the result is shit.

I seem to have no ear or else too much. it smoothes out to a drone or it doesn't have any even rhythm at all. I think of Saroyan[503] and how beautifully and effortlessly he puts words together – I feel hopeless.

Yes, of course I am hopeless, hopeless, <u>hopeless</u>!!!

And youth is gone.

And I am sick and weary and only sleep is simple.

Pity of self? No. A savage contempt for self.

Yet I shall go on. Necessarily. Helplessly. That's how it goes. And try to get A. here to go to bed with. And fill my belly. And put on a shabby little performance for people. <u>En Avant</u>!

And now I must make a sensible plan of action unless I am determined on messy destruction.

I must quit the effort to create for a while and retrench on something like mere endurance. Make a solemn compact with myself and on no account break it – to relax for a while and vegetate and let my nerves feed up. I don't dare do otherwise for death or madness are nearer than a myth.

Later – Better mood.

We read over the play to check the final draft which Paul has finished typing, and while it is rather shabbily contrived – or maybe <u>very</u> shabbily contrived – still I feel it may very well have the elements of a successful play. In other words, I have hope it will sell.

About style – I think I should work for the simplest. All this concern for rhythm may work out in absolute simplification and only writing when I am damn sure I have more than a vague wish to do it to escape ennui. Of course the wish is usually desperate but a desperate wish ought to be backed up by a clear conception to start with. In other words, fewer and better subjects. One big project – a play or a truly challenging story.

Shall I go to the beach? I think so. It hardly seems feasible and yet [*page missing*]

504.   *Look Homeward, Angel* (1929) is the story of Eugene Gant, who grows up in Altamont, Catawba (Asheville, North Carolina). Gant is the youngest of six children of a father who is an eccentric stonecutter and an unhappy mother who leaves the family when Gant is young. Gant's feelings of aloneness are tempered after he goes to college and becomes more adjusted to the world outside of Catawba. The novel ends with Gant breaking with his family and not returning home.

505.   *You Touched Me!*

506.   Williams had written Audrey Wood (21 July 1942, HRC) that he was considering grouping three plays "about the deep South, under the composite title 'Dragon Country.'" He noted that the third "may expand into a fairly long script."

507.   In a letter to Windham ([11 August 1942], Yale), Williams wrote:
       I put Holt Gewinner on the train for New York. He was wearing sort of a picture-hat, amber transparent straw with an enormous brim, a bottle-green sport coat and pale yellow trousers. . . . My friendship with Holt annoyed Paul and made Andrew furious. Andrew said, If you must have affairs, why don't you have them with interesting people? — My answer to that created a definite coolness.

Notebook Williams began in August 1942

*The Macon Period and St. Augustine ?*

*Saturday, 1 August 1942*

So I have filled one whole notebook with this period and am starting another.

A pleasant evening alone. Read from Wolfe's first novel.[504] A wind came up and cooled the attic. I go out for a bite to eat at the Pig'n Whistle. Now to sleep.

My room is neat – I cleaned it this afternoon.

Well – I am capable of nothing but sleep – head like an empty pea pod.

Cold hangs on everlastingly. H. has just about taken A's place and all in all – A. being such a delectable but cultivated young lady – it is a fair exchange.

Paul being distant again. Ho-hum! Goodnight.

*Sunday, 2 August 1942*

Sunday Aug. 2. A.M.

I wake. And blow the loathesome mucous from my nose.

It is tediously bright and I think wearily – This will be a gloomy Sunday. Perhaps ingenuity might devise something better but I will go to the Pig and drink coffee and probably won't even pretend to write.

*Wednesday, 5 August 1942*

Wed.

A week ago today I mailed the play[505] to New York and I haven't heard of it yet.

Seems like most of my ~~life is~~ vital energy is consumed in waiting for letters. I write mediocre verse (rhymed) nothing more. But I have good material for long play in <u>Dragon Country</u>.[506]

H. is gone and A. is mad at me over H. so the old libido is likely to have rough going – worse than usual.[507]

I swam and now I am back in ye olde attic smoking, feet on desk and stripped to my drawers.

If nobody likes play I may as well just go on sitting here as long as they will let me.

The ocean seems a rain dream. (poem).

508.  Two poems Williams wrote in August in Macon:

### THE IMAGE OF THE BELL AND DOVE

I.

Did ever you behold
a walnut shell
pretend to be a temple
with a bell

Or have you, Gentle Masters,
ever known
a universe within
a cherry stone,

An artifice for all
who would not enter
worlds of which they cannot
be the center?

But to dispense with
ambiguity,
let us suppose you came upon
a tree

Among whose leaves' abundance
you did see
the snowy dove, the silver bell,
and me!

IV.

But recognition must
acceptance be:
the bell, the dove, and I
forsook the tree.

We left it furnished as
it was before,
a universe within
a narrow door,

An artifice for all
who would not enter
worlds of which they cannot
be the center.

Now, Gentle Masters, was it
vanity
that builded such a nest
in such a tree,

Or, to dispense with
ambiguity,
is God still sitting in
that lonely tree?

. . . . . . . . . . . . . . . . . . . .

### THE DRUNKEN FAUN OF HERCULANEUM

I, good citizens, have come
from buried Herculaneum

To promulgate in sober states
the culture of inebriates,

To raid your tedious sheepfolds
and, so to speak, unsave some souls.

Now for your sakes, who look askance,
I shall perform my lewdest dance,

With my wine-sack on my shoulder,
not one August morning colder

Than the golden one in which
a drunk Etruscan in a ditch

Saw me leap across a pond
into centuries of bronze!

My sculptor was no blue-nose, but
he only dared to hint of what

He found consequent upon
his meeting with a beardless faun.

But you who have acquired a copy
of my young, disturbing body

Are at liberty to guess
what happened when I came to rest

On my elbows and my knees
in luxurious heaps of leaves,

Much too drunk to break away
from what, begun as lusty play,

Surprizingly enough resulted
in a deed which catapaulted

Me, the young wine-drinker, plumb
to here from Herculaneum!

The point of this apostrophe
improbable as it may be

Is that most immortal art
stems neither from the head nor heart

But from, respecting privacies,
above and just between the knees!

*Thursday, 6 August 1942*

Thurs. Midnite

Letter from Donnie – No mention of play.

Today more bad poetry.[508] <u>Pas de plus.</u>

Usual routine. but mind is calm – no neurosis. Home this evening with <u>Time</u> – a late snack at the Pig. Return under big brooding trees. It was a hunger for those big overhanging trees that brought me down here. Crickets. Well, here they are and here I am and the summer ebbs away. While in Europe the Titanic death-struggle goes on. But all in life seems – vain? – a dream? – I will not try to find a new phrase for it.

I suppose life will notice me again bye and bye and pick me up and hurl me onward again. But for a while I am drifting, drifting. Yes, the days, the days, the nights, the nights – one knows what he will do in the morning before he goes to bed at night and what he will do in the evening before he gets up in the morning. The sad truth of it is that this is a merciful thing and that a stale peace is one of the pleasanter things this brilliant adventure of life has to give us. All is pinned now on "You Touched Me" but if nothing comes of it, probably I will find there was, after all, another bone in the cupboard, even if it is only the familiar old dry one of endurance.

Endurance – My supreme faith is in thee. Goodnight.

Postcard Williams sent to Donald Windham

509. On 5 August 1942 (HRC), Audrey Wood wrote to Williams:

> The script of "YOU TOUCHED ME" arrived safely. I . . . will write to you more fully when I finish it. I am very happy that the play really is a full-length script (for a change) and am grateful to your typist for putting the script in professional shape. . . .
>
> Also, who do you see in the part of Matilda? As I have been reading it I've thought of Lillian Gish but ideally it should be a woman who is even younger. What are your ideas on this?

510. Douglas Moore (1893–1969) was a composer who studied at Yale and in Paris and is best known for his operas *The Devil and Daniel Webster* and *The Ballad of Baby Doe*. Moore's interest in folk culture prompted Wood to send him Williams' collection of folk verse "Blue Mountain Blues." Wood commented that Moore liked the folk verse "immensely," but nothing seems to have come of his interest. Later Paul Bowles set to music four of the poems, "Heavenly Grass," "Lonesome Man," "Cabin," and "Sugar in the Cane," which were published under the title *Blue Mountain Ballads* as sheet music in 1946.

511. On 9 August 1942 (UNC), Williams had written to Paul Green (1894–1981), a playwright and professor at the University of North Carolina at Chapel Hill, to organize a visit: "I have heard so much about your dramatic department that I would like to stop over for a few days on my way to New York — if you are going to be there." There is no record of Williams having visited Green in Chapel Hill.

Green received national recognition for dramas portraying life in the South, often set in his native state of North Carolina. His most important plays are *In Abraham's Bosom* (1926), a Pulitzer Prize–winning drama about a mulatto who tries to establish a school for blacks in a North Carolina town, *The Field God* (1927), and *The House of Connelly* (1931). Thomas Pawley, a classmate of Williams' at Iowa, noted that the plays of Paul Green were frequently produced. Green was on the panel of judges that awarded Williams a Rockefeller Fellowship in 1939. At the time of his death, Williams had a copy of Green's *Wide Fields* (1928).

512. The novel *You Can't Go Home Again* (New York: Harper & Brothers, 1940) is a sequel to *The Web and the Rock* (1939) in which George Webber writes a successful novel about his family and hometown. When he returns he is disillusioned by what he sees. This experience is believed to parallel Wolfe's own experience in his hometown of Asheville, North Carolina.

513. George Webber returns home for the funeral of his aunt and is met at the train station by his great childhood friend Randy Shepperton, who is embarrassed that he is only able to offer George a room over the garage and not their guest room because his boss, David Merrit, is staying with him and his sister in their house. George visits his friend at work and witnesses a scene in which he hears Merrit address Randy in a tone that is "a foul insult to human life, an ugly sneer whipped across the face of decent humanity. . . . But what was most dreadful of all was Randy's voice, humble, low, submissive, modestly entreating" (pp. 137, 138).

Excerpt of a letter Williams wrote to Paul Green (17 August 1942)

*Last summer I had money and I was on the ocean. This summer, alas, I am penniless.*

*Monday, 10 August 1942*

Monday –

A letter from Audrey produced a brighter outlook Saturday.

She appeared to be interested in the play.[509]

Douglas Moore, a Columbia University professor, plans to set some of my Blue Mt. lyrics to music.[510]

The tedium here becomes barely tolerable.

A. has been horrid – haven't seen him for a week and now I'm not sure I want to.

One can understand such things, analyze them to the point where bitterness is absurd. But reason doesn't remove the bitterness. One goes on composing hurt and angry speeches. Only a change of scene, a new, clean slate, removes the knot of fury.

So get me out of here, somebody – something!

Vite, vite, mes enfants!

Voila le tramway!

En Avant!

Chapel Hill?[511]


Later

I read Thomas Wolfe's "You Can't Go Home Again."[512]

Scene after scene has the stamp of genius on it.

Whether the total effect will be as powerful as the parts is a question that doesn't modify the fact that here is a man who has left his stamp on our human consciousness – and a very <u>great</u> stamp it is.

The picture of Webber's homecoming – particularly Randy and his boss – are as fine as anything of the kind I have seen – <u>finer</u> – Men like Wolfe – and the mess of this world – how do you reconcile it?[513] You don't – can't. The world is ruled by Randy's bosses. The Tom Wolfe's are observors – but their work makes them a threat to these evil masters. They lift the scales from the slaves' eyes – if the slaves dare to let them.

514. On the night of 16 June 1942, four Nazi saboteurs from a German submarine paddled ashore onto Ponte Vedra Beach, Florida. As part of Operation Pastorius they were carrying explosives to blow up defense plants and destroy important transportation arteries. They were disguised as tourists but were captured.

515. The first two lines of the third stanza of Hart Crane's "Emblems of Conduct." Williams chose them as an an epigraph for an early version of the short story "The Poet," titled "Meridian" or "Pillar of Smoke," but they did not appear on the published version.

```
E'en before noonday, neighbor,
. I tired of my labor,
dropped from the loft and hacked
at the wall with a sabre.

E'en before twilight, neighbor,
I rode from the stable,
and through the sierras, fast
as my staillion was able.

E'en before midnight, neighbor,
our quarry was lost in vapor,
my stallion raced back to the ranch
and fell dead in the stable.

E'en before daybreak, neighbor,
I tasted eternity's flavor,
I writhed in the meadows and burnt
my heart like a taper.


10. Wms.
Macon, Ga.
July, 1942.
```

*St. Augustine, Fla. —*

*Thursday, 13 August 1942*

Thursday Eve. –
    First day here, went immediately to beach –
    Oh, how good it was to meet the ocean again!
    I swam and swam and gargled the cold salt water and plunged and capered.
    Alone. Boys on beach but I talked to no one. A rain came up. I put my clothes under boat and swam. Rain flattened water – Silver sheet to plunge around in. Walked home across causeway.
    Disagreeable aspect here is suspicion of strangers because of saboteur scare.[514]
    I was stopped on bridge for identification and I feel self-conscious walking about town.
    My capital is about $1.70 to last till hypothetical letters arrive. Sunburned, tired, but will walk around a bit. So long.

Later – Read Crane – Now bed.

*"The wanderer later chose this spot of rest where marble clouds support the sea"*[515]

*Friday, 14 August 1942*

Friday –
    Up early about 8:00 and out on square for coffee. 1 cup – Tomorrow none. A gloriously bright cool morning. I feel well – the spectre of destitution is, of course, not far distant. It will take a letter today or tomorrow to circumvent it. Pigeons are muttering at window. They say "Tennessee – get off your ass and go to the beach!" which is what I will do. Will try the main beach today and report on it when I return. So long – (I will try to meet some people today – solitude is the bogey-man)

Evening –
    Agony with sunburn – worst I've ever had – whole upper body flaming.
    Day at beach a fiasco. Walked endlessly in hot sun to reach it.
    found it deserted and unattractive – No good for swimming only surf – fine sand and blazing sun an annoyance.
    But nothing is fun when you are lonely. I met no one. Talked to nobody. And again coming home I was stopped & questioned on bridge.
    Capital = about 50¢. No money tomorrow I will really be in for it. No kidding.

"Where Marble clouds support the Sea"

Thurs. Eve.

Dear Pavlovich:

A scribble to give you news of my safe arrival. I am at 246 Charlotte Street, care of S.E. Worley.

Did letters come? God, I hope so. I paid a weeks rent, $2.50 and am down to #170 Did you impress Dr. mail must be forwarded instantly care of General Delivery?

No sleep last night but nevertheless I went immediately to beach and swam all day. Got sunburned badly but cold

P.S. I will be thinking of you in N.Y. so good luck.

is already better — and, oh, how good it is to meet the ocean again! Water cold, excellent swimming

Town full of sailors but their clothes don't fit and they look almost as sloppy as those Camp Wheeler privates. But ——

I love the town. Has charm. Sweetest place in Fla. feel lonesome but guess that will work off. Many, many thanks for packing & everything. Will write a real letter soon as rested. Hello to Jordan. love — Tenn.

Letter Williams sent to Paul Bigelow on 14 August 1942

I said to Bigelow, "I have an evil premonition about this trip." just before leaving. Well, the place is o.k. – it's me. I didn't have a prayer.

A man cannot face the sun until he is steeled against it. The blasting kiss I received is proof of my punity. I came to it white and soft and it gave me a withering rebuke. I must leave it dark and hardened – one of its own kind. The kind of the sun. The sun's kind. It will confirm me. Place its fiery brand on my body. Mark me for its own. I will leave here with the sign of the holy author on my naked flesh. A sun child. A sun man. A savage. Lonely. Maybe speechless. Bitter, perhaps, but one who bears the kiss of fire on him. A survivor. One who has gone in and passed through and come out on the other side. <u>En Avant</u>!

A copy of "Time" has kept me occupied till after midnight – Now a mebral and attempt to sleep – and a prayer!


*Saturday, 15 August 1942*

Sat. A.M.

Getting up – sunburn <u>better</u> – Now to try my luck at that usually reluctant and recalcitrant instrument of divinity, the gen. del. window at the P.O.

Later –

A Telegram from Paul said special delivery letter mailed that morning. "Hold on, Toots."

food today – 1 doughnut 1 hamburger.


*Sunday, 16 August 1942*

Sunday 11:30 A.M.

Well, I am still holding on – Weak as a kitten. My cough shakes me like a dried leaf. I don't see how I can get through the day without food, but the chances are I will have to. Perhaps I will be very cavalier and go to the beach. No cigarettes either but don't miss them this A.M.

When you wait for something pretty desperately it will use every trick of evasion before it finally comes.

Eve.

It <u>came</u> – a few minutes after above entry. Since then I have been eating, eating! Also the extravagance of a movie.

Solitude continues.

I come home about 9:30 with nothing to do but sit on the porch till sleepy. But I have cigs. so it is not too dreary.

Tomorrow I think I will renew my acquaintance with Cuban coffee at the Spic joint down the street – work a while – go to beach – rest of week, the rest-cure.

516.  Herbert Berghof (1909–90) was an actor, director, and, most notably, an eminent drama teacher. He was born in Vienna and performed in numerous roles in Austria before fleeing Europe in 1938. Berghof was associated with the Dramatic Workshop at the New School, and Williams references him in a letter to Piscator (2 February 1942, HRC). He received critical acclaim for his role as the protagonist in *Nathan the Wise* earlier in the year. Brooks Atkinson's opinion in the *New York Times* (12 March 1942) confirms Williams' choice:

> As the sagacious Nathan, Herbert Berghof is giving one of the most radiant performances of the season. He manages to be compassionate and humble without losing his self-respect as a person and without wallowing in sentimentality.

517.  Probably the poem beginning "I wounded a man I knew."

I wounded a man I knew
for I hated and loved him, too.
His wound was fresh and it bled a lot
and the blood of his body was red and hot,
I wounded a man I knew.
He dripped remorseless dew.
His foot was white and his hand was white
and we slept in the crook of a tree that night.
I wounded a man I knew.
The veins of his throat were blue.
He was tender and wild with the faith
of a child,
and a penny for luck in his shoe.

St. Augustine, Fla
August, 1942.

My face is peeling. – Mail? I hope I hope!

*Monday, 17 August 1942*

Monday –
    Another lonely day.
    I get up early, read at the library. The Spick refuses to serve strangers so I go to a hotel for coffee. I do some good writing on the play which I am making from "The Malediction". It has a promising look, so I write H. Berghof[516] that I have a play for him to act in. Then the beach, and I am spurned by the kid I tried to talk to – he is painting his boat and is not inclined to be friendly. I can feel only a little pleasure in the beach alone. Alone, I return home, and walk the whole long way. Alone I eat and alone I wander a long ways, through an ancient cemetery, around the old fortress. I go and sit in a bar – alone. Return home alone. I ~~read~~ write down a new poem[517] in my collection, I smoke a cig., I brood – gloomily.
    Now I prepare to sleep. Alone. The cold, I believe, is better but the nerves are worse. When will the cool, white time of healing arrive? When will the fingers of peace be laid on my forehead? Oh, days ahead – give me a sign! Give me a candle – to walk by! Oh, it's so bewildering – uncertain – where I stand.
    Courage, my lad – <u>En Avant</u>!

*Tuesday, 18 August 1942*

Tues.
    The nerves continue their offensive.
    Blue devils in full force.
    Still no companionship which is what I need.
    Let me record once and for all the sad fact that the beach, which I am always regarding as the supreme benediction is not much good without companions. That it is not the cure-all I think it is when I am leading a hectic urban life. The beach itself is nice – lovely – but loneliness makes even that useless as a restorative.
    The cold, however, is better. But I keep on drinking coffee which I'd resolved to quit.
    I am so weary of introspection and it is carried to manic extremes here.
    Well, we will be more sensible now. Maybe move in a house where I will be thrown with people. My body is peeling – not very pretty. head feels funny – pops when I swallow – tight and ragged. Ah, well, I am not in the army. I suppose this is better than that would be. And so to bed – <u>Bon nuit.</u>

518. Brooks Atkinson reviewed *Across the Board on Tomorrow Morning* and *Talking to You*, which Saroyan
also produced and directed, for the *New York Times* (18 August 1942):

"Across the Board on Tomorrow Morning" is a comic, spontaneous stage gambol that Mr. Saroyan
has neglected to bring to life in the theatre; and "Talking to You" is a kind-hearted modern allegory
that leaves nothing but a generalized, stammering impression. Although Mr. Saroyan is an affable
chap with an attractive slant on people, his stage direction is like the compounding of a felony. He
needs a professional director.

Williams enclosed the review, together with one by Howard Barnes in the *New York Herald Tribune*, with
a letter to Paul Bigelow (postmarked 25 August 1942, Columbia) in which he wrote: "Saroyans plays were
panned in Times and Herald Trib, only rev. I've seen. Goody!"

519. Williams had written Windham ([20 July 1942], Yale) about the $60,000:

Saroyan is in New York now. . . . New Yorker says he is staying at "Hampstead House" — No —
correction! — "Hampshire House", a suite on the 28th floor. It seems that he swindled Mr. Mayer
(Hollywood) out of $60,000. on some kind of legal fraud. We must find out how he did it. There is
no trick to low for my present nature. Or yours, I hope. — Kid him along about his genius and our
sufferings. Both of us starving, selling our souls and trying to sell our asses.

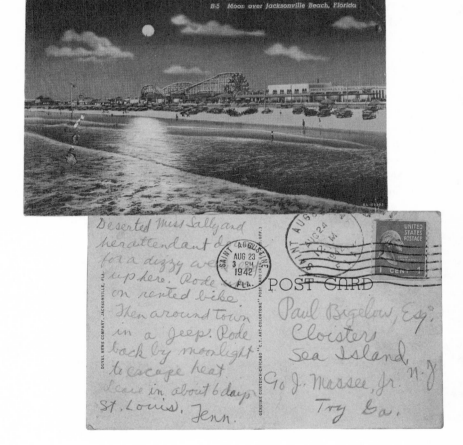

*Wednesday, 19 August 1942*

Wed

As days go, this one was good.

Roamed and roamed around looking for places to stay a little less lonesome than my present quarters. All too high.

Pardon! (Just spat up some bloody mucous)

~~Went out~~ Read N.Y. reviews of Saroyan's plays. I was pleased to find the critics took him to task.⁵¹⁸ The son of a bitch had it coming. Writing is not that easy even for a genius with $60,000.⁵¹⁹ – yes, I am envious and malicious.

I went to the beach. A boat anchored out beyond my usual range offered a challenge which I finally took – to prove my guts.

Nothing more but all that was better than yesterday.

Now, shaved, rested, I'll pace about the streets again. Byebye!

*Sunday, 23 August 1942*

Sunday –

Yesterday I rode my bike 30 miles up to Jacksonville beach and even further back, by moonlight – a physical ordeal but it was good for me. I saw a white horse standing motionless in a clearing, the moon just brightening and a little stream bubbling in the ditch. The horse was large and it stood there like a marble statue looking at me, around it great trees, moss-draped, and dusk falling.

Later the smooth white highway like silk under the tires and weariness and thirst making it so good when I finally reached a place to buy cold drinks. I drank a coke, an orange soda, and two glasses of water at one sitting.

The beach made me lonely, all those people I didn't know. I had too much timidity to speak to anybody.

I have written home for bus-fare to St. Louis. It appears the die is cast and I go back <u>again</u> – Can't I ever get away? – and under the worst circumstances. How can I face them, answer all their questions? My father – how to meet him again? – Will I be able to do it? – Or will I run away again? – New York? – And cheat my poor Mother who goes without a servant to keep me going? Oh, but this business of dragging myself back before them, again unsuccessful, again dependant, it is very, very hard for me to accept. Can I? – Will I? – Je ne sais pas.

This trip here was a sorry idea. I am wretched with loneliness and ennui – It begins to have a very stale, fetid atmosphere, this continual wretchedness, self-pity, and weariness of mine. My head and my heart are heavy with it. I must learn to cast it off. To be manly. In that direction I make progress slowly.

Crane, you have been there before me.
You have been all the places before me.
You are like me, traveller born –

520.  Robinson Jeffers (1887–1962) was a poet, educated in the classics, who led a reclusive life in the coastal
town of Carmel, California. He is known for his belief in extreme individualism. He based many of his
narrative poems on biblical and classical sources and dealt with such subjects as sexuality, incest, violence,
and intergenerational conflict. By 1942, he had published several volumes of poetry, the most recent being
*Be Angry at the Sun* (1941).

Charlotte Street, St. Augustine. The first house on the left is number 246 where Williams stayed.

Excerpt of a letter Williams wrote to Donald Windham
(21 August 1942)

Stranger and traveller.
I am thy frail ghost-brother.
The meek blond one with the blind left eye.
Take me now by the hand.
Lead me. Let us go together
Travellers born. Strangers. Friends.

O Hart. Dead Hart. No, living deathless Hart. Drunkard brawler. I cannot
follow entirely. I cannot burn so purely. Know my voice, however. Recognize me
and take me with you when my courage fails. Even to the final place. The resting
place. The dark. I am thy frail ghost-brother. Thy equal wanderer. Guide me.

What taunts me worst is my inability to make contact with the people, the
world. I remain one and separate among them. My tongue is locked. I float
among them in a private dream And shyness forbids speech and union. This is
not always so. A sudden touch will release me. Once out, I am free and
approachable. I need the solvent which hasn't come to me here, this time.


*Monday, 24 August 1942*

Mon. Night

This evening a stranger picked me up. A common and seedy-looking young
Jew with a thick accent. I was absurdly happy. For the first time since my arrival
here I had a companion.

I took him all over town, bought him a beer, found him a place for the night.
He was a hitch-hiker with a bag of cheese and rolls for food.

It was like cool water after hot thirst, just being <u>with</u> somebody. Left me quiet
and relaxed.

I went home and read Robinson Jeffers' extraordinarily good-and-bad verse.[520]

This afternoon I wrote and it was no fun but I got some probably not so bad
work done.

No mail. Tomorrow?

The New York silence disturbs me. I guess it will have to be home for a while,
at least.

Feel not bad tonight.

Hungry – very little to eat.

Salad for supper.

Milk for lunch.

Coffee for breakfast.

<u>Bon nuit</u> –

521. George Woodberry (1855–1930) was a distinguished poet, critic, and teacher who was professor of literature at Columbia University from 1891 to 1904. In the postscript to a letter to Paul Bigelow (postmarked 25 August 1942, Columbia), Williams asked:

> Do you think one could dramatize "Don Quixote"? Selected parts of it? The death of the chivalric ideal — fall of knight errantry, a play of the disaster of all ideals? I am reading — starting the book — the Introduction by Geo. Woodberry to the Knopf (1926) edition is what gave me the notion — brilliant essay!

Williams went on to include Don Quixote as a character in "Ten Blocks on the Camino Real," which was expanded into the full-length play *Camino Real*, as well as in the novella "The Knightly Quest."

522. Latin for "about to die." Interestingly Williams wrote a speech entitled "Te Moraturi Salutamus or An Author's Address to A First Night Audience" which he intended "to deliver . . . before the next production" of *Battle of Angels*. He tells the members of the audience who have an "allergy to serious sex drama" that "the kindest thing that you all can do is to leave the theatre." He concludes the address by asking those members who have a negative reaction to the play not "to impose themselves upon the reactions of other people, sitting next to you or near you" who if "not distracted [may] discover something in the play . . . that purges their own confused emotions through its very seriously-intended vivisection of the human heart."

523. The next day Williams drafted a response to Robert Lewis in his notebook: "I am sorry I haven't heard from Libby [Holman] as I have written a rather beautiful poetic play in four scenes, with a singing part for her — 'The Beetle of the Sun' is the present title." "The Beetle of the Sun" was a dramatization of "The Malediction." The prologue follows:

```
                NARRATOR'S PROLOGUE                                    人


                                        (STAGE LIGHTS, EMPTY ROOM, SINGING)
    A woman singing can fill an empty house

    with the shadows of leaves and color the air with lanterns.

    No room is bare with in it a woman singing.

    A lonely man, a man whose home is nowhere,

    stops on the street because of a woman singing.

    Because of a woman singing he climbs the stairs

    and recognizes a place for habitation.
          He finds
    Behold a furnished room, and furnished barely,    (DOOR OPENS, MAN ENTERS

    a bed, a chair, a table, a room that views

    a region suited only for skinny cats!
                                                 (HE MOVES TO THE WINDOW)
    Cabbages stud the yard like static fountains

    of bluish-green seawater. An odor of naptha

    comes from the laundry next-door. The bristling stacks

    of factories limit the distance. Toward the East,

    from which the sun has risen, the man can see

    the hills of the cemetary.  Still he remembers   (HE TURNS TO FACE A WOMAN IN
                                                           THE DOORWAY)
    the sound of the woman singing. He dares to believe

    that here is home and a certain allowance of peace....

    (THE WOMAN ENTERS THE ROOM)
```

*Tuesday, 25 August 1942*

Tues. A.M.

Basis of Zero! – We shall retreat to that line, the basis of zero – and there, with no ground to lose, we will stand impregnable because no enemy will have anything to get from us.

Later –

I have returned from reading at the library Geo. Woodberry's (who is he?) brilliant introduction to Don Quixote.[521]

The tragedy of the ideal –

The truth of the matter is that all human ideals have been hats too big for the human head.

Chivalry – democracy – Christianity – The Hellenic ideal of ~~Purity~~ Intellectual purity (the one I find most appealing) – all too big a hat! –

Undoubtedly the Fascist "ideal" of force which we are <u>supposed</u> to be fighting – is a closer fit.

But will not the immemorial Don Quixote of the race – Consciousness rebell at wearing a hat that fits with such humiliating precision?

No, the hopeful thing is still that we wish we had bigger skulls, not smaller hats to wear.

Maybe the bone will expand. If the world lasts long enough.

Well – Mystery, I salute thee! –

And I am very much "Moraturi"[522] today.

My head reels – the cold is again worse – the neurosis, the spectre of all defeat, is my hound-at-heels. I have about $1.50 and today no mail.

(As usual I use this journal mostly for distress-signals and do not often bother to note the little and decently impersonal things which sometimes have my attention)

A hard, clean rain is commencing to fall – cool wind sweeps in the curtains – I lie on the bed – Smoke – read – wait! – with what I can manage of patience for life to embrace me again. Such is the "basis of Zero." Simple endurance. There are worse things than this. The physical agonies of men at war, this existence would appear lovely to them. I think, however, it is all about on the same level – a diseased will and a sick mind – a life at the battlefront.

Night – still on the bed –

Smoking – waiting – a little devil of violence is under my skin. I looked at the big stupid white water pitcher a moment ago and thought how nice it would be to smash it against the wall. But I will not indulge that whimsy yet a while.

Mail came – a letter from Paul, a letter from Holt, a card from Bob Lewis.[523]

The blue devils have still got me by the balls.

It's just grit my teeth and hang on till I can move from here and be shocked back into a more normal state of mind by change of situation.

Good luck.

Don — Hope you haven't written me at home as I am not going there. I have a job. In the U.S. Engineers office (War Dept.) operating teletype machine at $120⁰⁰ a month, working night shift, from 11 P.M. to 7. A.M. At last moment couldn't endure prospect of St. Louis, so I abandoned my ivory tower which never was much anyhow. Let me hear from you.

Tenn.

Postcard Williams sent to Donald Windham on 31 August 1942

Williams' ID badge at the U.S. Engineers

*Wednesday, 26 August 1942*

<u>Wed. P.M.</u> – Aug. 27, 1942.
    Money has come!
    We prepare to blow out of this town!
    <u>En Avant!</u>

*Friday, 4 September 1942*

Friday – Sept 4. Jacksonville, Fla.
    The evening sky is pale pink and blue. So what?
    For over a week I have been working on the night shift at the U.S. Engineers. The job becomes tolerable. My nerves remain in shattered condition. Social neurosis and every kind of spook in the belfry. Not getting any swimming and not enough sleep and no sex may be responsible. Sensible thing is try to get all three.

*Sunday, 11 October 1942*

Sunday – Oct 11, 1942.
    Been here nearly a month and a ½.
    2 things have happened.
    1. The hope of immediate salvation from play dispelled by news I have to rewrite – from Audrey. Wants me to return to N.Y.
    2. Sex – a rather tender but not quite adequate relation with a simple adolescent. Puppy love sort of thing, which I only press as far as the limit of prudence. Still, an attachment exist, and this is an act of God, as it provides my sole comfort. That is, aside from having money for an abundance of food.
    The town is horribly dull. But the life I can bear.
    The blue devils have barely left me for a day since St. Augustine.
    I have not tried to bridge them.
    Done, attempted no work. Well, it will soon end, this period.
    I will accept Paul's and Audrey's suggestion and quit job and go back to N.Y., probably the sixteenth. <u>En Avant</u>.

524.  Lincoln Kirstein (1907–96) was a significant figure in the arts in the twentieth century. The author of thirty books and hundreds of articles on art, architecture, and literature, he is best known for his pioneering efforts in the development of ballet in the United States. With George Balanchine he co-founded the School of American Ballet in 1934 and the New York City Ballet in 1948. In 1942 he founded the magazine *Dance Index*. Kirstein arranged a meeting for Williams with James Laughlin, founder of New Directions, in his apartment. Laughlin went on to become the main publisher of Williams' work.

525.  Williams refers to Carly Wharton's interest in *You Touched Me!* Wharton was married to the prominent theatrical attorney John F. Wharton. With the backing of John "Jock" Hay Whitney, they had produced several successful Broadway plays, including *Life with Father* (1939), *Charley's Aunt* (1940), and *Cafe Crown* (1942) directed by Elia Kazan.

Lincoln Kirstein, 1946 (photograph by George Platt Lynes)

/ / / / / / /

Manhattan : Period VIII

*Early November 1942*

The little slants at the top of the page are my computation of the times I've been in N.Y. with periods abroad being the separations. This is the eigth period, now under way for over a week.

I am well, I am somewhat more than reasonably in good spirits. The 2 mos. employment in Jacksonville, a regular life with plenty of food and the fairly pleasant circumstances, gave me a new lease on life, badly needed after the hellishly close call in St. Augustine and the dragging summer in Macon, in that stifling attic. Still, even Macon with its prolific work and its rich material and Paul – was good for me in non-physical ways.

I don't know if I shall keep a journal. Probably not much of one, for I hope I shall be too busy for much introspection.

Lincoln Kirsten, through Donnie, has taken a sudden interest in my verse, though not, perhaps, a very judicial one. He may be helpful.[524]

The play re-write, third and final, is complete.

So, dear journal – my comforter – you may let me go for a while. I will come back again, crying no doubt, and tell you all about it.

For sex – two affairs, a beautiful cold prostitute from Texas, and all that implies – and a solid mature, rather Rubenesque person met in the steam room of this establishment whom I fucked twice both ways but probably won't look up again.

The sweet thrill of merely Caressing my little one in Jacksonville was better than any of these.

About myself, an opinion? I must and see, but I think I will manage to come through with a measure of decency still.


*Saturday, 12 December 1942*

Dec. 12 – about 1:00 A.M.

Been here over a month now. Nothing really has happened – to alter the ~~outlook~~ situation.

The play has been on the rounds for about 2 weeks. One producer has shown an interest.[525] The others not heard from. I worked 2 days and quit – too dreary – teletype operator at British Purchasing Commission. Could not sit still.

All day I went about looking for hotel jobs. Morbid timidity made it difficult for me.

Now I have about 50¢ (borrowed from Donnie) and nothing definite to depend on.

526.   Charles Henri Ford (1908–2002) is generally regarded as the first American Surrealist poet, as well as an innovative artist, writer, editor, and filmmaker. From 1929 to 1930, he edited *Blues: A Magazine of New Rhythms*, which published Gertrude Stein, e.e. cummings, and Ezra Pound. The magazine was not well received in America, and in 1931 Ford moved to Paris for four years where he established himself in the literary community.

Ford was admired for his imaginative and technically brilliant use of language, and he co-wrote with Parker Tyler *The Young and the Evil* (1933), considered to be the first gay novel. Ford went on to found and edit *View* magazine and View Editions in New York City (1940–47). During his lifetime he published sixteen collections of poems and had numerous one-man exhibitions of photographs, collages, paintings, and drawings in London, Paris, and New York.

Portrait of Charles Henri Ford by Pavel Tchelitchew, 1937

Sexually – a good deal.

Tonight my Oriental returned – not very exciting this time.

Oh, let's not talk about sex.

It seems rather empty now.

All I can do is wait. It will not be good here till I am settled – work I like or find tolerable – or play sold – a typewriter and time to create.

I see Donnie every day, nearly – I feel a deep fondness for him and the resentment about sharing the play seems trifling now.

I have been happy, I suppose. Health good enough, no neuroses. An animal pleasure in things.

But there must be more important things to come.

I wait for them –

I am waiting.

In the meantime I must be patient and wise – and <u>good</u>.

I must be a good boy.

Goodbye.


*Monday, 14 December 1942*

Dec. 14 –

Time roars quietly along.

I have about $2.00 left and no job and the room rent over due.

Donnie and Charles Henri Ford[526] swam with me at the "Y" this afternoon. Afterwards D. and I joked and invented imbecilic absurdities, walked along Broadway to Times Square looking at sailors, Etc.

I return early and sit about the "Y". I am restless tonight.

Yesterday afternoon a pretty unfortunate sexual experience with D.G. a new acquaintance. The nervous obstruction appeared and it was a bit awful.

This evening – craving, unsatisfied, in spite of all the promiscuity of this period. It is stupid and ugly. Or is it? It has begun to seem as simple as wanting a drink or food. That casual and unimportant. But that's not good, is it? No. But why protest? What's the use?

Tomorrow – lunch date with a producer – Miss Wharton.

Then I'll probably make some effort to get employment at hotels.

As usual life in N.Y. seems diverting but formless. And not really very much life-like.

I don't think I can sleep yet. Coffee about 10. ~~Will~~ May dress and go out for a bite. So long – Cross your fingers.

527.  Margo Jones (1911–55), a native of Texas, was a director, producer, and advocate of the regional theatre movement. In 1936 Jones had founded the Houston Community Players and served as its director. In 1942, she had recently accepted a teaching position in the drama department of the University of Texas at Austin.

In December Audrey Wood gave Jones copies of *Stairs to the Roof* and *You Touched Me!* Despite her enthusiasm, it was not until November 1943 that she directed *You Touched Me!* at the Pasadena Playhouse, followed by "The Purification" at the Pasadena Playhouse in 1944. In 1945, with Eddie Dowling, Jones co-directed *The Glass Menagerie*. She went on to direct *Summer and Smoke*, first in Dallas in 1947 and then on Broadway in 1948. When "The Purification" was published in *27 Wagons Full of Cotton and Other One-act Plays*, Williams added a dedication to Margo Jones. Williams borrowed his nickname for her, "the Texas Tornado," for his character Trinket Dugan in the play "The Mutilated."

Margo Jones

*Wednesday, 16 December 1942*

Tuesday Night –

It must be nearly 4 A.M. I can't sleep. Nerves I guess. Wharton seems on verge of buying play. Bigelow and I had lunch with her today.

Some changes must be made to satisfy her.

I then went to Employment agency. May go out of town for hotel work. Tomorrow. Unless Wharton buys play immediately –

80¢ left, room rent 4 days overdue.

Supper at Lincoln Kirstein's with Donnie – Fun – I am closer to D. than anyone else. Paul and I seem to be drifting apart. A mutual distrust seems to come between us. I hate distrust. I want so badly to believe in people. Their affection and honesty and good faith. I must try to be the things I want in others.

Well, I am honest. Much as I like Paul, I don't believe he is. I hope this feeling is an illusion and will pass away. It frightens me. We were so close last summer and he has been so good to me.

A miserable night in the Y. When D. leaves I am suddenly forlorn. The sordid itch of desire returns and the old shameful seeking.

The only purity, and rarely even then, is in work.

Crane. Dear Hart –
I embrace you
goodnight.
And keep those fingers
crossed.

*Friday, 18 December 1942*

Friday –

Wharton still cagey – no money – Another dinner date with her Sunday.

Margo Jones[527] writes long, enthusiastic letter from Texas. Hopes to produce "Stairs to the Roof".

I wake up this A.M. sick with cold and penniless and the two above items not yet apprehended.

The phone calls cheer me and I go out to Bigelows and the Author's League where Audrey has arranged a $10.00 loan to tide me over the next few days. I think perhaps I will try to go home for Xmas. It is a year since I have seen the home folks and a year is such a perilously long time as the old folks get older. It would hurt, it would be very sorrowful but I want it – to see them again. I should. After all, it is the only bond in my life. Otherwise I am just a loose plank on the flood. If Wharton kicks in with any cash I'll do the rewrite down there.

Bigelow was very nice today. He feels the separation and I think there is an affection in him, at least considerably genuine. The photograph of Isadora

528.   Arnold Genthe (1869–1942), born in Germany, emigrated to America in 1896 and specialized in dance and theatrical portraits. He took numerous photographs of the dancer Isadora Duncan and the Italian actress Eleanora Duse, which illustrate his characteristic painterly quality.

Notebook Williams began in November 1942

Duncan by Arnold Genthe – the one of Duse[528] – From five o'clock on I am alone. I swim, exercise, and go out alone to the movie. I return and the floor is quiet. My former friend, the dancer, is in a room with someone else. Desertion!

But last night I had a sudden and hot affair with a party from Wisconsin. I was told that I had a lovely body and the compliment was apparently sincere. As we increase the distance from our youth, such speeches have more and more pathetic value to us. It used to be taken for granted, that we were as desirable to the other as that one to us. Now we seldom are or we do not see how we could be, for we pursue the younger and lovelier than ourselves – Why do I write in the plural? It is too sad to say "I"? But I don't think much about losing my youth. It happens and is accepted gradually. I feel very young. In a way. And in a way very old. I do not feel the time sense of much longer living. No, it seems as though it would not be long to the finish. But I started feeling that a number of years ago.

I want to go back to <u>creation</u>.

Strongly, brightly, with a fresh and free spirit and a driving power.

To do the monument.

So long.

Photographs of Eleanora Duse (1924) and Isadora Duncan (circa 1915–18) by Arnold Genthe

529.  Donald Windham noted that during a period of four months in 1942–43 neither Williams nor he had lovers and often cruised together (interview with Margaret Bradham Thornton). The incident happened when they were cruising. Windham waited at the bar of the Hotel St. George while Williams went to his room with sailors and was beaten up.

530.  Paul Bigelow was living at 14 West 48th Street in New York.

531.  In a letter written in late December 1942 (HTC), Williams told his parents:
      I have been engaged in hot disputes and negotiations with a producer [Carly Wharton] who has finally come across with two hundred dollars to support me for the next two months while I make some further changes in the new comedy.
      A month later (25 January 1943, HTC), Williams commented on his progress in a letter to his mother:
      I have had to continue work on the play. Mrs. Wharton expects a lot of changes for her money and I can tell you it is quite a job satisfying her without making dangerous changes in the script.

Postcard Williams sent to his mother

*Tuesday, 5 January 1943*

Tuesday – Jan 5, 1943.

This is the first time that anybody ever knocked me down and so I suppose it ought to be recorded.[529] Unhappily I can't go into details. It was a case of guilt and shame in which I was relatively the innocent party, since I merely offered entertainment which was accepted with apparent gratitude until the untimely entrance of other parties. Feel a little sorrowful about. So unnecessary. The sort of behavior pattern imposed by the conventional falsehoods.

Donnie comforted me when he arrived on the scene. Now he is upstairs with another party procured in the bar. Why do they strike us? What is our offense? We offer them a truth which they cannot bear to confess except in privacy and the dark – a truth which is inherently as bright as the morning sun. He struck me because he did what I did and his friends discovered it. Yes, it hurt – inside. I do not know if I will be able to sleep. But tomorrow I suppose the swollen face will be normal again and I will pick up the usual thread of life. And go to Bigelow's[530] and write a bit. Poor Bigelow is ill.

*Thursday, 7 January 1943*

Wed. Night – (4:20 A.M. Thurs.)

Can't sleep – slept till 5 P.M. today.

Did nothing but visit Bigelow who was too ill for typing script. We have grown closer again. I am on excellent terms with both he and Donnie despite their enmity for each other. I play a somewhat deceptive rôle, since I must amuse each at the expense of the other, though I remain fundamentally faithful to both.

The life here in Brooklyn at the St. George hotel is comparable for sexual incontinence only to the early summer period at the Hotel Woodrow, Manhattan, summer, 1941. This is happier because of brighter prospect.

My face is still swollen from blow – the donor will remain in my memory always, and as a lover, not antagonist. There was something incredibly tender and sad in the experience. So much of life at its most haunting and inexpressible. Not that I like being struck, I hated it, but the keenness of the emotional situation, the material for art — these gave a tone of richness to it which makes the affair unforgettable among many that melt out of sight.

"Give me time for tenderness."

What is to come is still unclear but it looks like the play will go on. I have received an advance of $200.,[531] half of which is already spent – but the final and fourth revision is complete – I have worked on the play 11 months now.

What's next? In life? In work?

The heart is kicking up a bit lately. Take it easy, Son.

Goodnight.

532.  Paul Bigelow's jaw was fractured when he was mugged in Philadelphia.

533.  James "Jay" Laughlin (1914–97) was an heir to the Jones & Laughlin steel and iron fortune. He founded the publishing company New Directions in 1936 and went on to become a noted publisher of literary modernism. Years later Laughlin recalled his first meeting with Williams:

> I was at a cocktail party in New York . . . being given by Lincoln Kirstein, then one of my idols. It was a pretty big apartment, and I could see this little fellow with baggy pants and a torn sweater sitting all by himself and looking very nervous. And I was a little nervous too, so I went over to talk to him. We started talking and we found out that we both loved Hart Crane, and we became almost instant friends. ("James Laughlin's Newest Direction Is Looking Back," *Avenue*, December–January 1985, p. 142)

In a letter dated 20 January 1943 (HRC), Laughlin reacted to the poems:

> I am very excited with the poems you sent. It seems to me you ARE a poet. Some of the stuff is rough, to be sure, but it's studded with nuggets. You have some of that wonderful quality of Eluard — strange insights that reduce to highly poetic images.

Williams dedicated the poem "Camino Real," subsequently retitled "The Jockeys at Hialeah," to Laughlin.

James Laughlin

*Saturday, 9 January 1943*

Friday Night (4 A.M. Sat.)

Cruising like mad the past 2 nights and no dice! Tonight I entertained three Italians in my room. They were interested only in material advantage and my verbal exposition of the peculiarities of my way of life – We parted on excellent terms at about 2 A.M. but nothing done to appease my appetite. I recited poetry to them and offered them rum but the junior membership which they referred to as Oscar remained in retirement. So I did the lobby and the streets of vicinity and now I give up and return to my room with shattered faith in the efficacy of my Seeking.

Seeking – what a pain it is when it isn't satisfied.

Tomorrow is Saturday night and I'll probably do better but the failure these past 2 nights is depressing.

Aside from this – Saw Bigelow and worked on play but he has not started typing. Saw Donnie who seemed more than usually steeped in his own advantage.

A bad day, all in all, and we'd better close it late but not any later.

All this is bitchery. Sad and sordid bitchery. I don't see much beyond it. <u>En Avant.</u>

Saturday Noon – I rise after not much sleep and take a swim – not much swim. The day appears reasonably bright. I will go out to Manhattan, to Bigelow's and see what is cooking about the play.

*Tuesday, 12 January 1943*

Tues. Night.

The play script had to be turned over to professional typist as Bigelow did not recover sufficiently[532] to get it done. She is still at it – embarrassing delay.

This evening, to get something <u>done</u>, I sent off a bunch of the poems to Laughlin[533] after working more on "The Dangerous Painters". It <u>could</u> be a fine poem with more work on it.

Saturday Night I had the most beautiful (looking) lay of my entire experience. Really flawless. Strange how little excitement I felt, however. Wanted money, paid $2. Then turned it over to Donnie who was waiting his turn downstairs.

I had better get away from all this, unless the play goes into production. It satisfies nothing more than the immediate itch. I remember when I first came to N.Y. a couple of seasons ago – 3 seasons ago – I kept looking for "the big, important thing" to happen. Well, that summer I had K. It nearly killed me. Since then there hasn't been anything but surface. Well, I ought to simplify my life, to make it clear for work. And to get back some dignity. I couldn't stand an isolated life without a lover. But a life in a small place, with simple, honest relationships

534. Ella Williams (1875–1958), the unmarried sister of Williams' father, who lived in Knoxville, Tennessee.

THE DANGEROUS PAINTERS

I told him about the galleries upstairs,

the gilt and velour  insulation of dangerous painters.

I said, If they let these plunging creations hang

where they sprung from easels, along cracked walls,

beneath the broken ceilings, the fingers of starving bodies

would point them out, explain the tensile fury that gave them birth.

I said, It is therefore necessary to patronize them,

to give them expensive surroundings, as if to say,

This madman slept in a gold-brocaded bed!

As if to say, This torrent of anger ~~walked~~ moved on a velvet carpet!

As if to say, His rooms were softly lighted!

We must not know how the morning struck his face,

slapped it red without pity!  It must be felt

that his rage was approved by the church and the academicians

and all felt tender chagrin  at his dissipations.

A bread of pity, as black as the nostrils of negros,

was given at supper, the old nurse carved it quietly

and handed it out to quiet and stupefied people.

The evening fell with cinders drifting, drifting,

everywhere cinders drifting.

    The spent and purified people sat on the pavements,

hunched against broken walls and were grateful for stillness,

grateful for effortless breathing now that the wind

had begun to freshen the city.

With hardly a sound, with hardly even a sigh,

the earth began to move again through space.

                        Tennessee Williams
                        Brooklyn, January, 1943.

Opening and closing lines from Williams' long poem "The Dangerous Painters"

(friends), <u>and</u> some sexual partner or outlet accessible is what I should seek out for myself.

It is Jan. 10 and I haven't mailed the Xmas presents home. Or written Auntie.534

Self, self, self – How wearisome and ugly. I think it poisons my work. I must purify it somehow before the end.

En Avant!

(I am going down to do a little cruising.)

Later – No luck. Wretched.

I don't think it's sex I want. There is no great hankering for that. It's the dread of coming up alone to this little room at night. And going to bed and turning my face to the wall. It is hard to sleep lately before 3 or 4 in the morning. Ah, well – change is imminent, of one kind or another. The hell with loneliness – When we wake up, we will swim. Good night.

(I saw 4 middle-aged men moving heavily and dully across the lobby in their dark clothes and I thought how little they were unlike 4 apes. It hasn't happened yet, the human race, it has not yet been created.)


*Thursday, 14 January 1943*

Late Thurs. Night –

Probably the most shocking experience I've ever had with another human being last night when my trade turned "dirt". No physical violence resulted, but I was insulted, threatened, bullied, and robbed – of about $1.50 and a cigarette lighter. All my papers were rooted through and the pitiless, horrifying intimidation was carried on for about an hour. I was powerless. I could not ask for help. There was only me and him, a big guy. Well, I kept my head and I did not get panicky at any point though I expected certainly to be beaten. I didn't even tremble. I talked gently and reasonably in answer to all the horrible abuse. Somehow the very helplessness and apparent hopelessness of the situation prevented much fright. I stayed in the room while he was threatening and searching, because my Mss. were there and I feared he might try to confiscate or destroy them. In that event, I would have fought, called for help, anything! He finally despaired of finding any portable property of value and left, with the threat that any time he saw me he would kill me. I felt sick and disgusted. I think that is the end of my traffic with such characters. Oh, I want to get away from here and lead a clean, simple, antiseptic life – Taos – the desert and the Mts.

535. Fidelma Kirstein (1907–91), whose brother was the painter Paul Cadmus, was married to Lincoln Kirstein.

536. In Jean Cocteau's novella *Le Livre Blanc* (1928), the narrator describes his love affairs with young men, all of which end unhappily. Cocteau ends the novella with a plea for homosexual love to be accepted, not merely tolerated:

> Instead of adopting Rimbaud's gospel, *The time of the assassins has come*, young people would do better to remember the phrase *Love must be reinvented*. The world accepts dangerous experiments in the realm of art . . . but it condemns them in life. . . .
>
> . . . I will not agree to be tolerated. This damages my love of love and of liberty. (*The White Book* [San Francisco: City Lights Books, 1989], pp. 75, 76)

Fidelma Cadmus Kirstein, 1941 (photograph by George Platt Lynes)

*Friday, 15 January 1943*

Today I delivered the play to Carley Wharton's office. Her decision should come along shortly. Then I can leave – go home, I am lonely for the old folks – or else lose myself in the production.

I spent a quiet, sweet evening with Donnie and Fidelma Kirsten.535 Nice dinner there, good companionship and reading Blake, Baudelaire, and Cocteau's Livre Blanc536 aloud.

Fidelma is lovely. It was good after the horror of last night.

I must write home. And Auntie.

I am not a good boy. No. No.

But we will say good night.

*Saturday, 16 January 1943*

Sat. Night – An experience just consummated twice – very lovely – makes up for the last unhappy episode. This was blissful.

*Monday, 18 January 1943*

Monday Night (about 3 A.M.)

What Bigelow calls my "occupational disease" – crab lice – is back on me. Only one discovered but I shall have to procure a bottle of "The Personal Insecticide" tomorrow. Who shall I blame? Who is the father of these bastards I am reluctantly bearing? Qui sait?

(Elizabethan humor!)

Tomorrow I see Carly Wharton and a verdict will presumably be handed down on "You Touched Me" – an occasion important enough to alter the whole future course of my strange term on earth.

And so we come to the end of another journal. We are not afraid. We are prepared to go on. So En Avant!

*Wednesday, 20 January 1943*

Tuesday – Jan. 20 (I believe)

(about 4 A.M. Wed.)

Well, we'll devote the remaining few blank pages in this journal to the last few days in New York, for La Wharton has turned thumbs down on the re-write and my castles have tumbled again. I will probably return to Clayton and live on the folks for a while. Worse things are possible, since I have been away so long I'm really longing for home a bit. Excepting, of course, the old man. Perhaps he is

Sat. Jan 24.

I guess this sorry little notebook
will serve to record what's left
of the apparently dwindling 8th
period in New York.

My money is running out
and I am unable to settle on a
course of action. I drift* on.

My heart just now acted oddly.

Now I must not look for happiness
but endurance. It is strange and
interesting to think that what is now
so unknown, so dark, the solution of the
situation I am in, will resolve
itself in only a few days time

Saturday **night** and no sex. The
night seemed hostile.

too old a dragon to be still very fearsome. We shall see. Mon devoir is to Grand and Grandfather – and Mother.

It was a blow at Wharton's. She is way up on the 29th story and from her window we could see the Statue of Liberty. I had an admirable composure for <u>me</u> and I took the medicine which she gave me straight in a manner becoming a "veteran of discouragement" which I told her I was. We parted on good terms. I shall make no outraged comments on producers. They are fools – like everyone else – only a <u>little</u> more so. Unfortunately they have the power to wring a poet's heart, if not his neck, when he comes into the theatre – or tries to. – See Audrey tomorrow. Then probably —

En Avant!

(I have a rendezvous at daybreak – Someone will come to my room.)

*(The rendezvous this (Wed.) morning was nice. Creamy blond body and amusingly childish mind.)*

*Thursday, 21 January 1943*

About 4 A.M. Thurs.

The talk at Audrey's cheered me a bit. She was very sweet. Bigelow was there and they seemed to feel things would work out, better than I felt. Bigelow will type the thing over again after we discuss it at Audrey's Friday. Then I may leave for home – frightening idea. I must steel myself for it. "I run, cried the fox, in circles!" Maybe Clark will still be there but a meeting with him now might be almost intolerably strange with all the water that's gone under the mill since the days of our companionship – the "literary factory" –

*Friday, 22 January 1943*

Friday Nite (very late indeed) – Pleasant encouraging evening at Audrey's, Bigelow at his conversational best, very brilliant. I may manage to stay on here – Audrey prefers it and home would be a retreat at this moment not very strategic. Home to Brooklyn Sans cruising. No more space in this little blue book. Time! Thou Errant Knave!

*Saturday, 23 January 1943*

Sat. Jan 24.

I guess this sorry little notebook will serve to record what's left of the apparently dwindling 8th period in New York.

537. Williams did show up for work at the Gotham Book Mart, but because, as predicted, he arrived late, he was fired after only one day by its owner, Frances Steloff.

538. Hotel St. George, Clark Street at Henry in Brooklyn, New York.

539. Jeanne Lawson (1918– ), a dancer, married Fritz Bultman in December 1943 in New York City. In an interview with Margaret Bradham Thornton, she remembered Williams' nickname as "Minna."

540. Horton Foote (1916– ) is an actor-playwright who had formed the American Actors Company (1938–44) with Mary Hunter. By 1943 Foote had already had two plays, *Texas Town* and *Out of My House*, performed Off-Broadway. Foote went on to become a successful playwright and screenwriter, winning the 1995 Pulitzer Prize for *The Young Man from Atlanta* and two Academy Awards for screenplays.

Williams did find employment as an elevator operator, but it did not last long, for as he wrote to his parents ([March 1943], HRC), the job required that he work fourteen hours a night and was "entirely too much" for him. Over the next few months Williams would also work as an usher at the Strand Theatre and as a night watchman and elevator man at the Hotel San Jacinto at 18 East 60th Street.

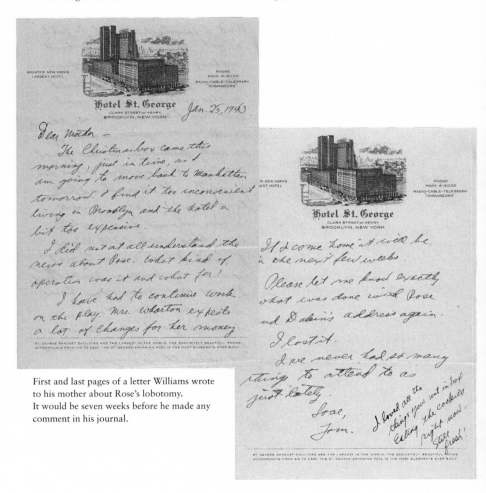

First and last pages of a letter Williams wrote to his mother about Rose's lobotomy.
It would be seven weeks before he made any comment in his journal.

My money is running out and I am unable to settle on a course of action. I drift on.

My heart just now acted oddly.

Now I must not look for happiness but endurance. It is strange and interesting to think that what is now So unknown, So dark, the solution of the Situation I am in, will resolve itself in only a few days time.

Saturday night and no sex. The night seemed hostile.


*Monday, 25 January 1943*

Sun. Night

Nothing has happened to change the situation except that I certainly won't get up in time tomorrow to try that job at the book store.537 It is 5 A.M. and I am applying "The Personal Insecticide" in the shower room. The little pets again.

Blank space is the future but if you don't dive you get pushed in anyway.

So here we go.

No cigs. Mood reasonably blue.

Hate this hotel.538 A sort of middle class Ritz.

Spent eve. with Fritzie and Jean. Jean is a tall blond fille de joie and a former burlesk dancer. Very fresh and clean looking and genuinely childlike. She loves "the girls" and likes to cruise with us.539 Has no money and just drifts through time as I do. I like her very much.

I am fed up with Paul at the moment and he with me. He is very anxious to get me out of town.

I rather think tonight that I won't go.

One lives a vast number of days but life seems short because the days repeat themselves so. Take that period from my 21 to 24 yr. when I was in the shoe busines, a clerk typist in St. Louis at $65 a month. It all seems like one day in my life. It was all one day over and over. Ben in "Stairs to the Roof." The best way to have new days is to travel or be sexually promiscuous or work with intensity on a long creation. The progress of the work gives time a perspective. Yes, we must not go over and over our same day unless that day is deeply satisfying which it rarely is. One cannot hope for a life of continual movement and change and so must devise a good and deeply satisfying day to repeat. A day involving love and creation and security and a beautiful open country. New Mexico.

Help me, dear God, to find what I need.

Goodnight.


Monday –

Well, at least a glimmer of light appears and the die is cast that I shall at least remain in N.Y. till the money gives altogether out.

Horton Foote540 the playwright told me about an elevator operator's Union

541.  In a letter to his mother (25 January 1943, HTC), Williams explained: "I am going to move back to Manhattan tomorrow. I find it too inconvenient living in Brooklyn and the hotel a bit too expensive."

542.  Contrary to Williams' opinion, the revival of the Chekhov play, starring Katharine Cornell (1893–1974) as Masha and directed by her husband, Guthrie McClintic, received enthusiastic reviews. Despite his negative reaction to *The Three Sisters*, Williams, as indicated in "notes for rewrite of Spinning Song" (dated February 1943), intended to rework parts in order to attract Cornell:

> As now sketched it is much too trugid and sloppy. Scenes must be chiselled finely. Build up all the mother's scenes to interest Cornell. Reduce the narrator's speeches to essentials. Suspect your lyricism — it's mostly bad. Try to build with more original material and more arresting plot or story, involving the parents, especially the mother. Her scenes with Father's death and the doctor the big scnes of play.

Within several years Williams would begin drafts of *A Streetcar Named Desire* and *Summer and Smoke* with Cornell in mind.

543.  In "West to Japan" (*Life*, 15 March 1943), journalist John Field reported the story of a successful patrol by an American submarine off the coast of Japan during which it sank "70,000 tons of Jap shipping."

544.  "The Playboy of Newark" by Ben Simkhovitch opened on 19 March 1943 at the Provincetown Playhouse, New York.

545.  Sanford Meisner (1905–97), a noted American actor, teacher, and director, was a member of the Group Theatre and appeared in a number of their productions. In 1935 he began teaching the Group's Method acting at the Neighborhood Playhouse School of the Theatre, where he became the head and stayed until 1959. After directing the new talent division of Twentieth Century-Fox Studios from 1959 to 1961, he returned to the Neighborhood Playhouse School in 1964.

546.  Mary Hunter (1904–2000), a talented director-producer, had founded with Horton Foote the American Actors Company.

547.  Lillian Green (1919–54), born in Clarksdale, Mississippi, was a blues singer who in the 1940s had a successful career touring theatres and clubs and recording a number of hits for RCA and other major labels.

Horton Foote, Mary Hunter, and the actor Joseph Anthony

which he thinks will get me a job. I will see in the A.M. Also will move from the St. George back to Y.541

Eventful day. Met William Saroyan and went to Cornell production of Three Sisters.542 Both disappointing. Saroyan is likeable enough with his somewhat calculated but fresh candor and probably has for many a charm. I felt too much space between us. As for 3 Sisters it just didn't have any effect whatsoever. Nobody connected with it seemed to feel the play as an entity.

So stupid tonight and the pen's no good. better quit. Let you know tomorrow how things work out.

So we light the last cigarette before sleep.

The air is pregnant with change, [unfinished]


*Friday, 12 March 1943*

New York Continued – March 12 1943
    What a long delay out of the sun!
    I live from day to day and days go on.
    I am dull but I go on writing.
    Yes, I am alarmingly dull, a wet match maybe won't strike anymore.
    Maybe the sun will dry it, it will still strike.
    Bad figure.
    Too sleepy to give any real information.
    This eve. Supper at Fidelma's with Donny. Nice walk across Park and along 5th Ave. Cool, clear night. Pleasant humors, fairly entertaining mystery movie. Home to Y to read "Life" account of submarine trip.543
    Fleet Munson called me last night. I was out.
    How strange!
    He was in prison for forgery last I heard.
    It would be nice to see him again.
    I associate him with that happy first season here at the Y. And the good luck.
    Maybe he's a bird of good omen, returning to change the luckless period since then.


*Sunday, 14 March 1943*

Sunday Eve.
    Last night rehearsal of Simkhovitches play "Playboy of Newark".544
    It has some charm but is rather on the weak side.
    I like him and the director Sandy Meisner.545
    Afterward – 2 Cuba libres and Ravioli with the cast at a Tavern.
    Then Mary Hunter,546 Horton Foote, and I went out to the Apollo in Harlem to see L'il Green. A Marvelous negro entertainer.547

548. Williams' comment about Foote indicates his feelings of rivalry which he would give voice to several months later. In a letter to Audrey Wood (9 July 1943, HRC), he wrote:

> It was not very smart of me to introduce him to Margo [Jones], for he is just as ingenuous as she is and I think he is much closer to her idea of a playwright. I regard Mr. Foote with a somewhat uncharitable reserve. Rivalry has something to do with it, I'm sure, but I find his great warmth and ingenuousness seeming a little spurious beside Margo's. — She doesn't. — The three of us get on well together, but I'm afraid I act like a Boston audience much of the time.

549. In his memoir *Tennessee Williams and Friends* (Cleveland: World Publishing, 1965), Gilbert Maxwell wrote:

> Meanwhile, in the Long Island hotel, my own problem with impossible night men had driven me to such desperation that I persuaded my boss to bring Paul Bigelow out to work with me.
>
> Paul had never set foot behind a hotel desk; nevertheless, he came to work one evening, learned how to operate the switchboard in five minutes flat and took over the desk like a veteran. . . .
>
> A few weeks later the hotel was sold; my amiable manager boss was fired, and I was gradually so sickened by what the new owners were doing to the place that I lost interest in the whole *enchilada*. . . . I complained to Bigelow night and day. He begged me simply to go on with my job and keep my mouth shut, as he was doing, but I found this procedure impossible. One day . . . I settled things for myself by losing my patience and my temper justifiably with the manager, and when he suggested that . . . I might better leave, I heartily agreed with him. (pp. 62–63)

550. Caleb Gray (1922–97) was a minor actor and writer. In a letter to Donald Windham ([July 1944], Yale), Williams gave a colorful account of his role in swapping sexual partners and noted: "Only KB [another name for Caleb Gray] could perform a better piece of diabolical strategy!" Windham explained that one night when they were all staying in the same house Gray had left Williams' bed in the middle of the night and come into his. Windham reported that Williams had denounced him and ordered him out of the house (DWL, p. 139n).

551. Williams returned to a manuscript he had described in a letter to Wood (circa 7 October 1941, HRC): "Completed first drafts (practically) of two new plays, one, mentioned previously, is now called 'A Daughter of the American Revolution' is predominantly humorous now, a sort of 'life with Mother'."

Only two fragments of "Daughter of Revolution" are known to exist. One comprises the scene in which Amanda Wingfield solicits magazine subscriptions of DAR members by telephone, a scene Williams would use in *The Glass Menagerie*. The other fragment contains only a title page and preface. On the title page Williams inscribed the play to "Miss Lillian and Miss Dorothy Gish for either of whom the part of Amanda Wingfield was hopefully intended." In the preface Williams disparaged the current popular war plays as shams and made a plea for the reconsideration of social dramas.

552. Williams would continue working on his dramatization of "The Malediction." A fragment entitled "Chaplinesque" (title taken from Crane's poem) reveals the influence of Charlie Chaplin:

> The play's intention is to create a sort of dramatic distillation of the quaintly appealing and lyrical elements of the early Chaplin screen comedies.
>
> Set, costumes, and make-up are black and white to suggest the effect of the early films. There is a piano accompaniment to the action and sub-titles.
>
> The sub-titles are projected on a screen above or to the side of the stage set.

In the published version of the play, Williams omitted the use of subtitles projected on a screen, something he would use later in *The Glass Menagerie*.

Williams eventually titled his dramatization "The Strangest Kind of Romance," changing the story's ending, in which the man drowns himself and the cat, to one in which the man returns from a mental hospital and goes off with his cat.

553. Williams and Windham were beaten up by two sailors in the Claridge Hotel.

554. Marion Gering (1901–77) was a former Broadway stage director who had successfully turned to films. He had hired Williams to adapt the story "Heart on the Sidewalk."

I find Mary delightful. Horton is a nice boy but I wonder how sincere.[548] No Donnie all weekend. No Bigelow since the Maxwell mess.[549]

This morning I woke up Cabey[550] for breakfast. Nice, Sunny walk downtown and I consumed 4 coffees in the course of the perambulations.

Got "Daughter of Revolution"[551] together – Don't think it's in a shape to show Audrey yet.

It's probably going to be a slight affair.

However "the cat play"[552] looks good – I got it back today and did a little good work on it this eve.

No sex in at least a week.

The violence at the Claridge[553] seems to have cured me of that particular type of waywardness. Probably not permanently, tho.

At any rate, the libido seems unusually dormant.

I'm due for a change, in fact long overdue. This period has surely just about run its course. Tho with Spring coming on, Manhattan is more attractive.

Mother suggests I come home. Grandfolks not well again –

Very possibly I will do it. In about a week.

What else is there to accomplish here? I'll probably have to go back to work, when poor Mr. Gering wises up to my neglect of his Story.[554] And I'd rather face that necessity in some other town. New Orleans. West Coast.

En Avant! – We'll see.


*Between Sunday, 14 March and Wednesday, 17 March 1943*

Reflections.

Something has gone out of me.

A degree of feeling?

Tenderness?

Is this only a necessary adjustment to circumstances that would otherwise be too much?

The longing for a place of my own – the ranch in New Mexico dream – is a hope to recover something being lost?

All these little incidents, places, people, the clutter of city life. The cynicism the ennui, the distrust. the repetition without any real deep, sustaining abiding rhythm.

These are the enemies of what's good in my being.

If only the play were sold. Succeeded. Well, that's not hopeless yet.

We go on hoping.


*Wednesday, 17 March 1943*

Wed. Night.

The reckoning with Mr. Gering is set for Friday.

555.  Eva Jessye (1895–1992) was one of the first black women to succeed as a professional choral conductor. She moved to New York in the 1920s, and by 1926 she had established the Eva Jessye Choir, which toured widely in the United States.

556.  In a letter to his mother a few days later (circa 22 March 1943, HTC), Williams reported: "The producer seems pleased with my work on his story, more so than I am. I only mind writing pot-boilers because it takes the time away from other things I want to work on."

A month later Williams changed his mind and wrote to Horton Foote (24 April 1943, SMU):

Did I tell you the pay-off with Gering? I had told him I would have to drop the war play. Then I discovered I hadn't money enough to get home on, so I had to tell him I had changed my mind and get another fifteen dollars out of him. Now I must pay back the fifteen or go on with the wretched business. When I think of it I could blow my brains out!

Williams never completed the work.

Williams and Donald Windham

I plan, more or less uncertainly, to leave for St. Louis. As early as Saturday.

It's all gone here.

The nerves washed out, the energy gone.

I can't even stir my body to exercise.

Can't swim even the minimum 10 lengths without effort.

Yet I go on placidly enough. Maybe because I still believe "You Touched Me" will come through.

Talked to Fleet on phone. We meet tomorrow. Somehow it seems a little momentous –

Last night dinner at Mary Hunter's and we went together to Eva Jessye (negro choir) in Brooklyn.555

Curiously intense self consciousness with Mary. I felt as though all the inner organs of my body were visible to her.

Self conscious whenever I like much. A bad fix to be in.

Last night a meaningless affair, after I got home. Not attractive party.

No particular libido.

Too generally done in I suppose.

So let's have a rest somewhere. No coffee. No society. No effort.

Home? The victrola, the dog, lonely walks at night, books.

But, on the other hand, my father – ugh!

We'll see, very, very shortly.

En Avant!


*Friday, 19 March 1943*

Very early Friday A.M.

Someone has just left and I am very glad.

How sweet it is to be alone. No danger, no demands. No questions. Just the old familiar presence of myself. I hear of the world bright with danger. I want to keep the dim little world which I keep in my own timid being. Excitement is dispensable, I think. Quiet and privacy is lovely. A bed to yourself is lovely. Sleep is better, really, than copulation. Cool, clean sheets should comfort even the dying and a drawn shade is like the soft touch of love.

Sleep. Sleep. It is early spring and the air so cool and fresh. The day not yet beginning.

Donnie will probably call to wake me and I shall see no one all day I do not love.

Yes, I will even try to love the Gering.556

Goodbye, old follower. Always be brave and patient. En Avant.

557.    Paul Cadmus (1904–99), an artist whose paintings often had satirical overtones and revealed an interest in the male body and hinted at homosexual themes. His brother-in-law, Lincoln Kirstein, wrote an essay in which he proclaimed Paul Cadmus, Jared French, and George Tooker "magical realists."

Cadmus' work is in a number of museums, including the Metropolitan Museum of Art, the Museum of Modern Art, the National Museum of American Art in Washington, D.C., and the U.S. Navy Art Collection.

558.    *Goodbye to Berlin* (1939), set in pre-Hitler Berlin, consists of six loosely connected pieces, of which "Sally Bowles" is the second. In "Sally Bowles," the narrator, Christopher, tells the reader that when he introduced Sally Bowles to his dowdy landlady, Fräulein Schroeder, she, "overflowing with politeness," addressed Sally repeatedly as "Gnädiges Fräulein." Earlier, Sally Bowles had told Christopher that she would "more or less" turn into a pitiful old landlady in "thirty years time." In the 1960s Williams would write a play entitled "The Gnädiges Fräulein" about two unattractive old women who run a rooming house.

Williams drafted a letter to Isherwood in his notebook:

Dear Ch,

Would you mind if I wrote a little article about you and would you help me with it? I would like it to be mostly about The Berlin Diary. (The more I think of it, the more amazing it seems that I had actually not heard of it till I met Lincoln) but also about your unique experiences here. And new writings. I am sure that Laughlin would be interested for New Directions.

Anytime you are out to this end of the beach, please use my shack, The Palisades, 1645 Ocean Drive. I do not lock the front door.

My nerves are very unsteady from readjustments or I would [*unfinished*]

In a letter to Windham dated 28 July 1943 (Yale), Williams wrote:

Nobody can honestly blame you for anything that you are. Blame or guilt is all mistaken and false. . . . There are a few of us who know this and feel it. I think it is what Isherwood says in Sally Bowles and it is what you hinted at in your phrase "the momentariness of truth".

Paul Cadmus, 1941 (photograph by George Platt Lynes)

*9/43 – Met Isherwood in Hollywood, my feelings about him were amazingly borne out. Reminds me – See him again.*

*Sunday, 21 March 1943*

Sunday Night. Very lately.

It seems funny at this particular time to think of the future. I have most surely come to the very near end of something but not to any beginning. I feel as though a gentle but wasting illness were in me most of the time lately. Weak, enervated. Even my legs strengthless. Always, nearly, tired and wanting to sit or lie down. The energy to write only whipped up for a few pages and none of it the old fire.

Still I feel it is all there and I need only a good, complete rest to restore me. And that there _is_ a future and some kind of a new beginning.

Fidelma's for supper with Donnie and Paul Cadmus.557

Charming as usual, those evenings with her, a little sadly.

It is not arranged, my leaving N.Y., but I believe it will happen. The only way to rest.

Reading Isherwood's Goodbye To Berlin. He interests me profoundly. Sally Bowles a brilliant study.558 A new something in it. How they can be lost and found again. And even their treachery isn't true, anymore than their apparent faith.

Isherwood seems strangely like me – his mind, his attitude. Only clearer, quieter, firmer. A better integrated man.

What is our purpose? To understand our lives and to communicate our understanding. Let's all join hands in the dark!

Drawing of Donald Windham
by Paul Cadmus, 1941

559. Venice-born actress and writer Elissa Landi (1904–48) had had a successful stage and film career in Europe before coming to Broadway and then Hollywood. Her film career failed to flourish in the United States, and after 1937 she only appeared in one more film, in 1943.

Apology, staged and produced by Lee Strasberg, was the first Broadway play by Charles Schnee (1916–63). In Apology, Albert Warner, who was born into affluence, marries wealth, becomes a robber baron, and in the process grows solitary and lonely. Apology received negative views, more for its unconventional narrative form than for its content. Schnee went on to become an Oscar-winning screenwriter and a producer.

Landi played the role of the commentator who introduced scenes and described what the characters were doing. About her performance the reviewer for the New York Times (23 March 1943) opined: "With long descriptive speeches, Miss Landi has a mountainous task which probably no one could fully accomplish."

Williams may have been interested in Schnee's use of the narrator, a device used successfully by Thornton Wilder in Our Town (1938). In limited form Tom serves as the narrator at the beginning of The Glass Menagerie.

560. Helen Thompson was the business manager for the American Actors Company.

561. Guthrie McClintic (1893–1961) was a distinguished and prolific director who was married to Katharine Cornell. By 1943 McClintic had directed the 1939 Pulitzer Prize–winning play, The Old Maid, as well as Maxwell Anderson's two New York Drama Critics' Circle Award winners, Winterset (1935) and High Tor (1937). Besides his success, McClintic's strong conceptual abilities would have appealed to Williams. Although McClintic had turned down Battle of Angels in 1940, Williams now wished to discuss You Touched Me! with him. McClintic would turn it down, but he would later stage it in New York in the fall of 1945.

Williams used McClintic's surname for the actor's manager in the short story "The Vine."

562. In his short story "The Short Happy Life of Francis Macomber," Hemingway deals with the crippling effect of fear on manhood. After Macomber overcomes his fear and kills a buffalo on an African safari, the hunter Richard Wilson thinks:

But he liked this Macomber now. Damned strange fellow. Probably meant the end of cuckoldry too. Well, that would be a damned good thing. Damned good thing. Beggar had probably been afraid all his life. Don't know what started it. But over now. Hadn't had time to be afraid with the buff. That and being angry too. Motor car too. Motor cars made it familiar. Be a damn fire eater now. He'd seen it in the war work the same way. More of a change than any loss of virginity. Fear gone like an operation. Something else grew in its place. Main thing a man had. Made him into a man. Women knew it too. No bloody fear. (Ernest Hemingway, The Fifth Column and the First Forty-nine Stories [New York: Charles Scribner's Sons, 1938], p. 132)

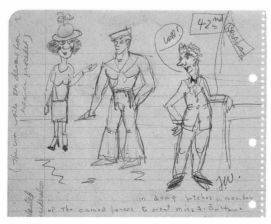

Sketch in Williams' notebook

*Monday, 22 March 1943*

Monday –

Just came from seeing Elissa Landi in incredibly bad play "Apology".559

Met Mary Hunter, Helen Thompson,560 Fleet Munson. We (including Donnie) went a couple of places to eat & drink and I walked Mary home. Cold, bright moonlight. Mary asked me in – I declined like an awkward schoolboy. I have been awkward and bashful lately a great deal.

Letter from Mother. Alarming news about Grand. She is gravely ill and won't go in hospital.

I plan to leave here about Thursday.

I called McClintic and made appt. to see him.561 Tomorrow at 4. Expect nothing.

All this is beside the point which is the new life I must make for myself. I guess it will have to encompass a job.

I talked earnestly to Donnie, while we drank wine in his office, about Grand and my lack of feeling, the numbness I have developed toward my family, even those who were the most to me. The love seems all there, but the capacity to feel about them seems nearly gone. Shameful that the news about Grand means so little. And whom do I love more? Or as much? Or has represented so much beauty? Nobody. Well – I've grown hard. There's no other answer to it. Turned into a crocodile. Of course I know that <u>being</u> there and <u>seeing</u> it will hurt almost exquisitely. So I don't want to go. I want to hide from it. But I <u>will</u> go.


*Tuesday, 23 March 1943*

Five thirty A.M. Tuesday

A surprise airraid blackout startled me out of sleep. Lights went out while I pulled on my drawers. And so dressed, I stood in the corridor with the others. I was informed it was only a test. The fencer from Virginia struck up a conversation and I asked him to have a smoke with me – but he doesn't smoke.

Hemingway is mistaken about fear.562 At least afterwards it is an aphrodisiac. And I think even during it might be.


*Wednesday, 24 March 1943*

Late Tuesday Night –

Conference with McClintic went off nicely.

He was cordial and kindly – and appeared to be rather substantially interested in the play.

Asked to hold script for further perusal.

After a blank beginning, I warmed up and became fairly eloquent. Probably seemed an odd but interesting character to the great McClintic.

563.  Williams was working on a dramatization of his story "Twenty-seven Wagons Full of Cotton," which he
      would send to Mary Hunter (circa mid-April 1943, HTC):
      About "27 Wagons", I gave it to you because Donnie and I nearly died laughing at Flora when we
      read over the last scene aloud. Was that pathological of us, and can a sadistic play be presented
      validly or successfully as a comedy? I am afraid that plays of sadism are a symptom of emotional
      exhaustion, the sort of thing that artists with exacerbated nerves are peculiarly subject to. And I
      wonder if there is not going to be a wave of violent if not cruel writing after the war. I was shocked
      when I saw [the St. Louis road production of] "Eve of St. Mark" to see them playing the horrible
      malaria scene in the cave for comedy and still more horrified that women in the audience howled
      with laughter. We are not soft people and the war is making us even harder.

564.  On 13 January 1943, a bilateral prefrontal lobotomy was performed on Rose. The lobotomy had been
      devised by a Portuguese doctor, Dr. Egas Moniz, as a positive treatment for such incurable conditions as
      schizophrenia and had been advanced in the United States by neurologist Walter Freeman and neurosur-
      geon James Watts. The procedure was described in the 30 November 1942 edition of *Time*:
      In their development of Dr. Moniz' methods, Drs. Freeman and Watts drill a small hole in the tem-
      ple on each side of the patient's head where two skull bones meet. Surgeon Watts then inserts a dull
      knife into the brain, makes a fan-shaped incision upward through the prefrontal lobe, then down-
      ward a few minutes later. He then repeats the incisions on the other side of the brain. No brain tis-
      sues are removed. (In two operations they have cut cerebral arteries. Both patients died.) . . .
      Purpose of the operation is to sever most of the nerve connections between the prefrontal lobes
      and the thalamus. The thalamus is lower, nearer the spinal cord. This part of the brain is widely
      believed to be the seat of emotions — fear, rage, lust, sorrow, other purely animal instincts. All ani-
      mals have a thalamus, but the higher animals — above all, man — developed superimposed layers
      of brain tissue which exercise some control over the thalamus. . . .
      After psychosurgery a patient requires months, sometimes a year or more, before he is mentally
      reintegrated and can lead a useful life. His personality is changed: he is neither his psychopathic nor
      his pre-psychopathic self.
      His capacity to project himself into the future is reduced. He is less self-critical, more extroverted.
      Say Drs. Freeman and Watts of their patients: "The freedom from painful self-consciousness, and
      also from preoccupation with former conflicts, repressions, frustrations and the like, and the asso-
      ciated elevation in mood, renders life particularly agreeable to them and they enjoy it to the
      fullest." . . .
      Of their 136 cases, Drs. Freeman and Watts regard 98 as greatly improved, 23 as somewhat
      improved, twelve as failures. Only 13 patients are still in mental hospitals; most are back at their
      jobs or housekeeping after one to six years of psychotic incapacity.
      Edwina had written to Williams on 20 January 1943 (HTC):
      Now that it is over, I can tell you about Rose, who has successfully come through a head operation.
      A letter from Dr. Hoctor and the surgeon said yesterday that she shows "marked improvement and
      has co-operated through it all".
      And Williams had responded on 25 January (HTC):
      I did not at all understand the news about Rose. What kind of operation was it and what for?

565.  George Jean Nathan, the well-known drama critic, wrote an article in the April 1943 issue of *Esquire* crit-
      icizing Lawrence Langner and the Theatre Guild for their choice of plays:
      The Theatre Guild has rejected Sean O'Casey's *Purple Dust*, to say nothing of the same author's
      *Within The Gates*, *The Star Turns Red*, and his latest, *Red Roses For Me*, and has highly admired
      and produced instead Tennessee Williams' cheap sex-shocker, *Battle of Angels*, which shut down
      after a few days' engagement out of town. . . .

566.  Presumably *You Touched Me!*

Curiously enough, his favorite was the tea scene. That was a pleasant surprise.
Palpitation just now –
Too much smoke, coffee.
I wrote alone at Donnie's office till two A.M. – from 7 – a 7 hour stretch –
longest at one stretch in a long time. On a short play. 27 Wagons. Not worth
much – amusing but a little nasty perhaps.[563]
Grand. God be with you.
A cord breaking.
1000 miles away.
Rose. Her head cut open.
A knife thrust in her brain.[564]
Me. Here. Smoking.
My father, mean as a devil, snoring. 1000 miles away.

*Sunday, 28 March 1943*

Sunday Afternoon. March 28
Very tired and blue. The situation might justify a degree of panic if I were not
too weary to feel anything that violent.
The season has converged into an aching wedge of nothingness. There is
nothing more here and I have not yet been able to root myself out. Home is the
only haven and what a haven that promises to be. I have nightmares about
meeting father. I dread the tragedy of seeing Grand so near to the end.
I am physically low, a ~~bad~~ cough, enervation.
Nathan's horrible comment in <u>Esquire</u> has been unreasonably depressing[565] –
the play which seemed the only way out is a fading promise and there is really no
good omen.[566]

Williams in Donald Windham's office at *Dance Index*

Dear Paul:

I've been home about two weeks and enjoyed it. It wasn't
nearly the ordeal I expected. Grand's condition has improved.
At any rate, she got out of bed to convince me she wasn't so ill
and has remained out ever since and is perking up considerably.
I've had a very quiet time, no entertainment, no people. Just
reading in the attic and writing in the basement and trying to
decide the next move in this baffling history of mine. A little
contemplation does the soul no harm, though it isn't so good for
figure. I have gained ten pounds since I got here due to no
exercise and three enormous meals and a few snacks between.
I have been reading Gorki's "Childhood" - what a magnificent
book! And 'Lady Chatterley's Lover'. The non-sexual parts of
it are Lawrence's best, though the fornicating sequences are
pretty boring. Poor David must have pulled his beard out
trying to think of something to have them do next! Like all
of Lawrence's women except his Mother, Lady Chatterley is rather
annoying. But the bitter portrait of Sir Clifford and the
housekeeper is really terrific. - Dear me! This would make a
good letter to Lady Abdy! - If I could think of something to say
about Mozart.

I go down-town tomorrow to apply for a job at one of the defense
plants. I plan to work a couple of weeks, save the money, and
buy a ticket somewhere. Very probably New Mexico. It has been
quite some while since the Indians have had the benefit of my
association, and it is high time that Mrs. Luhan and I got togeth
together for a little Panic Renaissance in the Lobos and among
the pueblos. Dakin has given me carte blanche with his civilian
wardrobe which I find to include a new pair of brilliant red
riding boots which fit me and an astonishing number of those
breezy little sport-effects which, as you know, have always
suited me so well. I haven't got Audrey's opinion on this
proposed excursion, though I doubt that anybody on the East Coast
will disapprove of it, with the morbid exception of Mr. Gering.

We drove out to see my sister yesterday and found the operation
on the brain had accomplished something quite amazing. The madness is still present - that is, certain of the delusions - but
they have now become entirely consistent and coherent. She is

full of vital and her perceptions and responses seemed almost
more than normally acute. All of her old wit and mischief was
in evidence and she was having great fun at the expense of the
nurses and inmates. She told me they were 'mentally lazy,
interested only in menial accomplishments.' She herself is
reading nineteenth century history and is particularly fascinated
by Victor Hugo. Before the operation she was unable to read at
all and was interested in nothing. She showed me about her
building and I noticed the other girls regarded her very
nervously. She said she had "publicly denounced them" that
morning. She had the impression that I had been in the
penitentiary and was sorry I wasn't, as she feels that an
institution is "the only safe place to be nowadays, as hordes
of hungry people are clamoring at the gates of the cities."
It was curious to see these delusions persisting along with
such a brightness and vivacity. To me mental therapy is the most
intriguing work there is, and if I could make a fresh start,
I'd take it up instead of writing. Unbalanced minds are so
much more interesting than our dreary sanity is, there is so
much honesty and poetry among them. But then, you wonder if
there is such a thing as sanity, actually. Our own behavior,
and especially our friends', does not provide a very good model,
does it?

Excerpts of a letter Williams wrote to Paul Bigelow (circa 10 April 1943)

I shy away from sex and it shies away from me. The cut lip was apparently a very deep wound. Last night Donnie and I cornered one piece of game but it was Donnie's prize and I went to bed with a headache. Today is sort of viciously bright. Tomorrow I must pull this battered being together, at least enough to pack and get going.

Any action is better than none.

<u>En Avant.</u>

Sensible program of action.

1. ~~Go ho~~ Leave for St. Louis tomorrow night.
2. Rest and cultivate a calm, detached attitude for a week or two.
3. Return to New York and get a job. Push the play, repair my "political fences".
4. By some means accumulate funds for removal to New Mexico.

Alternative programs –

Go to Florida.

(Remember St. Augustine)

Stay here.

(Wear self out, sacrifice probably the last chance to see family in God's knows how long.)

Put all action off –

(Make it more difficult, lose self respect, appear idiotic, encourage inertia, have no money left.)

The best of these is probably Florida. That, however, would wound the family and court a mess.

So – Train or bus for St. Louis tomorrow night.

Pack tonight.

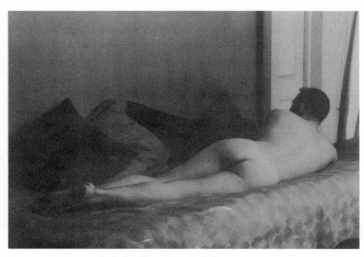

*Tennessee Williams, 5 St. Luke's Place, New York City,* 1943
(photograph by Jared French)

567.  The play "The Gentleman Caller" would eventually evolve into *The Glass Menagerie*. In mid-April (HRC),
      Williams had written Audrey Wood from Clayton:

> I have been able to do some sustained writing for the first time since last summer. The Gentleman
> Caller is developing into a full-length play.

Toward the end of April (24 April 1943, SMU), Williams had written Horton Foote:

> I have been working with tigerish fury on "The Gentleman Caller", it has become a fully-developed
> play almost of usual length. It has at least one part in it for you and maybe two, if you can imagine
> such a thing.

No complete manuscript of "The Gentleman Caller" is known to exist. There are, however, a number of
overlapping fragmentary drafts.

Opening pages of a letter Williams wrote to Donald Windham ([12 May 1943])

*Saturday, 22 May 1943*

Resumé: two months.
A pleasant visit home.
Dad left after the first week and the remainder was peaceful.
Grand got better and was around the house.
I worked pretty well and continually on The Gentleman Caller.567
About a month passed.
Then toward the end –
A telegram that I had been sold to Hollywood.
Return to N.Y.
Excitement and some pleasure. No sex all this time.
So I leave for the Coast.
And here I am.
I have been here 2 weeks now.
I am wretchedly lonely and sick.
All the symptoms of TB except no blood spitting. Had cough several months
now.
Since I've been here alone nearly all the time – every night –
Feel unlike myself or maybe it's just me exagerrated.

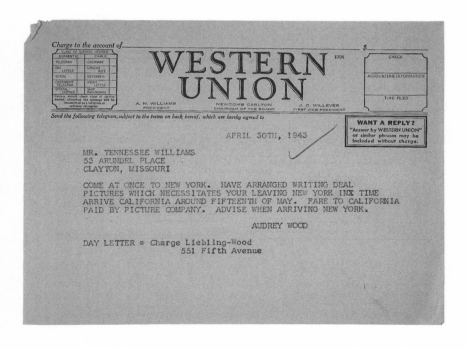

568.    Zola Godino, Williams' landlady at 1647 Ocean Avenue, Santa Monica.

569.    In a letter to Paul Bigelow dated 23 May 1943 (Columbia), Williams wrote:
[T]he land-lady has already provided material for an amusing one-act. She belongs to "the movement" but confuses it with sex. We get along fine — her first name is Zola and on her table she has
Zola's book "The Human Beast". When she entertains soldiers she tells them it is her biography and
the fools believe her — Well, she is rather beastly-looking, you know. Drinks a quart of beer for
breakfast — usually in my kitchen.
No manuscript of "Two Conceptions of Movement" is known to exist, but in September 1943 Williams
began a short story, "The Mattress by the Tomato Patch," about his landlady, whom he gave the name
Olga Kedrova.

570.    Blond, buxom Lana Turner (1920–95) was an established glamorous actress whose first role, at age sixteen, earned her the nickname "the Sweater Girl" for the tight blue sweater she wore in the film. Williams
had been asked by Pandro S. Berman to work on the script of the film *Marriage Is a Private Affair* for her.
Williams had little interest in this idea. A few days earlier he had written a letter to Audrey Wood (received
23 May 1943, HRC):
I am grateful that the news about Lana Turner made somebody happy. It is an ill wind that blows
no good!
    I think it is one of the funniest but most embarrassing things that ever happened to me, that I
should be expected to produce a suitable vehicle for this actress. Poor thing, she is now having a
baby and at the same time, her next picture is supposed to be written by me! As misfortunes usually come in pairs, if not triplets, this coming child of hers seems likely to be a monster.
    It would be useless for me to describe the script I have to work with, a scenario prepared by
Lenore Coffee. It contains every cliche situation you've ever seen in a Grade B picture. They want
me to give it "freshness and vitality" but at the same time keep it "a Lana Turner sort of thing".
    I feel like an obstetrician required to successfully deliver a mastodon from a beaver. A bad com-
parison, as the beaver is a practical little animal who would never get herself into such a situation.
In a letter ([29 May 1943], Yale), Williams told Sandy Campbell, Donald Windham's companion and lover:
The studio is very well pleased with my work which is making a sort of celluloid brassiere for Lana
Turner to appear in. It is derived from a Harper's Prize novel called "Marriage Is A Private Affair"
but we are using practically nothing but the title and a general air of "just got out of bed, let's get
back in!"
    I visited the producer just now and she looked at me with a dreamy sigh and said, "Oh,
Tennessee, you get the sex-values so clearly!" — I said, "Jane, if you lived right across from muscle-
beach you'd get them, too!" — Muscle-beach is where weight-lifters take their girls on week-ends
to toss them around for exercise of a most comprehensive nature. There is a big platform and sand-
pit across from my apartment reserved for this practise.
Earlier, Williams had written his parents ([11 May 1943], Columbia) that he would try to sell Berman an
original script of his own "as that would be much easier to work on."

*Sunday, 23 May 1943*

Sunday –

    Woke up with horrible taste in mouth as usual and a sickish feeling in stomach. Made coffee.

    Zola[568] come in for long conversation, bringing her quart of beer.

    Intimated sex. Talked Communism.

    Gave me idea for Comedy which I wrote when she finally left
        "Two Conceptions of Movement".[569]

    She is rather wonderful.

    I wrote hard & pretty well, drinking the strong coffee.

    Then weakness and tension.

    Went out and bought $1.25 dinner on beach – couldn't eat much of it.

    Caught car to Culver City intending vaguely to write but arrived here as weak as a kitten and incapable of anything but resuming this languishing journal.

    Really a bit frightening, isn't it?

    To be so ill and so lonely

    And supposed to work on something abominable – a script for Lana Turner.[570]

    Can barely whip myself into touching it

    And I don't need anymore whippings.

    I need rest and relief desperately.

    Perhaps I had better pray a little.

Lana Turner in *They Won't Forget* (1937)

571. Christopher Isherwood (1904–86) was a member of the talented group of young English writers of the
     1930s that included W. H. Auden, Stephen Spender, and C. Day-Lewis. Isherwood is best known for his
     novels *The Last of Mr. Norris* (1935) and *Goodbye to Berlin* (1939, reissued as *The Berlin Stories* in 1946),
     which formed the basis for John van Druten's play *I Am a Camera* (1951) and the Broadway musical
     *Cabaret* (1966). Isherwood emigrated to the United States in 1939, and during the 1940s his interests
     turned to Hinduism, about which he wrote *Essentials of Vedanta* (1969).
         In a letter to Donald Windham ([12 May 1943], Yale), Williams wrote:
         I met Christopher today. I invited him to lunch at the Brown Derby. I recognized him at once, just
         by instinct, and he does look just the way I imagine myself to look — it was funny.

         I like him awfully, and I think he must have thought me rather school-girlish about his writing
         which I place with Chekhov's.
         On 13 May 1943, Isherwood wrote in his diary:
         Yesterday, I had lunch with Tennessee Williams, the writer. He's a strange boy, small, plump and
         muscular, with a slight cast in one eye; full of amused malice. He has a job with Metro. He wanted
         to buy an autoglide to ride to work on. I tried to dissuade him, but he insisted. We went to a dealer's,
         and he selected a very junky old machine which is obviously going to give trouble. (*Diaries*, vol. 1,
         *1939–1960*, edited by Katherine Bucknell [London: Methuen, 1996], p. 290)
     Christopher Isherwood appears as a character in Williams' 1975 novel *Moise and the World of Reason*
     who asks another character, Miriam Skates, for an explanation of "non-portraits" (pp. 36–37).

572. Williams presumably is reacting to a caustic letter he must have received from Bigelow. On the same day
     as this journal entry (23 May 1943, Columbia), Williams responded to Bigelow's accusations of having
     "forgotten how to spell":
         I truly meant to write this sooner. . . .
             . . . I haven't forgotten how to spell, or read too many letters from Donnie — I am just too tired
         to hit the right keys. . . .
             Are you really coming to California and when? Of course you could stay in my apartment if I
         am still in it. Though it would not please you at all, being the sort that contains a plaster model of
         Mae West on the mantal piece and a picture of Saint Theresa over the sink. . . .
             Our friendship was a bit languishing in N.Y. — which is not the place for any sustained relation-
         ships — but you know I think of you always with much affection, though you may be a little baf-
         fling at times.
     Despite his words to Bigelow, in the postscript to an earlier letter to Audrey Wood (received 17 May 1943,
     HRC), Williams had said:
         And do try to keep Bigelow at that end of the country until I can afford to keep him in a becoming
         style. As soon as he got here I am sure he would require the attention of specialists. I have also tried
         to discourage Donnie, who is better off than he knows right where he is. Some day I will found a
         colony for dissatisfied writers, but the time is not ripe. One must have something to sell out here,
         and lots of good things don't.

I met Cristopher Isherwood.[571]

Liked him, he was so much as I had thought he would be.

But he has ignored me since the one meeting, in spite of a letter I sent him.

It was foolishly done, the letter.

But I wanted someone to be with and talk to So badly.

Donnie finally wrote me – yesterday got letter –

a bit snotty sounding not really affectionate.

I think his friendship wore out under the corrosion of our two rather competitive vanities.

I miss him but not as I missed Bigelow when I was so dependant on him for fellowship.

Now, alas, Bigelow is destroyed as a friend to trust.[572]

Justly?

Maybe I have been unfair.

But that is what comes when people aren't frank with each other.

I know that this period will change

or I will crack up.

Sex = o

Friends = o

Tennessee is on the Spot.

Behind the ⑧ again.

<u>Help</u>!!! (En Avant)

Christopher Isherwood, 1946 (photograph by William Caskey)

573. David Greggory, whom Williams had met in New York. Williams wrote Paul Bigelow (4 August 1943, Columbia): "He is out here doing publicity work for the radios. He has the Hollywood territory and I the Santa Monica and between us both we lick the platter clean."

574. Robert Lewis, who had moved to Los Angeles, directed a production of Maxwell Anderson's war drama featuring Lockheed workers.

575. "S" is Sandy Campbell (1922–88), a minor actor who became the devoted companion and lover of Donald Windham. In August 1948 Campbell joined the original company of *A Streetcar Named Desire* as the Young Collector. He would go on to play the same part in the 1956 revival, starring Tallulah Bankhead, which previewed at the Coconut Grove Playhouse in Miami. His collection of letters to Windham, published as *Twenty-nine Letters from Coconut Grove* (1974), chronicles the five-week period from the time they arrived for rehearsals on 2 January 1956.
    "C" is Paul Cadmus. According to Donald Windham (in a letter to Margaret Bradham Thornton): "Behind C's back" is true but TW's view of life. I was living in Cadmus's place while he was largely on Fire Island. He was in love with Sandy, who, already inducted into the Army, was at Princeton on the student deferment plan. Sandy, who was about to be called up, and was the next month, didn't want Cadmus to know he was interested in me, nor did I. But he was told when Sandy went to Fort Dix — and after he came out of the Army he lived with me for the rest of his life. A longer life than Romeo's or Juliet's.

576. On 31 May 1943 (HRC), Williams had written Wood:
    I am sending you herein a hastily prepared synopsis or film story treatment of "The Gentleman Caller". I have worked this out in spare time since I've been here, but as you know the stage version, in a rough draft, is already written before I signed here.
        I feel that this could be made into a very moving and beautiful screen play — much better than the stage version could be — only it would have to run unusually long, about as long, I should think, as Gone With The Wind — I think the theme and treatment is sufficiently big in scope to justify such a length and long films are better anyhow. . . .
        The stage version, as it now stands, is not up to the potentialities. It is still too rough to turn in.
        I think I should get that into shape first, before I tackled the screen scenario in full.
    Influenced by the film *Gone with the Wind*, Williams described the opening shot of his film as including "wide flat fields, the dark cypress brakes, the river and the levees and bluffs along it. Negro share-croppers' cabins and immense Greek revival mansions."
        Williams had envisaged the film would have a "lighter and more cheerful conclusion" than the stage version. One film story treatment ends with Laura sitting on the front porch with "almost a regiment of young soldiers" approaching. "Perhaps even — at the very end — the first Tom Wingfield or the second returns from his travels. At any rate — Amanda has finally found security and rest. What she searched for in the faces of gentlemen callers."

577. Williams is anticipating the publication of a group of twenty-nine poems, "The Summer Belvedere," in the third volume of the New Directions series *Five Young American Poets*.

578. Irene Dunne (1898–1990), a renowned stage and film actress, made her screen debut in her early thirties. She had great versatility and appeared in musicals, melodrama, and high comedy. She was working at the time on the MGM film *The White Cliffs of Dover*, the story of an American woman who marries into the English aristocracy and loses her husband in World War I and her son in World War II.

579. A few days earlier ([12 June 1943], HRC), Williams wrote to Wood:
    I have completed a long short story, 28 pages, which is another use of the material of "The Gentleman Caller" and may give you a clearer impression of what will be in it, the stage version. As you will see, the climactic dinner scene has great possibilities for a quietly impressive sort of drama, though you may be terrified at my attempt to project so special a character as the sister is. However the person who tells the short story also acts as a narrator in the play and his comments

*Friday, 4 June 1943*

Friday. June 4 or 5 –

Things considerably ameliorated since last report.

Loneliness ended, at least.

Ran into David Gregory[573] from N.Y. quite fortuitously and he spent last week-end with me in Santa Monica.

We met F.S. on Palisades who has supplied a sex interest, palliative if not exciting.

However have been having devilish time with sinus trouble. Comes and goes like that long spell I had in Key West, which tortured me for weeks with ear-aches.

Tonight I meet D.G. again and we go to see Bobbie Lewis prod. of "Eve of St. Mark" at Lockheed Air Plant.[574] Will meet some new people doubtless. The Social Situation is expanding rapidly now and probably the period of real loneliness is over.

Margo Jones writes she is coming to Pasadena & will try to put on "You Touched Me" – Expects to do it.

Letters from Don.

He and S. enjoying a Romeo and Juliet affair behind C's back.[575]

Think I'll devote the week-end to intense writing on something. I hope "The Gentleman Caller".[576]

Nice friendly letters from Laughlin.

Comes here for a visit soon.

The verse coming out is the pleasantest prospect I own.[577]

The California sky is blue and sunny today.

Sparrows chirp.

Terriers arf-arf.

Typewriter clickety-clicks.

My forehead aches a little and writing gets up no steam. So I may as well wander about the lot a bit, visit the Irene Dunne set[578] and knock off early. Maybe pick up my scooter at the repair shop.

En Avant.

*What a curious change of scene & circumstances from N.y!*

*Wednesday, 16 June 1943*

June 16 –

Writing is high on "Portrait of a Girl in Glass"[579] last few days. But today gone out again – way out. Dull as ditch water.

— memories — give a clarification and dramatic emphasis to the action. I will not enclose the story
with this letter, want to read it over and maybe get it typed here.

The "long short story" was "Portrait of a Girl in Glass," which Williams had expanded from an earlier
1941 draft.

Williams' return to the short story underlines the way in which he relied on the form as the basis for
many of his plays. Typically Williams worked out an idea as a short story, then dramatized it as a one-act
play, and later developed it into a full-length play.

580.   In a letter to Donald Windham ([25 June 1943], Yale), Williams wrote: "[T]here has been a big shake-up
at MGM. I am removed bodily and spiritually from the Lana Turner script, it being decided that my character was 'too fay' for Lana to deal with."

Williams posing with David Greggory

I throw little cheesy scraps to the movie producers and they remain curiously patient.

A good affair night before last, first satisfactory one in a long time. Felt pretty well and light-hearted since. Saw David last night and we spent a pleasant, laughing time together.

May as well knock off early this P.M. & get a swim at the club.

Hope "Portrait" gets back in the groove tomorrow.

Would like it to stack up with "The Malediction" or better.

But I am dissipating too widely.

Sunny weather –

I feel different – sort of a new character.

Not an exciting one this afternoon.

So long.


*Wednesday, 23 June 1943*

June 23 –

Just read over the typed copy of "Portrait".

A failure – dismal.

Worse than the thin little story it was before, with awkward, splashy writing, straining for effects it never achieves – a few good paragraphs only.

Read over "The Malediction" for comparison.

The artist would seem to have dwindled, though "Malediction" itself starts off pretty badly. So you see it isn't safe or simple.

You don't just work the steam up and write.

I've gotten into a pretty mess, haven't I?

What's to do?

Leave it alone.

Go on playing the cat's game.

Get on the scooter and ride home in the sun and take a swim and meet Margo.

Maybe it isn't as bad as it seems right now.

But it is a failure.

Don't touch anything but the play and whatever the studio requires.

Off the Turner script.580

I'm afraid the ego was too ambitious and optimistic.

I'm not much of an artist, even at best.

So long. Take it easy.

Always be brave and patient.

Now and again our honesty and effort prevails over weariness and the negation and something comes out that isn't wholly abortive.

581. A sixteen-page manuscript of "Portrait of a Girl in Glass" (dated June 1943, Santa Monica) is most likely the copy Williams sent. He wrote Audrey Wood (29 June 1943, HRC):

> Here is the story I promised you some time ago. I regret to say that the earlier version which ran for thirty-five pages was a bloody mess. However I think the present version may have an effective simplicity.
>
> It is a minor excursion into the same material I am using for the stage version of "The Gentleman Caller". I am sure you will think this material too slight for a long play, but the play will necessarily embody a good deal more than the story would suggest, and the character of Amanda should sustain it.

582. In a letter to Paul Bigelow (postmarked 9 June 1943, Columbia), Williams described the Palisades:

> The Palisades, by the way, are very amusing. They are a long park on a bluff over the ocean. There are two winding pathways, among palm trees and summer-houses and verdant arbors — and during the long twilights or when the moon is in its brighter phases — (there is an almost complete electric black-out on the coast) — a great many solitary figures stroll about them — nature-lovers and admirers of the ocean — pausing frequently to lean poetically against the balustrade or muse in solitude among the tangled vines — all of them so deeply moved by beauty that it has actual internal repercussions and they have to retire with amazing frequency to the rest-room, a pagoda-like building nestling among palms and bushes in the middle of the park. These influences make residence along the Palisades very elevating and would bring out the poet in one less impressionable than I. One might also observe that a love of nature is one of the most enduring passions, as the vast majority of these solitary admirers of the ocean appear to be fairly superannuated, even in the dark of the moon. Matings beneath a palm-tree are frequently very suddenly dissolved under the first arc-light, on the inland side of the park, by mutual agreement. My front room window is a fine observation post and I find it better than going to the movies. — Once in a while, when some intrepid blue-jacket crosses into the park, the palm trees sway and the very earth is shaken. A gregarious instinct suddenly develops in the solitary strollers and the white cap on the dark path is like a candle in the center of many capriciously flitting moths.

583. Williams wrote to Donald Windham about David Greggory ([12 July 1943], Yale):

> [P]oor David Gregory spends every week-end with me and the house we run, modest as it is, has a terrific overhead on Saturdays and Sundays. I remind myself more and more of a character I am writing about in a story called "The Rich and Eventful Death of Isabel Holly".

No manuscript of "The Rich and Eventful Death of Isabel Holly" is known to exist. It is presumably the story which became "The Coming of Something to the Widow Holly," about a rooming-house owner, Isabel Holly, whose paying guests had become dependents.

584. Nickname for Caleb Gray, also written as "Cabey."

Entrance to the MGM lot

*Tuesday, 29 June 1943*

Tues. June 29, 1943
 I prepare to mail the final draft of "Portrait".
 The short version, improved a lot but still no gem.[581]
 A rising dilemma of nerves will make a social life difficult, for a while.
 Mounting gradually for a week, the same that plagued me in Macon.
 On the other hand, sex life has been phenomenal, virtue of Palisades.[582] David and I ran quite an establishment last week-end.[583]
 Can't see it does you much good. Obviously frustration of that sort not the root of my difficulties.
 Must catch bus now to Pasadena and meet Margo.
 En Avant!

*Friday, 9 July 1943*

July 8 or 9 – Friday.
 The "crise des nerfs" fell off but last night returned. An evening in Hollywood with Margo, Horton Foote, David, a pair of Lesbos, and some actor belles. Nerves got very tight indeed as the evening wore along and I retired stiffly into my shell.
 Margo and Horton fairly drooling over each other. I have been supplanted in her heart, I fear, by the starry-eyed ingenue, Mr. Foote.
 I spent the night with David and he says I muttered aloud, calling my sister's name and the name "Gertrude". God only knows who Gertrude could be. I remember this sentence from my dreams.
 "When two naïves get together one always turns out to be less naïve." Quite true and well-put. *(what did it mean?)*
 David seemed perceptive of my dilemma without, of course, penetrating or prying. And I felt more brotherly toward him than usual.
 A hot bright hazy morning and I can hear a scythe on the lawn outside my Venetian (office) blinds. It is always such a grateful sanctuary, especially during these nervous spells and now that I have no picture assignment to be supposed to be working on.
 Can hardly be expected to go on indefinitely, but I drift along from one bright day to the next and make no move.
 I am not badly off at all, relatively speaking, even though I am only temporizing.
 Writing has been fiddling lately. I must throw myself back into "The Gentleman Caller" –
 Delightful letter from Bigelow.
 A love letter from K.B.[584]

585.   On 22 June 1943 (Maryland), Williams had written to Porter:
>    Through the agency of Donald Windham and the photographer I have come into possession of a photograph of my favorite living American author, one Katharine Anne Porter, and I want to thank you for being the subject of it. You are sitting, or perhaps I should say curled up, in what appears to be an enormous chair of straw that is practically a cabana and you appear to be looking out at the world from the shadowy recess of this big chair with a smiling warmth and knowingness that is very endearing.
>
>    Well, I am putting the picture up with the other two on the walls of my study. You will be a triumvirate that includes Hart Crane, and Anton Chekhov, besides yourself. I hope you approve of your company as much as I do!

On 30 June (HRC), Porter had replied:
>    Which one have you, facing out or profile? It doesn't matter. I was blissful in both.
>
>    You may be certain I am very pleased with the company in which I find myself. When I think of Hart Crane — do you know, I have some pictures I made of him in my garden in Mexico, on a good day too, with him being jolly and pleased with himself, wearing a woven silver bridle around his neck, posing for the fun of it; and that is a true record, too, as true as some other things too much insisted on, since the end was what it was: and I am glad to have these pictures now, for he was many times in such moods, though it is hard to remember now. . . . . I believed then and believe now that if there had been one person able to persuade him to be cared for for a while in a sanitarium, to take a disintoxication, he would be living yet and the great poet he began to be. But this may be only the long shadow of my own regret that I was not able to do anything. . .

A few days later ([12 July 1943], Yale), Williams wrote to Windham:
>    I got such a sweet letter from Katharine Anne Porter in response to my note. Which reminds me I must write her and ask for the pictures of Hart Crane she has.

In 1931, when Porter and Crane were in Mexico as Guggenheim Fellows, she took several photographs of him. Porter sent Williams the pictures, and they were in his possession at the time of his death.

586.   Obviously a direct reference to Rimbaud's poem "Le Bateau Ivre." In *Memoirs* (p. 123), Williams acknowledged Clark Mills as having written "the best translation (in [his] unbiased opinion) of Rimbaud's *Bateau Ivre*," citing the penultimate verse: "Of Europe's waters I seek none, except / a cold black pool where one unhappy child / kneels and releases towards the balm of dusk / a boat frail as a butterfly in May."
>    Early in 1944 Williams would write James Laughlin (31 January 194[4], Houghton):
>    Here is the list of books I wanted. All you have of Rimbaud, the Kafka, anything you recommend by E.M. Forster. Lately my enthusiasm has divided between Crane and Rimbaud but I don't think Crane would resent the division. . . . Do you think one should write a play about [Rimbaud]? A motion picture would be the ideal medium starting with "Morte a Dieu" and ending with the pitiful conversion in the hospital at Marseilles.

Williams did write a two-act play (untitled) about the last days of Rimbaud's life. The play alternates loosely with separate scenes depicting Rimbaud dying of cancer at the age of thirty-seven in a hospital in Marseilles in 1891 and Verlaine living a dissolute life in Montmartre in the same year. Williams made heavy use of flashbacks depicting Verlaine and Rimbaud's first meeting in 1871, as well as various subsequent points in time in their doomed and complicated relationship. Williams also included the ghost of Rimbaud in "Will Mr. Merriwether Return from Memphis?"

587.   Williams had met Eugene Loring (1914–82) at the California home of a former Iowa classmate, the highly regarded theatrical designer Lemuel Ayers. Loring, a choreographer and dancer who went on to found the American School of Dance in Hollywood, had by 1943 choreographed several major works, including *Billy the Kid*. Williams had hoped to work on a film version of *Billy the Kid* with Ayers and Loring, but it never got the backing of the studio. In a letter to Audrey Wood dated 9 July 1943 (HRC), Williams wrote:
>    Yes, Lem and Loring and I have been hatching the Billy idea. [Arthur] Freed is supposed to call me in for a conference on it. I see it as a sort of folk-opera with a fresh approach to the western material, songs and ballads and dances, predominating, with Loring as Billy. Possibly a use for my folk-poems, as lyrics. The story is beautiful and epic and could be given a very fresh and tender treatment if we were given a free hand with it.

A treasured letter from Katharine Anne Porter in response to my note about her picture that Donnie sent me.[585]

Well, the ventilators hum softly and benignly.

I suppose I will have some coffee – it is high noon – and peck away at the friendly old typewriter a while.

Ah, a rooster crowing!

The loveliest sound in the world, the sound I try to make when writing from my heart.

Shit, 10.

*Oh, yes, there has been a little blighted but crudely consummated affair. E.L. Stirred feelings.*

*Tuesday, 13 July 1943*

Tuesday – July 13, 1943

The scythe is chopping again on the vivid green lawn among the borders of brilliant M.G.M. flowers, the ventilators humming.

Last night I was couched with Eros who moaned like a wounded beast and flopped like a drunken boat – a <u>bateau ivre</u>.[586] but I was glad at parting as I so often am. We came in all the way from L.A. on the bus and only spoke about twice but as soon as the lights went out in the dim-out area, we clawed at each other. Curious, brutal thing, this kind of Eros.

I must invoke another.

One involving more of the retiring heart.

So I wrote a letter to E.L.[587]

Today work seems out of question. Debility and a slightly sickish feeling at the stomach.

But the office is nice and quiet. I can write K.A.P. and maybe Bigelow. And Dakin.

I was rude to Horton last week-end. Left word I was out of town which was not true, and I suppose he knows it. I have been altogether too harsh in my attitude toward him. I am sure he is to be classed among the gentle people and whatever he does to annoy me is not enough to make me so petty. I would like never to be petty, and never hurt feelings. My nerves are always being scratched and twisted, so that I am rarely ever quite my natural self.

Two months have slipped by, one third of my term here.

I had better start slugging at something. This is no time for leisure that is unproductive.

Get back at The Caller soon as I get a little steam up.

Tomorrow night Margo's – tonight an open date – I hope not to be devoted to the further desecration of the little god.

<u>En Avant</u>.

Williams confided in Windham ([12 July 1943], Yale):

> I have been having an affair with a famous dancer. This is <u>entre nous,</u> so if you guess who it is, don't tell as the character is terribly afraid of such publicity, as well he may be with my transcontinental reputation to think of.

Williams wrote a poem for Loring which is similar to the first half of "Mornings on Bourbon Street" (dated July 1943, Santa Monica):

```
          Poem for E.L.

I thought of my life.

I thought of the innocent            As though my blood had turned a different color,
mornings on Bourbon Street,          as though an original season had entered the air!
the sunny court-yard and the iron
                                     I thought of belief
Lion's head on the door.             and the gradual loss of belief.

                                     I thought of the repitition
I thought of the quality             of days and days, and the wanting to stop
light will not have again  is not likely   but having still to go on.
in the late afternoon
                                     When wisdom became
when I stood beneath the stone arches   a black root under the pavement.
around the Cabildo, and first thought

Love, love, love!

                            and then gold gleaming
```

588.  Williams had written Windham ([18 July 1943], Yale):

> I am sitting at my kitchen table waiting for my lover to arrive with lettuce and tomatoes and rum and sherry wine and a big floury loaf of bread in the fading sunlight. Coffee is percolating gently, and my mood is mellow. I have been very happy lately, just wallowing in it selfishly, knowing it will not last very long which is all the more reason to enjoy it now. I suppose life always ends badly for almost everybody. We must have long fingers and catch at whatever we can while it is passing near us [a paraphrase of lines in *Battle of Angels* (act 3, scene 3)].

589.  A few days later, in a letter to Windham (28 July 1943, Yale), Williams confirmed his feelings of apathy toward "The Gentleman Caller" and added: "It lacks the violence that excites me."

590.  Williams elaborated that day in a letter to Windham (28 July 1943, Yale):

> My nerves are tied in knots today. I have plunged into one of my periodic neuroses, I call them "blue-devils", and it is like having wild-cats under my skin. They are a Williams family trait, I suppose. Destroyed my sister's mind and made my father a raging drunkard. In me they take the form of interior storms that show remarkably little from the outside but which create a deep chasm between myself and all other people, even deeper than the relatively ordinary ones of homosexuality and being an artist. It is curious the various forms they take — someday, when I have the courage, I will sit down and face them and write them all out. Now I can only speak of the symptoms, for if I look at them too closely, I feel they would spring at me more violently. Now for instance all contact with people is like a salty finger stroking a raw wound. My office is merciful, but when ever the phone rings and someone raps at the door, I shudder and fairly cringe. Back of this craziness is a perfect sanity, untouched and wholly separate, a wise counsellor that looks for causes and tries to side-step effects and says patiently and comfortingly, Hang on, it will pass away! But knows that it will always return another day. Ever since I was about ten years old I have lived with these blue-devils of various kinds and degrees, they come and go, all of them at their crises achieving about the same intensity, none of them ever quite reaching the innermost me.

*Monday, 26 July 1943*

Monday – July 26 – 1943

Arrived at office and flopped helplessly in chair. Quite lifeless. Bitter taste in mouth and legs very weak.

An empty tiresome week-end with dull sort of depression yesterday. My little "wife"[588] came over for supper and later we walked the Palisades, but didn't pass the night together. I was glad to be alone when she left.

Don't know why all my vitality is gone. Maybe this climate, maybe lack of creative interest. The Caller doesn't excite me and nothing else does.[589]

But there is nothing worth recording in this familiar humor of ennui. I had better say nothing till I can talk as a man.

This pussilanimous whining, it disgusts me!

So – En Avant!

(We notice an alarming consistency in the reports of fatigue & dullness lately. Would suggest systemic. I still have a cough and spitting phlegm.)

I don't have the strength to move my literary pawns around the stage anymore. They are too heavy to push and they used to spring so lightly. And they have fallen into a sullen dumbness, after all their excited speech. Poor dummies! They sit and stare at me resentfully from the Shadowy Stage of my heart, and I can't help them today.

Some day I will again.

Some day everything will stop for always.

*Wednesday, 28 July 1943*

Wed. July – 28

The month of July appears to be devoting itself largely to a particularly obnoxious "blue devil" as I call my neuroses.[590]

It is one affecting social behavior and making it an ordeal. I am tense with it more or less continually, with little intermissions. It saps my energy and fills my stomach with burning gas.

It is difficult even to use the telephone and I cringe a little when someone knocks at the office door.

Whether it the cause or effect of nervous depletion, I don't know. I try to throw it off, and I know it is silly.

But fear can always – I am fear! And you can't really contradict him. You can only say I have out-lasted you many times before and there is a part of me that spits in your face!

591.  Ruth Ford (1920– ) is the sister of Williams' friend the poet Charles Henri Ford. Williams hoped she would play Matilda in *You Touched Me!* He wrote to Audrey Wood a few days later (2 August 1943, HRC):

> Margo and I showed the script to Ruth Ford, the actress, and she has actually duplicated Margo's enthusiasm for it. She will probably play Matilda. I wonder if you know her or her work. Her Broadway experience was with Orson Welles and she has played in 22 movies, but never gotten a real break out here, her featured parts being in Grade B films. . . . I have given her a script which she is showing to various people she thinks might be potential backers of a Broadway production — she has great charm and a world of contacts out here.

Ford eventually chose film work over the role of Matilda, but in 1946 she played Matilda in the Mt. Kisco production. In 1964 she played the Witch of Capri in *The Milk Train Doesn't Stop Here Anymore*.

Peter Van Eyck (1913–69), an actor who had emigrated from Germany in the 1930s, had begun a successful film career in 1943, with roles such as a hysterical Nazi lieutenant in the screen version of John Steinbeck's play *The Moon Is Down*. Williams described him as "excruciatingly beautiful."

592.  A few days earlier, Williams had written to Wood (received 11 August 1943, HRC):

> The lion is showing his claws! Tennessee is not cowering in a corner, but he is considerably confused and taken aback.
>
> I have just received a note informing me that I am to be laid off for six weeks without pay because there is no present assignment for me. This came up without any warning. The lay-off starts today — Monday. I have no copy of my contract but I assume the action is legal or they wouldn't take it.
>
> As you know, I was taken off the Lana Turner horror-play when Lillie Messenger talked to Berman and told him I was not happy about it. Since then I have had only one contact with official-dom here, which was an interview with Arthur Freed. He seemed quite sympathetic, and it was agreed that I would try to work out a story-outline on Billy The Kid as a sort of folk-opera. This I have been doing somewhat desultorily for the past couple of weeks, waiting for Lem Ayers who has an equal interest in the material to have time to confer with me about it and give me his suggestions. As you know, I have had plenty of my own work to occupy my time here, and felt that I was very gainfully employed from any reasonable point of view.
>
> The Scenario department, however, says the tentative Billy The Kid idea does not constitute an actual assignment. And just now a very curt young man has entered my office, without even knocking, to inform me that I should move my stuff out as I could not hold this office during the lay-off — which is extremely inconvenient because of the large store of Mss. books, Etc. that I have here. I shall have to give up my Santa Monica apartment, as I will have one week's pay to live on during the lay-off period and could not afford to keep that place. . . .
>
> Where I shall go during this period I am not sure yet. I may take a little trip, Frisco or some place, and will use the completely free time advantageously to get this work of my own out of the way.

593.  At the beginning of August (2 August 1943, HRC), Williams wrote to Audrey Wood that he had devised a new ending for "The Gentleman Caller" which was "considerably lighter, almost happy." In the manuscript (fragment) of "The Gentleman Caller (A Gentle Comedy)" the potential for a romance between Laura and her gentleman caller remains. Although Tom decides to leave home, his mother, Amanda, helps him pack and sends him off with a gentle plea for his return:

> I hope that you will forget my scolding tongue, and when you've found whatever it is young men go looking for about the world — Come home, and I'll be waiting — no matter how long!

A letter from Donnie just arrived. I will take it to commissary and read over milk – instead of coffee. A little reform.

Tonight Society – ordeal – Ruth Ford & husband Peter Van Eyck.591 Both charming but all the more frightening to me.

En Avant!

*Thursday, 12 August 1943*

Aug. 11 or 12

Thursday –

    6 weeks lay-off from Studio. Started Monday.592

    I am down here packing Mss.

    Dreary occupation.

    So much worthless scribbling I've done – It's rather horrifying.

    Last night J.C. the dancer.

    I was sort of dumb & helpless all evening. J. was remarkably nice & understanding.

    On way home walked into a plate glass door and shattered my false front tooth. Idiotic accident! Replaced this A.M. for $5.00.

    What to do? Probably a little trip on my thumb.

    Hope I'll lay off writing and get my wind back. En Avant!

*Saturday, 11 September 1943*

Sept. 12 (about)

    Sat. night and a moon nearly full.

    The unprecedented sex activity continues. The night that I don't desecrate the little god all over again is exceptional.

    As F.S. remarked it's about like a dog pissing on a tree. Why do I set that down. Why record it? because there is really nothing else.

    The life is so barren otherwise – but all my complaints are old ones, so old I ought to stop making them.

    My period away from Studio draws near close. I've really done nothing with it – I've worked every day, writing on this or that, better off doing nothing.

    I keep draining creative energies that don't seem to build up again. been back on the gentleman caller lately, and it has turned into a comedy bordering on fantasy – And is probably an abortion.593 No deep urge to create it. but all I desire in the world is to create something big and vital. If only I could make myself – find some groove that would permit it – Stop for a while and get fresh for a major work on Some strong theme. The blue devils eased off – only nip at my heels now and then.

594.  A few days later, Williams wrote to Audrey Wood (14 September 1943, HRC):
      I have had a good rest from the studio. Lately a distant relative of mine Jane (Lanier Brotherton)
      Lawrence who had the ingenue lead in "Oklahoma" has been visiting me with her fiance. She is a
      wonderful girl and will probably make some pretty big pictures out here with Columbia. Both I and
      the fiance were broke for a while and Jane supported us both with the most cavalier attitude — now
      I have your check and Tony a job so everything is okay. I presume I go back to the studio next week.
      Jane Lawrence's (1915– ) fiancé was Tony Smith (1912–80), who would become a major sculptor, archi-
      tect, and painter. Williams had met Smith in Provincetown in 1942 through Fritz Bultman, with whom
      Smith had studied at Chicago's New Bauhaus. A pioneer of Minimal sculpture in the 1960s, Smith's large-
      scale works were geometrical in shape, often in steel, and sometimes painted. He taught at institutions
      throughout the United States and received many prestigious art awards. When Lawrence and Smith were
      married shortly afterward, Williams acted as their witness.
          Jane and Tony Smith are referred to in Williams' novel *Moise and the World of Reason* as Moise's "last
      resource in this world" (p. 23).

595.  The "bad little play" may be "Two Conceptions of Movement" or possibly "The Spinning Song," which
      by October Williams had turned into a verse play.

596.  Presumably *Psychology of the Unconscious* (1916). Williams wrote Windham ([3 November 1943], Yale):
      I am reading Jung now, the man with the cosmic-unconscious theory — you should try him — and
      I think he explains logically what Lawrence felt intuitively, that the dreadfully conscious and will-
      ful people with the over-developed minds are peculiarly dead and away from the only really warm
      and comforting things in human life. Competitive groups such as Hollywood and Manhattan sets
      make a high degree of conscious will necessary. The unconscious that wants other things is more
      and more lost and thwarted and so the hearts wither up. It must be kept away from, these Lemuel
      Ayres and Ruth Fords with their fearful conscious egos saying, I will, I _will_ all the time. I have
      instinctively done the right thing out here, kept away from them all and petered out of the studio. I
      usually feel more or less damned but sort of purely damned, not nastily the way I would be if I got
      caught in this shit. It is so important, now, that we do sell the play and make some money out of it
      to build a free life on. But nothing can be counted on. Endurance is all. Anything we squeeze out of
      bourgeois society in the way of support is a little miracle to be sure! My distrust of the world, how-
      ever, has plumbed the depths and from time to time I make little discoveries that are surprisingly
      pleasant. — Enough confessions and self-analysis!

Tony Smith, Jane Lawrence, and Williams

Tony and Jane from N.Y. are my companions now and I find them a comfort.594
Read them a bad little play tonight which sent them quickly upstairs.595

All this would seem to represent a desperate situation. It isn't that bad. Everything I've ever had is still here – I'm just stale from a long, long seige of striving. The Coast has probably been a healthy change and while the sex promiscuity is a bit sluttish it is probably a good thing to get my fill of it. It seems to do no harm physically. And it doesn't violate the heart, not really, for it is very much like a simple indoor exercise. And without that diversion – what release would I have? The things I can find a thrill in are sex and creation.

Creation usually disappoints me now because I am in the grip of no theme strong enough to call into play the main artillery. It will come, I will recover all lost ground. Just stick around. We will come thru. <u>En Avant</u>!

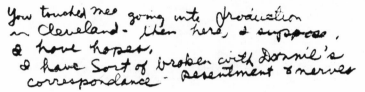

*You touched me going into production in Cleveland - then here, I suppose, I have hopes, I have sort of broken with Donnie's correspondance - resentment & nerves*

*Sunday, 26 September 1943*

Sunday –

Very comfortably propped upon an arrangement of pillows, I lie on my bed after the usual effort to write has ended with the revision of 1 page. A shuddering glance at the play had convinced me not to touch that today.

The room is full of California's gay sunlight and noise of voices on the walks and traffic.

I am about to smoke and read Jung.596

Tomorrow if I get my check I will take a trip somewhere.

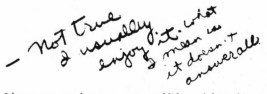

*– Not true I usually enjoy it. what I mean is it doesn't answer all*

I have accepted sex as a way of life and found it empty, empy, knuckles on a hollow drum.
No.
It is only because creation holds off from me, makes faces at me.
And everything is distant, not in me, that surrounds me.
To paint! Would that help?
Christ, why all this outcry? You know failure is.
That isn't news. Why make it out to be?

597. A passage from John Dos Passos' descriptive narrative of places traveled, *Journeys Between Wars* (New York: Harcourt, Brace and Company, 1938), in which he reflects on the outcome of the Spanish Civil War (p. 393). The last phrase, "how can the new world win?" was added by Williams.

598. Williams' six-week lay-off had expired on 24 September, and he was now able to collect a pay check from MGM.

599. Film adaptation (1943) of Lillian Hellman's play about a German refugee and his family who are pursued by Nazi agents in Washington.

Notebook Williams began in September 1943

Sun. Night.

blue and brown sometime good together. A little Cherubic party. Makes 3 this week-end.

I took a Mebral tablet this afternoon and am very quiet and serene. There was a moment of real clean happiness as I stood on the palisades and watched the searchlights on Catalina. Supper with Jane and Tony was nice, too. Sometimes an evening, an hour, walls off, withdraws from yesterday and tomorrow and you taste it purely and the taste is good. good.

> "How can the new world full of confusion and crosspurposes and illusions and dazzled by the mirage of idealistic phrases win against the iron combination of men accustomed to run things who have only one idea binding them together, to hold on to what they've got; how can the new world win?"
> Dos Passos.[597]

The answer is. We have got to straighten out. We will.
(Thank you, Mr. Williams, for solving that problem)

> My world is a world of a few simple ideas and a few simple feelings to which I try to be faithful.

Wednesday, 29 September 1943

Santa Monica   9/29/43

The time is come to commence another journal.

I hope it won't be as blue as the cover.

It does not start off auspiciously. The situation is menacing. but let us leave that till later.

Today I picked up my check at Metro[598] & went into L.A. Very nervous and – Etc. but I went to a bar on Main Street and heard some ravaged old bags sing sentimental ballads. Then to Watch on the Rhine[599] which was dull and false, one continuous fart from beginning to end.

600.    Frederic McConnell (1890–1968) was the director of the Cleveland Play House, which was, along with the Pasadena Playhouse, one of the two leading national little theatres. Margo Jones had written McConnell, who served with her on the executive council of the National Theatre Conference, an association of nonprofit theatres which had begun sponsoring national release of specific plays, and had recommended that the conference release *You Touched Me!* nationally. McConnell agreed, and *You Touched Me!* was scheduled to open in Cleveland on 13 October and in Pasadena on 29 November.

Williams' reaction to McConnell's letter of 24 September (Cleveland Play House Collection) appears overly negative. McConnell had written Williams:

> We are still much interested in the basic philosophy and basic beauty of your play, but we do find that there is a lot of doctoring to be done to make it play and to give it a professional presentation. All concerned are doing their best. Margo and I are working closely together and are in agreement about everything. I am not hesitating to give the production the benefit of my ideas and experience and Margo for her part is collaborating very generously. In other words, this is going to turn out to be a dual job insofar as production and direction is concerned.

601.    Bertha Case had recently moved to Hollywood to work for the A. S. Lyons Agency but remained in touch with Audrey Wood. On 14 September 1943 (HRC), Williams had written Wood:

> Today Case returned the script [*Spring Storm*], I submitted for Teresa Wright, saying that Duggan [a story editor] wanted it but couldn't sell it to Goldwyn. She suggested I make some changes and return it to her for submission to other studios. I have just now done this, building up what I think is the best selling-point. Will suggest to Bertha that she have copies typed up and send you one, as I think it makes a pretty good film story.

602.    As mentioned previously, there are numerous fragments of "The Spinning Song," but no complete manuscript of the play is known to have survived. An outline of "The Spinning Song or The Paper Lantern" dated September 1943 reveals a three-act play about the disintegration of a southern family through adultery, incest, murder, and mental fragility. The family live on their plantation, Belle Reve, and have complicated relationships with their black servants. The play, which deals with three generations, focuses on sixteen-year-old Ariadne who falls in love with Luke, the son of Jessie, her father's past mulatto mistress. Unbeknownst to her, Luke is her half-brother. When Paul, Ariadne's father, discovers her relationship with Luke, he kills Luke, not realizing that Luke is his son. The play ends with Paul being bound to a column of Belle Reve and being stabbed to death by Jessie's lover.

A painting by Williams

How right I am to leave Hollywood! Congratulations, Pal.

We won't bring up the subject of where you are going – yet. Sufficient unto the day.

Letters from Margo & McConnell and a one-night stand who addresses me as "Dearest Tee" & has two tickets to Ice Follies for friday Night. One of those lonely creatures who are so seldom the least bit pretty and this one no real exception. But lately I seem to have brightened the corner where I am in a number of cases, which is being useful on a rather low level and small scale.

Margo & Mac both blue over production, so that possibility dims.600 Also Bertha rejected scenario today.601

Now if something wipes out my N.Y. savings the picture will be complete. I dug out The Spinning Song602 and may attack it again, though only two or 3 scs. as it now stands are any good. <u>En Avant!</u>

The reason we can't grow up is there aren't enough new things to turn to. It does so good to learn you are cheated if there aren't any honest dealings anywhere obtainable.

*Thursday, 30 September 1943*

Thursday – 6:25 P.M.

(by the big clock tower out my kitchen window. The golden sun is setting in the west (not in the east, this time).)

M.G.M. called to inform me "things had not turned out as well as expected" and they were not renewing my option.

Dim as that possibility was, the complete removal of it is an additional strain to the psyche. If the play was a washout I would have stayed on here if they had let me. Now the play will probably washout anyhow and me and the 8 ball will resume our rarely interrupted liason.

So be it. En Avant!

I'm going swimming then eating then probably chasing nightingales.

A siren races weirdly along the streets, receding. Fire or crime somewhere. Everywhere. A dull sort of sick feeling in me, cough & cold.

Work pretty well, though, on The Spinning Song, which flowers into a newer, freer conception that might work out but would never solve an economic problem of the author. Never mind that. The author can bloody well take it.

603. Dick Cuthbertson was the long-term companion of David Greggory and was involved in the entertainment industry.

604. David Greggory.

605. Dick Cuthbertson.

606. Tony Smith.

607. Williams obliquely refers to his years of homosexuality since his relationship with Bette Reitz ended in 1938.

Tues. nite

Clean linen on the bed
and a good book.
Today no writee
too sickee
went in Hollywood
dragged around my
tired ass x came home
about sundown
no cruisee
no parkee
too tiredee
went to bedee
clean linen on bedee
kind of good bookee
Shittee

Later – The lyric quarry was overtaken and enjoyed.

4 of us dished & rode about, a bit of romantic feeling has developed for the 19 yr. older with the "snakey" eyes.

D. Cuthbertson[603] who was not the nightingale tonight but Sat. we meet again.

Sleep is knocking.
Tomorrow more
spinning & singing
I hope.

### Sunday, 3 October 1943

Sun. Oct 2 or 3

With virtually no will and little enough consciousness I drift from one day to another, with energy that ebbs and flows within a shallow estuary. For quite a while I have had the same thought or feeling every night, that the shroud is already cut, that this period is sort of a final temporizing. There is no very sound reason for this. To a somewhat lesser degree, I've had the feeling before.

Last night David[604] came over and so did young Dick.[605] I steamed up a little gaiety for them and we had supper on the pier. The neurosis was a fifth at the table but tolerably borne. We came home and danced then wandered out to the Palisades. There we divided. And I sat about or strolled in a stupor and only the dullest of incidents occured.

I returned alone to bed and was awakened later by David's return with a lovely chicken. I was too tired to mind my exclusion from the party very much.

So day came – day, that old, old visitor – bright Sunday. D. and I rose in a desultory way with desultory talk and cigarettes and comparison of notes and went out for a desultory breakfast at a drugstore. The continuum, to produce a word, is somewhat deathly. Surely one can arrange a more various existence than this is! Oh, but it's the mind, the heart that never really wakes up. Tony[606] says "Your hat is not in the ring!" "You're too young to be so outside of things."

Only 5 years of it since B.R.[607] and I said goodbye to all that. What an eternity! But now everything seems running sand through tired fingers.

I go tonight to Pasadena to see Othello.

### Tuesday, 5 October 1943

Tues. Nite
Clean linen on the bed
and a good book.
Today no writee
too ~~dul~~ sickee.

608. In a letter to Margo Jones (circa 4 October 1943, HRC), Williams wrote:
I will probably have to travel by coach to Cleveland but will time my departure so I can get a good sleep before the opening performance. Right now I've got a dreadful cough and a fever, but unless I get very much worse, I will make the trip.

609. Williams wrote to Windham ([22 October 1943], Yale): "I am mostly working on The Spinning Song, which is now all in verse." Most likely, Williams turned this into the "tragedy in verse called 'The Columns of Revelry'" about which he wrote McConnell (15 November 1943, Cleveland Play House Collection). Only fragments of a verse play based on "The Spinning Song" are known to have survived. In one fragment the Mother addresses the bridegroom of her daughter Blanche:

> Paul, you have married into a very old house.
> The house of Revelry has been twice destroyed.
> Once by cyclone in eighteen hundred and four,
> again by fire in the War Between the States.
> But the Columns of Revelry have remained as they are,
> immaculate and unshaken, for three hundred years.
> They're older than the nation. They seem to stand
> for something more enduring than the house.
> What is it? I've often wondered.
>     I like to think
> it is something of the spirit which they stand for,
> some quality of the heart,
> for that, as an old woman knows peculiarly well,
> is longer surviving than the body is.

610. *Five Young American Poets*, third series, including twenty-nine poems by Williams, and *New Directions Eight*, including Williams' play "Dos Ranchos, or The Purification," were not published until September 1944.

611. In May Williams had attempted a one-act based on his landlady Zola, but there is no evidence to suggest that he completed it. A few months later ([20 September 1943], Yale), Williams had written Windham that Zola would be the subject of a "tremendous short story" for either Windham or Isherwood:
Zola the landlady has given me a bowl of ripe tomatoes from the garden back of the house. They are big as your fist, bloody red, and spurt between your teeth when you bite into them. Bits of brown earth are still clinging about the spikey leaves and stems and the taste like the sweetness and pride of all unconscious life which we put so shamelessly to our own uses. Zola is a wonderful character, a lecherous communist woman of about forty-five with a great blown-up body. She sleeps with any man in the house who will have her, and has a frail, sour little husband named Ernie who does all the house-work, bed-making, Etc. while she soaks up the sun on the porch steps or a big raggedy mattress she has flung out in the back-yard near the tomato patch, with a cocker spaniel resting its head on her belly. Right now the wrestling champion of the Pacific coast is stopping here, a big monolith of a body. He stalks down the hall in an electric blue satin robe clinging like a kiss to all the lines of his body and lounges in the hall telephoning his women. While he phones he shift his body in the glittering robe lasciviously from right to left, the big buttocks jutting out and rolling as he croons into the mouth-piece. He fairly fucks the wall. I always pretend to be waiting to make a call so I can watch, and tonight Zola finally and reluctantly introduced us. Either she has gotten all of it she can take or can't get it. There are two things we agree on, and one of them is communism. The other is our most ardent point of agreement but we only discuss it in knowing smiles at each other and the shyly understanding exchange of drinks and tomatoes, Etc. The little husband is polite and furious and is always trembling a little. There is a tremendous short story in the place for you or Cristopher, especially the woman on the raggedy mattress by the tomato patch with the great rocking days of California weaving in and out while she ages and laps up life with the tongue of a female bull.
Williams would soon act on his suggestion and write "The Mattress by the Tomato Patch."

Went in Hollywood
dragged around my
tired ass & came home
about sundown.
No cruisee
no parkee
too tiredee.
Went to bedee.
Clean linen on bedee
kind of good bookee.
Shittee.

Last night character from Ocean Park – writer and drunkard. Sweet. We talked about Tahiti where we both think of going après la guerre.

Tried novel position in bed. O.k. till I came, then awfully tiresome.

Tomorrow pick up check at Metros and complete plans for Cleveland trip.[608] Anticipate it despite bad reports on play rehearsals.

Dull boy tonight. Excuse please.

very weak all day.

*Wednesday, 6 October 1943*

Wed Nite
pretty good work
on verse play[609]
got check
Swam at Y.
big swell dinner
with Cousin
Jane (Lanier) Lawrence
and Tony.

Tony read Thoreau's Walden which impresses me enormously. Not cold, not Puritan. An Elizabethan richness of language and deep lonely perception. I can use it in play.

No sex tonight. Home too late.

Cold bad, bad – but this evening I feel fairly well – not plagued by anything – a spirit of hope is being reborn about play for no apparent reason.

brochure & nice letter from Laughlin. I am crazy about Jay. He has become my little shiney god. Why does he bother with me? It is so easy to ignore a squirt like me. My name listed in brochure of forthcoming works but Jay says they will be out late.[610]

I will send him The Mattress Story.[611] It glows, I think. It has my richest heart

612. Williams continued working on his screen version of "The Gentleman Caller," first mentioned at the end of May in his letter to Audrey Wood (31 May 1943, HRC). In a letter (circa 26 June 1943, HRC), Williams told Wood that his next assignment at Metro would probably be something he himself selected as material. "I have done some more work on the film story treatment of 'The Gentleman Caller' and am showing it to Lillie [Messinger, MGM executive] as potential material."

Williams' "chance" may have been wishful thinking, for there appears to be no record of his or Wood's attempting to sell the film story treatment to Metro in the autumn of 1943.

613. On 21 October 1943 (HRC), Williams wrote to Audrey Wood:

I went on with my own creations . . . a group of stories I'm preparing for Laughlin to maybe publish. Incidentally, I do want you to have three or four of my best stories typed up right away and sent to me to add to this collection. . . . The ones I want are The Vine, The Red Part of A Flag, In Memory of an Aristocrat, Miss Rose and the Grocery Clerk, The Lost Girl, A Tale of Two Writers.

Williams wrote Windham ([22 October 1943], Yale) that he was working on a collection for Laughlin entitled "ALICE'S SUMMER HOTEL for this place I stay in." No such collection is known to exist, and despite Williams' efforts it was not until 1949 that Laughlin published eleven of Williams' short stories under the title *One Arm and Other Stories*. None of the above-mentioned stories was included in that collection.

614. Of the four short stories mentioned only three would eventually be published. "Portrait of a Girl in Glass" and "The Malediction" would be published by Laughlin in *One Arm and Other Stories* (1949), and "The Mattress by the Tomato Patch" would be published by Laughlin in *Hard Candy: A Book of Short Stories* (1954). "Blue Roses" refers presumably to the story "Blue Roses and the Polar Star" (begun in 1941) and not the story "Blue Roses" (written 1935), which was also never published.

"Blue Roses and the Polar Star," significant in its use of fantasy, consists of two vignettes. The first, "Blue Roses," set in the South, is the story of Laura Jean Logan, nicknamed Blue Roses when a boy misunderstood her when she described her condition of pleurosis. Laura Jean drops out of school, is wild with boys, leaves home, and mails a card with the brief message "Hello — goodbye!" Williams would reuse this line in Tom's opening monologue in *The Glass Menagerie*. About his father, Tom reveals, "The last we heard of him was a picture postcard from Mazatlan, on the Pacific coast of Mexico, containing a message of two words: 'Hello — Goodbye!' and no address" (scene 1).

"The Polar Star" begins six years after the first vignette ends. Laura Jean now lives in the French Quarter of New Orleans and has a lover, John, a merchant seaman whose ship is named *The Polar Star*. John dies at sea, but they have a son together, John II, who is a remarkable child. One day he slips into the water, rides on the back of a dolphin, and returns to shore spitting out a fountain of jewels.

Williams felt the need to write a lengthy note of explanation about the story:

What ("BLUE ROSES AND THE POLAR STAR") is about.

It is a fable of a prodigal's life, its penalties and its rewards, and it tries to approximate through fantasy, through a fairly gradual progression from realism to fantasy, the way that the prodigal receives rewards not through reality which has a tendency to become increasingly harsh as its demands are longer ignored — but through the gaining of an immaterial wealth of feeling and experience, departments in which the prudent soul, the niggardly, remains with empty-pockets. "Some people", says the sailor's message, "don't even die empty-handed." As for the rather remarkable infant, that infant is a "State of grace" that one comes to in triumphing over disgrace. And he does spit out rare jewels into your lap — He does incredible things, rides on the back of a dolphin, Etc. He comes after the sorrow and the purification of loss. He is the prodigal's katharsis, his last removal from "circumstantial evidence". This prodigal infant-of-a-prodigal is a miracle and he has a relationship with the mystery that surrounds the light-spot of life. One feels that he has memorized "secret instructions" — that he is a link to infinity — that he is entering the world with a superior knowledge and a purer plan. Blue Roses's bastard brat is that essence of wisdom, of serene knowledge, of surrender to truth which is what the person who dares to feel extravagantly at the risk of his skin finally gets when the skin is about all gone. — I don't mean to say the story is all alleghory. It isn't. Some things are put in merely for the charm of their strangeness and because as Saroyan has said "When you go deep enough into reality you find that the core of it is fantasy." In other words fairy-tales aren't nearly as odd as life.

Every life is waiting for a miracle. It has the eery, mystifying atmosphere of an initial gesture or incantation that will finally be completed and result in some piece of magic.

in it, not my drizzle puss self. I like some people, some. I like Jay, my brother
Dakin, Jane, Margo, Tony, even Donnie a bit. I shall more. Then many past. Oh,
well. I must stay on my feet, finish verse play, bang up job.

Tight-assed – Tony's expression for anything good. He calls Thoreau a "tight-
assed old girl". So wonderful, I will probably use it. My contribution to our
vernacular is bloomer girl. All the piddling literati I call bloomer girls. Wonder if
I am one? – Noooo! Not me! I am tightassed. (with bloomers) We were saying
tonight writing will finally be more and more a projection of personality direct,
organic, less just writing.

Tony says may finally stop being writing & just be person.
funny. Could be.
Writing disappear
into life.
the right direction.
Begonia, big heavy
flower – rots when
in full bloom.
Toes itch.
Hello, tomorrow
How will you be?
Be good!

## Thursday, 7 October 1943

Thursday Night.
blond loveliness in bed.
I came first, as usual, and the beauty lost its thrill.
but was sweet natured and the experience a good one.
More good work today on verse play.
Still sickly with cold. Chance I may sell treatment to Metro.[612]
Tomorrow I will get some stories off to Laughlin.[613] The Mattress isn't good
yet. Sloppy like everything I write.

## Friday, 8 October 1943

Friday
All arrangements set for depart. tomorrow. Coach to Cleveland – an ordeal I
hope I live through – feel better maybe because of bright note from Margo.
God bless her!
How I wish I could make this a triumph for us both.
Shaping some stories for Jay, Portrait, Mattress, Blue Roses, maybe
Malediction.[614]

615.   Almost two weeks later Williams explained in a letter to Audrey Wood (21 October 1943, HRC) why he
       had chosen not to travel to Cleveland for the opening on the 13th:

> About You Touched Me. I gave it up as a lost cause when I read Margo's last letter five hours before
> I was to catch the train. I know the impossibility of creating anything without an almost fanatical
> faith in what you are doing — when I heard the circumstances surrounding the production I knew
> that nothing but lifeless exercises upon the stage could come from it, and that too much of my dear-
> est feelings and thoughts were bedded in that awkward little play for me to enjoy looking at such a
> mutilation.

616.   The situation in which a prostitute takes a client's money and, instead of providing sex, assaults him.

617.   In the short story "The Angel in the Alcove," in which Williams included biographical elements of both
       himself and his grandmother, the narrator recounts his stay when he was a twenty-year-old struggling artist
       in a rooming house in the French Quarter of New Orleans. He remembered the appearance now and again
       in his room's alcove of a "misty grey figure . . . the tender and melancholy figure of an angel." The angel
       has a "gentle, unquestioning look" that the narrator recognizes as belonging to his grandmother, and he
       finds the angel's presence very comforting.

       After another rooming-house tenant, a tubercular artist, enters his room and joins him in bed, the nar-
       rator remembers feeling that the ghost of his grandmother "had permitted the act to occur and had nei-
       ther blamed nor approved." When the dying artist is evicted from his room, the narrator remembered that
       the angel failed to appear, and he interpreted her absence as a warning for him to leave the rooming house.

       The short story, which would be published in *One Arm and Other Stories*, would form the basis of
       Williams' 1970s play *Vieux Carré*.

Williams on the beach, Santa Monica

Later

Got feeling sick on Palisades and turned home early. lay on bed reading New Yorker. And drinking cream of tomato soup till my faintness passed. I am not a well boy lackaday!

Now I feel sleepy and peaceful – tomorrow = choo choo. remember how you doted on them way long ago in Mississippi?

*Saturday, 9 October 1943*

Saturday

Trip off – gloomy letter from Margo changed plans at last moment.[615]

Instead I went out and rented a bike and will devote the week to more healthful pursuits than a coach trip to Cleveland to see a messy performance.

I had no coffee today – feel a bit listless but not really low – I guess I'm toughened up prettily thoroughly.

Spect I'll land back on the family doorstep bye and bye, way things are going. Oh, well. Endurance is all, my pet.

*Sunday, 10 October 1943*

Sunday –

What was that about healthful pursuits? I was kidding. Spent entire bright day in the kitchen working on stories. Nicholson came over tonight and we hied to the Palisades where we ran into Bob & Vaughn – Vaugn had been clipped the night before[616] and was a bloody sight. Hair was saturated in 3 brands of scent, Christmas Night, Tabu and My Sin.

Too much for Nicholson but I found it redolent of New Orleans and was amused.

No amour – felt weak and sickish. So have come home alone to bed. Alone is right. I grow rather lonely these nights even when I am not alone. Deciduous atmosphere this period is getting. Soon it ends. Soon it ends. I wonder if I am really ill or just very depressed. The Angel in The Alcove[617] today was improved also Mattress. They go to Laughlin next week. Where do I go next week? To blazes? Me, me, me, me, me. Oh, I am so tired of me, me, me, me, me. I am unloved even by me. I love nobody.

I am being deliberately childish. I was a sweet child. Child murdered. I have slid through thousands of hands like a fish. This is too much. I must quit. Goodnight.

618. *You Touched Me!* was uniformly well received by the Cleveland critics (14 October 1943). The *Cleveland Press* noted that the "two young authors . . . write with considerable beauty and power of expression and are uncommonly adept at creating characters with down-to-earth, human qualities." The *Cleveland News* declared *You Touched Me!* "a thoughtful and interesting drama beautifully acted and produced . . . essentially a series of brilliant character sketches blended with overtones of humor, tragedy, and Saroyanesque poetic fancies." The *Cleveland Plain Dealer* noted that Williams and Windham had written a "sensitive, intelligent and interesting play." The play received only a small amount of mild criticism for its occasionally artificial and verbose dialogue.

The Reverend Walter and Rosina Dakin in St. Petersburg, Florida

*Tuesday, 12 October 1943*

Tues. Night

No sex since last Thurs. probably my longest period of continence since early summer. Partly weakness – I am really near to collapse. Then, luck when I go out is bad. I am not the radiant star of everybody's libido nowadays. My hair has gotten sort of ratty looking, my face dull and sallow, and my front teeth have two visible black cavities that I am too lifeless to have fixed. It surprises me that even by moonlight I still sometimes attract a good party. These years, how does one go through them? Yet the loss of youth is never more than a peripheral concern of mine. My sorrows are all more phantasmic than that. I do not put much down even here, and so these notebooks despite their attempt at merciless candor about my life fall short, give very little, perhaps really distort unfavorably for I seem inclined to note only the seedier things. Still they are companionable things. They talk to me from the past in a comforting way, make the links more real. The past gets lost so sadly. This will be the past, but what will the future be? I have never found it less conceivable.

Grand and Grandfather still alive – the falling monuments of all the sweet things in my childhood and later. Yet I don't write them. Tomorrow night the play goes on in Cleveland.[618]

> I will absorb
> anything that
> can happen there
> with singular
> sang froid.
>
> All of this is false,
> false, says nothing.
> I am a little batty
> here of late.
> Cold – Sick –
> one more cigarette
> and a little reading
> lights out then.
> Tomorrow then.

*Sunday, 17 October 1943*

Sun. Night –
> I haven't talked to you these past 4 nights.
> I have been a good boy.
> Outdoors on the bike. And no coffee, no writing –

619.  Set in the winter of 1939 in New Orleans, "One Arm" is the story of Oliver Winemiller, a hustler who had been the light heavyweight champion boxer of the Pacific fleet before he lost an arm in a car accident. On death row for the murder of a wealthy broker in Miami, Oliver is described as having "the charm of the defeated." This characteristic, combined with his youth and physical charm, made him "a person impossible to forget." While in jail, Oliver receives a number of letters which he describes as "bills from people I owe. Not money, but feelings." The day before Oliver is executed, he is visited by a young Lutheran minister who has been drawn to his case from newspaper reports. Oliver stirs homoerotic feelings in the minister, who flees to escape having to acknowledge his feelings. Oliver's body is left unclaimed and donated to a medical college.

   As he revealed in a letter to Windham ([31 May 1942], Yale), Williams had begun a story based on "the 1-armed blond hustler in New Orleans" at the end of May 1942.

620.  Echoes of Rimbaud, *Les Illuminations*, II Enfance, [part] iv. "Ce ne peut être que la fin du monde, en avançant," which Crane used as the epigraph to his poems "White Buildings" (Part 2 in *The Collected Poems of Hart Crane*), and Williams used as the epigraph to the play "The Last of My Solid Gold Watches."

   Je serais bien l'enfant abandonné sur la jetée partie à la haute mer, le petit valet suivant l'allée dont le front touche le ciel.

   Les sentiers sont âpres. Les monticules se couvrent de genêts. L'air est immobile. Que les oiseaux et les sources sont loin! Ce ne peut être que la fin du monde, en avançant.

   I might be the child left on the jetty washed out to sea, the little farm boy following the lane whose crest touches the sky.

   The paths are rough. The hillocks are covered with broom. The air is motionless. How far away the birds and the springs are! It can only be the end of the world, ahead. (Arthur Rimbaud, *Collected Poems*, edited by Oliver Bernard [Harmondsworth: Penguin Books, 1986], pp. 238–39)

Yesterday was foggy so I stayed home and went back to work. Worked well on short story about the 1-armed youth in N.O.[619] It has power. David came over and we entertained three sets, the second set was a circus – third stayed the night. I was no good really, lacked or lost interest till late in the night but then the nightingales sang nicely in a sleepy way.

Dear David – always with him I am especially shy and his understanding and caring seems only to make it more embarassing. He bought a copy of Crane whom he has caught my passion for.

I was glad to be alone again this afternoon. I had clean sheets on the bed – I read The New Yorker which always delights me – then a deep, sweet sleep till after dark. A movie – A hot beef sandwich – now bed.

Margo returns tomorrow and I will get the news on the play.

How indifferent I am or appear to be!

Oh, I do care, but relatively little, not as a man with his hat in the ring should care.

Today no coffee –
a victory – I
can get along without
it and the
abstinence definitely
improves my
nerves & heart.
Write tomorrow –
finish up stories
for Jay. Will he
like them?
Good Night.


*Wednesday, 20 October 1943*

Wed Nite.

Cold, cold.

My feet icey.

Fin du monde cold.[620]

Margo didn't like my new 3rd act – Sad. I was rather excited about it. Nothing happens – I see a little blood in my spit this morning.

Also heart bumpy – was back on coffee.

Tomorrow got to prepare Scene for McConnell.

621.  Pétrouchka, a version of Pierrot, is a character in the Russian folk tale. Three puppets of a Russian puppet master, the sad Pétrouchka, a beautiful ballerina and an opulent Moor, come to life in private. Pétrouchka falls in love with the ballerina who is oblivious to his interest and flirts instead with the Moor. When the Moor kills Pétrouchka, the horrified fairgoers mourn his death, but the showman picks up the broken puppet, explaining that it is just a doll. The ghost of Pétrouchka returns, however, proving his immortality.

622.  Presumably "The Pretty Trap." The "comedy in one act" ends with Laura and Jim, the gentleman caller, going for a walk. Amanda reports to Tom that Jim has already kissed Laura. The play ends with Amanda saying to Tom:

> Girls are a pretty trap!
>
> That's what they've always been, and will always <u>be</u>, even when <u>dreams</u> plus <u>action</u> — take over the world!
>
> Now — now, dreamy type —
>
> Let's finish the dishes!

THE PRETTY TRAP

(A Comedy in One Act)

by

Tennessee Williams

CHARACTERS

Amanda Wingfield.....A perennial southern belle,
transferred to more rigorous climate and conditions.

Laura Wingfield......Her daughter, a shy and sensitive
girl of eighteen who "needs to be pushed a little."

Tom Wingfield........Her son, the dreamy type, who
also needs pushing a little.

Jim Delaney..........A gentleman caller, who represents
dreams plus action, the man coming toward us. Needs
pulling.

Note: This play is derived from a longer work in progress,
The Gentleman Caller. It corresponds to the last act of
that play, roughly, but has a lighter treatment and a different
ending.

*Saturday, 23 October 1943*

Saturday.

"I only recently learned of the death of Miss Florence."

So Mother wrote today. All those Saturday afternoons, Hazel and Miss Florence and I. It was really Miss Florence who was most tender toward me. She always spoke of "your talent" when nobody else did. And in those time, dark, desperate days of adolescence, that meant something. Those afternoons were the bright spots of my life. Well, now she's dead. It brings death home.

I thought of death as I lay on the sun-roof this afternoon beneath that angry old golden lion the sun and among those chattering belles. I have been further from death than I am now.

Today I couldn't write on "One Arm" or anything.

Tomorrow I have to see my father at his hotel in L.A. Thank God Margo will go with me.

Petrouchka Petrouchka[621]

I wish I had a lovely little clown for a friend. One that had sorrows but made me sunny. My friends are all so much of the world though less than other people are. I want to be friends with some wild thing. All next week I'll be good – no coffee, I mean, and lots of out-doors. I will get something good to read. Jung seems a little too pretentious and a bit of a charlatan right now. All these involved dreams – I am sure nobody ever really had them! Or that they mean everything the Doctor says.

The unconscious – yes. But not like that. It should be but I fear it isn't.

I must go to Jane's and Tony's – So long.


*Tuesday, 26 October 1943*

Tues. Night

Thought you were lost Mr. Blue Book. searched high and low till I found you between some newspapers.

Just read over the one fairly long thing I've done out here, the 1-act version of Gentleman Caller.[622] It is appalling. Something has definitely gone wrong – that I was able to write such shit. Hysterical and empty. First the emptiness I suppose. Then dread of it. Then the hysteria pouring more emptiness.

What shall I do?

Be bravely patient and try not writing a few months?

Wisest thing to do.

But how will I keep up my spirits even tolerably without work?

I will only write after this when I feel something really there and not just to be writing.

But resolutions – how little they help me.

623.  Only one poem, "Goofer Song," is known to be dated October 1943.

```
                      GOOFER SONG

              I am admiring the body
              but trying to read the mind.
              Its humor is class entertainment
              but not my favorite kind.

              It hasn't the stops of a trumpet
              but neither, I think, has the lark
              who still is a potent dispensor
              of lyric appeals to the heart.

              The bar will be closed in a minute,
              and drunkards adjourned to the street.
              If old Saint Oscar is with me
              its problem is where to sleep.

              This last drink is a dilemma
              to conjure the Gloomy Dane!
              Where is the remark that maneuvers
              our talk to the intimate vein?

              Or wouldn't it really be wiser,
              with minimum reticency,
              to let my fingers address
              the heart in care of the knee?

              The silver of adolescence
              may be disdainful of brass,
              but just admiring this body
              is getting me nowhere fast.

              O Princess of Coney Island
              who reads all thoughts in a glance,
              is this a rising libido
              or, merely the presence of ants?

              Look in your crystal, dear sister,
              this is a hurry-up call,
              and tell me if thirteen buttons
              wear green lights in the ball!

              The body is stamped with approval
              but what in hell comes next,
              a So long, Mac on the Square
              or an uptown train to sex?

                         Tennessee W
                         Oct. 1943.
```

624.  Williams was reading *Rimbaud: The Boy and the Poet* by Edgell Rickword (London: William Heinemann, 1924). He wrote to Windham ([3 November 1943], Yale) and quoted the beginning of chapter VI (p. 39):
The tendency of education has been to create in the young mind the illusion that Nature is kind and Man benevolent, which is as it may be, but there comes a time when so much evidence has been accumulated to the contrary that the inexperienced youth bounds to the opposite conclusion.

Am I all spent? only time can answer. The pity is there was so little to spend – ever. In the way of real ability only the choking heart.

Messed around Pasadena. A dreary time of it, Margo and casting and two more or less arduous meetings with Dad. He appears very chastened and today we made talk alone for the first time in probably ten or fifteen years. A pathetic old man but capable of being a devil –

This must change this interim – it will for better or worse.

Dentist – Must.

Well – good night.

(We have clean sheets to give a little comfort.)

Tomorrow I may resume my little scratching about for some truth. Tired as the fingers are, they will go on digging.

*Wednesday, 27 October 1943*

Wed Nite

Yes, I did some scratching. A reasonably nice poem[623] and some repairs on <u>One Arm</u> of doubtful merit. Done delightfully on the Palisades when I went out on my bicycle just now. Have gone to bed with cigarettes and book, A life of Rimbaud.[624]

Feel good. Ruin is still in abeyance. Good night. En Avant, wherever you are!

Zola's daughter received a record of a sailor's voice. Her mother came in with it and played it before the girl was up. Then both of them returned and played it again.

He talked about the weather and a movie in a sad young voice. Said he was shipping out before a letter could reach him.

Later Zola gave me a plate of cookies. We are friends again.

I think I will stay on here till I leave California.

*Sunday, 31 October 1943*

Sat. Night

Happy state of mind continues and fairly creative too. <u>One Arm</u> grows.

Went to Elvira Street and Chinatown with Jane and Tony. Tired me dreadfully with all their shopping but we jested and camped merrily along. Tony in a berêt and blue turtle neck sweater with his red beard. Sensational. Jane gave me a tube of KY as a halloween present. They are good companions and real friends. I bought a lovely Chinese poster picture to hang in my room. Now home in bed about four A.M. hitchhiked in from end of car line.

feel phenomenally
well. why?
Irresponsibility!

625. Williams was hoping that Hunter would produce *You Touched Me!* in New York and was anxious to hear if she had been able to secure any backers. Williams would soon hear from Hunter, who had just seen the Cleveland production of *You Touched Me!* She wrote (29 October 1943, Yale):

> I find myself caught in a rather odd predicament — that I am being asked for the script by an interested backer and do not feel that I can submit to him either the version I have and certainly not the version as played in Cleveland. I know that you and Margo are working on revisions and I hope that you will send me a script with the main changes as soon as possible.
>
> Where the natural gaiety warmth and wit shine through, the play is electric and I believe more than ever in its fine qualities and its prospects for success. So I devoutly hope that you are clarifying and strengthening all those elements in the play and that you will not permit any interpretation of Aunt Emmie along the lines of making her a dour, puritanic New England woman but will insist on the line which to me is so surely established in the play that she is a flustered, frustrated somewhat confused maiden lady who hasn't the faintest notion that she is hostile toward the world and men in particular but thinks rather in terms that they do not understand her pure and delicate femininity.

626. Presumably Williams' reference to Crane's poem "Recitative":

> Look steadily — how the wind feasts and spins
> The brain's disk shivered against lust. Then watch
> While darkness, like an ape's face, falls away,
> And gradually white buildings answer day.

Tony says I am a
Chinaman.
Last night
the sweet writer who
pushes wheel barrows
at a nursery.
I have always
loved wheel barrows.
Tony & Jane say they do too.

We all rode in them as kids. Writer pushing wheel barrow made me happy somehow. We lay on sofa and heard symphony, quiet and warm. Room lighted only by gas range.

No word from Mary Hunter.[625]

So long. Tomorrow?

If bright ride or the roof. Lay off writing.

Mail stories Jay Monday.


*Saturday, 6 November 1943*

Saturday – Nov. 6th

God!

I see!

The Ape's face![626]

I've stopped writing.

If I am careful this moment and from now on I can maybe save myself from madness.

It is worth while doing anything to avoid that.

So I will if there is any chance.

Wanting the limitless I am ruined by limits. My work breaks down into the squirmings of a crushed worm.

If anything can break me this thing will. If it doesn't I can die of attrition or turn into a watch tower.


*Sunday, 14 November 1943*

Sun. Nov. 14

Last Sat. I seem to have been a little upset. Was working on "One Arm" – read it over and discovered that I had destroyed it. Tant Pire. but no call for hysterics. It is quite true that 90% of my work lately is abortive. Why? Can't say. It may be temporary – functional. It may be organic – incurable. All we can do is maintain our endurance – wait and see.

627.   Monogram was the name of a small B-movie studio. For the most part Monogram made low-budget movie series, such as the Charlie Chan detective films and the East Side Kids and Bowery Boys comedies, as well as B westerns. In a letter to Donald Windham dated 8 November 1943 (Yale), Williams described a story editor at Monogram, to whom he had read aloud a story of Windham's, as a "night companion."

Williams on the beach, Santa Monica

I went on writing this past week. Returned to Gentleman Caller limiting my efforts to Cautious patchwork.

Margo and Pasadena rehearsals of "You Touched Me" the main business. Not well and — Suffering from some intestinal disorder – diarrhoea and sore rectum. A little alarming. Especially since one dreads consulting a doctor about anything so — intimate.

Still no dentist.

Time and money pour away and nothing is decided.

I dreamed last night about J. Laughlin. That he had snubbed me when I called on him and the books left me out. Such appalling misery. I felt such desolation.

A symbol of my worry about my weak writing.

Today I spent with Ed Doane, my fat friend. We drove to beach and listened to radio. Then saw his films. I wound up at a movie.

glasses are lost!

This week coming on is portentous. Matter of health and moving will come to a point.

En Avant!

Later – I have just surrendered my bed to the friend from Monogram[627] who has brought in a pick up from Palisades and they are having a party while I wait in the kitchen for them to finish. They are taking their name – gasping and puffing like a pair of excited dogs.

Sex seems so silly when you're a spectator or audience. Well maybe the pick up is pretty.

I am told to respect shyness and remain out of sight. Rather presumptuous. Think I'll walk in presently and introduce myself. I'm out of cigs.

Monogram pokes head in to request a towel. Then more puffings. At least I bummed a cig. off him. The puffings now become climactic so I trust it will be over shortly. I feel like a soured old Madam. My bed will be a mess.

I always fuck so quietly. Don't I enjoy it as much?

The puffings stop and rustlings begin.

Over I hope.

No, they've started again.

Monogram whispers "I'm exhausted."

Answer – a breathless snicker. Now definite sounds of conclusion. Wonder if I'll get a look at the guest of honor? Probably not.

628. Williams would continue working on "The Gentleman Caller" over the next year. It would eventually emerge as *The Glass Menagerie*.

629. There exists in fact a letter from Williams to his grandparents dated 15 November 1943 (HTC).

*Nov. 15, 1943*

Dear Grand and Grandfather:

I have been commuting between Santa Monica and Pasadena ever since the play rehearsals started there which has made me even worse than usual at correspondance. I think of you all every day even though I so rarely have the leisure to write. I should have moved to Pasadena but the town is so crowded with war-workers there was literally not one vacant room. The trip is two hours each way and my attendance at rehearsals is necessary as I am still revising the script. While it was pretty successful and attracted a good deal of favorable attention, the Cleveland production showed some weaknesses in the script which I have to patch up during the present production. I think it will come out a lot better. The producer in Cleveland cut thirty pages out of the last act, including one whole scene, without consulting me, which made the last act rather inconclusive. Margo couldn't do anything to stop him without getting fired. However the affirmative spirit of the play was highly praised by everybody and passages were even quoted in the editorials ections of the Celveland paper, one editor basing an article on "twelve great lines" from one of the speeches about the post-war world. Margo has the only copy of this but I am writing for another so I can send it to you. I am hoping the play will be sold to Broadway, but the interested producers are waiting to see what happens at Pasadena and get the final revised script following that try-out.

I have received a letter from Dakin at Fort Dix. He is certainly getting around. I am sure all this is very good for him, and it now looks as though the allies are in a position to end the war before he has much chance for participation. - Resassure Aunt Ella about Hollywood. Everybody here is too busy to get into mischief. Actually it is the quietest place I've lived. All the night-life stops at midnight, people stay at home more than they do in Saint Louis. I personally have too much to do and think about to be influenced by Hollywood society even if it had any dangerous charm.

My plans are not certain yet, and won't be for a couple of weeks. If I decide to return East, I will get through Saint Louis for a visit.

                Dear love to you both,

                        Tom

*New address - Go Margo Jones, Pasadena Playhouse — I will, or may, find a place there this week.*

*Monday, 15 November 1943*

Mon. Night. Nov. 15 –

I am always alarming bed partners by having palpitations. "My God, how your heart is pounding!" Tonight my pulse was taken by the alarmed guest and it was counted "over 100". Considerably over I guess. I am so used to it it doesn't disturb me except when it makes me breathless. Well, tonight was worth palpitations. An almost ideal concurrence of circumstances and a record for me of 5 times perfectly reciprocal pleasure.

So now I play my Hawaiian records and smoke my second pack of cigs for the day.

This is hardly the behavior for a cardiac case but maybe my instinct tells me a long life would be evil and so puts the coffin nails in my hand and points to the hammer.

Today for the first time in a month or so I wrote pretty nicely. On the last scene of "The Gentleman Caller".[628] I have returned to the original version of it. It won't be a total loss after all. But it is very, very sentimental. Ah, well, I am not Dostoevsky nor even Strindberg. I must work within my limits.

Tomorrow I will take a bike trip through Hollywood to Pasadena. I have bought a new pair of glasses.

Hungry! And happy?

I will ride over to the "Quick and Dirty" for a midnight meal. Heigh Ho!

(No letter to Grand.[629]

Disgraceful.

I will, I will!)


*Tuesday, 16 November 1943*

Tues.

Diarrhoea and burning continues – disgusting business!

Too dull to work after last night's excesses. Also too feeble. I read and lie in bed. To see David. presently in Hollywood.

Will try to be agreeable.

But I am bleak enough. God knows.

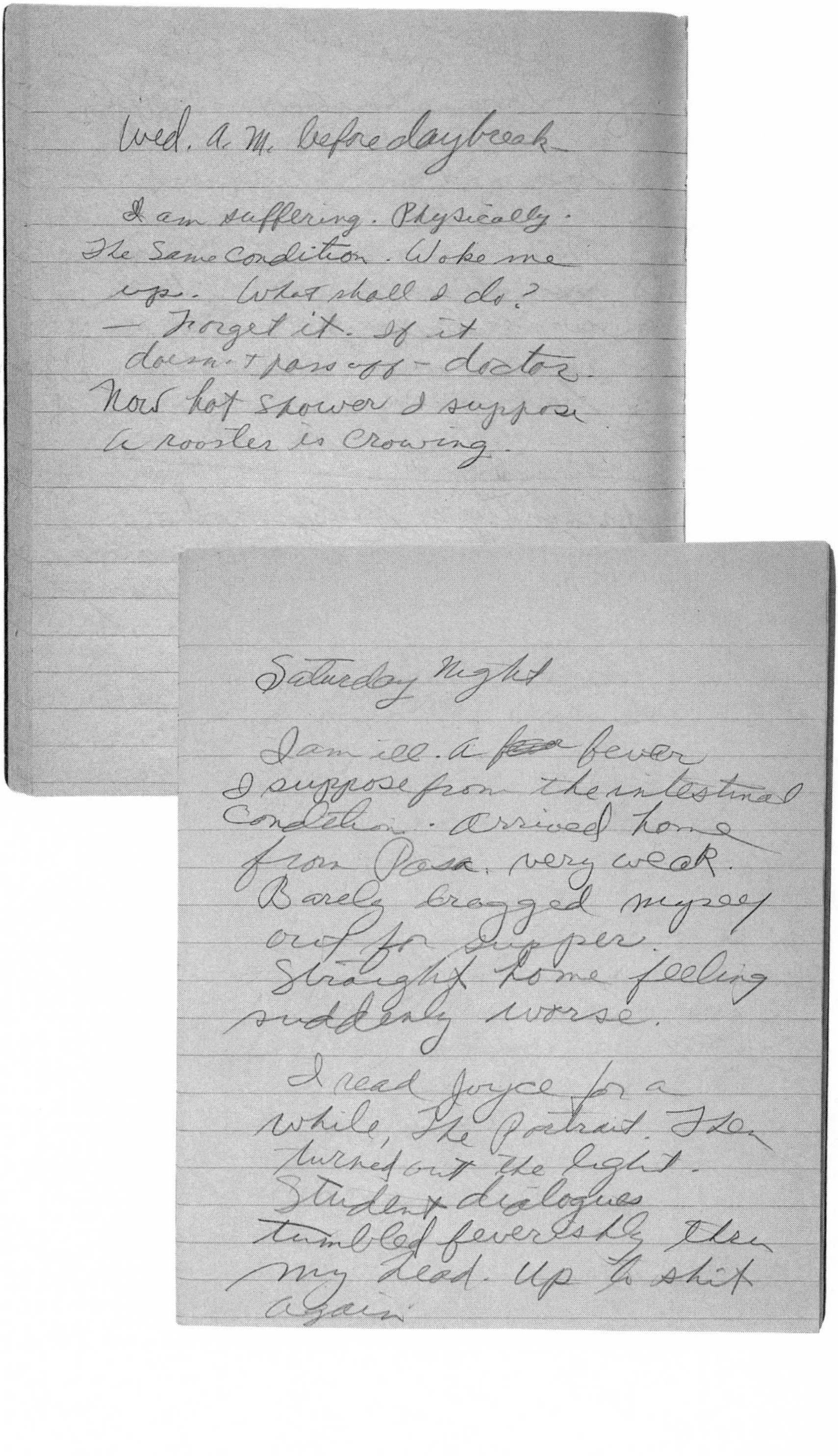

Wed. A. M. before daybreak

I am suffering. Physically.
The same condition. Woke me
up. What shall I do?
— Forget it. If it
doesn't pass off — doctor.
Now hot shower I suppose.
A rooster is crowing.

Saturday Night

I am ill. A fever
I suppose from the intestinal
condition. Arrived home
from Pasa. very weak.
Barely dragged myself
out for supper.
Straight home feeling
suddenly worse.

I read Joyce for a
while, The Portrait. Then
turned out the light.
Student dialogues
tumbled feverishly then
my head. Up to shit
again

*Wednesday, 17 November 1943*

Wed. A.M. before daybreak –

I am suffering. Physically. The Same condition. Woke me up. What shall I do? – Forget it. If it doesn't pass off – doctor. Now hot shower I suppose. A rooster is crowing.

*Saturday, 20 November 1943*

Saturday Night

I am ill. A fever I suppose from the intestinal condition. Arrived home from Pasa. very weak. Barely dragged myself out for supper. Straight home feeling suddenly worse.

I read Joyce for a while, The Portrait. Then turned out the light. Student dialogues tumbled feverishly thru my head. Up to shit again.

Now my feet are icey and my head burns.

Perhaps I shall be very ill. I have quite at the bottom of the world so much lately.

Being unable to write anything decent is no help. My brain seems feeble, my nerves shot.

It would be nice to be home, now. St. Louis. In a clean quiet place among old ladies. Obviously if I remain able to get around and exercise any volition, I must do something to improve my position.

No self pity. I feel none of that. Not much fear. Just weariness.

I pray somebody will call on me in the morning for I may be in a bad state.

Let us hope! En Avant!

Sunday Night

No, it is still Saturday night. My Monogram friend dropped in with another lover and I was once again privileged to function as audience. However I was grateful for the visit as I was feeling a bit abandoned – and now I have perked up. They have just departed. Monogram brought a bottle of wine and 2 packs of cigs. as tribute but he and his guest drank nearly all the wine.

*Sunday, 21 November 1943*

Sun. It is a bright, sunny morning. The diarrhoea continues but I feel better and will dress and go out. Tomorrow I shall see a doctor.

monologue – Introduction

1. The birthday celebration & apple.
2. Portrait commission
3. "I see her as —"
4. Discuss families – army in Spain. (aft I)
   Lisabetta – "Vocation – I thought not."
5. "You will live to something while
   in window – Song "How doth my love." You
   will live to be very old. Intercede with Cardinal –
   Pope – Lisabetta – Incest _____ Dungeon?
6. Defeat of brother's army – failure of intercession –
   Portrait is finished – Ariadne! – embrace.
7. Wedding anniversary supper –
   unveiling – death – End.
   monologue – epilogue

Out line for
"A Balcony In Ferrara"

J.W. 3/4/44.

*November 1943 ended with the successful opening of* You Touched Me! *in Pasadena.*

*In December Williams traveled from Hollywood to see Frieda Lawrence in Taos and then on to St. Louis to spend Christmas with his family and to be with his grandmother, who died on 6 January 1944.*

*While in St. Louis, Williams wrote a rough first draft of "A Balcony in Ferrara," a "romantic tragedy . . . suggested by Robert Browning's dramatic monologue, 'My Last Duchess'," returning to a subject on which he had written at the University of Iowa. He also, as he noted to Margo Jones, "did a complete re-write of the nauseous thing I read you in Pasadena,* The Gentleman Caller" *(2 March 1944, HRC).*

*In mid-March 1944 Williams left St. Louis for New York City, where he soon learned that he would receive a grant of $1,000 from the American Academy of Arts and Letters.*

*The grant allowed him to spend part of the summer in Provincetown, where he worked on "The Gentleman Caller." By early September Williams traveled to New York and remained there for approximately six weeks. He wrote Margo Jones (September 1944, HRC):*

> *I am having "The Glass Menagerie" (formerly The Gentleman Caller) typed up here right away and will send you a copy. It has some interesting new techniques and all in all I am not displeased with the out-come. That is, when I consider the terrible, compulsive struggle it was to do the thing and what a frightful, sentimental mess it might well have been, and was at some stages. It needs a good deal of pruning, condensing, possibly some rearranging even in this version. . . . I think it contains my sister, and that was the object.*

Rose Williams                Williams in Provincetown

630.  Williams described the visit to Fire Island, a beach on Long Island, New York, in a letter to Margo Jones (circa 9 June 1944, HRC):

I have been shuttling back and forth between [New York] and my cottage on Fire Island. . . . I had the place for three weeks, a lovely five room cottage on an island in the Atlantic. I meant to get away from the world but actually had more society than usual as all my New York friends, and most of Donnie's, flocked over for week-ends that lasted all week. It was fun but hardly describable as a retreat, Christian or otherwise.

631.  *The Leaning Tower and Other Stories* (New York: Harcourt, Brace and Company, 1944). In the title story, Charles Upton has come to Berlin to become a painter. After a drunken night with other boarders of his rooming house, he comes to see his landlady's small, mended statue of the Leaning Tower of Pisa as a reminder of the "infernal desolation of the spirit, the chill and the knowledge of death in him" (p. 245).

Notebook Williams began in October 1944

*Monday, 2 October 1944*

Monday Oct 2 – 1944
     I lost my last journal on Fire Island in May[630] and haven't kept one since –
     Too bad – the summer deserved recording – it was a psychological tempest –
but summers usually are –
     Here on the further shore of it I linger a while in Manhattan – there isn't
much wind in my sails –
     I am suffering a severe case of nerves – physical manifestations – I have
attacks of panic – mostly on street – must rush into bars for drinks to steady
myself – I get breathless – I have a weight on my chest – how much is sheer
anxiety, how much real cardiac symptoms I don't know –
     All I know is I can't afford to slip into the ghastly neurotic state of ~~those years~~
the time before.
     I sent home for trainfare but I've already spent most of it without leaving
for home.
     I wonder if home will help.
     Well, there is no sure answer to that or any question right now.
     So we come back to our old friend endurance – and hope he remains on our side.
     It's funny – I have intervals of feeling quite well and easy – very brief ones –
     A week or so ago I spit up a mouthfull of blood.
     What charming notes!
     So nicely integrated.
     I'd better let this go.


*Tuesday, 3 October 1944*

Later –
     A Manhattan night –
     I suppose it is about 2 A.M.
     I lie in bed having just finished the title story of K.A. Porter's new book[631] –
curiously unliving piece for her to produce –
     traffic rumbles distantly
     the elevator now and then groans up – and down –
     showers run somewhere –
     Reminds me that I have lost my swimming-cap –
     a real calamity –

Still later –
     this will be one of the famous nights –
     I feel myself close to ~~~~~~
     the shapeless black thing one smells at the back of a cave –
     I turn the light back on –

632.  Jon Stroup (1918– ) was an art editor at *Town and Country* and a friend of Donald Windham's.

    As a music student at the University of Texas in 1943, Charles Paul Moor (1924– ) first came across Williams' work when Margo Jones had shown him a copy of *Battle of Angels*. Moor went on to write an article about Williams, "A Mississippian Named Tennessee," for *Harper's* (July 1948). Williams attempted to stop its publication, describing it as a "direct contradiction of most of the known facts about me, worst of all it is terribly dull" (letter to Audrey Wood, 19 April 1948, HRC).

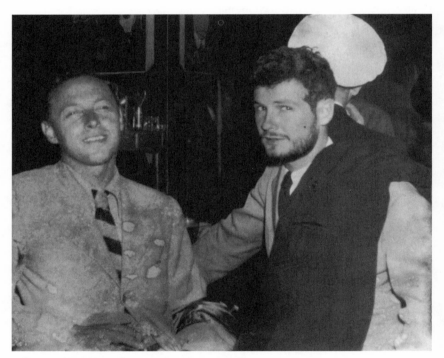

Williams and Donald Windham in Jack Dempsey's Broadway Bar

On the dresser is the bottle of elixir of sodium bromide but there isn't much of it –
I should save it for tomorrow – but I can't sleep –
And the situation is so thin –

I shall, of course, be a man.
Always when my back is really against the wall I recover a little manhood.
Enough. Just barely enough to cover up – and go on –
This I will do again –
And again and again if need be –
I shall act a little manlier than the terror in me suggests –

All right. What now?
Another hot shower?
Dress and go out?

Or shall I be as one who dines with such a dark, ambiguous beast that neither mind nor matter quite divines which one is feast which the beast.

Still later –
Remain wakeful – imagine it's about 6 A.M.
the place begins to stir –
Suppose I'll take another shot of the elixir and another shower – In God we Trust.
the state is less concentrated, at any rate – more general –
and I continue to find it silly as well as dreadful.
yawning but not at all sleepy –

Morning –
I am <u>up</u> – that is all I will say at this point – Some sort of bovine philosophy or attitude may pull me through the day. We'll see – <u>En Avant</u>!

*Monday, 9 October 1944*

Monday Oct. 9 –
Seems to be a week later – feel a whole lot better – no particular crise de nerfs this week –
Today got another check from home.
Made appt. to see Stroup, Laughlin, and Paul Moore tonight[632] – that's a big social dose for one evening – don't exactly look forward to it – feel a bit less than socially brilliant –
May see Doubleday-Doran tomorrow about a book-selling job to keep me here till I'm spiritually ready for Clayton and renewed creation.

633. The Men's Residence Club at 317 West 56th Street was a less expensive and shabbier version of the YMCA.

634. Audrey Wood sold *The Glass Menagerie* to Eddie Dowling, who would co-produce the play with his backer, Louis J. Singer. In addition, Dowling would play the part of Tom both in Chicago and in New York.

Cover of the playbill of *The Glass Menagerie*, with Laurette Taylor (left), Eddie Dowling, and Julie Haydon

Read K.A.P. again last night – the first few stories in the book altogether redeem the weak impression of the title one.

They are awe-inspiring. So warm, so tender – and yet with an astringent quality that precludes sentimentality –

I don't touch her – I'm afraid – ever!

Still no swim cap –

as for sex – it occurs with sufficient regularity – barely sufficient glamor however.

I make myself an infernal nuisance to poor Donnie – wearing his shirts – lounging in his office – drinking his rum –

On Sundays I give him a holiday – and stay away.

He is remarkably sweet tempered about it.

So – we do go on –

Right now I am a little home sick for almost every place I've been –

Santa Monica, Provincetown, Florida, even home.

Manhattan is so furious and impersonal. Still – It offers adventures! And I'm not yet ready for anything but motion-diversion.

Some sort of test is pending.

I have to pass it.

En Avant!

*Tuesday, 10 October 1944*

Another sleepless night in the M.R.C.[633] too much society perhaps – anyhow don't feel a bit sleepy at 6 A.M. – just went out to eat – cream of wheat – Chilly little moon still in the sky.

Whore at newstand telling the newsie a couple of sailors stole her purse – but she had her big money hidden and all they got away with was 15¢ – good for her!

Newsie says: "If they had played along with her they would've gotten a good screw."

So I smoke – and loll on the bed – while another day commences – must see about a job or buy ticket home pronto.

*Wednesday, 18 October 1944*

Wed. Night –

Sold play to Dowling.[634] Should be happy – but seemed to be the signal for another Crise.

Awful bad time of it –

little better now after stiff shot of bromide,

however up till today I've been mending

this will pass quickly

I'll go home and rest – dear God! – Goodnight.

635. Phenobarbital is a barbiturate that would have been prescribed to relieve anxiety. The prolonged effects of frequent use include sluggishness, difficulty in thinking, poor comprehension and memory, slowness and slurring of speech, exaggeration of basic personality traits, irritability, and moroseness. In Williams' play *Not About Nightingales*, Mrs. Bristol takes phenobarbital tablets to calm her heart palpitations.

636. Harold Norse (1916– ), poet and novelist, had spent part of the summer of 1944 with Williams in Provincetown. In *Memoirs of a Bastard Angel* (1989), Norse described the evening he and Williams visited Lynn Riggs (pp. 136–37). In the early 1960s, Norse lived in Paris in the "Beat Hotel" with William Burroughs, Allen Ginsberg, and Gregory Corso and there wrote his experimental cut-up novel, *Beat Hotel* (1975). *Hotel Nirvana: Selected Poems, 1953–1973* (1974), which was nominated for the 1974 National Book Award, established Norse as one of the leading Beat poets.

Rollie Lynn Riggs (1899–1954) was a playwright and poet whose most well-known work is *Green Grow the Lilacs* (1931), the play on which the musical *Oklahoma!* (1943) was based.

637. Ramon Naya, playwright and painter, had been a protégé of Lynn Riggs' and had lived with him in the late 1930s in Sante Fe, New Mexico, where Riggs had built a studio for him and helped him organize an exhibit of his paintings.

Rollie Lynn Riggs                    Harold Norse

*Thursday, 19 October 1944*

Morning –

I wonder if anyone has ever dealt more skillfully with a more vicious and deadly opponent than have I with the beast in my nerves?

I cannot kill him, nor ever <u>entirely</u> escape – I can only dodge him, evade him, put him off.

This I do with the most astonishing cunning, developed over 20 years of practise. I am now an old master of the game. He remains as he was – deadly, implacably malignant, treacherous, huge.

But he cannot increase in Craft –

His advantage Comes only when I dissipate mine.

Of course it is not fun, this game – this being relentlessly pursued.

But we see that we have this beast –

We live with him till the day we die – that is the sentence strangely passed upon us –

So we perforce accept it and keep our wits sharp –

Yes – really everything in my life, even <u>work</u> – the little spasms of love – all human relations, all preoccupations – have been peripheral, incidental to this huge, dreadful game of fox and hounds with neuroses.

This morning I think that we have slipped by again –

<u>En Avant!</u>


*Saturday, 21 October 1944*

Saturday Evening –

A Somewhat controlled situation –

I am taking phenobarbital[635]

Swimming –

keeping socially occupied.

Last night Harold and I went to Lynn Riggs[636] and his friend Murphy – "ideal juvenile"

four or five Scotches –

excellent –

animated talk.

I really like Lynn.

Saw Ramon Naya's paintings – almost as impressive as his plays. We talked mostly of Ramon.[637]

Last heard of, he was in Ojai, California.

going to Fidelma's for supper –

resumed sex last night after a week off due to strain. probably go home Monday.

So long –

638. Jane Owens had visited Williams on Fire Island with Paul Moor. In his letter to Margo Jones (circa 9 June 1944, HRC), Williams wrote:

> I have decided that Jane is second only to you as a verbal spell-binder. Her anecdotes and reminiscences kept us entertained the whole time. As if that wasn't enough, she and Paul washed a whole week's accumulation of dishes and got the place looking better than any time since I struck it.

639. Rosina Dakin died on 6 January 1944. In "The Man in the Overstuffed Chair" and "Grand," Williams gave moving accounts of her last hours.

Williams' grandmother and mother

*Wednesday, 25 October 1944*

Wed. A.M. –
five o'clock –
 The object was 19 – & lovely!
 I'll talk tomorrow.
 Exhausted

Wed. midnight
 Supper with Jane Owens[638] and Paul Moore – in a stuffy little French
restaurant, felt a sort of claustrophobia – had to get up and wait for them outside
on the walk –
 Pains in chest – earlier in afternoon – nerves pretty bad again this eve – took 3
or 4 phenobarbital tablets in course of evening –
 now home for apparently sexless night –
 but last night with the love child was one for the books.
 this little room is depressing –
 I usually become attached to rooms I sleep in but this one remains a gloomy
closet.
 Well, the big wide bed in the attic in Clayton is going to be nice.
 Hope I'm moderately in control –
 And can write!
 Think I'll work on stories – but no coffee since I got back from the Cape,
nearly 2 months ago – and I'm not sure I can go back on it – writing without it?
– Not likely.
 Mother has been so swell! Wrote today I should hurry home – "there are
pheasants in the ice-box" – And she's gotten the attic all made ready for my return.
 Donnie has been awfully good to me, too –
 well, everyone has.
 I am fond of people lately – especially some –
 I don't suppose I was ever misanthropic, but my attitude toward humanity
has become rather tender – actually.
 I haven't deserved as much from friends as they've given. Such as Donnie –
Laughlin, Mary Hunter, Margo.
 Others – lots of them – for years and years –
 So I must pull myself together, Conquer my nerves, phobias, dread of the
makeshift body I live in – and its various quiverings of apprehension –
 be manly and serve those who love me.
 <u>Give!</u> – to life – and love.
 Yes, I have got to be a man again – this little cowardly recession must stop.
 Good night.

 I suddenly thought of my grandmother – and her death – and covered my face
with mourning for her, as if it had happened just now.[639]

640.    William Inge (1913–73) was the drama and music critic for the *St. Louis Star-Times* and also wrote feature stories on public personalities passing through St. Louis. His interview with Williams was reported
the next day, on 11 November, in "St. Louis Personalities: 'Tennessee' Williams, Playwright, Author."

Inge went on to become a highly regarded playwright himself. He wrote about small-town life of the
American Midwest with compassion and understanding. His most well-known plays are *Come Back, Little
Sheba* (1950), *Picnic* (1953), which won the Pulitzer Prize, *Bus Stop* (1955), and *The Dark at the Top of
the Stairs* (1957), for which Williams wrote the preface (1958). His works of the late 1950s and 1960s did
not receive critical acclaim and failed to draw much of an audience. Inge suffered from alcoholism and
depression and committed suicide in 1973.

William Inge

*Saturday, 4 November 1944*

Clayton –
Late Saturday Night Nov. 4, 1944

Home appears to have been bad strategy –

More or less wretched since my arrival – Not so much cardiac as the other physical neurosis –

Never quite panicky but a continual plague – almost continual –

So we face Sunday – usually, traditionally, the black day at home.

I have made two feeble efforts to write – Either the material didn't really excite me or I just couldn't get off – very slow, dull going so I quit. I allow myself nothing stronger than café au lait.

The confidence quite knocked out of the old boy –

One cannot give in so one has to go on – this is not a battle in which one ever dares to let go.

Manhattan where one could always turn to a friend or a lover for distraction was better for a period like this. Here there is no reliable diversion – with work ~~at least~~ temporarily blocked off.

I can only grit my teeth and wait for the summons to return to N.Y. and hope that there I will win over the mysterious enemy in my skull.

~~I wonder if I have mentioned that Dowling has bought play?~~

Well, I feel a bit quieter now in the attic than I did downstairs. And I have gone thru the day and eve. without sedatives – only some drinks downtown – I have joined the Y and have my daily swim – 16 lengths today without stopping. Don't think my physical shape could be seriously wrong and do that.

Anyway you look at it, I'm in a tight spot – but I am the new Houdini!

En Avant!


*Friday, 10 November 1944*

Friday very late –

Just returned from a cocktail party given me by Bill Inge, drama editor of the Star.[640]

As Bill remarked, "Il y a beaucoup de beauté."

"Yes," said I, "but what could be more useless?"

And useless it was except as social diversion (as distinguished from sexual).

As usual I was attractive to the wrong party and the right one was not attracted to me.

So I came home a bit frustrated – though the evening was valuable as establishing my first real contact with such society in Saint Louis –

I'm afraid they were rather a dull lot – but there <u>were</u> a couple of <u>beauties</u> – if I hadn't failed to get my gun off – I would doubtless speak more warmly of their charms. Well, it has been a strange time here –

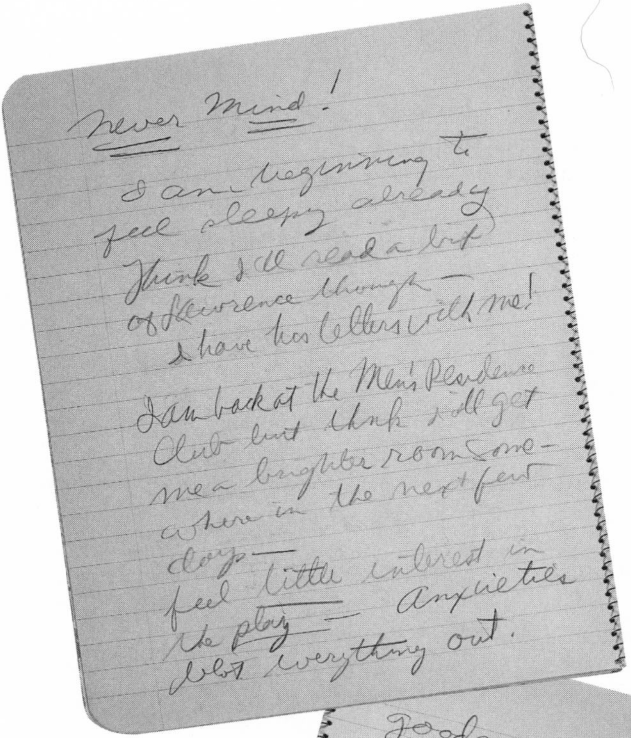

Never Mind!

I am beginning to
feel sleepy already
Think I'll read a bit
of Lawrence though —
I have his letters with me!

I am back at the Men's Residence
Club but think I'll get
me a brighter room some-
where in the next few
days —
feel little interest in
the play — Anxieties
blot everything out.

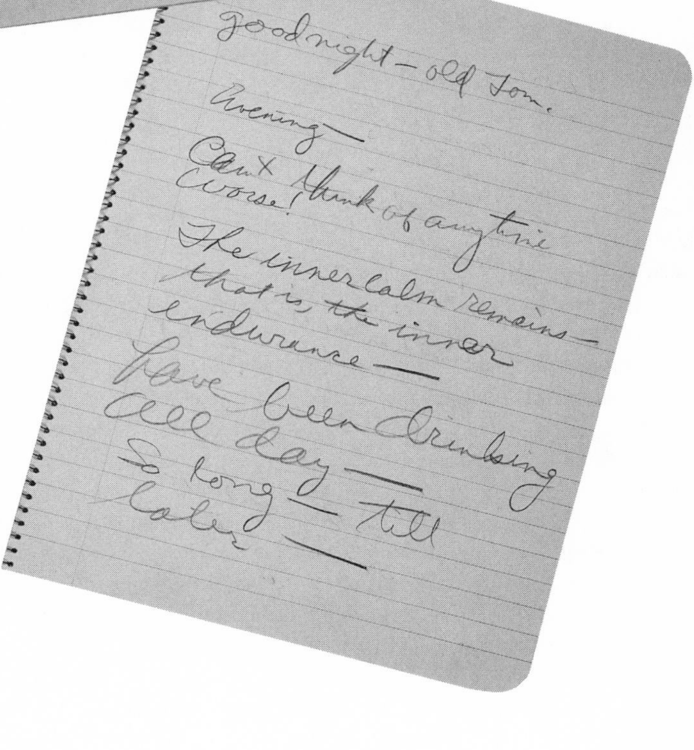

Goodnight — old Tom.

Evening —
Can't think of anytime
Worse!
The inner calm remains —
that is, the inner
endurance —
Have been drinking
All day —
So long — till
later —

Quite unhappy, really – there's no denying it –

I doubt if the family failed to notice that.

the really vicious neurosis let up a bit the past few days –

but about two days ago – I guess Wed. – there was a really awful <u>crise de nerfs</u> –

And I've been walking on eggs all the time –

drinking quite a bit – I guess this is how alcoholics get started – their nerves crack & liquor gives them artificial security –

So it's about over here –

We leave tomorrow or Sunday night –

I feel a bit sad about the way I've acted here –

too wrapped up in my own anxieties to be really nice to the family –

I've only eaten supper with them <u>once</u> –

barely exchanged six words with the old man –

last night I got home early and talked to Mother a bit – I've tried to be agreeable with her but my torments kept me too preoccupied.

Ah – well – We go on from here – Again – Good Night.


*Monday, 13 November or Tuesday, 14 November 1944*

Manhattan

The fox has completed another one of his circles – got back ~~later th~~ this Eve. – trip not bad till last few hours. Then the blue devils started – reached a crescendo about 4 A.M. on my way home from a fruitless quest of sex. I have taken a sleeping tablet and feel some quieter – must ~~see~~ call Dowling and God knows what all tomorrow when I will probably be a real wreck.

Right in the middle of the "crise" – I smiled at myself and said, Tom, what an ass you are!

Why are there Two of me?

Why can't there be just one? – Single, sensible, sane!

from now on there is – remember that – just one! And he says <u>never</u> <u>mind</u> – he says – <u>Never</u> <u>Mind</u>!

I am beginning to feel sleepy already. Think I'll read a bit of Lawrence though – I have his letters with me!

I am back at the Men's Residence Club but think I'll get me a brighter room somewhere in the next few days –

feel <u>little</u> interest in the <u>play</u> – Anxieties blot everything out.

goodnight – old Tom.


Evening –

Can't think of anytime worse!

The inner calm remains – that is, the inner endurance –

have been drinking All day –

So long – till later –

641.  Possibly the beginning of scene 4, in which Tom comes home drunk one evening and is greeted by Laura.
       In *Memoirs* Williams described its genesis:

> Julie [Haydon] was quite fond of the late George Jean Nathan and so Mr. Nathan, appreciating her
> devotion, took a certain interest in *Menagerie*, and that night he got together with Eddie [Dowling]
> and between the two of them they composed a drunk scene for Eddie which they thought was the
> only possible salvation for the play. This scene involved such things as a red, white, and blue flask,
> a song for Eddie — "My Melancholy Baby" — and other unmentionables.
>
>    This "drunk scene," obviously composed in a state that corresponded, was given me as a *fait
> accompli* the next day, when I crept into rehearsals.
>
>    I said to myself, "This is the living and dying end." (p. 82)

642.  "Who knows."

Later –
   an oasis
   a calm in the storm
   a green isle
   a gull's wing poised without
   motion
   peace
   repose
   a water lily
   a deep green lake
   a bottomless well –

After hours of unmitigated hell.

It descended, the lull, after a satisfactory fuck I left the bordello hardly believing it was _me_ – so curiously quiet I was –

I hardly dared think about it, it was so merciful.

Now I am home – I have taken my sleeping pill –

Tomorrow may resume the hostilities – or perhaps the truce will continue – anyhow I say to myself, "What will be, will be."

Of all that is precious in this world, peace is supreme – even an hour of it.


_Friday, 8 December 1944_

Dec. 8 or 9 (?)

Rehearsals been in progress about 10 ten days.

Nerves better – no critical situation since the first few days here –

but I am torpid –

fairly lifeless.

Had a new scene to write for play[641] – should have been easy – I did two weak pages – with difficulty. I get little or no pleasure out of the production. The social aspect is embarassing. The sudden prominence – the false esteem – simply embarassing.

Margo of course is a God send. If she hadn't met me at that train in Saint Louis – I can't imagine how I would have proceeded.

It's a pity I have so little to say. Really feel as though my brain had shrunk and dried up.

Perhaps it is simply hiding from my nerves.

Couldn't blame it for that!

Me, me, me – as usual!

Let's find a pleasanter subject.

Just had my gun off.

Sleepy – but will go out – village – Don – or a Show. Quien Sabe![642]

643.  In *Memoirs of a Bastard Angel* (New York: William Morrow and Company, 1989), Norse described the bistro on Morton Street, the Beggar's Bar, run by Valeska Gert, a dance-mime who had fled Nazi Germany:

> From dirty street steps with an iron railing, cluttered with overflowing garbage cans by day, you entered a tiny ill-lit smoke-filled cellar, crowded and noisy, where coffee and beer were served. You ran into every poet, painter, actor, and intellectual in New York. The lights would suddenly go out, plunging you into darkness, and after a long delay Valeska would appear in a blinding white spotlight, her puckish face carefully smeared in flour, with mauve eye shadow and glitter on her lids and cheeks (anticipating hippies and punks), and some outlandish harlequin costume. In a German accent she delivered political satires in singsong poetry to thunderous applause.
>
> Derived from Berlin cabarets of the 1920s, Valeska's style was called *Sprechstimme* . . . , characterized by musical speech, rather like the tone of wonder and awe that grown-ups employ when narrating fairy tales to children, but heightened and intensified by sudden dramatic variations in pitch, volume, and duration, punctuated by eerie cries. Its spooky appeal went over big in the 1940s. . . . She became a celebrity, and the tiny foul-smelling dump was packed nightly, including the uptown carriage trade. (p. 126)

644.  Ad Astra was a "sort of sanatorium" in Vence, in the Alpes Maritimes of France, where D. H. Lawrence had gone to rest a few weeks before his death in 1930. In *Memoirs* (p. 102), Williams described Lawrence's collected letters as the "greatest" of his work and recalled the sentence "This place no good." Later in his journals, Williams would use the phrase himself, in describing London in 1951 and Munich in 1952.

645.  Laurette Taylor (1884–1946), the well-known stage actress, had come out of retirement to play Amanda in the Chicago and New York premieres of *The Glass Menagerie*.

Laurette Taylor in *The Glass Menagerie*

Later – I chose the village – looked up Harold Norse and we did the spots together – such as Valesca's.[643]

Wound up with someone whom I left with Harold and pursued my lonely way home with the morning paper and The New Republic.

My mind is clear though sorrowful and prescient of sorrow to come – if not catastrophe.

It seems as though life had somehow stepped from behind a flattering screen these recent months. Or is that the old illusion of memory?

Tomorrow I will see Donnie – there is no one else who would know what I meant if I ever was able to say it. That is, among my present associates.

Le Fin – what they put after a french film – what is it, and where?

Rose, my Grandmother – Can I doubt that ends come?

Am I altogether selfish? How does one find out – weigh his decency?

how much fortitude have I? Enough for le fin?

Will I write again – ever – strongly?

I have taken a sleeping pill and will read Lawrence's letters till I get sleepy.

Later –

Ad Astra –

those last letters of Lawrence – really heartbreaking!

"This place no good." the last words.[644]

If I write another play – I would like it to be about a sick man – an invalid – going to a friend for comfort. the story of basic human decencies. The story of the Samaritan.

It is all we have left. It would be too grown up I suppose – for people – if I wrote it. or could write it.

I am terribly, terribly grown up now!

So – goodnight.


*Saturday, 9 December 1944*

Saturday Eve.

What a bad rehearsal – and time so short.

Poor old Laurette[645] can't get her lines down.

She still fumbles and mumbles and practically nothing is done on interpretation, mood, inflection, Etc.

Well, it looks bad, baby.

But keep the fingers crossed. going to swim –

then to see Donnie –

Maybe we'll have some mischevious fun tonight.

On *16 December Williams traveled to Chicago to attend the rehearsals of* The
Glass Menagerie *and reported to Donald Windham ([18 December 1944], Yale):*
> *I thought the situation was hopeless – as [Laurette] Taylor was ad libbing prac-*
> *tically every speech and the show sounded like the Aunt Jemima Pancake hour.*

The Glass Menagerie *opened on 26 December 1944 to great acclaim from*
*Chicago critics, including Claudia Cassidy of the* Chicago Tribune, *who wrote*
*(27 December 1944):*
> *[I]t is a dream in the dusk and a tough little play that knows people and how*
> *they tick. Etched in the shadows of a man's memory, it comes alive in the-*
> *ater terms of words, motion, lighting, and music. If it is your play, as it is*
> *mine, it reaches out tentacles, first tentative, then gripping, and you are*
> *caught in its spell.*

*Initial public response was lukewarm, and by the second week the producers of*
The Glass Menagerie *were considering closing the play. By the end of the third*
*week, however, the enthusiasm of the Chicago critics had caught on, attendance*
*had dramatically increased, and the producers were soon discussing when the play*
*should transfer to New York.*

*Shortly before the New York premiere of* The Glass Menagerie, *Williams had*
*already begun work on another play, one that would evolve into* A Streetcar Named
Desire. *On 23 March 1945 (HRC), Williams wrote Audrey Wood a long letter:*
> *I have been buried in work the last week or so and am about 55 or 60 pages*
> *into the first draft of a play which I am trying to design for [Katharine]*
> *Cornell. At the moment it has four different titles, The Moth, The Poker*
> *Night, The Primary Colors, or Blanche's Chair In The Moon. It is about two*
> *sisters, the remains of a fallen southern family. The younger, Stella, has*
> *accepted the situation, married beneath her socially and moved to a south-*
> *ern city with her coarsely attractive, plebian mate. But Blanche (the Cornell*
> *part) has remained at Belle-reve, the home place in ruins, and struggles for*
> *five years to maintain the old order.*

*Williams spent June and July in Mexico where, as he wrote Audrey Wood (20 June*
*1945, HRC), he met:*
> *Leonard Bernstein, Dolores Del Rio, Rosa Covarrubias, Norman Foster . . .*
> *Balanchine, Chavez, and many lesser notables of the International Set (!) all*
> *of whom have invited me places. But it is not like Chicago and New York,*
> *that is, the society is not at all exhausting and I have plenty of time to work.*

*While in Mexico, Williams almost completed "One Arm," a story he had begun*
*three years earlier.*

*By July,* The Glass Menagerie *had won the New York Drama Critics' Circle*
*Award, the Sidney Howard Memorial Award, and a Donaldson Award. At the end*
*of September,* You Touched Me! *opened in New York to a fairly indifferent public*
*reception and closed on 5 January 1946.*

646. Williams completed the short story "The Interval" (and its variant "A Travelogue of Stars That Fall"), an account of an ill-fated marriage with hints of homosexuality, in October 1945 and the poems "A Liturgy of Roses" in October 1945 and "The Chart" in November 1945. The one-act play is very likely the beginnings of "Camino Real, or The Rich and Eventful Death of Oliver Winemiller" (a source for "Ten Blocks on the Camino Real").

647. *You Touched Me!* opened in New York on 25 September and suffered from comparisons with *The Glass Menagerie*. It "survived" until 5 January 1946.

Guthrie McClintic, Donald Windham, William Liebling, Audrey Wood, and Williams at a dress rehearsal before the Boston opening of *You Touched Me!*

Donald Windham and Williams with Edmund Gwenn as Captain Rockley in *You Touched Me!* 1945 (photograph by George Platt Lynes)

*Monday, 29 October 1945*

Oct 29 – 1945

Taking this up again after lapse of nearly a year – although I made a few Chicago and Mexican entries in another book – Reading this over – Seems my nerves are infinitely better than last year – Should be – I have been living on the fat of the land, pampering, indulging myself. Only problem is lack of creative energy and productivity. Nothing I've written – and I've written very little, relatively – stacks up to my better periods. Some improvement just lately. A pretty fair short story, one, maybe two good poems – a 1-act I'm now working on may turn out fairly well, though it is repetitive of a familiar ~~theme~~ material and characters.⁶⁴⁶

Sex remains fairly plentiful here and less neurotic. This week-end abstemious – reluctantly, but the nightingales have piped sweetly of recent times. The Mexican idyl, for instance. And that night in Laredo, Texas. And F. who stayed with me a while – white marble turned to flesh. Never sunk my shaft in sweeter ground! Yes, the sorrow is creative dullness, only that. Which is partly just laziness I suppose. Too much comfort. Too little drive. But we have 2 card tables in the room and the typewriter and many mornings – Coffee doesn't bother me now. 2 or 3 cups every A.M. – No <u>crise de nerfs</u> in a long time.

As for friends – Oliver has left town, to teach at a prep school. I don't see much of Donnie, though he has behaved pretty well.

Oh, yes – "Y.T.M." has opened. Rather a failure.⁶⁴⁷ That was a disappointment but apparently not such a great one. It is still running but declining fairly sharply the last 2 weeks. Doubt it will survive two more.

The sleep neurosis troubles me a little every night.

And I have been going to a doctor about diarrhoea, lack of energy, etc.

I have 12,000 white blood ~~vessels~~ cells – normal 8,000.

No specific cause yet determined.

B.C. a new lover – interesting but not really right.

The Polack an occasional and always agreeable party.

Things in general? Good – comparatively. Mind is quite remarkably peaceful. And clear. And uninspired. Feel a healthy curiosity about what's coming.

Good night.

*Tuesday, 30 October 1945*

<u>Morning</u> – 30 Oct.

~~Read~~ Assembled and read the 1-act – another fiasco. weak as picnic punch – has a few faintly pleasant touches – plastic details – but is trite and gutless – bloodless – had depended on it to revive my confidence so I could tackle a major project but it is just another in the fairly unbroken succession of diminuendos.

Thank God I have money and can go out and amuse myself – while Rome burns.

See you later, kid.

648.   Jane Lawrence Smith.

649.   The manager of the Shelton Hotel, New York, had written Williams (23 November 1945, private collection):
       It has been called to our attention you have been in the habit of doing considerable entertaining in
       your room. . . . We wish to call attention to the fact that under no consideration do we allow any
       entertaining in the rooms after twelve midnight.

650.   Rosamund Gilder (1891–1986) was the editor of *Theatre Arts*. As early as July 1942 Audrey Wood had
       tried to place a one-act, "The Purification," with *Theatre Arts*, which occasionally published short distin-
       guished plays. *Theatre Arts* never published any of Williams' plays, but in a letter to Wood dated
       19 September 1944 (NYPL), Gilder referred to Williams as "a remarkable talent, but just how it can find
       its way onto our professional stage without blowing that conventional institution up, would be hard to say."

651.   *Strange Fruit*, the ill-fated love affair between a white man and a black woman, was the dramatization of
       the 1944 novel by Lillian Smith (1897–1966). Williams' positive opinion of the play may be due to the fact
       that the plot of *Strange Fruit*, in which the black woman's brother kills her lover and father of her child,
       has similarities to his play "The Spinning Song or The Paper Lantern." Williams' criticism of the play's
       dramatic composition was shared by critics.

652.   George Jenkins (1908– ), a stage, film, and television designer, had been assistant to Jo Mielziner in
       1937–41. In 1946 he won a Donaldson Award for the sets of *I Remember Mama* (1944).

653.   No record of what poems Williams read at the Poetry Center of the Young Men's and Young Women's
       Hebrew Association is known to exist. A draft of his introduction, however, suggests that he may have
       read an early poem written in high school and "Sonnet for Pygmalion," begun in 1935. A later version of
       the poem was published in the *Washington University Eliot*, November 1936.

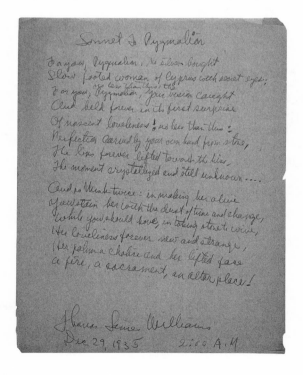

*Wednesday, 28 November 1945*

Wed Nov. 29 –

That 1-act has been developing into a full length play and to it is now attached my hopes of at last getting something new done.

I leave for New Orleans very soon – perhaps in a week or 10 days.

Winter is closing in on N.Y. Very grey – very bitter – I need a soft climate and softer people –

Time and its running away depresses me lately –

the days have little substance – just go, go, go!

I work or try to work a few hours each day and a formidable amount of paper has been covered.

Don and I seem really estranged though each enquires of the other through Jane[648] or Fritz.

Quite a lovely sex party last night. Milk fed chicken on toast!

Met in the swimming pool – advantage of this place.

They want me to move out.[649] So providing the needed push – packing will be fun – all these papers, 2 trunks, 2 victrolas – all my junk –

Sleep neurosis quite bad lately – stay awake till around 5 or 6 A.M. & sleep till noon.

N.G. – Time for change.

En Avant!


*Friday, 30 November 1945*

Fri. night

The mick just left – sweet person but no thrill and I was disappointing as a partner. Supper & Theatre with Rosamund[650] who is a love. Strange Fruit – best new play of season[651] – bad dramaturgically – lovely sets by George Jenkins[652] – would be good designer for my new play – when & if I finish it. I will finish it.

Tomorrow read poems Y Poetry Center.[653]

St. Louis Cathedral, New Orleans, as seen from Williams' apartment

> I get an Apt. in the
> Old Quarter on Jan. 1st with
> 4 rooms and a balcony
> right behind the cathedral.

Excerpt of a letter Williams wrote to Donald Windham ([20 December 1945])

*In December Williams traveled to New Orleans where he found an apartment at 710 Orleans Avenue. Pancho Rodriguez y Gonzales moved in with him. At the end of February, Williams wrote Paul Bigelow (27 February 1946, Columbia) that he had "completed a Mexican fantasy," "Ten Blocks on the Camino Real." And a month later he noted to Donald Windham (25 March 1946, Yale) that he was "working slowly on a longer play." The play, which Williams had begun almost a year earlier, would develop into* A Streetcar Named Desire. *Williams also finished the short story "Desire and the Black Masseur," begun four years earlier, and by April he had begun the short story "The Night of the Iguana."*

*At the end of April 1946, Williams bought a used Packard convertible roadster and drove to St. Louis. He planned to leave soon for another trip to Taos where he would meet his lover Pancho. On his trip to Taos, Williams suffered from abdominal pain, and on 16 May he was admitted to the Holy Cross Hospital in Taos to undergo surgery for diverticulitis and appendicitis.*

710 Orleans Avenue, New Orleans

654. In a letter to his parents dated 23 May 1946 (HTC), Williams described his car breakdown and operation:

> The experiences since I left Saint Louis have been so unpleasant that I don't even like to write about them. I took sick the first day on the road, started having sharp pains. I was immediately afraid of appendicitis and saw I called in a doctor that evening when I arrived at Springfield, Mo. He said it was just cramps from nervousness, so I went on the next day. Fortunately the bearings burnt-out which compelled me to stop in Alva, Okla. I saw another doctor who thought I had a kidney stone and advised me to take the train up to Wichita to see a specialist there, which I did. He put me in a hospital for a couple of days. I had X-rays and while nothing seemed to be revealed the doctor there diagnosed it as low-grade appendis but dismissed me from the hospital thinking an operation was not necessary. I had to leave the car as it would not be ready for several weeks, parts being difficult to replace. So I went on to Taos by bus, continuing to suffer. When I got here I had a fever and a blood-count of 18,000 which indicated a serious infection. The doctors here put me right in the hospital. The pains had suddenly stopped so they suspected the appendix had burst. Naturally I was quite alarmed at this news. They decided they had better operate immediately, and did that evening. According to the doctors (there were two of them) the appendicitis was a lucky accident, for when they made the incision they discovered another acute condition which might not otherwise have been suspected. Something called "Meccles diverticulum" (phonetic spelling) which is attached to the small intestine was seriously infected and at the point of rupture which would have caused peritonitis. Had to be removed. Also appendix. I was on the table about two hours as they had to talk things over. They are very young doctors, the surgeon being just 31, and recently out of the army, but they seem to be quite modern and capable. They told me there was nothing malignant in the condition. I don't suppose they would tell me if it was, so I thought it might be a good idea for Dr. Alexander to call or write them for a fuller account of their findings. If it was anything more serious than they represented to me, it might be better for me to go to New York where the best treatment is available.

655. Amado "Pancho" Rodriguez y Gonzales (1920–93) was a lover of Williams' during 1946–47. They had a stormy relationship full of temper and violent outbursts. According to Fritz Bultman, "Tennessee behaved very badly toward Pancho . . . by using Pancho for real-life scenes which he created — and then transformed them into moments in *A Streetcar Named Desire*" (Spoto, pp. 123–24). Rodriguez died in New Orleans, a retired salesman and buyer for a men's clothing store. Williams named the violent father in *Summer and Smoke* Papa Gonzales, and the object of Emil Kroger's infatuation in the short story "The Mysteries of the Joy Rio" Pablo Gonzales.

Williams and Pancho Rodriguez

*Wednesday, 5 June 1946*

June 5, 1946 – Wednesday.
  So sick of Alva, Oklahoma!
  Car broke down here a month ago – bearings burnt out.
  I left it here and went on to Taos where I had a major operation.[654]
  Now have returned – car still not ready. Been here three days with Pancho[655] –
we have both descended into a nearly speechless gloom and apathy – fail even to
comfort each other anymore. We've been through such a fantastic succession of
misfortunes! I've never had quite such a freakish run of bad luck in my life. Yet
I've survived so far. But I wonder how much more I can take. If the operation
had not knocked me out nervously I would bear up better. As it is I'm a quivering
mass of anxieties – Will try to continue a bit more coherently after a while.

*By the end of June 1946 Williams had fully recovered and had decided to spend
the summer on Nantucket in a rented house at 31 Pine Street. Williams was joined
by Carson McCullers. Their friendship, which lasted through McCullers' life, began
shortly after Williams had read her novel* The Member of the Wedding *and wrote
to her of his admiration. On learning that McCullers was a distant cousin of Jordan
Massee's, Williams invited her to Nantucket. She arrived mid-June and they got
along so well that she stayed for the summer. Years later Williams would recall
(*Saturday Review of Literature, 23 September 1961):*

> [W]e worked at opposite ends of a table, she on a dramatization of "The
> Member of the Wedding" and I on "Summer and Smoke," and for the first
> time I found it completely comfortable to work in the same room with
> another writer. We read each other our day's work over our after-dinner drinks,
> and she gave me the heart to continue a play that I feared was hopeless.

> When I told her that I thought my creative powers were exhausted, she
> said to me, wisely and truly, an artist always feels that dread, that terror,
> when he has completed a work to which his heart has been so totally com-
> mitted that the finishing of it seems to have finished him too, that what he
> lives for is gone like yesteryear's snow.

656.  Carson McCullers (1917–67), southern novelist and short-story writer, had written two novels by 1946. *The Heart Is a Lonely Hunter* (1940) is the story of a deaf-mute in a small southern town, a portrait of human isolation and thwarted love. *Reflections in a Golden Eye* (1941) is a morbid tale of murder, infidelity, bisexuality, and sado-masochism set on an army post in the South. In 1946 she published *A Member of the Wedding*, a novel about the feelings of a motherless thirteen-year-old at her brother's wedding. McCullers' dramatization of this novel opened on Broadway in 1950 and received several major awards. She went on to write two other novels, *The Ballad of the Sad Café* (1951) and *Clock Without Hands* (1961), and the play *The Square Root of Wonderful* (1958).

Williams wrote the introduction to the 1950 edition of *Reflections in a Golden Eye*. In addition, he dedicated the poem "Which Is My Little Boy?" to McCullers. He also wrote "Three Songs for Carson" of which only a fragment exists and was published as "Her Head on the Pillow."

Carson McCullers (photograph by Karl Bissinger)

Map showing Martha's Vineyard, 1941

*Saturday, 14 September 1946*

Sept. 14, 1946 (1 A.M.)
   Am I dying?

(About Noon)
   Ship stopped at Martha's Vineyard. I suddenly feel a bit better – less nauseated. Sit up and wash my face – I have a little private state room, procured from a kind lady by Pancho. I do not think much. Brain really seems sort of anesthetized. Carson is with me and she has been an angel.[656] Though I have only really felt like seeing Pancho. He has <u>not</u> been an angel. That is not his nature or habit. But I think we love one another.
   The boat has started again leaving Martha's Vineyard and the Boston train is waiting for us in Wood's Hole. I guess I will survive this trip. Beyond it I do not look.

657. Williams wrote Wood from the hospital (letter received 17 September 1946, HRC):
    I am getting along O.K. here. Will try to continue revisions on "Summer and Smoke". [Postscript] Have not yet heard when they will turn me loose.
    Almost a month later Williams wrote his grandfather (letter postmarked 10 October 1946, HTC):
    I was sick when I arrived in New York, so I went straight into the hospital. . . . I had been over-working and it had affected my stomach. I couldn't eat anything solid for about a week.

658. "A Garden in the Rain" (lyrics by James Dyrenforth) was sung by Perry Como.

659. An early draft of *Summer and Smoke*.

632 St. Peter Street, New Orleans

*September 1946*

A Dream

Last night I dreamt that my house (on the West Coast) was searched three times by the police, each time entering in pairs. This went on all night. Toward morning other men <u>disguised</u> as policemen (really burglars) entered to search the house – No longer in pairs but individually in numbers that over ran the premises. I dropped a glass: it cracked. Windham took glass and smashed it because he said it was dangerous to drink from a cracked glass. I was chagrined by smashing of the glass.

Today I have entered St. Luke's hospital for purgation of a tape worm. A rugged ordeal tomorrow salts and medicines all day.[657]

*Williams spent the autumn of 1946 in New Orleans at 632½ St. Peter Street, in the apartment with a skylight that he would remember so fondly in* Memoirs.

*Sunday, 27 October 1946*

Sunday – Oct. 27 – 1946

A doctor talks over the radio about phagocytes – and their battle with bacteria.

How casually they talk about the immense mysteries of organic life!

Cells – anti-bodies – atoms –

And at the other extreme of magnitude – solar systems.

And not one sign to betray the presence of a reason.

Lately the sense of this mystery has filled me with a barely controlled panic. Perhaps because signs within me indicate I may be near to that collapse into the inorganic which every individual goes to after an unbroken chain of organic being that extends all the way back to the first living cell!

*Monday, 28 October 1946*

Monday –

How could it be true?

How could it be not true?

A tenor singing "It's just a garden in the rain"[658] on my new radio which takes the place of thought in the place.

I read over bits of the play[659] and it seems grotesque, a creation of disease. I have Crane's picture propped against my typewriter cover on the writing table. I suppose my experience somewhat parallels his.

660.  In a letter to Margo Jones dated 17 October 1946 (HRC), Williams had written:

I have been feeling well and getting a lot of work done. Miss Alma and her wild young doctor are coming to life in their native climate. For a while the silent film sequences were only tentative and I was careful to keep the main body of the play independant of them, but now I'm going whole hog and making them an integral part of the script. I know it can be done, the question is — Will anybody do it? (Don't mention this to anyone till the play is finished).

Numerous fragments of silent film sequences with captions exist and include a confrontation between John and his father, a reading group, a Sunday morning in church, a confrontation between John and Jessie's lover, a scene in which Alma calls the police over disturbances at the Buchanan house, and a scene in which Alma helps John give inoculations to cotton pickers. By the end of November, Williams decided to eliminate the silent film sequences. He told Jones ([19 November 1946], HRC), "I'm afraid they would break the poetic unity."

```
                        ENVOI

    When I took sick I fastened my will on the resolution to
finish this play. Perhaps that was a mistake. It is hard
to create with one eye on your work and one on approaching
dissolution. It is hard to judge how much this division of
attention may have affected my work on the play. I am afraid
the play is more like a withered flower pressed in the pages
of a book than a stone monument.

    Vanity is the necessity of artists. I have been vain
enough at times but between those times I have felt very
keenly the limitations of my talent. I have admired artists
like Chekhov and Crane and Lorca who had not only intensity
but the power to organize and control it - at least for a time.
I don't know that I have ever had that power. If my strength
my physical strength had held out long enough I might have
found it. I had a strong will to do so.

    Today as I feel my life-blood flowing from some deep
internal wound, the thing I could talk about most easily
is dread. But there is no use in that for me or anyone else.
I have much to thank the world for. I have been lucky in
this respect, that I have received more in the way of unex-
pected kindness and tenderness from people than I have lost
through expected indifference or harshness.

    It is impossible to say who won the argument in the play.
Neither of them did and both of them did, and that is how it
has seemed to me. Perhaps I could have made it clearer. That
can be said of almost all my work. But to be clearer is not
necessarily to be more truthful. Enveloped as all of us are
in the inscrutable....
```

*Tennessee Williams*
*November, 1946.*

Except I haven't written "The Bridge".

I seem to be trying to make sense or order out of it. A useless undertaking.
And the wish to make drama never quite fails.

Write an "Envoi" to accompany script –
Put all material you are now unable to handle into the silent film sequences.[660]
My vanity and egotism are inescapable. It is the human condition.

There is always the desire to dignify myself and to lend significance to my
experience and my works and stature to my personality.

If only I could lose myself in "Karma" – the universal being – and cast off
personal will and ambition. I suppose that is the way to learn to accept the
organic dissolution.

If I had kept my physical strength five or ten years more I might have purified
myself.

Because I have shown an aptitude for learning which comes with an open,
acceptive mind. I think I have gone as far toward release from dogmatic
strictures as anyone goes. There again, the desire to dignify myself! But the
human condition, as I remarked before, is that impulse.

*Wednesday, 30 October 1946*

Wednesday –
Blood in my bowels this morning.

*Friday, 1 November 1946*

Friday
Took the script to the typist yesterday.

I read it over first. It is still wanting. I think I over-elaborated it. Should
perhaps return to the simple earlier treatment, keep it in the three sets. Some
progress made in developing the old scenes. I suppose considering the
psychological state in which I was working I did pretty well.

A beautiful letter from Carson yesterday.

*Friday, 15 November 1946*

Nov. 15 –
Still working on play.

The situation of my psyche remains nightmarish.

The iron jaws of a trap seem to hold me here in a little corner, backing away
from panic.

661.  "A Chart of Anatomy" was an early alternative title for *Summer and Smoke*.

662.  First published in 1932 in the United Kingdom and in 1946 in the United States, *The Memorial* portrays the conflicts felt by Eric Vernon, who is torn between his desire to emulate his father, a heroic soldier of World War I, and his desire to follow the bohemian gay life led by a friend of his father's.

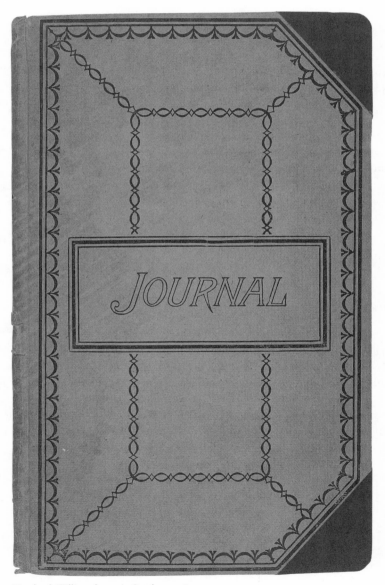

Notebook Williams began in October 1946

I cling to little palliative devices – the swimming pool – the sleeping tablets – reading in bed – sometimes movies – the familiarity of Pancho.

Always before these recessions into craven misery have passed after a while and I have forgotten each fear in turn and taken up some other fear in turn and taken up some other.

This hangs on and on, seemingly interminable.

The doctors continue to tell me I do not have cancer, but their talk, their attitude is ambiguous and my own symptoms, the weakness, the abdominal twinges, burning stomach, diarrhoea at times, seem to register something umistakably more than a state of neurosis.

Still if the dread is true, I should be grateful for not yet having been brutally told it is true, so that when I feel better I can still believe the dread is unjustified. If only the oblivion which I think is death did not seem so horrible to me!

If ever I rise again from this fear, how careful I shall be, must be, to fortify my spirit against another such surrender to cowardice.

Now I think I will write a letter to Carson to reach her before she sails for Europe.

*Tuesday, 19 November 1946*

Nov. 19 –

Grey rainy day, one of the first of that kind we've had here.

I worked a little. Feel a bit better than the last few days. See doctor Thursday. If he is encouraging I'll take a trip. This place, the day to day dragging reiteration, must be interrupted somehow.

*Sunday, 1 December 1946*

Dec. 1.

Still here, still working on "Chart".661

Sometimes it seems just a grade or two superior to a radio soap-opera.

I have committed some astonishing lapses of taste in this play.

Health improved rather distinctly this week and state of mind correspondingly. Partly due to reunion with an old friend Bill Richards who was passing through N.O. before sailing for Europe.

If I can make it – I think Europe is the place for me now. Still I'd hate to leave Pancho.

This week coming – Margo will visit here one night on her way to Dallas.

I'll finish up this 3rd draft before she gets here and let her read it. If she is encouraging it will help.

Am reading new book by Isherwood "The Memorial".662 It is disappointing, wonder if it isn't really an old one.

663.  In a letter to Audrey Wood (22 November 1946, HRC), Williams wrote:

As for my health, that has been ever since the operation a disturbing problem, in fact a constant shadow. I don't have the severe attacks of pain that I had just before the operation, but keep on having discomfiting symptoms and a general weakness which continually remind me of it. The doctor here, like the ones in New York, tell me that I do not have a malignant condition but there is a certain ambiguity in their attitude which does not reassure me and I don't know what to make of it. And my nature is not bold enough to be sure that I want to. I have never had a particle of physical courage about anything!

664.  Presumably Maurice Zolotow (1913–91), a show business writer. In a letter to Audrey Wood (3 January 1947, HRC), Williams confided: "Zolotow apparently heard I was finishing a play for he wired both me and the city editor of the [New Orleans] Times-Picayune for details about it. I told him as little as possible." Williams obviously responded to Zolotow's wire and may have avoided telling his agent about Zolotow's "negative reaction" by claiming reticence.

665.  Laurette Taylor died on 7 December. In "An Appreciation" for the *New York Times* (15 December 1946), Williams wrote:

I have always been so awkward and diffident around actors that it has made a barrier between us almost all but insuperable.

In the case of Laurette Taylor, I cannot say that I ever got over the awkwardness and the awe which originally were present, but she would not allow it to stand between us. The great warmth of her heart burned through and we became close friends. . . .

Gallantry is the word that best fits those human qualities which made Laurette Taylor so intensely lovable as a person. I do not think it is realized how much she sacrificed of her personal comfort and health during the year and a half that she played in "The Glass Menagerie." She remained in the part that long because of a heroic perseverance I find as magnificent as her art itself.

The race track at the Fair Grounds, New Orleans

*Wednesday, 4 December 1946*

Dec. 4. Woke up with a belly-ache and carpenters hammering on the adjoining apartment walls. Something like what is going on inside me, perhaps – only rats instead of carpenters.

Went back to work on play in spite of decision to let it go.

Yesterday afternoon I spent at the race track and possibly I shall go out again this afternoon.

It is a lovely place, and the races give me a bang. I love the kids in their silks.

It is a good day for races – clear, cool, sparkling – if only I felt somewhat better.

Pancho and I made up after another silly misunderstanding. He thinks I have other boys. Alas, I barely have energy for one!

Now shave – dress – take to the streets or the races and try to forget the "shadow".663

*Monday, 16 December 1946*

Dec. 16 –

Have slipped a bit lately. The nausea has returned. Only vomited a couple of times but feel continually sickish and no interest in food.

However I've purchased a car and spent my days out in it. Virtually quit writing, did a little more feeble patchwork on "Chart" today.

Maurice's negative reaction664 and Margo's unexpressed but suspected disappointment took whatever was left of the wind from my sails and I don't even feel like sending the ms. off.

But I shall.

If I pick up a bit or at least remain level – I'll undertake a motor trip to St. Petersburg.

The nightingales can't sing anymore. They just died on the branches. And it's all a bit useless here.

Laurette died a week ago – that affected me badly.665 In fact, seemed to start the present decline.

I haven't caught sight of my old guardian angel in a long time lately.

Where are you, Angelo mio?
Can't you hear my little cries of distress?

I have hung up my Japanese wind-chimes in an open window and they tinkle all the time, quite companionably, during the long, lonely periods in the apartment.

If I were well, I feel that I would be writing my best work now.

If!
One of Mr. O'Neill's pipe-dreams.

666.  Pancho's twin brother, Juan.

Pancho Rodriguez, Margo Jones, and the Reverend Walter Dakin

*Thursday, 19 December 1946*

Dec. 19

Nausea persists. Dr. Sullivan seems bored and impatient and offers no suggestion except that I see a psychiatrist.

I feel pretty desolate.

Quarreled with Pancho last night. He brought his brother[666] home with him for the second consecutive night which would be all right if I were well but I don't want anyone around when I'm sick except Pancho. So we quarreled and slept in separate rooms.

Is it possible that I am losing my mind?

On top of all this, the weather has turned dismally grey – cold.

En Avant, Amigo!

Later – I managed, remarkably, to go down town and mail "chart" to Audrey. Had an oyster stew on the way home. No appetite but no nausea. Now back home in bed with newspaper and Crane and Hemingway. Two of the best bed-partners a sick old bitch can have.

(One must regard suffering and fear as the natural state of man, punctuated by anguish and terror.)

*Sunday, 22 December 1946*

Sunday Dec 22.

It has come! The knife-like pain that I had just before the operation has recurred. It was that which I have lived in dread of these seven months past.

The rest must be whatever it will be, and I can only pray for some courage if the supreme test is now here. Unfortunately that has never been one of my salient virtues.

Sullivan declined to see me himself but sent young doctor whom I like a lot better. The same old story – they have nothing to offer – I feel a bit calmer now after reading a long story of Hemingway's. And the pain is now dormant. I wait to see if it will return tomorrow.

So the nightmare is all but confirmed. I must cherish the last little shred of uncertainty.

Funny – I had been feeling better today. Riding around in the car with Pancho – visiting the zoo – when all at once the 7-months wait ended and the pain exploded inside me.

The point of my pencil is broken and my brain has become quite dull.

Manana

667.    "The Poker Night," an early alternative title for *A Streetcar Named Desire*. Williams, however, would keep the title for scene 3, the only named scene in the play.

668.    Williams considered several endings for *A Streetcar Named Desire*, which included Blanche throwing herself under a train and Blanche being forcibly removed from the stage, before deciding on the final ending, which was "physically quieter."

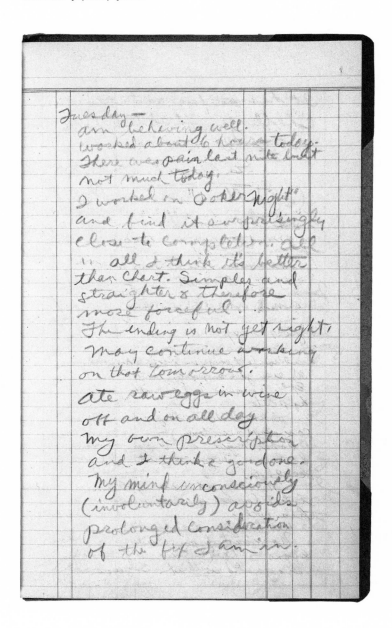

*Monday, 23 December 1946*

Morning – I slept pretty well and so far this A.M. the pain has been absent. I will try to decide on some formula of behavior and follow it as stoically as I can. I will probably not alter my usual routine any more than necessary. Will go out and take care of some errands, such as the bank, telegram or gift to grandfather. I feel quite sleepy – May sleep a while before I get up. Pancho and his brother have left. I continue to feel unreasonably annoyed over the brother's presence over-night.

Had intercourse 3 times yesterday and night before, after a considerable abstinence, which had encouraged and heartened me – until the pain struck.

I hope if I continue this sickening journal I will stop indulging in all these clinical details.


*Tuesday, 24 December 1946*

Tuesday –
   Am behaving well.
   Worked about 6 hours today –
   There was pain last nite but not much today.
   I worked on "Poker Night" and find it surprisingly close to completion.[667] All in all I think it's better than Chart. Simpler and straighter & therefore more forceful.
   The ending is not yet right.[668] May continue working on that tomorrow.
   Ate raw eggs in wine off and on all day. My own prescription and I think a good one. My mind unconsciously (involuntarily) avoids prolonged consideration of the fix I am in. It has so far met the challenge and acted like a gentleman.
   <u>En Avant</u>.
   (It is Christmas Eve. Pancho is home with me and preparing a nice supper.) There are clean sheets on the bed. I read, write, smoke and am tolerably peaceful.

Williams with Pancho Rodriguez (right) and his twin brother, Juan (left)

669.  As previously noted, numerous fragments of the play "The Spinning Song" (alternatively titled "The Paper Lantern") exist and relate to *The Glass Menagerie* and/or to *A Streetcar Named Desire*. In some fragments a woman named Blanche lives on the plantation Belle-Reve and, like Blanche in *A Streetcar Named Desire*, talks about dying from eating an unwashed grape and being "buried at sea, dropped overboard in a sheet of snowy canvas" (scene 11).

670.  Audrey Wood had wired Williams about the play, but he had apparently not received it and wrote to her on 3 January. She responded with a letter on 7 January (Columbia):

I just read your letter of January third. However, I can't tell from that whether or not it was sent before you received my wire in which I asked you quite a few questions pertaining to the play I still want you to call SUMMER AND SMOKE. If you didn't get it, the wire went like this: PLEASE DON'T THINK I HAVE LET YOU DOWN. I HAVE READ PLAY FULLY ONCE AND AM HALF WAY THROUGH IT AGAIN. STILL WANT TO FINISH SCRIPT AGAIN BEFORE WRITING IN DETAIL. WHILE I FEEL THIS DRAFT MUCH BETTER AM STILL CONCERNED ABOUT MANY THINGS IN IT. WOULD YOU BE WILLING USE ORIGINAL LAST SCENE WHICH IS MY PREFERENCE. ALSO FEEL REMAINING MOTION PICTURE SEQUENCE SHOULD BE ELIMINATED. WILL FINISH RE-READING OVER WEEK END AND BE IN TOUCH WITH YOU BEGINNING OF WEEK.

Grandfather has bought a pith helmet and a pair of swimming trunks covered with palm-trees - you cannot imagine what a fantastic sight he is!

Williams with his grandfather in Key West, and an excerpt of a letter Williams wrote to Pancho Rodriguez ([31 January 1947])

*Thursday, 2 January 1947*

Jan. 2 – 1947

Have felt surprisingly well this week. We even gave a party New Year's Eve. No pains and a pretty good appetite.

I am still working casually (desultorily) on "Poker Night" or "Paper Lantern".[669] Title not yet decided.

Thinking of driving down into Florida if I remain this well.

Waiting for Grandfather.

No word from Audrey about "Chart". She is probably disgusted with it.[670] So was I. Maybe it will seem better after a while.

Oh, how dull I am!

Goodnight.


*Sunday, 16 March 1947*

March 16 –

Have broken down again after a remarkably good period and much travel – Key West in car with Grandfather – Boston and New York with Pancho –

But now I am having the nausea – vomiting – and a little blood in the bowels again – So I turn to my journal. I always do when things look bad. That's partly why I seem such a morbid guy in these journals.

It looks like P. and I may have reached the hour of parting – He has been increasingly temperamental. Has quit his job. Is crazily capricious. I still care for him but right now I feel a hunger for peace above all else.

And I have my grandfather with me for companionship. I love him so much I did not think it would be possible for me to feel so tenderly toward anyone again. But he is a rare and wonderful person. <u>90</u> next month – I hope we can remain together from now on out.

"Poker Night" finished. A relative success, not pleasant but well-done. I think it will make good theatre, though its success is far from assured.

Margo here now – alas, I am in no shape to make her enjoy it, let us hope I snap out of this and can take another little trip in my jalopy with Grandfather.

Goodnight, kid.

671.  Windham sent Williams the short stories "The Warm Country," "The Seventh Day," "The Starless Air," "Flesh Farewell," "New Dominoes," "Single Harvest," and "Night." The stories were not published in a collection until 1960 when they appeared in *The Warm Country* with an introduction by E. M. Forster.

Royal Street, New Orleans

Victor's Café, on the corner of Toulouse Street and Chartres Street, New Orleans, where Williams, "spent from the rigors of creation," would revive himself

*Friday, 28 March 1947*

March 28 –

Spent practically all day in bed. Not exactly sick but so tired.

Finally went out to a movie with Pancho. Returned to bed and read another one of Don's stories. He sent me a bunch of them to write a foreword. They are fine. I wonder if I will be able to write about them. Hardly feel up to it right now.[671]

Got to decide pretty soon where we go. That is, if we go anywhere.

Grandfather has left me. I didn't want him to but he was determined. Started to cry as we parted at the train. I think he felt it was for the last time.

The news, the radio commentators, the idiocies and vicious rabble-rousing tactics make the country seem like a mad-house now.

If I were well-enough I would leave for Europe – or China.

Last night – however – for the first time in ages – I had an erotic adventure of the first magnitude – a child of the gods. It did me good, spiritually. I warned P. that I must have a little license this Spring, as it may be my last. But P. is not reconciled.

*Saturday, 29 March 1947*

Saturday Night –

The great cleanliness and relief after vomiting! The calm that comes over your soul when your sick belly has purged itself of all the sour bile – your very sickness seems to have spewed out and you feel quite pure again inside. It is nice, then, to retreat to bed and write a few lines or read until you are sleepy enough not to think. To breathe quietly – how sweet! Oh, how sweet it would be to exist altogether without this tired old fabrication of flesh – Such a mess of impurities and disintegrations – such a pitiful mess. But where is existence except in this ruin?

Let us dream of tomorrow being quiet and sweet without sickness.

The days still come and go.

En avant.

Jackson Square, New Orleans

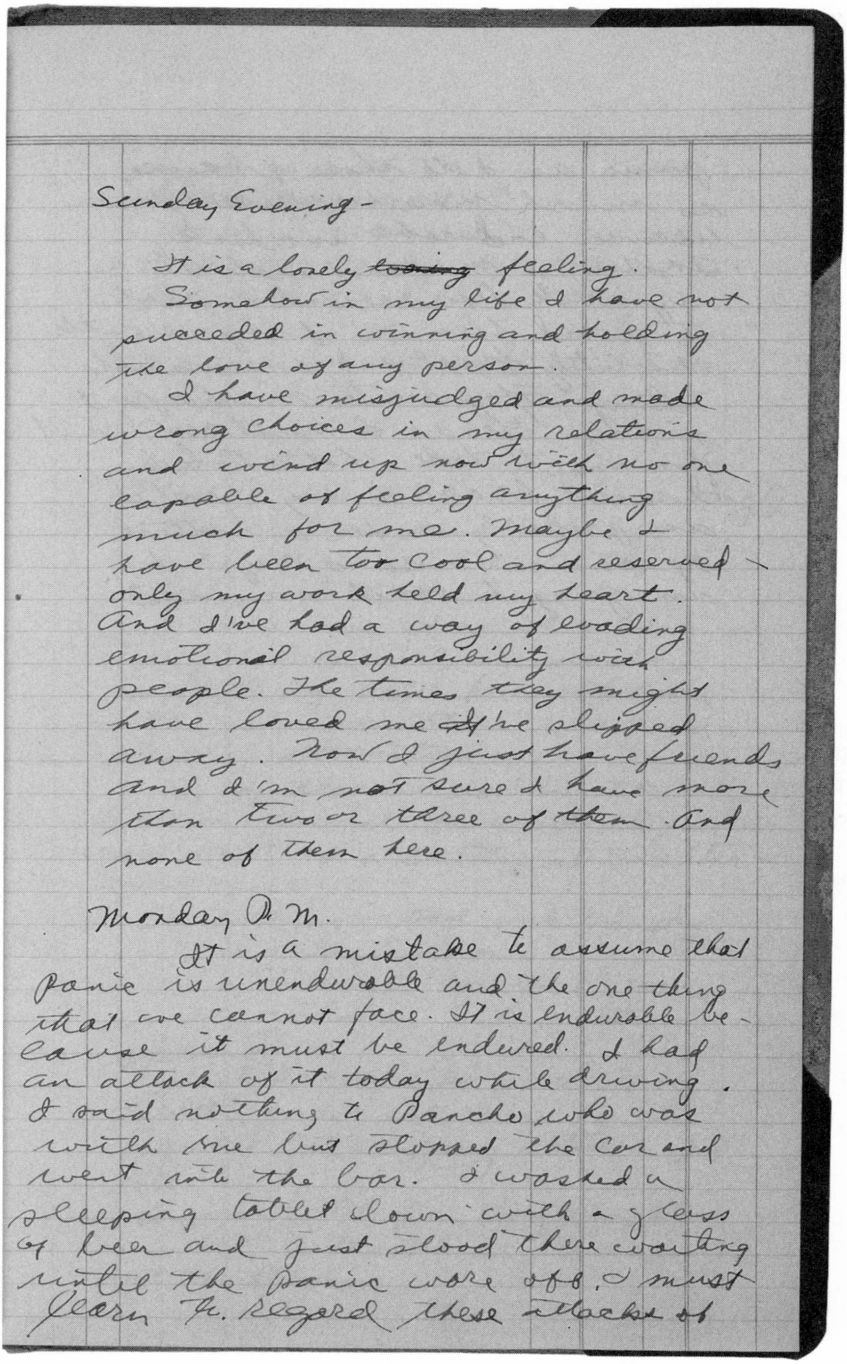

Sunday Evening —

It is a lonely ~~losing~~ feeling.

Somehow in my life I have not
succeeded in winning and holding
the love of any person.

I have misjudged and made
wrong choices in my relations
and wind up now with no one
capable of feeling anything
much for me. Maybe I
have been too cool and reserved —
only my work held my heart.
And I've had a way of evading
emotional responsibility with
people. The times they might
have loved me I've slipped
away. Now I just have friends
and I'm not sure I have more
than two or three of them. And
none of them here.

Monday A. M.

It is a mistake to assume that
panic is unendurable and the one thing
that we cannot face. It is endurable because it must be endured. I had
an attack of it today while driving.
I said nothing to Pancho who was
with me but stopped the car and
went into the bar. I washed a
sleeping tablet down with a glass
of beer and just stood there waiting
until the panic wore off. I must
learn to regard these attacks of

*Sunday, 30 March 1947*

Sunday Evening –
    It is a lonely ~~evening~~ feeling.
    Somehow in my life I have not succeded in winning and holding the love of
any person.
    I have misjudged and made wrong choices in my relations and wind up now
with no one capable of feeling anything much for me. Maybe I have been too
cool and reserved – only my work held my heart. And I've had a way of evading
emotional responsibility with people. The times they might have loved me I've
slipped away. Now I just have friends and I'm not sure I have more than two or
three of them. And none of them here.


*Monday, 31 March 1947*

Monday P.M.
    It is a mistake to assume that panic is unendurable and the one thing that we
cannot face. It is endurable because it must be endured. I had an attack of it
today while driving. I said nothing to Pancho who was with me but stopped the
car and went into the bar. I washed a sleeping tablet down with a glass of beer
and just stood there waiting until the panic wore off. I must learn to regard these
attacks of panic as I do those of nausea, as much more unpleasant but likewise
endurable incidents. That is, I must not elaborate my whole life around a plot to
avoid them as if they were the absolutely final and irreconcilable thing. They are
too much a part of my life as I must now live it for me to take that attitude. I
must be able to say, "Now I am probably in for an attack of panic" – as I say, "I
am going to vomit in a while."


*Friday, 4 April 1947*

Good Friday – April 4th
    A charming young friend from Nantucket visited us today. I made more than
my usual social effort. It tired me but perhaps on the whole did me good.
Especially the embrace in the back room, while mixing drinks. P. was curiously –
I mean surprisingly – undisturbed. And even talks of bringing the friend home for
the night. I think I would be content to leave it as it was. Lips, bodies – only
occasionally, rarely, do they catch fire with each other. Even when there is a good
deal of attraction.
    Today the window in the hall is open and the wind-chimes have kept up a
continual chatter – very nice.
    The evening is cool and windy.
    I am relaxing now.

672.   Williams was in discussion with Laughlin about the short stories to be included in his first collection, which would be published as *One Arm and Other Stories* in early 1949.

Williams and Irene Selznick on the set of *A Streetcar Named Desire* (photograph by Ruth Orkin)

Some twinges here and there in the abdomen but nothing special.

Think I may take a sleeping tablet – go out and moon on the Square. Till company returns if it does.

A nice letter from Jay Laughlin. He is still interested in bringing out the stories.[672]

---

*Williams spent the next few months finalizing details on his two plays. In July 1947 Margo Jones would direct the premiere of* Summer and Smoke *in Dallas. By mid-August, in Provincetown, he had already started work on the play that would become* The Night of the Iguana. *Williams wrote Jones (15 August 1947, HRC):*

> I started working on another long play today: just the opening shot. But I shall not push hard until after "Streetcar" is in. I call it <u>Quebrada</u>, meaning The Cliff. The scene is a hotel at Acapulco built on a cliff over the Pacific which will be used symbolically as the social and moral precipice of our times, the characters some intellectual derelicts: will be able to use Mexican music!

*By the second week of September, Williams was back in New York to finish the casting of* A Streetcar Named Desire, *which was scheduled to open in December in New York after a tryout in New Haven. He ended what had become an increasingly emotionally tempestuous relationship with Pancho Rodriguez.*

---

*Monday, 20 October 1947*

Monday –

I shall not try anymore to express my feelings for I don't feel able to say anything so it is better, if I want to keep a journal, to be as stupid as I comfortably can, and that is very stupid. This was a lost day. I went to bed at 9 A.M. and got up when it was getting dark and did nothing but attend rehearsals. Tonight I made the mistake of drinking coffee. My belly aches a bit in a dull way and my mind seems to imitate that feeling. Today I was particularly aware of missing Pancho. Now I am back in bed, alone, in the room that does not take on the feeling of home. Perhaps it will when I have managed to be less miserable in it or shared it with someone for more than a night.

673. In *Memoirs*, Williams recalled the setting in which he wrote *Streetcar*. He fondly remembered Dick Orme's apartment at 632½ St. Peter Street, describing it as "one of the loveliest" he had ever occupied:

> What I liked most about it was a long refectory table under a skylight which provided me with ideal conditions for working in the mornings. I know of no city where it is better to have a skylight than New Orleans. You know, New Orleans is slightly below sea level and maybe that's why the clouds and the sky seem so close. In New Orleans the clouds always seen just overhead. I suppose they are really vapor off the Mississippi more than genuine clouds and through that skylight they seemed so close that if the skylight were not glass, you could touch them. They were fleecy and in continual motion. I was alone all day. (p. 109)

674. Jane Lawrence Smith.

675. *Blood Wedding*, or *Bodas de Sangre* (1933), is one of Federico García Lorca's (1898–1936) well-known tragedies. It is the story of a young bride who runs off with a former lover who is then murdered by her husband. Williams would have been interested in Lorca's *Blood Wedding*, not least because it has similarities in plot with his 1940s play "Dos Ranchos, or The Purification." In Williams' play the husband of Elena murders her brother, who has carried on an incestuous relationship with Elena.

676. *The Journals of André Gide*, vol. 1, *1889–1913*, translated from the French, with an introduction and notes by Justin O'Brien (New York: Alfred A. Knopf, 1947). André Gide was awarded the 1947 Nobel Prize for literature.

677. In Williams' 1975 novel *Moise and the World of Reason*, the narrator, a struggling writer, remembers the intense physical relationship he had with the previous love of his life, Lance, "a light-skinned black, skater by profession, who referred to himself as 'the living nigger on ice'" (p. 13).

678. In a letter to Pancho Rodriguez ([November 1947], HRC), Williams explained his feelings further:

> In my life there has been so much <u>real</u> tragedy, things that I cannot speak about and hardly dare to remember, from the time of my childhood and all the way through the years in between that I lack patience with people who are spoiled and think that they are entitled to go through life without effort and without sacrifice and without disappointment. Life is hard. As Amanda said, "It calls for Spartan endurance." But more than that, it calls for understanding, one person understanding another person, and for some measure of sacrifice, too. Very few people learn until late in life how much courage it takes to live, but if you learn it in the beginning, it will be easier for you. . . .
>
> Of all the people I have known you have the greatest and warmest heart but you also unfortunately have a devil in you that is constantly working against you, filling you with insane suspicions and jealousies and ideas that are so preposterous that one does not know how to answer them. It is a terrifying thing. You must face it and make a determined effort to master it now before it becomes too well-established.

Portrait of Williams by
Buffie Johnson, 1947

Portrait of Pancho Rodriguez
by Williams

*Monday, 27 October 1947*

Oct. 27 –

This is very much like last Fall. Remember?

The long table under the skylight[673] and the miserable labor on "Summer and Smoke" and the panicky times when you thought you would not survive the coming winter. Never quite <u>panicky</u>, no. But grim and wretched enough for all practical purposes. Then you bought the car and began spending the nice afternoons out – things picked up a little, gradually. But not till Grandfather came and you escaped with him to Florida did you really seem to catch hold of life again – And wrote "Streetcar". All in about 6 weeks, that is, the final draft of it. You recovered your lost manhood!

Well, this time I am also in a low state of body. A little nausea nearly all the time and such fatigue! I don't even feel like looking around for sex.

I haven't written anything to speak of – in that respect it is worse than last Fall. Perhaps it is worse in more respects than I fully realize but I do not wish to be morbid about it, do I?

The Phoenix may still rise again.

The dream of the "Benevolent Captain" – Remember.

Tomorrow the "Streetcar" and I depart for New Haven where we open on Thursday.

This evening I spent pleasantly with Jane.[674]

Now I am back in bed and feeling not too badly. What shall I read? – "Blood Wedding"?[675] or finish Gide's Journal?[676]

Reading in bed has been for some time my chief comfort.

<u>En Avant!</u>

(Miss Gide seems to have been an old auntie all her life! Her writing has never moved me though I observe its excellencies. She is a bit dry for my fruity tastes. I doubt that she and I would have hit it off – still, she has some qualities I would enjoy. However I don't have the impression, from her journal, that she liked anyone really very deeply except Miss Gide, whom she pretends to deprecate but whom I think she regards as a girl of destiny pretty nearly all the way through.)

(Perhaps I envy the length and felicity of her days.)

(She seems to invite envy.)

(She declares, at one point, that she spends 5 hours a day practising Bach and Chopin – That girl's ass and fingers must have been something prodigious! To sleep she drinks a "libation of orange water". <u>Girl</u>!)

I have not had a really exciting lay since July in California – that epic ice-skater.[677] My feeling for P.[678] has more or less definitely fallen from desire to custom though my affection is not lost. I don't think it was time or repetition. It was partly that but other things, a spiritual disappointment, was the more important factor. He is incapable of reason. Violence belongs to his nature as completely as it is abhorrent to mine. Most of all, I want and now must have –

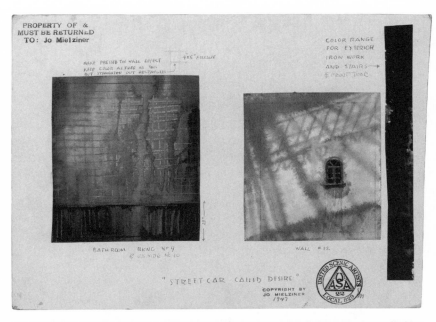

Set designs by Jo Mielziner for *A Streetcar Named Desire*

Dear Jo:

I am awfully happy to have your sketch
of the set. I fell in love with it at
first sight, and I still get a bang
every time I see it. Thanks, and my
best wishes to you, Jo.

I hope you will keep an eye on the show
while I am gone.

Regards,

simple peace. The problem is to act kindly and still strongly, for now I know that my manhood is sacrificed in submitting to such a relationship. Oh, well — it will work out somehow.

———◆———

A Streetcar Named Desire *opened in New York on 3 December 1947 and was an instant success with praise from numerous critics. Howard Barnes in the* New York Herald Tribune *(4 December 1947) declared Williams "the Eugene O'Neill of the present period," and Wolcott Gibbs in the* New Yorker *(13 December 1947) described* A Streetcar Named Desire *as a "brilliant, implacable play about the disintegration of a woman, or, if you like, of a society." Brooks Atkinson, writing for the* New York Times *(4 December 1947), wrote one of the more thoughtful reviews:*
> *Tennessee Williams has brought us a superb drama, "A Streetcar Named Desire." . . . Like "The Glass Menagerie," the new play is a quietly woven study of intangibles. But to this observer it shows deeper insight and represents a great step forward toward clarity. And it reveals Mr. Williams as a genuinely poetic playwright whose knowledge of people is honest and thorough and whose sympathy is profoundly human.*

———◆———

Marlon Brando and Jessica Tandy in *A Streetcar Named Desire*

679.  Before leaving Paris for the south of France on or about 20 January, Williams had spent several days in the American Hospital in Neuilly, a suburb of Paris, for hepatitis and mononucleosis. About his stay he wrote Carson McCullers ([late January 1948], Duke):

> I left Paris soon as I got out of the hospital where I was for two or three wretched days. Honey, I did not like that doctor of yours one bit! I don't know what was the matter with me, some kind of toxic condition. I felt like I couldn't stay awake and I couldn't eat anything. I think it was brought on by the poisonous liquor and food I had to consume in Paris and the depressing weather which never let up. Myers said I was threatened with a couple of awful sounding things like Scylla and Charybdis but I didn't like him or the hospital so I got out of bed and left town.

680.  In a letter to Carson McCullers ([late January 1948], Duke), Williams mentioned he was reading *The Age of Reason* (1945) by Sartre: "It is badly written, in a way, but there is a terrifyingly keen analysis of mental processes and emotions or lack of emotions."

> Five years later, Williams would remember having read *The Age of Reason* (letter to Brooks Atkinson, 25 June 1953, HRC):

> I catch flashes of a "tortured sensibility" in the best of Sartre. I don't mind a work being dark if it is rooted in compassion. In a notebook I once copied the following bit from Sartre's "Age of Reason": — "Various well-bred moralities had already discreetly offered him their services: disillusioned epicureanism, smiling tolerance, resignation, common sense, stoicism — all the aids whereby a man may savor, minute by minute, like a connoisseur, the failure of a life." — The sadness in this reflection is a genuine thing, truthful and therefore moving. Of course there must be more comfort in his existence than in his "existentialism" or he couldn't endure it, I agree with you about that. I'm sure he is comforted by the esteem of his followers, for instance, and by the excellent French wines and restaurants and the civilized freedom of thought that still prevails and is the great tradition in his country. Apparently he has no use for me. In the summer of 1948 I gave a cocktail party for theatrical friends in Paris and sent him a long wire, inviting him, to which he didn't respond, and during the party I heard he was in a bar nearby and dispatched a French writer to bring him over. He assured the writer he would come, but a short while later he strolled by my hotel without even looking up.

> In *Memoirs* (pp. 68–69), Williams recorded a meeting with Sartre in 1959 in Havana.

681.  Williams wrote Donald Windham and Sandy Campbell ([9 March 1948], Yale):

> While in Paris — you ought to stay there a night or two — be sure to visit Madame Arthur's where they have a really excellent drag show and the most beautiful male whores and the boys dance together.

682.  In a letter to Oliver Evans dated 31 January 1948 (HRC), Williams wrote:

> My first night on the Boulevard I met a young Neapolotan who is a professional lightweight boxer. How I thought of you! Thick glossy black hair and a small but imperial torso! The nightingales busted their larynx! And Miss Keats swooned in her grave! . . . I wish I could tell you more about this boxer, details, positions, amiabilities — but this pale blue paper would blush!

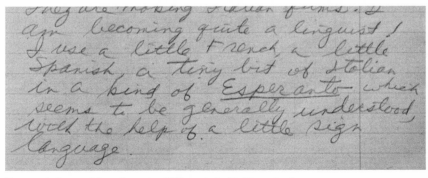

Excerpt of a letter to Margo Jones that Williams drafted in his notebook

*Tuesday, 27 January or Wednesday, 28 January 1948*

Nice –

Train now pulling out for the Italian border – I am on my way to Rome. The sun – glorious sun – is on my face, in my eyes, and I love it. There has been almost continual rain since I arrived in Europe the sixth of this month. Spent two weeks in Paris – got sick there and was very low in spirits when I left.[679] But a week spent quietly at St. Paul de Vence, resting and eating good food, has evidently restored the damage and I feel pretty good now – knock wood! However I am not very bright and my writing does not catch fire. I am pecking away at "Summer & Smoke" for lack of other inspiration. I think I will make a good play of it before I'm done for I have some fresh ideas and a climax.

Europe? And I have not yet organized my impressions.

Travelling alone is a bit frightening at times.

At other times it is a bit exhilerating.

Sartre's freedom![680]

The wine of solitude.

I look forward to Rome as to some mystery with good portents.

I had two lovely affairs in Paris, one a piece of living sculpture and the other a charming little chick. I frequented a nice dancing place called Madame Arthur's[681] and Mon Jardin!

When it is warmer, if all goes well, I will return to Paris and really enjoy it next time.

En Avant!

Later – we are now pulling out of Ventimiglia and there is a fair weather sunset in the Mediterranean. The country is full of flowers and the sea is turquoise. Snow-covered alps are visible way off. (I probably wrote the same things when I passed through here at 16!) I am sharing my compartment with a pleasant English couple of middle years.


*Circa Friday, 30 January 1948*

Rome –

"Jeeno" has just left and I have ordered "latta" and a sandwich brought to my new room at the Albergo Ambasciatori.[682] The new room is much better. It has a large balcony over the Via Venuto. Lying in bed with the French doors open I can see the night sky as I grow sleepy. But sleep seems tyrannical tonight and I resist it. I have a weird dream. I am taking a class of some kind. While I am out of the room – my coat is mysteriously slashed. This has happened to 3 other coats of mine. Someone in the class hates me and uses this revenge. The natural object of suspicions seems – for some reason – a good-looking, tall young negro. But I shake hands with him to assure him I don't blame him. In a burst of

683. Williams' dream was based on reality. By the end of 1947 McCullers had suffered her third stroke and had been hospitalized in Paris.

684. Gordon Rollins was an American who eventually moved to the Greek island of Mykonos and opened a restaurant.

685. Williams expressed his enthusiasm in letters to a number of friends. On 7 January 1948, in a letter to Paul Bigelow (Columbia), he identified one of the books he was reading as *The Mysterious Universe* (1930) by Sir James Jeans. He wrote James Laughlin the same day (7 January 1948, Houghton):

> I am on a scientific kick right now, I took with me a little library on physics, mostly atomic and astronomic, some thrilling stuff. I am so stupid I have to read each page twice and sometimes twice again to latch on to the abstractions but it is worth it. Sir James Jeans, Einstein, Selig & Hecht, DuNouys. Relativity and the Quantum theory are still somewhat beyond my comprehension but I am getting at least a poetic concept. They seem to feel, at present, that the universe is just an abstraction in the mind of a pure mathematician. I find it difficult to reconcile this with my personal experiences.

A few weeks later, Williams wrote to Carson McCullers ([late January 1948], Duke):

> Do you like physics? I am reading a lot about astronomical physics and relativity and so forth as it really exercises the mind and the imagination to think about those things, such as curved space and the electrical particles that matter is made of, all of them dashing around at the rate of thousands of miles a second, and everything being made of them.

Williams outside his apartment at 45 via Aurora, Rome

gratitude he tells me who the real culprit is, a white student – name "Prophyl" or something like that. Later I tell my brother – he suddenly changes the subject by informing me that Carson is in a hospital dangerously ill and in great pain.[683]

At this point I wake up, not feeling well and not inclined to return to sleep. The dream seems to contain Freudian images but I'll be damned what they are! I like Rome. I must limit my activities, however, to stay well. My inability to release any steam in writing makes me want more society and diversion than is healthy. Also I must arrange to take some form of regular exercise. The swimming pools are not open.

*Thursday, 5 February 1948*

Thursday –

I am supposed to fly to Sicily tomorrow but I doubt that I shall. I can't get over my dread of planes and I do not feel like pulling up stakes here. Life goes pleasantly enough. I walk a great deal. For the past 2 days I have abstained from sex and today perhaps only coincidentally, I managed to do some work on "Summer & Smoke". Fairly competent, perhaps. I spent the evening in the company of Gordon Rollins,[684] the most agreeable (non-sexual) company I've had in Europe. He startled me this evening by saying he'd had an operation for tumor of the brain last Fall. I wonder if that is so. I am not yet certain that he is not a fabricator of tales. I am not as trustful as I used to be, especially with charming boys who don't support themselves. Still it interested me. If it is true – remembering Kipp – I must be kinder to him.

Could it be that he and I both – !

Tonight a bit depressed. And nothing to read but my "Physics"[685] – I make so little sense of it with my dim brain.

So long.

## My Current Reading

**Tennessee Williams**, playwright, author of that Broadway smash hit, "A Streetcar Named Desire," provides us with the following list of his reading:

THE MYSTERIOUS UNIVERSE, by Sir James Jeans (Macmillan)

HUMAN DESTINY, by Lecomte du Noüy (Longmans)

EXPLAINING THE ATOM, by Selig Hecht (Viking)

THE STRANGER, a novel by Albert Camus (Knopf)

CALIGULA and CROSS PURPOSE, plays by Albert Camus

LA FOLLE DE CHAILLOT, a play by Jean Giraudoux

NO EXIT and THE FLIES, plays by Jean-Paul Sartre (Knopf)

LIONS AND SHADOWS, by Christopher Isherwood (New Directions)

THE IDIOT, by Feodor Dostoievsky

THE THEORY OF RELATIVITY, by Albert Einstein

*Saturday Review of Literature*, 6 March 1948

686.  American-born Donald Downes (1903–83) lived in Rome and had worked during World War II for British and then American intelligence. In addition to his work as a secret agent, he had been a schoolteacher, political writer, and foreign correspondent. In 1953, Downes published *The Scarlet Thread*, his memoirs of his espionage activities.

According to Windham, in 1948, Downes' lover was Franco Zefferelli (1923– ), who was working with Luchino Visconti as assistant director on *La Terra Trema* (interview with Margaret Bradham Thornton).

A week later, Williams wrote about his trip to Sicily in an article he sent to Audrey Wood titled "A Film in Sicily." In the article, he gave the trip a completely different gloss:

I am in Sicily to watch the making of La Terra Trema, an Italian film which will be known in English as The Earth Shall Tremble. I became interested in this film while I was in Rome, when I was shown a collection of stills which were the most beautiful photographs of the most beautiful faces I had ever seen. These pictures were in the possession of Mr. Donald Downes, a gentleman of international connections who looks like a pleasantly depraved Roman emperor such as Tiberius and talks like a character out of Dashiel Hammett, and who is now engaged in raising money for the picture. Practically everything about this picture is being done "on the cuff" as we say in the States. They are raising the capital as they go along. Compared to Hollywood picture-making it is inexpensive, about a hundred thousand dollars. They are also "shooting on the cuff" — I believe that is our term — which means that the script is being written while the picture is being shot. Each day's sequence is prepared the night before. There are no script writers. In fact there are not even any actors. The performers in the picture are fishermen and their families in the little Sicilian village of Aci Trezza, and the story is a simple chronicle of their lives. The director of this film is an Italian nobleman named Count Luchino Visconti. Visconti is a member of one of the great historical families of Italy but he is now associated with the Italian proletariat. He was the man who directed "The Glass Menagerie" in Italy where it was known as "Zoo di Vetro", and it made a tour of all the big Italian cities.

Wood submitted the article to the *New Yorker*, where it was rejected for being "mannered," "phoney," and "unbelievably bad." It appeared, however, as "A Movie Named *La Terra Trema*" in *'48: The Magazine of the Year*, June 1948.

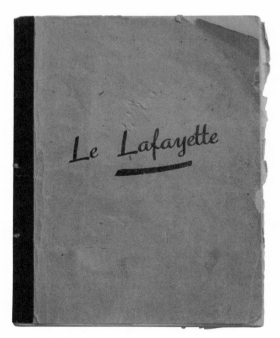

Notebook Williams began in January 1948

Yes, I am going, after all!

And it makes me feel good to act in spite of the fear – an exhileration – so is the spirit liberated in the only way possible on this perilous sphere –

*Saturday, 7 February or Sunday, 8 February 1948*

Catania, Sicily –

A letdown – the place, the people seem dirty – the film-making tedious – an hour for a single shot – And I an outsider. Why did Downes want me along? He has his lover here, and his business but there is nothing here for me, and I was at home in Rome.[686] Ah, well. I'll make the best of it. Maybe I'm just feeling tired and tomorrow will prove more interesting. The dining-room and one of the waiters have charm – however a bath tub is indispensable to sex in Italy (for one of my effete tastes) and this room has only a sink with cold water.

I suppose I may take a look at Taormina and perhaps Naples & Amalfi on the way back. I really must stop complaining like such a tired old maid when I'm really having the time of my life.

Am I not? Ha-ha!??!

"Spring in Tuscany is like everybody's romantic dream of spring" said Mr. Downes! His lover is a beauty.

And he himself is a character second only to Bigelow, I'm sure. I feel rather well & comfortable tonight in spite of diarrhoea and disappointment in Sicily.

My interior (lower section) has been behaving rather suspiciously of late. Trouble may be brewing but we must not expect it. The worst, by far, is the dullness of my mind. I cannot write a letter, even, with any ease. But if I keep hammering the old watchman may wake up and at last respond. A letter from Grandfather and Donnie – both faithful. And one from the little Yanuck who made my last week in New York so happy. I am sleepy now – the air is sweet and cool and the street sounds are pleasant – All except the streetcars which are the noisiest in the world I'm sure!

*Sunday, 15 February 1948*

Sunday – Feb. 15 or 16

Sunday is a bad day for me. Fairly consistently so. Such little things as getting no mail make a difference.

The diarrhoea has increased lately and has now become really debilitating though my stomach is still functioning more or less normally and I am not reduced

687.   Although Williams had written in his journal at the end of January that he was "pecking away at 'Summer & Smoke'" he may have been already working on the one-act sketch from which *The Rose Tattoo* was derived, "Il Canne Incantado delle Divina Costiere."

688.   In *Those Barren Leaves* (1925), one of Aldous Huxley's (1894–1963) early novels, he exposes the shallowness and pretentiousness of those who regard themselves as belonging to a cultural and sophisticated elite. It is a satire of a group of English gathered in the Italian villa of Mrs. Aldwinkle, who sees herself "unofficially a princess, surrounded by a court of poets, philosophers and artists." Her guests fail to live up to the high aims she sets for them.

689.   Salvatore Moresca was a lover whom Williams disguised as Rafaello in *Memoirs* (pp. 143–45). Williams first met him in 1948 and for a time they spent every other night together. In the poem "The Blond Mediterraneans (A Litany)," dated February 1982, Williams would write: "Salvatore would meet me faithfully twice a week, / always punctually, always very discreetly, / until yesterday afternoon when he didn't appear at all." In "The Negative," the last story Williams is known to have written (dated November 1982), he would name the fragile, failed, destitute poet, who is employed in London by Lord Amberly to perform sexual favors, Tonio Moresca.

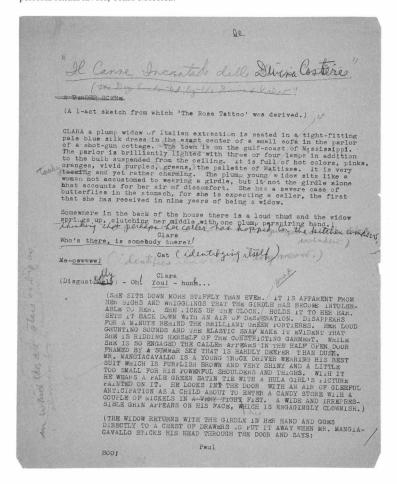

to the condition I was in at Paris. But today I feel particularly weak & listless. Only stared at my Mss. and put them wearily away.[687] Drove about Trastevere in a cab and was outrageously over charged. Walked feebly around the Borghese gardens and when the sun had lost its vigor, as I had mine, returned to the Albergo Ambasciatori, removed my clothes & collapsed onto my bed again. Ah, me. Of what interest is all this! Only for brief intervals do I live like a light bulb turned on for a few minutes. My dullness other times is phenomenal. I do not know myself. What is this creature I live with? What does he want? What is he trying to do?

Perhaps it would be better to light a cigarette & return to my moderately good book by Huxley "Those Barren Leaves".[688] Really better than moderately though it is too lacking (Huxley) in sensuality to be truly my dish. The satire of character seems lacking in compassion though sometimes it makes you laugh quite heartily.

If only – once more for a while – I could get the colored lights going in my brain! – And create with power and certainty as I have at rare times when I was loved by the gods!

En Avant.


*Tuesday, 17 February 1948*

Tuesday

"Poor Tom's a-cold."

It is really cold here tonight. I am half way between apt. & hotel – moving – will probably miss this pleasant little room at the Ambassador. The apt. was an impulse of doubtful virtue.

The diarrhoea has stopped today – paregoric. Some faintly disquieting sensations in the bowels but nothing very notable.

As for work – zero! The usual grade here.

Tonight I have another date with Salvatore "The Piccolo"[689] – which I don't want to keep, but will. My affections are transient these days & it's better that way. This is a fugitive time in my life – En Avant! – will return here for my last night at the Ambasciatori.

Salvatore Moresca, Williams, and Sandy Campbell

690. Presumably "Cabeza de Lobo (the dramatization of a Mexican myth)," of which only an outline and multiple fragments are known to exist. In "Cabeza de Lobo," Oliver, the main character, meets the daughter of a professor of anthropology who is traveling in Mexico (in one variant the professor is on a Guggenheim fellowship). The daughter (in one variant she is an anthropologist, too, in another a Smith College student) explains to Oliver that the father is investigating a "myth, a fantastic story" which belongs to Cabeza de Lobo. Cabeza de Lobo is both the name of the town as well as the name of the woman "with the head of a wolf who's supposed to have cast a spell on the town." "She drinks human blood, and once every month she demands another victim. The people in the town are said to have no emotion. They make sounds like laughing and sound like crying, but they don't really laugh or cry, they don't really have any feelings of love or fear or pity. Because if they felt any real emotions the spell would be broken and the Cabeza de Lobo would die."

In one variant the victim is selected by drawing a card. In another, Esmeralda, the beautiful sister of the werewolf, picks a victim, dances with him, gives him the privilege of "lifting her veil," and then surrenders him to her sister to be devoured. The spell can be broken only if the beautiful Esmeralda sheds a tear.

As the story progresses, the myth (which the anthropologist and his daughter dismiss) is performed with Oliver as the victim. As suggested by the outline, Esmeralda, the beautiful sister, sheds a tear and Oliver escapes.

Brian Parker, in his article "Documentary Sources for *Camino Real*" (*Tennessee Williams Annual Review*, 1998), identified an untitled version of this play and designated it an important source for *Camino Real*.

Williams had referred to this play as early as July 1945. In a letter to Margo Jones ([early July 1945], HRC), he wrote:

I am writing a play about a <u>were-wolf</u> — <u>Cabeza de Lobo</u> — inspired by a Mexican painting of one. It will be a bit longer than Purification and I hope it may finally be good enough to use on a program with it. It is full of <u>horror,</u> so after working on it I have to sleep with my light on.

691. Williams wrote one poem, "Testa Dell' Effebo," and an early draft of "Rousseau: Bord de l'Oise" in February 1948.

> TESTA DELL' EFFEBO
>
> Of Flora did his lustre spring
> and gushing waters bathed him so
> that strings of instruments were held
> until his turning let them go.
>
> Then gold he was when summer was,
> unchangeable this turning seemed
> and celebrants with strings have told
> how golden then his temples gleamed.
>
> But finally as metals will
> the lustre of his body dimmed
> and that town burned wherein was turned
> this slender copper cast of him.
>
> *TW.*
> *Napoli, 1948.*

*Friday, 20 February 1948*

Friday – Feb. 2?, 1948

I am still dating "The Piccolo" begins to be a problem as I can't help feeling a certain responsibility.

The tender web. Better slip out of it before you're tied.

The apartment seems a pretty good arrangement. Except there is no hot water. Fortunately The Piccolo is a clean child.

I have a masseur who comes in 3 times a week – gives me exercises – and I have discovered quite a lovely swimming pool.

Should I not be content?

I am reasonably so. But it plagues me not getting a new work under way.

I have made several faint starts. The latest about the Professor & his daughter may go somewhere.[690] The signs are not especially encouraging. I am not even sure I have done much to improve "Summer & Smoke".

Health? Rather surprisingly good. No more diarrhoea. Occasional twinges here & there in the guts.

Sexually it's a bull market. I have never been so full of manly vigor. My cock actually seems to hang an inch longer and the fear of impotence has not occured at all lately.

Tomorrow a new caller – a student in the afternoon. The Piccolo that night.

I have a bedside radio.

This is a list of my blessings.

What am I trying to sell myself?

Get to work, baby. That's the only blessing will do you much real good.

The coffee here is swell. Big steaming white cup big as a soupbowl. Drinking too much of it. Heart a bit jumpy tonight, and that is not one of my blessings. Neither is time, which is still always passing no matter how much or little a boy does with it. And someday — En Avant!


*Thursday, 25 March 1948*

March 25, 1948

Tomorrow will be my birthday. It has been an almost totally static period here.

The work problem grows gradually and continually more acute. I have actually not done a fucking thing – except one poem and some little scratches at a new play which still has no plot and shows no sign of catching fire.[691] I have had static periods before but I don't think any in which the creative self seemed quite so thoroughly under blankets if not under sod.

692.   Presumably the surname of a sex partner.

693.   Williams first met Gore Vidal (1925– ), the prolific novelist, essayist, and playwright, in Rome in the spring
of 1948. In *Memoirs* Williams remembered:

> One evening at a dinner party given either by Henry McIlhenny of Philadelphia, the famous cura-
> tor of art, or by Sam Barber, the celebrated composer, in a baroque apartment at the American
> Academy — I met young Gore Vidal. He had just published a best-seller, called *The City and the
> Pillar*, which was one of the first homosexual novels of consequence. I had not read it but I knew
> that it had made the best-seller lists and that it dealt with a "forbidden subject."
>
>     Gore was a handsome kid, about twenty-four, and I was quite taken by his wit as well as his
> appearance. We found that we had interests in common and we spent a lot of time together. . . . we
> made some trips in the jeep to places on the "Divina Costiera" such as Sorrento and Amalfi. (p. 146)

Vidal would write the screenplay for the film version of *Suddenly Last Summer* (1959) and for *Last of the
Mobile Hot-Shots* (1969), based on Williams' play *Kingdom of Earth (The Seven Descents of Myrtle)*.
Williams dedicated the poem "The Form of Fern" to Vidal.

```
         THE FORM OF FERN

         (For Gore Vidal)


   The form of fern, whether it trembles wetly
   Near to the touch, or sleeps secure in limestone,
   Is very stuff of reason.  See how strictly
   Its pattern is fulfilled, how passionless
   And pure it is, how delicate and just. ·

   The form of fern, because it seems so slender,
   Knows constant threat, has many enemies
   (The powerful sun among them) but it knows
   How it must live, and has a green transcendance.
   No form is half so tough, nor half so tender.



                              Barrytown, New York
```

694.   Frederic Prokosch (1908–89) was an American novelist and poet. His first novel, *The Asiatics* (1935), was
a huge critical and popular success, drawing praise from literary figures such as T. S. Eliot, André Gide,
Thomas Mann, and Albert Camus. His next novel, *The Seven Who Fled* (1937), won the Harper Prize. In
a letter to Brooks Atkinson dated 29 March 1948 (NYPL), Williams described Prokosch as "simple and
friendly, which is certainly not the impression you get from the austere pictures of him that usually appear
on the back of his books."

695.   In *Memoirs*, Williams recalled the meeting with George Santayana (1863–1952):

> [O]ne afternoon Gore took me to the Convent of the Blue Nuns to meet the great philosopher and
> essayist, by then an octogenarian and semi-invalid, Santayana. He seemed like a saintly old gentleman.
> He had warm brown eyes of infinite understanding and delicate humor and he seemed to accept his
> condition without the least bit of self-pity or chagrin. It made me, this meeting, a little more at ease
> with mankind and certainly less apprehensive about how the close of a creative life might be. His gen-
> tleness of presence, his innate kindliness, reminded me very strongly of my grandfather. (pp. 146–47)

No neuroses except this anxiety which is perhaps itself a major one.

Mind seems torpid. I find social relations difficult for the simple reason that I seem too dull for conversation. A piece of jelly is my present state of consciousness. What to do about it? Just complaining and worrying does no good. The sex life continues to flourish.

La Primavera is golden and warm.

Each day has its pleasures. <u>Piaggi!</u>[692] – the Roman god. Salvatore – Gore[693] – Fred Prokosch[694] – Gordon Sager – others that drift around as I do – fish in a sunny acquarium.

Donnie comes in a week or so – he is on the boat now. This afternoon I go out to St. Peter's. Vatican with Gore. Yesterday we saw Santayana at the Convent of the Blue Nuns.[695] As I have read none of his work the meeting meant less to me than it did to Vidal who practically worships the old man.

He had an air of serenity that was lovely.

I will now go eat.

2½ cups of coffee have not enlivened my fancy.

Salvatore comes over again tonight.

Gore Vidal and Williams

696. Peter Latrobe was a destitute Englishman who was friendly with Williams during his time in Rome in 1948 and 1949. In *1948: Italy, Letters to Sandy [Campbell]*, Windham mentions an episode in Rome in 1948 with Williams, an Englishman (Peter Latrobe), and himself (p. 73). They had parked after midnight in the Villa Borghese and were arrested and detained overnight by the police. In 1949 Williams kept Windham informed about Peter Latrobe.

> Peter and I celebrated by picking up three golden panthers disguised as Italian sailors. When Peter discovered that I had chosen the nicest he flew into a rage and declared that this sailor had confided to him, privately, that it was really, he, Peter, that he had desired. ([20 February 1949], Yale)

> Frankie's passion is clothes, and this week we have been on a haberdashary kick. . . . Also a suit for Peter La Trobe who is still wearing the same old rags he slept in that night in the bull-pen. (8 April 1949, Yale)

> Peter La Trobe has really gone out of his mind. He claims that Irving Rapper has offered him a job as dialogue director for the Menagerie, that Irving was madly infatuated with him, continually squeezing him arm or pressing his knee. I think we shall soon have to send him to Ischia with Auden and Chester [Kallman] and Truman [Capote]. ([10 June 1949], Yale)

697. The "great election" between the Christian Democratic Party and the Front (the Communists and Socialists) represented the first election of the Italian Republic. Prior to 1946 Italy had been governed by a monarchy.

698. In the short story "Rubio y Morena," the writer Kamrowski, "essentially a lonely man" who "had never been able to believe that anybody sincerely cared much about him," picks up a young Mexican prostitute, Amada. She lives with him, but he eventually loses interest and treats her badly, and she leaves him. He misses her, searches for her, only to find her dying. Williams' writing of this story is coincident with his break-up with Pancho Rodriguez. Two months earlier (11 February 1948, HRC), Williams had written Oliver Evans about his break-up with Pancho, "life is supportable without [love] and loneliness is sometimes quite pleasant."

Williams in Italy, 1948

*Sunday, 11 April 1948*

April 11 – Sunday

    Still the same – A sticky do!

    Gore & Prokosch have left Italy –

    Only Peter La Traube[696] of my English speaking friends remains here with the great election a week off.[697]

    Peter and I do the Galleria nights when Salvatore isn't with me. Tonight we had a pair that we sent home immaculate as they arrived – too young!

    Afterwards I worked a bit on the story of Amada and it remained cold.[698] Writing seems to have become a forgotten art. Why? I can't figure it out. The will, the want, even the force seems there, but it won't flow.

    The body remains well – in spite of 3 coffees a day and most irregular habits.

    Tomorrow S. and I may drive to Florence – Adios!

Donald Windham                Sandy Campbell

699. Williams' reference to Priapus and cherries obviously has sexual connotations. Priapus was an early Roman god of fertility. The Romans often placed a statue of Priapus, painted red and with an enormous uncovered phallus, in gardens.

700. The following day, Williams wrote Audrey Wood (19 April 1948, HRC):
Send me any good books on the frontier days (colorful anecdotal atmospheric) about the frontier days of the Texas oil-industry as that is the background of my latest attempt at a comedy. I've started three or four different plays but this is perhaps the most promising.

701. *Guasta*, "broken down."

702. On 3 May, Williams received a telegram (Delaware) from the president of Columbia University:
HAVE HONOR TO ADVISE THAT UNIVERSITY TRUSTEES HAVE AWARDED PULITZER PRIZE TO A STREET-CAR NAMED DESIRE FOR ORIGINAL AMERICAN PLAY.
Earlier in the year, on 31 March, *A Streetcar Named Desire* won the New York Drama Critics' Circle Award for the best play of the year.

703. Margo Jones had arrived in Italy at the end of May. Williams had invited her to Italy to discuss *Summer and Smoke*, which she was scheduled to direct in New York in the autumn. Jones then planned to travel to London with Williams for the opening of *The Glass Menagerie*. Williams wrote Windham ([7 June 1948], Yale):
Margo's visit has been a strange one. I would not think it possible that anyone could react as little to Italy as she has. If you tell her something is beautiful she agrees with you without even turning her head to look at it. We took a trip in the Jeep to Capri and Sorrento. On the way back we took a wrong turn and got lost in the mountains and a rainstorm. It was quite indescribably beautiful . . . and when we had to stop for the night in a mountain village named Frosinone (which name you should remember) she was afraid to occupy a room by herself because the town had been heavily bombed and she was afraid the vengeful natives might attack her. We all three slept in one room, which bewildered Salvatore no end. He never quite understood the situation and every few minutes he would pop up on his elbows to look across at her and then flop down again with a startled giggle. In the morning he told me, "This Donna multo strano. This donna like parlare, like mangare, like drink, pero no like amore, no like poesia!" However this donna is very useful and obliging in such matters as packing for trips and making arrangements. We have our tickets and reservations straight through to London without my lifting a finger.

704. In a letter to Carson McCullers (8 June 1948, Duke), Williams wrote:
Honey, the news of Pancho is terrifying! He is in New York with some mysterious travelling companion staying at a very expensive hotel on Central Park, has called Audrey and everybody to inform them that he is sailing for Europe June 11th, the day I arrive in England. He lands at Liverpool and presumably will come directly to London to look me up. It gives one a feeling of inescapable doom!

Postcard of Salvatore Moresca and Margo Jones sent by Williams from Capri to Donald Windham on 3 June 1946

*Sunday, 18 April 1948*

Election day – April 18.
"The immaculate pair" returned tonight and there was a great festival of Priapus. Cherries fell.[699]
Rome was quiet today – no election disturbances reported.
I started a new play but that ceases to be a notable event.[700]
the Florence trip a fiasco. Jeep guasto.[701] Now laid up in garage.

*Friday, 7 May or Saturday, 8 May 1948*

May 7 or 8
The period has gone beyond where it should have stopped. I have quit trying to work. Mind seems utterly torpid except for the nightly anxiety over falling asleep.
Now my health has broken. Diarrhoea and no appetite as when I first came here. No crisis of nerves just a continual depression. felt practically no elation over winning Pulitzer prize.[702]
My work was more of my life than I knew and – now –
Why? Maybe it is just a matter of not being young anymore.
Windham & Campbell are here. I'm afraid they must find me an awfully dull companion. I talk less than ever. Rarely more than two sentences at a time and it frightens me to search for words. The sex, abundant as ever, has become rather stale, routine. The Romans are all pretty much alike – gentle, affectionate, easy – no surprises. Still sex remains the one great solace. I try not to become too fond of Salvatore for I must leave him here, and soon.
    <u>En Avant!</u>

*Sunday, 6 June 1948*

June 6 or 7 – Sunday –
Leaving here with Margo[703] Tuesday morning. She has made the departure a lot easier for me – packed my stuff yesterday, made the travel arrangements. Lucky thing. I am scarcely able to function on the most rudimentary level. Close to panic a few times lately at thought of the imminent demands. Instinct to withdraw entirely away – where I am unknown & unseen. Anonymous. But it is better, it is wiser, to go forward ostensibly as if nothing had happened. One must expect deliverance when none is in sight.
Windham is in Venice.
Letter warns me that Pancho may be coming to Europe.[704] I would probably fall dead at the sight of him – with terror. How did I get into that? In a way the past seems almost as obscure as the future.
The Marble Arch. I wonder what that will be like? A change may be salvation, after all.

705.  A few days earlier (5 July 1948, Duke), Williams had written to Carson McCullers about his stay at Kelvedon Hall in Essex, the country estate of Sir Henry "Chips" Channon, who had married Lady Honor Guinness in 1933 and divorced her in 1945:

> I returned to the hotel just now from a rainy weekend at one of the great manor-houses of England where I was guest of an immensely wealthy old member of Parliament who married into the Guinness beer fortune, got rid of the lady but kept the fortune. The place is of Georgian period and somehow I felt suddenly as if I had walked into the setting of an Isak Dinesen tale, one of the Gothic ones. . . . The house was built so long and it seems to have absorbed the lives of many strange and wonderful and rather secretive people. For a while, after the owning family died out, it was turned into a nunnery. Then two young nuns were found drowned in the little swan-lake. This tragedy blighted the place: everyone said it was haunted. Ghosts were certainly walking the night I was there!

706.  Despite Williams' pessimism, *The Glass Menagerie* opened in London on 28 July to generally positive, although, in the words of the producer Hugh Beaumont, "not terribly impressive," reviews. Despite some reviews that criticized the structure and pace of the play, the *Daily Telegraph* (29 July 1948) described Williams as "a poet who writes in prose, an artist in giving a magic quality to ordinary words and very ordinary — even tiresome — situations" and lauded John Gielgud (1904–2000), one of Britain's finest classical actors and directors, for his immaculate production. Helen Hayes (1900–93), in her first appearance in London, was consistently praised in her role of Amanda Wingfield, and *Tatler* (11 August 1948) went so far as to describe her "beautiful performance" as "the making of the evening."

707.  "The Big Time Operators" and either a precursor to *The Rose Tattoo* or a precursor (in play form) to *The Roman Spring of Mrs. Stone*.

Williams and Helen Hayes

I have done a good turn this month, anyhow.
Maybe several.
Now if only —
En Avant!


*Thursday, 8 July 1948*

July 8 – London –
 The Marble Arch and everything else (practically) was a bitter disappointment.
One rather delectable red-head served me occasionally but has now gone to sea.
An air of hopelessness on this island, the people grim, cold, unpleasant. The
upper society quite heartless. Snobs and hypocrites to a shocking degree.[705] My
interest in the production not been enough to offset these impressions – now
nearly all gone owing to lack of participation. Gielgud too difficult to work with
a~~cold personality~~ somehow antipathetic. Hayes has flashes of great virtuosity
but her performance lacks the heart and grace and poetry of Laurette's and
sometimes it becomes downright banal.[706] The others are so-so, and the
mechanical direction is no help. I hope that I shall have to retract some of these
judgements after the opening – or this whole English adventure will be a fiasco. I
must stop doing things because I am told to.
 The work has picked up a little. Two interesting beginnings of plays are in
progress.[707] I am not really on the ball. Not by any means. But the signs are less
utterly bleak than they were the last couple months in Rome. After I get through
Summer & Smoke there will be a real showdown, I guess. Cards on the table! No
more evasion – We will look Tennessee squarely in the face and see what we can
make of him.
 Tonight little Salvatore would be a great comfort. I feel lonely and the
approach of sleep is never any solace to me.
 Oh, to be clear of all this, quite clear of it and still <u>alive</u> but in some other
world, some younger and sweeter being!

---

*Williams returned to New York in August for the rehearsals of* Summer and Smoke,
*which opened in New York on 6 October 1948. The play met with a mixed recep-*
*tion, with reviews the next day ranging from describing the play as "a pretentious*
*and amateurish bore" (*New York Herald Tribune*), "a juvenile and sadly delin-*
*quent effort" (*New York Daily News*), to being described by Brooks Atkinson*
*(*New York Times*) as "tremulous with beauty . . . the gift of a poetic and creative*
*writer." It closed three months later on 1 January 1949.*

---

708.  Paul Bowles.

709.  Williams met Frank Phillip Merlo (1921–63), a second-generation American of Sicilian descent from New
      Jersey, a navy veteran, and former lover of the lyricist John Latouche, in Provincetown during the summer
      of 1947 where they spent a night together in the dunes. In the early autumn of 1948 Williams accidentally
      ran into Merlo in New York City, and by October of that year they were living together as lovers.

      About Merlo, Paul Bigelow remembered:

      We were all very pleased when Frank moved in with Tenn. . . . Frank was a warm, decent man with
      a strong native intelligence and a sense of honor. Those of us who cared about Tenn realized that
      Frank wanted to care for him and to provide some order in his chaotic life. Tenn had what I call
      "artist's order," which is something else — but he needed someone to look after the ordinary logi-
      cal structure of everyday life. And with great love, this is what Frank did. (Spoto, p. 153)

      Williams and Merlo's relationship became strained in the 1950s, especially toward the later half. They
      remained together but lived rather separate lives. When Merlo was diagnosed with inoperable lung cancer
      in 1962, they became closer again.

      Williams dedicated *The Rose Tattoo* to Merlo. In the short story "The Night Was Full of Hours,"
      Williams remembered happy times with Merlo, and he included the ghost of Merlo in the play *Something
      Cloudy, Something Clear*. Poems written by Williams either for or about Merlo include "Little Horse,"
      "Death is High," and "A Separate Poem."

      LITTLE HORSE
      *For F.M.*

      *Mignon* he was or *mignonette*
      *avec les yeux plus grands que lui.*
      My name for him was Little Horse.
      I fear he had no name for me.

      I came upon him more by plan
      than accidents appear to be.
      Something started or something stopped
      and there I was and there was he.

      And then it rained but Little Horse
      had brought along his *parapluie.*
      *Petit cheval* it kept quite dry
      till he divided it with me.

      For it was late and I was lost
      when Little Horse enquired of me,
      What has a bark but cannot bite?
      And I was right. It was a tree.

      *Mignon* he is or *mignonette*
      *avec les yeux plus grands que lui.*
      My name for him is Little Horse.
      I wish he had a name for me.

710.  Maria Britneva (1921–94), born in St. Petersburg, Russia, was brought up in London and became Lady
      St. Just when she married Peter Grenfell, Lord St. Just, in 1956. As an aspiring actress, she first met
      Williams in London at the end of June 1948, and they soon became very good friends. During the 1950s,
      Williams secured minor roles for her in several of his productions, but she was primarily known for her
      energetic spirit and sharp wit. In 1991, she published *Five O'Clock Angel: Letters of Tennessee Williams
      to Maria St. Just, 1948–1982.*

711.  By 1948 Arthur Miller (1915–2005) had not achieved the prominence he soon would with *Death of a
      Salesman* in 1949. In the spring of 1947, however, Williams had seen *All My Sons*, Miller's first successful
      play, set against the backdrop of World War II, about an individual's responsibility to society. It was
      directed by Elia Kazan. Williams had been so impressed by the play and the director that he was deter-
      mined to engage Kazan for *A Streetcar Named Desire*.

# THE LOG BOOK.

*Saturday, 4 December 1948*

Third day out on the Atlantic on the steamer Vulcania. The weather is pale grey and warm. I spent an oddly peaceful but almost sleepless night. I had a mystic feeling of faith as I lay in my comfortable bunk and listened to the steady sound of the ship and the sea and the rain. A mysterious affirmation of something. I am trying, now, to remember just what it was. It was as if the Mysterious One Himself had crouched beside me and was whispering something reassuring into my drowsy ear. This was especially good on account of the fact that I had been troubled by anxieties the two days since sailing, and perhaps, less consciously, for a good while preceding. The immediate cause of this depression was a report given me by Paul[708] and Frankie[709] of what Maria[710] had said about me to Laughlin. She had told him (and presumably others) that in her opinion I was washed-up – "Finit" was her fancy word for it. She meant as an artist. She said that I had exhausted my material, my old material, and that my life, particularly my circle of friend and "contacts", was too narrow and special for me to discover new or more significant subjects. She held out one possibility of salvation which was, by implication if not direct statement, herself. This was of course only an extension of what she had said to me. That I associated so much with special cases or freaks that men like Arthur Miller[711] – for whom I had

Donald Windham, Maria Britneva, and Sandy Campbell seeing
Williams and Frank Merlo (far left) off on S.S. *Vulcania*

712.  Hugh "Binkie" Beaumont (1908–73), managing director of H. M. Tennent Ltd., the well-established British theatre production company, was from the mid-1930s to the early 1960s one of the most powerful theatrical producers in Britain. Tennent had recently produced *The Glass Menagerie* and would go on to produce *A Streetcar Named Desire* in 1949 and *Summer and Smoke* in 1951.

713.  The three play manuscripts most likely were "The Big Time Operators" and precursors to *The Rose Tattoo* and *The Roman Spring of Mrs. Stone*.

714.  *Battle of Angels* (1940), *The Glass Menagerie* (1945), *A Streetcar Named Desire* (1947), and *Summer and Smoke* (1948).

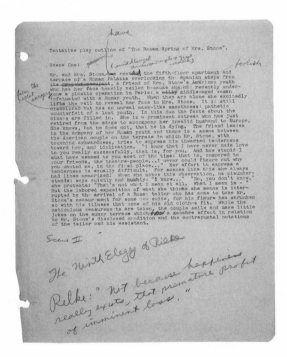

Hugh Beaumont (photograph by Cecil Beaton)

John Gielgud (photograph by Dorothy Wilding)

expressed a great admiration – did not feel at ease with me and could make no vital contact: that I was building a barrier between myself and the real world and its citizens. Coming from a girl whose social background appears to have been all but exclusively the smart theatre set of London – the elegant gentlemen of Shaftesbury such as Gielgud, Binkie[712] – this criticism seemed a bit incongruous. Nevertheless I couldn't dismiss it altogether. I felt it was honestly meant and there was a grain of truth in her warning. But to discover that she had been saying this, and so much more, to other people about me seemed a distinct betrayal of friendly trust. And it did not improve any further my recently improved relations with women. As for that grain of truth: the truth doesn't lie so much in the fault of the company I keep. That company is good, and stimulating. The fault, the danger, which she had partially correctly foreseen, lies in the over-working of a vein: loneliness, eroticism, repression, undefined spiritual longings: the intimate material of my own psyche is what I have filled my work with, and perhaps built it on, and now I have got to include, perhaps predominantly, some other things, and what are they? There is a dilemma, but I am not refusing to face it, and this Cassandra is a little bit premature in her cries of Doom! After all my world, the world of my representation, has more latitude than most: my experience is special only outwardly: the heart of it is more or less universal. My energies have suffered some attrition, just as my body has. My face and my body have aged and I don't have the spontaneity in any way that I had when I was beginning this decade of my thirties. And a great deal of work is behind me and in that work is a great deal of expression which leaves a great deal less to be expressed hereafter and I shall certainly never turn to hack work which is writing without the need to write other than economic. On the other hand, clarity and wisdom and the critical faculty have grown: probably discipline is also more evident. I feel no cynicism but on the contrary a deeper respect for life and humanity. There are voices in my heart and hands beating at the doors of it and a great desire and will on my part to answer the calls they are giving. My mood is not elegiac. It is not heroic, but it is not elegiac. It is always interesting to assess the odds. With three play manuscripts[713] in various stages of incompletion tucked into my portfolios I would say that the odds are approximately six to four in my favor, that is, in favor of my returning by next Fall with a good new play to produce. None of these scripts is over the hump. At least one of them is in sight of it. So far I have never failed to push a thing through to some kind of completion if I determined that I should. Not even "Summer and Smoke" the whole history of which was fraught with the most abysmal discouragement: abandoned five or six times, I nevertheless picked it up again each time and went doggedly on with it, and the result is a play that is good enough to impress some people – not myself and not many but <u>some</u> – as the best of the four long plays I've had presented.[714] Someday, somewhere is the end. There is always an end somewhere. But I will probably die before I finish. Maria, when I am washed up – or <u>finit</u>, as you put it – you won't send me a cablegram. You may send me a box of roses!

715.    "The Delicate Prey," "A Thousand Days for Mokhtar," and "By the Water," the one "laid in a Turkish bath." Although Williams had taken on horrific subjects before, such as death by crucifixion in the early story "My Father's House" and cannibalism in the story "Desire and the Black Masseur," Williams remembered in *Memoirs* (p. 159) being shocked by "The Delicate Prey," in which a thief slices off a boy's penis.

716.    *The Plague* (1948), *La Peste* (1947), is a novel about an outbreak of bubonic plague in the Algerian port of Oran. Through the eyes of Dr. Bernard Rieux, who does his best to alleviate suffering, the reader witnesses the devastation caused by the epidemic. Albert Camus (1913–60) was one of the intellectual leaders of the Resistance movement, and the imprisonment by the plague is a metaphor for the Nazi occupation. The novel is a story of courage and hope against the arbitrariness of human suffering.

717.    Very likely the beginnings of "The Diving Bell," which would be published in the collection *Androgyne, Mon Amour* in 1977:

```
I want to go down to the sea in a bubble of glass

where Thought the father and Action the son are slow

but Sensation, the ghost of the two, is subtle and quick.


It's only a dare-devil's trick,

the length of a burning wick,

between tu-whit and tu-whoo!


Oh, it's pretty and blue, but not at all to be trusted.

The ceilings and walls are encrusted

with counterfeit moons and doubloons

and choir-boys with false golden hair...


I want to go down to the sea in a diving-bell

and rise again to the surface with much to tell.

I want to give warning: "It is an overcast morning."


Or: "I have gone over the works,

and whether you kiss it or give it a couple of jerks,

it doesn't matter..."


"If the fireman has broken his leg and his hook and his ladder

and the plumber can't stop the drip in the kitchen sink -

Baby, could it be earlier than you think?"



                    Tennessee Williams
                    The Atlantic, December, 1948.
```

A melodious bell in the corridor announces the lunch-hour. I am not hungry but I shall have a martini and a piece of non-fattening meat or a salad. And I hope that I shall have strength to take a work-out in the Gym this afternoon. There is danger of hitting 160 pounds again before we land at Gibralter, and it may be some time before I get acquainted with a new swimming-pool. <u>En</u> <u>Avant!</u>

Saturday night: We are supposed to be getting out of the Gulf stream but it's still as moist and warm as those afternoons when my sister and I used to sit on the backsteps in Mississippi blowing soap-bubbles out of old spools. I feel relaxed. The whites of my eyes are actually white for a change. I visited the gymnasium in the afternoon: sat in the electric cabinet and then had a massage: weighed in at 150 pounds which is surprisingly little, if the scale is correct. The wide cabin is full of wind tonight and the ship full of creakings for the sea is getting heavier, the roll more perceptible. Paul has given me three stories about Morocco, including one that is laid in a Turkish bath.⁷¹⁵ Merlo is reading Sartre so I shall read Bowles. I have also been reading Camus' The Plague⁷¹⁶ and have a much higher opinion of it this time: the finest prose style of our time, perhaps. I did little work today: mostly on a poem.⁷¹⁷ But feel that tomorrow I shall accomplish more. In a couple of days we shall be along the Azores. Beautiful name. I hope we shall come close enough to see them. Paul said that once he could see them waving from the shore, that is, the natives. Many beautiful places and names in this part of the world that I have never been before. I must stay out of myself: not in too deeply: so that I can look and see and enjoy and feel and know. There has been too much of the other. Well, movement is good for that. It helps to open the doors and the windows wide. It is not for frightened people, but neither is life. For frightened people there is really nothing but gas on the stomach – and gremlins. Okay. I am not making much sense so I will go to bed.

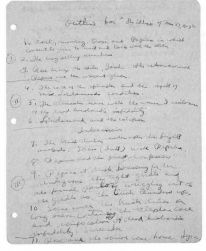
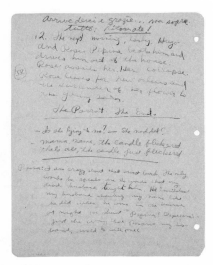

Outline for a precursor of *The Rose Tattoo*, "The Eclipse of May 29, 1919"

718.  In a letter to Audrey Wood (18 November 1948, HRC), Williams wrote:
      Since I got here I have been working on the average of six or eight hours a day. This evening even
      working on the graveyard shift! And have accomplished, I think, a good deal. It now looks as if "The
      Big Time Operators", which is the present title of play, might have a fairly complete first draft some-
      time this Spring, and I hope it won't take more than one re-writing. The story is not at all biograph-
      ical but the material is drawn mostly from Huey Long, showing the main character in a mostly
      sympathetic light as a man very close to the people, fantastically uninhibited, essentially honest, but
      shackled with a corrupt machine and machine-boss. As a good half of the play deals with him as a
      young man (about 29, when first elected Governor) — though actually Long was a bit older than that
      — I am thinking now about Marlon Brando as in every respect but age the part fits him perfectly. . . .
            I would like . . . the following reference works. Two biographies which I now have from the St.
      Louis library. "Huey Long: A Candid Biography" . . . and "The Kingfish — Huey P. Long, Dictator".
      . . . Also two books written by Long himself which are called "Every Man a King" and the other "My
      First Days in the White House". . . . I have avoided, and will avoid reading, all fiction about Long as
      I don't want any unconscious coloration to creep into the play, and my character, Père Polk, will be
      pretty much my own creation with just as much of the Kingfish as I find theatrically enticing. For one
      thing he has plenty of sex-appeal, and that's what made me think of Brando for it.

719.  "Flesh Farewell," a title Williams borrowed from a short story of Windham's, was an early title for a man-
      uscript that would evolve into *The Rose Tattoo*. More than ten years later Williams also considered using
      it for the film version of *Orpheus Descending*.

720.  Irene Mayer Selznick (1907–90) produced *A Streetcar Named Desire* in 1947. About her Williams had
      written James Laughlin (9 April 1947, Houghton):
      [W]e already have a producer "in the bag". A lady named Irene Selznick (estranged wife of David
      Selznick and a daughter of Louis B. Mayer). Her chief apparent advantage is that she seems to have
      millions. Audrey says that she also has good taste. Of course I am skeptical. But I am going half-
      way to meet her. She is flying down to Charleston and I up and we are to have a meeting-conference
      tomorrow evening at the Hotel Fort Sumter.

Irene Selznick

*Sunday, 5 December 1948*

SUNDAY: The usual day of unpleasant revelations. I review the idea for the
political play,[718] that is, the ghost of an idea and it doesn't seem very like me. It
seems forced, outside my real sphere of interest and aptitude. So far I have not
written anything – except certain scenes in You Touched Me – that did not come
out of my heart, but this would be like those scenes that didn't, that is, most of it
would. It is a big and important theme that doesn't really interest me very much:
gets too far away from my own experience. How could I hope to handle it and
invest it, under those circumstances, with any vivid reality? I read over the
various stuff (dramatic) that I have been working on lately and the only stuff that
has any fire in it is the stuff I was just playing with for my own entertainment: a
lot of the script called "Flesh Farewell".[719] If that story opened up as a real story
then I could make something out of that. The trouble is that I am being bullied
and intimidated by my own success and the fame that surrounds it and what
people expect of me and their demands on me. They are forcing me out of my
natural position as an artist so that I am in peril of ceasing to be an artist at all.
When that happens I will be nothing because I cannot be a professional writer.
The Lieblings and the others are standing over me too much, without any
comprehension, I'm afraid, of what I am or am not. I guess I made the right
move when I caught this boat. Get out of reach of them. It would probably also
be smart to put Dakin on guard at home so that he can protect my financial
interests. It doesn't look like I'm going to hit another jack-pot anytime soon: this
has got to keep me for a long while, until the wounded gladiator recovers. Until
the heart finds a new song and the power to sing it. Openings come quickly,
sometimes, like a blue space in running clouds. That's how it has always been. A
complete overcast: then a blaze of light: and there is heaven again. And I am in it.
But it must be a real heaven, not a painted backdrop, not blue gelatine on the
cyc. In the meantime there is life, and it may be wise to practise a little deception
with those people on the shore behind me who think I am a little machine
making money. I must give them the slip. Oddly I think Irene[720] when she said:
"Don't play it safe" and kept repeating that to me, drunkenly, again and again – I
think she may have meant this. She may have, with her peculiarly sharp insight,
have seen that I was trying to do something that wasn't myself – out of fright –
and known it wouldn't work well. And been advising me not to. Very rich people
who are not fools can sometimes see beyond money. Poor Audrey. She is simply
in an impossible position, married to a poor little mess of a guy – and apparently
loving him – who can't see more than five blocks north or south of Times Square.
– For me the important, thing, now, is not be paniced. To see my position and
hold it. And move with calm and vision. And to learn how unnecessary are all
the little prides and conceits that came to me with my success.

721. Williams borrowed the name of a classmate at University City High School, Phil C. Beam. The character Phil Beam appears in a number of incomplete play fragments, including "The Big Time Operators," "Brush Hangs Burning," "The Pink Bedroom," "The Puppets of the Levantine," "The Cutting of a Rose," and "Virgo," all of which relate to *Sweet Bird of Youth*. These fragments include aspects of two story lines: an unsuccessful dreamer who tries to win back his former sweetheart and a corrupt political boss with an unhappy mistress. Williams would combine these two story lines in *Sweet Bird of Youth*.

     In "The Enemy: Time," Williams' one-act play he developed into *Sweet Bird of Youth*, Williams named the main character Phil Beam, but he eventually changed it to Chance Wayne in the full-length play.

722. Italian version of the American film *Pittsburgh* (1942), which starred Marlene Dietrich and John Wayne and told the story of a coal miner who makes a fortune, breaks with his business partner, rejects the woman who loves him (Dietrich), marries for social standing and wealth, loses everything, starts over again, and is reunited with his friends.

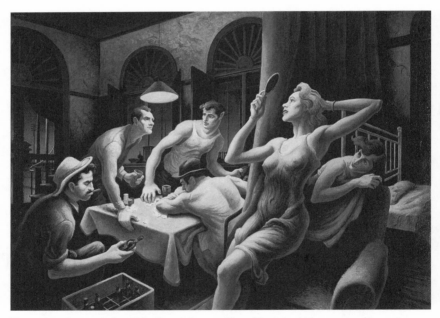

Thomas Hart Benton, *Poker Night (from A Streetcar Named Desire)*, which was painted in 1948 and given as a Christmas present to Irene Selznick by her estranged husband, David Selznick

*Monday, 6 December 1948*

MONDAY AT SEA:

    This morning for the first time there is sunlight flashing on the waves though the sky is still colorless, and the sea is rougher than usual. I remained in bed after breakfast: had only one cup of coffee and did no work but read over the Phil Beam script[721] with very limited satisfaction. Perhaps the elements of a play are there but the story line has not emerged and the dialogue is way below par except for a few brief passages. A fin du monde feeling came over me as the morning wore away: not exactly a blue funk, at least not a passionate one, but I found myself wondering if I would ever come back across this ocean. – Last night was beautiful, as such things go, animalistic and wild. Later I dreamed of my sister. Woke up. Then went to sleep and dreamed of her again. At one point I was lying in her bed, the ivory-colored bed: but it was not a dream of incest, although I am at a loss to explain it. I was standing naked in a room. Heard footsteps. Jumped in the bed to cover myself. Discovered it was my sister's bed. She entered the room. Spoke to me angrily and pulled back the covers. I struggled not to expose my nakedness. She turned away crossly while I got hastily up from the bed. There I woke up. Another time during the night I woke up gasping for breath: had a feeling of dying: but when I woke my heart was not disturbed so perhaps it was only a nightmare. But during the film yesterday afternoon when I was laughing at something I had much the same sensation: a breathless panic. Better to think it is nerves! Early tomorrow morning, at eight, we are supposed to be in sight of the Azores, and this afternoon there is to be an Italian film called La Febbre Dell' Oro Nero[722] – now the chimes are announcing lunch. I have no appetite but will go to the table with my Sartre – probably spend the afternoon taking the sun in the deck chair. So we go on – with our comfortable little mercies . . .

Benton's pencil and ink sketch that Irene Selznick gave to Williams

CABEZA DE LOBO.  (the dramatization of a Mexican myth.)

Outline:

Oliver's arrival and the theft of his wallet.
scene interior of hotel and the werewolf's shadow.
Scene with professor's daughter by fountann.
Professor and daughter exeunt to get wife.  Oliver sees Esmeralda.
Oliver decides to stay and the tourists leave.
Scene between Oliver and Esmeralda: balcony.
Oliver goes to pawnshop.
Cabeza de Lobo on street: behind pillar: shadow.
Oliver and the street people, his terror.
Oliver and La Gitana: the card.
Oliver and Esmeralda: the lifting of the veil.
The Gitana's return and the howl of the Cabeze de Lobo outside.
Oliver goes outside.  Shadow of Cabeza from column.
He starts toward the arch.  She follows in reboza.
He gasps and staggers along collonade.  Falls to knees.
Esmeralda : Una Lagrima!  Una Lagrima verderada!
Adios, Esmeralda!  Adios Oliver.

Outline for a precursor to *Camino Real*

*After arriving in Gibraltar, Williams and Merlo traveled with Bowles to his home
in Tangier where they stayed for two weeks. From there they spent a week in Fez
before returning to Rome. Williams remained in Rome but toward the end of
March wrote Windham (23 March 1949, Yale):*

I have been in a state of depression lately and have not written for that reason. The life in Rome has gone stale. I tried a few days in Florence. That was
worse. . . . Tomorrow Frank and I are going over to Ischia to try that.
Truman [Capote] and his new lover, whom he imported here from the States
— Jack Dunphy — are already there. We drove them to Naples but I fell out
with Truman last night. . . .

My own efforts recently have been middling to poor: I have two plays,
perhaps even three, pretty well mapped out and one of them in rough first
draft form but that sounds considerably better than it actually is, for the writing lacks fire. I have had very few good writing intervals since I came to Italy.
Perhaps it is the debilitating climate and perhaps when I go to Paris, soon, I
will be stimulated again as I was last year. But I am worried and depressed
and I don't feel at all well.

Williams and Paul Bowles in Morocco

723.    Eyre de Lanux, born Elizabeth Eyre (1894–1996), a painter, writer, and designer, studied art at the Art Students League. A minor poet and writer from the 1920s to the 1970s, her work appeared in *Story*, the *New Yorker, Harper's Bazaar, New Directions*, the *Transatlantic Review*, and *Nouvelle Revue Française*. In 1918, she married Pierre de Lanux, a diplomat and former literary secretary of André Gide. They moved to Paris and in 1948 she moved to Rome, had a romance with the Italian writer Paolo Casagrande, who was half her age, and met Tennessee Williams. At the time she was working on large fresco paintings and portraits and, in October 1948, Williams sat for her. In her diary she made the following note about his portrait: "Tennessee — mix burnt sienna (light) with the mixture / one grey blue eye? a white scarf?" On 8 April 1949 (Yale), Williams wrote Windham, "I have completed . . . the first draft of a short story about Eyre de Lannux which won't be good for a long while yet." According to a friend of de Lanux's, she destroyed the fresco of Williams after the publication of *The Roman Spring of Mrs. Stone* in 1950.

724.    As a young New York debutante, Caresse Crosby (1892–1970) distinguished herself by inventing the modern brassiere which she patented and sold to Warner for commercial production. She went on to become a minor poet who, with her husband Harry Crosby, founded the Black Sun Press and published and promoted many of the early modernists, including Lawrence, Proust, Pound, Joyce, and Crane. After her husband and his lover shot themselves in a sensational suicide pact in 1929, Crosby continued to publish American and European writers. She also supported avant-garde artists such as Salvador Dalí at her Crosby Gallery of Modern Art in Washington, D.C. In the early 1950s, in response to the atom bomb, she organized "Women Against War" and bought a ruined castle in Italy, the Castello di Roccasinibalda, which she restored as a retreat for pacifists.

725.    Having worked on dramatic and film versions, Williams developed a narrative account of his story, which he initially titled "Moon of Pause" but would later publish as *The Roman Spring of Mrs. Stone*. In this novel, a wealthy actress, recently widowed and retired from the stage, lives an aimless life in Rome. She reacts to aging and the loss of her beauty and career by having an affair with a self-absorbed young gigolo:
>    And yet Mrs. Stone could not deny to herself what she felt in her body, now, for the first time, under the moon of pause which should have given immunity to such feeling but seemed, instead, to have surrendered her to it. She felt incontinent longings, and while they repelled her, they gave her a sharply immediate sense of being. (p. 46)

The affair ends badly, and the novel concludes with Mrs. Stone taking a new lover in order to stop "the drifting that was nothingness" (p. 110).

726.    Peter Latrobe.

727.    Wood had written Williams two letters dated 18 May 1949 (HRC), one addressing Williams' concerns about the film script of *The Glass Menagerie*, including its length, his financial interest in the film, and choice of the director, Irving Rapper. In the second letter Wood addressed Williams' concerns over a road tour of *Summer and Smoke*.

*Monday, 23 May 1949*

May 23 – 1949

Why have I not kept a journal in so long? Perhaps it is because I've been less lonely, or perhaps only that I grew tired of talking to myself about myself, which is what my journals were mostly. However it is good to keep one. Serves some excellent purposes. I hope I will continue this one.

I felt better today after a neurotic spell of finding society very uncomfortable. There is still a little strain but it is wearing off.

This evening cocktails at Eyre de Lannux[723] where I met the well-known Caresse Crosby[724] but Eyre was the only interesting person there.

Afterwards we, Peter and I, picked up Frank who had a temperamental fit of some kind – disappeared from the supper table and is still at large. The boy mystifies me, sometimes.

I have about finished <u>Moon of Pause</u>[725] – prefer not to have any opinion of it yet.

Life ranges between tolerable, barely tolerable and fairly pleasant. I go on. Endurance is something of which I become increasingly tolerant.

Renato. A beautiful boy with hair a little darker than honey. Peter[726] gave him 5 thousand lire to pay his rent and he made a speech, warning Peter that he must not expect any sexual ~~returns~~. reparation. Peter indignant and I quite agree. Weather soft and lovely – barely warm. Hot water shower has started working. I read Sartre & Cris. Marlowe. Odd pair.

*Tuesday, 24 May 1949*

Tuesday –

The day that <u>Time</u> magazine comes out – our link with the American scene.

Today I was stupid as a pig. I made no further progress on the novella. Literally nothing happened except that the Roman rut was worn a little deeper. Frankie, however, seemed to be in bright spirits and we were closer than usual. Discussed going to Sicily for beach life – rest – swimming – And for Frank to visit his relatives.

Good mail. A long letter from Paul Bowles and two from Audrey.[727] A fairly entertaining American film of ancient vintage, tonight. Now bed again with <u>Time</u> and my Sartre. I don't suppose the nightingales will sing as they did last night.

728. An area of Rome along the banks of the Tiber.

729. Frank Merlo.

730. Kip Kiernan.

731. Williams and Merlo had traveled with Paul Bowles to Morocco earlier in the year. In a letter to Windham dated 23 March 1949 (Yale), Williams wrote:

   I am terribly fond of Frankie but I am afraid "it will end in tears" — to quote Maria [Britneva]. He hates the dependance involved in our relations. I make a sorry companion these days, and when I see him enjoying so much more the company of others, such as Truman, it is naturally a bit hard on me, since I believe that I love him.

Eyre de Lanux

*Wednesday, 25 May 1949*

Wed. –

My God, how the nightingales sang tonight! Enough to break their little hearts. It was a fine day – soft, balmy May weather – the news of my sister – out of the asylum 3 days a week – some work, not too bad – dinner at Santa Maria in Trastevere[728] – Palatina wine – driving about the streets – Peter picked up a boy –
Goodnight.

*Friday, 27 May 1949*

Friday –

Read over first part of novella and it seemed so bad – so artificial and lifeless – that I closed it quickly and put it away. I can so ill afford to lose this creative battle as well as so many others but there is no point in hiding from the stark fact that the fire is missing in almost everything I try to do now. Is it Italy? Is it age? Who knows. Perhaps it is just the lack of any more deep need of expression but I have no satisfactory existence without it. without it I have nothing but the animal life that is so routine and weary, except for the moments with F.[729] when we seem close.
What to do now?
Niente? We will see.

*Sunday, 29 May 1949*

Sunday –

I love F. – deeply, tenderly, unconditionally. I think I love with every bit of my heart, not with the wild, disorderly, terrified passion I had for K[730] that brilliant little summer of 1940. But doesn't this finally add up to more? If it doesn't it is only because of the mutations – time – in me.
But it is amazing that I who've become so calm and contained about other matters could feel as much as I do when F. is sleeping beside me. If only I could give F. something beside clothes and travel – something that would add to the content of heart and life, make a difference in his state of being. If he left me, and perhaps he will, I would go on living and enduring and I suppose turn him into a poem as I've done with others. But the poem is already there in his actual presence – Enough. I said to Paul,[731] "I am afraid it will end badly." – Will it? The best way is to let everything alone – as it is – accept – and give – stei tranquillo.

732.   When Williams had expressed concern to Wood over the choice of Irving Rapper (1898–1999) as director
       for *The Glass Menagerie*, she responded (18 May 1949, HRC):

   At Warners in the past, Rapper has directed THE CORN IS GREEN, NOW VOYAGER, with Bette Davis,
   and ONE FOOT IN HEAVEN. As a matter of fact when Greta Garbo saw NOW VOYAGER, she liked it so
   much, she wanted Rapper to direct her in Balzac's DUCHESS OF LANGAIS, which was supposed to be
   started in Rome in August, but Rapper turned it down, since it was going to interfere with
   MENAGERIE. Also, Rapper comes out of the theatre, and when I was just beginning to represent writers in New York as a young girl, he was looked upon as a coming theatre director. His very good
   friends are people you know and with whom you can check, among them are Leonard Bernstein,
   Kazan and John Huston. The more I think about it the more I think there is a good point in Rapper
   coming to meet you abroad.

       Rapper directed the film, produced by Warner Brothers and Charles Feldman, which premiered 7 September
       1950. In a letter to Irene Selznick (14 June 1949, Boston), Williams described his reaction to Rapper:

   Irving Rapper was here to consult with me about the film-script for "Menagerie". I took quite a lik-
   ing to him and perhaps we will be able to come to some fairly dignified compromise on the script.
   I read it again in Paris and was terribly shocked by the ending. I don't know why, but I didn't remember its being quite that bad, and in response to my howl of dismay which reached Mr. Feldman by
   way of Audrey, they dispatched Rapper to pacify me. I rashly agreed to resume work on the film-
   script. Hate going back to it, but I couldn't let it be filmed that way without some effort to save it.
   I have been busy on that for the past couple of weeks. Unfortunately the only true ending was the
   one in the play, and the one I have now worked out, to satisfy their demand for "an up-beat", is the
   lesser of various evils — at best.

733.   "No more, perhaps."

734.   Thomas Heggen (1919–49) was an Iowa-born navy veteran who used his experience in the Pacific to write
       the best-selling novel *Mister Roberts* (1946). He collaborated with Joshua Logan to turn his novel into a
       Broadway hit. He was found drowned in his bathtub after taking sleeping pills on 19 May 1949.

735.   Maria Britneva.

Thomas Heggen

*Monday, 30 May 1949*

Monday

Today went to the outdoor piscina – just opened – also did, for the first time since return from North, some good work on novella – conquered the first section and part of the last – wonder if it will help much, or will it continue to stink?

Frankie and I have been happy lately in Rome. I am particularly glad that he is.

Rapper arrives this week to discuss screen play of "Menagerie" with me.[732] Tomorrow a little more work and an afternoon swim.

Niente piu. forse.[733]

The recent tragic death of Tom Heggen should focus attenttion and more on the problems that beset successful young writers in the theatre Inc.[734] I don't believe that Mr. Heggen committed suicide as the paper reported. He was suffering from the psychological shock of sudden fame. Personally I did not know him but have heard so much ~~intimate~~ about him through a young English girl actress[735] seeking parts on Broadway, one whom he had befriended and taken into his house, when she was without funds for purely humanitarian reasons, that I feel I have considerable knowledge and understanding of him. He was accustomed according to this friend, to the constant use of barbiturates in ~~careless~~ dangerous quantities. It appears to me that he simply fell asleep in the bathtub which can easily happen to a tired and frightened young man who is leaning too much on or has been forced to rely on drugs. The tragedy points up once more the crying need for a different sort of theatre in America, one that will be a cushion to both fame and fortune which will provide the young artist with a continual, constructive contact with his profession and a continual chance to function in it. Otherwise these losses will be repeated then, and there is no field of creative work in which they can be less afforded.

Tom Heggen was a gifted young man. The theatre needed him badly, for he had heart and vigor and freshness.

I feel that the existence of powerful, active non-commercial theatre, sustained by the state or federal government or the profession itself could have kept him in touch with the right sort of fellow-workers, provided him with the right kind and degree of appreciation and activity, and saved him from the panicky loneliness and isolation with which fame had unnerve him and so contributed very largely to his death and our loss.

736.   In the early drafts of *The Rose Tattoo*, including "Stornello," Williams named the Serafina character Pepina Quarino, "a type ideally suited to the Italian actress Anna Magnani."

737.   Most likely "Counsel," which Williams had begun in Paris in May. "Counsel" appeared under the heading "Three Poems," together with "The Soft City" and "The Eyes," in *New Directions in Prose and Poetry Eleven* in December 1949.

738.   Lago di Garda, located in northern Italy near Verona, is considered to be one of the most beautiful lakes in Italy and is a popular resort.

Postcard of Lago di Garda sent by Oliver Evans and Williams
to Marion Vaccaro (postmarked 7 July 1949)

<u>STORNELLO</u>

BRIEF OUTLINE OF PLAY IN PROGRESS: TENTATIVE TITLE "STORNELLO"
(Italian name of a type of dramatic-narrative song, usually in
dialogue form between a male and female singer.)

BACKGROUND.

    The play is laid in a very small shrimp-fishing community on
the Gulf coast in America, a little town settled predominantly by
Sicilians.

    The date is not fixed too definitely, but is modern, and the
entire action takes place in twenty-four hours of a day in late
spring, which happens to be the day of a solar eclipse and of the
local highschool graduation ceremonies.

    The "star" part is that of a Sicilian widow (between 30 and 40)
a type ideally suited to the Italian actress, Anna Magnani - who is
incidentally said to be learning English.

    The widow's name is Pepina. She is the widow of Rosario Quarino
a truck-driver who was killed in an accident on the highway about 8
years before the start of the play.

Excerpt of an outline of "Stornello," an early draft of *The Rose Tattoo*

*Friday, 3 June 1949*

Friday
– Several days and nights of accumulative tension between F. and me – tonight a blow-up. Violent (verbally) scene on the Streets, with shouts of four-letter words a bit reminiscent of the late unlamented ordeal by Pancho, but we talked it all out and though I guess the basic tension is still there, indissolubly, I now feel better for the explosion.
Maybe tonight I will sleep. Conference with Rapper tomorrow.

Friday –
I suspect that we are only temporizing. I've never made a go of it for very long. The loneliness is rooted too deep in me. And F's is a member of a darker race. To admit to myself that I can never be loved? Is that the necessity? Perhaps only a woman could love me, but I can't love a woman. Not now. It's too late. The wise thing now is to draw my heart slowly back into my own cage of ribs. Is it? Watch for a while. wait. Stei tranquillo! A lot of this may be only the strain of work – without the satisfaction of knowing the work is good. Perhaps you're only imagining F. matters that much.

*Tuesday, 7 June 1949*

Tuesday –
The blue devils have been playing a return engagement. But tomorrow Mr. Rapper leaves and I can take it easier. Of course Maria is coming which may or may not be a help. F. is acting up again. Ugly, violent scene in car with poor Peter who had said something a little indiscreet. Another little reminder of Pancho. On the other hand, there are the nightingales which probably never sang much sweeter. Today I did a tiny bit of work on the Pepina play.[736] Very ragged nerves, Body – Hypertensive.

*Sunday, 19 June 1949*

Sunday June 19 –
I have recently completed a long poem and mailed it to Laughlin.[737] The only thing I've really completed here although I've been working and trying to work continually.
I feel all screwed up.
Tomorrow I take to my heels again, with Oliver Evans in the Buick – We go North to Lago di Garda.[738] Perhaps the change will restore me a bit.

739.  Elia Kazan (1909–2003), the pre-eminent American director whose intense collaborative relationship with Williams began in 1947 when he directed *A Streetcar Named Desire*. Kazan went on to direct three other plays by Williams, *Camino Real* (1953), *Cat on a Hot Tin Roof* (1955), and *Sweet Bird of Youth* (1959). In addition, Kazan directed the film of *A Streetcar Named Desire* (1951) as well as the film *Baby Doll* (1956). About Kazan, Williams wrote in *Memoirs*: "I don't think anyone has ever known, with the exception of Elia Kazan, how desperately much [my work] meant to me and accordingly treated it — or should I say its writer — with the necessary sympathy of feeling" (p. 102).

Kazan and his wife Molly Day Thacher had written Williams about "Stornello." Williams responded (12 July 1949, Wesleyan):

> I thank and love you both for the honesty of your letters and for the trouble you took to write them. . . . I had already done some pretty brutal stock-taking of myself and accomplishments, or rather lack of them, on my trip through the lake country and by the time I got back to Rome, yesterday, the vapors of illusion were pretty thoroughly dispelled. . . . The simple truth is that I haven't known where to go since Streetcar. Everything that isn't an arbitrary, and consequently uninspired experiment seems to be only an echo. This was true last year in Rome when I started and gave up at least four plays. When I went back to the States I seemed to be finding my way out of the predicament and I worked on a new play there, about a southern demagogue and with a social emphasis ["The Big Time Operators"], which I thought I was seriously interested in and would push through to completion. But no sooner did I sail out of New York than my interest in it dissolved. I couldn't convince myself that I cared enough about the character and ideas involved to put any fire into the writing. Then I began to be badly frightened, and as always happens under that condition, I lost my objectivity. I wandered into work on "Stornello" simply because it seemed to demand so much less of me. It would have been more sensible to stop working, and just wait, with the hope that there would be a resurgence of energy that would allow me to continue the stronger themes that I had undertaken before I became so devitalized. But to wait is hard, when there is much uncertainty, so I began to work again without really having the power. You will be glad to hear, though, that I hadn't gone very deep into this work, not even to a point where it would be difficult to give it up, and now that the whole problem has come to a head, and there is no more possibility of delusion and evasion, I feel strangely much calmer and less anxious about it. . . . I don't need to tell you that the synopsis was not a real picture of the play that I had in mind. My efforts to make it sound lively made it sound cheap, but in the character of Pepina there was a lostness which I could feel and write about with reality, and would have, if I wrote it. The trouble was that I had already written so much about the same thing. In many ways writing is the most perilous and ephemeral of the talents, and you never know whether an impasse is only temporary or final, and the only real help lies in honesty with yourself and from others and keeping alive your interest in life itself.

Elia Kazan

*"a well-written story should always contain one or two sentences which are intelligible only to the author."*

*(epigrammatic literary rule)*

*Wednesday, 6 July 1949*

Wed. July ?
  Sirmione –
  Troubled by my failure to feel settled even for a brief spell. Though I am weary I am continually restless.
  Of course this place is dull – only conventionally pretty – the lake insipid – the swimming poor.
  But – Will probably leave tomorrow for Venice.


*Tuesday, 12 July or Wednesday, 13 July 1949*

Rome
  Approaching a crisis.
  Kazan's letter[739] – the dissolution of play project –
  Nerves – the fear of talking – society almost intolerable.
  Nervous impotence.
  Concern over F.
  Bodily weakness – fatigue – sloth.
  Today wrote two letters & went back to bed.
  Tonight barely strength to hold this pencil.

740. The barbiturate Seconal is a highly addictive depressant prescribed in the late 1940s and 1950s as a sleeping pill. The prolonged effects of frequent use may include sluggishness, difficulty in thinking, poor comprehension and memory, slowness and slurring of speech, exaggeration of basic personality traits, irritability, and moroseness.

741. In his introduction to the 1950 New Directions edition of Carson McCullers' novel *Reflections in a Golden Eye*, first published in 1941, Williams wrote:

    *Reflections in a Golden Eye* is one of the purest and most powerful of those works which are conceived in that Sense of The Awful which is the desperate black root of nearly all significant modern art. . . .

    . . . I have found in her work . . . such intensity and nobility of spirit as we have not had in our prose-writing since Herman Melville. (pp. xvii–xviii, xxi)

742. A beach on the west coast near Rome frequented by Romans.

743. Mita Corti was the daughter of Nina, Duchessa Colonna di Cesaro. Williams had sat next to the duchess at a dinner in March, and she had invited him to have cocktails. Nina was an acquaintance of Maria Britneva's mother, and her two daughters, Simonetta and Mita, were friends of Maria's.

744. Williams misspells Passato, a well-known restaurant in Rome.

Oliver Evans

Left F. at theatre with "his gang". Came home alone under influence (waning) of a secconal[740] taken right after supper.

Something has to break soon.

– Hope not me –

Poor little Maria – Hurt her by odd behavior at supper. She went home in tears.

*Thursday, 14 July 1949*

Thurs.

Innovation – a pitcher of ice water by the bed –

Today better – except for a little crise after coffee in P.M.

Meant not to work but did – a little on Carson's preface.[741] Tonight the neurosis lifted with only company of F. who was very sweet and close to me.

Did not see Maria. Oliver only for a few minutes.

*Saturday, 16 July 1949*

Saturday –

Oliver and I drove out to Fregene beach[742] – moderately pleasant. O's good humor prevails as long as he is being entertained.

Niente Maria –

Saw Frank only in morning –

He disappeared before I got back tonight – first time we haven't dined together in Rome.

Peter working on me again about Rapper-Hollywood deal – Had dinner with him – Nerves quieter but the trauma is there. And work remains useless.

*Monday, 18 July 1949*

Mon.

A pleasant day. Cancelled beach trip & rewrote Carson's preface with some progress. swam with Oliver and Maria.

Frank joined us for dinner – also Contessa Corti (Meeta)[743] – charming film & supper Palsetos[744] and wine later at a garden restaurant on the Via Appia Antica. Then F. and joined his gang – I was relaxed – enjoyed it. Now home – waiting happily for F. to join me in bed.

745. Irene Mayer Selznick.

746. In 1949, Swedish-born actress Ingrid Bergman (1915–82) left her husband for the Italian director Roberto Rossellini (1906–77), whom she married the next year. She acted in six of Rossellini's films, beginning with *Stromboli* (1949). Williams would dedicate his poem "Les Etoiles d'un Cirque" to her.

747. A hotel and restaurant.

748. Poems Williams was writing that summer include "Faint as Leaf Shadow" and "The Eyes" (early draft dated July 1949, published version dated August 1949).

Frank Merlo and Williams in St. Mark's Square, Venice

*Wednesday, 10 August 1949*

August 10 –
    afflicted with huge hemorrhoid, big as a walnut. Exquisitely painful for a couple of nights. Now seems responding to treatment, at least the soreness is greatly relieved.
    Last night dinner with Irene,[745] Ingrid Bergman and Rossolini[746] – exciting afterwards the nightingales sang very sweetly for Frank and I despite my imperfect health.

*Thursday, 11 August 1949*

    Bergman-Rossolini rushes – disappointing – sore ass – we all went to Quirinale[747] afterwards. Nobody even seemed to notice Ingrid was there — May leave for Capri tomorrow if the condition of my ass hole permits – Wrote a pretty good poem[748] this A.M. Was happy.

*At the end of the month Williams returned to the United States, and by mid-November he was in Key West. From Key West Williams wrote Paul Bigelow (4 December 1949, Columbia):*
    *Working very hard here, and I think pretty well. Did 40 pages of a new novella [“The Knightly Quest”] and several scenes of an old play [The Rose Tattoo] that I brought back from Italy are re-written. The new novella is my first attempt at an extended piece of humor in prose. It is a fantastic satire on a southern town that has become the seat of “A Project”.*
*For the majority of the time, Williams remained in Key West until he departed for Europe with Merlo on 20 May 1950.*

Williams, Irene Selznick, and Oliver Evans

749.  Williams finished the first complete draft of *The Rose Tattoo* in Key West in January 1950 and by the summer of 1950 was working on his third draft.

The new first scene is set at "prima sera" beginning with mothers calling their children home to supper. Williams decided to eliminate the first scene, in which Rosario, Serafina's husband, gives a lift to a dying old man before he crashes his truck. Williams decided to begin the play after Rosario's death because, as he explained in a letter to the producer Cheryl Crawford dated 26 June 1950 (NYPL), "It gives the play the classic unity of time and a great deal more compactness." He noted that "[Kazan] originally said he thought Rosario was better as a memory and a legend and he felt the play broke into two parts with his death." The "priest scene" is presumably the first scene of act 2, in which Serafina and Father De Leo quarrel.

A few weeks later (14 July 1950, HRC), Williams wrote Crawford about the new ending:
I have worked into the story a new element which changes the ending. It is now established in the story that Pepina received a supernatural sign when she conceived her two children, Rose and the son who died at birth the night of her husband's death. On the occasion of each conception she felt a burning pain on her left breast and saw, or imagined she saw, a stigmata, the rose tattoo of her husband appearing on it. Now in the end of the play, when she is kneeling to gather the ashes from the broken urn, the stigmata returns. She cries out. The ancient woman (La Fattuchiere) and others rush into the yard in response to her wild cries. She kneels with her breast exposed as the old woman enters the house, crying out: "The tattoo, the tattoo has come back! It means in my body another rose is growing!" The old woman, to comfort her, tells her, Yes, I see it, I see it clearly, Pepina — and envelops her in the grey shawl of pity as the curtain comes down. — It should be felt by the audience that Pepina may be right, that she actually has received a sign that she has conceived by Alvarro.

750.  In his letter of 14 July 1950 (HRC) to Cheryl Crawford, Williams wrote:
I have gone to Vienna for a few days to escape the fierce heat of Rome, the hottest summer in 100 years. It is cooler, here, but the city has a feeling of profound desolation, for the first time making me feel the psychic, as well as material, ruin of western Europe. The city was far more destroyed than I had expected. They are tearing down the ruins and a great deal of re-building is going on so that the atmosphere is filled with an odor of dust, as if you were actually breathing that quality of ruin-beyond-repair which Vienna has. There is nothing hopeful or vigorous about the re-building. I watch the workmen from my hotel window, and they seem to be working in a kind of disgust, as if they knew it was useless. They work in a sort of stupor and sometimes they kick the wheelbarrow over and sit down on it with their face in their hands. Italy is like the wonderfully wise singing clown in King Lear, sad but making songs out of it, but here you see the different melancholy of the Germanic spirit, the lightless, graceless surrender to total defeat.

751.  *The Seven Pillars of Wisdom* (1926), by T. E. Lawrence (1881–1935), better known as Lawrence of Arabia, is an account of his exploits directing a successful rebellion of the Arabs against the Turks during World War I.

*Tuesday, 18 July 1950*

Tuesday July, 1950

Read over most of revisions of <u>Tattoo</u> – discovered the "great progress" had been illusory. There was obviously no revival of energies in the work. Decided to return to old script, keeping only the priest scene and the new ending and probably the new first scene – and the elimination of the Rosario section.749

Now comes the violent test – forced rest! – without accomplishment behind me. But it is obvious that the only hope is to try to recover my energy, some freshness, through a period of repose.

Too bad Vienna didn't work750 – perhaps Positano or Sicily will.

Anyway – desperation is out of style. And I have "The Seven Pillars of Wisdom"751 to read and a fair supply of sleeping tablets left – not much cash but I own a house, now, in Key West where the nights have quiet and coolness and many stars –
<u>En Avant!</u>

*Wednesday, 19 July 1950*

Wed. 4 AM.

A continual restlessness plagues me here – I am either too sleepy to read in bed or too nervous. Cruising, even, has lost its power to interest or distract me. The wire that will probably hasten our departure from Europe was therefore welcome – this Roman period has all the defects of the one before and very little of the occasional charm. I blame this on myself, my failure to lose myself in really satisfactory work, lack of accomplishment, disappointment in the play overshadowing the whole ambient of my present life. Rest is only solution and somehow so terribly difficult to take.

Williams' house, 1431 Duncan Street, Key West

752.  The opening lines of an incomplete poem, "The White Café." In the version reproduced, Williams compares the bird's fate to his sister's.

```
The bird that tastes the weather may not fall
but he is risking fall.
Over all
his silver of adolescence may fall and fall.

A perch upon nothing may be the safest of all.

Security never was reconciled to the bird.
His cries are heard
by all whose fond admonition, Too high, too high,
was disregarded the moment he took the sky.

Explorer, my sister, with impotent sorrow I watched
you descend the abyss of lunacy, world without end,
without end, without end!
               In glittering disarray I watched you descend,
clutching and letting go, plummeting like a stone,
the feathers of tragedy all, all senselessly blown!

A range of membranes peopled by magic lice
glows purple.  The golden sparks
appear to be motionless.  In God's time
they move.

From reason's escarpment I, the survivor, watch
with hands held over the passionless face of a clock.
```

Williams would use the image of a fragile bird flying too high in *Orpheus Descending* (act 1, scene 2): VAL: They fly so high in gray weather the goddam hawks would get dizzy. But those little birds, they don't have no legs at all and they live their whole lives on the wing, and they sleep on the wind, that's how they sleep at night, they just spread their wings and go to sleep on the wind like other birds fold their wings and go to sleep on a tree . . . They sleep on the wind and . . . never light on this earth but one time when they die!

753.  Fritz was the nickname for Frederic Prokosch. Williams did find something to say about *The Asiatics*, his highly acclaimed first novel about a young American who travels from Beirut across Asia to the southern border of China in vague pursuit of happiness. Williams wrote to Prokosch ([late August 1949], Columbia): Last year you gave me a copy of your book, The Asiatics, but I have only just now read it, while crossing back to the States, and I want you to know that I think it a great, an extraordinarily great, book, jewelled with wonderful images, with a wild and beautiful sort of freedom, almost anarchy, about it which I had certainly not expected, not even from your poetry, fine as that is but generally, maybe only because it is a shorter form, more subject to order. It has a feeling of freedom from usual form such as I remember finding only in Kafka or Joyce but it differs in richness of sensuosity, in pure luxury, from both of those writers. It is quite marvelous the way it surges along, breaking, foaming, and then continuing like a wave washing right over its shores, a sense of flow, continual passage, richness, excitement unlike any other piece of writing I've known. I am still reading it, have not yet finished, but wanted to let you know immediately, though this letter may not reach you for quite a while, how very much it has moved me.

754.  *The Rose Tattoo.*

755.  Nembutal is a barbiturate which was prescribed as a sleeping pill.

*Saturday, 22 July 1950*

Saturday

No, it's no go, no go!

Too much writing and not enough fire in it to warm a single chestnut! Then quit! – but what after that?

Is there any life for me without it – at my age? nearing 40.

Love – the companion of desperation.

I have been twisted by a world of false values – And the talent died in me from over-exposure, a sort of sun stroke under the baleful sun of "success" – naturally I will go on trying to live as well as I can and the probability is that tomorrow, or the day after tomorrow, I will begin to edge back into the state of illusion. And hope.

At a certain point, the only dignity left is that of silence.

"The bird that tastes the weather dares not fall."[752]

*Sunday, 23 July 1950*

Sunday – I could hardly feel worse. The real bottom of the world, it always comes on Sundays. Having to read Fritz's novel, as well, and think of something to say about it besides Poor boy, I know how you feel.[753]

How infinitely <u>wrong</u> this Roman period has turned out! – Key West seems like heaven in retrospect – the morning energy for work – the cool, sweet rooms – the night rides along the ocean highway. And Frank's friendliness. That's quite different here. I wonder if I have a single friend left? – Sounds suspiciously like self pity, all this – but it is only a comment. I don't feel sorry for myself since I feel I deserve nothing much better. Certainly not from people –

*Sunday, 30 July 1950*

Sunday – another Sabbath commences blackly. I drank a very weak cup of coffee and at 4 A.M. I am still unable to sleep and too restless to read. Frank sleeps blissfully.

I churn over tired thoughts about the play.[754] I have taken two phenobarbs and a nebutal.[755]

756. In a postscript to a letter to Paul Bigelow a month earlier (3 August 1950, Duke), Williams explained his reasons for returning to the United States:

> Charlie [Feldman] wants me to come to Hollywood and has offered to pay our transportation and living expenses, so we will probably be returning to the States about the middle of the month, that is, starting back. They have sent me a final shooting script of "Streetcar", as assembled by Gadg [Kazan], and he has done a really marvelous job on putting it together with great directness and economy of style. I think I have been unjust to Gadg about "Tattoo", that his reservations have been sincerely based on a lack of satisfaction with the script for reasons that were probably sound. It seems to me that trust in a person, if it is given after enough consideration, is practically never misplaced. Of all things it is the hardest for me to give, much harder than love, but I don't think I am ever wrong when I give it. I think about the play I will finally be guided by his decisions. And Audrey's.

Set design by Boris Aronson for *The Rose Tattoo*,
and a letter from Williams to Cheryl Crawford

*Friday, 1 September 1950*

Sept. 1 –

    On the sea, returning. To what?756

*Williams spent the autumn working on* The Rose Tattoo, *which opened on 29 December 1950 in Chicago and received constructive criticism from* Variety *(10 January 1951):*

    *Tennessee Williams is still continuing his study of frustrated, introspective women. In "Rose Tattoo" he deviates from his usual more ethereal creatures, to try and depict a warm, earthy female. . . .*

    *If the first act undergoes a strong rewrite and cutting (it ran close to an hour and 15 minutes), and other acts are tightened, with a strong climax, this might fare well on Broadway.*

Williams, Maureen Stapleton, and Frank Merlo at the Club DeLisa
during the Chicago run of *The Rose Tattoo*

757.  Williams began his journal entries for 1951 in the blank pages of a notebook dating from 1947. The previous entry in the notebook, for 27 October 1947, concluded:

> Most of all, I want and now must have — simple peace. The problem is to act kindly and still strongly, for now I know that my manhood is sacrificed in submitting to such a relationship [with Pancho Rodriguez]. Oh well — it will work out somehow.

758.  After opening in Chicago, *The Rose Tattoo* moved to New York, where it ran from 3 February to 27 October 1951. In the journal entry for 27 October 1947, Williams was anticipating the opening of *A Streetcar Named Desire* in New Haven. Hence "and again I wait."

Eli Wallach as Alvaro and Maureen Stapleton as Serafina in *The Rose Tattoo*

*Tuesday, 30 January 1951*

Jan. 30, 1951
  It did![757]
  Beside me the Little Horse is sleeping, the gift of the "Benevolent Captain" –
after Pancho.
  and again I wait for the opening of a new play "The Rose Tattoo".[758]
  Anxiety over all these weeks has made me ill and sleepless – the Little Horse
looks haggard, too.
  Tonight I am full of cold tablets and secconal. I am listening to F's quiet
breathing beside me. He feared that he might not be able to sleep but he is
sleeping soundly now. Grandfather is waiting for us in Key West.
  Four days now, and we will know. It seems like the whole future hangs on it. I
mustn't ever again permit myself to care this much about any public success. It
makes you little. and altogether too vulnerable. I wonder if I can try to concentrate
on becoming a new, free person after this thing is over. It is mostly for Frank's
sake that I care. Alone, I could run away from it. But with Frank I will have to
face the possible failure more or less squarely. God be with us! now godnight.
  P.S. What do you think is going to happen? – <u>I don't know!!</u>

*Thursday, 1 February 1951*

Feb. 1
  Two more days, and we will know.
  Last night we had our first New York audience, invited – the show was down
and I felt the response was not as good as Chicago.
  This A.M. I had an attack of extreme weakness when I got out of bed, felt as
though I would pass out. Took a couple of stiff drinks and returned to bed. The
cold has gone down on my chest. No coffee today.
  The sunshine and the stars of Key West will be good regardless of how this
crucial event turns out. The sea will comfort me, and perhaps it will even restore
my power to work. I think a physical weakness and exhaustion is the deterrent
right now. It would be wise to rest completely for a while.

759.   In the summer of 1928, Williams had traveled to Europe with his grandfather and a group from his grand-
       father's Episcopal church.

760.   *A Farewell to Arms* (1929).

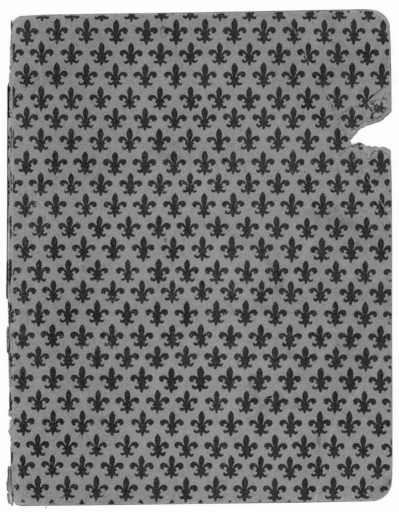

"Journal of the Summer 1951"

*Despite Williams' fears,* The Rose Tattoo *opened on 3 February 1951 to a positive audience and received reviews from such critics as Brooks Atkinson of the* New York Times, *who described the play as "original, imaginative and tender. It is the loveliest idyll written for the stage in some time" (5 February 1951). While all the reviews were not as positive as Atkinson's, by the time Williams returned to Key West at the end of February the play was well on its way to becoming a success and received a Tony Award in March. Williams and Frank Merlo left for Europe on 18 May.*

———

*Journal of the Summer 1951*

*Sunday, 22 July 1951*

Venice,
Hotel Excelsior, Lido –

For the first time since 1928 I feel the enchantment of this city.[759] Didn't feel it at all the time in between (1949) when Oliver and I came here.

But I arrived here terribly exhausted, almost panicky with depression, from Munich. Perhaps it was Frank's unexpected phone call that made Venice suddenly so beautiful to me – that delicacy, that lightness, which I love most in things – people or cities – happening all at once for me. when last time it had seemed just wet and heavy.

Now I have a little room with a balcony over the beach, and the sea sings to me and a freshness grows in the room, gradually as the night advances, cooler and cooler, fresher and fresher, while the sea keeps singing.

Three big snowy pillows on the bed.

A book of Hemingway's.[760] A glass of milk coming. Don't think I'll need a sleeping pill.

Worked fairly well today for the first time in at least a month.

*Tuesday, 24 July or Wednesday, 25 July 1951*

Tuesday or is it Wednesday?

If it was Frank's phone call that relieved my state of mind the day before it was his behavior yesterday that plunged me back into gloom. Yesterday was the first time in our lives together that I've known him to act like a bitch, and a rather usual one at that. Of course there have been "signs", now, for a number of

761.  John Blair Linn Goodwin (1912–94) was a wealthy writer and poet and friend of Paul Bowles'. Goodwin often wrote about the places he visited. His published work includes *The Idols and the Prey* (1953), a novel about Haiti, and *A View of Fuji* (1963), a novella about Japan. One of his many short stories, "The Cocoon," was included in the 1947 volume of *Best American Short Stories*.

762.  Harold Clurman (1901–80) was a renowned director, critic, author, and teacher. He was a founding member of the Group Theatre. Over the course of his life he directed plays of Odets, Miller, O'Neill, and McCullers, as well as Williams' *Orpheus Descending* (1957). During the period 1949–80, he was a theatre critic for several well-known publications, including *The Nation* and the London *Observer*.

  In his introduction to *Eight Plays* (Garden City, N.Y.: Nelson Doubleday, 1979), a collection of Williams' major plays from *The Glass Menagerie* to *The Night of the Iguana*, Clurman began:

> One day, at a rehearsal of *Orpheus Descending* . . . Tennessee Williams remarked, "If I did not write, I'd go mad." . . . Williams' writing saves him from obsessive fears and guilt, and it may be said that his work is a permanent struggle to overcome these traumas by making drama of them.
>
> Williams has always felt himself a dweller in Hart Crane's "broken world," fearing those personal and social sins that render life infernal: falsity, cruelty, corruption, violence, and the even greater fears of age and death. (p. ix)

Clurman went on to comment:

> It is the "peculiar people," the unprotected, the innocently sincere, the injured, the estranged, the queer, the defenseless, the abandoned, and the maimed whom Williams redeems for us by his compassion. It is no simple humanistic virtue but the expression of his blood tie with all those who suffer the scorn, indignation, indifference, or misunderstanding of the safe and sane, the comfortable majority. (p. xii)

Clurman's wife, Stella Adler (1901–92), was an actress, director, and distinguished acting teacher. She was a member of the Group Theatre and, in 1949, founded the Stella Adler Theatre Studio in New York City. In the 1960s and 1970s, she taught at the Yale School of Drama and New York University.

Harold Clurman                    Stella Adler

months, but the resentment, the discontent – whatever it is – and he is still an
enigma to me – are more and more exercised and displayed, now even publicly,
adding humiliation to confusion, insecurity and sorrow. I can only wonder . . .

Of course when I discussed this with him, there were the customary vehement
denials of any alteration in his attitude toward me. He is very convincing. Then I
think it over <u>afterwards</u> and I wish that I were still convinced but I am <u>not</u>. This
much is self-apparent, plain as my nose or his, he is not at all keen on seeing me
at present. It is unfortunate for me that this emotional dislocation had to come at
a moment in my life when I most needed someone to give me the security that I
used to feel in thinking myself cared for. If it is dishonesty, it is an extremely ugly
example of it and a cruel one. He goes on to Vienna – probably today, and I
don't think Goodwin[761] intends to be easily discouraged. I had hoped F. might
propose my joining him in Vienna. <u>That</u> was a vain wish!

So I suppose I will have to resume my own solitary travels tired and listless as
I am, and dangerously depressed as I often become, and God knows how it is all
going to work out. But I must try to be a little bit prudent, a little bit wise, and
start drawing the sails of my heart back in, for the wind is against them. Isn't it a
pity? It usually is, but feeling it for yourself is no good. I should be able to work
better to fill up the gap at a time like this. The work <u>has</u> improved a little since I
left Rome.


*Wednesday, 25 July 1951*

<u>Later</u> – Dreadfully hung over, can't even remember when I made that last entry –
evidently sometime <u>after</u> last night but it's surprising I didn't mention, among my
complaints, how very ill I am feeling –

I called F. He made or suggested <u>no</u> appointment to meet. I feel as alone as a
man must feel at the moment of his death.

I know he will never really <u>say</u> – I will just have to try to guess what's
happened, what I've done, what's wrong between us.

I have no home but him. Can I find another? Can I live without one?


*Thursday, 26 July 1951*

Next day 6 A.M.

For the second consecutive night I haven't been able to sleep, partly, I think
because of drinking too much – last night entertained Clurman, Stella Adler[762]
and number of their friends and in order to bear up I had to drink excessively as
I was too nervous for such a large gathering. I have taken a secconal and a big
draft of my liquid medicine, which is almost gone, still tense and sleepless.

This day is going to be a tough baby!

763. In a letter to Gore Vidal dated 13 August 1951 (SHSW), Williams wrote:
Rome was disappointing this summer, especially the car was kaput so early in the season, and it was fearfully hot. I also took in Munich (good cruising and 3 very good gay bars!) and a week at the Lido of Venice.

764. Peggy Guggenheim (1898–1979), born into a wealthy American family, was a great patron of the arts. She lived in the eighteenth-century Ca'Venier dei Leoni in Venice.

765. At the time of this journal entry, Hemingway's most recent book was *For Whom the Bell Tolls* (1940).

766. Williams completed the first draft of "Three Players of a Summer Game," which he titled "Three against Grenada," in Venice.

Peggy Guggenheim on the roof terrace of the Palazzo Venier dei Leoni, Venice, 1950 (photograph by David Seymour)

10 A.M.

After second seconal still no sleep.

"Willy" from Munich[763] just called! What next?

*Friday, 27 July 1951*

Thurs. (I believe)

Embarking on another sleepless night – the seconal taken at 11:30 did nothing. I am now at 1:10, drinking wine –

3 sleepless nights in a row may just about finish me.

I don't understand it, to say the least.

I had to receive Guggenheim[764] and a Swiss producer on the beach this P.M. My social manner verged on hysteria. Think I offended them both – talked crazily.

In spite of my wretched condition, which I suspect is almost a nervous breakdown, I have put on weight. 150 lbs. today – the drinking, I guess.

Well, Frank is gone. Would he have stayed if he fully understood my condition? I doubt it, now.

Later –

– Wine did no good – it is now 2:30 and I've just taken a slug of the liquid sedative. So far no <u>crise</u> – just wide awake, and worried.

2:45 – the second secconal. Am continuing "Farewell to Arms" –

The writing is good but the book superficial. The man seems brutal and stupid, or false. In a way, I prefer H's last book.[765] Still this one is very readable. I'm glad to have it right now, anyway.

One good thing about all this is that I shall be more content to resume the old life in Rome when I get back there, especially if Frank behaves a little more considerately.

tomorrow – doctor. also massage and haircut. and all the sun and swimming I am able to take – <u>no</u> coffee, no work unless I manage, after all, to get a really good night's sleep.

*Sunday, 29 July 1951*

Sunday – 5:15 A.M.

Last night (Fri. night) a good sleep, about 8 hours, without any sedation but tonight sleep eludes me again. A cold is developing and I have the dull prospect of a call from Willy.

Yesterday A.M. I wrote a nice but very brief little story.[766] First thing I've done in a long time, that is, completed.

This evening a charming American lady, a stranger, invited me to dine with

767.   A well-known hotel in Venice.

Williams with Wifredo Lam (far left), Truman Capote, and Peggy Guggenheim
at the Palazzo Venier dei Leoni, Venice, and Peggy Guggenheim's guestbook

her, as her guest, when I wandered onto the verandah of the Gritti Palace.767 I was able to talk without my usual nervousness. She was warm, natural. About 52, I would guess, but still pretty.

1 2:3 0 P.M.

Finally slept in all about two hours. I believe there is some physiological, more than psychic, cause of this insomnia, for being nervous has never taken this form with me before. I think it may be hypertension.

The prospect of an afternoon with the German appals me, but I can't give up the beach on that account.

I think I'll try to leave Venice tomorrow. I've had it! Everything is seen through a glaze of sickness. Like a term in Purgatory this summer. What's the way out of it, besides the one I don't want to take?

Is there anything sadder than places dedicated to the pursuit of pleasure like this big Miami Beach type of hotel!

Sunday night –

Dinner at Peggy Guggenheim's surprisingly helped to lift my spirits a little. But I am most anxious to escape from this place early as I can, tomorrow if possible. Albert ("Nellie") Laschia a really sweet old queen was at Peggy's and spoke kindly of "Mrs. Stone".

Now we shall see if Morpheus is willing – after reading a bit.

*Monday, 30 July 1951*

3 A.M. was <u>not</u> willing.

Have taken the first secconal, ½ hour ago and am drinking a little Scotch and tepid water – Feel relaxed, however, just not sleepy.

If I had a bed partner, would this strange affliction disappear? or if I were back in familiar surroundings?

I am going to apply discretion and wisdom to my life for what is left of this tormented season. I am going to be reasonable and patient. I am going to be adult. I am not going to indulge in useless despairs, however plausible they may be. And I am going to go out of my way, as I have here, to be sweet to acquaintances and so to make friends, for I am desperately lonely, and so are many others.

Oh, if only Via Venuto will be a river of coolness at night and I can drift up it into the Villa Borghese in a trance-like quiet, and come down it again, if Frank is away, with someone warm and lovely. One more little prayer, that there will be occasional cool mornings when I am able to work. And that Grandfather keeps well, and waiting for me in America.

768. Williams would adapt this line for his short story "Happy August the Tenth" (1970), about a day in the life of two middle-aged women who live together in an apartment in New York City. The day begins unpleasantly when Horne awakens Elphinstone by shrieking, "Happy August the Tenth!"

769. On 14 June 1951 (NYPL), Williams had written Cheryl Crawford:

Apparently Binkie [Hugh Beaumont] is serious about doing <u>Summer and Smoke</u> in London. I am doing a <u>completely</u> new version, even changing the title as it now takes place in winter, and I think I have a straight, clean dramatic line for the first time, without the cloudy metaphysics and the melo-drama that spoiled the original production.

770. On 22 July 1951 (HRC), Williams wrote to Audrey Wood about the loss of his car:

The last few weeks have been fraught with misadventures. First of all, I smashed up the new car, the Jaguar. I was driving North, intending to spend someweeks on the Costa Brava of Spain as the Roman summer was taking my energy and I couldn't work. About one hundred miles out of Roma I became very nervous. I took a couple — or was it three? — stiff drinks from a thermos I had with me, and the first thing I knew there was a terrific crash! The car had gone into a tree at 70 miles an hour! — It had to be towed back to Rome. One side was virtually demolished. Repairs will take a month and one thousand dollars! But they say the car will look like new. — It was amazing that I was not seriously injured. My portable typewriter flew out of the backseat and landed on my head. Only a small cut, no concussion, but the typewriter badly damaged! — Ever since, from the shock, I suppose, I have felt very tense.

Williams in Rome

*Tuesday, 31 July 1951*

Tuesday –

Well, I am back in Rome after a night containing one hour's sleep, but no "crises", on the train. Frank is still away but a suitcase and some of his clothes remain in the wardrobe, so I presume he will return sometime.

I tried to take a nap but sleep didn't respond. The apartment is cool, the streets blazing. I may stroll down to the baths after while, for I have a very active libido these recent days. If sleep doesn't fail me again tonight, I will slam back into the typewriter tomorrow.

I have made up my mind to keep one step ahead of the doldrums and depression, even if only by jumping out of bed or walking around a block. Useless black thoughts must not be tolerated, other things must, the facts must be tolerated, but surely not all of the unpleasant fancies which drag me slowly down into a pit of inertia. I must remain active. I want to stay alive. And I want to feel able to live and act independently, with a dignity of self-reliance. The crustacean world for a while! Patient back of its armor. And staying if possible out of boiling water.

Later – the first night here was dull. A fair movie, however – but the Venuto was almost as tired as me and I left the baths this afternoon without satisfaction. Cruising requires some energy even in Rome this summer. I could barely keep my eyes open in the movie but now that I'm in bed I am wakeful.

*Thursday, 2 August 1951*

Rome August 2

A man on the street said to me today "Happy August Second!"[768] – he was drunk.

The streak of insomnia broke with Frank's return. Slept normally last night. Slept 3 hours already tonight.

Will close the windows when the birds start waking. The big room is cool. But the ennui and the inertia continue and no work seems worth doing.

*Saturday, 4 August 1951*

Saturday night – August 4 or 5

Piled manfully into work yesterday and again today on the new "S. and S."[769] and I feel it will be ready for typist next week as a first draft.

No, Rome is not really tolerable in August without a car.[770] Soon as I get play to typist will take another trip. Possibly to France.

F. has all the warmth and charm of a porcupine here lately. Would a kind or intelligent person behave in that way?

771.  Le Boeuf sur le Toit, which had taken its name from Cocteau's 1920 ballet about the carnival in Rio de Janeiro, was a popular nightclub in Paris. In 1948, Williams had recommended Le Boeuf sur le Toit, which had been the cradle of café society in the 1920s, to Donald Windham as a place where he might see Jean Cocteau and Jean Marais.

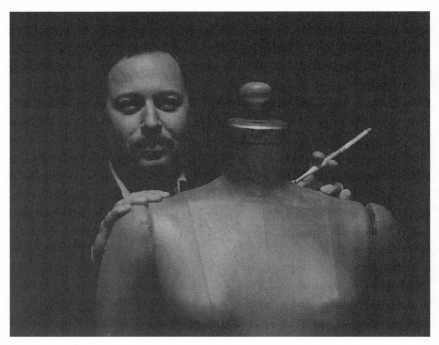

Photograph by Sanford Roth

Sketch for the set of *The Rose Tattoo* by Boris Aronson

*Thursday, 9 August 1951*

Thursday –

The experience of reading over the "New S. & S." was a staggering blow. Probably the worst job I've ever done. Quite pitiful.

of course as usual I concluded that I had better abandon the world of letters altogether.

In any case, I think I had better give up work this summer except as a diversion now and then.

Rome gets hotter each day, and now even the nights are heavy. The river of coolness fails to flow after dark.

*Wednesday, 15 August 1951*

Paris Aug. 14 or 15 – (Early Wed. A.M.)

Having a pretty rough time of it the last few hours.

Suddenly broke out in an itchy rash. Immediately presumed I had scabies. Then gastro-intestinal upset commenced. Green liquid pouring from my bowels. No pain but a gassy stomach. The rash appears to be fading so I now wonder if it was not connected with the other disturbance. Have not yet called a doctor but feel very nervous in spite of 2 secconals. However I think I'm relaxing a bit now and may be able to sleep it off.

Until this happened, the trip was going well. No despondency, no insomnia, some agreeable society and the prospect of a very attractive "lay" met tonight at the "Boeuf"771 – Could all this be a violent case of anticipation? At my age?

A very nice Jewish man, middle-aged, named Ben Something is the present protector of the prospect but is sailing tomorrow and urged me to take over. Declares the body to be "the most beautiful in the entire world" – a large order. I said I thought "the most beautiful body" was waiting for me in Rome.

Yes, I feel better now.

I do hope it wasn't and isnt the 7-year-itch!

Wed. 5 P.M.

No, it wasn't scabies, if the doctor at the American hospital is right but an allergy, nettle rash, due to, he thinks, food poisoning.

The rash disappeared this A.M. but has now returned on my arms – the diarrhoea continues and I feel in low spirits. Ate a bowl of soup and ½ glass milk for lunch which was a slight violation of orders – to eat nothing for 24 hours. A bit lonely, too. No one calls me, if anyone knows I am here, beside the pair met last night – And no word from them. It was a relief however to learn I don't have "the itch" – would be more of a relief if I stopped itching.

772.  "The Night of the Long Knives," taken from an early Nazi marching song, was the phrase given by Adolf Hitler to his massacre of Ernest Roehm and his associates on 29 and 30 June 1934. While this phrase is applied to ruthless deeds and actions, Williams adapted the phrase to refer to the summer when a number of people (Audrey Wood, Maria Britneva, Paul Bigelow, and Oliver Evans) underwent surgery. As a result of his car accident, Williams included himself in the group. A few days earlier (13 August 1951, SHSW), he had written to Vidal:

> This has been what the Chinese would call "The summer of the long knives!" No one has been spared, not even the divine bird. Some of its brightest feathers are scattered upon the floor of the cage. . . .
>
> My operation occured on the Via Aurelia between Rome and Genoa in my new Jaguar. I was driving it at 70 miles an hour, fortified by a couple or three stiff martinis, when a capricious truck came out of a side road and I decided to hit a large tree instead. One side of the car was demolished. My portable typewriter flew out of the backseat and crowned me just over the hairline. I have not had a bigger or more excited audience since the opening of "Menagerie". No one could believe that the divine bird was still able to flutter!

773.  John Perry (1906–95) was a director of H. M. Tennent Ltd. Tennent did produce *Summer and Smoke*, which opened in London at the Lyric, Hammersmith, on 22 November 1951. *The Rose Tattoo*, which had opened in Chicago on 29 December 1950, was not performed in London until 1959. It was produced by a group that included Sam Wanamaker, who also directed it.

Williams on a terrace with Ken Scott (left), Count Elia Zorsi, and Peggy Guggenheim

in a bottle because, she said, they made your fingers smelly. I once
contradicted her on this point. But she seized my hand, held it to her
nose for a disgusted second. Then pressed it to my nose. Smell! she
commanded. See? Your fingers are smelly! But she would not mind looking
at the lightning bugs that were already caught in the bottle. Any little
amusement at all was pleasant to Mary Louise, for she had no friends except
me. I was not forbidden to visit her and yet I had the impression that
mother would rather I didn't.

        Once I asked about this, and of course you know the answer.
Her mother was not a lady!

                        Tennessee Williams
                        Venice, July, 1951.

Ending of the story "Three against Grenada"

*Thursday, 16 August 1951*

Thursday 3 A.M.
  The rash is much worse, though the intestinal symptom has gone. I can't quite believe it's a simple food allergy. If it continues today, I'll try to find a dermatologist. Naturally feel quite miserable. Sleep fairly impossible again tonight, though I dozed a couple hours very lightly with unpleasant phantasies.
  The "summer of the long knives"772 rolls along.

*Tuesday, 28 August 1951*

London – The Cavendish
  A pleasant and productive stay here, over a week, with Maria and work going well and some good bed partners.
  Tomorrow return to Paris. Need a rest. My general nervous state seems much improved but the ticker a bit irritable – too much liquor, coffee, social activity.
  But very, very grateful for the remission in nervous state.
  Too sleepy – no insomnia at all here – sleep like a baby.
  I miss Frank in spite of his disturbing behavior this summer. Hope the weeks apart may make it easier for us to be together again.
  En Avant! (Aug. 28 or 29)

*Wednesday, 29 August 1951*

Tuesday – noon –
  Very, very tense, my dear, very tense –
  And a plane trip coming up this evening – Heigh-ho!
  But working well on a poem, perhaps so well it gave me this inner convulsion –
  Just taken: 2 phenobarbs, 1 secconal, 1 martini.
  Now already the magic begins to work.
  But I know it isn't right, it isn't well, this cycle of sedation.
  And I do want to finish that poem, not go to sleep.

Later –
  the plane trip was pretty nerve wracking the first 20 minutes but then I settled down and really didn't mind the rest of it, thanks to liberal libations from my flask.
  Now back at the Pont Royal, and the usual letdown after a plane flight. Hungry – shouldn't be since I am almost 150 lbs again and have had 3 meals today.
  The interview with Perry at Tennents was discouraging. Obviously they are not going to do "Tattoo" and I doubt they are very serious about the new version (or old one) of "Summer" – oh, well.773 As long as I'm able to work, all that's

774.  Beatrix Lehmann (1903–79), an English actress known for her power and intensity, first appeared on stage in 1924. She was recognized for her performance as Ella Downey in O'Neill's *All God's Chillun Got Wings* in 1929 and by 1936 was one of London's major actresses, appearing in productions from Shakespeare to Ibsen. In the September 1958 London production of Williams' *Garden District*, she played Mrs. Venable in *Suddenly Last Summer* and Grace Lancaster in "Something Unspoken."

McCullers spent August–October 1951 in London and, during that period, was hospitalized in a state of near collapse from excessive alcohol consumption and physical exhaustion.

775.  Valentina Sheriff was, according to one of Carson McCullers' biographers, Virginia Spencer Carr,

a wealthy Russian who came to Paris by way of Shanghai, then California and New Orleans, where she had found herself a rich, Louisiana-born husband. Now a divorcee and admittedly addicted to drugs, she was also a very warm, gentle, and generous person. Miss Sherriff was a cosmopolite the likes of which Carson had never known before, and Carson was intrigued by her. A friend, also, of Tennessee Williams, she traveled in an orbit of upper-Parisian society and introduced Carson and [her husband] Reeves to a strange and sometimes motley assortment of Europeans and Americans. (*The Lonely Hunter: A Biography of Carson McCullers* [Garden City, N.Y.: Doubleday, 1975], p. 398)

During January 1952 she loaned Williams and his grandfather her house in New Orleans. In summer 1955 Williams wrote to Merlo about the death of Sheriff in a New Orleans hotel from a drug overdose.

776.  Williams was either preparing poems, including "The Interior of the Pocket," for submission to *New Directions Thirteen* or assembling poems for his first collection, which he eventually submitted to James Laughlin in February 1952.

777.  On 8 September 1951 (NYPL), Williams wrote to Cheryl Crawford from Copenhagen:

I have been doing a tour of "Tattoo" openings in Scandinavia. There are to be eight, altogether; so far I have only seen one (very fine) in Copenhagen and another one, nearly as good, in Goteborg, Sweden. . . .

The Danes are just as warm and lovable, in their own Northern way, as the wops. The Swedes are a little too serious and shy for a quick communication. All are fine actors, and I have never had such a warm-hearted welcome anywhere as I've had here. I needed it badly, for this has been a bad summer. I have been ill the whole time, I don't [know] whether in body or spirit or in both.

Valentina Sheriff and Carson McCullers

o.k. Carson and Maria saw me off. Was worried over Carson in London. She does nothing but drink and moon over Beatrice Lehmann, and seems a bit dislocated to say the least.[774]

What next this curious summer? – Will decide about that tomorrow. Now a short walk and a wee bite to eat.

*Thursday, 30 August 1951*

Wednesday Night (Thursday 4 A.M.)

Spent evening with old friend Valentina[775] – wore me out. Am now too tired to sleep, and very jittery.

Talked to Frankie over long distance – He sounded very sweet and in a good humor but no report as to progress on repair of car.

Morning 10 A.M. –

Entrancing beauty at "Boeuf". I am invited to drop in for a drink in the afternoon. Just think. Last night so fatigued that I declined a chance to avoid sleeping alone.

Slept six hours. Have to finish poems for Jay[776] – also get to bank. Dine with Valentina at a Russian restaurant and call Maria tonight and come to some decision about my next move, which will be Rome only if the car will be completed on schedule.

The morning is grey. I wake up with enough gas on my stomach to elevate a fair sized balloon.

Ah, here comes my coffee.

*Sunday, 9 September 1951*

Sunday

Sometimes I find myself in a place and don't really know why I'm there, and that is the case with this visit to Copenhagen.[777] Why did I come all this way?

778. At the time of his death, Williams had two books by Gertrude Stein (1874–1946), *Three Lives* (1946) and *The Autobiography of Alice B. Toklas* (1933).

779. In a letter dated 15 September 1951 (Wesleyan), Williams wrote Kazan of the lack of harmony in his relationship with Merlo:

> Frank has not been himself either this summer, and that has not helped any. He has been cagey and irritable and sullen.
>
> Long-term relationships are infinitely complex things, they get more so with each year, and the best solution is mutual independence, the best assurance of keeping it going. This is far more true of two men than of a man and a woman, where one is appointed by nature to a more passive role. . . .
>
> Frank is not here at the moment, he is out like a cat on the town.

780. In his letter dated 15 September 1951 (Wesleyan), Williams wrote Kazan:

> Please let me know how serious you are about the one-acts, and which ones, if you are serious about them, you would like to do. My choices would be, in order of what I think is their quality, The Unsatisfactory Supper, 27 Wagons, This Property is Condemned and Camino Real. I think the final one has a kind of "lift" at the end that would be good as a tailpiece to the program. On the boat coming over I did a little work on it, building up the "Quixote" — that is, bringing him into it earlier — but have not read it over since then.

781. Presumably "Three Players of a Summer Game," aspects of which Williams would use in *Cat on a Hot Tin Roof*.

*Tuesday, 11 September 1951*

Tuesday Sept. 10.

At times in life there is a big two-letter word that says "No!" and you must learn how to read it. It's the most difficult of all short words to read, and perhaps the most important. It may not always be there but it is there now and if I don't read it and believe and accept it, at least for a while, I'm going to crack in so many pieces you couldn't find one of them!

*Sunday, 16 September 1951*

Sunday – Sept. 16

Rome again, not much cooler than when I left it, and things are not changed much. But the car is back from the repair shop looking, if not acting, good as new, and although my work hasn't really revived, and although they didn't like the new version of "S. & S." and are doing the old one – still the world is tolerable, and even pleasant sometimes. I enjoy reading Gertrude Stein at night.[778] I love the cold wine at supper. I like being with Frank when he is friendly to me, which is only part of the time, I don't think I can say most of it.[779]

I have an odd little new pain, off and on, in the right side of my neck, a peculiar twinge that is disturbingly mysterious, feels like the sort of pain that might get worse instead of better. But it doesn't come often and is not now at all severe.

A wire from Audrey that Kazan may do my one-acts this year, but do I believe it?[780] Well, hardly. Possible, just possible, in my cynical opinion. If he did it would be as remarkable as if I really managed to write something good for a change or felt really well for a change.

Well, it's a sunny Sunday, and temperate. A good afternoon to have a couple of martinis and then go for a swim and lie in the sun.

*Monday, 1 October 1951*

Sept. 30 (Sunday night – No, Monday – 3:00 A.M.)

Sort of at the bottom of the world – again.

Brought home a divinely beautiful dancer – so intimidated I couldn't do anything – After two nights of frustration in Paris. But the real jolt was when I read through my long story[781] this A.M. (yesterday). Had thought that might be the <u>one</u> accomplishment of the season. But it was <u>dull, dull!</u> And I hit the bottom!

The old familiar rock bottom –

A plane trip tomorrow, God help me.

782.  Most likely Greene's *The Third Man* (1950), written originally as the outline for the screenplay of the 1949 film of the same title. In this slight novel, Rollo Martin, a pulp fiction writer, arrives in Vienna to visit an old school friend, Harry Lime, only to find that his friend has been killed under suspicious circumstances.

783.  Williams had used this description in his short story "The Night of the Iguana" when Edith Jelkes and the writer discuss the tablets they are taking.

```
                                                                    25

        dark glasses his face looked older and the eyes, which she had not

        seen before, had a look that often goes with incurable illness.

            She noticed that he was looking about for something.

            "Tablets." he muttered.

            She caught sight of them first, among a litter of papers.

            She handed them to him.

            "Thank you. Will you have one?"

            "I've had one already."

            "What kind are yours?"

            "Secconal. Yours?"

            "Barbital. Are yours good?"

            "Wonderful."

            "How do they make you feel? Like a water-lily?"

            "Yes, like a water-lily on a Chinese lagoon!"

            They both laughed. "So you were just being friendly..."

            "I was lonely and ill," said Miss Jelkes. "I have no life

        but what I can catch from strangers."

            "You travel around?"

            "Constantly."

            "Me, too. Does it help you?"

            "It seems to."

            "Yes, it's like the tablets. Trouble is, it wears off same

        as they do, and each new place has a little less novelty for you.

        Are you a writer?"

            "Why, no, I paint," said Miss Jelkes. "Haven't you seen me

        painting?"

            "I suppose I have, I'm too absorbed in myself to notice much."
```

784.  Malcolm Cowley (1898–1989) first published *Exile's Return: A Literary Odyssey of the 1920s* in 1934. In 1951 he revised and expanded it to include new material on Pound, Fitzgerald, and Crane.

And London. Thank God for Maria, if she still likes me. I wonder if <u>anyone</u> does, and <u>why</u> if they do. Paris is really the end of the world. Unless America is. They are running neck and neck for that distinction. The dancer was kind. I must remember that.

And take my sleeping pill and say goodnight –

10. A.M.

Slept four hours and woke up feeling depressed. Took another pill and a drink of Scotch but didn't feel like sleeping so I just lay here and stewed. Put in long distance call to Rome – thought I'd tell Frank to leave car there & keep the apartment as I'd like to go back soon – after the obligatory appearance in London.

Nothing to read, damn it, except an incredibly bad mystery novel by Graham Green,⁷⁸² and the prospect of the day is beastly. So far no plane reservation. This hotel (Montalembert) is totally inept. Like one of my works this summer.

*Tuesday, 2 October 1951*

4 A.M. Tuesday – Oct. 2.

Back in my old rooms at the Cavendish. They are nice to return to. But the plane trip was an ordeal. 40 minutes before it even took off – cooped in with a full load of passengers. Flight 1 hour and 20 minutes. I endured it by benefit of a seconal and my flask. Much drinking before flight. Wine afterwards. No wonder I woke up just now feeling rocky. I really should never take a plane. The demands on my already ravaged nerves are too much. I must try to be easy on them for a while, And that's for sure. But trying doesn't always work, does it?

The enormous silence of this place. 3 rooms. Took a nembutal. wonder if it will make me feel like a water lily on a Chinese lagoon?⁷⁸³

I do hope so. Right now I feel like a hornet up a cat's ass. I have a good book, and that helps – Malcolm Cowley's book about writers of the 20's.⁷⁸⁴ They seem almost as ravaged as I and that makes them good company for me. In a book. I don't suppose our common sufferings would have created the same sympathy in life. Our common vanities, suspicions, insecurities, irritabilities, rivalries would have got in the way. What a pity it's like that among the few who can understand and could help and we have to go to the ones who may have a degree of warmth or sympathy but without real comprehension and in the end it wears out, the little tenderness they gave us. They get tired of our freakishness and indifferent to our continual crises, so meaningless to them.

Sex in Paris was a fiasco – a real fiasco.

Just now saw an abhorrent object – a big cockroach crawling from under the bed – no doubt attracted by the remains of my midnight tea. Well, back to the book. En Avant!

785. Peter Glenville (1913–96) was a British director hired by H. M. Tennent Ltd. to direct the London production of *Summer and Smoke*, which premiered on 22 November 1951. He went on to direct the film version (1961).

786. In scene 7 of *Summer and Smoke*, John Buchanan's father is shot by Rosa Gonzales' father.

787. Alexandra "Sandra" Molostvova, Maria Britneva's cousin, who was raised by Maria's mother, suffered from childhood diabetes. By 1951 her condition had deteriorated so much that she had to be hospitalized. She went into a coma on 27 September.

788. Williams continued working on *Summer and Smoke*. Two days later (8 October 1951, Wesleyan), he wrote to Kazan:

    [R]ehearsals started yesterday on "Summer & Smoke" and I do think now, finally, I have gotten the sort of play there that I wanted to make it, not the complete new version I did this summer past but the original much altered, without the phoney melodrama, and it is superbly cast. A great young actress, Margaret Johnson, is playing Miss Alma and the level of all the performances is very high compared to the one in America and I dare say the direction will also be more resourceful since Peter Glenville is doing it.

    At the end of the month, however, Williams would complain in a letter to Audrey Wood (27 October 1951, HRC) that Glenville and Johnston had "put the murder back into it. In fact, all my changes, practically all of them, have been discarded and they have reverted almost entirely to the original script."

789. George Painter, author of *Proust* (two volumes, 1959 and 1965), copies of which Williams would later acquire, confirmed the identity of the book as André Maurois, *Proust: Portrait of a Genius*, translated by Gerald Hopkins (New York: Harper & Brothers, 1950). Painter expressed surprise over Williams' failure to recognize Maurois' word choice "inversion" as a euphemism for homosexuality (letter to Margaret Bradham Thornton):

    Maurois (1950) fits in every way . . . and is the only possible candidate for his comment . . . its reticence and staidness and caution are noticeable and explain and justify Williams' verdict in this context that it was (for him) "rather dull". It's puzzling, all the same, that he ignores Maurois's frequent and full accounts of Proust's homosexuality, Maurois tactfully avoiding names, but astonishingly and at that time almost uniquely explicit. . . . In Maurois' text "inversion" as also in Proust's own vocabulary is a merely stylistic verbal choice without difference from the less polite "homosexuality".

790. Williams gave the title "The Enemy: Time" to "the one-acter which became *Sweet Bird of Youth*."

791. The Festival of Britain was a grand exposition held throughout the country from 3 May to 30 September 1951. It marked the centenary of the Great Exhibition of 1851 and was intended to be a "Tonic to the Nation" following the devastation of World War II and the austerity of the postwar years. The festival celebrated the country's past achievements in the arts, industry, and science and looked ahead to a future of progress and prosperity. The London centerpieces of the festival were the South Bank Exhibition and the Festival Pleasure Gardens in Battersea.

*Wednesday, 3 October 1951*

Wed. 2 A.M.

Soooo! – dinner with Glenville[785] and we tore the play to pieces. The murder scene[786] must go out. – one way or another.

Sandra[787] – a terrifying thing! – why? a lovely child like that.

dreadful scene at "Y" between Maria and I and a "Y" Secretary –


*Saturday, 6 October 1951*

Sat. 5 A.M.

On the carpet, remnant of a crushed cockroach, and the horrid suspicion I may have stepped on it in my barefeet – must get slippers.

Think I have solved "murder" scene[788] but have to get Glenville's o.k. tomorrow.

No sex here in London. The constant attendance of Maria and the unhappy recollection of Paris have accounted for this unprecedented chastity, as well as, of course, the great difficulties of London as a place to cruise even when you feel like cruising.

Sandra remains in a nightmarish state. Shakes one's faith in the ultimate mercy even of nature. And as for medical science! –

Still reading this rather dull book about Proust which never mentions his homosexuality.[789]

No word to indicate that Frank has left Rome. I wonder if he is going to be nice this season. That is, nicer than last. I would also do well to wonder if I am going to be nice, or nicer than last.

I must get back, soon, to one of my new long plays since it is very unlikely that I will be able to force myself to take the long rest I need.

Meanwhile the enemy, Time,[790] eats away at the biscuit.

I don't like London this time. The sky is grey as an old woman's dress or bare skin. People are sharp and bitter now that the Festival[791] is over and the poor dull imitation of summer.

There is an absolute greyness – people don't even wear evening clothes or dinner jackets as they did formerly.

The island isn't big enough for a society that doesn't get bored with itself. Yes, I think even New York may be a bit better.


*Tuesday, 9 October 1951*

Tuesday 5:25 P.M.

A panicky feeling, the familiar one of imminent extinction, jarred me out of sleep just as I was slipping into it. Needed a nap very badly. Only 4 hrs. sleep last night and feel terrible. The wire is pulled too tight, as tight as it will go. without breaking.

792. On 8 October 1951 (Wesleyan), Williams wrote Kazan, "The prospect of another Kazan production is a good enough reason for any living playwright to go on living and <u>even</u> return to America." Of the four one-acts about which Williams had written to Kazan on 15 September (Wesleyan), two ("Ten Blocks on the Camino Real" and "27 Wagons Full of Cotton") were chosen for production as a double bill.

793. Williams wrote a poem, "A Wreath for Alexandra Molostvova," inscribed "For Maria Brit-Neva," which was published in *In the Winter of Cities*. An early version of the poem "Orpheus Descending," published in *Panorama* in spring 1952, was dedicated to Molostvova.

Sketch in a letter Williams wrote to Andrew Lyndon (June 1977)

A letter from Kazan. He is really serious about doing "Camino Real" and that makes me feel much better about going back to America.[792]

Frank will be here tomorrow and I must say I'm glad. I hope that will improve the situation as much as it used to before last summer – and even then, when he was not in a mood.

Perhaps I am not — what was I going to say?

Too weary to think.

Think I shall stay in bed.

A call from Valentina. She has forgiven me for describing her as "an adventuress" – the highest compliment I could pay a lady, perhaps. She too is having a time with her nerves. Maria has gone to see Sandra. Perhaps I will have dinner with Val. Then a quiet movie. or a drink at the Festival. En Avant!

*Wednesday, 10 October 1951*

Wed: 12:40 A.M.

Dinner at a disgustingly pretentious and exorbitant place called "Club 21" – fake Russian atmosphere – with Valentina. I was in too low a state to be congenial but Val. seemed undisturbed about that and though her interminable chatter bores me, when I'm tired already, I like her. She is going to get me 100 seconals tomorrow. 100 seconals and the return of the Horse is not a bad outlook for domani. I think of grandfather & feel guilty and a bit sad. I wonder if I will sleep?

*Sunday, 14 October 1951*

Sunday 6:30 A.M.

Even before daybreak, or just after, Sunday hits the customary stride. Black thoughts creep through this irritable vegetable that I call my brain. I don't think I can endure London, the life here, through the opening of the play. Yet the demands of a return to America are frightening. If it weren't for grandfather I would retreat to Italy again or to N. Africa or Greece even though the car is here.

Frank is also here, of course, with a bad cold and we are sleeping in separate rooms.

Sandra died Thursday night, just as I was arriving at the hospital.

A shockingly bleak story, her life and the end of it.

The Greek orthodox service was deeply moving. I wept uncontrollably all through it. The music, singing, Chanting, the candles and the bearded bishop in his bell-shaped robe of purple and gold swinging the censor with ceremonial gestures. All so much richer than poor little Sandra's life. Her face in death was angelic.[793]

I thought, of course, of Rose.

For a long period today I literally did nothing. Just sat in a chair, nothing seeming worth doing. Finally dragged myself out to swim at the very dull

794. John Lehmann (1907–87) was an English writer, poet, publisher, and editor who joined the Hogarth Press in 1938 and went on to found his own publishing firm in 1946. Another of his sisters was the novelist Rosamond Lehmann. From 1948 to 1952 John Lehmann Ltd. acted as Williams' British publisher.

795. The Athenaeum Club, located at 107 Pall Mall, was founded in 1824 as an association of individuals known for their scientific and literary achievement and patronage.

796. In the play, Miss Cornelia Scott, a sixty-year-old southern spinster, waits at home with her fragile secretary, Miss Grace Lancaster, for news of whether she has been chosen unanimously to be Regent of the Confederate Daughters. Cornelia brings up the fact that she feels that there is something unspoken between them that ought to be discussed. Grace eventually concedes:

> You say there's something unspoken. Maybe there is. I don't know. But I do know some things are better left unspoken. Also I know that when a silence between two people has gone on for a long time it's like a wall that's impenetrable between them!

797. Williams conveyed his enthusiasm for the potential play production in a letter to Maria Britneva on 17 November 1951:

> Right now we are suspended in air, waiting breathlessly for Marlon Brando to make up his mind. He is the only one that seems right to play the male lead in both short plays, and he is interested but claims that he needs a week in which to consult his analyst about it and make the proper spiritual adjustment. (*FOA*, p. 49)

Despite Williams' tentative optimism, the plan for the two one-acts would fizzle due to lack of financing and Kazan's unwillingness to commit. Williams would soon turn to developing "Ten Blocks on the Camino Real" into a full-length play.

John Lehmann

International Sportsman's Club and that will probably be the high point of the day now beginning, as well. No, "this place no good". <u>En Avant</u>.

*Monday, 15 October 1951*

Mon. 6:30 A.M.

The noises of Jermyn Street have started.

Today I will drop by rehearsals and unless I am terribly pleased by the way the show is shaping up, will immediately make bookings for America, first available ship.

Last night dinner with John Lehmann. Of course I was indiscreet and spilled all my resentment over treatment (or lack of it) by H.M. Tennent, in the presence of the actress-sister, Beatrix, who shot out of the house right afterwards with an air of satisfaction.[794] John was pleasant. we dined at his club The Athenaeum[795] and had a lovely white Alsacien wine called Tarmenter (1949), but poor food.

Frank was recovered enough to go to a movie and afterwards the nightingales gave a concert.

A better Sunday than most. But the standard of Sundays in my life is not at all a high one.

I worked not badly early in the day on a 1-Act "Something Unspoken"[796] – just about finished. So – till later.

*Tuesday, 20 November 1951*

Nov. 20 – I think

Back in Manhattan – Gladstone hotel – So far so good – except that I am too busy, and consequently too tired most of the time, to be very friendly to my old friends – and some will take offense.

Work on "Camino" seems to be going well.[797]

Knock wood!

Summer and Smoke *premiered in London on 22 November. It was well received with favorable comments from the press.* Punch *(5 December 1951) called it "a moving commentary on the tragic side of love and a delicately understanding treatment of emotional panic." Williams wrote to Peter Glenville, the director of the English production ([late November 1951], HRC), "The report on 'S. & S.' is the most gratifying thing that's happened to me in a long time."*

798.  James Laughlin and Gertrude Huston (1919–98). Huston designed book jackets for New Directions. She became Laughlin's third wife in 1990.

799.  On 29 February 1952, Williams delivered to James Laughlin a group of fifty-eight poems, which Williams had graded A to E. While most of the poems had already been published, some of them he described as "reworks." The majority would be chosen for the volume *In the Winter of Cities*, which did not appear until 1956. With a few exceptions, the rest would be included in the collection *Androgyne, Mon Amour* (1977).

800.  Williams wrote "A Moment in a Room" in Key West in March 1952.

A MOMENT IN A ROOM

Coarse fabrics are the ones
for common wear,
the tender ones are those
we fold away.

For time's not cheated by
a moment's quiet,
the heart beats echo to
eternal riot,

And so I watch you quietly
comb your hair.
Intimate the silence,
dim and warm.

The cock must crow his fading
stars among,
the lie is only waiting
on the tongue!

I could but do not break
a thing so still,
in which almost a whisper
would be shrill.

But while it waits, I speak not
false to you,
something unspoken in
the room is true,

It is delusion that
this quiet could bloom
a timeless something in
one little room,

And still it goes as though
it longed to stay,
this tender moment we
must fold away.

Williams would include approximately half the stanzas of "A Moment in a Room" in the two distinct poems "Across the Space" and "We Have Not Long to Love."

801.  Williams was adding a studio and swimming pool to his Key West house.

802.  Williams was attempting to write a film script based on the four one-act plays that Kazan had considered directing six months earlier. On 10 February 1952 (NYPL), Williams had written to Cheryl Crawford about the film's progress:
> The film is going great. . . . I think it is going to be a very original and strong picture. We're using "Wagons" "Solid Gold Watches" "Property Condemned" and "The Unsatisfactory Supper" and the transitions have worked very smoothly so that it all seems to be of one piece.

The film script for *Baby Doll* (1956) would be based on two of the plays, "27 Wagons Full of Cotton" and "The Long Stay Cut Short, or The Unsatisfactory Supper." In a 1971 interview, Kazan explained the evolution:
> Then I began working on the movie, a little bit here and a little bit there, just to feel it out, and I kept facing the problem of structure, and instead of doing what I first thought, an anthology movie, I decided to make a unified movie. I threw out *This Property is Condemned* and *The Last of My Solid Gold Watches*, but I used *The Unsatisfactory Supper*, that is the old lady and the scene of the supper. (Michel Ciment, *Kazan on Kazan* [London: Secker & Warburg, 1973], p. 74)

*February 1952*

Key West, Fla

Spent evening with Jay and Gertrude.[798] F. and Bigelow joined us in bar and we saw a dull strip show. F. took off by himself as usual and I came home to read over a bunch of my old poems that Jay wants prepared for a volume.[799] They're pretty thin & dull, most of them. I'm a dull boy. have been for a long time. Can't really blame F. for not desiring my company anymore.

Mother left yesterday – a sad visit. I was too shy to be pleasant.

Grandfather is languishing.

I am sad and lonely.

It is 3 A.M. and Frank is still out –

I've taken a sleeping tablet but I'll find it hard to sleep tonight. The same old dull tedious resentment and hurt – why do relationships have to be turned into duels. I dont want to fight – I want to trust and love and feel loved. or at least liked – not barely tolerated – Oh shit – what's the way out?

Still trying to figure.

I'm afraid my brain is suffering from chronic fatigue – I just don't seem capable of clear, incisive thought except at rare moments – mornings lift the cloud a little – but evenings – I can't hardly put words together. And life seems more preposterous all the time. Well, there is never any harm in trying to keep your head, a cool one, in any situation. Rage, explosions are simply destructive. There is always a reason. No one is really guilty. You've said that often and believed it. Or is it an aphorism of yours? You know that whether or not guilt is real – some people do behave meanly and brutally whatever the reason may be and others try not to and more frequently are kind. Are you sure which you are? Well, I'm sure that I try to be kind, and that I do have love in my heart for Frank, which he seems to despise. Why? Because he feels confined by me – his dependance. And isn't reasonable enough to understand that that circumstance was and still is his choice.

That balcony bedroom on the Lido in Venice – I think of it tonight. Nothing has changed much – but time goes on. I go on with it still.

*Friday, 7 March 1952*

Fri. 2:30 A.M. (March 6)

A fairly pleasant day

the sea perfect for swim

some work on poems[800]

a fairly entertaining film – Frank in a good humor for a change.

He picked up a sailor at the Cayo Hueso but didn't make out, it seems.

Work on studio progressing rapidly.[801]

Everyone seems pleased with the film script.[802]

No complaints for a change. Goodnight

803.   Williams had written to Cheryl Crawford on 10 February 1952 (NYPL) about being encouraged that she
       was interested in *Camino Real*. He added:

> I have gotten hold of the unabridged (12 volumes) Memoirs of Casanova and Dumas novel
> "Camille" and the material in the play is now based on the real histories of those characters. I think
> the play is essentially a plastic poem on the romantic attitude toward life.

Jacques Casanova de Seingalt (1725–98) was an Italian adventurer who, after being expelled from a
Venetian seminary for misconduct, led a life as a charlatan, gambler, and lover who traveled around
Europe. His fortunes vacillated, and he ended his career as librarian at Count Waldstein's castle in Bohemia.
His *Mémoires* (1826–37) are considered unreliable but of great historical interest.

804.   A few days earlier (14 April 1952, HRC), Williams had written Audrey Wood about the story which he
       started the previous summer in Venice:

> I think it has the situation and characters for a play or a film, eventually. I spoke of it to Jay while
> he was here and he thought it would make a good title story for a collection of stories that he wants
> to bring out along with the selected poems.

Paul Bigelow and Williams with sailors

Dinner on S.S. *Liberté*

*Saturday, 8 March 1952*

Sat. March 8 4 A.M.
> Shit!
> drunk – sleepy
> a moderately pleasant encounter with a ¾ German.
> Piddling work on a poem this A.M.
> dull, rainy P.M.
> movie –
> Now Casanova's memoirs[803] –

*Wednesday, 16 April or Thursday, 17 April 1952*

April 16 or 17
> We're breaking camp now. Frank and grandfather leave in the Jaguar tomorrow for New Orleans. Oliver and I proceed a couple days later in Oliver's new Cadillac, a happy consequence of his father's demise. I've been working on "3 Players of a Summer Game" – The writing is stiff.[804] But "Camino" seems to be getting under control and if I have some good days in New Orleans or Columbus, it will be out of the woods when I arrive in New York, though I wonder if any producer could raise enough money for it.
> I am not restored, but I feel fairly self-possessed.
> My ass-hole is sore. Piles again. I look worn and faded. I think the trip will pick me up and I am not depressed. I shall keep the flag flying bravely as I can. So <u>En Avant</u>!

Later –
> a series of queer feelings as if close to extinction – ~~brea~~ air hunger? – just as I am about to fall asleep, the last one with a twinge of pain in the chest – alarm me so much that I get up and go downstairs for a drink and take a seconal tablet.
> This occured after fucking.
> Now I feel fairly calm but don't want to sleep for a while if I can help it.

*Tuesday, 10 June 1952*

June 10 – Sail tomorrow on the Liberté but without the car, owing to negligence on part of Liebling-Wood. Fucks up the whole trip – adds enormously to our difficulties.
> I have been on edge for quite a while – very narrow margin indeed.
> Breathlessness at night, tension daily – diarrhea every A.M.
> F. has been pleasant enough but sort of separate.

805.  José Quintero's (1924–99) production of *Summer and Smoke* opened at the Circle in the Square, in Greenwich Village's Sheridan Square, on 24 April with Geraldine Page as Alma. It was the surprise hit of the season and ran for over a year. It was a pivotal point in the careers of Quintero and Page and is credited with launching the Off-Broadway movement. "The day after *Summer and Smoke* opened," Quintero, who had co-founded the Circle in the Square, wrote in his autobiography *If You Don't Dance They Beat You* (Boston: Little, Brown and Company, 1972), "we became a success. I had never known what success was, but somehow in the United States things happen overnight. They give you no time for preparation" (p. 119).

In a letter to Maria Britneva dated 27 May 1952, Williams wrote that José Quintero was his "new enthusiasm in the world of drama." "If Gadg quits the theatre, which seems likely, now, Quintero will be, at last, another director that I could work with" (*FOA*, p. 56). Quintero went on to direct *Camino Real* (1960, Circle in the Square at St. Mark's Playhouse, New York), the film version of *The Roman Spring of Mrs. Stone* (1961), and the Broadway premieres of *The Seven Descents of Myrtle* (1968) and *Clothes for a Summer Hotel* (1980).

806.  Williams' landlady at 45 via Aurora. In "A Terribly Sad Story," a short story set (and most likely written) at this time, Williams named the landlady Mariella and described her as having "greeted [Robert] with her usual slightly mechanical but nevertheless warm-hearted effusiveness."

807.  Anna Magnani (1908–73), the Italian stage and film actress, starred in the film version of *The Rose Tattoo* directed by Daniel Mann which premiered on 12 December 1955. She won an Academy Award for her role of Serafina, and five years later she would star in *The Fugitive Kind* with Marlon Brando. In a letter started on 8 July 1952 and modified on the 14th (Wesleyan), Williams wrote Kazan: "Tomorrow I'm having lunch with Magnani's lawyer. She is not only willing but eager to do 'Tattoo' in America in May."

Despite Williams' optimism, Magnani, fearful that her English was inadequate for Broadway, declined, and the role of Serafina was given to Maureen Stapleton (1925–2006).

808.  In a letter to Kazan started on 8 July and modified on the 14th (Wesleyan), Williams explained his reason for traveling to Hamburg:

You can't believe the heat here in Rome unless you are sitting right in the middle of it! I have made train reservations for Hamburg. . . . It will be easier to think and work there.

809.  According to Gore Vidal, Frank McGackin was in the antiques business and later settled in Greece.

José Quintero                                    Anna Magnani

"Camino" typed up – I haven't dared read it yet. My biggest hope now is Quintero. The village success of "Summer & Smoke" best thing that I've had this year.[805]

*Tuesday, 8 July 1952*

Rome – July 8.

Back in the Eternal City.

Work continues to go well which is, after all, most important.

Rome about the same but hotter than usual this summer. We're back at Mariella's.[806] I get awfully tired at night. Last night two superb young Italo-Austrians from Cortina came home with me. We all took a shower and it was gay. But alone with one, I was too Conscious of the other alone in the parlor where I keep my money, so it didn't quite come off. Frank was out till 5 A.M. "Pleasant but sort of separate" describes the situation still. Am I morbidly suspicious? My attitude is that "romps in the hay" – "trade" – no matter how often – within reasonable limits – is fair and sensible in a homosexual alliance of long standing but that if one or the other starts cultivating close and extended intimacy with a third party, then it becomes a cheat, and someone is "The Patsy".

I had practically no trade in Key West, literally none in N.Y. – but two adventures here, which is the right place for it.

Smashed the car again yesterday – hit a concrete post in the Villa Borghese. But driving slowly and only the fender was smashed. However, I'm worried about my reflexes or eyesight. The right eye is getting undependable.

Seeing Magnani's mgr. this eve. about "Tattoo".[807] <u>En Avant</u>

*Tuesday, 15 July 1952*

Tuesday July 15 (?)

Reached that point here when work stops and I just stare at the machine in the mornings.

But I have a membership at the Country Club now, and the water in the pool is sparkling cool. This improves the afternoons which had become so tedious. However it's a long ways out and I can never find my way easily about Rome.

Leave for Hamburg on Friday.[808]

*Friday, 18 July 1952*

Friday – On the train, 2 hours out of Rome, drinking some chianti & taken a secconal as I got little sleep last night. The night was pleasant. Spent with a sweet American Frank McGachan,[809] while "The Horse" was laying Italian in

810. In a letter to Oliver Evans (5 August 1952, HRC), Williams elaborated:

> My dear, I was in Hamburg last week and guess who was staying in the same hotel! Miss Otis Taylor, the last of the Edwardian Aunties! We did the town together several nights, and I must say she is the most agreeable and charming company and I like her extremely much. There are three or four bars in Hamburg where the boys dance together and your sister did not miss a dance! She was the belle of the balls! Great strapping blonds whirled her about the floor to the Waltzes of Strauss, pursued her along the waterfront, kissed her among the ruins and seduced her incontinently between the cabarets. They would not allow her to rest. If they could not enter the hotel with her, which was, alas, often the case, owing to the manly roughness of their apparel, such was the heat of their passion that nothing would do but she must retire with them into the bushes. At one point she had to remain quite immobile, as if turned to marble, for about twenty minutes, in a peculiarly intimate pose with a Herculean blond who was resting his forehead on the trunk of a tree, while a policeman smoked a cigarette not ten yards away on the banks of the Alster. Eclogues and bucolics!
>
> Why have you removed Athens from your itinerary? Miss Taylor says it is not to be believed, especially a certain park in the center of town. . . . I am about ready to take another trip. Rome is cool and lovely, now, and trade is abundant. . . . I walked and taxied all about Hamburg from midnight till five in the morning looking for a room where I could have a private conversation with one of my dancing partners. Not a room anywhere. At daybreak and after, we wound up in a whore house that rented us a bed for half an hour. You can't bring people into the good hotels after dark.

811. After the failed production of *Battle of Angels* in Boston in 1940, Williams was given a check for $200 by the Theatre Guild and "told to get off somewhere and rewrite the play" — an assignment he attempted in spring 1945 but did not begin in earnest until the early 1950s and would not finish until 1957. In an essay published on the eve of its production (*New York Times*, 17 March 1957), Williams gave his reasons for "sticking so stubbornly" to this play:

> [N]othing is more precious to anybody than [the] emotional record of his youth, and you will find the trail of my sleeve-worn heart in the completed play that I now call *Orpheus Descending*. . . .
>
> . . . [Y]ou see it is a very old play that *Orpheus Descending* has come out of, but a play is never an old one until you quit working on it. . . . About 75 per cent of it is new writing, but what is much more important, I believe that I have now finally managed to say in it what I wanted to say, and I feel that it now has in it a sort of emotional bridge between those early years . . . and my present state of existence as a playwright.

Despite the "new writing," the story of *Battle of Angels* and *Orpheus Descending* remained the same — "the tale of a wild-spirited boy who wanders into a conventional community of the South and creates the commotion of a fox in a chicken coop."

Photograph given to Frank Merlo by Mariella, Williams' landlady

apartment. Have been sexually cool toward "Horse" lately – not sure why. Think I'll enjoy this trip – change should be stimulating. After heavy atmosphere of Rome. So far it's better than last summer, although the summer neurosis – fear of speech – still plagues me a good deal at times. It always comes on me in summer for some unknown reason.

Reading Cervantes. Love him. En Avant.

Later – 11:30 P.M. We are stopped at Basel and I don't know whether that is Swiss or German. The people look like Krauts to me. Taken a seconal but doubt I get much sleep. Suspect I'll have a bit of a scrap with my nerves on this excursion. They feel tight. Still, you never can tell. I may all of a sudden relax and be a perfect angel. When I get away from The Horse I realize how much he represents "home" to me. Feel unsafe without him. Therefore these trips are good for my morale. Now more Cervantes as the train goes on. Hamburg 10 A.M. We must hope for the best.

*Saturday, 19 July 1952*

First day in Hamburg. Not too good. 3 gay bars where the boys dance together but there is something hard and cold about it. Real Prostitution and "clipping". No warmth. Made date for tomorrow afternoon with a beauty but I suspect the character is N.G.

Feel more lost here than I did in Munich or Venice. Much more. Neurosis, and also the quality of the place.

*Monday, 21 July 1952*

Monday – Now in more attractive quarter – The Atlantic hotel – neurosis lifted.

*Monday, 28 July 1952*

The remainder of the trip was pleasant. I stayed six days and had 3 lays – none memorable – but enjoyed the dancing in the gay bars and the companionship of an elderly American queen Otis Taylor,[810] a young German, Reinhart Wolf – who took some photos of me for the papers – and a young Brazilian Ruy Duarte who says he is the Vicomte d'Orleans et Burgundy.

Traveling alone in a 1st class wagon-lits compartment is one of the pleasantest things that you can do in Europe. It was delightfully cool in Hamburg – the hotel was charming – all in all, since I did some good work there, the trip was a good change, although a short one, now back to Rome, with renewed interest. The pool at the club and the new impetus on "Battle of Angels"[811] will help to pass the time

812.  Williams responded to Kazan (29 July 1952, Wesleyan):

Your letter gave me a jolt when I found it this morning on my return from Hamburg. I'm not so disturbed over Jo's reactions, disturbing as they are, as I am by the feeling that you have been seriously affected by them. What with his "very negative reaction" and Cheryl's disappointment and confusion, I think it is remarkable that your own interest and faith in the play still survives. Mine is indestructible. . . .

Now about Jo: do you still think he ought to design this show? I don't think he is "with it" in body or spirit, and I don't see how he can move from a "v. negative" reaction to a "v. positive" reaction, and unless he does, how can he contribute the sort of passionate enthusiasm and conviction out of which a really good piece of work has to come?

813.  Jo Mielziner (1901–76) was the most influential American theatrical set designer of his generation. He was noted for his use of simultaneous settings that allowed the action to flow uninterrupted from one set to another. Mielziner had designed sets for three of Williams' plays, *The Glass Menagerie*, *A Streetcar Named Desire* (for which he won a Donaldson Award), and *Summer and Smoke*. Mielziner wrote Williams a month later (26 August 1952, HRC) about the set design:

Now in regard to "Camino Real". I felt like an ungrateful dog to criticize a script that is so packed with excitement and beauty! I suppose it was my desire to have this be your greatest script of all.

Gadge and I have talked over some general scenic ideas based on an extreme simplification. Perhaps the basic set might take a physical form which suggested some sort of a bear pit, as though Kilroy were trapped in a place where there is no obvious physical escape. Perhaps some sort of a "labyrinth". I hope we could find ways of using projected images and patterns and colors to fulfill your suggestion of the constant changes in the various blocks. Of course, physical props that actors dealt with would have to be three-dimensional, but I am convinced that some style in physical production must unite these ten blocks.

The following month ([September 1952], NYPL), Williams wrote Mielziner:

[*Camino Real*] is an intensely romantic script, and it needs a magic background. . . . I think the plaza should have the haunting loveliness of one of those lonely-looking plazas and colonades in a Chirico.

He did not understand Mielziner's "bear pit" idea and eventually rejected it. Lemuel Ayers was ultimately chosen to design the sets.

814.  Frank Merlo's local lover.

815.  James Merrill (1926–95), son of Charles E. Merrill, one of the founders of the investment bank Merrill Lynch, moved to Rome in 1950 after his first book of poems was accepted for publication. Merrill, who once described his poetry as "chronicles of love and loss," would go on to become one of the leading poets of his generation, known especially for his skillful use of rhyme and meter.

Set design by Jo Mielziner for *Camino Real*

pleasantly and I feel that I must be more understanding of F. What else have I got, after all, but the "Horse" and my memories? and my work. Pulling the petals of a daisy to find out if he loves me will do no good. It is more important to love than be loved. Just passed Como – descending, now, into the hot northern plains. <u>En Avant</u>!

### Tuesday, 29 July 1952

Tuesday – July 29

Rome. No change except the fairly important one of being cooler – rain twice since I got here. And, oh, yes, a discouraging letter about "Camino" from Gadg[812] – reporting Jo's[813] "v. negative" reaction and reflecting some discouragement of his own. I had hoped for too much, but I am not crushed by this retrenchment. My health seems better. I got up at 8:20. But only wrote a letter to Gadg. F. still asleep. His intimacy with Alvarro[814] seems to occupy his whole life here. It goes on a day and night basis. I exist rather separately. No friends here. But Oliver may be approaching. The pool at the club is my great daily comfort – ice cold, sparkling clean water in which I swim 20 lengths a day with ease and pleasure.

### Saturday, 2 August 1952

Aug. 2 – Situation unchanged. But today I feel even more discouraged about work. I didn't get enough sleep – woke at eight. Had coffee but it gave me no stimulation and when I read over yesterday's work it seemed bad. No word from anyone in New York since Gadg's negative letter and I suspect the project is in a process of dissolution.

Irene supposed to arrive in Rome today. I don't feel like exposure to her penetrating gaze. Perhaps in a few days I will take off for somewhere and Alvarro can move into the apartment. Now I'll get dressed, visit Amexco, have a bite of solitary lunch – then the flight to the cold pool in the country. What else can I do?

### Saturday, 9 August 1952

Aug. 9 –

Woke up last night from a dream in which I had missed a bus. My sister was on it. I managed to stop the bus, but the case containing my Mss. wasn't on it.

Madness in place of art?

The bus was a low, red vehicle, shaped like a racing car.

Today I'm supposed to meet a young poet named James Merrill, who is said to be very wealthy, <u>and</u> a good poet!!?[815] This is part of a policy to make some sort of society for myself here. After this last desperate attack on "Camino" I will need to divert myself with somebody or something, if I can.

816. On 24 July 1952 (NYPL), Kazan had written Williams a long letter with detailed suggestions for the reorganization and rewriting of the play. He finished the letter by noting that he would be in Munich in August (to work on the film *Man on a Tightrope*), and he urged Williams to meet him there to continue working on *Camino Real*.

A number of the suggestions Kazan made in his letter were adopted. For example, Williams substituted Marguerite for Jacques in the scene with Kilroy in Block Fourteen as an opportunity for Marguerite to develop compassion for Jacques.

Kazan's active role in the development of *Camino Real* would be repeated in subsequent collaborative efforts. Williams' response to Kazan's participation would remain ambivalent and complex. While he welcomed the clarity of vision of a great director, he at times resented Kazan's intrusion and attempts to dominate the creative process.

In his letter, Kazan made some general points, including emphasizing that the Kilroy story should remain the emotional center of the play and that the central theme of the play was "How to get out of this place! . . . Symbolically . . . how to die with dignity and honor and gallantry?" Kazan's specific points related to a suggested rearrangement of material and inclusion of parts of the December 1951 script.

*Saturday, 16 August 1952*

Aug. ? –

In Munich with Kazan. His latest notes on Camino, a virtual return to the original script, are a depressing blow as they show the deterioration of my position. I have fallen off remarkably in the esteem of my co-workers when they start dictating my work to me.[816] I must try to be calm and reasonable. Take whatever good ideas are offered but hold the line when a demoralizing retreat is proposed.

The city is cool – at least – left Rome and Frank under strained circumstances.


*Sunday, 17 August 1952*

Sun. night –

"Quelle misère! "This place no good." Not even worth talking about. Doubt that anything can be accomplished with Gadg. Too discouraged to do good work. It seems that I am falling back on all fronts – see no end to it. Retreat is limitless this side of death. That doesn't make much sense – days go by so fast. fading, fading. Leave no mark but fatigue. It becomes so huge. It blocks out everything. Self pity? No. I say that with conviction. Perhaps I am even too tired to pity myself. I live quite alone really – a single cell. Lost among many. Curiously calm though. Not deeply "engagé". "Your hat is not in the ring" Tony Smith said to me eight years ago – no, nine. That is now even truer. I work as hard as I can but there is an inner dissociation. A bleak detachment. Maybe it makes me unreal to people & that is why they can't love me.


*Wednesday, 20 August 1952*

Wed.

Yesterday eve we read over the work I've done on Camino under Gadg's direction. He kept snorting and exclaiming, oh, this is wonderful! the way a doctor tells a dying man what perfect condition he's in. It seemed to me like one long agonized wail and I couldn't go out to eat with him. Said excuse me but I think I'll go cruising now.

I found somebody, but such halitosis my interest expired. drank 4½ Scotches. Took 2 sleeping tablets. Dreamed of failure. dreamed that I was examining a Ms. to find out why It didn't read right and concluded that too many words were underlined and syllables extended! Perhaps the unconscious mind provided a good analysis. Excessive intensity may be the reason it doesn't come off – that and insufficient pure impulse or energy.

817.  Literally "holiday in August." *Ferrogosto* begins on 15 August and marks the part of the summer when businesses close.

818.  Henry R. Luce (1898–1967) co-founded *Time* in 1923 and six years later became editor-in-chief (1929–64). He went on to start *Fortune*, *Life*, and *Sports Illustrated* and soon was considered to be the most influential magazine publisher in the United States and also one of the most controversial. His critics believed that *Time* reflected his personal leanings which tended toward Republicanism, anti-communism, and internationalism.

819.  Williams expressed his ire by giving the name of this country club, the Circolo de Golfo, to the retreat of a corrupt general in the September 1952 draft of *Camino Real*.

820.  In 1952, Whittaker Chambers (1901–61) had published *Witness*, his best-selling account of his life leading up to his participation in the trial of his friend Alger Hiss. Chambers accused Hiss, a polished State Department lawyer and head of the Carnegie Endowment for International Peace, of being a Soviet spy. Chambers had earlier been a Communist and served as a spy for Soviet intelligence. He became disillusioned with communism and left the party in 1938 and joined the staff of *Time*. Chambers was adamantly opposed to liberalism and felt any "New Deal" type of social reform would bring about totalitarianism.

Richard Nixon, then a young congressman on the House Committee on Un-American Activities, was very involved in the prosecution of Hiss.

821.  Williams wrote to Kazan on the previous day (23 August 1952, Wesleyan):
Current issue of "Time". . . . They are taking the gloves off. The Divine Nixon is on the cover! He looks like the gradeschool bully that used to wait for me behind a broken fence and twist my ear to make me say obscene things. Quote from "Time": "The ordinary man may be less confused than many an 'intellectual' . . . It is part of Nixon's job to show that if Americans want to rid themselves of Communism and left-wingism at home, they must throw the Democrats out." — Out in the open at last: the sneaking raid on all liberal thought and feeling under the transparent pretext of stamping out reds. What does "left-wingism" mean to the Luce gang except a free and enlightened and humane and articulate voice of America? Finished "Witness" with a feeling of awe. The episode of the microfilm in the pumpkin, the receptacle with lethal chemicals and damp-towel, somehow missing fire — couldn't read the directions because of bad eyesight, towel fell off in his sleep — is quite sufficient in itself to put the whole business in the "Ritz Men ONLY." Jesus, what's going on?! Nixon has also come out for McCarthy! Will support his candidacy without necessarily endorsing all his views, and says Eisenhower will, too. We must get to the States for this election, Brother . . .
[Postscript] Burn this letter, or hide it in a pumpkin!

822.  In his diary, Noël Coward (1899–1973), British actor and playwright, wrote:
*Monday 25 August*
Lunched at the Capriccio. Wandered about Rome — it is an exquisite city but, at the moment, trampled flat by Americans. Called on Tennessee Williams, who has an apartment of desperate squalor. We went out and sat outside Rosati's and watched the world go by. It was pleasant enough, but I longed to be alone, so took a *carrozza* and had a short drive before going home to bed.
*Tuesday 26 August*
I dined with Tennessee, and we drove out along the Appian Way and looked at all the ruins — lovely except for the horror of Tennessee's driving. I cannot imagine how he got a licence — he admits cheerfully that he cannot see with one eye and cannot drive at all, and yet he has a Jaguar. On the way back we ran out of *essence*, but were able to coast to a petrol station. After this we got lost and drove about wildly in several different directions! It was all very light-hearted, although a trifle dangerous. Not really so, however, because I made him drive slowly. We missed a few trams and buses by inches and finally, at long last, I got to my bed. (*The Noël Coward Diaries*, edited by Graham Payn and Sheridan Morley [London: Phoenix, 1982], p. 197)
Coward would play the role of the Witch of Capri in *Boom!* (1968), the film version of *The Milk Train Doesn't Stop Here Anymore*.

*Sunday, 24 August 1952*

<u>Sunday in August</u> – Ferrogosto[817] – Last night was pleasant. Went to see Carmen at Terme de Caracalle – thrilling opera – interrupted in Act III by a violent windstorm which blew over the mountain scenery. Was with Salvatore, Gil Phillips, Jetti Preninger and her young husband from Clayton and the relations were pleasant – S. spent the night with me. The sex was agreeable but hardly ecstatic and I felt indifferent, basically. There's a touch of the courtesan about him now. The innocense isn't there anymore. Of course he has no reason to show me another side of his nature. He does rather nice little "nature morte" oil paintings and is by no means reluctant to sell me one of them. No money was exchanged between us.

Today, Sunday, was dreary enough. Work was out of the question – I had drunk too much last night – but I bought "The New Yorker" and Mr. Luce's revoltingly interesting publication[818] and lay in bed reading and napping all the P.M. Dreams of loneliness and rejection, involving my sister, but in a curiously changed personality as though she was a disguise for someone else. Scene in a hospital room. My dreams indicate that I am deeply lonely and unsure of myself – F. and my work – frustration.

Tomorrow a lot to do. Rewrite a scene – then get off several letters. No word from F. who is reported to be in Sicily. Alone? A street boy Filippo told me some disturbing things but may be lies. I don't know.

Unpleasant scene at the club where I swim.[819] The Mgr. called me from the pool to say "guests had protested that Salvatore had gone in swimming without taking a shower". Shouldn't have taken him out there. May result in loss of the pool which was my great and almost only comfort here this summer. Hate rich Italians! Prosperity doesn't seem to benefit their natures. Perhaps it is the upper middle class or "new rich" that give this impression – S. was perfectly clean – always is.

Still reading Whittaker Chambers hideous book[820] with loathing and fascination. Current issue of "Time" extolls him and attacks "Left Wingism" – must be eliminated![821] Intellectuals and liberals are more and more openly the real target of Luce gang.


*Tuesday, 26 August 1952*

Tues. Eve

It should be mentioned that I have been happy these past few days. Noel Coward[822] in town. Find him good company. He praises my work! Perhaps he praises everyone's work, but that is better than despising everyone's work as some other writers I know.

F. still away. And no word. I feel a bit rancorous about it, but I shall not be tiresome and beat my breast. If he doesn't get back Tomorrow, Thursday, I shall drive to Naples on Friday and let him wonder where <u>I</u> am, if he cares. Nothing, perhaps, would suit him better than that.

On the other hand, I hope he is having a good time, since I'm not having a bad time – work <u>seems</u> to be going well.

823.  Several years earlier, Williams had written to Carson McCullers (18 June 1949, Duke):
      Truman and Auden and Chester [Kallman] and various other of the spiteful sisterhood were all clus-
      tered on the little island of Ischia for several months but all at once there was some convulsion
      among them and they all came off at once. Truman and his paramour passed through town for a
      few days last week, Auden and Chester also at the same time. There was a great collision in the pub-
      lic rooms of the Inghilterra (hotel) all hissing and flapping like geese, and there are rumors that the
      island of Ischia has dropped back under the sea.

824.  Sam Langford (d. 1958) was the Irish-born companion of Brian Howard (1905–58), English poet and aes-
      thete who became friends with Auden at Oxford. After serving in the British navy during World War II,
      Langford lived abroad with Howard.

W. H. Auden and Chester Kallman

*Thursday, 4 September or Friday, 5 September 1952*

Thurs. or Fri. Sept. 6 or 7 –

There is the usual sun. 3 days ago wired Audrey that I was mailing final script of Camino but it's still here and I'm trying to read through it. No wings apparent in the text so far. And such a long time on it! What a terribly tired old boy I've gotten to be.

Stopped now. Will go out to pacify my spirit with vino and a bit of lunch and the pool at the club. Crowd of decadent English here. Ran afoul of them at Toto's and they called me a "3rd rate writer" – Said I'd settle for sixth. They are the "Ischia shits"[823] who suck the ass of Auden. One of them, a boy named Sam Langford,[824] is interesting and nice. Maybe only because he wants me to buy him drinks. A little friendliness means a great deal now. Frank being very sweet, lately. We leave Oct. 2nd. I'm so tired. Hope something will revive me. <u>En Avant</u>

---

*Williams returned to the United States and spent the remaining months of the autumn in New York working on* Camino Real *with Elia Kazan. He returned to Key West for the Christmas holidays. By the second week of February Williams was back in New York, where he stayed for the opening of* Camino Real.

---

Elia Kazan reading the script of *Camino Real*

825.   Williams refers to the journal entry for 1 February 1951 in which he had anticipated the opening of *The Rose Tattoo* in New York: "Two more days, and we will know. Last night we had our first New York audience, invited." *Camino Real* previewed in New Haven and Philadelphia and opened in New York on 19 March 1953. It ran until 9 May 1953.

826.   Williams named his dog after Mr. Moon, the night porter at the Cavendish Hotel in London.

827.   *The Denton Welch Journals,* edited by Jocelyn Brooke (London: Hamish Hamilton, 1952). Denton Welch (1915–48), writer and painter, was born in Shanghai and educated in England at Repton and the Goldsmith School of Art. In June 1935, aged twenty, he was knocked off his bicycle by a car and suffered injuries from which he later died. Welch's published work includes the autobiographical novels *Maiden Voyage* (1943), *In Youth Is Pleasure* (1945), and *A Voice Through a Cloud* (1950), an account of the accident and the months spent in a hospital, which was not quite finished at the time of his death. In addition, two collections of his short stories were published posthumously, *Brave and Cruel* (1949) and *A Last Sheaf* (1951).
       The journals cover the period 1942–48 and record, for the most part, spontaneous impressions of daily life and, increasingly toward the end, Welch's feelings of the transitory nature of existence.
       In the postscript to a letter ([11 March 1945], Houghton), Williams recommended James Laughlin read *Maiden Voyage* "to understand Charles Henri [Ford] Etc. — a lovely book!"

828.   In the 1950s, Paul Bowles spent time in Ceylon and, for a brief period, owned Taprobane, a small island off the southern tip of Ceylon. In his autobiography, *Without Stopping* (New York: G. P. Putnam's Sons, 1972), Bowles wrote about his first visit to Ceylon: "I was constantly exhilarated by the light, the climate, and the vegetation; this euphoria kept me walking most of the day" (p. 298).

829.   Williams did dedicate *Camino Real* to Kazan.

830.   According to Vidal, Monty Delmar was a boxer who aspired to be a writer.

Williams with his grandfather and Mr. Moon

*Tuesday, 10 February 1953*

Feb. 1953.
  A lot of empty pages remain in this book so I will use it again.
  The situation is very parallel to the one at which the journal left off. Once again I'm awaiting the opening of a new play <u>Camino Real</u>.[825] Yesterday we had our first run-through of 2 Acts – profoundly depressing. But Gadg remained strong – apparently confident and his spirit bolstered mine.
  A few nights ago I had a very frightening attack of the kind that occurs sometimes when I'm falling asleep or in sleep – the feeling of "imminent extinction" – A real scarey one – as if my heart had stopped beating – Usually occurs when I've over exerted. Too much strain coupled with drinking parties, used for relief.
  Grandfather, once again, is waiting for us in Key West. And once again I feel that the sea, the sun and the stars will be a most agreeable anodyne to this period of suspense.
  Oh, yes, we now have a pet – an English bull, remarkably homely creature – Mr. Moon.[826] But lovable. He is now snoring beside me. I have a book, Denton Welch's journal.[827] A drink – Scotch & soda and my secconal tablets should anxiety recur.
  Tonight dined with old friend Valentina Sheriff. I was sleepy but she seemed not to mind. A lonely woman. Lonely people always touch me and appeal to me. This summer the plan is Greece – and the Levantine – possibly even Ceylon! – recommended so highly by Paul Bowles.[828] Is it presumptuous of me to plan anything at all? <u>En Avant</u>!


*Friday, 20 February 1953*

Friday –
  A bad infection developed suddenly on my right leg. Doctor said it looked "worrisome" and shot me full of penicillin which makes me feel both tense and dopey. Very much on edge a while ago but Scotch & secconal are quieting me now. Mr. Moon snores beside me. I asked Frank to sleep in the other room as I like to be alone when I get very "edgy". The rehearsals are shaping up much better now. I feel hopeful again. Very close to Gadg and fond of him.
  I plan to inscribe the play to him.[829]
  Still reading Welch's journal which is delightful.
  Tomorrow – Monty Delmar.[830]
  Tonight – just dreams.

Hurd Hatfield as Don Quixote in *Camino Real*

Camino Real *opened on 19 March, received mostly negative reviews, and closed less than two months later. Walter Kerr wrote in the* New York Herald Tribune *(20 March 1953) that* Camino Real *was "the worst play yet written by the best playwright of his generation." In a long letter the following month (13 April 1953), Kerr responded to Williams' protest of his opinion. Kerr explained that* Camino Real *failed not because*

> *people are appalled at what is actually in the play; but . . . people are simply not able to get through it to your intention at all. . . . What terrifies me about "Camino Real" is not what you want to say but the direction in which you, as an artist, are moving. You're heading toward the cerebral; don't do it. What makes you an artist of the first rank is your intuitive gift for penetrating reality, without junking reality in the process; an intuitive artist starts with the recognizable surface of things and burrows in. Don't swap this for the conscious, rational processes of the analyst, the symbolist, the abstract thinker. (DLB, p. 139)*

Set design by Lemuel Ayers for *Camino Real*

831.  In a letter to Kazan (postmarked Le Havre 10 June 1953, Wesleyan), Williams wrote: "We had a curious embaracation. Frank's closest friends and mine assembled for drinks in the stateroom. A girl-friend of Frank's whom I had not met before became hysterical over his departure and had to be supported off the boat."

832.  William S. Gray (d. 1992) first met Williams in New York in 1948 and then in 1952 when he was a graduate student at Tulane University in New Orleans. Gray went on to become a professor of English at Randolph-Macon College in Ashland, Virginia. In his introduction to *A Look at Tennessee Williams,* by Mike Steen, Gray recalled Williams' faultless ear and eye for detail.

833.  Skipper McNally, a minor actor, was a good friend of Elia Kazan's and had a small part in Kazan's award-winning 1954 film *On the Waterfront*. In the postscript to a letter to Kazan dated 31 March 1954 (Wesleyan), Williams wrote about McNally's visit to Key West:

> Skipper was here and should have had him a ball. For some reason this year the island is over-run by beautiful nymphos, really attractive ones, who almost rape the men in public, let alone what they may do in private. They grope you at the bar and literally howl to be fucked. Won't take no for an answer if they can possibly get any other. I think Skipper was scared. He left mighty quick.

834.  George S. Kaufman (1889–1961) was a playwright and director, considered to be one of the founding fathers of the American popular theatre. Many of his plays had long and successful runs on Broadway. On all but one play, Kaufman collaborated with partners, including Marc Connelly, Edna Ferber, and Moss Hart. Two of his plays, *Of Thee I Sing* (1931) and *You Can't Take It with You* (1936), won Pulitzer Prizes. Williams borrowed the title of a play Kaufman wrote with Hart, *Once in a Lifetime*, a comedy about panic-stricken Hollywood trying to cope with the new talkies, for his 1939 play fragment about a tourist couple in Taos.

Kaufman's second wife was the actress and playwright Leueen MacGrath (1914–91). In a letter to Kazan (postmarked Le Havre 10 June 1953, Wesleyan), Williams added: "Became very friendly with the Kaufmans, George and Leueen, they are great fun."

Frith Banbury (1912– ) was also an actor and producer.

Postcard Williams sent to his mother from S.S. *United States*

*Friday, 5 June 1953*

June 5th 1953

Sailed today on the "United States" thus beginning another one of our summer's abroad and not auspiciously. A neurosis is worrying the ragged edges of my nerves and I was disturbed by a tearful scene put on by F's friend Ellen[831] in front of others. These suspicions of mine are tiresome. I must at least cut them out of my list of torments this summer. This summer! Hard to believe it's come around again – after "Camino" and all . . .

But here it is and has to be coped with. F. is sleeping. It isn't yet time for dinner so I'll go up for a martini or two and a look at the boat.

Bill Gray[832] cried a little as he said goodbye to me but by no means so copiously as Ellen did over F.

How could anyone manage to feel much concern over my coming and going I really don't know.

Have thought of death a lot lately –

Must try to "play it cool" as Skipper McNally[833] advised me in his letter from the Coast.

Yes, play it cool and have a cocktail now. En Avant!

*Saturday, 6 June 1953*

Saturday –

A rough time with the blue-devils close at my heels but me running hard still. Awful last night for a while and early this A.M. but letting up a bit now. And I'll go up for a light lunch & wine and a movie and swim later. Tonight dinner with George Kaufmann and his actress wife & Frith Banbary, the British director[834] – An amusing book to read and plenty of liquor aboard – But I'm putting on weight.

William S. Gray

835.  "Kingdom of Earth" is the dramatization of Williams' story begun in 1942 about the bastard son who, jealous of his tubercular brother who has inherited everything, seduces Myrtle, his brother's wife, and when his brother dies, marries her. Williams would eventually lengthen the title of the play to *Kingdom of Earth (The Seven Descents of Myrtle)*.

836.  *Baby Doll.*

837.  Robert Soule (1926– ) had designed the sets for the 1952 production of *The Glass Menagerie* at the Lenox Hill Playhouse, New York. He went on to design the set for the 1958 world premiere of *Garden District* (York Theatre, New York) and the set and costumes for a 1959 production of *Orpheus Descending* (Gramercy Arts Theatre, New York). In 1963 Soule designed a revised version of *The Milk Train Doesn't Stop Here Anymore* (Barter Theatre, Abingdon, Virginia).

Williams' "new apartment" at 11 via Firenze, Rome (first building on left)

*Saturday, 27 June or Sunday, 28 June 1953*

June 27 or 28 –

a new apartment in Rome with a terrace that catches the sun. A steep climb up four floors but an agreeable neighborhood next to the opera. work picking up after a bad time with it. F. has resumed his summer routine, days with Alvarro. At night we dine together at home or at Capriccio's or the Tre Scalini and the ½ litre of wine makes me so sleepy that I sometimes doze through the movie we usually go to after dinner.

Trade is brought in two or three times a week but the baths have been closed by police "for immorality".

Right now I'm sitting in the sun on the terrace, waiting for Salvatore who called this A.M. I told F. he was coming, shouted it down from the terrace to him on the street as he went off with Alvarro, and he struck his forearm with his hand, meaning "Fuck You!" – nothing serious!

*Monday, 29 June 1953*

June 29 –

I've just about run through this Roman period already. Everything is just a little too familiar. I think I need the shock of something new to keep me from sinking into the old summer lethargy and stupefaction. So! Probably I will take off for Spain in a few days now. Will look into boats & planes tomorrow at Amexco. Tonight we went to the ballet. I left after the first half – Frank remained. I had my usual 2 drinks on the Veneto, where I ran into Irving Rapper – extricated myself quite nimbly and sat alone in front of the "The Golden Gate" – It's getting warm here – no breeze tonight. Mr. Moon is snoring by the foot the bed. He greets me very cordially when I come in alone but pays me no attention when I enter with Frank.

Nothing good to read. The work is petering out again. Just a re-write of an old story "Mattress by the Tomato Patch". Must soon decide whether to work on "Battle of Angels" – "Kingdom of Earth"[835] or the film script.[836] Perhaps the wisest decision would be no work at all, but Spain would have to be awfully fascinating to make that tolerable.

Was thinking of Bobby Soule[837] today – wondering how he is, a bit wistfully. Also that I am a son of a bitch. Why? Don't know. but I am. Not the only one, though. Will I ask Maria to join me in Spain?

*Wednesday, 1 July 1953*

July 1 –

Today applied for booking on a boat from Naples to Barcelona, sailing July 8. Won't be confirmed for a day or two – myself and car. A good move – in fact,

838. Most likely "The Mattress by the Tomato Patch," which Williams started in 1943.

839. Marc Lawrence (1910– ) was a Hollywood actor who, between 1933 and 1951, appeared in more than one hundred films, establishing himself as a well-regarded and versatile character actor, especially in crime and suspense films. Blacklisted by McCarthy in the 1950s, he moved to Italy where he continued his career. In 1960 he returned to Hollywood where he began to direct films as well as continued to act. About him, Williams wrote Kazan (undated, Wesleyan):

> I have become good friends with Marc Lawrence in Rome. He is a vital guy and has been through a lot of what you went through with. He found me a new swimming pool there and we've had some good talks, which have been a welcome change from the chit-chat of visiting royalty in Rome.

840. "Better to be alone than in bad company."

841. Luchino Visconti (1906–77) had asked Williams to write the English dialogue for the film *Senso*, based on a novella by Camillo Boito. Williams did not wish to do it and instead suggested Paul Bowles. Williams wrote Bowles (22 June 1953, HRC):

> Today Luchino Visconti came to see us. . . . I am simply not in condition, nervously, to undertake a job of this sort but I told him that you would be a perfect choice for it if you would be interested. He wanted me to write you at once and see if you'd like to. I dare say there would be a sizable increment. This he did not go into but there is American backing with stars such as Farley Granger involved. It might be worth your while if you are looking for "loot". He does not know your work as he cannot speak nor read English but I spoke of your books. He wants me to act in a "supervisory" capacity, which means that I would lend advice and assistance if needed. He wants to pay both of us but since I would not be doing any of the actual work I would — confidentially — turn over whatever I received to you.

842. Walter Baxter (1915–94), author of *Look Down in Mercy* (1951) and *The Image and the Search* (1953). In the spring of 1952, Williams read *Look Down in Mercy*, a novel that would have interested him, given the similar reactions of guilt and despair of Blanche's husband in *A Streetcar Named Desire* and Tony Kent, the main character in *Look Down in Mercy*, to their homosexuality. Kent, a British colonel, leaves a conventional married life for war service in the Far East. Along with another soldier, Anson, Kent is captured by the Japanese but escapes. The trauma and intensity of this experience cause him to recognize homosexual feelings for Anson. Besieged with guilt, Kent turns to alcohol and attempts suicide.

Baxter's handling of the theme of homosexuality may have influenced Williams in the suggestion of a homosexual relationship between Brick and Skipper in *Cat on a Hot Tin Roof*. Such a relationship did not exist in the 1952 short story "Three Players of a Summer Game," which was an important source for *Cat on a Hot Tin Roof*.

843. In his article titled "A Film in Sicily," Williams described the plane trip to Sicily:

> I hate flying and hate it even worse when you are flying over water in a converted Douglas bomber which has more patches in it than a pair of Sicilian pants. . . . We flew from Rome over the Apennines and down to the toe of the boot, during the course of which flight I washed down three quarter grains of phenobarbital with three shots of Cognac. Then I lit up a cigarette. Hardly was it lighted when [Donald] Downes turned round in his seat and remarked, "Be careful how you dispose of that cigarette. This plane is highly inflammable." But it seemed more likely that we would go down in water than up in flames, for just at this point the plane entered a region of capricious air-currents and began to make surprising dips toward the Bay of Naples which we were flying over. . . .
>
> At the toe of the boot we came to rest in a very rough field of small yellow flowers where a second plane was waiting for us. It looked like a poor country cousin of the first. . . .
>
> I thought it was extremely tactless of Mr. Downes to tell us that this "cheap plane" was going to take us directly over the fiery crater of Mt. Etna which is the highest volcano in the western world. However that's what it did, exactly as Downes had predicted, and we landed safely on the other side only about twenty minutes away from the village of Aci Trezza where [*La Terra Trema*] was being made.

about necessary as the situation here has deteriorated with shocking speed. I feel indifferent, this time quite genuinely I'm afraid. One gets tired of begging for crumbs under the table. A period of separation is the only answer, and maybe that only half one. For several days now I have labored over <u>two</u> <u>fucking</u> <u>pages</u> in a story.[838] Brain is sharp as Mr. Moon's nose. A nice talk with Marc Lawrence[839] this evening before dinner. I dined alone and went to movie alone. Just as well. "Meglior solo que mal accompagnato"[840] as they say here. If I get the July 8 booking may spend a couple of days on a beach near Naples. Here is Kaput. But goot! <u>En Avant</u>.

*Wednesday, 8 July 1953*

July 8 –

This is the day I was supposed to sail. Had to cancel bookings because the car documents had expired – Today will look into plane flights as it is the same here, only more so, and there is no point in prolonging it. Only trouble is Paul Bowles may be coming here in a few days and I <u>should</u> be on hand to greet him, as I arranged the film (writing) job for him.[841]

It is hot and heavy now.

But I've had two pleasant evenings with Walter Baxter, the English novelist whose book I loved,[842] and his young lover, B. Whitman, an actor.

Now the streets & a bite & a bottle somewhere under an awning – Then Amexco and the travel agencies again.

*Journal July 10, 1953*
*The trip to Barcelona*

*Friday, 10 July 1953*

My first European air flight since the one to Sicily in 1948.[843] A nice Italian 2-motor plane and fair weather. now over a blue body of water, I suppose the sea.

Only slept 2 hours last night as F and I had one of our periodic cathartic discussions. His manner toward me had been fairly insufferable for a couple of weeks and I voiced my protest when he showed no inclination to stop reading last night although it was our last night before I departed for Spain. It is much like summer before last and I never know how much, or how little, is settled or clarified in these show-down talks but they usually relieve the tension for a while. I said I was tired of being treated like a stupid, unsatisfactory whore by a bad-tempered pimp. Bubu de Montparnasse stuff. Etc.

844. In an undated letter to Kazan (Wesleyan) that Williams wrote from Barcelona, he recalled Charles-Louis Philippe's 1901 novel *Bubu de Montparnasse* in describing his relationship with Merlo:

    I had to leave Rome as Frank's behavior toward me became almost insufferable. He seemed to be playing Bubu de Montparnasse and to expect me to accept the role of one of Bubu's less satisfactory whores. I mean that conversation had fallen to the level of grunts with barely varying inflections and simply coming into a room with him seemed to constitute an abuse of privelege. This went on for two weeks. Then I had it out with him, verbally, and flew to Barcelona the next day. I don't think the poor bastard is even aware of what I protested about. He is sunk into such a pit of habit and inertia and basic contempt for himself or his position in life which I think he, consciously or unconsciously, holds me responsible for and almost if not quite hates me for. That old cocksucker Wilde uttered a true thing when he said, Each man kills the thing he loves. The killing is not voluntary but we sure in hell do it. And burn for it. I have given up faith in happy solutions to problems between two people but I shall try to think of something just the same and to work it out if it can be this coming year. . . .

    . . . And maybe it will all clear up again as it has before and we'll go right along as we have been going. So far I haven't thought of anything else.

845. Williams' "new" *Battle of Angels* would soon emerge as *Orpheus Descending*.

846. Franz Neuner who, according to Williams, was the "impresario sexually" of Barcelona.

847. San Sebastian was a popular beach club at the Barceloneta beach where mostly middle-class youths were members. In *Suddenly Last Summer* (scene 4), Catharine tells Dr. Cukrowicz:

    In Cabeza de Lobo there is a beach that's named for Sebastian's name saint, it's known as La Playa San Sebastian, and that's where [Cousin Sebastian and I] started spending all afternoon, every day.

848. Antonio de Cabo managed, together with Rafael Richart, the Teatro de Cámara. *El Zoo de Cristal* and *Un Tranvía Llamado Deseo* were performed in 1947 and 1948, respectively.

Antonio de Cabo (second from left) and Williams (center)

Well, a trip was indicated and is being taken.[844] I look forward to Barcelona with fairly pleasant expectations as Irving Rapper and his friend said there was much in the way of diversion.

Have been working (only so-so) on the new "Battle"[845] – completed "Mattress" story in pretty good style. Will continue tonight in Barcelona.

*Saturday, 11 July 1953*

Sat. Noon

Sitting in my room at the Hotel Colon (Barcelona) waiting for an unknown gentleman named Neuner[846] to call for me. Rapper gave me his name as someone who could give me entrée to the interesting society here. We shall see. Usually such contacts are disappointing. He is already late. But the plan is to go out to the beach for the afternoon and he mentioned a Danish boy with him.

Later –

The afternoon was quite good and the contact an exception. I spent 6 hours on the San Sebastian beach[847] and had an affair in my Cabana with someone procured by Franz. Had a Paella on the beach, a good swim in a salt water pool. When I returned I found Antonio de Caba waiting for me. He is the young director of the little art theatre here that put on "Streetcar" & "Menagerie"[848] and is very good looking probably the loveliest eyes I've seen in a mortal face. Tonight he is taking me to the "China town" – Quartier Chinois he called it – we talked in French. Evenings start late here and I'm afraid I shall be sleepy long before it's over. He says there's a place for dancing and I'm reasonably sure he means what I hope he means.

*Monday, 13 July 1953*

Mon. Night

A very active and agreeable time here. Some really good work (4½ hrs.) this A.M. on "Battle". A Paella for lunch, a swim at St. Sebastian and afterwards open house in my room for about 6 hours. A totally disastrous "lay" with the last remaining guest, who stripped very badly. A bad dinner in the hotel and an evening listening to nostalgic old American records at the apt. of the leading critic here, who put on 4 different drags during the evening. But the life here is good and I could like Antonio very much indeed. Que peut je faire? or is it – puis je faire? I talk in nothing but French here.

849.  Jean Cocteau (1889–1963), French poet, novelist, artist, and director, had staged *A Streetcar Named Desire* (*Un Tramway Nommé Désir*) in Paris in 1949. In 1937 Cocteau had discovered the struggling twenty-four-year-old actor Jean Marais (1913–98) and soon became his surrogate father and lover. In 1950 Cocteau adapted his play *Orphée* (1926) for film and Marais played the lead. Marais went on to become one of France's most well-known actors.

850.  Angel Zúñiga (1911– ), a well-known Spanish literary, theatre, and movie critic, published a number of books, ranging from collections of short stories to travel, biography, and history. In *Mi Futuro es Ayer* (1983), he noted that Williams was involved with Spanish actors when he stayed in Barcelona. At the time of his death, Williams had Zúñiga's book *Una Historia del Cuplé* (1954), which was inscribed to him.

851.  Two years later, in a letter to Kenneth Tynan (26 July 1955, Yale), Williams would reveal the connection between his operation in 1946 and *Cat on a Hot Tin Roof*:

> About the operation and the "shadow of death" that hung over me from 1946 till —
>
> My recent history dates from that occasion . . . and I think it has an interesting bearing on all my work since then, romantic pessimism, preoccupation with mortality, Etc. Of course it only became explicit, something I finally dared to deal with directly, in "Big Daddy" in "Cat".

Jean Marais and Jean Cocteau, and Cocteau's book jacket
design for the French edition of *Streetcar*

Angel Zúñiga and Williams

*Tuesday, 14 July 1953*

Tues. A.M.

The room is full of flies, and noisy, too. – The filthy flies are intolerable so I demanded a flit gun be used when I go out presently to the beach.

Not enough sleep last night and consequently morning's work suffered. Still better than usual.

But I've quit at 1:10 and can't eat here before 2:30 or three. Saw Cocteau a couple of times here with his "fils adoptif" the beautiful youth of "Orfée"[849] – less golden now and rather enigmatically silent. Cocteau is astonishing in his ageless vitality. Drugs? I like him.

Can't make up my mind to send for Maria. She's really so expensive and there's quite enough society here now. But I feel guilty because I said I would ask her to join me.

Am not aware of missing F. so far.

Well, I'm too selfish to be aware of much but myself and my own little quotidinal variations of mood or circumstance. En Avant.


*Wednesday, 15 July 1953*

Wed. 5 A.M.

A sleepless night. dressed and went downstairs to enquire if a bar was open around here and the night clerk graciously volunteered to send some liquor up to my room & some hot milk. So I have now taken a Seconal (nembutal earlier) – one of, if not my last of the pinkies. I hope I shall be able to continue work tomorrow.


*Friday, 17 July 1953*

Friday –

Woke this A.M. frightfully ill with a gastrointestinal attack of great severity, and a good deal of fever developed during the day. Angel Zuniega[850] comes to look at me every one or two hours which is extraordinary but a little too much. I am too stupid to talk. I wired Maria that I was ill and could she fly down but now I wonder if that was wise. I will be going back to Rome soon as I'm able and the simpler the situation there the better.

Of course I don't know if this is just a little "tourist" trouble or some organic crisis. I felt a sudden wave of loneliness for Frank. And pity and love – What a sorry companion I make for anyone young & alive. The way down is a long one and it seems to continue. I think I have been living in a sustained, repressed state of panic since 1946 or longer.[851]

Now the organ grinder has started his evening serenade – it's after seven.

852.  Sulfanilamide was used as an antibiotic.

853.  Ahmed ben Driss el Yacoubi (1931–8?) was a Moroccan painter born in Fez. He became a close friend of Paul Bowles' and traveled with Bowles to numerous destinations. Bowles' chauffeur was another Moroccan, Mohammed Temsamany.

854.  Kif, the fine chopped leaves of the common hemp plant, is usually mixed with tobacco and smoked in a long wooden pipe with a small clay head.

855.  "For lack of something better."

Mohammed Temsamany, Williams, Frank Merlo, Ahmed Yacoubi, and Paul Bowles
in front of the Trevi Fountain, Rome

*Saturday, 18 July 1953*

Later

I was resting lightly as a bird in a dreamless sleep when Angel arrives at 12:30 A.M. to wake me for more pills. He is killing me with kindness. Then a phone call from Antonio. But Bowles wired that he is coming tonight and perhaps he will take me out of this curious exhausting world – but I have never known a kinder man than Angel.

Rest is something they have never heard of.

The diarrhoea continues but I had a light supper of clear broth, chicken and ice cream which did not apparently bother me. My mind is very dull but fairly peaceful and I hope I can sleep again I think there is less fever.

Later

Woke at five of my own accord this time. The hour for another dose of pills which I will now take although I don't really think they (Sulfanilimide)[852] is indicated in my condition.

This is the first time I've slept well since I left Rome.

Sat.

Bowles arrived this morning, with Ahmed, Jaguar, and a uniformed chauffeur.[853] Continued after lunch leaving Ahmed to fly with me on Mon. as he didn't have French visa. We went to the "Toros" but I left after the first half as blood made me sickish and for the first time the spectacle offended me. No doubt the bad figures of the matadors had something to do with that. Spanish men are not beauties, at least not in this province.

I have been scarcely civil to my social entourage here. Their attentions are too constant and the labor of conversing in my French is too much in my present low state.

I have retired at 11, leaving Ahmed to his own devices which he indicated might include some kif.[854]


*Sunday, 19 July 1953*

Sunday Noon

A black Sunday though the sun is yellow as butter. Slept well and was geared for work when I woke but several little things went wrong. I couldn't find my glasses and some papers were misplaced. I went to pieces and couldn't do a thing – totally impotent. Sometimes an experience like this throws me off for days and days after. But I'm going out to the beach and try to relax in yellow butter sun and maybe get sucked off by one of those beach whores. faute de mieux.[855]

Company = Angel & Ahmed

856.  Barrio Chino, the old quarter next to Barcelona's harbor, was well known for its cheap restaurants, hotels, brothels, and nightclubs.

857.  The class of bullfight in which bulls must be at least four years old and fought by qualified matadors.

858.  Ellen Adler (1927– ), a painter, who was living in Europe.

Ellen Adler

Maria Britneva and Williams

*Monday, 20 July 1953*

Later –
   did just that – a full day & night
   San Sebastiano and Barachina[856]
   just now returned under Angel's escort at 12:30 A.M.
   Smoked kif with Ahmed in the bordellos of Barachina and along the streets.
   This afternoon saw a good corrida[857] – 2 goodlooking young matadors held
my interest through all 6 fights.
   Tomorrow – plane to Rome – <u>En Avant!</u>

Monday
   gay time on streets smoking kif with Ahmed. We rode in open horse carriage
from the Columbus "Colon" to the Cataluna plaza, whole length of Rambles.
But dinner was no good and the boy we brought home was strictly for the birds.
   Smoked more kif. Then Ahmed & boy left and I retired with Time magazine.
Slept a while. Woke up at 3 – face all puffy but still feeling good.
   Ahmed is charming company but I don't envy Paul his attachment. Of course
Paul is capable of more detachment in his attachments than I am. I feel no sexual
attraction to Ahmed but he is the first person to make me laugh and feel gay since
Maria. "The Horse" and I never laugh together. Why? He has a sense of humor.
   With him what I find is composure – when he is on his good behavior – Wrote
well in morning –

*Circa Tuesday, 28 July or Wednesday, 29 July 1953*

   Rome again for a week now.
   Bowles & Ahmed staying in another apartment on same floor.
   Only mornings are live. And they only when the work goes.
   I drift on a sluggish stream that seems to go gently down, and how can I stop
the flow?
   Last night a ghastly supper party with a group of hostile squares and Stella
Adler with her daughter[858] who resembles a dainty young cobra. I was annoyed
with Bowles. He ignored my repeated suggestions that we leave. Although I
scarcely think he enjoyed the party more than I. I don't get along at all with
normal men.
   Last night they made overt remarks which I had to ignore.
   Today no energy for work. Hot. Glaring – Sopranos shrieking at Opera across
the street. Nothing to do now but go out for lunch on foot or in cab as the car is
still being repaired.

859.  *Orpheus Descending.*

860.  Williams directed Donald Windham's play "The Starless Air" at Joanna Albus' theatre in Houston, Texas, which premiered on 13 May 1953. The Theatre Guild then optioned it for a summer production in Westport, Connecticut, and Williams agreed to direct the play there also. Langner's option for a June production was extended three months, but as time passed Williams seemed less interested in returning to direct the play, and Langner believed that without Williams it would be hard to secure backers.

861.  Marc Lawrence.

Franco Zeffirelli, Williams, and Luchino Visconti in Rome

*Friday, 7 August 1953*

Friday Aug 7

The summer is wearing rapidly away. Paul and his entourage are still here and now Maria has arrived and I feel a bit trapped. I love them but the social demands are excessive in my state of depletion.


*Thursday, 13 August 1953*

Thursday Aug. ?

Today the dreaded occasion of reading over the work and the (almost but never quite) expected fit of revulsion.

Off-key, forced, hysterical. What could I expect? It's been a long time since I've been in a condition to work calmly and strongly – or wildly and strongly either.

Today there are flutes instead of bad sopranos at the opera house. The air's cool. The sun very bright.

It's earlier than I would choose. Not late enough for the solace of lunch and vino. But perhaps I'll drive out early to the pool with Maria.

Of course tomorrow I'll start re-writing again.[859] Unfortunately the first 2 acts had already gone to the typist.


*Monday, 17 August 1953*

Monday –

Fearful cold – one of those flash colds that come on me like a violent allergy – I think from fatigue more than anything else.

Last night a bad attack of suffocation – "air hunger" – whatever it is – felt very close to extinction. feared to sleep again – awake till long after sunrise. But worked again today on Act 3 and perhaps improved it a bit. Letter from Windham who is also having a rough time with a play[860] – Langner has apparently called off his production.

Tonight went to Lawrence's[861] for supper. The food was good but the evening a bore and I was wretched with cold – once again Bowles was reluctant to take me home when I wanted to go and I feel quite "put out" with him. Would hate ever to be dependent on him. Perhaps Ahmed's misbehavior is not, after all, so remarkable. I am getting to be sort of crotchety.


*Wednesday, 19 August 1953*

Wednesday –

The ugly monument unveiled again. But I kept at it.

862.  The short story "The Mattress by the Tomato Patch," which would be included in *Hard Candy: A Book of Stories* (1954).

863.  When Williams wrote to Bowles to offer the job of writing the English dialogue for *Senso* (22 June 1953, HRC), Williams described the standing of the director, Luchino Visconti:

> Visconti made the latest Magnani film, "Bellissima", which is a great success now in America, and also a much greater film, "Terra Trema". He also has directed "Streetcar" and "Menagerie" in the Italian theatre, and is by far the greatest director in Italy as well as a "grand Seigneur", the Viscontis being one of the three oldest families in the country — this is irrelevant but interesting, I think, since he is also very "leftish". I like him and I think his dealings would be completely equitable — this is relevant.

A few months later, when Bowles did not do "a satisfactory job," Williams "felt obliged" to take over since Visconti had hired Bowles at his recommendation (letter to Audrey Wood, 19 September 1953, HRC).

*Senso,* the story of an illicit and doomed love affair between a married Italian countess and an Austrian military officer during the Austrian Empire's evacuation from Italy in 1866, was well received when it came out in 1954.

Williams and Bowles shared the credits on the film.

864.  Literally, "spa." Williams is very likely referring to the hot water baths at Terme di Caracalla.

Causes of defeat: first, age. The spontaneity of youth is lost which swept me over many past obstructions. Physical deterioration and a mental fatigue that makes me ~~almost inco~~ downright stupid. Inability to rest which might restore energies. I can't somehow. I can't face a day without the few hours of escape into the intensities of work, no matter how futile it becomes. Emptiness. Nothingness of my world outside of work. For instance in Santa Monica (1943) which I was writing about this morning,[862] when work failed, as it sometimes did even, then, I could hop on my racer bike and work off tensions in free physical exercise. Now my body is bankrupt. Mind, too. A great storm has stripped me bare, like one of those stripped, broken palm trees after a hurricane passes. Under these conditions, how does one continue? Simply by continuing, I guess. Or not. Depending on what happens to you, no longer on what you do.

Full scale rehearsal at opera, voices and orchestra. Meaningless noise to me.

Sent last of new "Battle" to typist yesterday and woke up this morning thinking how clinically mad it probably will seem when I read the Ms. over.

Cold dryer – down on chest. Maria just phoned me to join her at club. I shall. Rien d'autre. En avant.

(What fearful admission do I have to make, that after "Streetcar" I haven't been able to write anymore except by a terrible wrenching of the brain and nerves?) (Now worn out.)


*Sunday, 23 August 1953*

Sunday –

That mood has passed again. Maria & I have just arrived in Naples. I drove the whole way. It is a moony night and we have rooms and balconies over the bay at the Excelsior. American battleships lie off shore and the town is swarming with swabbies.

Tomorrow must work on the Visconti film script[863] – never stopped on "Battle" – which did seem a fiasco when I started to read it over. I still hope to salvage it – At least till the next black mood comes along –


*Monday, 24 August 1953*

Mon. A.M.

Maria wants to go to Sicily. I am timid of such an undertaking, and in summer. Also I'd possibly get my throat cut. Also I've lost my letter of credit.

Sitting here waiting for coffee. Will take a whack at "Battle" and then I suppose I'll have to resume work on that dreary film script.

Last night an al fresco adventure – Felix of the "Terme".[864]

865.  *Heimweh*, "homesickness."

866.  In *Calypso* (1953), by the British writer Humphrey Slater (1906–58), a wealthy middle-aged widow living in Florence unwittingly becomes involved in trouble that ends in murder. Slater had achieved international success in 1948 with the publication of *The Conspirator*, which was then made into a film.

Positano

*Tuesday, 25 August 1953*

*Positano*

Tues. Night –

A pleasant day, quite unusually pleasant. Worked well both on film script &
Battle.

Good swimming in P.M.

At supper Maria and I laughed our heads off.

Afterwards ran into an American painter, Peter something & a pretty middle-
aged lady from Houston and we went up the Mt. behind a horse that farted
every few steps of the way. There was nothing to do but laugh & so we laughed.

Later, alone, went down on the beach and had a crazy little adventure with a
young lunatic – no satisfaction but contact. We both took flight when someone
approached. Now – very late – about 2 but I had a nap before dinner. En Avant.


*Wednesday, 26 August 1953*

Wed.

Another pleasant day. Just about completed film work this A.M. and spent the
P.M. rowing Maria about in a little "barchetta" which was light as a cork and we
swam various places. Met Gordon Sager who has promised to introduce me to the
sexual mysteries of the place tonight at the beach where there is to be a dance.

A gentle sadness, "heimwehr"[865] or something of the sort, came over me as I
tried to take a nap before dinner and a corn on my little toe ached. So I got up &
shaved & dressed and prepared for dinner – ravenously hungry. But M. is not
ready. And I don't want to face those people downstairs alone. Started a book
Calypso[866] which is promising but this place wont do until the nightingales have
offered at least one serenade. Peut-etre ce <u>soir!</u>?

En Avant

*Yes, they sang
that night!*

867. The hotel Le Sirenuse in Positano. Alida Valli (1921– ), born Baronessa Alida Maria von Altenburger, was an Italian actress of haunting beauty. Her film career began in 1936 when she was fifteen. After World War II she worked in Hollywood for David Selznick. Her best work is considered to be her roles in *The Paradine Case* (1947) and *The Third Man* (1949). She played the countess in *Senso* opposite Farley Granger.

In the play *Orpheus Descending*, the character Carol Cutrere has "an odd, fugitive beauty which is stressed, almost to the point of fantasy, by a style of make-up with which a dancer named Valli has lately made such an impression in the bohemian centers of France and Italy, the face and lips powdered white and the eyes outlined and exaggerated with black pencil and the lids tinted blue."

868. La Buca, a restaurant.

869. In "Man Bring This Up Road" (the precursor to the play *The Milk Train Doesn't Stop Here Anymore* and the film script *Boom!*), Flora Goforth, a wealthy, eccentric lady in her seventies who lives alone in a villa on the Amalfi coast, is visited by a talented but down-and-out poet, Jimmy Dobyne, who seeks shelter and possibly a job. Mrs. Goforth taunts him with food and when he doesn't respond to her sexually, she dismisses him, giving as her reason her belief that he offended her with what she believed to be a sarcastic remark.

870. Peggy Guggenheim and Libby Holman. A month earlier (28 July 1953, Yale), Williams had written Windham:

[Paul Bowles] has two Arabs with him, his lover Ahmed (stolen but now relinquished by Libby Holman) and a chauffeur. . . .

. . . Ahmed is torturing Paul by not sleeping with him. It seems that Libby told him that such relations were very evil and the opinions of a lady with thirty million dollars cannot be taken lightly by a young Arab whose family live in one room.

Alida Valli

*Thursday, 27 August 1953*

Thurs. Eve

Rain this P.M. and a great rainbow, violet, green, yellow, orange & rose over the sea.

We bathed late in the rain and now I'm resting before dinner. Maria is such a charming companion, like one of those dear little girl friends of my childhood or Rose.

Worked well this morning on "battle".

Maybe we leave tomorrow.

*Saturday, 29 August 1953*

Friday eve. (Sat. 2 A.M.)

Still here but planning to leave tomorrow. good work again today, on a new story and on the Visconti film.

Dinner at a couple of old ladies up the mountain. Saw Valli dance at the Sirenusa.[867] Rather a dull day with no sex on the program. I think I've had this place, though it has indeed been pleasant & productive.

Maybe Sicily? – Not if this famine of the libido continues.

Sat. Eve

Still here. Although I may not be quite aware of it now this little period is probably one of the happiest and most peaceful in years.

Gordon sent me a little messenger at dinner who turned out to be the message. I was, luckily, dining late and alone, as I had left Maria at a party and come home for a nap and she didn't return till the messenger was delivering the message and I told her, called through the door, that I would meet her down at the Buca,[868] but instead I've taken a sleeping pill and am reading my book, Calypso, which is only just readable. Maybe we <u>do</u> leave tomorrow but I'm not at all sure. It's warm tonight – no wind – and the music from the Sirenusa sounds next door and very tedious. I miss the Horse. After all, there's nothing quite like him, is there? But — absence lends and so forth.

first draft of a story today about the place where I had lunch, 3 Easter egg villas between here and Amalfi[869] but the hero is <u>not</u> Gordon and the lady is sort of a composite of various vampires I have known. but <u>not</u> Peggy & <u>not</u> Libby.[870] It is not good yet, in fact it is sort of cheap, but perhaps I will be able to elevate it tomorrow.

871.  Margaret "Lorna" Ashton Stimson Lindsley (1889–1956), a freelance writer, was an indefatigable fighter for those she considered repressed. She supported the Loyalists in Spain, the Zionists in Palestine, and the underground Free French Resistance during World War II. In 1943 she published *War Is People*, an account of her experiences in Spain, Palestine, and France, and the effect of war on the ordinary people.

872.  Marquis Paolo Sersale, the mayor of Positano, whose family owned the hotel Le Sirenuse.

873.  Possibly Peter Grenfell, Lord St. Just (1922–84), who, according to Maria Britneva, had come to Italy and proposed to her. She married him in July 1956.

874.  "Let's go."

MAN BRING THIS UP ROAD

Mrs. Flora Goforth owned three Easter egg colored villas that perched on a seacliff some hundred feet over the Northern skirts of Amalfi. She was a fantastically rich old lady who *had been* ~~was~~ disappointed in her children and even more disappointed in her grandchildren and now beginning to be disappointed in her great grandchildren, and so for the past twenty years or more she had consoled and diverted herself by taking an interest in "young people who did things", a term that distinguished them from all but one of her own ~~descendants~~ *relatives*, her ~~grandson~~ *nephew* Chapell who did line-drawings so delicate that they were scarcely visible on *the* ~~the~~ *white* paper. But it was Chapell nowadays who seeded the ~~prodigies~~ *young people* for her and introduced her to the right ones among them and let her know when they had fallen out ~~of~~ *from* fashion. Presence at one of her parties, a place at her table at a benefit ball, was almost as gratifying as finding ~~their~~ *ones* photograph, all in one season, ~~transferred~~ *risen* from ~~college~~ *the Harvard* yearbook to Harper's Bazaar, and so Mrs. Goforth enjoyed a sort of social renascence after that melancholy period in which mortality and fatigue and disappointment had severed most of ~~the~~ *her* old associations. She was once more sought after, so *flatteringly*

*Sunday, 30 August 1953*

Sunday.

Re-wrote Story today. Starting slow but picking up after a double Scotch. Still needs work.

Rather gay and pleasant P.M. at the other beach with Lorna Lindsley[871] for lunch and afterwards a long boat ride with a handsome young Italian Marquis[872] and Maria's "Count".[873]

Too sleepy tonight to accompany Maria to the noisy 'Sirenusa'. Rumor that Paul Bowles is coming here tonight or tomorrow. I am rather eager to get back to Rome, Frank and Mr. Moon now. But have offered to go to Verona if Visconti needs me. Now will probably go in town for cigarettes – or will I? Hard to say. goodnight.


*Monday, 31 August 1953*

Monday –

Yes, it's time to go.

Another good day's work but the place palls on me and I long for the old life in Rome. Maria has picked up a couple of titled gents who are okay for her but "niente per me", and another night and morning seems about the limit I want to take. No sign of Paul yet. And the nice lady from Houston, Mildred, has gone. Still it's been a good stay here – productive and peaceful and, on the whole, quite pleasant.

A faint Autumnal sadness drifts in the air this evening. far away cries of children, fading sky, buses honking around the Amalfi drive far off. And now and then a distant splash of the sea – bird voices – fading light – running footsteps – a subjective sadness, to be sure – and not at all deep. In fact just a little affected, I suppose. Hope I can sleep before supper so that after supper I'll feel like going out.

Later – I did, slept almost 2 hours but was still tired after supper. My fatigue perhaps comes from intense early morning work, from about 7:30 or 8:00 till noon – which is an hour or two longer, I believe, than I lasted in Rome. Also the wine makes me sleepy. But I did go out. Had a verbal set-to with a drunken woman who thought she could needle me with impunity and was corrected on that score. Being with Maria has sharpened my tongue these days & nights. A friendly stranger said "BuenaSera" and I strolled on the beach, not alone. And later to the hotel, not alone, and the nightingales sang, not at the top of their pitch, but with a fair sweetness.

Now alone in bed and the tide is washing in loudly below the cliff. Another morning's work – then <u>andiamo</u>![874]

Bowles is here in Positano but has not yet descended the hill to look us up. I

875. "Man Bring This Up Road."

876. A paid lover.

877. Very likely Hemingway's *Death in the Afternoon* (1932).

878. Flora Goforth, protagonist in "Man Bring This Up Road."

suspect he's annoyed either with me or Maria or both. He is inclined to think himself abused on any pretext but I am terribly fond of Paul and rather annoyed at Maria's attitude toward him. I think she's made some trouble between us which I hope Paul will be willing to discuss. He is rather the sly one.

*Tuesday, 1 September 1953*

Tuesday.

Behaved rather disgracefully today – liquor, I'm afraid. The intense writing has blown my nerves and the liquor on top of that makes me act a fool. I gave the two old ladies a tongue lashing for last night's snub and now it appears they were probably quite guiltless. It is obvious however that Paul for some reason was reluctant to see us. I don't suppose I shall ever feel quite the same toward him, or about him, which is too bad, for me, as I had a sort of hero worship for him before this last meeting.

Perhaps I'm getting a bit like Hart Crane in his last days – a bit mad.

Changed the story[875] today – removed the melodrama but probably too much of the substance with it and it would surprise me to read it over sometime soon and get one of those nasty shocks my creative life has been so full of in recent times.

Crave a drink.

Marco[876] was here – afterwards an agonizing feeling of embarassment and shame, I don't know why.

*Wednesday, 2 September 1953*

Wed. A.M. (11:20)

If I've done nothing else this summer, and I suspect sometimes that I haven't, I have certainly "kept at it". Sometimes when I read the work over it seems like the work of a lunatic or drunkard, at ~~lea~~ best the second. But each time I recover my blind hope or faith and go on again the next day. Now the beach for a swim and lunch and then we hit the road back to Rome with flags still flying – <u>En Avant!</u>

*Saturday, 5 September 1953*

Sat. Midnight

Rome again – the energy didn't hold and the two mornings since I've been back have been duds. Tonight I barely had strength to climb up the stairs to bed. But now I have a tall glass of ice water beside me and a pretty good book about a doomed matador[877] – Tomorrow I'll waste another day on old Mrs Goforth,[878] I'm afraid. Soon we leave for Verona, perhaps all of us. goodnight.

(frightened)

879. *Orpheus Descending.*

880. Jenny Crosse (1919–64), a journalist, was the eldest child of Robert Graves and Nancy Nicholson. In 1952, she had married Patrick Crosse, head of the Reuters bureau in Rome.

881. Martha Gellhorn (1908–98), one of the first female war correspondents, covered more than a dozen major conflicts over a period of sixty years. She was also an accomplished fiction writer and published five novels, fourteen novellas, and two collections of short stories. She was married to Hemingway from 1940 to 1945.

882. Truman Capote (1924–84), New Orleans-born writer best known for his novels *Other Voices, Other Rooms* (1948), *Breakfast at Tiffany's* (1958), and *In Cold Blood* (1966), the telling of the horrific murder of a family in Kansas in novel form. With the publication of *In Cold Blood*, Capote was credited with the creation of a new genre, the nonfiction novel.

   Williams and Capote knew each other quite well, and in *Memoirs* Williams recounted several amusing incidents with Capote, including a transatlantic crossing during the summer of 1948:

   > He returned with me to the States on the *Queen Mary* and it was an hilariously funny crossing. In those days Truman was about the best companion you could want. He had not turned bitchy. Well, he had not turned *maliciously* bitchy. But he was full of fantasies and mischief. We used to go along the first class corridors of the *Mary* and pick up the gentlemen's shoes, set outside their staterooms for shining — and we would mix them all up, set them doors away from their proper places. (p. 150)

   Capote included an unkind and unflattering portrait of Williams as Mr. Wallace, "the most acclaimed American playwright," in an extract from his novel-in-progress *Answered Prayers* published as "Unspoiled Monsters" in *Esquire*, May 1976. Wallace is described as "a chunky, paunchy, booze-puffed runt with a play moustache glued above laconic lips," who has a "corn-pone voice." Wallace's description of himself as "a dying man . . . dying of cancer" causes the narrator to observe: "[H]ere's a dumpy little guy with a dramatic mind who, like one of his own adrift heroines, seeks attention and sympathy by serving up half-believed lies to total strangers. Strangers because he has no friends, and he has no friends because the only people he pities are his own characters and himself."

Truman Capote visiting the *Senso* set, Verona

*Sunday, 6 September 1953*

Sunday midnight

Another poor morning and afternoon dull as piss carting Maria around with a camera in the car – we've seen a little too much of each other and a separation would be advantageous to us both.

Dreary old Sunday – but we did visit a charming convent near the Colisseum –

Tonight she took F. & I to dinner and we did more driving around afterwards. the day was really a total blank, the sort of day that you might as well not count. But I have a good book, and now the day is over – En Avant.

*Monday, 7 September 1953*

Monday Midnight –

A strange nightingale took wing – from Bari.

Mailed play[879] to Audrey today.

Maria angry at Frank so we dined without her.

Nothing else to report except that I am worried over this continual stiff neck and that I think I've discovered my first grey hair but hope it is just a blond one. Mr. Moon is snoring by my bed, after a frantic game of "who's got the biscuit" and I have finished my good book which turned out a bit disappointingly. And now I'm reading some of Hemingway's old stories again.

*Tuesday, 8 September 1953*

Tues. Midnight

A blank A.M. A dreary P.M.

And an evening not so bad at Jennie's[880] with Maria. We met Hemingway's former wife Martha Gelhorn[881] who had a sharp tongue and a keen mind but I'm not sure I'd like her over a long haul. She discussed Capote[882] with devastating humor & malice.

Jennie's husband had a rarely beautiful and sensitive face. I have such a hunger for faces like that. and gentle manners and soft speech, getting old, I guess.

Tomorrow evening Verona

883.    Presumably *Cat on a Hot Tin Roof*. Six months later, Williams would write, "Why did I despair of [*Cat on a Hot Tin Roof*] so in Madrid, in this same journal?"

884.    Contrary to his fear, Wood did write Williams. His pessimism, however, about her reaction was borne out in the letter. Williams responded (14 October 1953, HRC):

> Since the script simply doesn't "come off", I don't know if there is much point in telling you what I was aiming at but I will try to. What always bothered me in it was the juvenile poetics, the inflated style of the writing, so I tried to "bring it down to earth", to give the characters a tougher, more realistic treatment. Also I wanted to simplify the story-line, to make it cleaner and straighter, by eliminating such things as "The woman from Waco", Val's literary pretensions, the great load of background and atmospheric detail, and the hi-faluting style of Cassandra's speeches such as "Behold Cassandra, shouting doom at the gates!" and all that sort of crap which seemed so lovely to me in 1940. Unfortunately in 1940 I was a younger and stronger and — curiously! — more confident writer than I am in the Fall of 1953. Now I am a maturer and more knowledgeable craftsman of the theatre, my experience inside and outside the profession is vastly wider, but still the exchange appears to be to my loss. I don't need to tell you how hard I have worked to compensate for that loss, devotion to work is something we have in common.

Visconti and Alida Valli rehearsing the opening scene of *Senso* in La Fenice theatre

*Wednesday or Thursday circa early October 1953*

Madrid

Quite a long lapse. From there I went to Venice, memorable chiefly for a gondola moored on a misty night in the middle of the lagoon and battleships floating barely in view and for the gondolier who sang like a nightingale should sing. And La Fenice theatre, the loveliest that I have ever been in, like sitting in the middle of a flower.

And Ravel's concerto which I had never heard before.

The return to Rome distinguished only by F's coldness which still persists. For some reason he has again decided to put the screws to me. And I mean the screws that you get in a hardware store.

Later – much better.


*Thursday or Friday circa early October 1953*

Thurs. A.M. or Friday

Anyhow the next day –

Looked through the new play script[883] and was so disheartened that I closed it and prepared to descend to the bar. What most troubles me is not just the lifeless quality of the writing, its lack of distinction, but a real confusion that seems to exist, nothing carried through to completion but written over and over, as if a panicky hen running in circles.

Some structural change in my brain? An inability to think clearly and consecutively. Or simply too much alcohol?

The prospect of returning to America with this defeat in my heart which only drink can assuage is a mighty dark one. If it were not for grandfather I would certainly remain abroad.

Later –

Took the Ms. down to the bar with me to read it quietly over my first drink of the day – but that did no good at all, it only seemed worse and I am now certain that the working apparatus is, at least for the present, totally disrupted. Probably the new version of "Battle" was such a mess that Audrey can't write me about it.[884] Now we must take this trip through Spain, dry tortured country as burnt out as I am and as dreadfully sick.

I have nothing more to work on. If I have any sense at all left in me, I will stop trying to work and will just try to find comfort in the little animal comforts of simple existence. What a blessing that I do have some money! Many don't even have that.

This will pass. One thing that I can be, if nothing else, is decently kind and

885.  Nickname for Seconal.

886.  *Perros*, "dogs."

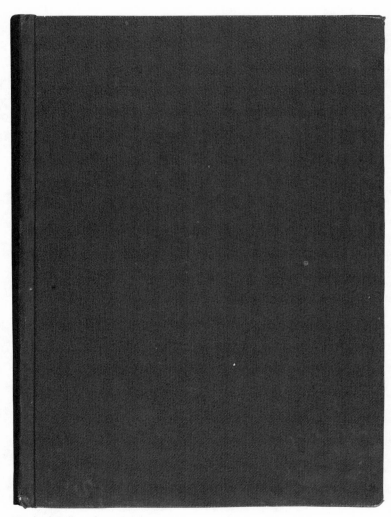

Notebook Williams began in July 1953

understanding. Everything else may go, but that doesn't have to go, too. Surely there is something that I can do in the mornings.

*Friday, 9 October 1953*

Friday night

A bad time of it.

Jolted out of sleep couple of times so took a pinkie[885] and read a bit. Astonishing amount of gas on the belly which has been acting up quite a lot this season. Read through this journal – how dreary it is! Not a spark anywhere of anything but endurance. And today I broke my resolution to quit work, I tried to work again. Tonight lovemaking and the high altitude of Granada created this little crise.

Roosters crowing all over the plain of Granada and the "peros"[886] howling so Aurora must be coming. F. sleeps tranquilly in the next bed and Mr. Moon on the floor between.

Goodnight.

P.S. Just had a slight earthquake – lasted a couple of seconds and did no damage, apparently, to anything but my already devastated nerves.

I wonder if I'll be able to get through those Mts. to Malaga tomorrow?

Portrait of Frank Merlo by Williams, c. 1952

887.   The novelist James Jones (1921–77) was known primarily for fiction that deals with the effect of World War II on soldiers. *From Here to Eternity* (1951), the story of life in the U.S. Army before the Japanese attack on Pearl Harbor in 1941, became a sensation with its powerful, vivid, and occasionally vulgar language. The film *From Here to Eternity* came out in 1953.

888.   *Stairs to the Roof* had been performed in March–April 1945 at the Pasadena Playbox and two years later at the Pasadena Playhouse. There appears to be no evidence, in the form of manuscripts or correspondence, to suggest that Williams continued working on the play.

*Friday, 16 October 1953*

Tangier – Oct. 16

Yes, I got through those mountains to Malaga, but these are higher and I can't get through.

The sun shines over the straits of Gibralter as I sit impotently before the portable Royal and my glass of Scotch, and a blank white wall.

*Saturday, 17 October 1953*

Oct. 17

I am sure that God will help me. Nothing else can.

*Monday, 19 October 1953*

Oct. 19

Reading a superb book James Jones' "From Here to Eternity"[887] – hard as a rock pile and he hits it with a great hammer and it's our world and time. Thought I wouldn't like it because it was so popular but it's one of those best sellers for the best reason. Surprised the critics bought it – guess it was too powerful to resist.

Cocks crowing all around at the false morning of the moon. I've dreamed of my sister, seeing her in a cream colored lace dress which I had forgotten. In the dream a lady who looked like my sister wore it – then I had it on and then I was struggling to sit down between two tables and was wedged so tightly between them I couldn't breathe. Woke up feeling breathless and started to read and washed down the pinkie with a drink of Scotch. Horse sleeps peacefully. So does Moon, snoring louder than Horse.

*Tuesday, 20 October 1953*

Oct. 20

Today was good, at least better, worked on "Stairs to the Roof"[888] and seemed to be getting along o.k., although there was a good deal of corn in it. A wire from Audrey. Made me feel better – Good fair day – may take to the beach and brave the chilly waters apres dejeuner. Sweet letter from Jane and Tony. Now must dress. Lovely clouds over Spain, mountains of Spain visible under them. Various ships in blue harbor. White laundry flapping on roof tops, always a rooster crowing somewhere here, children's voices same as anywhere else in the world. Lonely wanderers on the enormous light tan beach and trucks' motors and horns of autos and much sun but the air a little too cool for comfort on my bare chest on this balcony five stories high. Many little noises. One begins where

889.  Presumably *Baby Doll.*

890.  Mike Steen (d. 1983), a minor actor, had been introduced to Williams in New Orleans by his roommate Bill Gray. They became friends and saw each other when Williams was in New Orleans. Steen played the Deputy in the film version of *Sweet Bird of Youth* (1962) and Max in the film version of *This Property Is Condemned* (1966). In 1969, Steen published *A Look at Tennessee Williams,* a collection of interviews and conversations with a number of well-known actors, writers, and directors.

891.  Cheryl Crawford (1902–86) was executive assistant to Theresa Helburn at the Theatre Guild in the late 1920s, co-founder with Harold Clurman and Lee Strasberg of the Group Theatre (1931), creator with Eva Le Gallienne and Margaret Webster of the American Repertory Theatre (1946), and co-founder with Elia Kazan and Robert Lewis of the Actors Studio (1947). She also pursued a career as an independent stage producer with a particular interest in musicals, including her biggest commercial success, *Brigadoon* (1947). She produced four of Williams' plays: *The Rose Tattoo* (1950), *Camino Real* (1953), *Sweet Bird of Youth* (1959), and *Period of Adjustment* (1960). Williams dedicated *Sweet Bird of Youth* to her.

Crawford's production of Edward Chodorov's comedy *Oh, Men! Oh, Women!* opened at the Locust Theatre, Philadelphia, on 30 November before moving to New York.

Lee Strasberg, Harold Clurman, and Cheryl Crawford, 1931

another leaves off, and they over lap and run together. This is life. Death has no sound or light in it, but this is still life.

*Friday, 23 October 1953*

Oct. 23.
   My dreams at night make more sense than my activities by day.
   Trying to work on the fucking film script.[889]
   Do I need more money?
   For what?
   To finance this luxurious decline, to maintain the luxury of it?

*Williams returned to New York in early November.*

*Friday, 4 December 1953*

Dec. 4 –
   Started today on the trek to St. Louis, Mike[890] driving and we made good time (70 an hour) stopping over at Philly to see Cheryl's play[891] and to visit the club.
   The N.Y. period was sweet with the Horse on his rare best behavior owing perhaps, to some extent, to his malaise. However the work continues to languish. I worked steadily, every morning, but the good days, and they were not too good, came seldom. maybe only three out of the month.

Williams in the studio of the East 58th Street apartment

892.    Robert MacGregor (1911–74) was Williams' editor at New Directions. In an interview in the *Paris Review* (fall 1981), Williams remembered MacGregor as "a very lovely young guy. . . . He'd been a patient of Dr. Max Jacobson. He only took little pills that Jacobson gave him. I was in a state of such profound depression [in the mid-1960s] that he thought anything was worth trying, so he took me to Jacobson. It was through this Robert MacGregor that I had those three years of Jacobson shots that he mailed to me in the various parts of the country."

893.    Born Johnny Bulica in St. Louis, Johnny Nicholson (1916– ) was the owner of the Café Nicholson on East 57th Street, a frequent haunt of high society and high "bohemia." Nicholson also owned a brownstone, 323 East 58th Street, where Williams was renting an apartment. In the play "A Cavalier for Milady," the first scene is set in an interior with "Victorian-chic" furnishings "that could be created by Johnny Nicholson."

894.    *Green Hills of Africa* (1935), Hemingway's second book of nonfiction, is the record of a month on safari in eastern Africa in which he describes the landscape, the local people, and the hunting of big game animals. In the form of dialogue, he shares his thoughts on various topics, including his idea that "all modern American literature comes from one book by Mark Twain called *Huckleberry Finn*" and his view that America destroys its writers by allowing them to make money and thus betray themselves by needing to sustain a certain standard of living or by creating the climate in which writers care too much about the opinions of critics and thus lose confidence when the opinion is negative.

895.    The apartment at 323 East 58th Street. A Columbia 360 is a phonograph.

Tanaquil Le Clercq, Donald Windham, Buffie Johnson, Williams, and Gore Vidal in the patio garden of the Café Nicholson, New York, 1949 (photograph by Karl Bissinger)

But I like the apartment and my friends were all remarkably nice to me. Jay and Bob McGregor,[892] Gore, Bigelow, Bill Gray and Mike and I began to like Johnny Nicholson[893] and the situation emotionally and nervously was controlled. No crise. F's sweetness had a lot to do with this. Do hope it will persist when we meet again.

Health about as usual. Troubled mostly by the suspicion that my work is far below the level I desire. We continue our trip tomorrow.


*Sunday, 6 December 1953*

Sunday 12:15 A.M.

Drove to Pittsburgh today along a marvelous turnpike and Mike drove up to 85 or 90 miles an hour. I didn't touch the wheel. Tonight we wandered about Pittsburgh looking for the gay places. I felt listless and heavy so I left Mike in a bar and came home to comfort myself with this journal and Mr. Hemingway's "Green Hills of Africa" which I'm reading again,[894] as I do all of his works. Miss Frank & Moon and the big brass bed at 323 and the Columbia 360.[895] But the die is cast and I am going home. I'm not sorry. Grandfather is waiting. I pray that he will be well enough for another season with me. So the earth turns and we turn with it. Or try to, just as long as we can, even at 96. and 42.


*Monday, 7 December 1953*

Monday – 5:30 A.M.

The city of Columbus Ohio gave us a chill welcome. Mike went to the Y and I am puting up in a wretched studio bedroom at a hotel called the Deshler-Hilton, a [*unfinished*]

Slept badly on a narrow folding bed, with unhappy dreams and a sour stomach and little zest for the morrow and the morrows. but desiring to go on. Painful reflections upon the express train – rapidity of time which is rocketing me into my 43rd year on this earth.

Johnny Nicholson (photograph by Karl Bissinger)

896. Edwina Williams, who had separated from her husband at the end of 1947, had recently moved to 6360 Wydown Boulevard in this fashionable suburb of St. Louis.

897. In *The Immoralist* (1902), a puritanical Parisian scholar, Michel, marries to please his dying father. On his honeymoon to North Africa, he is drawn to an exotic world and succumbs to erotic sensations. When his wife falls gravely ill Michel neglects her to gratify his own desires. After the death of his wife, Michel confesses to his friends, "I have reached a point in my life where I can't go on. . . . Knowing how to free oneself is nothing; the difficult thing is knowing how to live with that freedom" (André Gide, *The Immoralist*, translated by David Watson [Harmondsworth: Penguin Books, 2000], p. 15).

New Orleans Athletic Club, 222 North Rampart Street

*I got reckless and invested half of my current cheque in a membership at this rather exclusive Club, but it is worth it as there is a marvelous salt water pool, Turkish bath, Etc., and the prettiest Creole belles in town. I am already well-established in their circles and*

Excerpt of a letter Williams wrote to Paul Bigelow (postmarked 25 September 1941)

but reading Hemingway's good book and will possibly wash down a secconal with a bit of Scotch.

A hotel is no good when you have to put the glass on the floor because there's no table by the bed. (a Hemingway type of sentence)

*Thursday, 10 December 1953*

Thurs. Dec ? 1953

Home in the new house in Clayton.[896] Work seems to prosper here but that could be illusion.

Happy to find Grandfather about as well as ever.

Tomorrow we drive out to see Rose.

Mike will co-pilot.

Saturday we leave for what I hope will be a brilliant holiday season in New Orleans.

So Long.

*Sunday, 20 December 1953*

*New Orleans Dec 1953*

Less than brilliant, though last night the nightingales were in good voice.

Tonight, Saturday, not going out as my dissipations gave me palpitations. Have slept three hours. It is 2:30 A.M.

Now reading Gide's Immoralist[897] again. Prissy but pretty at times. It rains outside slowly and gently, in the New Orleans way, and I have a card to the athletic club. So pleasant there! Saw Pancho today and bought some gifts from him at the haberdashery he works in.

*Tuesday, 22 December 1953*

Tuesday Dec. 23

The nightingales have just sung – an old sea chanty. Only moderately good as I was embarassed afterwards and there were long sentimental speeches and expressions of gratitude that I had to appear to relish. My post-orgasm reaction is pretty dreadful sometimes. I only want to be left alone in my little white bed with my book and my seconal and my last libation. Tonight I've drunk inordinately, at least a dozen hi balls during the past eight hours. And tomorrow must work hard again on film play. It seemed to go well today.

"A cool hustle" – term a kid named Tony used tonight. I wish I listened more

898.    The Rendezvous was a bar on the corner of Bourbon Street and St. Peter Street. In a letter to Oliver Evans dated 5 December 1955 (HRC), Williams wrote:

> Remember Frank of New Orleans? The leather-jacketed ex-truck-driver who was bar man at the Treasure chest and hung out at the Rendezvous? He is tending a side-walk hot-dog-and-chili stand in Miami. Ran into him a few nights ago and he's much the same in appearance and manner. Promised to call me today.

899.    Joan Crawford (1908–77), one of Hollywood's leading film stars of the 1930s, revived her career with her performance as a temperamental musical comedy star who falls in love with a blind pianist in *Torch Song* (1953).

900.    The British actor Michael Wilding (1912–79), married at this time to Elizabeth Taylor, played the role of the blind pianist. Over the course of her acting career, British-born Greer Garson (1903–96) was nominated for seven Academy Awards, and in 1942 she won in the title role of *Mrs. Miniver*, the story of a British housewife during World War II.

901.    Williams and Kazan were working on the film script *Baby Doll*.

The Rendezvous, 640 Bourbon Street, New Orleans

Dixie's Bar, 701–707 Bourbon Street (diagonally across from The Rendezvous)

to these kids. Their lingo is my stock-in-trade. But I am self conscious and concentrate on myself.

The wind is moaning and whistling.

Talked to Frank last night. My heart is full of love for the little horse and only for the little horse.

And grandfather. And for Rose. Alas, much too much of me is concerned with myself.

*Thursday, 24 December 1953*

Christmas Eve.

Just fancy! I am spending it in bed despite a call from Oliver (very drunk) reporting that "The Rendezvous"[898] is brilliant. But then came another call, the one that talked of "a cool hustle" and he came to pay me a call. The nightingales were on key. though their tone has been sweeter on occasions. But those girls are costing me plenty: $40 for the past two concerts. I always relieve my embarassment by over paying perhaps – I mean probably – because the whole thing seems offensive to the inextinguishable Puritan in me still. I am peaceful. moderately. Mike returns 2 days after Christmas and on the 28th we'll start the trip to Miami in the car. Work on film goes with apparent ease and satisfaction. And I have the use of the N.O. Athletic club pool, so heavenly!

Oliver acting strangely – a little madder than usual which is mad enough. Today we had a delightful lunch given us by the officers of a visiting French warship tied up at Toulouse Street Wharf. They are so civilized, charming and urbane compared to American navy brass. Oliver brought one home with him. I didn't. But the occasion was very agreeable. ~~Only one complaint~~ I'm suffering from piles! (No connection)

*Friday, 25 December 1953*

Christmas day 1953

Shit! – no other comment so far.

Not as bad as all that, though it seemed more like any Sunday than the day of Christ's birth.

Work rather languid today in spite of good night's rest. Took Grandpa calling on some old parishioners, The Fluornoys. I was shy and uncomfortable. Later we dined well at the Pontchartrain, Oliver as guest. And I went to the movies alone, to see Our Joan (Crawford) in "Torch Song"[899] which I enjoyed though Michael Wilding does remind me a bit of Miss Greer Garson.[900] Frank had called, but I wasn't in when he called. Still I am pleased that he called. I have washed a "pinkie" down with Scotch and am naked on the bed with my journal and that tiresome book by Miss Gide. A nice wire from Gadg.[901] Goodnight –

902. In May 1946 Williams suffered a ruptured appendix and an infected diverticordium.

903. The Ochsner Clinic was a state-of-the-art, privately run hospital started by the Ochsner family in New Orleans. In *Cat on a Hot Tin Roof*, Big Daddy undergoes extensive tests at the Ochsner Clinic.

The Reverend Walter Dakin and Oliver Evans

*Sunday, 27 December 1953*

Sunday –

Something perhaps quite serious has developed suddenly. A rectal swelling, hemmorhoidal, but much more painful than any previous attack of that disorder. It has woken me up an hour after I got to sleep (with seconal) and hot bath, which relieved it before, doesn't help this time. Must see a doctor tomorrow. The possibilities frighten me.

Supposed to start for Miami tomorrow but it seems unlikely I'll be able to travel – not in this pain.

*Monday, 28 December 1953*

Later – 4:15 – A.M.

Don't think I ever spent such a night of pain not even at the time of the operation in 1946.[902] It is relentless, constant, burning, aching, and the lump at the anus is the size of a walnut, at least.

Frightens & appals one to think what misery, what anguish, our bodies are capable of. And this one such a sordid one, too. It might at least be in a decent place!

Later – It is now 5:45 and the pain, if anything, has gotten worse despite another or two other hot baths. The ointment was worse than useless, seemed to increase the irritation.

I must go to Ochsner Clinic[903] or hospital soon as morning. Must be an acute infection.

Nobody I can really count on here – Oliver is behaving like a spoiled, capricious child, or worse, and no other acquaintance, except possibly Mike, could be reasonably expected to feel any concern. Grandfather is also a problem, and the fact we're supposed to vacate these rooms tomorrow.

Quelle desastre! En Avant!

*Tuesday, 29 December 1953*

Monday or rather Tuesday A.M. about 3.

All hell is descended on me, retribution for all my misdoings and the things undone —

I am in a shabby little hospital outside N.O., sleepless with pain, unable to pee. Awaiting surgery in the morning.

So far nerves controlled but feel pretty desperate. God be with me!

There must be more to say but this pain eclipses thought.

Perhaps that's a mercy. The one.

904. In *Summer and Smoke* (scene 12), Alma takes tablets that make her feel "like a water lily on a Chinese lagoon."

905. According to Thomas K. Griffin, a New Orleans journalist and cultural historian, Williams had called him and asked for his help in moving to the Touro Infirmary for "emergency surgery."
    "But the real reason," according to Griffin, "was that at Ochsner they were very strict about alcoholic drinks, and he wouldn't do without. I didn't know that until I had taken extraordinary measures to have him transferred to Touro. So they did this relatively minor operation there, and he had his liquor." (Spoto, p. 192)

Williams and Mike Steen in Key West, 1967

Later – 3:55

Just let them give me a hypo on top of 3 seconals and several whiskies. Perhaps a mistake but I'm beginning to feel like Miss Alma's water lily on that chinese lagoon.⁹⁰⁴

If anythin goes wrong. I want Frank to have the film play in addition to other items – I think he is loyal to me and possibly even loves me. Who else does? Audrey. Grandfather, Rose (as I was) and Mother in her way.

The injection does not kill the pain – but makes me less concerned with it. But I do wish I could pee. That would be a blessing.

Oliver was sweet tonight – after last night's and this morning's bad behavior. I think I will try once more to pee now –

It rains, the rain, but still no pee for me.

Tuesday P.M.

Transferred to Touro Infirmary, at my insistence, for the operation.⁹⁰⁵ Much nicer here but as zero hour approaches my manhood is hard tested.

Nothing more to be said about that now. Long only for Frank's arrival but that, alas, will probably be hours after the big ordeal. Though there will be others that he can see me through.

Tues. Midnight –

Operation called off or at least postponed till tomorrow. Thank God. I was in no shape for it.

Frank is here. Just left. A great comfort.

I've had a hypo of morphine but feel little effect so far. May also take a seconal to insure rest but slept about 3 hours before Frank arrived.

Will try to sleep again.

Rugged, this thing – Nothing so terrifying or agonizing since Spring of '46. Oh, to be just a little bit well again, for a while!

*Wednesday, 30 December 1953*

Later – That hypo has made me feel very strange –

rather panicky which I must now control.

I won't take them again. Anything strange upsets me. And fear is the worst pain. (You can say that again.)

Rain coming down hard now. I'll be okay in a while. I will, I will. Yes, better now. The old ~~fear~~ terror of anesthesia with me a real phobia –

906.   A sitz bath is a tub in which one bathes in a sitting posture and is used after hemorrhoid surgery.

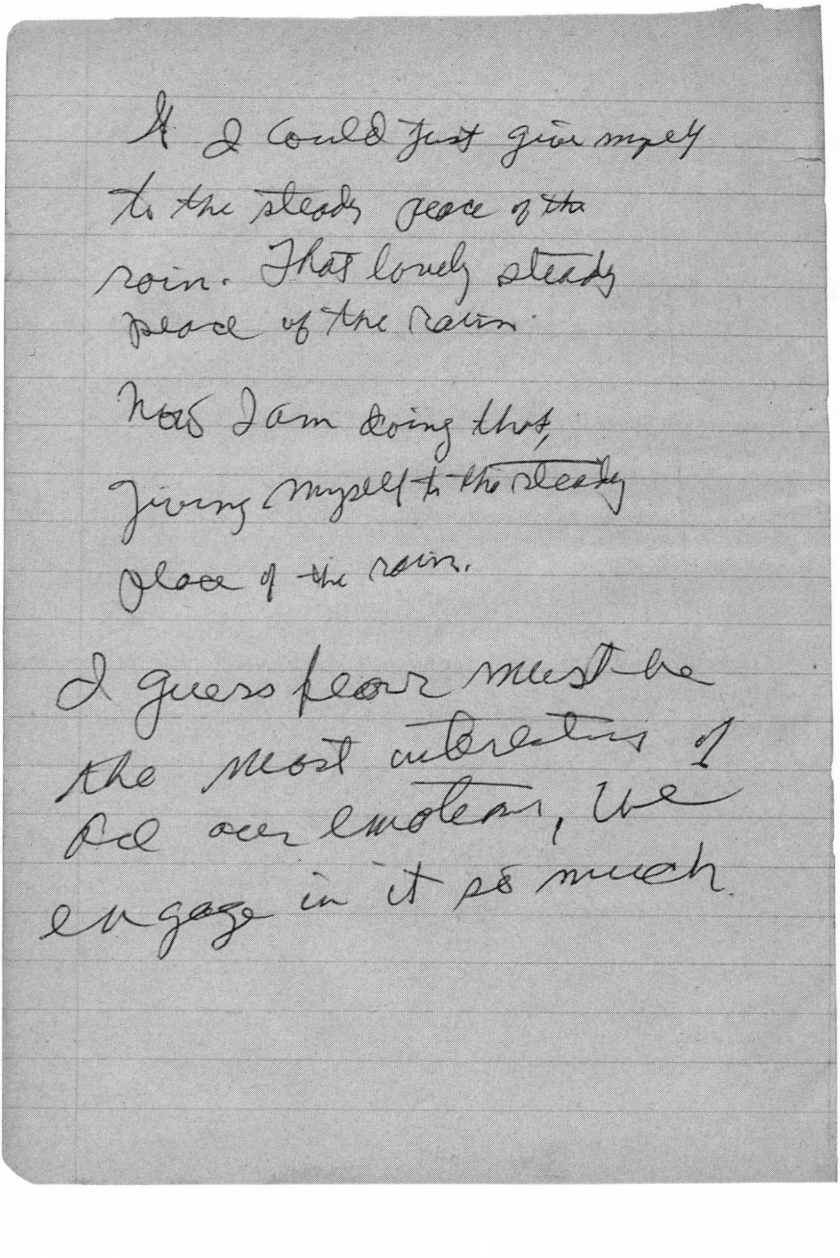

If I could just give myself
to the steady peace of the
rain. That lovely steady
peace of the rain.

Now I am doing that,
giving myself to the steady
peace of the rain.

I guess fear must be
the most interesting of
all our emotions, We
engage in it so much.

If I could just give myself to the steady peace of the rain. That lovely steady peace of the rain.

Now I am doing that, giving myself to the steady peace of the rain.

I guess fear must be the most interesting of all our emotions. We engage in it so much.

Called for a glass of hot milk which I am now sipping.

It seems to me that once upon a time I must have had an ancestor or two who would despise this craven behavior. I don't know which they are, these dauntless ones, but I bid them join me now.

I'm such a coward, oh, such a damned snivelling coward. It does disgust me so.

Wednesday –

Woke up feeling much better after my first sleep in 3 nights and the pain was gone but the edema still there – not much reduction, if any, is apparent to me.

The drug kept me dozing all forenoon but Frank, Grandfather and Mike came at noon and after their visit the drugged state wore off. I have no good book and the hospital won't give me a TV or radio.

Have just been transferred to another room which has a private tub but I don't like it as well.

However I must count my blessings today among which are certainly Frank's presence in town and not having to face an operation. But the future aspect of things is not clear . . .

No, not a bit. The prospect of golden afternoons and calm moonlit nights on the little island is a dream that may be only the stuff that dreams are made of.

Later –

getting nervy and the damn thing hurts and nothing in the new room is quite right. Too big and too much hard grey light. Think I'll retire to the Sitz bath⁹⁰⁶ although all that hot water does weaken me.

Evening – Waiting for Frank like a dog for his bone and his master! – so lonely in here with just my piles and television.

Some damned fool doctor came in here to cross-examine me about my cardiac history. So many doctors are so stupidly unimaginative in their dealings with anxious patients. Of course there are also some like my doctor Smith in New York who are divinely aware I know all about myself but I don't want anyone else to tell me. I mean I know but prefer <u>not</u> to know, especially when, as usually is the case, knowing does no good.

907. In the 1950s late-night television programming ended with the playing of the "Star Spangled Banner."

908. In Paul Bowles' novel *The Sheltering Sky* (New York: New Directions, 1949), Port says to Kit:
"I think we're both afraid of the same thing. And for the same reason. We've never managed, either one of us, to get all the way into life. We're hanging on to the outside for all we're worth, convinced we're going to fall off at the next bump. Isn't that true?" (p. 101)

909. Harold Mitchell and Jim Connor.

Williams and Frank Merlo in Key West

Later – It must be 9 and F. still hasn't come.

Sickness and pain are the loneliest things in the world. They belong to another world. The well people are far away.

If I am ever even relatively well again and free from pain I hope I will remember how this was well enough to take a new pleasure simply in the absence of pain and in the freedom to move.

Later

Frank is here and I've taken my hypo and am in a state of nerves about it again. It is milder than the one last night. they say. Well, I'll be all right in a while. This fear of hypos has got to be conquered.

Actually this one is milder than last night's. my reaction is just plain old scaredy cat.

But this does it. I will just refuse to take them again.

Now I'm through with this silliness.

Not quite through with it I guess but almost through with it. A man can be scared and calm at the same time.

Frank was so sweet to me tonight.

This pill (hypo) would be wonderful if I had not been scared of it.

Absolutely no pain in the ass!

Ah, well – Frank has gone home now. The TV has quit with "The Star Spangled Banner."907 Time for me to appeal to the Sandman.

No. Not quite yet time. Frank said they will permit me to have a drink.

I have a drink beside me and there's more of the same in my suitcase. I've only had one drink a day for the past 2 days and actually that's better perhaps than being quite calm.

But I'm beginning to level off, now.

How sweet it will be to get back to work again. No matter how badly. After this I won't make any extravagant demands of myself. That's done. I will be content with the little that I'm still able to do. I would like to see Bill Inge tonight, for some reason. Also Paul Bowles and Janie. They're all as frightened as I am, you know.908 Just as frightened, only about other matters. There is a tender comradeship in fear when others have it.

But my "Horse" is my little world. How can I tell him? How can I tell my world? I know how bad he can be but I understand why and finally it doesn't matter. In my life there were the two Roses, Grand and my sister. There was Hazel. There was Mitch and Jim.909 Grandfather. Mother. And the Little Horse. I don't say Kip as that was violent desire, not truly love. The Horse I love truly. The hours before he arrived at the hospital tonight were almost as difficult as the hour after the hypo. I think the thrombosed hemorrhoids are reducing a bit tonight but I still can't pee which is troubling. Suppose someone said to me, Tennessee, you have cancer? How would I take it? Probably not well. And yet I suspect that I do. I whisper it to myself. But then, remember the panicky night at the American

910.   In *A Streetcar Named Desire*, Stanley, in describing Blanche's situation when her affair with a high-school student was revealed, tells Stella: "But they had her on the hook good and proper that time and she knew that the jig was all up!" (scene 7).

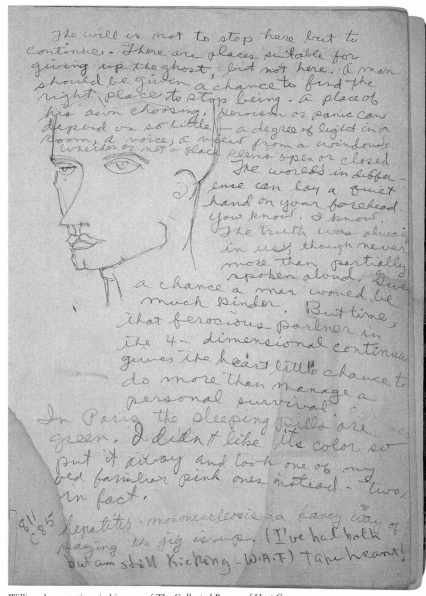

Williams' annotations in his copy of *The Collected Poems of Hart Crane*

hospital in Paris. I said (wrote on a fly leaf of Crane's "Bridge") – "the jig is up."[910]

And it wasn't by a long shot. Here I am, six years later! in another hospital in another land.

Sometimes wanting to survive hard enough does it.

*Thursday, 31 December 1953*

Morning 7:15

Not a good night. Sleep interrupted twice by diarrhoea and only got about five hours at most.

Extremely anxious over continued inability to pee except a little bit, now and then, in hot water.

The day stretches before me its grey infinity. It will be hours before Frank comes. This is a hard thing for him, too.

I shall try not to be any gloomier than necessary today, no matter how things go.

Later – the day improved a great deal, the weather turned bright. The TV programs were amusing and I suffered no pain comparable to the exquisite torments of a few days ago.

The morning, or rather afternoon (2 P.M.) call of grandfather and Frank was ruined by the presence of Mike. I had to ask him to leave. Silly of me to find him so repugnant all of a sudden. It's that complacent way he beams at himself, I suppose.

Oliver came, drunk, after being out all night. Wept over his problems which seem so little to me – compared to mine.

The doctor warns that I shall eventually require surgery but that it needn't be now. Well, it is New Year's Eve, and I face the coming year with more hope in my heart than circumstances may warrant. I am glad to be alive and hope to remain so yet a while.

Frank Merlo

911.  Jo Van Fleet (1919–96) was starring in an episode of *Campbell Playhouse* called "Reville for Two Angels."
She had played Marguerite in *Camino Real* and went on to play Bessie in the film version of *The Rose
Tattoo* (1955).

912.  Presumably *Baby Doll*.

Jo Van Fleet in *Camino Real*

life! Why did I spoil it for
myself with all those
fierce demands and
disappointments? If
I get out of this, I think
I'll know better. I will
ask little of myself and
less of others. Of life
only a spell of quiet
in the sun, freedom to
move without pain in
that sweet quiet.

*Friday, 1 January 1954*

New Year's Eve – later –

Wouldn't take hypo tonight. Slept a couple of hours without one, woke at 2 A.M. feeling less than terrific. Maybe call for the hypo after all, as it does seem to relax the anal area at night, however it may and does disturb the higher man. But so far have only called for a hot water bottle and a glass of hot milk.

New Year's day – 9:20 A.M.

Not a good beginning.

I managed to get enough sleep without the hypo but there is more discomfort this morning. I am depressed. It isn't clearing up at all quickly and I'm restless and bored as well as anxious and uncomfortable. Oh, how I long to be loose again, entering the Key West studio for morning work, with the sky and the Australian pines through the sky light and clear morning light on all four sides and the warmth of coffee in me and the other world of creation. And driving out to the beach in the afternoon, the slow, easy, meditative drink on the pink terrace there, the long easy swim in the buoyant, pleasantly cool water. Grandfather lounging on the porch as we drive home and Mr. Moon. Or just the luxury of walking and sitting down without pain and being able to pee without lying in a hot tub.

How sweet is simple life! Why did I spoil it for myself with all those fierce demands and disappointments? If I get out of this, I think I'll know better. I will ask little of myself and less of others. Of life only a spell of quiet in the sun, freedom to move without pain in that sweet quiet.

Night – 8:15

Managed to pee standing at toilet for first time since this started.

Oliver came over today and said, "I talked to your doctor. He says you should have an operation as it could become malignant."

I thought the remark at least unnecessary.

He has impulses of shocking cruelty sometimes because? – ?

Just saw Jo Van Fleet on TV and she was great. I find some comfort in knowing that my recent failures have been helpful to the players in getting jobs.[911]

Herbert Brown – actor in TV show, v.g. as possibility for Val.

*Saturday, 2 January 1954*

Morning –

Would have been good, I expect, if I hadn't drunk coffee and attempted to write in the hospital bed. No go. Too many irritations especially the seating arrangement. Now feel a bit edgy from frustration but after a seconal and a drink I may go through the Ms.[912] with pen and make notes and corrections or I may just lie there watching TV or reading James Joyce, "The Dubliners" which is

913.    Carl Butts attended Ben Blewett Junior High School with Williams. He received a ninth grade citizenship award in 1926. In the 1970s play *A Lovely Sunday for Creve Coeur*, set in St. Louis, Williams named a "nice old" butcher Mr. Butts. Over a sizzling skillet, Bodey enthusiastically tells her roommate Dorothea, a civics teacher at Blewett, about him (scene 1):

> The fryers are sizzling so loud I didn't catch that, Dotty. . . . I think that Roosevelt did something for the country when he got us half Saturdays off because it used to be that by the time I got off the streetcar from International Shoe, Piggly-Wiggly's on the corner would be closed, but now it's still wide open. So I went in Piggly-Wiggly's, I went to the meat department and I said to the nice old man, Mr. Butts, the butcher, "Mr. Butts, have you got any real nice fryers?" — "You bet your life!" he said, "I must of been expectin' you to drop in. Feel these nice plump fryers." Mr. Butts always lets me feel his meat.

914.    End of scene 6 of *A Streetcar Named Desire*.

Page from a manuscript of *A Streetcar Named Desire*

truly superb and which I somehow had missed till now. A lyric talent which is controlled by intellect, the rarest of happy accidents in the world of letters. Lyric, intellectual and "noble". probably the greatest writer since Shakespeare – It's odd. I have a strange feeling of insouciance, a sort of witless insouciance today, perhaps because I was unable to write and didn't much care that I wasn't able to. Could it be that I have given up that old breast-beating? If so, that would be worth all I've been through lately. Breast-beating, self castigation for failure outside your control is the ~~fatal~~ error that makes a hell of an artist's life.

### Sunday, 3 January 1954

Sunday P.M.

My attempt to resume work this morning was not too fruitful but my general condition seems steadily better so I feel encouraged. The day is hot as summer and as bright. After two and no visitor yet but the doctor. He's nice but I feel shy with him. A good book. But T.V. is Sunday dull with preachers and patriotic costume dramas. Well, it looks like the road goes on from here, after all, for which I give praise to the Lord, and much Thanksgiving! I cried out for survival when it seemed that the walls were starting to close in.

Line from TV drama "Here comes general Le Marquis de Lafayette!"
A good excuse to turn the fucking thing off but I'm too lazy to get up and do it.

Carl Butts. – an old schoolmate who played the piano at "aud sessions" at Junior Hi.[913] My best friend (only one) there. Just now remembered him, seeing "Liberace" at the TV piano.

### Monday, 4 January 1954

Monday –

Distinct improvement happily noted today. The swelling has very definitely gone down and the soreness almost completely disappeared now.

I should think I could get out tomorrow.

Then flight to Miami Wed. with grandfather.

Key West soon as Frank brings Moon down.

"Sometimes there's God so quickly!"[914]

915. On 6 January 1954 (Wesleyan), Williams replied to Elia Kazan: "You always write me directly and truly about what is going on in your head and heart and it makes me feel a lot less alone anywhere that I am."

916. Marion Vaccaro.

Williams in his studio, Key West

Frank Merlo, Marion Vaccaro, and Williams in the Bamboo Room, Key West

*Tuesday, 5 January 1954*

Tuesday –

Another thwarted effort to pick up work. I'm afraid I'll slip back into gloom about that if I don't watch out and remember, carefully, what I resolved when I was so sick a few days ago. That I would make no more incontinent demands on the exhausted artist. Let him rest. Even let him expire if his term is over. But since I want life, even without Creation, I must not whip myself for not doing what I've stopped being able to do. Whether the failure be only a while, or longer, or always.

*Wednesday, 6 January 1954*

Wed. Evening

Arrived by plane in Miami, Grandfather and I, after an incredibly long flight that made 5 stops on the way and took 3 hours longer than a flight from New York. I am cross with The Horse about this as he should have enquired before booking us on this "milk" plane. But I am happy to be here, all in one piece, and my "trouble" seems to be not adversely affected by the journey – in fact better.

Tomorrow I hope to work like a son of a bitch!

Desire nothing else.

A sweet, very sweet, letter from "Gadg" that warms the cockles of my heart. I answered it right away.[915] Goodnight.

*Thursday, 7 January 1954*

Thurs. Eve.

The sort of day that I dreamed about in the hospital. I lay in the sun by the pool. I worked in the morning. I moved about freely without pain . . .

So life goes on again. No word from Frank. He could arrive late tonight but I rather doubt it. The room's hot. Reading matter only so so but I have a Scotch beside me and I feel no pain. I would rather like a companion, however, and am entirely unlikely to have one. Marian[916] warned me that the town is "hot". The streets are notably dull. Last night a horrid cockroach appeared on my bedside table. I hope he doesn't return.

*Friday, 8 January 1954*

Later – 5:45 A.M.

Slept 3 hours, then woke and took a hot bath to relieve itching. Hope the day's activity didn't cause a setback. Must take it easy today. Dreamed that a wealthy old lady, entertaining me and grandfather, read my journal and had her

917.    Gilbert Maxwell, who was living in Miami.

Williams and Gilbert Maxwell

Frank Merlo and Williams outside 1341 Duncan Street, Key West

colored maid put it in incinerator, whence I rescued it twice, and very irate, prepared to leave the mansion. Apparently meaningless dream. Why this innocent journal? What did the old lady represent? Among her guests was a man named Taft! Grandfather was impressed at meeting him.

6:15 – Whew! Scared Shitless! Just turned over in bed and became so dizzy I nearly blacked out!

Don't know what form of treatment is indicated but I took a panicky drink and a seconal just now and will try to read till I'm calm. A queer thing!

I do feel that work, with its present tensions, is contra-indicated for a while now. I do wish Frank were here. There's no one I can turn to. I am lying here picking a scab on my right knee.

The old machine is getting very cranky.

I would finish my drink but I feel a touch of nausea.

Day is beginning now. Birds chattering somewhere distant and the sky turning a paler blue.

I will go to sleep after while as if this hadn't happened.

I had a short, sharp attack like this one morning in N.Y. about two months ago, sitting at my typewriter. Then I thought it was related to the work tension. I would like to go to the window and get some fresh air but am a little timid of moving much now.

Just now vomited – sitting in chair at window. Feel better now but wonder if I'll have to take another seconal. May have tossed the other.

Friday evening –

Frank has come and gone again, by plane to New York. I have been feeling odd, light-headed, all day. A little better tonight after dinner. But wish The horse hadn't gone off again so quickly. However –

I may call Gilbert.⁹¹⁷ On the other hand I may just read my magazines and hope for a good night's sleep to restore me.

Just now – a painful jolt in my heart. I got up to get my Scotch. This does not bode well for the night in progress. Dialed Gil's number. No answer. It is only 9:30 – a long night is before me. Ah, how I wish that damned doctor at the hospital had not alarmed me about my ticker!

I suppose on the whole I am reasonably calm. I have taken a seconal and am having a drink. Actually the incident would not have disturbed me were it not for the vertigo last night and faintness today.

There is one thing to do, one thing and one only – put it out of my mind and pass the night as though it hadn't occured.

I have opened the door between my room and grandfather's. Goodnight.

918. In *The Deep Blue Sea* (1952), by the British playwright Terence Rattigan (1911–77), a judge's wife attempts suicide when she is rejected by her ex-RAF lover. It was staged at the Studio M Playhouse in Coral Gables.

919. Possibly a scene from *Orpheus Descending* or *Cat on a Hot Tin Roof*.

The Reverend Walter Dakin in Key West

*Saturday, 9 January 1954*

Saturday night

Seeing Gilbert was a good move. He charmed me out of my panic. I forgot my anxieties most of the evening and felt well. We went to "Studio M" and saw 2 acts of "The Deep Blue Sea"[918] then came home and had a couple of drinks in the hotel bar. I also took a seconal and felt a bit high and very relaxed and had a nice easy conversation with a lady in the bar.

Tomorrow I hope there will be sun and a pleasant afternoon by the pool.

*Sunday, 10 January 1954*

Sunday

One of those notoriously bad Sunday's at least so far.

Woke up so light headed I could hardly let in "room-service". Had a cup of coffee but remained on bed. This persistent giddiness is exceedingly troubling. I may try to write, just a bit, now, then go down to the pool. If I am able to navigate.

Later –

wrote a tired little scene,[919] as tired as I am. now I will take grandfather down to eat. There is no sun. It is warm and grey as an old chicken feather on a dirt road in the Delta. I feel like I had given all my blood to Red Cross, all but one and a half pints of it.

*Wednesday, 13 January 1954*

Wed. Miami

These past few days were too sad to talk about. Last night I picked up a little and drove out to the university theatre to see "Death of a Salesman" done there and I felt better. Had a night of broken sleep but was able to work a little this morning. It's a cool day but the sun is bright and perhaps I can swim and lie by the pool after lunch. Frank may arrive today. or tomorrow. I can't remember which day he told me he was coming back from New York. I am still light-headed.

*Saturday, 16 January 1954*

Key West – Sat. Jan. 16 –

I am doing what I dreamed of doing again. Clear mornings, coffee, the studio – quiet, serene.

But the Muse is not attracted.

Not today.

920.    In a letter to Maria Britneva (22 April 1953), Williams described the atmosphere of the studio:
        [T]he Key West studio! It is so lovely! A sky-light with delicate bamboo curtain, palms, banana trees
        and fern-like Australian pines through the windows in all four walls, a Japanese lantern over my
        head with glass-pendants that tinkle in the constant trade-winds, a silver ice-bucket, gin, and oranges
        for pauses in occupation. Wonderful sounds, the palms and banana trees make, like ladies running
        barefooted in silk skirts downstairs, a constant flickering of light and shadow, a table that's five feet
        long, theatrical posters stuck all over the lemon yellow walls, my own bathroon, a comfortable lit-
        tle bed, driftwood, a fan that belonged to Hart Crane, shells, solitude, peace! (*FOA*, p. 75)

Gore Vidal and Williams in his studio, Key West

*Sunday, 17 January 1954*

Sunday
    Today the same. Only more so.
    The sky is cloudless and the wind-chimes barely tinkle.[920]
    I shall go looking for the usual temporary solace of sun and sea.


*Monday, 18 January 1954*

Monday
    Woke up feeling light-headed. Couldn't finish my coffee, had to wash a
"pinkie" down with a martini and only wrote 2 pages.
    The day is fair. I suppose I'll keep drinking and take the sun on the beach.
    I feel weak and silly.


*Thursday, 18 February or Friday, 19 February 1954*

Feb. 18 or 19 or 20
    Assembling the Ms. of the new "Battle" again and again – defeated.
    Intensity no longer makes anything but a quality of hysteria.
    The days have been relatively easy but each night there is panic or a threat of it.
    The way out, or even on, is obscure. I must simply go along with the days and
nights in this place and try not to feel more desperate than I have to.


*Saturday, 20 February 1954*

Late – Sat. Night
    Panic twice today, both times assuaged by a seconal and bourbon.
    But the cardiac neurosis is in full flower again and looms as a fearful spectre.
    After all, what threatens life, threatens everything that is.


*Sunday, 21 February 1954*

Later – slept a while and woke, F. still out, Moon scratching and snoring.
    I'll probably go downstairs for a drink – don't feel sleepy, alas, so may remain
awake till F. returns. I hope no more pills will be necessary.

921.    Vitamin B12 injections are sometimes given for exhaustion caused by anemia.

922.    The Reverend Walter Dakin often stayed at the Hotel Gayoso in Memphis, Tennessee.

923.    Early drafts of *Cat on a Hot Tin Roof* included the title "A Place of Stone," a title Williams took from Yeats' poem "To a Friend Whose Work Has Come to Nothing." Williams considered using its last four lines as the play's epigraph:

> Amid a place of stone,
> Be secret and exult,
> Because of all things known
> That is most difficult.

When the play was published this epigraph was replaced by well-known lines from Dylan Thomas:

> And you, my father, there on the sad height,
> Curse, bless, me now with your fierce tears, I pray.
> Do not go gentle into that good night.
> Rage, rage against the dying of the light!

924.    Burt Lancaster (1913–94) had recently received an Academy Award nomination for best actor in *From Here to Eternity* (1953). In the film version of *The Rose Tattoo*, which premiered on 12 December 1955, he was playing the part of Alvaro Mangiacavallo.

Hotel Gayoso, Memphis

*Tuesday, 9 March 1954*

March 9 or 10 – Tuesday
    My feet have been numb for 5 days.

*Wednesday, 17 March 1954*

Wed. March 17
    Consulted a specialist here about the alarming symptoms of dropsy. He told me it was not that but something he called "early peripheral neuritis" which he ascribed to a toxic condition induced partly by liquor. He gave me Vitamin B12 in the ass and I'm to continue these shots every other day in Key West.[921]
    Of course I would love to believe the good doctor but I don't quite believe him.
    We shall see what we shall see. There's nothing I can do but try to worry about it the least that I can.
    Bigelow is with me and we fly back to Key West today.

*Saturday, 3 April 1954*

April 3, 1954
    In New Orleans with grandfather, taking him back to the Gayoso in Memphis.[922]
    Symptoms last described still persist. But otherwise I feel no worse than before. Can't get in touch with Dr. Hanley at the Ochsner clinic today so I guess I'll stay over here, at the St Charles hotel, at least till Monday. Talked to Oliver last night but haven't seen him yet. or anybody. We have a date for lunch. I wrote sort of messy today on "Place of Stone".[923] The intrusion of the homosexual theme may be fucking it up again.
    Well, anyhow I better get dressed now and play it cool today. Maybe can enjoy this stay a little.

*Sunday, 4 April 1954*

Sunday –
    "Had big nite of fun!" in Quarter with Oliver.
    The town was brilliant. I got a little drunk and hired a nightingale to serenade me in a small hotel close to the St. Charles. By no means a memorable concert but an acceptable "faute de mieux".
    Circulatory – symptoms – arms, legs going to sleep during the night – and of course the feet are still a couple of sponges (dry) today – but I'm getting used to that now and I try not to think about it and sometimes don't.
    I'm in the middle of a big row between Magnani and Lancaster[924] over precedence in billing.

925. Charles B. Hinch, "Tennessee Williams Has New, Unusual Titled Play," *New Orleans Times-Picayune*, 6 April 1954, p. 22.

926. Alexander Fedoroff (1927–79), a native of New Orleans, had worked in the theatrical field, and in 1953 his play "Day of Grace" was produced at the Westport Country Playhouse in Connecticut. He went on to write another play and several novels.

Monday —

And so I leave Grandfather today and I'm fairly certain I'll never see him again. I think he's fairly certain of it, too. It breaks what's left of my heart. Time's relentless. Of course we may meet in Ohio sooner than I know. An interminable train trip before me as I chickened out of the 4 hour non-stop flight to New York. Feared claustrophobia would attack me with no stop

*Tuesday, 6 April 1954*

Tuesday –

Photo and write-up in paper and a TV date in an hour. I am still (or more?) susceptible to the flattery of public attention.

Work somewhat blocked today – but the design is clearer and seeing the play "Cat on a hot tin Roof" named in print[925] made it seem realer to me.

Why did I despair of it so in Madrid, in this same journal? When was I seeing it clearer, now or then?

Tomorrow & Thursday – Ochsner clinic.

Friday – Memphis –

*Wednesday, 7 April 1954*

Wed.

Saw the heart-specialist at Ochsner Clinic. He said the condition was not circulatory but his diagnosis was not at all specific. He used a vibratory pitchfork to test sensory reaction. I felt it distinctly on my wrists but not at all on my ankles. This is by no means reassuring, I guess. And I took a dim view of "Cat on a Hot Tin Roof" when I read it over, the first act, this A.M. It doesn't really seem to have the essential ~~clarity and~~ force and it still lacks a clear, strong line. It is low voltage, and not pure enough to make up for that. Alex Federoff[926] called and I am to see him at 5:30 this afternoon. Perhaps that will be pleasant. I may as well seek the pleasures the flesh may still offer, while, Etc.

Last night a pick up that was beautiful and cold and no satisfaction and very little sleep afterwards. <u>En Avant!</u>

Wed. Night.

Nothing to report of interest except two sex adventures. The matinée was fine, the soirée a fiasco. Was impotent – should never attempt sex twice a day now that I am in my forties and far from well.

*Monday, 12 April 1954*

Monday –

And so I leave Grandfather today and I'm fairly certain I'll never see him again. I think he's fairly certain of it, too. It breaks what's left of my heart. Time's relentless. Of course we may meet in Ohio sooner than I know. An interminable train trip before me as I chickened out of the 4 hour non-stop flight to New York. Feared claustrophobia would attack me with no stop.

927.   Hal Kanter (1918– ) is a television and film writer, producer, and director. Williams' collaboration on the screenplay of *The Rose Tattoo* with Kanter became so unpleasant and unproductive that Williams rejected Kanter's request to share the screenplay credit with him. In the final version, Williams received sole credit for the screenplay and Kanter received credit for the screen adaptation.

928.   Johnny Nicholson.

929.   James S. Elliott (1925–81) would produce "27 Wagons Full of Cotton" and Raffaello de Banfield's opera *Lord Byron's Love Letter*, which de Banfield (1922– ) based on Williams' one-act play, and for which Williams wrote the libretto. Both pieces would premiere on 17 January 1955 in New Orleans.

James S. Elliott and Williams, and a poster for the double bill Elliott produced in New Orleans

*Saturday, 17 April 1954*

6:20 A.M. Saturday

Sleepless night – abdominal discontent, and fury over the "Tattoo" script I was given by my "collaborator" Kanter:[927] He couldn't write "I see the cat" and I may be stuck with him. My fury extends to the whole bunch of them –

I want to shut a door on all that dreary buy and sell side of writing and work purely again for myself alone. I am sick of being peddled. Perhaps if I could have escaped being peddled I might have become a major artist. It's no one's fault. It's just a dirty circumstance, and now's maybe too late to correct it.

Drinking a soothing glass of cold milk.

Saturday Night

Liquid diarrhoea (green) continues and I had to spend the evening out. So weak, tired and stupid, barely spoke. Must work on "Tattoo" script tomorrow. Then another social occasion in the evening. I already loathe New York and the life here – Moon is sick as I am. I accused F. of neglecting him – probably not fair. But F. seems totally absorbed in Johnny[928] – seems to have no other concern.

*Sunday, 18 April 1954*

Sunday night –

The little dog just died – so quickly!

A single heart breaking cry – another, softer, and he was gone.

Frank hysterical – I feel cold and desolate.

They've gone to a hospital with his body – our little Moon, goodbye!

*Monday, 26 April 1954*

Sun. Night – (week later)

Yes. watch out for these Sundays. This is a mean one, too.

Can't relax – it's 4 A.M.

*Friday, 7 May 1954*

Friday May ?

Sailing date draws near. a week from tomorrow. Work has hit an all time low – that's something, man! – Today this A.M. a real <u>crise</u> – felt close to collapse. A seconal pulled me through. Pleasant P.M. with Jimmy Elliot who is going to do Rafaello opera version of "Lord Byrons Etc" and "27 Wagon" next season[929] – perhaps my sole production.

930. Williams was most likely reading *The Selected Letters of Lord Byron*, edited with an introduction by Jacques Barzun (New York: Farrar, Straus and Young, 1953), although he owned at the time of his death *Byron: A Self-portrait, Letters and Diaries 1798 to 1824*, with hitherto unpublished letters, edited by Peter Quennell (London: John Murray, 1950).

931. Paul Bowles and other residents of Tangier could not identify Jennie. Possibly Williams wrote Jennie but meant Janie Bowles.

932. Tuinal, a barbiturate made from amobarbital and secobarbital, is a sleeping pill. Both seconal and tuinal are prescribed for the short-term treatment of insomnia. Small doses relieve tension; large doses may produce blurred vision, impaired thinking, slurred speech, and impaired perception of time and space.

Drawings of Williams' bulldog Buffo by Anna Magnani

I am not unhappy – we have an adorable new puppy, Signor Buffo. Frank is being remarkably agreeable. Big party (farewell) planned for Sun. Eve.

### Monday, 31 May 1954

Tangier – May 31

No recovery in work. Physical condition alarming.

Bad attack on street day before yesterday and since then, very anxious. Haven't worked for two days. Got new 3rd Act Battle back from typist today and decided not to send it to New York. Virtual surrender, at least for the present. Will try to lay off work for a good while and see if some recovery comes from rest. we leave here day after tomorrow.

### Thursday, 3 June 1954

Tangier – June 3 –

Still here. Anxiety fairly continual and I'm just holding on. Liquor and secconal are my only refuge and they not unfailing.

The thing to do is adopt, forcibly, an acceptive, stoic attitude, quite deliberately and resolutely "let go"! Be limp. Drop everything.

Anal irritation has also developed again and I am afraid of another serious attack in that quarter. Tonight slept only 2 hours.

Frank came in at 3:30 and from then on no sleep and Byron's letters[930] fail to divert me enough to provide much comfort.

but En <u>Avant</u>.

(Ramadan is over. Cannon saluted 20 times at 3:30. The beach at the foot of the hill is already overrun by holiday Arabs – perhaps the sky will clear and the afternoon may offer me entertainment as well as the narcotic wine at Jennie's.)[931] But I've been a sexual dud lately. (Among other things)

### Saturday, 5 June 1954

Saturday 7:40 A.M.

The plane for Madrid is taking off, now, and I am calmer than I expected to be, in view of my general condition which is <u>nearly</u> as near collapse as one could go . . . . But the day is clear, the plane is not overcrowded. I have 5 secconals and a tuinal[932] in my pocket and a pint of liquor. and I am seated just forward of the lavatory to which I shall doubtless retire soon after the plane takes off – which it is now doing. En Avant!

Take off slow. Scared me a bit. But now we're up and cruising close to the sea.

Seated next to me is a handsome young man with those dark eyes which are

12 via Corsini, Rome, where Williams stayed in summer 1955

51 via del Babuino, Rome, where Williams stayed in summer 1956

more expressive in Spain than other dark-eyed countries. I hear the stewardess bustling about with metal containers. I trust that she will provide me with a receptacle for liquor – Approaching Madrid now – a good flight – nerves calm after first ½ hour, a seconal and a drink.

Saturday 3 P.M.
A good start here. Room at the Palace, lovely.
Seat for a big corrida this P.M.
Had a Paella for lunch and a bottle of Palomar.
Now will take a nap till 5.
The Toros begin at 6.
Thanks Allah! – as Ahmed would say.

*Sunday, 6 June 1954*

5:10 A.M. Sunday –
Work after a 3 hour sleep feeling rather seedy and depressed, the usual let-down after a plane flight. It's always more of a strain than I know. Reading Lawrence's masterpiece "Sons and Lovers" again. A book that should have moved the earth to pity. It reminds me of my own heartbroken home, Mother. The sad distance come between us. My desperate old father. And the fate of Rose. And my soul, if I have one still, sighs. And shudders and sickens. I get up and pour myself a drink and wash down a seconal with it. Ah, God, God!
Dark violet light of daybreak but no bird voices.

Sunday – Can't work today. Concentration impossible. A bell hop brought cigarettes and tried to seduce me. I was not responsive – physically or emotionally.
Now I'm dressed. Probably not in my right mind, but dressed, and going down to the bar and to enquire if there's another bull-fight.

( *there was* )

*Monday, 7 June 1954*

Monday 8:30 P.M.
Plane to Rome delayed till 10. Having dinner at airport in Madrid after a frantic ride out in a broken down hack – the driver misunderstood and took me, first, to the TWA office in downtown Madrid and I thought sure we'd never make it.
Countless things doubtless lost in the madness of packing.
I really don't know why I'm making this trip. I have nothing to show Audrey and can't imagine what she has to discuss with me so soon after New York. But I rarely know why I do things anymore. I just go along in response to various impulses, in or outside me.

933.   Isa Miranda (1905–82), the Italian stage and screen actress, would play the part of Lady Torrance in the London production of *Orpheus Descending* (1959) at the Royal Court Theatre.

Opening pages of a letter Williams wrote to Jane and Paul Bowles

9:57 P.M.

Plane now about to take off. I have the last seat back, my choice, a single right by the men's room to which I will doubtless retire as soon as the plane is off. They are pressurizing the cabin and that disturbs me.

It is exactly 10 P.M.

I was pretty shaky back there a bit. Consequence of what I'm not sure.

Pressurizing? Long wait at airport? General nervous debility?

Ah, well. I am not exactly the world's most tranquil person. But they serve drinks on this plane and in the air I find that time has a way of slipping by faster.

This notebook is falling apart – will have to have it bound in Rome. I'll need it for company in the days to come. If I decide to give up the creative struggle, I think I will go to the Orient – Ceylon or India or Japan – I think perhaps the time has come. I wonder if Frank would go with me? A lot depends on what sort of money comes in from the films. Next year, unless the films pay, I'll be in a much lower income bracket.

I'm being stupid, aren't I? Really just chattering to pass the time but I do think "Middle aged man, go East!" is a good idea. And I do think Frank would go with me. He has his own kind of gallantry, you know, As much as I have mine and he would never "ditch me in a hitch".


*Tuesday, 8 June 1954*

Tues. 3 A.M.

Arrived! Rome again – and oh, it's good to be back, even with business, matters over my head! A solitary walk from the Boston hotel up the wide cool river of Via Venuto, a Scotch at the Strega, and back to my "little white bed". Good night and Thank God.

Tuesday 11:50 P.M.

Have moved to Inghilterra. 2 pleasant rooms but I feel lonely in them. After my nap this P.M. I felt very shaky indeed. Had to use liquor and seconal to get through the evening with the Lieblings and Miranda.933 Isa rather disappointed me. Her social manner is artificial. Tomorrow I have to deliver the play to them (Orpheus). I must resume swimming somewhere.


*Wednesday, 9 June 1954*

2 A.M.

Had to close windows to keep the noise out. Fortunately the rooms are cool. I had forgotten how noisy Rome can be. Don't feel sleepy. Vague, oppressive anxiety dogs me. There's a glass of liquor and 2 capsules by the bed but I wish, I would prefer to, avoid them – Feel dreadfully alone, especially since my heart jolted a few

934. *Kingdom of Earth (The Seven Descents of Myrtle)* would end up having only two acts. The "good stuff" may refer to the additional elements Williams gave to his dramatization. In the play Williams added a flood, a plot by Lot and his wife, Myrtle, to destroy the written agreement between Lot and Chicken dealing with inheritance, and, in the final scene, the appearance of Lot wearing a wig and dressed in his deceased mother's gauzy white summer dress. For the play, Williams would also modify the ending of the story. At the end of the short story, Lot dies and Myrtle and Chicken marry and expect a child; at the end of the play, Lot collapses and Myrtle and Chicken run off together to escape the imminent flood.

935. *The World in the Evening* (New York: Random House, 1954), set against the backdrop of World War II, follows the emotional development of Stephen Monk, an Englishman living in California. After the end of his second marriage, Monk stays with a relative in a small Quaker town in Pennsylvania and recovers from being hit by a truck. With much time to reflect about his past relationships, including an earlier affair with a younger man, he comes gradually to understand his bisexuality.

Unidentified man, Audrey Wood, Williams, Isa Miranda, and William Liebling
in Piazza della Repubblica, Rome

minutes ago. I've got to work out some plan for myself, some means of restoring my balance because otherwise — Smash! Stomach erupting, great burps of acidity.

I shall look for place tomorrow on the warm yellow streets. And this summer I will look for courage in my heart and God somewhere, somewhere. Maybe Frank can help me. Maybe Maria will help me. Maybe God will help me. Maybe I'll help myself. Anyhow things will change. The decline can't continue since I have arrived at just about the pit.

3:50 – I remain sleepless, despite secconal. No other comment occurs to me. I suppose as a last resort I might take that block-buster tuinal. Well, read a while first.

*Friday, 11 June 1954*

Friday –

We have moved into a new apt. and it's gone sour on me already. I am not in a state to like anything now. Was off coffee and work for about 5 days but it made no appreciable difference in my nerves so I started both again yesterday. Work almost totally blocked. Sex and work have followed same course lately. Last two days I have taken secconal before noon. Today it rained. I walked about in it for 2 or 3 hours after lunch on Piazza Nervona. Now back alone with the dog who sleeps his lonely hours away, a call from Mark Lawrence. I felt tongue tied. He's going to send over a masseur for me tomorrow. Tonight I plan to ~~see~~ hear "Carmen" the only opera I like very much. I think I will soon take off for another place – Sicily? Portofino? Hamburg?

*Saturday, 3 July 1954*

Sat. – July 3 (or 4th?)

Imagine not knowing whether or not it's the Fourth of July?

Been better here, the anxiety lifted.

Stopped taking secconals during the day, swimming at club pretty regularly. Shaken off the blue devils pretty successfully for the present. Work picked up a bit. I've been assembling first draft of "Kingdom of Earth" and it does contain some good stuff, though it runs too short and its philosophical content is hardly important.934

Reading Isherwood's new novel.935 Disappointing, doesn't seem to be anything deeply personal or creative, but still has passages that are good prose.

Have had some good sex lately – the best with F., of course.

Maria is with us. I am getting adjusted to the situation but at first it seemed a rather trying complication, fond as I am of her. A girl in the house is a strain! And Maria does need attention. and I am selfish . . . mostly the last item is relevant.

Goodnight

936. On the following day (10 July 1954, HRC), Williams wrote Audrey Wood about the actions he had taken to prevent losing artistic control over the film of *The Rose Tattoo*.

I had to write [the director Danny Mann] a very strong letter yesterday. <u>I don't like the smell of things!</u> I reminded him that I finally signed with [the producer Hal] Wallis because I was assured that his association would give me the equivalent of artistic control, and I don't like the changes in script that are being made without my consent or even knowledge. I don't want to create a bad atmosphere but am resolved to be tough about this. It's <u>that</u> important to me, and also to <u>Magnani</u>. "All hell will break loose" if they start fucking (pardon!) up <u>this script</u> on me. . . . . I will devote the remainder of my days to a real old fashioned Sicilian vendetta! — the butcher knife in the purse will be comparatively genteel. Because there is <u>no</u> excuse for it! I <u>can</u> give them, <u>if</u> they'll <u>let</u> me, a beautiful and successful film.

937. At this time Williams viewed *Kingdom of Earth* as complementary to *Cat on a Hot Tin Roof*. In his letter to Wood (10 July 1954, HRC), Williams wrote:

I expect to return with complete (rough) drafts of two plays "Kingdom of Earth" and "Cat on a Tin Roof". They could be done together in the shorter form and both contain parts for Brando. . . . Although totally different in background, the plays are complementary in <u>theme</u> and would go well together.

Williams on the beach near Rome

*Friday, 9 July 1954*

Friday
    down beat again.
    Rage with Hollywood people over suspected Cheapening of "Tattoo".[936]
    Cardiac anxiety.
    Boredom and depression.
    Routine existence here.
    Enormous expense and nothing much to show for it.
    Oh, well. I got to keep on going.
    A note of hope – I seem to be slowly getting "Kingdom" in some sort of
shape.[937]
    Dilapidation of typewriter, which is in almost as collapsed a state as myself, is
a considerable handicap.
    Now out – Amexco & club with Maria.


*Saturday, 10 July 1954*

1:15 A.M.
    Left company on roof and descended to bed.
    Pains in chest and enormous fatigue.
    Too tired to read or write.
    Like hearing the voices upstairs.
    <u>Assez pour maintenant</u>! – mon cher.
    So, so tired!

later – not too tired for fucking. And it was damned good.
    Today we decided to go to Vienna.
    I hope that I will fall under a golden spell.

(apparently left when
notebook in Rome when
we took the Trip to Vienna
and Venice. no
entries on that
excursion.)

938.  Esmond Knight (1906–87) was a well-regarded British actor who had been temporarily blinded while serving in World War II. He regained enough of his sight to continue acting after the war and appeared in a
number of films, including Olivier's *Henry V* (1944) and *Hamlet* (1948), and *The Red Shoes* (1947). He
was married to the actress Nora Swinburne (1902–2000).

939.  In *The World in the Evening*, Stephen Monk's first wife, Elizabeth Rydal, a writer with a weak heart, dies:
That was the night Elizabeth died — at about three o'clock, the doctor said. She died only a few feet
away from me, and I never woke; so she couldn't have cried out, or made any loud noise. . . . [T]here
was no trace of pain on the smooth waxen face of the thing she had left. (p. 248)

940.  The first two lines of Rilke's Tenth Duino Elegy.

941.  "May God be with you."

*Sunday, 11 July 1954*

Sunday

About what you'd expect of a Sunday. 2 seconals, one before noon, another about 6 PM on way back from Fregene when claustrophobia developed in the car, driving Maria, Mr. & Mrs. Esmond Knight[938] back from the beach. The remainder of the evening was not unpleasant, but I hardly need state that work has been stalled lately.

Cardiac anxiety returned, apparently set off by description of a death in Isherwood's book[939] and some attacks of air hunger a few nights ago. The plane trip to Vienna is a formidable venture but I will probably go through with it, as the routine here doesn't suit me, and there is no good place to work in this apartment.

*Monday, 12 July 1954*

Monday A.M.

Here's the dilemma, let's face it. I can't recover any nervous stability until I am able to work freely again, and I can't work freely until I recover a nervous stability.

Solution? – Much less clear.

Just not working doesn't solve the matter for the need to work, the blocked passion for it, continues to tear me inside.

Working against exhaustion bit by bit wears me down even further.

Then there is no way out? None except through some bit of luck – another name for God. Of course it is true that I go through these cycles repeatedly, constantly, but now the downward curve is fiercely relentless and the little upturns are very little indeed, relatively insignificant, little circles inside a great descending arc which is still descending.

"Someday, emerging at last from this terrifying vision, may I burst into jubilant praise to assenting angels!" Rilke[940]

*Saturday, 31 July 1954*

Saturday July 31 –

Motor tuning up for take-off to Barcelona. Back seat. A flask of Bourbon. Maria beside me. A movie mag. A copy of Hemingway. And some pinkies in case the going is rough. I am not nervous now. we saw Magnani before leaving and the meeting was gay and friendly.

Still hot. Still on ground. Now we're on the strip and the two motors are roaring. It's a 2¼ hr. jump to Barcelona. Non-stop. "Vaya con Dios"[941] – I trust that Oliver will meet us when we land and tomorrow there will be good "Toros".

942.   About the trip to Sitges, Maria Britneva wrote in her diary:
         Arrived today alone at three. That fool Oliver mucked it all up. I had to go with Oliver to meet his
         boy Sebastian who is much too good for him. I don't know why I went except Tennessee let him
         down in not going, so I felt I had to go for Tennessee. (*FOA*, p. 95)

943.   Isidro Sola had played Jim in *El Zoo de Cristal* at the Capsa Theatre in 1947.

944.   In an interview in the *Paris Review* (fall 1981), Williams developed his thoughts further:
         Hemingway had a remarkable interest in and understanding of homosexuality, for a man who
         wasn't a homosexual. . . .
             Have you ever read "A Simple Inquiry" by Hemingway? Well it's about an Italian officer in the
         Alps during the First World War. And he's of course deprived of female companionship. He has an
         orderly, a very attractive young orderly. He desires the orderly. And he asks the boy, rather bluntly,
         "Are you interested in girls?" The boy panics for a moment, and says, "Oh, yes, I'm engaged to be
         married." And the boy goes out of the room, and the Italian officer says, "I wonder if that little
         sonofabitch was lying?"
             The final line in Hemingway's *Islands in the Stream* is one man saying I love you to another.

945.   Williams refers to the last sentence of chapter 17 of Hemingway's *Death in the Afternoon*: "Viva El greco
         El Rey de Los Maricónes [the king of the queers]."

Williams, Maria Britneva, and Oliver Evans in Europe

*Sunday, 1 August 1954*

Sunday –

The good expected pattern except that morning work was desultory. But San Sebastiano beach was up to its good standard. Oliver and I both enjoyed the same Eros. Now Maria is dressing. When she is dressed we'll take off for the Corrida. The room is quiet and cool. So far Oliver has been on his good behavior, altho upset over a contretemps with his love, Sebastiano. Blue devils threatened me when we arrived but appear dispersed for the present.

*Wednesday, 4 August 1954*

Wed.

Alone here now. Maria and Oliver went to visit his Sebastian below Sitges,⁹⁴² where we spent last night. I returned alone to Barcelona and find my solitude restful. A bit worried over the re-appearance of some rectal irritation. Made this my excuse for not going with Oliver & Maria.

Someone may call at 8. An actor who played Jim in "Menagerie" here.⁹⁴³ Had a sweet concert (Nightingale) yesterday, before we went to Sitges. Arranged and provided by Franz Neuner, whom I met here the time before and who is the M.C. in this town, sexually.

Toros again tomorrow. And again day after. Then probably Madrid. Working with interest and some progress on "Kingdom of Earth".

*Thursday, 5 August 1954*

Thurs. A.M. – A bright day without the weight of Roman summer. I woke too early, about 6:30, and applied medication and sat in hot water (bidet) to relieve rectal trouble, which is not serious, so far, except as an apprehension. Read "Death In the Afternoon" by Hemingway with ever increasing respect for it as a great piece of prose, and honest acknowledgment of a lust which is nearly always concealed. H's great quality, aside from his prose style, which is matchless, is this fearless expression of brute nature, his ~~almost~~ naively candid braggadocia. If he drew pictures of pricks, he could not more totally confess his innate sexual inversion, despite the probability that his relations have been exclusively (almost?) with women. He has no real interest in women and shows no true heterosexual eroticism in any of his work.⁹⁴⁴

(I don't think this is just the usual desire to implicate others in one's own "vice".)

Hemingway calls El Greco, whom he greatly admires, "El Rey de Maricones"⁹⁴⁵ – perhaps in literature H. deserves the same crown.

946.    In addition to playing Tom in the 1947 Barcelona production of *El Zoo de Cristal*, Adolfo Marsillach (1928–2002) played Mitch in the 1948 Barcelona production of *A Streetcar Named Desire* (*Un Tranvía Llamado Deseo*). He went on to become one of the most important stage and film actors in Spain.

947.    Possibly Williams' reference to the underlying friction and irritability that, on occasion, plagued his and Merlo's relationship and caused Merlo to go off on his own. In 1951 Merlo had traveled to Vienna and failed to ask Williams to join him.

Adolfo Marsillach

*Saturday, 7 August 1954*

4:45 AM Saturday

A terrific flash cold has made me wretched and sleepless. Came on me yesterday morning with great violence. But I was imprudent, as ever, had sex in the P.M., and went to the bullfights with a depressingly pretty-pretty waxdoll like Spanish actor who played Tom in "Menagerie".946

Fortunately he had a screen test at 9 so I got rid of him and had a pleasant dinner with Maria in the hotel.

Now I lie here sweating, after a second pinkie and I had a deliciously cold bottle of milk and now a tepid glass of Spanish whiskey & water. I shall be, oh, so grateful when I shake off this cold. I may even forget to complain about other trials. Is it a punishment for enjoying the brutal poetry of the Toros? 3 times in 1 week!

I miss the Horse and dreamed a sad dream of my sister till I woke up at 2:30.

*Thursday, 12 August 1954*

5:10 AM Thursday

Cold has gone and work picked up. Four hours steady today (yesterday).

But Maria and I are getting a bit too much of each other. Such constant propinquity would be a strain even on lovers, and I don't feel inclined to adjust my ways and wishes to hers. Oliver has been good company here. but I'm afraid he is running short of funds and I'll be expected to make up the deficit. It's hard for my friends to realize that my economic resources are less than infinite.

I'm feeling cross tonight. Nembutal didn't work and this Spanish whisky is really sort of foul. Tomorrow Toros again, and after that, Madrid is contemplated. By plane. Not a happy thought. Sex has been a bit disappointing here, especially at San Sebastiano. My appeal, even to the hustlers, seems to have suffered a decline this summer. I believe Oliver is having the same experience. Middle age . . . .

I think often and fondly of my little friend, The Horse.

Often and anxiously of the Vienna problem.947

Noon –

Evans woke me too early (to borrow money for his trip) so work was spoiled. I wrote 1 page, gave up, and got off a letter to Carson. Now nothing to do till the Toros at 6. The beach doesn't promise much this year and the city itself is not "Romantic Spain" – will call Frank this eve.

Eve – "Nessuno responde".

948. Alcide De Gasperi, the Italian premier, suffered a heart attack and died on 19 August at the age of seventy-three.

woke at 4 AM – couldn't get back to sleep. It is now 6:30. I've given up Madrid but we're being called at 7:30 so it's no use taking a pill. I have only 12 seconals left, a larger bunch of nembutals but they seem to have a stupefying effect next day – woke Maria, informed her of my decision and gave her 2000 pesetas so she can go without me – one ticket wasted. But I've spent money like a drunk sailor this summer. And got nothing for it but boredom. And irritation.

*Friday, 13 August 1954*

Woke at 4 AM – Couldn't get back to sleep. It is now 6:30. I've given up Madrid but we're being called at 7:30 so it's no use taking a pill. Have only 12 seconals left. A larger bunch of nembutals but they seem to have a stupefying effect next day – woke Maria, informed her of my decision and gave her 2,000 pesetas so she can go without me. One ticket wasted. But I've spent money like a drunk sailor this summer. And got nothing for it but boredom. And irritation. Nerves are a bit better, however, physical shape better, too, I believe, than when I arrived in Tangier in June. The nightmare phase has passed over. At least for a while. I'll try Rome again in the next few days, soon as I can get us plane passage back there.

9:10 P.M.

Just talked to Frankie long-distance. My emotion was real. The realest thing that I have felt this summer, including those moments of panic.

Love. Yes, love. I can say that I've known it. Am I worthy of it? Is anybody ever? We're all such pigs, I am one of the biggest. Was I kind to Oliver? I seemed to be more concerned with what he might cost me than his problems and sorrow. I am usually nice to Maria, only usually, but would I be if she didn't flatter me and amuse me and provide good companionship, Etc? However I do love the Horse, that much is certain. But isn't it rather disgraceful that I've only written Grandfather once this summer? Exhaustion and illness might be pleaded, but they're not enough excuse.

*Monday, 16 August 1954*

Monday 7 AM

Actually Spain stinks. I suppose that's true of any Fascist country.

*Monday, 23 August 1954*

Monday

Back in Rome for about a week.

Work goes not badly but the blue devils are back. It took no more than the account of De Gaspari's death to revive my cardiac neurosis, in prodigious flower.[948] Last night a crise at movie, barely stemmed by 2 double scotches and a pinkie when I staggered, pale and shaking, into the nearest bar. How disgusting! I must rise above it. I will.

949. Harold "Hal" Wallis (1899–1986) was a highly successful and prolific film producer. Of his 138 films, including *The Maltese Falcon* (1941) and *Casablanca* (1942), nominated for Oscars, thirty-two received Academy Awards. Wallis produced the film version of *The Rose Tattoo*, which received eight Oscar nominations and won three awards. He would go on to produce *Summer and Smoke* (1961), which received four Oscar nominations.

950. Austrian-born Sam Spiegel (1901–85) was one of the most successful independent producers of American and British films. In 1933 Spiegel fled Germany, first to Vienna and then in 1939 to Hollywood. On arriving in the United States he changed his name to S. P. Eagle and produced a number of films including *The Stranger* (1946), directed by and starring Orson Welles, as well as *The African Queen* (1951). The very successful *On the Waterfront* (1954) was the first film Spiegel produced under his real name. On the morning of 27 August 1954, Williams sent a wire to Wood (HRC) asking her to airmail the latest draft of *Orpheus Descending* to Spiegel. He did not produce the film version of *Orpheus Descending* (titled *The Fugitive Kind*), but in 1959 he produced the film version of *Suddenly Last Summer*.

951. *Passeggiata*, "walk."

952. Tachycardia is an abnormally fast heart rate.

Williams, Hal Wallis, and Anna Magnani on location in Key West during the filming of *The Rose Tattoo*, fall 1954

Sam Spiegel, Maria Britneva, and Williams

*Thursday, 26 August or Friday, 27 August 1954*

Friday – or Thurs.? –
 Last night, a gala.
 Nightingales gave 2 concerts, and the second was rare and lovely.
 This morning – even less than the usual steam for work so I'm quitting early and hope to revive at the pool before cocktails with Magnani and Hal Wallis[949] at 6:30 and afterwards, dinner with Sam Spiegel.[950]

*Friday, 3 September 1954*

Friday Sept 3
 Of work. Nothing today, nothing yesterday, nothing the day before yesterday and nothing the day before that.
 Score – 0.

*Tuesday, 7 September 1954*

Taormina, Sicilia

 A bad experience tonight. I sat with my friend Franco till he closed his bar and then, thinking we might take a picturesque passageato[951] over the sea, I went along with him when he started home. But we stayed on the main street. I was reassured by the music of the late nite-club so I walked him past there and all the way up to the piccole piazza with the fountain about a mile from the Main Square. Then we separated. The evening was my third (not bitter but somewhat but somewhat annoying) disappointment. I started back. I noticed that the nightclub music had stopped. Apprehension began. I found what I suspected was true, the bar had closed. Panic began to advance. I walked quicker. My chest felt constricted. I breathed hard and fast. I wanted to break into a run but didn't have the breath to. The street was empty. Its length seemed to stretch forever. Every step built up my panic and I seemed to be going further rather than closer to my hotel. Twice or three times I had to stop for breath. But there was no apparent tachycardia,[952] just the panicky breathlessness. Less than ½ way I swallowed a secconal but my mouth was so dry (from panic) that it was hard to get it down. Even after I reached the main square, in sight of Hotel Temio, my sanctuary, the panic persisted. In fact reached its climax when I was half way up the gradient, about 50 yds. in length, to hotel gates. I stopped and leaned against bank and plucked a leaf of wild geranium and tried to admire the stars which are said to calm fear. Still no tachycardia (noticeable) but I could hear my breath whistling and I breathed like an exhausted runner. Now in my room, the seconal is taking effect (my second today) and I have

953. *The Journal of William Beckford in Portugal and Spain 1787–1788*, edited by Boyd Alexander (London: Rupert Hart-Davis, 1954). William Beckford (1760–1844), an English novelist, eccentric, collector, and hedonist of extraordinary wealth, wrote his journal after he was forced to leave England when his scandalous romance with the Hon. William Courtenay, later ninth Earl of Devon and eight years his junior, was exposed. Beckford's journal recounts his struggle with Robert Walpole, the English ambassador to Portugal, over whether he should be given an introduction to the queen. When Beckford could not defeat Walpole he traveled to Madrid and became simultaneously entangled with an older married woman, a young married woman, and a twelve-year-old "Mahometan" boy. Again he was engaged in a "Walpolian" contest to be presented to the Spanish royals, but again he was defeated, and he left Spain in June 1788. Beckford returned to England, and a few years later built a grand Gothic edifice, Fonthill Abbey, to rival Salisbury Cathedral.

Beckford is also known for his oriental tale, *Vathek* (1786), the story of the deranged caliph's debauched life and final descent into hell.

954. In his foreword, "Some Words Before," to Gilbert Maxwell's *Go Looking: Poems 1933–1953* (Boston: Bruce Humphries, 1954), Williams compared his difficulty in writing a foreword to Maxwell's poems with O'Neill's difficulty in writing a foreword to Crane's poems:

> A poet once asked a playwright who was his friend to compose a foreword to his first volume of verse. The playwright, having enormous admiration for the verse, though he acknowledged an incomplete understanding of it, gladly assented to the request. However, time passed and the foreword remained unwritten, although the publication of the poems was waiting only upon the foreword's completion. Poet and publisher began to press the playwright a little; and at last he made his shamed confession. He simply couldn't do it. He didn't know how to. The mere attempt of it made him feel a fool . . .
>
> The poet was Hart Crane. The playwright was Eugene O'Neill. The volume was *White Buildings.* . . .
>
> I find myself understanding Mr. O'Neill's predicament. What makes it so difficult to write a preface to a collection of verse is that it doesn't require one, and that is even truer in the case of Maxwell and Williams than it was in the case of Crane and O'Neill. There were possibly things in the eclectic idiom of Crane that a foreword might helpfully introduce to his first startled readers. But Gilbert Maxwell presents no such difficulties. He rises entirely fresh from the spring of tradition.

Williams, Natalia Murray, Frank Merlo, and Anna Magnani sailing to the United States on S.S. *Andrea Doria* at the end of September 1954

my liquor and I am quite calm and comfortable. But someday, I fear, one of these panics will kill me. And not at all kindly or agreeably, to say the least. Was anyone ever so scared of death as I am? So craven? I do wonder. (I had my first affair in Taormina, today on a little island near beach. That was when I took my first seconal. A bit scared of distance but not panicky, perhaps because of impending sexual satisfaction with a very attractive party.)

*Wednesday, 8 September 1954*

Wed. (next day)

Got through it. But had to change hotels and the new room is an airless closet facing the side of a hill instead of the sea. Stifling. Have descended to plaza in cab (at 12:30 A.M.) and washed down second pinkie with a glass of milk (to ease acid stomach). Two bus-loads of Germans were taking off at midnight, (fighting for seats on buses) for Palermo. Their vigor and toughness is more appalling than heroic somehow. Well, I am ¼ hun so I can say it.

Now back in my (still airless) chamber and the pill takes little effect but I can read more of William Beckford's Portuguese Journal,953 an enchanting book. (Talked to Maria in Rome and that cheered me up a bit. Sorry I didn't take her on this trip, though I could hardly afford to, the way my money's been going this summer.) Well – En Avant. –

*Saturday, 27 November 1954*

Saturday (after Thanksgiving)

As I said to Frank, yesterday, when I started out on this trip, "when you feel like retreat, charge is indicated!" Have sometimes, maybe – but rarely, I'm sure – felt less in condition for a "sally forth." But I am now on the way. Tampa . . . about to take off on 3rd lap of the journey – (Key West to L.A.)

A double neurosis, 2-barrelled, the fear of speech, and the cardiac neurosis (augmented by fairly frequent palpitations, "jolts", and general anxiety which made it necessary for me to carry a flask of whiskey with me wherever I went). Wakings at night, usually after 3 hours sleep and oppresive dreams, with that feeling of being near panic, sometimes just going downstairs for a drink seemed like a challenging, perilous undertaking. –

So! Here we go. I feel better than I did just before we landed and it's only an hour to New Orleans from here. I have Gilbert's poems, "Go Looking" with me.954 I can tell by my ears that they are now pressurizing the cabin as they did in Madrid last summer before the take off for Rome. Ah, yes. After all, what older friend than anxiety do I have? Or should I say acquaintance? Yes, I should!

Now taking off! – I hope! Still on the ground! No! We're in the air now. So!!! The rest (after New Orleans) will be relatively easy, but I am sorry that Oliver

955.   In an undated letter to Elia Kazan (Wesleyan), Williams explained his rewriting:

> I shot off a rewrite of the new ending to Audrey last week. . . . So I'm wiring her today to hold your copy till I give her another re-write on it. This I started today. I was blue about it last night but as somebody said, Never judge the day by the evening of it! Today I am again full of hope and determination! . . . I am also, at the same time, rewriting a lot of Act One, putting it in a tighter, straighter-line, frame and concentrating on the character of Margaret with emphasis on those things about her which make her human, understandable and likeable. Some one who's always crouched at the feet of the rich and lucky with the smile of a beggar, and the claws of a cat. Expecting a kick, but begging for something better and willing to give it plenty! — A normal, though desperate, person. A fighter . . . After all, . . . the play was not just negative, since it was packed with rage, and rage is not a negative thing in life: it is positive, dynamic! I share your feeling about Brick, want to kick him. . . . But he's got to be understood, too. He's one of the rich and lucky. Got everything without begging, was admired and loved by all. Hero! Beauty! — Two people fell in love with him beyond all bounds. Skipper and Maggie. He built one side of his life around Skipper, another around Maggie. — Conflict: Disaster! — One love ate up the other, naturally, humanly, without intention, just did! Hero is faced with truth and collapses before it. . . . Maggie, the cat, has to give him some instruction in how to hold your position on a hot tin roof, which is human existence which you've got to accept on any terms whatsoever . . .
>
> Vitality is the hero of the play! — The character you can "root for" . . . is not a person but a quality in people that makes them survive.
>
> [Postscript] Read Isherwood original version of play. He loves it. Tomorrow will read him the re-writes and see if he finds it improved.

956.   Presumably *Cat on a Hot Tin Roof.*

957.   Galatoire's, at 209 Bourbon Street, and Antoine's, at 713 St. Louis Street, were two of Williams' favorite restaurants.

958.   Kolb's, at 125 St. Charles Avenue, was a very popular German restaurant which closed in the 1990s.

Postcard of Antoine's Restaurant, and
Kolb's Restaurant, New Orleans

and I are no longer friends. I am still <u>his</u> friend but he's not mine. I am sitting by a window that lets in the sun.

Professionally – excuse me, I mean <u>artistically</u> – things look bright. A wire from Gadg this A.M. expresses pleasure with re-write.[955]

Just had a highly disagreeable shock! Forgot there was a time difference (Eastern-mid-western) between Florida & N. Orleans. my schedule said we get there at 3:10 but the pilot just announced it will be <u>two</u> <u>hours</u>. Okay. That's it. Okay.

Time passes quickly in planes. It's just a question of knocking off the time to the point where I feel safe in it, every passing moment is in my favor, you see, and peace descends as it did in the N.O. hospital, when the terror of the unexpected effect of the morphine began to pass and I told Frank (waiting down the corridor, I didn't want him watching the ordeal) that he could go home now.

Now I am back in the men's room with a glass of water & my flask and 2 secconals in my coat pocket) took one before flight, Okay?!

<u>Much</u> <u>sun</u> outside! – <u>Tonight</u> <u>the</u> <u>gay</u> <u>bars</u>, Trade! the best I can get! And I promise myself I will get some. Okay? Sure. Think about the new play[956] and Magnani in "Tattoo", and look at that old familiar face in the mirror. Grandfather took <u>much</u> longer flights than <u>this</u>! Must have my hair trimmed soon. At 3:10 I can take another seconal if I feel it is necessary. I feel better now. Will soon settle down. Yes, much better now. It is already 2:50. I can get thru another hour. the last 20 minutes don't count. Imagine that you are crossing the channel, old boy! Where shall I dine tonight? I believe at Antoine's, if it's not too crowded, otherwise perhaps at Galatoire's.[957]

Later – New Orleans –

Slept 3 hours after dinner (at Kolbs)[958] then did the bars, running into my old friend Don Langley. He is here now. (at the St. Charles)

I've taken a seconal but don't feel truly relaxed. Don's gone now. We spend a rather sad, quiet evening together. No sign of Oliver. Rumor hath it that he has sold his house and is going to the Canary Isles.

Poor boy! I miss his friendship, especially tonight. I feel pretty lonely with just my anxiety for companionship in this hot hotel room.

*Sunday, 28 November 1954*

Sunday 11:45 AM

We took off late in a wind. <u>Very</u> <u>rough</u>, tossing the plane about like a flapjack – nerves? Not too good but not too bad. I had 2½ Martinis before the take off. I hope we will climb above this weather. There's a lot of sun now. but the erratic motion is not altogether gone. Sitting next to me is a scared looking boy about 14 with that curious sophistication about him that kids have before they are

959. Williams traveled to Los Angeles to watch the shooting of the interior scenes of *The Rose Tattoo* at Paramount Studios and to confer with Elia Kazan about *Cat on a Hot Tin Roof*.

960. Rainer Maria Rilke's *Duino Elegies* was an important work for Williams. He used the opening lines of the First Elegy as the epigraph for *Summer and Smoke*: "Who, if I were to cry out, would hear me among the angelic orders?"

On one draft of the play "The Youthfully Departed," Williams described it as a "Scenario for a ballet with dialogue based on the tenth of Rilke's Duino Elegies." The play was included with "A Cavalier for Milady" and "Now the Cats with Jewelled Claws" in the grouping "Three Works for the Lyric Theatre."

In the autobiographical play *Something Cloudy, Something Clear* (part 2, scene 2), August recalls the Tenth Elegy (lines 76–79):

See how light the sky is? Light as clear water with just a drop or two of ink in it. Note to end on? How did it go, that bit of Rilke? "The inscrutable Spinx? Poising forever — the human equation — against the age and magnitude of a universe of — stars . . ." The lovely ones, youthfully departed long ago. But look [*He points.*] very clearly here, and while this memory lives, the lovely ones remain here, undisfigured, uncorrupted by the years that have removed me from their summer.

Williams considered using lines from the Ninth Elegy as an epigraph for *The Roman Spring of Mrs. Stone* (as well as for the precursor in play form): "Not because happiness really exists, that premature profit of imminent loss" (lines 7–8).

Self-portrait

coarsened by late puberty. We <u>are supposed</u> to land at 1:05 in Dallas. I hope there is not a time difference as there was on the last flight. I <u>hope</u> that I will feel able to fly straight thru to L.A.⁹⁵⁹

12:37 P.M. – Have retired to lavatory for a drink. weather is now fine. I feel relaxed. After drink may try to read a bit, wish I had something really absorbing to read. wish I had the Duino Elegies⁹⁶⁰ with me or my Crane. Miss Maxwell's verse is <u>very</u> personal, most of it. Now we are rocking a bit.

2:15 Am going on from Dallas, having been "cleared" the rest of way through to L.A. Have to sit in Lounge as plane is full. Stewardess says flying time is app. 2 hours. I wonder if they serve liquor in El Paso? or <u>sell</u> it? Not sure my flask will serve 5 more hours.

Time's all screwed up, but now we have taken off from El Paso – Yes, I did have the guts to go on, altho I had a bad headache and there was no bar in the El Paso airport nor bottles for sale. However!

I guess I will manage. And the sooner this trip is finished, the better. Maybe can't land in L.A. because of smog. I have gone to the lavatory for a nip of my precious elixir, which must be husbanded most prudently now.

Debating whether or not I should take a pinkie now. Or save it till I really feel I have to. Rugged! Tonight at the Beverly Hills hotel I will make some comment on this interval, this little piece of eternity which I am now passing through . . .

Have decided to take the pinkie in 5 minutes. Meanwhile another look at the old puss in the glass. What good does that do? Quien Sabe! Nobody else to look at right now, baby. except those rugged Mts. in the sunset.

One of the worst hour & ½ I've ever been through with only about 2 inches of whiskey in the flask and what I thought was 2½ hours of flying. God extended his white hand of mercy! – Seems that we were actually only one hour out! (The seconal did no good – nerves burned right through it!) Never again take a plane without a <u>full bottle</u> on me!

See you later – after 2 martinis at the airport bar, I trust, and a happy long ride to the hotel, thanking God every inch of the way.


*Monday, 29 November 1954*

It is 4:45 AM. in Beverly Hills hotel. I have wakened from a deep, exhausted sleep and taken a seconal so that I can resume it after reading a while. The heart does a flip now and then but I came through remarkably well. Sent F. a funny wire, "Tell Miss Simone (Tours) there is time difference between East and West Coasts and ½ pint whiskey does not cover it on Sundays. Love. Tenn." My suite is <u>lovely</u>. I have a TV set. I think my nerves are going to be better tomorrow. Thank you, my father!

961.  Don Bachardy (1934– ), an American painter, was Isherwood's companion from 1953 until Isherwood's death in 1986. Jimmy Charlton (1919–98) was an American architect who shared a casual friendly-romantic attachment with Isherwood in the 1950s.

962.  Williams responded to Kazan a few days later (letter dated 31 November 1954, Wesleyan):
I "buy" a lot of your letter but of course not all: possibly I "buy" more than half, and after a couple of nights studying it out, I think I understand it.
To be brief: the part I buy is that there has to be a reason for Brick's impasse (his drinking is only an expression of it) that will "hold water".
Why does a man drink: in quotes "Drink". There's two reasons, separate or together. 1. He's scared shitless of something. 2. He can't face the truth about something. — then of course there's the natural degenerates that just fall into any weak, indulgent habit that comes along but we are not dealing with that sad but unimportant category in Brick. — Here's the conclusion I've come to. Brick did love Skipper, "the one great good thing in his life which was true". He identified Skipper with sports, the romantic world of adolescence which he couldn't go past. Further: to reverse my original (somewhat tentative) premise, I now believe that, in the deeper sense, not the literal sense, Brick is homosexual with a heterosexual adjustment: a thing I've suspected of several others, such as Brando, for instance. (He hasn't cracked up but I think he bears watching, he strikes me as being a compulsive eccentric). I think these people are often undersexed, prefer pet raccoons or sports or something to sex with either gender. They have deep attachments. . . . Take Brando again. He's smoldering with something and I don't think it's Josanne! . . . he's the nearest thing to Brick that we both know. Their innocense, their blindness, makes them very, very touching, very beautiful and sad. . . . But if a mask is ripped off . . . that's quite enough to blast the whole mechanism . . . knock the world out from under their feet, and leave them no alternative but — owning up to the truth or retreat into something like liquor . . .

963.  Christopher Isherwood.

Notebook Williams began in November 1954

Monday –

Got through most of the difficult business today.

Spent pleasant eve. with Isherwood & his friend and another (Jimmy).[961] Got a 5 page letter from Gadg elucidating, not too lucidly, his remaining objection to play. I do get his point but I'm afraid he doesn't quite get mine. Things are not always explained. Situations are not always resolved. Characters don't always "progress". But I shall, of course, try to arrive at another compromise with him.[962]

*Friday, 3 December 1954*

Friday 5:35 AM

<u>ghastly</u> time here, loathe every minute of it.

9:00 A.M.

Lay sleepless in bed for four hours. Never felt <u>much</u> more depressed, anxious, <u>bored</u> with anxiety than I have here. No one has made any effort to entertain me except Chris.[963] And in the vital respect of getting me someone to go to bed with, not even he has made any successful effort at that. I suppose I must seem dreadfully unattractive right now.

Williams during the filming of *The Rose Tattoo* in Key West
(photograph by Sanford Roth)

964. Barbara Bel Geddes (1922–2005), a well-known stage and film actress, played Maggie in *Cat on a Hot Tin Roof*, which opened on 24 March 1955 in New York.

965. Burl Ives (1909–95) was a successful folksinger and actor who had recently played the sheriff in Kazan's film *East of Eden*. Ives played the role of Big Daddy in *Cat on a Hot Tin Roof*, both in the play and later in the film (1958).

966. *A Streetcar Named Desire* was staged by Joanna Albus at the Originals Only Playhouse in Sheridan Square. Brooks Atkinson's review in the *New York Times* (4 March 1955) was critical of Maria Britneva's performance:

> Although Joanna Albus, chatelaine of the Houston Playhouse, has staged a thoroughly intelligible performance, there is no point in pretending that the acting conveys the intricate mysteries of the script.
>
> In the part of the desperate Blanche du Bois, Maria Brit-Neva, an English actress, is not able to express the inner tensions of that haunted gentlewoman. She does not miss the moments of pathos or the distaste for rude people and wretched surroundings. She tells the story clearly. But there are furies sweeping through Blanche's mind. She is always close to the breaking point. Miss Brit-Neva is not able to bring those terrors to the surface of Blanche's personality.

Williams and Audrey Wood

*Tuesday, 22 February 1955*

Feb. 22, 1955

    A black day to begin a blue journal –

    "Cat on a Hot Tin Roof" in rehearsal. The leading actress (Bel Geddes) inadequate, the play not coming to life enough.[964] I'm tired and a bit drunk and I have a beastly cold – I am already making plans for a far away flight (perhaps as far as Ceylon) the night the play opens in New York!

*Wednesday, 23 February 1955*

Wed. 7:30 AM

    Woke feeling ill and exhausted so took a pinkie and hope to resume my sleep.

*Saturday, 26 February 1955*

Saturday

    Last night the first run-through – devastating. Bel Geddes improved but Burl Ives[965] acted like a stuffed turkey. Another tonight which Audrey and Maria will attend. Maria opens tomorrow in "Streetcar" in Village.[966] I feel hellish – just about hanging on by the skin of my teeth. The old top-piece not working so I'll let this go till later.

Jordan "Big Daddy" Massee and
his son, Jordan, Jr.

Burl Ives as Big Daddy and
Barbara Bel Geddes as Maggie

967.    *Cat on a Hot Tin Roof* was previewing at the Forrest Theatre in Philadelphia. Christopher Isherwood would see the play on opening night, 7 March, and he, too, was not pleased with the set. On the following day he noted in his diary:

> I still think it's a very good play, but the performance was awful. An awful arty expressionistic set by Jo Mielziner. This play absolutely demands realistic staging. It is not symbolic. It means exactly what it says. (*Christopher Isherwood Diaries,* vol. 1, *1939–1960*, edited by Katherine Bucknell [London: Methuen, 1996], p. 479)

968.    The Reverend Walter Dakin died in St. Louis on 14 February 1955, aged ninety-seven.

969.    In his review for the *New York Times* (25 March 1955), Brooks Atkinson declared *Cat on a Hot Tin Roof* to be a "stunning drama." He went on to say:

> "Cat on a Hot Tin Roof" is the work of a mature observer of men and women and a gifted craftsman. . . . [O]ne of its great achievements is the honesty and simplicity of the craftsmanship. It seems not to have been written. It is the quintessence of life. It is the basic truth. Always a seeker after honesty in his writing, Mr. Williams has not only found a solid part of the truth but found the way to say it with complete honesty. It is not only part of the truth of life: it is the absolute truth of the theatre. . . .
>
> The acting is magnificent. . . . Barbara Bel Geddes, vital, lovely and frank as the young wife who cannot accept her husband's indifference . . . Burl Ives as the solid head of a family who fears no truth except his own and hates insincerity . . . give marvelous performances.

Set design by Jo Mielziner for *Cat on a Hot Tin Roof*

*Wednesday, 2 March 1955*

March 2 –
    Another blow. arrived in Philly to find the set a meaningless piece of chi chi – no atmosphere, no relation to the play.[967] Why is luck so resolutely against me of late? Did it die with grandfather?[968]

*Thursday, 3 March 1955*

March 3 —

*Monday, 28 March 1955*

March 28 – Monday
    Too many birthday celebrations – woke feeling ill. Anxiety developed and was not easily diverted.
    The success of the play still seems a bit unreal.[969] All these weeks of apprehension and strain are bound to exact their toll.
    My bowels have been disturbed a good deal lately.

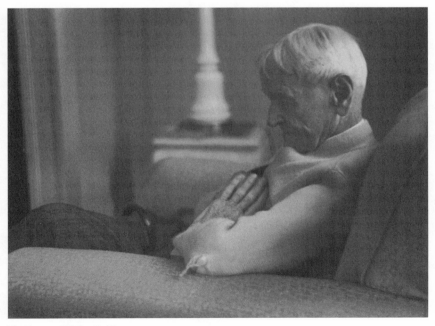

The Reverend Walter Dakin

970. In response to self-doubts expressed by Williams following the premiere of *Cat on a Hot Tin Roof*, Brooks
     Atkinson wrote to him on 30 March 1955 (HRC):

> Since I know you don't lie or pose, I believe you when you say that the success of this play was a
> life-or-death affair to you and that you had doubts of your capacity as a writer. But, my God, how
> can you get so mixed up about your abilities? I should think your popular success, if nothing else,
> would give you a feeling of command, for you, Arthur Miller and Bill Inge are the only contempo-
> rary playwrights who have been everywhere accepted as theatre artists of first rank. Of course, every
> production is a gamble in which a thousand things can go wrong, and I'm happy, as you are, that
> nothing went wrong this time. But as for the long range point of view, you would have no misgiv-
> ings if you could believe the facts. I suppose the whole upset is the aftermath of the cruel torment
> of getting a play on the stage.

**Columbia University**
**in the City of New York**
NEW YORK 27, N. Y.
ADVISORY BOARD ON PULITZER PRIZES

May 2, 1955

Mr. Tennessee Williams
Morosco Theatre
45th Street West of Broadway
New York, New York

Dear Mr. Williams:

    I take very great pleasure in confirming the fact
that the Trustees of Columbia University, on the nomination
of the Advisory Board on the Pulitzer Prizes, have
awarded the Pulitzer Drama Prize, established under the
Will of the late Joseph Pulitzer, to you for CAT ON THE
HOT TIN ROOF, for the year 1954.

    In accordance with that award, I enclose the University's
check for $500 as tangible evidence to you of the selection
of your work.

    With renewed congratulations, I am

                    Sincerely yours,

                    John Hohenberg
                    Secretary

JH/cl

Enclosure

*Friday, 1 April 1955*

Friday –

Fatigue is the keynote of this interval – You see, I have nothing to say, the play production and its tensions drained every thing out of me.[970]

I have nothing to record but the continuity of days. They do continue, and I continue with them. Tonight, a radio appearance with (and for) Maria. Then a night in the Village and a sadly hopeless (I fear) beguine for F.O. who is married and indifferent to me, all because of once beholding F.O. in the showers at the "Y".

We drove home <u>after</u> the bars had closed, and I was anxious for I had no liquor on me. Took a second pinkie in the cab. Tomorrow comes Mama, I presume. A big party for her on Sunday.

Notebook Williams began in February 1955

971.   Presumably Monty Delmar, mentioned in the journal entry for 20 February 1953.

972.   Williams and his grandfather traveled to Europe on S.S. *Homeric* in July 1928.

973.   In a letter to Audrey Wood (14 October 1953, HRC), Williams had written:
     Just before I sailed for Europe this time, Bill Inge said to me, Tenn, don't you feel that you are
     blocked as a writer? I told him that I had always been blocked as a writer but that my desire to write
     had always been so strong that it broke through the block. But this summer I'm afraid the block has
     been stronger than I am and the break-through hasn't occured.

Williams on the deck of S.S. *Homeric*

*Thursday, 26 May 1955*

May 26 3:15 A.M. – Sailing day.

Tomorrow, little blue book, we go to sea again and start another one of our strange, haunted summers in lovely Rome – in desperate Spain with the bull-fights – with <u>what</u>? Only God knows.

Tonight the Nightingales gave a spectacular concert. (Del Mar)[971]


*Saturday, 28 May 1955*

Saturday May 28 –

Sit feeling somewhat dazed and just a tiny bit sea sick before the Olivetti, waiting for the steward to deliver a "double dry".

First time I've felt sea sick since 1928.[972]


*Circa 6 June 1955*

Europe – Summer of 1955

Rome again, in a hideous modern hotel in Parioli, at least till tomorrow. F. on road with the MG and Buffo. No pleasure in return this time, due to hotel location, heat and inability to do any work for a week or so. Internal state: ominous. I am now faring forth into the heat and glare to see if a taxi is accessible to Amexco for any possible word from the other Side.


*Monday, 20 June 1955*

June 20 (?) 7:50 A.M.

Wakened twice, by Frank closing shutters with a typical bang, then, a while later, by a griping pain in my belly. Gastric and intestinal symptoms have increased markedly of late. This could be reaction to the intense strain of the past season. On the other hand, it could be a return of the organic difficulties that were announced so violently in the Spring of 1946. Anyhow, they are not welcome. Another possibility lies in the fact that I haven't been able to work since I got here. An almost total impasse. (I avoid using the word 'block' – Inge scared me with it too badly)[973] – But I am booked on a plane to Athens tomorrow and the chances are, unless I get sicker, I'll take it. Only some radical change can divert the downward course of my spirit, some startling new place or people to arrest the drift, the drag. A call for courage. Can I answer it? En avant.

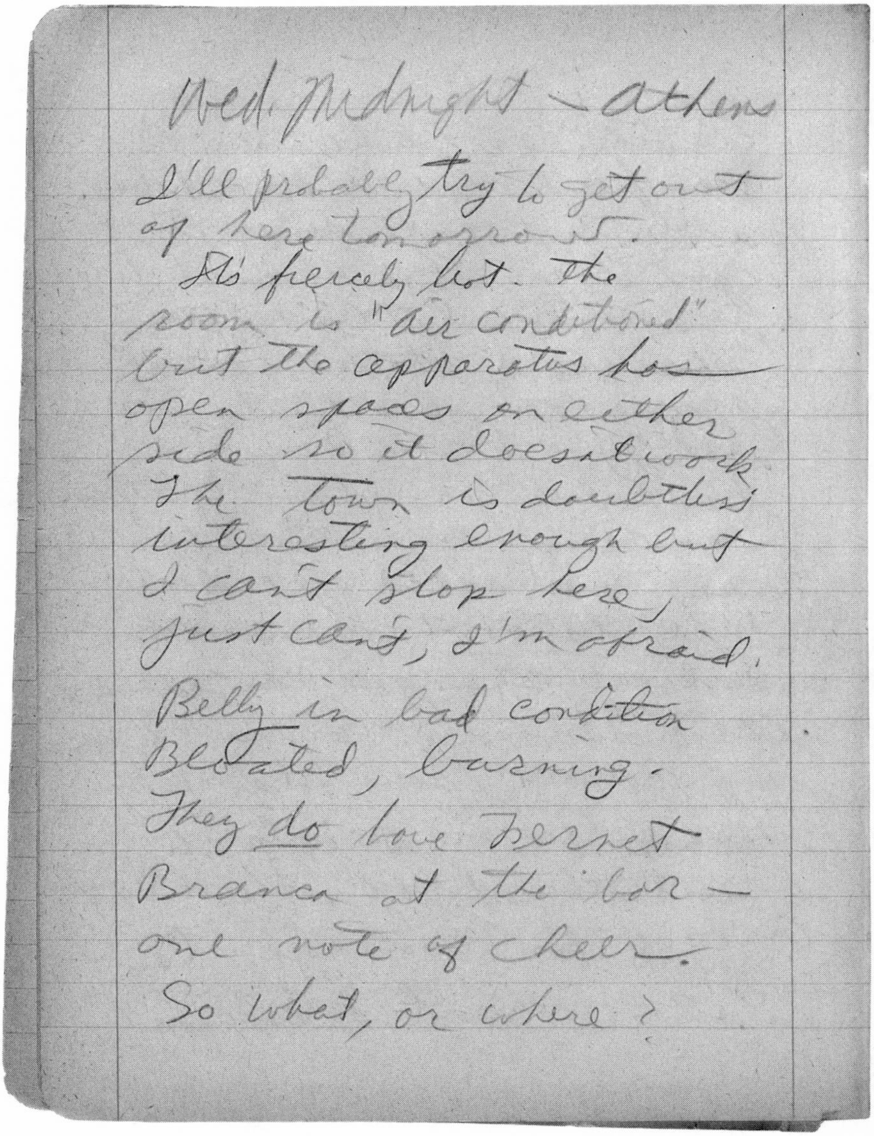

Wed. Midnight — Athens

I'll probably try to get out
of here tomorrow.

It's fiercely hot. The
room is "air conditioned"
but the apparatus has
open spaces on either
side so it doesn't work.
The town is doubtless
interesting enough but
I can't stop here,
just can't, I'm afraid.

Belly in bad condition
Bloated, burning.
They _do_ love Fernet
Branca at the bar —
one note of cheer.
So what, or where?

*Wednesday, 22 June 1955*

Wed. Midnight – Athens

I'll probably try to get out of here tomorrow.

It's fiercely hot – the room is "air conditioned" but the apparatus has open spaces on either side so it doesn't work. The town is doubtless interesting enough but I can't stop here, just can't, I'm afraid.

Belly in bad condition

Bloated, burning.

They <u>do</u> have Fernet Branca at the bar – one note of cheer.

So what, or where?

North, I guess, almost anywhere north. Maybe all the way up to Hamburg. Then maybe Berlin. Who knows? Anyhow I guess I'd better keep going if I can, as long as I can. – No work tomorrow, not even if I sleep well tonight. En avant.

Later – This will be a memorable night, a "night of the long knives". I feel as if I'd swallowed a few billiard balls.

*Thursday, 23 June 1955*

Thursday: Athens, June 22, 1955

Better today – a bit of good work after a double gin and a pinkie to relax me – It's crazy how I used to rely on stimulants to work, now on sedation.

Went by very expensive ($8.00) cab along Coast road, swam one place, (bad water and no "hunting") and explored another, much better but much further out, where I may swim tomorrow.

Have not yet visited the Acropolis which I see clearly from hotel window. Think I'll skip it, unless I come back through here. Flying to Istanbul tomorrow. This isn't my cup of tea. It looks like Havana, but Havana is better! No trace of Hellenistic glory in these modern Greeks. Of course they're okay as folks but — I want something more voluptuous, Yes – and decadent. Maybe I'll find it on the Bosphorus?

Thurs.

– I <u>did</u> work today.

And maybe will tomorrow.

Feel much better no belly ache tonight. A bit lonely – but that's okay.

I have Haig's Scotch and a bottle of ice cold mineral water and am booked on a plane to Istanbul tomorrow.

No sex here. The trade is homely and not aggresive. The Square is lovely at night – the pale blue neon Greek letters are enchanting. Should have had some in "Camino".

I hope there'll be good swimming and lovely corruption in old Constantinople. ~~tomorrow night.~~

974. In a letter to Paul Bigelow (circa 10 April 1943, HTC), Williams wrote that he had been reading *Lady Chatterley's Lover*:

> The non-sexual parts of it are Lawrence's best, though the fornicating sequences are pretty boring. Poor David must have pulled his beard out trying to think of something to have them do next! Like all of Lawrence's women except his Mother, Lady Chatterley is rather annoying. But the bittter portrait of Sir Clifford and the housekeeper is really terrific.

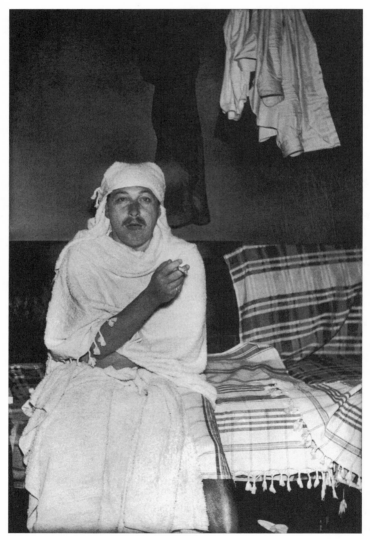

Williams in Istanbul (photograph by Ara Guler)

*Friday, 24 June 1955*

Friday

Now aboard plane for Istanbul – dusk falling. I am in a placidly "triste" melancholy but fairly comfortable mood, less anxious, perhaps, than I've ever been in, in a plane about to take off. And no "pinkie" to account for it, either. Well, I slept well in Athens, had no fun, no bedroom sport, the nightingales were silent, and the creative difficulty was not very remitting — but I am going on from there, a small, self-contained, somewhat dead, cold person, a sort of a lunar personality without the shine. But kind! Yes, I think I am such. (as Rose would say) such! It's lovely this hour, I have a feeling that Istanbul will offer more than Athens to this bird. Hope! En Avant!

(we are still on the ground but rolling into position for the charge. Now stationary, poised – motors repped! – )

(lots of empty seats, always a comfort on a plane, to the claustrophobic)

OK – here we go! –

We're up! – over water – lights of fishing boats, a young crescent moon –

8:35 –

Reading Lawrence, Lady Chatterly, his best novel, but I think how tiresome it must have been to put down so many words about things.974 Is it because words fail me that I think this?

They are passing out dinner trays – got mine – looks good – and fattening – alas!

*Saturday, 25 June 1955*

Friday A.M. Istanbul

Luck is not favorable to the bird on this excursion. Istanbul appears to be the ugliest, dullest city in the world. And this, after the disappointment of Athens, is very disconcerting, especially since it's so distant, even by plane, from every where but a return to Athens. I have waited ½ hour for them to bring my coffee – still waiting!

Had a press interview while waiting.

*Sunday, 26 June 1955*

Sunday 7:45 AM.

Woke at Six and read myself practically blind although I have nothing interesting to read. Lady C. bores me this time, never can get interested in Graham Greene and I'm not in the mood for Whitman. I don't guess anything would please me, now, but escape from this ghastly place, surely the ugliest and most dispiriting I've been in eight summers abroad (or is it only seven?) Jesus,

975.  *Baby Doll.*

Williams at his typewriter, Rome, 1955 (photograph by Ara Guler)

and not able to work, and no sex! Not since Rome. Booked on Air France flight back to Athens tomorrow morning but this Sunday now in progress will be a ball-buster. (Telephone operator called to announce it was 7:30 – I had not requested a call. Characteristic of this new Hilton monstrosity to which I came under the delusion that it had a swimming pool.) All this sounds merely cross – the surface of desperation. Any diversion, any comfort, any solace, now, is vastly important. So are all irritations.

*Saturday, 2 July 1955*

Saturday – Rome
    The most embarassing of all relations is with a whore. At least, after the act, when you suffer the post-orgasmic withdrawal anyway. a good whore, in the sense of a really wise one, knows how to create an atmosphere that obviates this hazard but the one this afternoon, though divinely gifted in the practise of bed, made me feel very sheepish afterwards. I didn't know how to offer the money or how to say goodbye. It is because of my Puritanical feeling that it is wrong, <u>wrong</u>! – to use another being's body like this because of having need, on one hand, and cash on the other – Still — I owe more pleasure to this circumstance in life than anything else, I guess. Can I complain? Breast beating is twice as false as the love of any whore.

*Monday, 4 July 1955*

Monday July 3 or 4.
    Woke up this morning with cramps and diarrhoea, the way things have been going lately, and there was a Turk at the door, someone I'd met in Istanbul, a photographer who brought me an album of photos he'd taken of me there, which showed me how ugly I've gotten, fat and neckless.
    He stayed and stayed so afterwards couldn't work, not till I'd settled my nerves with a pinkie and a martini.
    Now – having done a couple of undistinguished pages of work on film-script[975] – I feel lower than whale shit – too tired to move. Oh, but I guess I'll move! – Call at Amexco for possible mail.
    But no swimming pool today. Couldn't possibly drag myself that far.
    Then what?
    Return to the sack?
    No, sally forth bravely while you can. And mail the new shit to Kazan.
    Wednesday – fly to Spain.
    Time and the body's rot are such atrocities!

976. In Aldous Huxley's entertaining satire *After Many a Summer Dies the Swan* (1939), Jo Stoyte, a Californian oil magnate, is afraid of old age and death and has retained Dr. Obispo, a personal physician, to work on a theory of longevity. An Englishman whom Stoyte has hired to catalogue one of his recent acquisitions, "the almost legendary Hauberk Papers," discovers that one of the Hauberks, the fifth Earl of Gonister, writing in the eighteenth century, had developed his own system of longevity by "ingesting each day not less than six ounces of the raw, triturated Viscera of freshly opened Carp."

   In the course of the novel, Stoyte learns that his "daughter-mistress" is being seduced by Dr. Obispo, and in a rage, intending to shoot Dr. Obispo, he mistakenly kills someone else. Dr. Obispo blackmails Stoyte, and they travel to England in search of the Earl. They discover him, aged 201, living in squalor, having developed, as he slowly aged, into an ape.

977. The *torero* name of Antonio Borrero (1935– ). His greatest success was among the Catalan fans who made him an idol in Barcelona. He was not considered to be a great *torero*, but he was beloved by the Catalans because he was very courageous. As a consequence, he was caught by the bullhorns numerous times, sometimes very seriously.

978. Williams reported to Frank Merlo ([22 July 1955], HTC): "Claude Marchand, the colored dancer, is . . . in Barcelona, with his English lover, and they are good company." Williams continued: "Society snow-balls here. More and more, till you scarcely have a moment to yourself. It takes real strategy to contrive some precious hours of solitude."

Williams in Valencia (photograph by Duncan Melvin)

*Wednesday, 6 July 1955*

Barcelona – Wed P.M.

A pleasant, short (3½ hour) flight here with practically no anxiety in plane. PAA Transatlantic Clipper. It's hot and bright in Barcelona. I'm in bed with a good book (Huxley's <u>After Many a Summer</u>, Etc.)976 and mineral water & Haig's Scotch which I brought from Rome, and tomorrow I have booked a barrera for the Toros – "Chamaco"977 – the beauty I read so much about last summer will appear on the program In the earlier afternoon I will try my fortune at San Sebastiano – sea and sun and maybe – Quien sabe!

Last night in Rome the nightingales were not silent. I'm sleepy now, and rather comfortable. So long.

Later –

On Las Ramblas ran into my dear friend Angel Zuniga, the one who sat up all night with me when I was ill here, year before last. He took me to the opening night of a new "Revue" – I left at intermission as only the dancing was passably good and I was pooped. Also ran into Franz Neuner who has been so good, in the past, at providing me with good "trade" – we have a date for tomorrow evening after the bulls.

My cold bottle of Solares has arrived – a drink, and slumber, now – Solares is the world's loveliest water! (in a bottle)

*Saturday, 9 July 1955*

Sat. 7:30 P.M.

Toros a bit disappointing and afterwards Neuner didn't show up so I struck out alone. A fairly attractive pick-up but disagreement over the pay envelope ended the encounter on a sour note. However I did discover a good place to take them, "Hotel Nacional" in Barrio Chino, clean & cheap.

Now a little reading and I hope some more sleep.

*Wednesday, 13 July 1955*

Barcelona July 13

for the first time in days <u>weeks</u> I feel a slight levitation of the spirit — due to what? My escape from the hell of Sitges? The pleasant party at Claude Marchand's?978 The prospect of having a date with the adorable little flamenco dancer on Sat.? The afternoons at San Sebastiano, particularly lunching, slowly with a bottle of cold white wine, in the hot sun on the beach?

Or just that I am beginning to feel more at home here? Now I must descend to see if my nightingale for this evening has shown?

979.   "Do not come in the mouth."

Kenneth Tynan in Valencia (photograph by Duncan Melvin)

Another contribution of Franz. I've had to buy a lady's bag and belt to recompense for these favors.

*Friday, 15 July 1955*

Friday

So! – to continue.

A routine is established which I can endure.

I wonder if the decay of the world didn't begin one summer in these dry Latin countries?

Yesterday I met Sylvestre Bella Vista, only event worth recording. We only talked. I felt that he somewhat despised me, as I do myself. All of the beach boys came by and asked me for cigarettes till my pack was empty. A mongrel dog came begging but wouldn't eat bread. I said, he isn't really hungry and Sylvestre Bella Vista replied, He is like some people, eats without being hungry. Then I knew he saw through me. That I was a dog living on scraps for which I was not even hungry.

The beach in the blazing afternoon is a savage poem of the heart's desolation. Now I will dress to go back there.

*Saturday, 16 July 1955*

Sat. July 16 or 17

The Gypsy is due in five minutes – ! Will report on this later. If I am not stood up, it should be something for the books. A pocket-size Flamenco dancer, built by Proxiteles – from the place next to Carrocoles is Bario Chino. Claude Marchand made the arrangement for me. Today some work on film script, better than usual, and a good time at beach. A green salad & wine and two good swims and much sun.

P.S. The Gypsy was divine in beauty and deportment except that one way was inadmissable and the other way met with the admonition "Non vene in boca"[979] or something like that. So — I am only ½ satisfied. But it's o.k. – I've had too much of it lately. And Junior is tired. Someone just called and said "I'm a friend of Senōr Neuner. I want your autograph" – I said "Come by tomorrow at noon" – Maybe this will be more satisfactory – but I made a date with the Gypsy for the bull-fights Monday afternoon – with a 2 hour margin for preliminaries. The Gypsy is really lovely, with skin like F's. Maybe I will be able to make the Gypsy like me?!

Aspero!

980. Leslie Eggleston was an acquaintance of Williams'. In a letter to Maria Britneva, Williams referred to Eggleston as his "bête noire," and in a letter to Merlo he wrote ([22 July 1955], HTC):

> Miss Egleston is back on the trail, now, she calls every day, almost, to announce she is waiting downstairs in the bar. I'm glad the fiesta Brava starts in Valencia this Sunday so I have a reason to cut out.

As the journal entry indicates, Williams failed to escape to Valencia without Eggleston.

981. The interview with Kenneth Tynan (1927–80), the British drama critic, resulted in "Valentine to Tennessee Williams," *Mademoiselle*, February 1956. Excerpts follow:

> In Spain, where I saw him last, he looked profoundly Spanish. He might have passed for one of those confidential street dealers who earn their living selling spurious Parker pens in the cafés of Málaga or Valencia. Like them, he wore a faded chalk-striped shirt, a coat slung over his shoulders, a trim, dark moustache, and a sleazy, fat-cat smile. His walk, like theirs, was a raffish saunter, and everything about him seemed slept in, especially his hair, a nest of small, wet serpents. . . .
>
> It is unmistakably the face of a nomad. Wherever Williams goes he is a stranger, one who lives out of suitcases and has a trick of making any home he acquires resemble, within ten minutes, a hotel apartment. Like most hypochondriacs, he is an uneasy guest on earth. . . . He says justly of himself that he is "a driven person." The condemned tend always to be lonely, and one of Williams' favorite quotations is a line from a play [*Orpheus Descending*] which runs: "We're all of us sentenced to solitary confinement inside our own skins." He says such things quite blandly, with a thick chuckle which is as far from cynicism as it is from self-pity.
>
> To be alone at forty is to be really alone, and Williams has passed forty. In a sense, of course, solitude is a condition of his trade. All writing is an anti-social act, since the writer is a man who can speak freely only when alone: to be himself he must lock himself up, to communicate he must cut himself off from all communication; and in this there is something always a little mad. . . . The theater, he once said, is a place where one has time for the problems of people to whom one would show the door if they came to one's office for a job. His best-loved characters are people like this, and they are all, in some way, trapped. . . . He is the most personal of playwrights. Incomplete people obsess him — above all, those who, like himself, have ideals too large for life to accommodate. . . .
>
> Though he does not need company, he does not shun it. Leaning back on a bar stool, one of a crowd, he can simulate ease with a barely perceptible effort. Mostly he is silent, sucking on a hygienic cigarette holder full of absorbent crystals, with a vague smile painted on his face, while his mind swats flies in outer space. He says nothing that is not candid and little that is not trite. A mental deafness seems to permeate him, so that he will laugh spasmodically in the wrong places, tell you the time if you ask him the date, or suddenly reopen conversations left for dead three days before. . . .
>
> He longs for intimacy, but shrinks from its responsibilities. . . . His friendships are many and generous, ranging from Mediterranean remittance men to Carson McCullers; but love is a sickness which he will do anything to avoid. If his deeper instincts crave release, you may find him at a bullfight — or even writing a play.
>
> . . . Williams' view of life is always abnormal, heightened and spotlighted, and slashed with bogey shadows. The marvel is that he makes it touch ours, thereby achieving the miracle of communication between human beings which he has always held to be impossible.

982. "Half past eight."

983. Toros en Jelves. Jelves is a small village not far from Valencia with a small bullring.

984. Joaquin Bernardó was one of the most highly regarded Catalan *toreros*. With incredible elegance and finesse, he was greatly appreciated all over Spain. He married a famous gypsy dancer, Maria Albaicin.

985. El Turia (the river that crosses Valencia) was the nickname of Francisco Barrios, a second-rate Valencian bullfighter.

986. Williams wrote to Kazan (letter received 28 July 1955, Wesleyan) about his outline of *Baby Doll*:

> Gadge Baby!
>
> My imagination, weary, jaded ole thing which it is this summer, was not exactly fired by your outline

*Tuesday, 26 July 1955*

Tuesday July 27 (?) Barcelona

Well, the Valencia bit was interesting but intolerable. Heat? Unimaginable! And the city's water – <u>cut off!</u> Everyone sweating and stinking and I had a hotel room right under the roof – Went down there by train, sharing a compartment with the remarkable Mr. Eggleston[980] who did a trick in the compartment while I dozed (for appearances).

Ken Tynan interviewed me.[981] I gave him my true birthdate and the story of the Spring of 1946.

His stammer made me v. nervous at first, as I feared I would catch it. I feel he and I could be great friends if we didn't expect much of each other and we <u>wouldn't</u>. Now I'm lying here in my shorts with Scotch and that divine Agua Solares, waiting for Manolo San Juan to arrive at ocho y media.[982] It is now ocho. I have a barrera seat for the Toros on Julves.[983] (Chamaco, Bernado,[984] and one called El Turia[985] that I've never seen.) Bernado is the prettiest, almost swish. In fact, you could scratch out the 'almost'. A little worried about "The Horse" – don't like the persistent reports of illness. Will wire him tonight to call me. I wrote Gadg that I could not follow or consider his ham outline for film.[986] Not even if this were a summer when I could write! Sometime soon I will sit down, or stand up, and have a good talk with God. I feel him with me, but we haven't made talk lately. I need Him bad. <u>Adios!</u>

Joaquin Bernardó

(which reached me yesterday . . .). On the contrary: it (my imagination) was somewhat chilled and dampened, and I will try to tell you why, without being unnecessarily expository. . . .

I feel that my own original conception of the film-story as a grotesque folk comedy of the modern South, with some serious over-tones, carefully kept within the atmospheric frame of the story, is still the only right one. The course which you indicate for the ending is far too heavy, at least for a work that is to have any sort of artistic unity. You are talking about Heavy Drama! — that winds up with a genteel woman's FULFILLMENT, Death for one man, prison for the other. I know that I have not been very fair with you because there was a point where I appeared to accept this sort of an ending, Meighan killing Silva, dragged off in chains, etc. But that was before I became really "engaged" in this material, I had a couple of plays and play productions on my mind so I gave it all too little serious consideration. If I had thought about it, I would have realized that to have tragedy on stage or screen you have to build up to it, everything has to be conceived and done in a way that establishes a premise for a tragic ending, mood and style of writing have got to prepare it. Otherwise, one thing defeats the other, the result is nowhere! So even before this summer, I discarded the idea of a heavy ending. . . . my knees ache with boredom at the thought of trying to take her, or make an audience take her, seriously as a "fulfilled woman"? You mention Pagnol. I am not sure I have seen a Pagnol film but the name suggests a lightness, a delicacy, a playfulness, in which case the film is now on the right track. . . . But I don't think a Pagnol atmosphere, if I am interpreting it rightly, can have an early Eugene O'Neil finish tacked onto it without the most serious disagreement between the two, each impaling the other upon a frog-gig!

987.    Antonio Ordóñez (1932–98) was one of the greatest *toreros* in the history of bullfighting. Recalling his first meeting with Ernest Hemingway in Cuba, Williams wrote in *Memoirs*:

We started talking about bullfighting. I was not an *aficionado* of bullfighting, not somebody who knew the fine technique, the fine points of bullfighting, but one who enjoyed the spectacle of it and I had become, the previous summer, a good friend of Antonio Ordóñez, who was, you might almost say, an idol of Ernest Hemingway's. I mentioned to Hemingway that I knew Antonio Ordóñez. Hemingway was pleased, I thought, and he was also pleased that I shared his interest in bullfighting. (pp. 67–68)

*Cogidas* are literally "caughts" or gore marks from a bull's horn.

988.    On 24 July 1955, Margo Jones had died accidentally of carbon tetrachloride poisoning, two weeks after a cleaning company had used the chemical on a carpet and sofa in her apartment.

989.    *Cat on a Hot Tin Roof*, like *A Streetcar Named Desire*, won every major theatre award: the Pulitzer Prize, the New York Drama Critics' Circle Award, and the Donaldson Award.

Antonio Ordóñez (photograph by          Antonio Ordóñez
Inge Morath)

*Friday, 29 July 1955*

Friday

Just now a man from the travel agency, young and personable, said on the phone, I am here at your hotel with news about your reservation on The Vulcania. (I have booked passage to Palermo, still tentative, for Tuesday) May I see you? I dressed and started to go down to lobby when he appeared at door, entered, <u>locked</u> it behind him, and took off his coat and sat down, saying, "The reservation is not yet definite" – the value of my reputation in Barcelona? It so happened I had something else in mind so I appeared to take no notice of the singular entrance and errand.

This P.M. drove out to a lovely hotel on a beach between here and Sitges with Carlos and the great Torero Antonio Ordonez, a charming "chico" but not a perfect model for Swim trunks. He showed us his six "cogidas" two of which were grave ones.[987] We had the best paella I've ever eaten in a terrace on the beach. A nice clean change from San Sebastian. Yesterday news of Margo's death[988] – shocked me.

*Monday, 1 August 1955*

Rome
Monday – August ?

Nothing to say except I'm still hanging on.

*Friday, 9 September 1955*

Hamburg – Sept. 9.

It seems to me that this summer is really a logical, predictable outgrowth of the others.

there was a slow, steady progression of creative exhaustion through the last six or seven, and though I am not sure "Cat" is a truly good play, still it's a bit uncanny that I was able to make it as good as it is.[989]

Now the block is fairly complete. I don't see any way over it, under it, or around it, without a visiting angel, of great sweetness and power.

I lie here, after a morning "pinkie" a double martini, and with a Scotch, waiting for a golden rose to arrive "after one" – (P.M.) – how long after remains to be seen. And how well tired "Junior" can rise to the occasion. Weather amazingly warm and fair but I've closed the drapes on the window so I can rest, and wait in a comforting twilight.

## Author's Note

What you are seeing tonight is the production of the first draft of a play, something that ordinarily I would only dare to show to my literary agent, and even then with grave trepidations: it is a work in progress. If it is now in a state that's fit to be exposed to the public, that fact is creditable to the stimulating faith and daring, to the quick imagination and insight, of its director and to his players' gifts, including their patience. All the while this work has been in rehearsal, it has also been undergoing continual changes in dialogue and structure, even in basic theme and interpretation of character. At times Studio M has looked more like a printing press than a theatre, with stacks of re-writes, newly mimeographed, covering the stage and actors looking like a group of dazed proof-readers. I doubt that they will get the script out of their hands more than a day or two before dress-rehearsals. All of this has been very hard on them: it has been of enormous value to me. I hope it is a precedent, not just one adventure.

Excerpt from the playbill of *Sweet Bird of Youth* at the Studio M Playhouse, Coral Gables

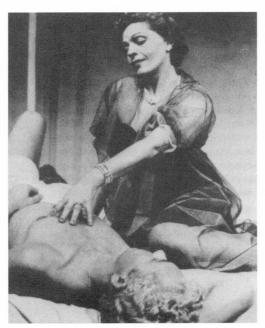

Alan Mixon as Phil Beam and Margrit Wyler as
Princess Pazmezoglu in *Sweet Bird of Youth*
at the Studio M Playhouse

*Williams remained in Europe through the third week of September. He traveled extensively because, as he explained in a letter to Maria Britneva:*

> The Horse [Merlo] gave me a very bad time in Rome; perhaps I gave him an even worse time. He was always with that cynical street-boy Alvaro. . . . The Horse's character, each summer with Alvaro, is hardened and cheapened so that I can't stay with him but must keep flying around on these sad little trips which are always so disappointing, to Athens, Istanbul, the month in Spain (I must admit that wasn't so bad, really!). And now Scandinavia and Hamburg, to be followed by Berlin, Paris, London before we sail the 22nd of this month, losing things wherever I go, being terrified in planes, swallowing pinkies, having dangerous dates with pick-ups and so forth. (FOA, pp. 126–27)

*Williams returned to New York in the autumn and completed revisions to the screenplay* Baby Doll. *On 16 April 1956, Williams' play* Sweet Bird of Youth *was produced in Coral Gables, Florida, as "a work in progress."*

*Williams left for Europe at the end of May, and by the end of June he was back in Rome.*

Williams, Jane Bowles, and John Goodwin with the Captain and First Mate of S.S. *Queen Frederica* crossing the Atlantic, June 1956

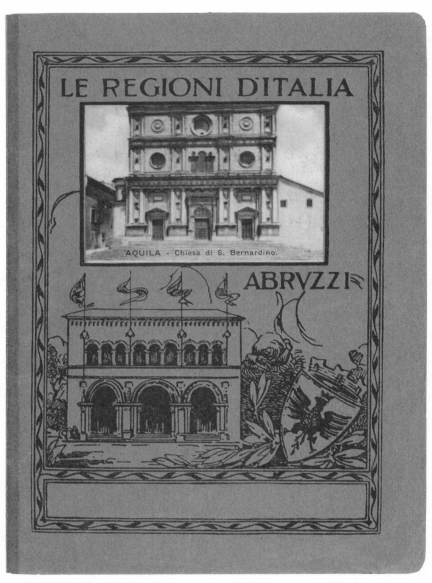

Notebook Williams began in July 1956

*Tuesday, 3 July 1956*

July 3 – A wretched day, most of which I spent in bed. This evening more pleasant. Had date with Amia on V. Venuto at 11:30 and also met a young American painter who has a villa in Positano. Perhaps I'll go there as he indicates the place is agreeable as it was in the past.

*Saturday, 28 July 1956*

Late in July, perhaps July 28.
  – An almost unbroken decline in health and spirits this summer, leading where I don't know. I presume it springs to some extent from the unprecedented weakness of my work. But perhaps that is mistaking the cause for the effect.

*Saturday, 4 August 1956*

Saturday Aug. 3 –
  Thin ice! For the first time a real concern for my sanity – obviously something has to be done, some drastic step taken but I feel immobilized.
  A little kindness, and warmth and affection, just a little, might have helped me this summer. None was offered, though the need of it was apparent to the most obtuse or indifferent eye that I can imagine.
  So? We go on from here, a little bit further, at least. But don't forget it!

*Sunday, 5 August 1956*

Sunday Aug. 4 –
  Ice cracking!
  If I can get through the next few days or weeks I'll make it the rest of the way somehow.
  It won't be easy and it won't be pleasant, but if I get by this next little interval I can go on from there.
  It may be necessary to retreat for a while to a sort of vegetable existence, at best.
  Then – Then – Perhaps New Orleans?
  <u>En Avant</u>.

990.   Marion Black Vaccaro and Vaccaro "Vacky" Hanover, a cousin of her husband's.

```
        HOW CAN I TELL YOU?

HOW CAN I TELL YOU?  WITH MY LIPS AND MY HANDS?
YOU MIGHT MISTAKE THEIR LANGUAGE.
IT ISN'T EASILY SAID.

THERE'S ONLY MOMENTS WHEN WE CAN BOTH BELIEVE IT.

IF WAKING I TAKE YOUR LEAN-BONED HEAD IN MY CLASP AND DON'T TRY TO TELL YOU
MORE THAN THIS TENDER HOLDING,

WOULD YOU BE WILLING TO UNDERSTAND WHAT THAT SAYS?

YOU MIGHT, THINK, OH,
THIS OLD FAMILIAR GESTURE!  I DON'T BELIEVE IT.

EVEN IF I BOWED TO YOU, YOU MIGHT THINK, OH,
HE'S STILL PRETENDING SOMETHING.

THE TROUBLE IS THAT DOUBT IS ALWAYS HALF TRUE,
THERE IS A HARD KIND OF ACCURACY IN DISTRUST WHICH IS HARD, VERY HARD,
TO LET GO OF.

STILL: WE STAY WITH EACH OTHER, WE KEEP RETURNING TO PLACES,
THE SEARCH CONTINUES.

WHAT ARE WE LOOKING FOR IN THE HEART OF EACH OTHER?
WILL IT EVER BE CLEARLY
THE OTHER AND NOT THE SELF WE SO WANT TO COMFORT?

                    L.W.
                  Rome, 1956.
```

*Monday, 6 August 1956*

P.S. Now it's 5:30 A.M. Heard the first bird notes. Have taken another seconal, my fourth in 24 hours, and now the intolerable desolation is tolerable. Some people think I like pain, suffering. That's bull! There is nothing more painful than pain and I long to escape it but my nature and the circumstances of my life imposed it on me, and I could find no escape. It may be, that with psycotheraphy, I can be liberated as person and artist and that my best work still lies before me. It may be that I can recover my lost decency, and deserve affection which I need most.

Monday – A fair sleep after daybreak and what seemed like better work. Then another big row with F., who's now quit the house. I will go out to buy my frugal lunch at the grocery near here, wine, cheese and a few slices of cold roast beef. When things open after the siesta, I will probably go to Bolliger and book the earliest possible flight to the States. This madness here is untenable, and hideous.

*Sunday, 12 August 1956*

Aug. 12 (Sunday)
    After a few, very few, days of calm, another storm broke with the same provocation.
    I trust that I will be leaving tomorrow for Sardinia (Cagliari) with Marian and her cousin.990

*Wednesday, 26 September 1956*

8 AM over Atlantic
    We have been in the air for 12 hours except for the stop at Shannon. I've slept fairly well with 2 seconals. Now I've begun feeling a bit of tension. Have poured myself a stiff drink of Scotch and may resort to a 3rd pinkie.
    I don't really think these long, long flights are for me, not on planes. However! – I may get used to it.

*Thursday, 27 September 1956*

Sept 27, 1956
St. Thomas, Virgin Isles
    Suffering from a little sunburn and a great deal of loneliness.
    My only friend is this town is the colored boy who carried my luggage into this hotel cottage.

991.   Gilbert Maxwell published one novel, *The Sleeping Trees*, in 1949. His novel "The Long Pursuit," alternatively titled "Stand on the Rock," was never published. According to Richard Leavitt (letter to Margaret Bradham Thornton): "Gilbert drove everyone crazy reading from it at the drop of a hat. Williams refused to read it, saying to Gilbert, 'You know my eyes are bad and I must conserve my sight for my own work.'"

992.   Williams' dream appears to have been partially based on fact. On 24 September 1956 (Columbia), he wrote to his mother:

It was a great shock to me to find a telegram saying you were in the hospital when I got back from visiting Rose in Hartford. However my phone conversations with Dr. Alexander and Dr. Gildea have been reassuring, as they say that you are only suffering from a nervous upset caused by worry and tension, and they feel that a short hospital rest is all that you need. I asked them if I should come to Saint Louis and they did not advise me to.

On the next day (25 September 1956), Williams wrote to Maria St. Just:

I had a wire to call the doctor in St. Louis and was informed that my mother had been put in a psychiatric ward, suffering from paranoia. She thought her colored maid was trying to poison her and the colored chauffeur to murder her, result of her disturbance over the anti-segregation violence in the South, and had not eaten for days and was in a state of hallucination. They say I should not see her now. That it would be too shocking for me. I couldn't suffer another shock now so I'm flying to the Virgin Islands to pull myself together and then coming back to St. Louis to cope with the situation. (*FOA*, p. 139)

993.   Miltown, the trade name for meprobamate, was introduced as an anti-anxiety agent in 1955 and was prescribed primarily to treat anxiety and tension. Excessive use can result in psychological and physical dependence.

Frank Merlo and Williams in Key West

The island is charming though, and if tomorrow some thing happens to relieve my loneliness I may stick around.

Otherwise the chances are that I'll fly to Miami "dopo domani" – and look up Lew and watch some TV in the Robert Clay or The Towers and hear some more of Gil's eternal novel.991

Sat out and looked at the stars tonight but I didn't feel the presence of God. I haven't felt it for a long time now. Somethings awfully gone away from here, meaning me.

But still we persist, like the cactus, and still say <u>En Avant</u>.

*Friday, 28 September 1956*

Sept 28
    Slept well about 7 hours but woke depressed – in hot bright morning feeling like a Convict on Devil's Island. I suspect I will attempt a get away within the next 24 hours.

*Saturday, 29 September 1956*

Sept 29 5 A.M.
    A dream woke me up just now.
    I dreamt I was giving a wild party, very sexual, involving negros. My Mother was suddenly brought home from a hospital.992 My grandmother gave me a shocking description of her condition – I was afraid to see her myself – even my father appeared red-eyed from crying. I dismissed the guests. My grandmother sank down on a long flight of stone stairs, breathless from her emotion. I was frightened for her and heart sick for Mother but still dreaded to see her. The most extrordinary element of the dream is my father's grief. I supposes it expresses my guilt-feeling about not going to St. Louis. Actually I would have been better off there than here at St. Thomas. Have not yet made any move to get away. Although last night was lonelier & more miserable than night before. Even the battery of my rented car went dead and I had to leave it at Virgin Isles hotel, where I could not enter the bar because I wasn't wearing a jacket.
    I'm drinking more here, and took 4 quarter grain seconals and 2 or three Milltowns993 yesterday. Physically I feel stronger and better, though –
    A single charming companion would change the whole picture.

994. "Mal de Merde," letter to the editor, *Time*, 22 October 1956, pp. 11–12. In a review in *Time* of an article by Robert Elliot Fitch, Professor of Christian Ethics and Dean of Berkeley's Pacific School of Religion (*New Republic*, 3 September 1956), the reviewer noted that Fitch identified the current "high priest" of the cult of the *mystique de la merde*, or the cult of the deification of dirt, as neither Ernest Hemingway nor Norman Mailer but Tennessee Williams and cited *Cat on a Hot Tin Roof* as evidence. In response, Williams sent the following letter:

> Sir:
>
> Much as I am flattered by your reference to me as "the high priest" of something, even something called "merde" [Oct. 1], I must put in my two cents' worth of protest. The gentleman quoted, Dean Fitch, may have gone to *Cat On a Hot Tin Roof*, but he went to it with a pair of tin ears and came out of it with a tin horn to blow. *Cat* is the most highly, intensely moral work that I have produced, and that is what gives it power. It is an outcry of fury, from start to finish, against those falsities in life that provide a good fertilizer for corruption. What it says, in essence, through the character of Big Daddy, is this: when your time comes to die, do you want to die in a hotbed of lies or on a cold stone of truth?
>
> TENNESSEE WILLIAMS
> Charlotte Amalie, V.I.

995. Louis Shulterbrandt (1907–96) was a teacher, government official, businessman, and real-estate broker. His wife, Eldra Shulterbrandt (1917–94), educated at Columbia and Harvard, was a teacher with a special interest in literature and drama. According to their daughter, Michele, Eldra enjoyed meeting accomplished people who visited the Virgin Islands and most likely learned of Williams' arrival and arranged a meeting.

996. According to Karl Malden, John Prisch had previously worked in the theatre as a stage manager (interview with Margaret Bradham Thornton).

Williams swimming (photograph by W. Eugene Smith)

*Sunday, 30 September 1956*

Sunday

Still no action on the front of Venus, and I am not irresistibly seduced by the morning cup-bearer, who sprawls in my chair with legs wide apart and hand in crotch and closed eyes, and talks languidly about a girl friend. Timidity and prudence have allied themselves with my sense of – what? Perhaps dignity, since I resent such overt provocation without a commitment from the other party. Color prejudice is not at all involved. In fact, that element, the color, is half of the provocation.

I find a little more energy for work, though I still rely on the liquor & pinkie to get going at it.

I wrote a letter of protest to Time yesterday about a prudish attack on "Cat" – was sorry, afterwards, that I mailed it.994

Today is grey. I haven't gone swimming. Am expecting the Shultebrandts, a negro intellectual couple and their child for lunch.995 Nothing else to mention – No definite plan.


*Monday, 1 October 1956*

Monday –

The day began fair and cool but is clouding. The same routine. I felt jittery from heavy drinking at "The Pink Barrel" bar last night. Lucien brought my coffee and ice cubes as usual and seated himself in a chair, as usual, in the usual position, and, as usual, I retreated to the typewriter without response to the provocation as work, even now, comes first.

I did three or four pages on "Sweet Bird" and it seemed strong to me, but then I could not say my state of mind was totally objective. Now a swim and the usual cheeseburger & cottage cheese.

En Avant.

Mon. P.M.

Broke the law of chastity tonight – didn't really enjoy it except as a release of the libido. The partner was highly desirable, Caucasian, and perhaps the youngest I've had outside of Morocco. But thoroughly experienced. Drove my rented car very badly and very rapidly down a steep chute-the-chute road and I couldn't even remember a Hail Mary. I was almost as bad, driving back drunk.

Ran into John Prisch996 at "The Gale".

Lo and behold, he is sleeping with the lady who owns it and she has made him the manager.

Ok. I'll leave this week. It isn't safe for me here.

En avant

997.  In 1956, Meyer Levin published *Compulsion*, a fictional account of the Leopold and Loeb case of 1924. Two affluent University of Chicago students, Nathan Leopold and Richard Loeb, who had kidnapped and murdered a thirteen-year-old neighbor, Robert Franks, were defended by the legendary attorney Clarence Darrow. In Levin's novel two Chicago teenagers, Judd Steiner and Artie Straus, kidnap and murder a young boy and are defended by a brilliant lawyer, Jonathan Wilk. The success of the book led quickly to a Broadway play and acquisition of screen rights in 1957 by Darryl F. Zanuck.

998.  Anthony Perkins (1932–92) was nominated for an Academy Award for his performance as a conscience-torn Quaker during the American Civil War in *Friendly Persuasion* (1956). He went on to win a Tony Award in 1958 for his starring role in *Look Homeward, Angel*. He often played mentally troubled and deranged characters and is best remembered for his portrayal of the sexual psychopath, Norman Bates, in Hitchcock's film *Psycho* (1960).

The Merlo family in Elizabeth, New Jersey

Frank Merlo as a teenager

*Saturday, 6 October 1956*

Miami – "The Towers"
Oct. 6
　　Last night a good lay at Gil's.
　　Today – tension – Unable to resume the dubious work on "Sweet Bird" so started a short one just to be doing <u>something</u>.
　　Now the pool – without pleasure – Called N.Y. but Frank was in new Jersey.


*Sunday, 18 November 1956*

Miami – Nov. 18
　　The old childish dread of falling asleep has come back on me tonight – despite a "tranquillizer".
　　This second Miami bit is going stale on me now.
　　Only the mornings are still agreeable. I continue to work about 3 hours a day but with the stimulants that have now become customary.
　　Last week I had two sexual adventures, one that cost nothing and with a sweet person but that person has disappeared.
　　Last night I gave a cocktail party – afterwards Gil slugged a dike and was thrown out and beaten up by the pair of them.
　　I'm reading a novel about the Leopold & Loeb case.[997] It's fascinating. I'll go back to it now.


*Friday, 23 November 1956*

Friday – Nov. 23 –
　　I guess sitting & watching TV is better than nothing.
　　Saw a good movie this PM "Friendly Persuasion" with attractive new kid Tony Perkins.[998] Found it was Ladies day at the "Y" and too late for hotel pool so I'll have to rely on a cold shower to pull me together for the evening. Someone may call at 7 but I don't trust such expectations in Miami nowadays. Got to break this <u>routine!</u> – but I don't want to go to Havana, at least not alone, and fuck whores.

## NEW YORK Herald Tribune

A European Edition is Published Daily in Paris

MONDAY, DECEMBER 17, 1956

© 1956, New York Herald Tribune Inc.

### Kazan, Tennessee Williams Reply

# Spellman Takes Pulpit To Forbid 'Baby Doll'

*Texts of statements— Page 15.*

**By Bert Quint**

Francis Cardinal Spellman exhorted Catholics yesterday to refrain from patronizing the motion picture "Baby Doll" under the "pain of sin."

"The revolting theme of this picture and the brazen advertising promoting it constitute a contemptuous defiance of the natural law," the Cardinal told worshipers from the pulpit at the 10 a. m. solemn Mass at St. Patrick's Cathedral.

Elia Kazan, producer and director of the picture, disagreed in a statement later that the film is immoral. He said, "It is the personal story of four small and pitiable people." In Key West, Fla., Tennessee Williams, who wrote "Baby Doll," said, "I cannot believe that an ancient and august branch of the Christian faith is not larger in heart and mind than those who set themselves up as censors. . . ."

A member of the cathedral staff said she believed the Cardinal "probably" had not seen a preview of the picture but had been informed of it by the Legion of Decency.

Cardinal Spellman, one of this country's four princes of the Roman Catholic Church, spoke "in the performance of his duty as Archbishop of New York, in solicitude for the welfare of souls entrusted to my care and to the welfare of the country.

Members of the cathedral staff could remember only two previous occasions on which Cardinal Spellman personally spoke from the pulpit in St. Continued on page 15, column 1

*New York Herald Tribune,*
17 December 1956

*Sunday, 25 November 1956*

Sun.

Up till midnight, yesterday, as I remarked to Gilbert, was the happiest day I could remember in recent years, due mainly to a singularly nice experience in bed.

But at midnight I made a drunken ass of myself because my greedy pursuit of another indulgence, I mean with another party, was somewhat rudely frustrated by the precipitate departure of the object.

———————

Baby Doll *was released on 18 December and was condemned by Cardinal Spellman, the Archbishop of New York, as a degrading picture that stimulated "immorality and crime," and he instructed those under his spiritual care to stay away from it "under pain of sin." Despite such condemnation,* Baby Doll *received four Academy Award nominations, including best screenplay.*

———————

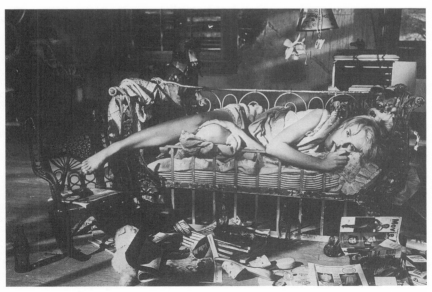

Carroll Baker in *Baby Doll*

999. *Orpheus Descending* opened in New York on 21 March 1957 and closed on 18 May. According to Maureen Stapleton, who played Lady Torrance, Williams and Harold Clurman, the director, were not working well together. Because she knew Williams so well she had been chosen to tell him that the entire prologue would have to be cut (Spoto, p. 212). The title "Something Wild in the Country" was replaced during the re-tryout tour.

1000. At the beginning of the year (5 January 1957, Yale), Williams wrote to Sandy Campbell: "I am planning to start analysis soon as I return the end of this month . . . as I am tired of living with myself as I am." Williams sought psychiatric help in June.

1001. Williams received negative reviews from such periodicals as *Variety, Time,* and *Newsweek. Variety* declared, "'Orpheus' is neither a cogent nor satisfying drama" (27 March 1957). *Time* concluded that the play failed for three reasons, "faultiness of structure, an obsessiveness of attitude, an empurpling theatricalism" (1 April 1957). *Newsweek* opined that while the play is "studded with scenes of humor, violence, passion, and poetry . . . they seem set pieces without any underlying pull to hold them together" (1 April 1957).

Even Brooks Atkinson, generally very positive about Williams' work, found significant shortcomings. In the *New York Times* (22 March 1957), Atkinson wrote:

"Orpheus Descending" is a loosely woven play — overwritten in some of the scenes, uncertain at times in its progressions. . . . [I]t seems to this playgoer that Mr. Williams has his story less thoroughly under control this time, and his allusive style has a less sturdy foundation. The purple patches that explode magnificently in his best work sprawl and crumple when they are not soundly motivated.

What we are left with is a discursive tale with an attractive locale, a sense of small-town realities, some original characters and several wonderful scenes.

In an article in the *New York Times* (17 March 1957), Williams responded to what he believed was a lack of understanding by the critics:

[*Orpheus Descending*] is a play about unanswered questions that haunt the hearts of people and the difference between continuing to ask them, a difference represented by the four major protagonists of the play, and the acceptance of prescribed answers that are not answers at all, but expedient adaptations or surrender to a state of quandary.

Set design by Boris Aronson for *Orpheus Descending*

*February 1957*

February 1957

Passing one of the wretchedest nights of my life. Tension over a bad rehearsal of "Orpheus" now called "Something Wild, Etc"[999] – Vodka and Scotch, real slugs and a supper of chili con carne – my stomach swole up like I'd swallowed a good-sized watermelon. I puked and puked and since then 3 sleeping tablets and 2 tranquillizers have had no effect. I begin, now, to get panicky about the play – But the die is cast – I've got to ride with it, now.

As for work, the report is pitiful.

Psychiatric help is imperative now.[1000]

Physical symptoms alarming. Have bled from bowels 4 nights in succession, enough blood to turn the toilet bowl bright pink.

Frank has been patient and sweet since the bad, nearly disastrous, quarrel in Key West.

Well, tomorrow we have to start picking up the pieces.

---

*On 27 March Williams' father died in Knoxville, Tennessee.*

---

*Sunday, 31 March 1957*

March 31, 1957

Those pieces are hard to pick up.

"Orpheus" was slaughtered by the Furies of the press.[1001] I still think the play had poetry and beauty.

Night of the opening I started to pack for Hong Kong. Pity I didn't go through with that wild impulse – Instead I've returned again to the "Towers" in Miami – a totally strange world might have jolted me out of this inevitable despondancy.

Of course some of the tension is gone since the opening is over – but it's left me rather lifeless. It will not be easy to resume work on anything of importance.

The moment has certainly come for psychiatric help, but will I take it?

1002. Soon after Richard Freeman Leavitt (1929–2003) met Williams in 1956, they became good friends. Leavitt edited the pictorial biography *The World of Tennessee Williams* (1978) and compiled *Ave Atque Vale!* after Williams' death. With Kenneth Holditch, he wrote *Tennessee Williams and the South* (2002).

1003. George Robison Black, Marion Vaccaro's brother.

1004. A game in which the players take turns asking each other questions that they have to answer truthfully. In *Twenty-nine Letters from Coconut Grove* (1974), Sandy Campbell records playing the truth game with Williams and Tallulah Bankhead in early 1956.

In *The Milk Train Doesn't Stop Here Anymore* (scene 5), Mrs. Goforth says to Chris Flanders: "Let's play the truth game. Do you know the truth game?"

CHRIS: Yes, but I don't like it. I've always made excuses to get out of it when it's played at parties because I think the truth is too delicate and, well, *dangerous* a thing to be played with at parties, Mrs. Goforth. It's nitroglycerin, it has to be handled with the — the carefulest care, or somebody hurts somebody and gets hurt back and the party turns to a — devastating explosion, people crying, people screaming, people even fighting and throwing things at each other. I've seen it happen, and there's no truth in it — that's true.

Williams and Richard Freeman Leavitt, 1978

*Monday, 1 April 1957*

April Fools' Day, '57

A little work in the A.M. and a long afternoon in the sun by the pool with Gilbert and his attractive friend Dick.[1002] Some tension later which I countered with liquor and a pinkie. Then had a cup of coffee to wake me up. Two queens came over, rather nice ones, seven years together and we left Gil's for the Starlite Lounge because we'd finished my Scotch. I had 3 double bourbons at the bar and for a change, Gil was happily drunk and the time was pleasant.

I announced that I was retiring from the professional theatre and going to devote myself to friendship and a good, simple life in New Orleans, with analysis . . .

Bull! – How on earth do I know what I'm going to do, except that it's fairly plain that I will go on drinking and drinking and <u>drinking</u>, and having a good time in bed whenever I can and hitting the keys of my new "Olympia" typewriter – a good one – Ah, well. Goodnight.

Mon. Eve.

Dinner at Marian's. She got drunk and I fell asleep watching TV. George[1003] drove me home after providing me with a list of gay resorts in Amsterdam just in case I do fly to England next week – I don't think I will.

My sleepiness left me as soon as I got back to the hotel and I felt lonely. I am still feeling lonely. There's nothing else to report.

*Tuesday, 2 April 1957*

Tues. Eve –

I behaved well, for a change, during the course of a pretty trying evening. Three charming kids & poor old drunken Gil and me, and the kids quite absorbed in each other. I refused to become annoyed, although I had bought all the groceries, and wine and paid the bar-bill later. However I shall know better tomorrow. Fortunately I had little libido to suffer, coming home alone.

I still think maybe Hong Kong Would have been better and still have not decided about the trip to London.

*Friday, 5 April or Saturday, 6 April 1957*

Friday 2:30 AM

A long, sweet talk with F. on phone.

At Gil's tonight we played the truth game.[1004] I suppose the consequences will be apparent tomorrow.

Still no decision on the flight to London –

1005. Peter Hall (1930– ), the eminent English director, producer, and artistic administrator, was directing *Camino Real*. It opened on 8 April 1957 and was performed by his own company, the International Playwrights' Theatre. Two years earlier Hall had directed the English-language premiere of Beckett's *Waiting for Godot*. Hall went on to direct the London premiere of *Cat on a Hot Tin Roof* (1958). In addition, he served as co-designer for both the world premiere (Spoleto, Italy, 1962) and the New York premiere (1963) of *The Milk Train Doesn't Stop Here Anymore*.

Williams did travel to London to see *Camino Real*. In a letter written from Paris (received 23 April 1957, HRC), he expressed to Audrey Wood his personal reaction to the play:

> On the whole, the Peter Hall production was a fine one, the new script is much better than the one played in New York. . . . The acting . . . was extremely good. Of course this play will always have a mixed reaction but the audience were absorbed and applauded with vigor.

1006. Lawrence S. Kubie (1896–1973) was an orthodox Freudian psychoanalyst who practiced in New York from 1930 to 1959 as well as serving on the faculties of six medical schools, including Johns Hopkins, Yale, and Columbia. By the end of June, Williams was seeing Kubie three or four times a week.

About his psychoanalysis Williams wrote his mother (28 June 1957, HTC): "I've been wanting to try it for a long time, and this seems a good time to do it, now that it seems advisable to stay at a safe distance from Broadway till the critics have a chance to forget my recent transgressions."

Lawrence S. Kubie

*Saturday, 6 April or Sunday, 7 April 1957*

Sat. 2:40 AM

Still no decision, waiting some word from Peter Hall about probable reception of play as I don't want to fly over to experience another fiasco.[1005]

A gay party tonight which went on from 4:30 P.M. till midnight and reached a peak of something with nude swimming in Marian's pool.

It isn't really such a bad life here.

*Saturday, 27 April 1957*

Rome April 27

No. And I'm going back to it. I fly out tomorrow (Alitalia) to Madrid.

*Circa Monday, 3 June 1957*

Harkness-Pavillion – New York.

Exquisite boredom, lying here in a hospital bed at command of Dr. Kubie,[1006] to be examined and "dried out". I don't think I can stand much of it. Can do without the liquor and that's undoubtedly a wise move, but — (interruption!?)

Well – the boredom vanished when the two Docs entered and I felt suddenly trapped. Heart began doing its flip-flops. I was nearly panicky.

Nurse just gave me some bitter liquid I'm too go through a lot of tests, it seems – starting in A.M.

I guess I've been hiding from this a long time, dodging, ~~cheating~~ kidding myself but maybe it's better, now, to have to collide with it, face to face, head on – Gosh, I'm downright incoherent.

*Thursday, 6 June 1957*

Thurs. 9:20 P.M.

*Friday, 7 June 1957*

Fri. 7:10 A.M.

Found nothing to say last night. This morning? Well, I guess they'll let me out of here for the weekend. Then perhaps I can think clearly about things and decide if to surrender myself, my will, to doctors, clinics, Etc. is my way of salvation or any hope of it. or whether flight, my only way before now, is not still the better.

1007. Williams was sent to the Austen-Riggs Center in Stockbridge, Massachusetts, for a period of psycho-therapy. He told his mother (28 June 1957, HTC):

> I stayed only five minutes in the Institute. I took one look at the other patients and told Frank to carry my bags right back out to the car. I checked into the local hotel and stayed there over the week-end to make sure that this was not the place for me, then drove back to New York. I think the psy-chiatrist Dr. Kubie who is head of the analytic institute in New York, is right in thinking I need some therapy of that kind to relieve the tensions that I have been living under, but I think it's unnecessary for me to live in a house full of characters that appeared to be more disturbed than myself.

1008. Williams reported to his mother (28 June 1957, HTC) that the only things they found in their physical check-up, "according to their report," was "an old scar on a heart-valve, probably result of some damage in childhood, and a thyroid deficiency."

1009. *The Loss of a Teardrop Diamond* is a screenplay about Fisher Willow, the daughter of a Mississippi Delta plantation owner. Fisher is a debutante of the Memphis season, but she is not accepted because of the dis-grace caused by her father. Mr. Willow blew up the south end of his levee to protect his plantation from flooding and caused severe flooding for farmers south of him, which resulted in a number of people drown-ing. Fisher falls in love with Jimmy Dobyne, the poor son of the manager of her father's commissary. Their romance is interrupted when she loses a teardrop-shaped diamond earring, and he believes she thinks he has stolen it. During the course of the evening Fisher is advised by her ill aunt Addie: "You want to be loved by somebody that you love but you don't know how to arrange it. And not all the teardrop dia-monds, lost or found, in this world can arrange that for you." The play ends with Fisher and Jimmy spend-ing the evening together.

1010. Reserpine was prescribed for the treatment of hypertension, mild anxiety states, and chronic psychoses. Its side-effects included lethargy, drowsiness, gastro-intestinal upsets, and vertigo.

1011. According to Richard Leavitt (letter to Margaret Bradham Thornton), Ramon was Williams' "procurer." He "kept a stable of boys for rent," which Williams referred to as Ramon's "Lending Library," and he would ask Ramon, "Do you have any, ah, new books in your li-br-ary?"

1012. Gore Vidal identified Joe Murphy as a waiter who worked at one of the better restaurants in Key West.

Williams with unidentified acquaintance in Havana

As for my work – I must accept the possibility that it may be over – finished. And try to devise some way to go on without it!

Miami between Airport & Beach –

Cab driver says it's the hottest day he ever felt here. I hope he's right.

I'm stealing a week between New York and the "retreat" "retreat" at Stockbridge, assuming I do go there.[1007] I was headed for Havana but missed the plane for there. Luckily, I guess. Already a bad omen. My driver's license has expired. This was discovered when I went to rent a car at airport. Suppose I'll manage to get one anyhow, though.

The hospital check-up was not very illuminating.[1008] I am still on a low alcohol ration which is just about the only good thing I have to report.

*Tuesday, 11 June 1957*

Tues.

Yesterday I goofed. With the plane trip as an excuse (not a good one) I had at least 8 drinks during the day and had 3 seconals, one before the flight and two later, combating an intense depression that had fallen over me.

Today I'm determined to resume the fixed quota. Perhaps by staying alone I can make it.

*Thursday, 13 June 1957*

Thurs Midnight Havana.

This A.M. (woke at 6 and read till room service started at 7) I was able, for the first time in months to do some satisfactory work. ("The Loss of a Tear Drop Diamond")[1009] – only a few pages but it picked up my spirits a bit.

Loneliness has begun to shadow me, though.

Tonight a fat drunk at the bar called me "Jew boy!"

Called two other (normal) men fairies and said "Go sleep together!"

I'm drinking a bit more than my quota. Two Scotches at bar. 3 drinks in morning. A daiquiri at Dirty Dick's, 3 glasses of red wine at lunch and 3 of white at dinner – Also two seconals so far, and a green tranquillizer whose name I do not know and a yellow one that I think is called reserpine[1010] or something like that. Well, tomorrow Ramon has promised me something special,[1011] and the sun may be out. I may be able to work again in the A.M.

Drifting a little farther out of reality all the time, perhaps. Wired Joe Murphy,[1012] said the weather was cool & the swimming great and please come for the week-end.

Touring cast of *Suddenly Last Summer* (1959) with Diana Barrymore as
Catherine (seated far right), Cathleen Nesbitt as Mrs. Venable (seated center),
and Richard Gardner as Dr. Cukrowicz (standing far right)

*Saturday, 9 November 1957*

Nov. 10, 1957
"Resting and waiting in a comfortable twilight" – how nice that sounds to me now.
I'm in a plane before take-off, bound for Miami.

*Sunday, 10 November 1957*

Nov Sunday 7:30 A.M.
Am back at Hotel Towers, my old suite #1007 looking over the Bay.
Brought in the TV set.
Coffee and orange juice will arrive at 8.
So I have returned to a familiar pattern for a few days.

---

*Williams spent the autumn in New York working on the forthcoming production of* Suddenly Last Summer *and continuing his analysis with Dr. Kubie. Williams wrote Maria St. Just in the autumn:*

> *The analysis is still going on, and it gets a bit dreary. It can be an awful drag, concentrating so thoroughly, day after day, on all the horrid things about yourself. If only we could turn up something nice, but so far nothing of that sort even worth mentioning, just envy, hate, anger, and so forth. Of course he is attacking my sex life and has succeeded in destroying my interest in all except the Horse. . . . I give it just one year. Then I start traveling again. Being tied down to New York is almost unendurable. (FOA, p. 150)*

*On 7 January 1958,* Suddenly Last Summer *and "Something Unspoken," grouped together as* Garden District, *opened Off-Broadway to generally positive reviews, none more so than Brooks Atkinson's in the* New York Times *(8 January 1958):*

> *"Suddenly Last Summer" is further evidence of Mr. Williams' genius with the language. Although his world is tainted with corruption, it is beautifully contrived. No one else can use ordinary words with so much grace, allusiveness, sorcery and power.*

*Two days after the opening, Williams returned to Key West to recuperate for several weeks. By 23 April, he was back in New York continuing his analysis. He wrote of his depression:*

> *The old doctor says that I am passing through "purgatory". . . . I had just about made up my mind to quit the doctor this week, in fact I'd written him a long letter of farewell, but instead of posting it I delivered it by hand and of course he talked me into going on with it again. (FOA, p. 151)*

Opening page of the notebook Williams began in February 1955 and resumed in November 1957

*Within weeks Williams had ended his analysis and traveled to Key West to see Frank Merlo and then on to New Orleans where he planned to work on the ending of* Sweet Bird of Youth. *In a letter to Elia Kazan dated 4 June 1958 (Wesleyan), Williams explained why he had ended his analysis:*

*I had to defy my analyst to continue my work this past year. He said I was over-worked and must quit and "lie fallow" as he put it, for a year or so, and then resume work in what he declared would be a great new tide of creative power, which he apparently thought would come out of my analysis with him. I wanted to accept this instruction but without my work, I was unbearably lonely, my life unbearably empty. And I didn't feel I could go on working with him while acting in total defiance of all his injunctions. So I quit for a while. I think maybe after this play I could do what he asks. Lie fallow. Recuperate my energies, slowly. The trouble, now, is that my personal life is all fucked up. Frank and I have drifted so wide apart and nobody else has come near enough to help me. I have a good constitution, a pretty strong one, but I am consciously breaking it down, bit by bit, day by day, by these methods of living and working, as if I thought I had to race against time.*

*By 22 June Williams was back in Europe.*

Sketch in Williams' notebook

1013. Eddie Berk (1929– ) was a close friend of Marion Vaccaro's who lived in Miami. According to Richard Leavitt (letter to Margaret Bradham Thornton):

> He was a flamboyant queen and best friends with Marion Vaccaro. He embarrassed people with his wild behavior and while Tennessee liked him early on, he avoided him later to the point of skipping Marion's funeral for fear of running into him. He could be amusing, but one only went to certain places with him. We usually referred to him as "The German Chef," but Marion always called him "Mam'selle."

1014. Anthony Franciosa (1928–2006), the American actor, played Pietro, who has an illicit love affair with his stepmother, Gioia, played by Anna Magnani, in the film *Selvaggio è il Vento* (1957). He would go on to play Ralph in the film version of *Period of Adjustment* (1962).

Anna Magnani and Williams at a festival

Anthony Franciosa

*Wednesday, 2 July 1958*

Lisbon, July 2, 1958

A corner room on the seventh floor of the hotel Embaxiador – great winds of Portugal blowing the dark green curtains, light that rises and falls. ·

Arrived early this morning with horse and dog by a Pan Am Clipper plane – Retired to read in bed – Comfortable, serene. A good beginning.

*Thursday, 3 July or Friday, 4 July 1958*

Barcelona – July 3 or 4

Just checked into Hotel Colon – have a room on the hot top floor. If it doesn't cool off by evening will request a change. But there is a corrida this eve. and I will have a barrera. I hope to sleep away most of the afternoon as last night was sleepless due to a fight with the Horse.

I have my Agua Solares and plenty of milltowns, pinkies, Etc. And a bottle of Scotch still unopened. If I weren't so beat and the room were a little cooler, I would be content – relatively. In any case I hope to avoid complaints and miseries for a while, if I can.

*Saturday, 12 July 1958*

Rome – July ? (Sat.)

Arrived here to find, so far, no trace of Frank. Have a pleasant room at the Excelsior but no interest in the city, and no interest in further travel, either. The moment is somewhat perplexing. Marian is suffering from an ear infection, giving her terrific pain. Eddie Berk ("Mademoiselle" of Coconut Grove) is also here.[1013] I do not lack company but it's depressing to find that F. has left – and left no word. I am partly to blame as I didn't call or write from Barcelona. And had been rather horrid in Lisbon because he read a book while I wanted to make the nightingales sing.

OK. No complaints, no miseries – en avant!

*Monday, 14 July 1958*

Mon. A.M. (6:00)

Finally saw Anna and met Francioso.[1014] I slammed a car door on his finger in Anna's tiny Alfa Romeo. Felt quite overcome with nerves. Calmed myself, finally, with Scotch and pinkies at Belvedere delle Rose where we went together – (The bill was 11,000 lire! which Tony paid) Franciosa rather thrilling especially between me and Anna in the tiny car. I felt as fluttery as a school girl. A really

1015. "Those tiny swifts the Romans call rondini had now returned to the city. During the day they hovered invisibly high toward the sun but at dusk they lowered a quivering net to the height of Mrs. Stone's terrace" (*The Roman Spring of Mrs. Stone*, p. 48).

1016. Presumably *Confessions of a Mask*, Yukio Mishima's autobiographical first novel about a homosexual adolescent who masks his sexuality. The English translation was published by New Directions in 1958.

1017. "The Mutilated" is a one-act play about two prostitutes, one dim and childlike who has been recently released from prison for shoplifting and the other who has had a mastectomy and is full of shame about her affliction. They treat each other with bitchiness as they reconcile their miserable friendship one Christmas Eve. "The Mutilated" was paired with another one-act, "The Gnädiges Fräulein," and produced under the title *Slapstick Tragedy* in 1966.

1018. John Foster Dulles (1888–1959), the U.S. Secretary of State from 1953 to 1959 under President Eisenhower, was a strong and active opponent of communism. Dulles took a major role in leading the Republican Party out of its tradition of isolationism in foreign policy into an era of internationalism. His philosophy of foreign policy included the concept of "brinkmanship": "The ability to get to the verge without getting into the war is the necessary art . . . if you are scared to go to the brink, you are lost." Dulles' belief that the Western Allies and their friends in Asia should oppose communism led to the formation of the Southeast Asia Treaty Organization (1954).

Another foreign-policy concept in which Dulles had a major role was the Eisenhower Doctrine (1957) which provided for the United States to use armed forces to support Middle Eastern countries against communist aggression. Under the terms of this doctrine, United States forces were sent to Lebanon in 1958.

1019. Iris Tree (1897–1968), poet and actress, was a daughter of Sir Herbert Tree, the highly regarded British actor-manager who founded the Royal Academy of Dramatic Arts. Her volumes of poetry include *The Traveller and Other Poems* (1927). In 1959 she played herself in Fellini's *La Dolce Vita*. Williams would later include Iris Tree among the group of ladies of the international set in Rome "who did writing that impressed me unforgettably" (*New York Times Book Review*, 15 January 1978).

1020. A week later, in a letter to Audrey Wood (24 July 1958, HRC), Williams elaborated on her condition:

Marian Vaccaro was with me, suffering from an agonizing ear-infection which she was doctoring with a quart of whiskey a day and never leaving her room. She's a very sick woman, still, and I hate heavy drinking in anyone but myself. . . . But Marion has been such a wonderful friend to me for so many years that I can't ignore her predicament. In addition to the quart-a-day, she has constant sedation and injections to keep her in a semi-somnolent state but this does not prevent her from picking up the phone at three or five in the morning to say she is dying. I suspect she may be right about it. She coughs all the time, doesn't eat, has to be supported along the street on the few occasions that you can get her out. Well, today she is out and I hope that she went out to book a passage back to the States as I don't feel able to cope with her problems as well as my own, I'm not even distantly related to Florence Nightingale, I'm afraid.

1021. Name of Williams' bulldog.

nice kid, too. But now I've been unable to sleep. The rondinelli are squeaking madly about the windows,[1015] it's daylight, I have only 2 more pages of Mishima's book[1016] which has turned out less brilliant than it started.

*Tuesday, 15 July 1958*

Tues. July 15 –
   Another virtually sleepless night and a feeling of imminent crack-up – yet I have ordered coffee (7:30 AM.) and apparently intend to follow usual morning routine.

*Wednesday, 16 July 1958*

Wed. – 11 A.M.
   Bad intestinal condition – diarrhoea with bleeding. But supper with Anna last night – her kindness, humanity, wisdom – lifted my cloud of depression quite a bit and I went to Bricktop's, after.
   This A.M. – the old routine but work on "The Mutilated"[1017] seems to go a bit better.
   Have cancelled my flight to Barcelona and made up my mind to wait for Frank's return to Rome and try to create an understanding between us that will make it possible to go on together.

*Thursday, 17 July 1958*

Thurs. 6:20 A.M.
   Not much sleep tonight since I had dozed so much yesterday. The world appears to be on one of Mr. Dulles' brinks of war.[1018] Very threatening indeed. Soon as I recover from this indisposition, assuming that I do, I think I'll fly back to the States and retire to Cuba or visit Bigelow & sweat out the summer back there.
   Tonight one of Rome's rare and lovely summer rain & thunderstorms. We had taken Iris Tree[1019] to dinner. She remains quite marvelous. But poor Marian! I think she is gravely ill, down the hall, under morphine all day to endure the ear (?) condition.[1020] What a nightmare world! Or have I said that before?
   Miss Brinda,[1021] now snoring, has already peed on both carpets here, disdaining the bathroom and the rainy outdoors. En Avant.

1022. Kubie, according to Williams, had advised him to give up writing for a period of time in order to rest. In a letter to Audrey Wood (9 July 1958, HRC), Williams wrote about his treatment with Kubie:

> Of course I will see Kubie, first, when I get back, and thrash out our differences. I don't think a patient should feel more depressed and uncertain of himself than ever, after a year's treatment, even though interrupted from time to time by an escape compulsion. I feel that he has been stubbornly obtuse about the need to continue my work when there's nothing to put in its place, and when I feel so strongly that I have so little time left in which to complete it.
>
> He did give me more insight into the dark side of my nature, but it increased my depression which was already about as much as I could endure. I resented him telling me that I must "go through hell" when I have been going through nothing but hell, with slight variations of temperature, for the past ten years of my wretched, diseased existence.
>
> I want to become a decent person. as I used to be, but I'm not sure Kubie's the one who can help me attain this.

1023. Williams had traveled to Sicily with Magnani. He wrote Audrey Wood (24 July 1958, HRC): "Anna is going to be presented, at Taormina, with the italian equivalent of an Oscar for her performance in 'Wild is the Wind'. [Frank and I] are to be her attendants. I hope to stay there, for the swimming, about two weeks."

1024. Williams wrote to Kazan ([11] August 1958, Wesleyan):

> [The] discussion of the play I had with Sam Spiegel in Taormina . . . shook me up quite a bit, as it made me face up to this important problem of cohesion in the script. I think the weak points, the ones that need tightening most, are the Finley house scene, the rally scene, and the lately devised telephone scene between Heavenly and Chance — I think, now, that their telephone talk is a mistake. They should never have any contact or communication with each other in the play. The material from that scene can be shifted to the scene between Chance and Scudder in the first scene of the play, and no contact between the two young people should ever occur in the play.

1025. Giorgio was "a very attractive young Roman gigolo" who escorted Marion Vaccaro when Williams was busy.

Marion Vaccaro, Giorgio, and Williams

*Friday, 18 July 1958*

1:30 Fri. A.M. July 17

Lying awake here in The Excelsior – some uncomfortable thinking about the course of my life which seems pretty declivitous.

But some lovely writing in Lawrence's "The Rainbow" which I am at last reading.

Have been reading myself blind these past two days, laid up with dysentery or colitis.

9:15 A.M.

Undertaking another day without coffee and work. Kubie would be pleased.[1022] Not sure I am – Nor am I sure that I won't revert to the routine in a while.

*Saturday, 26 July 1958*

Taormina –

A room at the San Domenico with a balcony overlooking the sea –

– A film festival[1023] –

– last night a talk with Sam Spiegel.[1024] He didn't like "Sweet Bird" – He said I'd brought in too many elements that were foreign to the main story, Princess and Chance. I agreed with him about it and will try to cut these extraneous things down before it goes into production.

Great lethargy today. No interest in the life here. F. is getting cross and unpleasant with me. I am trying to be as nice as I can.

Marian and Giorgio[1025] are with us. She's drinking heavily and in constant pain from her ear – infection, if that's what it is. My sympathy is a fairly perfunctory sort. Just did 3 pages today, slowly, without inspiration. Have paid $1300. for a 2 months lease on an apt. in Rome. (Including deposit) but doubt that I will spend more than 2 or 3 weeks in it. I think Barcelona suits me better. I may cable Maria to visit me somewhere this summer. I need her spirit.

*Sunday, 3 August or Monday, 4 August 1958*

Taormina –

It must be after midnight. I am lying here burning with fever which suddenly came on after my day at the beach.

A.M.

Still burning. Just took a cool bath. Some abdominal pain, not severe.

1026. On 3 August 1958 (HRC), Williams wrote Audrey Wood about the article that appeared in the 26–27 July weekend copy of *Il Paese Sera*:

> A nasty Roman journalist made a vicious personal attack on me in Paese Sera (Communist paper) while I was with Magnani in Taormina. She and Frank want me to sue the paper but I don't intend to, of course. It is too hot for a law-suit or anything of an active nature. The article claimed that I was so drunk I could barely speak, that I kept the Mayor of Messina waiting for an hour and when he asked me what I had written, I told him that I was the author of The Divine Comedy. Also that I had greasy, hairy hands that looked as if they were accustomed to picking up dirty male under-wear! — the article was removed from later editions of the paper and has not been quoted. Since it appeared in a Communist paper I don't think it's sufficiently damaging to justify legal action. In fact, it's so nasty it's almost funny.

1027. Born in Indianapolis, Janet Flanner (1892–1978) was the *New Yorker*'s Paris correspondent from 1925 to 1975 and was a member of the Left Bank American literary colony that included Hemingway, Stein, Crane, Pound, Barnes, and the Scott Fitzgeralds. Her reportage of European cultural and political life under the pen name Genêt brought her many awards.

Natalia Danesi Murray (1901–94) was born in Rome and came to the United States to marry an American. She worked as a broadcast journalist as well as for two major Italian publishers. Her friendship with Flanner began in the 1940s, and they remained intimate friends until Flanner's death.

Williams' relationship with Murray dates back much earlier. In a letter to Cheryl Crawford (26 June 1950, NYPL), he wrote that he was going to seek Murray's help with the Italian for *The Rose Tattoo*: "I want nearly all the first dialogue in the knife scene to be in Italian. The action is explicit enough and the emotion would make Pepina revert to her native tongue."

Murray's sister, Lea Danesi Tolnay, who worked for Rappresentante di Autori Drammatici, was Williams' literary agent in Italy.

1028. The British actress Margaret Leighton (1922–76), who had won a Tony Award in 1956 for Terence Rattigan's play *Separate Tables*, was starring in Rattigan's new play, *Variation on a Theme*, at the Globe Theatre. She was highly respected, both in London and on Broadway, and also made numerous screen and television appearances.

The following day (31 August 1958, HRC), Williams wrote to Audrey Wood about Leighton:

> Last night I saw Margaret Leighton in her closing performance of the Rattigan play. She invited me backstage after the show and told me that she is to see you all in New York Friday, on her way to the Coast to make a film that she will finish in the late Fall, and so would presumably be available for us. I think she's a wonderful actress and could play the pants off the Princess! Please do get Kazan to see her and all of you consider her carefully.

Williams added that Leighton distinguished herself from other actresses by generating a "neurotic power . . . which is right for the Princess."

Leighton was not chosen for *Sweet Bird of Youth*, but she did play Hannah in *The Night of the Iguana* in New York (1961) and won another Tony Award. She went on to play the Fräulein in "The Gnädiges Fräulein" (1966) and Trinket in "The Mutilated" (1966).

1029. In a letter to Kazan ([11] August 1958, Wesleyan), Williams described the changes he was making:

> As for the scene at Boss Finley's, I think it is too cluttered up with peripheral bits. It should drive straight into the conflict between the girl and her father, after opening strong on Chance's return to Saint Cloud and the possible complications which that involves. Perhaps Aunt Nonnie should be cut out of the play, maybe even Tom Junior. Begin Finley house scene with the horns blowing (on Princess car) and HEAVENLY rocking, rocking on the bone-white verandah against the sea-blue sky. Boss Finley coming out as Heavenly answered the phone. It's Chance. He, Boss, knows it is. She says someone called the wrong-number and he makes her sit down with him at the verandah table and goes straight into the strong scene between them: hit hard and get out fast! — for this bit.

In the final version of the play, Williams did not exclude Aunt Nonnie and Tom Junior. The Finley house scene begins with Boss Finley and George Scudder on the porch while Heavenly is lying on the beach. Chance Wayne drives by briefly in his car and later does telephone the house, but his phone calls are intercepted by a servant.

The "Paese Sera" business[1026] probably disturbed and hurt me more than I knew. Feverish dreams about it last night. Program? – a little hard to plan. I can only hope that I will be in a condition to catch the train to Rome tomorrow. I doubt that I would find it comfortable, or even tolerable, to remain there more than a few days but I have no idea where to go.


*Circa 20–28 August 1958*

Positano

The summer began with the sting of a Medusa in Barcelona and that seems to have set the keynote to practically all that has followed.

I have been here about two weeks, maybe more. There were a few relatively good days. Then work petered out and depression deepened so that I suppose I would have left days ago if I'd had the energy to pack my gear. Now a return of diarrhoe, hemorrhoids and right eye swelling up with another big, ugly sty.

Today Janet Flanner & Natalia[1027] came over from Capri. I managed to make agreeable – I hope.

Tomorrow I must get moving, and I shall. Trouble is that no where on earth would really please me now.

It's 4 A.M. and all is not well. En avant!


*Friday, 29 August 1958*

London Aug. 29 '58.

My room at Claridges is full of mirrors and bright overhead lights which do my undressed figure no charitable deed.

Maria is expecting me at her flat. She is preparing a chicken and about to receive an old wet hen. En avant.


*Saturday, 30 August 1958*

Sat Aug 30

A nice walk about town in one of those rare sunlit days in London. Then lunch with Maria. She looked very pretty and was very nice but my state of tension was still in flower and I couldn't shake it off, despite the wine.

Now 2 hours nap and I pick her up for a 5:30 matinee to see Margaret Leighton.[1028]

I miss the horse & dog that I live with in Rome.

I think I did a little good work today on Sweet Bird, condensing the Boss Finley scene.[1029]

The climate here seems to pick me up a bit.

1030. *Sweet Bird of Youth.*

1031. *Ariadne,* by the French philosopher Gabriel Marcel, was followed by *Garden District* at the Arts Theatre in Great Newport Street. Ariadne is a rich and complicated hypochondriac who sets out to win the affections of her husband's mistress, the proud and struggling musician Violetta. Because her marriage is a failure and because she wants her husband, once a homosexual, to be happy, Ariadne appears to support the liaison. Violetta becomes confused as to whether Ariadne is uncommonly generous and unselfish or a master manipulator. The play ends with the liaison irretrievably broken due to Ariadne's meddling.

1032. Trevor Howard (1916–88), a British actor who made a career of playing English officers and gentlemen. His work in film spanned from 1944 to 1988.

1033. Williams had initially conceived the role of the Princess for a foreign actress and traveled to Paris to hear several French actresses read for the part.

1034. By the 1950s, Peter (Stephen Paul) Brook (1925– ), the well-known avant-garde British director, had directed plays by Jean Anouilh and Christopher Fry in London's West End as well as Shakespeare at Stratford. In 1955 he had staged *Titus Andronicus* with Laurence Olivier which featured Brook's own set designs and *musique concrète.* In 1957 he directed the Paris premiere of *Cat on a Hot Tin Roof* (*La Chatte sur un Toit Brûlant*).

1035. Natasha Parry (1930– ), British stage and film actress, who was married to Peter Brook.

1036. In a postscript to a letter to Audrey Wood (18 September 1958, HRC), the producer John C. Wilson described his frustration over Williams' non-appearance at the London opening of *Garden District*:
> P.S. We had a little trouble with Tennessee, who came to rehearsals in the <u>middle</u>, stayed a few days at Claridges . . . and then went back to the South of France with the professed intention of returning for the opening and a Press Conference here. The day before the opening he sent us word he was ill with sunstroke and would be unable to get to the Press meeting; and on the day of the opening another message saying that he would not be able to come <u>at all</u> as he was full of anti-biotics. . . . [W]hen I telephoned the Carlton in Cannes, he had left. <u>Not</u> for London, but for <u>Barcelona</u>.

In a letter to Wood dated 19 September 1958 (HRC), Williams gave his own account:
> I did not go to London after all, as I took very ill the day before I was to fly up there. I had a high fever and constant coughing and heart palpitations. Finally called in the hotel doctor, at Cannes, and he said I had Flu and also said, "You know, your heart's very bad," which scared me so that I stayed up all night to guard against the Reaper. Remained in bed all the next day and the day after that I flew down to Barcelona. I suspect the play did badly as I have had no word of its critical reception. I'm glad I wasn't there.

Frank Merlo, Williams, Janet Flanner, and Natalia Danesi Murray

*Sunday, 31 August 1958*

3:00 A.M.

Slept 2½ hours and woke with a burning stomach. Room service just delivered a whole bottle of cold milk. Had violent diarrhoea before I went to bed. The insides are pretty fucked up this summer –

So now it's Sunday, a day I've always hated, especially in London with all the pubs closed and no theatre.

Impulse: to fly away.

*Tuesday, 2 September 1958*

1:15 A.M. Sept 1.

Not at all a bad day. Progress on "S.B."[1030] Lunch with Maria & a long walk about the Serpentine in Hyde Park. Napped for 2 hours.

Woke very tense – social neurosis – and took Maria to Arts Theatre – an old fashioned but interesting play, "Ariadne".[1031] Supper at Little Acropolis – a small pinkie and liquor put the neurosis away. We met Trevor Howard[1032] and a couple from Hamamett, Tunisia, and I have begun to think of taking a trip there, right after my little stay here. <u>En Avant</u>.

Tues. Sept 3 –

Departed London for Paris.[1033] via BEA in company Peter Brook,[1034] Sam Spiegel and Natasha,[1035] all of whom I like. At first the social neurosis was very, very severe but it subsided after champagne and whiskey on the plane – However I declined invitation to dine and go on the town with their party and retired to my room on the roof of the Pont Royal, feeling lonely but having some good books to read.

*Monday, 15 September 1958*

Cannes –

Took some very bad coals to New Castle which I threw out this morning in a very ugly scene of jealous rage.

Ill for past two days with summer flu – that's what the hotel doctor calls it. Ticker acting up badly and the stupid Dr. succeeded in alarming me about it. Consequently now pretty tense and each palpitation, of which there are no small number, gives me a scare. <u>Mustn't</u> turn cardianeurotic, on top of everything else this beastly summer.

Was to fly to London today – Cancelled and am booked on plane to Barcelona Wed., day after tomorrow.[1036]

Lonely! Very lonely!

1037. *Garden District* opened on 16 September and the reviews were for the most part neutral to slightly positive. *The Times* (17 September 1958) called "Something Unspoken" a "straightforward study of character" and *Suddenly Last Summer* a "highbrow thriller." The reviewer went on to say:

> Nobody can complain that as a thriller writer Mr. Williams takes things easy. On the contrary, he sets himself a dénouement so startling that it is only with difficulty that he can create the idea of a character wicked enough to sustain its dreadful burden. Sebastian is torn to pieces and eaten by a rabble of hungry black boys. Even to appear to deserve such a fate he has to be painted in pretty queer colours, and Mr. Williams's gifts for portraiture and for eloquent and expressive dialogue have to work at high pressure. Hard as they work we can hardly say when the dénouement comes that we are thoroughly seized of the nature of Sebastian's wickedness.
>
> We are in no doubt, however, about the wickedness of Sebastian's mother.

1038. *Novilleros* are apprentice matadors.

1039. Herbert Machiz (1923–76), director, producer, and acting teacher, had previously directed a summer theatre production of "Something Unspoken" (1955) and the disastrous New York revival of *A Streetcar Named Desire* (1956) with Tallulah Bankhead. In addition to the London premiere of *Garden District*, Machiz had successfully directed the New York premiere at the beginning of the year. Machiz's association with Williams continued and he went on to direct both the world premiere (1962) and the New York premiere (1963) of *The Milk Train Doesn't Stop Here Anymore* and *In the Bar of a Tokyo Hotel* (1969).

Herbert Machiz directing Beatrix Lehmann and Patricia Neal in a rehearsal for the London production of *Suddenly Last Summer*

*Tuesday, 16 September 1958*

Tues. A.M.

Got through that night.

Flu symptoms and fever seem to have subsided after antibiotics and the ticker is calm right now.

Just ordered coffee.


*Wednesday, 17 September 1958*

Wed. 2 AM.

I gathered from Maria's guarded report that the London opening of Garden District was far from triumphant.[1037]

Leaving tomorrow AM for Barcelona if I can pack and get to the plane.

Condition not bad, not good. En Avant.


*Thursday, 18 September 1958*

Thurs. A.M.

Woke up at Hotel Colon racked with coughing.

Spent day mostly in room – some work in A.M.

Corrida in P.M – pretty good, a pair of Novelleros[1038] that I enjoyed watching. Afterwards, cocktails in the Ritz bar with Carlos Lombarde and his very handsome Greek friend. I was so tense that I had to take a pinkie – Later, took them to dinner at Hotel Colon but was too exhausted afterwards to go out. Retired and woke up now and then feeling lousy.


*Friday, 19 September 1958*

Fri. A.M.

Felt like death when I woke up this morning but, surprisingly, after coffee, double martini and pinkie, I felt pretty good and took a sanguine view of my work on Act Two of "Sweet Bird". Have just put through a call to Machiz[1039] in London to enquire about fate of "Garden District". He will probably lie a good deal. Afterwards, I will go out to the beach and probably be foolish enough to swim in those cold, not clean, pools. En Avant!

1040. Two verses from *The Dhammapada*, perhaps taken from the translation by F. Max Müller (verse 103 [ch. VIII] and verse 54 [ch. IV]), first published in *The Sacred Books of the East* (1881).

Marlon Brando and Williams on the film set of *The Fugitive Kind*

Card Williams sent to Donald Windham,
December 1958

*Sunday, 21 September or Monday, 22 September 1958*

Sunday – 2:00 A.M.

A child of love – dined on the terrace with the cathedral spires lit up and a mass choir singing Catelonian folks songs on the Square below. Then love – came twice, both ways, and divinely responsive as if a benign Providence, or shall we be frank and say God, had suddenly taken cognizance and pity of my long misery this summer and given me this night as a token of forgiveness.

Quotation from a sacred book of Buddhism:

"If one conquer in battle a thousand times one thousand men, and if another conquer himself he is the greatest of conquerors."

So true!

Another: "The scent of flowers does not travel against the wind, neither that of sandalwood, but the scent of good deeds travels even against the wind."[1040]

---

*There are no known notebooks for the period October 1958 to March 1979. The only indication of an intent is Williams' comment at the end of his journal covering the period October 1946 to April 1947. On 29 November 1966, Williams wrote:*

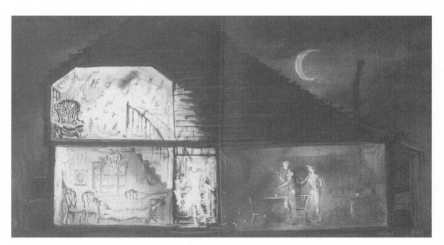

Set designs by Jo Mielziner for *Sweet Bird of Youth* (top), *Period of Adjustment* (center), and *The Seven Descents of Myrtle* (bottom)

*But it was only an intent and sixty-three pages of his journal remained untouched. Whether or not Williams wrote in other journals during this period is not known. Perhaps he did, as a habit of over twenty years is hard to break, and the journals are now lost. Or perhaps, despite his intentions, he was, as he wrote to friends, too exhausted to write at the end of the day.*

*In an undated letter to Oliver Evans at the end of 1961 (HRC), Williams explained why he had not written:*

> *I have almost entirely given up the practise of letter-writing which used to be one of my great pleasures in my vernal years, that is, if I ever had any years that could be so described. The trouble is I am no longer able to write anything at all in the evenings which is the time when I wrote letters.*

*Despite a declining physical condition, Williams continued working. Over the period 1959–69, Williams had nine new plays produced as well as a number of revivals. He also published* The Knightly Quest, *a collection comprising a science fiction novella and four short stories. Williams' play* Sweet Bird of Youth *premiered in New York in March 1959 and was damned by a number of critics. Robert Brustein described it as "disturbingly bad — aimless, dishonest, and crudely melodramatic" (*Encounter, *June 1959), and John Chapman wrote that Williams was a "dirty-minded dramatist who has been losing hope for the human race [and] has written of moral and physical decadence as shockingly as he can" (*New York Daily News, *11 March 1959). The review in* Time *(23 March 1959) was equally harsh:*

> *Sweet Bird of Youth . . . is very close to parody, but the wonder is that Williams should be so inept at imitating himself. The sex violence, the*

Geraldine Page as Princess Kosmonopolis and Paul Newman as Chance Wayne in *Sweet Bird of Youth*

Kate Reid as Molly and Zoe Caldwell as Polly with the Cocaloony in "The Gnädiges Fräulein"

John Huston and Williams on the film set of *The Night of the Iguana*

*perfumed decay, the hacking domestic quarrels, the dirge of fear and self-pity,*
*the characters who dangle in neurotic limbo — all are present — but only*
*like so many dramatic dead cats on a cold tin roof.*
*In response to the criticism he received for the subject matter of* Sweet Bird of
Youth, *Williams told a* Newsweek *reporter (27 June 1960), "I don't want to write*
*about [bestiality] any more," and he described his next play,* Period of Adjustment,
*his slight comedy about two young married couples, as being "kinder" and "more*
*upbeat." Despite Williams' efforts to appease the critics,* Period of Adjustment
*received lukewarm reviews when it premiered in New York in 1960 and failed to*
*gather the critical approval Williams sought.*

*By the end of the year Williams was beginning to doubt himself. He wrote to*
*Maria St. Just:*

> *I had planned to stop work in the sixties. I am so far out of fashion, now,*
> *that I am almost back in. Withering attacks from all critical directions, they*
> *even hold me responsible for the corruption of other playwrights.*
>
> *. . . I am sick of my work myself. Besides I'm too tired to continue.*
>
> *I've kept forcing myself to work when any sane person would know that*
> *I ought to stop for a while and try to be human again. The recent work isn't*
> *worth burning the candle at both ends for it, maybe not even at one end. I*
> *think I am finally losing my critical faculty and don't know any more if the*
> *work is good or awful. (FOA, pp. 168, 169)*

*Despite his observations, Williams could not discontinue his habit of writing every*
*day. He spent 1961 in Key West revising and expanding* The Night of the Iguana,
*which had had its world premiere in Spoleto, Italy, in the summer of 1959. When*

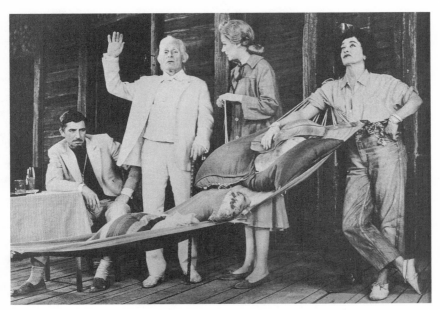

Patrick O'Neal as the Reverend Lawrence Shannon, Alan Webb as Nonno, Margaret Leighton
as Hannah Jelkes, and Bette Davis as Maxine Faulk in *The Night of the Iguana*

Williams, Richard Burton, and Elizabeth Taylor during the filming of *Boom!*

Gene Fanning as Monk and Williams as Doc in *Small Craft Warnings*

*it opened in New York at the end of 1961, the critical acclaim was uneven, but it won the New York Drama Critics' Circle Award for best play, and* Time *magazine put Williams on the cover of the 9 March 1962 issue, proclaiming him America's greatest living playwright.*

The Night of the Iguana *was followed by the New York premiere of* The Milk Train Doesn't Stop Here Anymore, *which opened on 16 January 1963 and closed two months later to generally negative reviews.*

*Williams spent 1963 reworking* The Milk Train Doesn't Stop Here Anymore *and caring for Frank Merlo, who had been diagnosed with lung cancer. Despite their strained relationship, Merlo's illness and death in September 1963 deeply affected Williams, and his dependency on drugs and alcohol increased.*

*After the failure of the January 1964 revival of* The Milk Train Doesn't Stop Here Anymore *starring Tallulah Bankhead — it closed after four performances — Williams fled to Jamaica "to recover as best I can from my latest professional disaster" (letter to Donald Windham, [13] January 1964, Yale). By early summer he told his mother and brother that he was still feeling "pretty depressed over the disastrous events of the year but I hope and suppose that feeling will gradually wear off" (circa June 1964, HTC). And in October Williams wrote them: "For the past four or five months I have been going through a period of deep depression" (9 October 1964, HTC). He noted, however, that Charles Bowden, the producer of* The Night of the Iguana, *was "going to put on a pair of short plays called 'Two Slapstick Tragedies' and we have a good chance of getting Margaret Leighton."*

*Despite Williams' optimism,* Slapstick Tragedy, *a combination of the one-act plays "The Gnädiges Fräulein" and "The Mutilated," which did star Margaret Leighton, opened on 22 February 1966 and closed four days later.*

*By the mid-1960s Williams was combining intramuscular injections of amphetamines with large doses of barbiturates. In* Memoirs *he recalled his routine: "liquor . . . nightly sedation of two Doriden tablets and a five-hundred-milligram Mellaril tablet, not to mention the morning barbiturate . . . I took immediately after the intramuscular injection [of amphetamines]" (p. 209).*

The Two-Character Play *made its world premiere in London in December 1967 and left most critics baffled. The critic for the* Daily Express *observed (13 December 1967):*

> *It would need a psychoanalyst — and preferably Tennessee Williams's own — to offer a rational interpretation of the enigmas that litter the stage like pieces of an elaborate jigsaw.*

The Two-Character Play *was soon followed by* The Seven Descents of Myrtle, *which opened in New York on 27 March 1968 but closed on 20 April. A year later* In the Bar of a Tokyo Hotel *opened in New York on 11 May and closed on 1 June.*

*The combination of hard work, drug and alcohol abuse, negative critical opinions, and lack of commercial success of his plays proved too much for Williams. In September, at the intervention of his brother, Williams was confined to the psychiatric division of Barnes Hospital in St. Louis to undergo a complete withdrawal of drugs. He remained hospitalized for three months.*

Williams at a benefit party for "Creve Coeur" in Charleston, South Carolina

*In one of his letters to Andrew Lyndon, Williams wrote (4 November 1969):*

*The Bin, Spooksville, De Profundis*

*11/4/69*

> _ _ _ _ _ _ _ _ _ _ _ way in Saint Louis?  The last thing I
> remember preceeding my confinement & the last thing I remember very
> clearly - is rising at two A.M. in Key West and making coffee - falling
> down as I removed a Silex of boiling water from the stove and spilling
> the water over my naked shoulder, second degbee burn.  The rest is not
> blank but is too fragmented and chaotic to be sorted out so far.  I got
> the cold turkey treatment.  Terrible withdrawal from Doriden.  Had three
> convulsions in one morning and chipped my left shoulder-bone so I can only
> lie on my right side these interminable nights without sleep for more
> than an occasional lucky bad dream hour.  ("Death, how do you like your
> beautiful blue-eyed boy?")  It's sort of fun writing you.  This typewriter
> haunts me.  Let me at it, baby, let me at it!  Ha!  I'll clackety clack out
> the goddamndest play some day - IF! - I get out of here let's pray...

*Williams was released from the hospital on 20 November and was back in Key West in December.*

*From 1970 to mid-1979, despite the numerous failures of the previous decade, Williams continued his prolific output. He produced six new plays and revised and expanded three earlier ones. In addition he published the novel* Moise and the World of Reason, *his memoirs, a collection of short stories,* Eight Mortal Ladies Possessed, *and a volume of poems,* Androgyne, Mon Amour.

*In July 1971 "Confessional" premiered at the Maine Theatre Arts Festival. Williams continued working on "Confessional" and expanded it into* Small Craft Warnings, *which premiered the following year in New York. In order to attract attention to his new play, Williams played the role of Doc for the first five performances. It was, at the age of sixty-one, his first professional appearance on stage. About the play Harold Clurman wrote that it "strikes one as a demonstration of an old posture, an overcalculated litany now bereft of poignancy" (*Nation, *24 April 1972). Clurman went on to say that the play "is not the Williams of today, whatever his spiritual condition may now be. The play is an encapsulation of past history, which in its original telling possessed authentic vitality. We can only hope that, when the playwright gets the residue of his toxic affections out of his system (I refer to the plays of his period of exhaustion), he can give fresh voice to whatever his recovery may dictate." Despite the mixed reviews,* Small Craft Warnings *ran for almost six months, the longest run of any of Williams' plays since* The Night of the Iguana *in 1962.*

*After its 1971 Chicago tryout,* Out Cry, *a revision of* The Two-Character Play, *premiered in New York in March 1973 and closed after twelve performances. Rex Reed called it a "bad," "boring," "pretentious," "static" and "all but incomprehensible" play and noted that it "should have stayed in Tennessee Williams' trunk" (*New York Sunday News, *11 March 1973).*

*By 1973, not only was Williams working on a novel and his memoirs; he was also working on an expanded version of "The Gnädiges Fräulein," which pre-*

A painting by Williams, 1974

Set design by Jo Mielziner for *Out Cry*

*miered in New York in May 1974 as "The Latter Days of a Celebrated Soubrette"
and survived only one performance.*

In May 1975 Williams published his second novel, Moise and the World of
Reason, *the story of a failed young writer and his eccentric friend, the old artist
Moise, and a "has-been" playwright. Both the failed young writer and the has-been
playwright bore a resemblance to Williams. It received mixed reviews. The critic
for the* New York Times *observed that "For the first time, [Williams] has dealt at
length . . . with the subject of homosexuality" (15 May 1975). Another noted that
the novel read less like a novel and "more like a series of notebook entries in which
the author muses at random on art and sex" (*New Republic, 24 May 1975*).*

The Red Devil Battery Sign *opened in Boston in June 1975 and was scheduled
to move to New York in August. Its Boston reception was so unfavorable that it
closed within two weeks and the New York production was canceled. In a review
titled "Dead Battery: The Streetcar Breaks Down" in the* Boston Phoenix *(24 June
1975), the critic began: "On the basis of this embarrassing exercise in ethnic hysteria, Tennessee might change his name to Missouri."*

*In November, Williams published* Memoirs. *Despite critics' negative reaction to
its nonlinear presentation, the focus on too much trivia and descriptions of sex,*
Memoirs *made the best-seller list.*

*In the second half of the 1970s, Williams' new plays failed to attract the success
he so desperately wanted. In 1976 "This Is (An Entertainment)," a disjointed farce
in which a cuckolded count and his sexually voracious countess remain in a hotel
in the capital city of a small European monarchy on the verge of being overthrown
by revolutionary forces, premiered in San Francisco on 20 January but closed in
mid-February. As one critic noted, "He is such a grand old man that I suppose no
one will tell him when a play simply stinks" (*Educational Theater Journal, October
1976*). In May 1977,* Vieux Carré *premiered in New York but closed after five performances. The critic for the* New Orleans Times-Picayune *wrote on 13 May 1977:*

> At times the play seems to be the tragic answer to the question this now aging,
> great master is perhaps most often asked in his autumn days: "Why don't you
> write a play like one of your earlier plays?" He has, but sadly it has little of
> the lyric qualities of "Glass Menagerie" or "A Streetcar Named Desire".

*In January 1978,* Tiger Tail *(the stage version of* Baby Doll) *premiered in Atlanta
to a positive reception, but it failed to garner enough support for a New York production. In June of the same year "Creve Coeur," a play about two unmarried
women who room together, premiered in Charleston, South Carolina. While it
received positive local press, New York critics such as John Simon spoke harshly:
"[T]he Williams work was an unmitigated disaster, and anyone silly enough to
bring it to Broadway deserves to lose even his torn undershirt" (*New York, 26 June
1978*). Simon's words proved prescient. "Creve Coeur," revised as* A Lovely Sunday
for Creve Coeur, *was produced in New York on 17 January 1979. The reviews
were unfavorable and it closed after thirty-six performances.*

1041. 1014 Dumaine Street.

1042. Mitch Douglas (1942– ) took over as Williams' agent when Bill Barnes left International Creative Management in 1978. He represented Williams until 1981. When Williams severed his relationship with Douglas, he wrote (August 1981, private collection):

> As representative and client we are simply not well cast. Don't let that bother you. You're an excellent agent for anyone but me. I can't reform, at my age, in my state of health, to the Olympic marathon jumper you want and deserve.
>
> Mitch, I'm winding things up and not with too much regret. I mean the career side of my life. You need much younger clients.
>
> Notice, please, that I have no protests, no complaints. Am just being realistic. And apologize for any embarassment that I may have caused you.
>
> Regardless of my age and infirmities I will be around a while longer and while I'm around, I will always be interested in the young friend [Mitch Douglas] who was also born on March 26th.

1043. Robert Lantz (1914– ) represented Williams' estate from 1985 to 1989.

1014 Dumaine Street, New Orleans

Mitch Douglas and Williams

# MES CAHIERS NOIRS

*Spring 1979*

Today I was released from a brief stay at the Southern Baptist Hospital in New Orleans.

All the doctors admitted they had found wrong, after an exhausting number of tests and x-rays, was a couple of gall-stones and a sclerotic condition in the left ventricle of my heart. They advised against surgery for the gall-stones unless they began to pain me, which they haven't so far. I dare say they regard me – as I do – as a bad surgical risk.

Soon after I returned to my New Orleans apartment[1041] I went to the Athletic Club and had a good swim. Just as I was leaving I encountered an extraordinarily handsome youth. I recognized his face but didn't recall the circumstances of our previous meeting.

He'd been about to enter the club for a work-out but accepted my invitation to dinner. We had two bottles of wine at Marti's. Somewhat inebriate, I invited him to accompany me to Key West tomorrow – which is now today. I wonder if he will go and how it would work out. He invited me to lie on the bed with him but would only remove his shirt and allow me to caress his chest. He may have wanted to see if I was just another sex-hungry 'john' – or maybe he's just another cool hustler. I seem not to be a good judge.

Insomnia dogs me tonight. I mean this morning.

--------------------------

I will try to sleep just once more, first taking a hot bath and then a 10 milligram valium.

I'll only remain in Key West a week, I believe, and then, with or without my beautiful but ambiguous new acquaintance, I'll head back for a confrontation with Mitch[1042] – I will insist that it be 'cards on the table'. I have hung on ten years to have one more success in the American theatre, if only to defy my detractors. If Mitch can't provide it, I think I am capable of demanding either another agent at I.C.M. or pulling out of that colussus altogether and going to someone like Robert Lanz,[1043] on whom little Audrey has never cast her large shadow.

--------------------------

And finally this summer, I will take a trip to Venice – with God knows whom.

Beyond that I can't conjecture. Surely there's someone somewhere and there are various places.

I have lost ten pounds. Perhaps I'll have a face-lift – a bit of counterfeit youth, well, at least middle-age, could improve my chances.

--------------------------

1044. Williams' comments are explained more by his tendency toward hypochondria, which had intensified during this period, than any serious medical condition.

1045. Edmund James Perret II (1945–91), from an established New Orleans family, met Williams in Washington, D.C., where he was the assistant director of the American Psychiatric Association. Perret returned to live in the French Quarter of New Orleans. He served as a pallbearer at Williams' funeral.

 Two years earlier, in a letter to Maria St. Just (1 September 1977), Williams had rejected the idea of Edmund Perret as a traveling companion:

> Despite his good breeding and charm, my friend Edmond won't do as a travelling companion. He got in touch with Bill Barnes (who happened to be in Washington the week-end we arrived there) and told him that I didn't trust him and that I was in a state of derangement. Of course I do have periods of questioning Bill's judgement in my professional life. An aging writer prey to . . . his own constant apprehensions, paranoiac or not, is bound to feel like a creature that is backed into a corner. (*FOA*, pp. 360–61)

1046. On 21 June 1979 Williams wrote to Maria St. Just about the house at 915 Von Phister Street: "Rose loves the house but wants to return to the Lodge. I will take her back when I go to Massachusetts in a week for a production of *Camino*. Rose is patient and sweet and so tragic" (*FOA*, p. 372).

 Rose returned to Stony Lodge in Ossining, New York, and spent the rest of her life there.

1047. Williams met Robert Carroll (1947– ), a Vietnam veteran with aspirations to be a writer, in 1972. In a letter to Maria St. Just dated 30 September 1972, Williams described him as his traveling companion.

 Maria believed the liaison between Carroll, who had a drug problem, and Williams was destructive. On 26 May 1973, Williams tried to explain his relationship with Carroll:

> You know, he has kept alternating between great sweetness to me — mostly in New York where I have the protection of Billy [Barnes] and others — and down-right beastliness of behavior which makes it all but impossible for me to go out with him in public. He goes out of his way to be rude to everyone. Yesterday we were invited to lunch at Zeffirelli's and he ignored the whole company — just lay there chain-smoking. Franco whispered to me, "Maria a ragione" [Maria is right]. Well, you have a pretty good batting average at perception and this time you batted one thousand.
>  The trouble is that he plays on my sympathies and on my acute loneliness. You really don't seem to know how awful it is to be alone at my age — and "gay." He makes himself so pathetic at times and I remember his years in Vietnam, his background as the ninth child of a West Virginia coal-miner, out of all touch with his family and with no friends to keep up with. (*FOA*, p. 292)

In the autumn of 1979, Williams and Carroll severed their relationship and Williams wrote to Maria St. Just (October 1979):

> Only positive accomplishment is getting the Twerp back to Boone County, West Virginia.
>  He gets $150 a month to stay away, which is just a fraction of his demands — well-worth the relative peace on the compound, even the creatures seem relieved. (*FOA*, p. 374)

Despite this falling out Williams and Carroll remained friends and saw each other intermittently for the rest of Williams' life.

Williams and Robert Carroll

Perhaps the title (<u>Black Pages</u>, in English) should be changed to <u>Mes Chairs Noirs Et Blancs</u>, since I hope I do not intend to restrict myself to comments of a dark nature.

Of course today it is difficult not to think blackly, since the disorder for which I submitted myself to the horrors of the Southern Baptist Hospital in New Orleans have now returned after only a two day respite.[1044] Bad surgical risk or not, I think that I shall take it, either here or abroad, unless there a lasting reassurance of a working intestinal tract.

I see no particular reason not to skip New York and just fly directly out of Dulles on the Concorde after a night at The Marriott across the street from it, and perhaps the genial company of Edmund.[1045] It is even possible that I might persuade him to accompany me to England for the hospital bit, if that's indicated. I understand if things go badly and you hang on, you are permitted euphoric drugs such as heroin near the end. And why not?

--------------------------

Did I die by my own hand or was I destroyed slowly and brutally by a conspiratorial group? There is probably no clear cut answer. When was there ever such an answer to any question related to the individual human fate?

Perhaps I was never meant to exist at all, but if I hadn't, a number of my created beings would have been denied their passionate existence.

This season I purchased a home on a lovely residential street in Key West and removed my sister Rose from Stony Lodge and placed her there: perhaps mistakenly, it remains to be seen.[1046] But will I remain to see it?

Today I must leave for New Orleans for medical examination and possibly for surgery: the chronic disease of my gastro-intestinal system has, for several weeks now, flared up alarmingly and there is no true relief. I suffer no pain. But I am observing my life and the approaching conclusion of my life and I see a long, long stretch of desolation about me, now at the end.

Or will I yet survive? In what condition, under what circumstance? Certainly I will not survive <u>sub regnum</u> Carroll.[1047]

The best I can say for myself is that I worked like hell. The Carrolls of this world are the little foxes who eat our grapes. We did not plant our vineyards for their small, ruthless teeth. I always observed that his eyes were somewhat inhuman: a curious stone-like color, not blue nor green nor gray, and his facial features not quite completely formed.

I don't believe in individual guilt: we have all been manipulated by forces unknown, unchosen.

Still, that which is cruel is cruel: and to me that which is consistently cruel is abhorrent.

I am old and ugly and that is abhorrent, but in a different way. My disease is abhorrent, but in a different way. When I was the age of Carroll I was not corrupted. I remained a kind person, or at least a person who respected kindness and struggled to retain it, for a long, long time.

1048. In the play *Something Cloudy, Something Clear* the ghost of Hazel as a young girl appears and speaks with August. He reminds her, "You said to me once, 'Don't you know, August, I'd never say anything to embarrass or hurt you.'"

1049. Kate Schweppe Moldawer (1932– ) met Williams in Key West in the late 1960s. They became good friends and occasionally traveled together. Her two sons were pallbearers at Williams' funeral.

    In a letter to Maria St. Just in March 1982, Williams wrote:

    Gave a public reading of a story I thought was finished a few nights ago. . . . The story is a scandal but very funny. It is called "The Donsinger Women and Their Handy Man Jack" — I don't think your grand-daughter should be exposed to it yet. It came out of my visit to Texas with the notorious Texas Kate. She had a young gigolo with her and insisted that we all go to "the ranch" on the Guadalupe. A nightmare! Icy cold and nothing to eat but venison *sausage*! (*FOA*, p. 386)

1050. Viola Veidt (1925– ), the daughter of the German actor Conrad Veidt, lived in Key West during the 1970s. In a letter to Audrey Wood dated 14 March 1970 (HRC), Williams wrote: "Viola . . . looks just like [Conrad] but is quite beautiful . . . is sleeping with the chief of police and says she could get [Bill] Glavin run off the Key." In a fragment of the play "The One Exception" (dated January 1983), Williams named one of the characters Viola Shield, a "smartly-dressed, energetic" painter, who visits her mentally ill friend Kyra to ask for a loan.

Williams and Viola Veidt

If I relinquish the struggle at this point and cry out, 'This and this, and so and so are abominable!' – it is the honesty of desperation.

One's mortal enemies should not be unnamed.

--------------------------

At random, I offer you a list, and the charges against them. Along with this list of enemies I place a sadly shorter list of those whom I hold dear.

First among those who still remain living is my sister Rose. She is the living presence of truth and faith in my life. She was rightly named for our grandmother, Grand. Extravagant though it may be to describe Grand as the angel of my life, I do describe her as that.

Both she and my sister defined a true nobility to me and gave to my life what I have known of grace.

I beg their pardon for the bitterness that now surfaces in my worn-out heart.

Grandfather was charmingly selfish, but he loved people and life and was loved in return by all who recognized the simplicity and warmth and child-like innocence of his nature. Don't mistake me. By simplicity I don't mean foolish.

I am fortunate to have lived through a time when such people could exist.

And then, of course, there is Hazel, the memory of her.

'Tom, don't you know I would never say or do anything to hurt you?'[1048]

There was Marian Black Vacarro who became my dear friend and travelling companion after the death of Frankie.

There is Maria. Since 1948 there has always been Maria. Perhaps she has become a little exhausted by the endless effort of trying to keep me going – but it isn't much further, dear child.

Now here in Key West there is beautiful Texas Kate.[1049]

She planned last night to accompany me to the Miami hospital: But I have changed my mind about going to a hospital on Miami Beach. After all, it is Ochsner Clinic that has my most complete medical records, and I have a lovely apartment there and still a few dear friends. Perhaps Texas Kate would accompany me there instead.

--------------------------

I still have in my heart a great sympathy for poor Viola Veidt.[1050] Why did she throw away her several talents and settle for a life of liquor and dependancy?

Now I no longer answer her phone-calls which is a failure of weakness.

--------------------------

What are artists? Desperate searchers after whatever can be found of truth and beauty, even when the two may be poles apart.

I am surely in no condition to arrange this material in any kind of sequence: but does it matter now?

The gospel-spouting, violence-oriented, import from New Orleans came into the kitchen at 2:30 A.M. last night and without the slightest provocation, without

1051. John Simon (1925– ) has been the theatre critic of *New York* continually since 1968, except when he served as film critic (1975–77). He has held numerous other positions, including theatre critic for the *Hudson Review* (1960–80).

For almost two decades Williams received a barrage of criticism from Simon. Writing for the *Hudson Review* in spring 1961, Simon described *Cat on a Hot Tin Roof*, *Suddenly Last Summer*, and *Sweet Bird of Youth* as "cowardly" and "untruthful" (p. 83).

Simon was especially negative about Williams' later plays. For example, in 1972, in a review of *Small Craft Warnings*, Simon wrote, "It is, clearly, the play of a man who has lost all sense of give and take with life, except for dimly recording the mumblings in bar-rooms from Tokyo to New Orleans" (*New York*, 17 April 1972, p. 84).

Five years later, in a review of *Vieux Carré*, Simon remarked about Williams, "A man who would steal and resteal from himself is the saddest of all failures" (*New Leader*, 20 June 1977, p. 21), and on 26 June 1978 in *New York* he wrote his most damning statement of all:

> The kindest thing to assume is that Williams died shortly after completing *Sweet Bird of Youth*, and that his subsequent, ever more dismal plays are the work of a lover of his who has learned to impersonate him perfectly in daily life, but only very crudely in playwriting. (p. 61)

1052. George Jean Nathan (1882–1958) was one of the most widely published drama critics during the first half of the twentieth century. With the exception of positive comments on *The Glass Menagerie*, Nathan wrote negatively about Williams' plays. In a review of *A Streetcar Named Desire*, Nathan wrote:

> While he has succeeded in making realistically dramatic such elements as sexual abnormality, harlotry, perversion, seduction and lunacy, he has scarcely contrived to distil from them any elevation and purge. His play as a consequence remains largely a theatrical shocker which, while it may shock the emotions of its audience, doesn't in the slightest shock them into any spiritual education. (*New York Journal-American*, 15 December 1947)

Less than a year later, in a review of *Summer and Smoke*, Nathan delineated what he judged to be Williams' faults:

> The first is his debatable character drawing; the second is his adolescent point of view; and the third is the ultimate impression that, though he obviously starts off with complete honesty, his still limited resources impel him in the end to purely theatrical fabrication. (*New York Journal-American*, 18 October 1948)

And about *Cat on a Hot Tin Roof* Nathan opined:

> Williams has here again concocted a theatrical evening that is interesting in the degree and to the extent that an auditor is willing to suspend his impulse to snicker at the playwright's fierce determination to pass off his wide-eyed wonder over sex for a searching gaze into it. One of these days, when and if he grows up, Williams will return to the humorously sympathetic delineation of less complexly beset and more normal characters which occupied him so successfully in the earlier stages of his playwriting career and we shall all, himself included, be the better and happier off for it. (*New York Journal-American*, 2 April 1955)

1053. In an article in the *Miami Herald Tropic Magazine* (1 April 1979), "Three Scenes from the Life of a Tormented Playwright: At Wit's End at Land's End," Madeleine Blais quoted from the police records:

> From the Key West police blotter, 1/28/79: "Mr. Williams and friend, Mr. Dotson Rader, were accosted by four or five white males in the 500 block of Duval Street. The attackers advised they knew who Mr. Williams was. At this point the attackers punched Mr. Dotson Rader in the jaw. Mr. Williams advised that he was thrown to the ground. Mr. Dotson Rader and Mr. Williams were then kicked at by the attackers. . . ."
>
> . . . "They were just punks [Williams said]. It happened quickly. There was no injury sustained. A lens fell out of my glasses. The publicity is ridiculous." Nevertheless, doesn't it bother him? "Of course not."
>
> Why not? He seems surprised by the question, and his answer is delivered regally, in his best Southern drawl, cadenced, liquid, honeyed. "Because, baby, I don't allow it to." (*DLB*, pp. 351–52)

Dotson Rader (1942– ) is a journalist, editor, and novelist whose book *Tennessee: Cry of the Heart* (1985) is an account of his friendship with Williams which began in 1969 and lasted until Williams' death. According to Rader, he was the model for Big Lot in Williams' novel *Moise and the World of Reason* (1975).

any liquor in him nor drugs, attacked me as viciously as I've ever been attacked except by the dedicated assailants Simon (of Esquire and New York Magazine.)[1051] and old G.J. Nathan.[1052]

'I been going around tonight tawking to the young people of the island and they gave me the low-down on you. You're a drunk and a has-been and they say you've ruined the island's reputation (referring, no doubt to Dotson Rader's wildly exaggerated account of our mugging incident on Duval Street last spring.)[1053] and they wish the hell you'd get off it for good.'

I gave Carroll a long letter to deliver to him, saying that my reputation here could do him nothing but harm and that he should utilize his open-dated first class return ticket to NOLA as early as possible that day.

But as far as I know he is still around here.

As Kate says, 'With someone like him you know you're not dealing with a full deck.'

As I say, he constitutes, if still here, one of the island's greatest hazards.

---------------------------

Williams, Kate Moldawer, and Rose

1054. In his will dated 11 September 1980, Williams named his attorney, John L. Eastman (1939– ), and Maria St. Just as trustees of his trust. He never named any literary executors.

1055. Brooks Atkinson (1894–1984) was the highly regarded drama critic at the *New York Times* (1925–42 and 1946–60) and was a great supporter of Williams' work. About *A Streetcar Named Desire*, he wrote: "[I]t reveals Mr. Williams as a genuinely poetic playwright whose knowledge of people is honest and thorough and whose sympathy is profoundly human" (4 December 1947). Atkinson judged *The Rose Tattoo* to be "original, imaginative and tender" (5 February 1951) and *Camino Real* to be "eloquent and rhythmic as a piece of music" (20 March 1953). About *Cat on a Hot Tin Roof*, Atkinson wrote: "It seems not to have been written. It is the quintessence of life. It is the basic truth" (25 March 1955). And in one of his last reviews of Williams' work, Atkinson proclaimed *Sweet Bird of Youth*, "a portrait of corruption and evil . . . [with] overtones of pity for those who are damned," to be "one of his finest dramas" (11 March 1959).

1056. *In the Bar of a Tokyo Hotel* premiered on 11 May 1969 in New York. The play received poor reviews. In his notes to the cast at the Eastside Playhouse, Williams wrote:

> It is about the usually early and particularly humiliating doom of the artist. He has made, in the beginning of his vocation, an almost total commitment of himself to his work. As Mark truthfully says, the intensity of the work, the unremitting challenges and demands that it makes to him and of him (in most cases daily) leave so little of him after the working hours that simple, comfortable <u>being</u> is impossible for him.
>
> . . . [A]s death approaches, he hasn't the comfort of feeling with any conviction that any of his work has had any essential value.

1057. Ray Stark (1915– ), a well-known Hollywood producer of films such as *The Goodbye Girl* (1977), produced the films *The Night of the Iguana* in 1964 and *This Property Is Condemned* in 1966. According to John Eastman, Audrey Wood did indeed try to persuade Williams to sell the copyrights to his plays. Williams was very opposed to the idea and never sold the copyright to any play.

Dotson Rader and Williams

Daylight is appearing through the dusty skylight.

Tomorrow I will be very busy, winding things up here as I can, getting scripts typed, naming my literary executors,[1054] booking myself away.

I would say the vocation is worth living and dying for.

Certain members of the critical profession in the theatre – I think particularly of John Simon and his ilk – are somehow committed to gratuitous brutality and insult.

George Jean Nathan was rather like that, although he had more presence. And stature.

Still, the time came in 1969 when they turned to assassins of a playwright who deserved better of them.

They closed in like wolves at the scent of blood.

Brooks Atkinson[1055] had long retired from the ~~pack~~ number, and at the time there was no one who seemed inclined to understanding and mercy.

Audrey Wood was quick to retire from her position as representative and defender.

I remember Stella Adler saying at the première of 'Tokyo Bar',[1056] perhaps a bit patronizingly: 'Who is going to look out for Tennessee now?'

(It had been quite a while since anyone really had.)

The question was addressed to Audrey who gave no reply.

And while I'm remembering these bitter things, a phone-call from Irene Selznick shortly after she'd acquired the rights to produce 'Streetcar'.

It was very cunning.

'Tennnessee,' she said, 'I will probably have to ask more of Audrey and Bill in the way of advise and assistance than agents are usually asked to give a producer, and so I have given them eight percent of my share as producer.'

I suppose I was also rather perceptive.

'But they are already getting their ten percent from my royalties. Do you really think, Irene, they ought to have nearly twenty percent of the play?'

Obviously this was the reaction that Irene wanted.

Not long after the Leiblings were obliged to pay for their extra piece and sometimes I wonder if they forgave me for it.

I must admit that I have often suspected Audrey of getting shares under the table.

I know that once she attempted to sell the copywright of 'Iguana' to that tasteless Hollywood producer, Ray Stark.[1057]

It was Luise M. Sillcox, then Secretary of the Dramatists' Guild, who apprised me of this plot.

'Tennessee, you mustn't sign the agreement. Ray Stark could do anything with the property, there could be dreadful sequels to the play, why, there could even be cartoons.'

I have the documents locked away, in case you doubt my word.

But it was after the death of Frank Merlo that Audrey showed how little I meant to her as a human being.

It was almost as if I ceased to exist in those seven years of almost clinical depression.

1058. MCA, one of the top Hollywood talent agencies, acquired Liebling-Wood in 1954.

1059. Williams wrote Audrey Wood several letters at the end of his stay. In one, dated 4 November 1969 (HRC), he wrote: "New Directions sent me the proofs of <u>Dragon Country</u>. Most of the stuff reads as if I must have been pretty tired when I wrote it and I guess I was." She replied five days later (9 November 1969, HRC): "You weren't tired my love — you were way out on a light beam in a world that didn't exist except in your own confused mind."

1060. Sue Mengers (1938– ) was an aggressive superagent in the 1970s. Known for her relentless pursuit of clients, she represented Barbra Streisand, Ryan O'Neal, and Gene Hackman, among others.

1061. When Williams and Audrey Wood severed their relationship in 1971, William E. Barnes (1932–89) became Williams' agent at International Creative Management and a good friend. Prior to becoming an agent, Barnes worked in the 1960s as a casting agent and story editor for Otto Preminger. Williams dedicated the play *Small Craft Warnings* to Barnes and added, "You said to go on, and I went." Barnes was a pallbearer at Williams' funeral.

1062. Milton Goldman (1914–89) was a highly successful actors' agent at International Creative Management and a good friend of Williams'.

1063. American-born agent, son of Cornelia Skinner and grandson of Otis Skinner, who worked in the London offices of International Creative Management.

1064. Lynda Huey (1944– ) looked after Rose in Key West from 1979 to 1981.

Bill Barnes and Williams

I had more respect for Bill Liebling in the end.

When Liebling-Wood dissolved, she went into MCA[1058] and poor Liebling had to function as casting agent out of their little suite at the Hotel Royalton.

When finally I was confined for three months to Renard Division of Barnes hospital in St. Louis, I received from her no word till I wrote her – near the time of my release – a long, friendly letter. To that she replied, saying 'For a long time you've been way out at the end of a laser beam.'[1059]

People act as if she had written my plays.

I remember Sue Mengers,[1060] at a London party, saying: 'Isn't it awful how Tennessee walked out on Audrey? Well, anyhow she had him in his good years.'

Well, that's how they think I feel . . . . .

Their clients are not artists but properties to them.

-------------------------

She passed me on to Bill Barnes when I finally quit her.[1061]

At least Bill had southern style and charm, and a lovely pent-house with terrace and a jacuzzi on the East Side.

Under his representation I worked desperately to ~~somehow~~ make a comeback, but somehow there was always a fatal flaw in the packages that he put together, not all of which could be attributed to mere negligence.

He entertained well: he gave nice parties.

I could only go up in the way of representation, and I have only good things to say of Milton Goldman,[1062] Mitch Douglas and my representative in England – where I now have better success – Dick Blodgett,[1063] who is wise and witty and charming.

-------------------------

My sister Rose, the living presence of truth and faith in my life. If I go abroad to die, I must not leave her, afterwards, in the custody of her present companion, a tasteless woman whose idea of giving Rose a good time is to take her to the Masonic Lodge.[1064] Her divorced husband was granted custody of her children and she admitted shamelessly, a couple of nights ago while our guest at dinner with Rose and others, that she did not correspond with the children.

Tonight she had dressed Rose for a party at Kate's in a livid green dress from Woolco's, as tasteless as possible and as unbecoming. I had said that Rose should have a green dress but I meant to buy it for her myself, in a pastel shade, such as lettuce.

-------------------------

Critics: I recognize them as potential assassins, before, now, and after.

Artists: the instruments of that ever fleeting and ambiguous thing called Truth.

Of Truth, what can we say but it is all that we can apprehend of the possibility of God, unseen, unknown and unknowable, but – as I have often remarked – without a Creator, how could there be Creation?

1065. Williams had a falling out with Windham over the publication of his letters to Windham. The specific cause was contained in a letter Williams wrote to the editor of the *New York Times Book Review* (published 15 January 1978). Williams maintained that he had been tricked into signing the copyright to the letters when he thought he was signing a document that only allowed Windham to publish his letters in an expensive and elegant edition that would have a limited market. Williams was upset to learn that he had signed the copyright over to Windham and that the letters could be and, in fact, were published by a major publishing firm and distributed widely.

Windham defended himself in a response published simultaneously:

As Mr. Williams's lawyer and my lawyer, and the lawyers for Holt, Rinehart & Winston, and all others involved in the commercial publication of the "Letters" know, TW signed two agreements, six weeks apart, granting me the copyright to the letters he wrote me.

1066. Williams praised Windham on several of his book jackets:

*The Dog Star* (1950) — "I think it marks the advent of probably the most distinguished new talent to appear in the last decade. Its theme is of profound relevance to a tragedy of modern youth. The writing is utterly pure without the affectation of purity."

*Emblems of Conduct* (1964) — "Of all our younger American writers, he shines like the morning star."

*Two People* (1965) — "Donald Windham has cast into dramatic juxtaposition the Anglo-Saxon and Latin character, and done it with such perception that the novelist would seem to belong equally to both breeds: a rare if not unprecedented accomplishment."

1067. In the appendix to *Tennessee Williams' Letters to Donald Windham, 1940–1965*, Windham wrote:

Kilroy's character and the best scenes of "Camino" were written . . . before 1948. . . . In rewriting, all the unpleasant characters in "Camino" were enlarged and yet not made understandable. . . . Up until "Camino", Tennessee's work (and life?) seems to me self-dramatization. From "Camino" on, it seems self-justification. The change occurs between the two versions of "Camino." (pp. 320, 321)

1068. On 20 November 1977 Robert Brustein (1927– ), then Dean of the Yale School of Drama, reviewed *Tennessee Williams' Letters to Donald Windham, 1940–1965* in the *New York Times Book Review*. In a letter to Windham (April 1946, Yale), Williams had referred to the "fundamentally stupid" professors who write criticism of Broadway "from the haven of the academy." Given this attitude, it is not surprising to see Williams referring to Brustein as a "Ya-hoo." Brustein commented on Williams' indifference to landscape, architecture, nature, food, politics, philosophy, and social climate. He noted what he believed was Williams' ruthlessness toward others, especially Windham. And his conclusion was that in publishing these letters Windham allowed "the glorious bird to dip his own tail feathers in a pot of tar."

In his reply to Brustein's review, Williams wrote (15 January 1978):

It may seem that I am ashamed of the letters, which I am certainly not. Less biased reviewers have praised them for their vitality and freedom and life-loving and life-enduring power of expression.

I am not alone in regarding them as a valuable documentation of a young writer's way to survive the difficult climb to achievement.

1069. The main character of *The Hero Continues* (1960), the writer Denis Freeman, was based loosely on Williams and deals with the corrupting influence of fame on creativity and personal relationships. About *The Hero Continues*, Williams had written Windham:

I was touched by the book's effort to understand and penetrate with sympathy the opaque and twisted nature of the continuing hero. I must admit I had expected . . . to find myself . . . dealt with less mercifully. What the book catches most truly is the solitude of Denis, a sort of self-imposed sentence to solitary confinement. A refusal to believe in almost any love or affection for himself, related, most likely, to a profound sense of guilt, shame, inadequacy, impotence. (4 April 1960, Yale)

I love the book because it's as beautiful and terrible as life. I did resent the bit about Dennis declining to believe that an old, dear friend was dying of leukemia in order to avoid the hospital expense, but then I thought, Well, maybe the factual untruth of such an implication is artistically defensible, just as Sebastian's being eaten up by those whom he had eaten was the poetic abstraction of a truth which is truer than any factual one. ([20 June 1960], Yale)

My old friend Donald Windham, a consummate liar and betrayer in his dealings with me, anent the Letters to him,[1065] but the author of several books (especially <u>The Dog Star</u>) that have great power: I never wrote to him of them, nor gave quotes for them, with anything but the truest[1066] [*tails off*]

---------------------------

What makes a Windham? Inherent cruelty, I would guess, and that invidious rage that comes from writing well without much financial reward. Does he truly believe that the sketch for 'Camino Real' is superior to its final form, and that between that sketch and the final form, I abandoned, or lost, my power and purity as a writer?

His footnotes and his appendix to my collected letters to him are remarkably venomous to his disadvantage, not mine.[1067] He did indeed deceive me about the papers he had me sign, giving him the copywright to my letters. He said I was only permitting him to have the letters printed in Verona. And yet soon after they were openly published in the States by Holt-Rhinehart, and although they are amusing and well-written letters, their effect on my reputation amongst the vast plurality of Ya-hoos such as Brustein[1068] in the States was as damaging as he intended.

Yet he loved to write and he could write very well and I never failed to give him just praise sincerely.

And what about his roman-a-clef <u>The Continuing Hero</u>? How little he ever knew me is illuminated most clearly in that work.[1069]

Why do I write of Windham?

A painting by Williams, 1976

1070. Princess Margaret, Countess of Snowdon (1930–2003), younger sister of Queen Elizabeth II.

1071. Williams' tribute to Rosina Dakin, entitled "Grand," was first published in a limited edition of three hundred copies in 1964. A teleplay entitled "Grand," by Trace Johnson, was optioned by Martin Poll and Associates from July 1979 to January 1980 but was never produced.

1072. Andreas Brown (1933– ) first met Williams after he had been hired by Wood to catalogue and appraise Williams' archives in the early 1960s. After Brown acquired the Gotham Book Mart in New York City in 1967, their friendship grew as Brown often sent Williams boxes of books and periodicals that he had selected for him.

1073. Williams meant Dick Blodgett, the grandson of Otis Skinner.

1074. After psychoanalysis, Williams' attitude toward his father changed and he became more understanding of him. In "The Man in the Overstuffed Chair," Williams wrote about his relationship with his father during the period 1932–35 when his father had forced him to leave the University of Missouri after his junior year and work at the International Shoe Company:

> [T]he ride downtown that my father and I would take every morning in his Studebaker . . . was a long ride, it took about half an hour, and seemed much longer for neither my father nor I had anything to say to each other during the ride. I remember that I would compose one sentence to deliver to my father, to break just once the intolerable silence that existed between us, as intolerable to him, I suspect, as it was to me. I would start composing this one sentence during breakfast and I would usually deliver it halfway downtown. It was a shockingly uninteresting remark. It was delivered in a shockingly strained voice, a voice that sounded choked. It would be a comment on the traffic or the smog that enveloped the streets. The interesting thing about it was his tone of answer. He would answer the remark as if he understood how hard it was for me to make it. His answer would always be sad and gentle. "Yes it's awful," he'd say. And he didn't say it as if it was a response to my remark. He would say it as if it referred to much larger matters than traffic or smog. And looking back on it, now, I feel that he understood my fear of him and forgave me for it, and wished there was some way to break the wall between us.
>
> It would be false to say that he was ever outwardly kind to his fantastic older son, myself.

Williams went on to add:

> A psychiatrist once said to me, You will begin to forgive the world when you've forgiven your father.
>
> I'm afraid it is true that my father taught me to hate, but I know that he didn't plan to, and, terrible as it is to know how to hate, and to hate, I have forgiven him for it and for a great deal else. . . .
>
> The best of my work, as well as the impulse to work, was a gift from the man in the overstuffed chair, and now I feel a very deep kinship to him. I almost feel as if I am sitting in the overstuffed chair where he sat, exiled from those I should love and those that ought to love me. (*CS*, pp. xiii–xv)

Williams painting in Key West

A definition of incomprehension and cruelty merits exposure at this length. And then, of course, I am an angry old man, though not, as Princess Margaret[1070] called me to my face at a London Party, 'a dirty old man'.

--------------------------

Those whom I would say never lied? Are they not those who understand and are willing to understand and to love?

In my life, extra-familial, what has happiness been but little fractions of experience, encompassing not much time. But, yes, there was work, and if I ran before death to perform it, this saying of truth as I felt it, then – whatever it comes to when completed – whatever was discarded on the way – friendship or love, sanity or that which is so regarded, I may deeply regret but would not wish to choose otherwise . . .

--------------------------

Bill Barnes – did he care sufficiently far beyond his bed and jacuzzi on his East-side pent-house roof? And is that a serious question? After all, charm and his unquestionable gestures of kindness and grace should not be forgotten.

Audrey: I bear her no ill will, I hope, but I remember seven years of the Sixties and a heart-shaped locket she wore on a chain about her throat: it contained nitroglycerin tablets, and surely must have served her husband Bill Leibling as a constant reminder of his death approaching. About her I also remember her lack of care and concern after the death of Frank Merlo: an event that cast me adrift and invisible from the shore.

Yet work. And some who continued to care.

'Grand': the mention of her suffices. Do they really want to make a film of 'Grand'? Then let them know her a little. I have tried to define her in a story[1071] but I'm afraid that their screen-treatment, unless it corrects its incomprehension of that delicate angel, is one that neither I nor my literary executors – who are my present representatives and my dear friend Andreas Brown,[1072] – and Otis Skinner[1073] of I.C.M. in England [*sentence incomplete*]

Grandfather: a gentleman and a man of true faith in his vocation – and yet endearingly worldly. 'Two cherries in my manhattan' – 'Oh, are we going out to a cocktail party? Ready in a minute!' – and always the delight of the occasion . . . .

My father, C.C. Williams? – the saddest man I have known. Please read my story of him ('The Man in the Over-stuffed Chair'.)[1074]

Edwina Dakin Williams, his wife? – came South from Ohio at eight, grew into a southern belle, approved for my sister to have one of the first pre-frontal lobotomies performed in the States because she was shocked by Rose's tastefully phrased but explicit disclosures of masturbation practised with Candles stolen from the Chapel, at All Saints in Vicksburg.

Such was the Puritanism imposed by Edwina that I did not masturbate till the age of Twenty-Six, then not with my hands but by rubbing my groin against my bed-sheets, while recalling the incredible grace and beauty of a boy-diver plunging

1075. Lemuel Ayers (1915–55), theatrical designer and producer, studied at Princeton and was awarded a Rockefeller Fellowship to attend the University of Iowa, where he received a master's degree in theatre arts in 1938. Ayers became a highly regarded designer whose work included the scenery for *Oklahoma!* (1943). He employed a painterly approach to scenery with settings depicted in a stylized realism. Ayers received Donaldson Awards for both his settings and his costumes for *Camino Real* (1953).

1076. In an interview in the *Paris Review* (fall 1981), Williams contrasted his single status to that of Norman Mailer's:

> I think it made it possible for me to practice my profession as a writer. You know what happened to poor Norman Mailer. One wife after another, and all that alimony. I've been spared all that. I give people money, yes. But I couldn't have afforded alimony, not to all those wives. I would've had to behead them! Being single made it possible for me to work.

1077. Thomas Lanier Williams II (1849–1908).

1078. Twice Oscar-nominated actress Sylvia Miles (1932– ) had played Mrs. Wire in the London production of *Vieux Carré* (1978). Williams was planning a production of *Goforth*, the revised version of *The Milk Train Doesn't Stop Here Anymore*, at the English Theatre in Vienna. The planned production only went as far as discussions with the managers of the theatre.

1079. In 1916 Williams suffered from diphtheria, a respiratory disease, followed by Bright's disease, an acute inflammation of the kidneys, which left Williams bedridden for a year. It is unlikely that either disease would have affected his heart.

1080. Wilbury was the name of the Palladian house in the south of England owned by the Lord and Lady (Maria) St. Just. Williams opened *Memoirs* with a reference to Wilbury:

> To begin this "thing" on a socially impressive note, let me tell you that one recent fall, before the leaves had fallen, I happened to be weekending at one of the last great country houses in England, an estate so close to Stonehenge that one of the stones was dropped on the lady's estate before it got to that prehistoric scene of druidical worship and, probably due to collapse or revolt of slave labor, it was not picked up but allowed to rest where it fell, and this bit of information has only the slightest and most oblique connection with the material which follows.

1081. Williams stated in *Memoirs*: "[A] codicil to my will provides for the disposition of my body in this way. 'Sewn up in a clean white sack and dropped over board, twelve hours north of Havana, so that my bones may rest not too far from those of Hart Crane . . .'" (p. 117).

Williams, in fact, never made such a codicil to his will, but he did give these lines to several characters. In *A Streetcar Named Desire*, Blanche says: "And I'll be buried at sea sewn up in a clean white sack and dropped overboard — at noon — in the blaze of summer — and into an ocean as blue as my first lover's eyes!" (scene 11). Williams had written almost exactly the same lines in the earlier play "The Spinning Song" (fragment). Williams' character Maxine Faulk, in the play *The Night of the Iguana*, describes her husband's sea burial: "[M]y husband, Fred Faulk, was the greatest game fisherman on the West Coast of Mexico . . . and on his deathbed . . . he requested to be dropped in the sea . . . not even sewed up in canvas, just in his fisherman outfit" (act 2).

1082. In *The Red Devil Battery Sign*, a play set in Dallas, the Woman Downtown, a rich former southern debutante, is stalked by her husband's henchmen. She has in her possession documents that reveal a sinister design "for surrendering a democracy to rule by power conspiracy." In the bar of the hotel where she is hiding she meets a swarthy musician, King Del Rey, who is suffering from a brain tumor. They fall in love, but King soon dies protecting the Woman Downtown from an evil pursuer and she escapes with a pack of wild young denizens. Despite three failures — Boston (1975), Vienna (1976), and London (1977) — Williams continued reworking the play.

naked from the high board in the swimming-pool of Washington U. in Saint Louis.

I could have been passably 'normal' – (I loved Hazel Kramer from the age of eleven till she married a likeable Irishman at the University of Wisconsin. Now both of them ~~deceased~~ are dead. At the University of Iowa I had my single consummated love-affair with a girl and while that went on, for several months, I lost all interest in boys, with the ~~possible~~ probable exception of Lemuel Ayres.)[1075]

But there's no doubt that homosexuality of a most sensual sort is my nature luckily, I would say – for otherwise I'd have an alimony problem as big as Normal Mailer's . . .[1076]

Most deeply (after Hazel) were two other extraordinary women: Marion Black Vacarro and Maria Britneva, now Known as The Lady St. Just. It is sadly true that the latter of these two ladies appears to me, now, to have settled for things ~~unacceptable~~ unimpressive to me: ~~grandeur of~~ title and wealth by marriage.

But dear Marian is dead. Maria is intensely and fiercely alive.

I am in transit, my work prematurely finished.

I will go to no man and no man would go to me. I am old, sick, and ugly.

At the end, now distinctly visible to me and by way of the malignancy that killed my grandfather Williams,[1077] I would take my seventeenth and final flight by Concorde, accompanied perhaps by the star of Vieux Carré (London) and of Goforth (Vienna's English-speaking theatre and hopefully of London, very hopefully of London if the work can accomodate itself to the small stage in Vienna.)[1078] It would probably be there in London, while we are preparing for GOFORTH, that I would take the long shot of an operation with a heart damaged by a year-long childhood disease.[1079]

If I should, by this long shot, manage to survive it, what better could I ask than to rest at Wilbury with Maria[1080] till it was time for the ambulance to remove me?

I wish a Greek Orthodox service: then a return to the States and the burial at sea (a day North of Havana) where my idol Hart Crane, feeling his work finished (as did Mishima at the end, and as do I), found refuge only in that vast 'mother of life'.[1081]

Now I must suspend these cahiers to see what I can do with the final bit of my last important dramatic work, 'The Red Devil Battery Sign'.[1082] (Remember to have it copywrighted as soon as typed.)

--------------------------

I must read the New Testament again where God is not savagely vengeful toward those whom the Old Testament informs us were made in His Image, but where in the New Testment he is the poem of forgiveness and mercy, suffering for our venalities on the Hill of Golgotha, crucified for us between two thieves whom He invited to dine with him that evening in Heaven.

A poem, yes, heaven not being a place but a state of grace.

Christ forgave whores and others prey to the venalities of the flesh. But did He forgive evil, as a being or as an element? That I doubt: I think he abhorred and condemned it in his <u>Cahiers Noirs et Blancs</u>.

1083. In *Memoirs*, Williams attributed this remark to Elia Kazan. Williams responded: "Gadg, I know very well that each of us dies but I don't think we all die alone" (p. 171).

In *The Two Cultures and the Scientific Revolution* (New York: Cambridge University Press, 1959), the English novelist and physicist C. P. Snow (1905–80) remarked:

> Most of the scientists I have known well have felt — just as deeply as the non-scientists I have known well — that the individual condition of each of us is tragic. Each of us is alone: sometimes we escape from solitariness, through love or affection or perhaps creative moments, but those triumphs of life are pools of light we make for ourselves while the edge of the road is black: each of us dies alone. (p. 6)

*Many Moons Ago* by Williams, 1980

The dread of oblivion is a natural dread, there is nothing disgraceful about it. ~~I think~~ It is universal among humankind. But there is a choice to be made between its craven and its stoic acceptance. I hope I have made the choice as I prefer to make it: and that I am not deceived nor alone at the end.

I, I, I! – a burden to be surrendered.

A dear friend once said to me: 'Each of us dies, and each of us dies alone.'

When the conscious being flickers out, then maybe one is alone but I shall not be till then.[1083]

*Williams spent the summer of 1979 in Key West. By the end of August he was encouraged by his new play and wrote Paul Bowles (31 August 1979, Delaware):*

> *Although my health continues to decline, I've finally written a play ("Clothes For A Summer Hotel" about Scott and Zelda Fitzgerald and their intimate circle) which has had auspicious reactions in manuscript and is booked into the Royale. Required enormous documentation, but I think it's worth it, as I feel in it a surging undercurrent of power that I've not felt in a long time.*

*During the later half of 1979 "Kirche, Kutchen und Kinder," a black comedy about a hustler in New York, and "Lifeboat Drill," a black comedy about an elderly couple on a cruise, had limited runs on Off-Off Broadway.*

*On 2 December 1979 Williams was honored, along with Henry Fonda, Ella Fitzgerald, Aaron Copland, and Martha Graham, at the Kennedy Center in Washington, D.C., for his contribution to the arts.*

*Rehearsals for* Clothes for a Summer Hotel *began in January 1980.*

Wilbury Park, Newton Tony, Wiltshire

1084. Robert Carroll.

1085. Leoncia McGee, Williams' housekeeper in Key West.

1086. Doriden (glutethimide) was prescribed as a sleeping pill. Glutethimide was introduced in 1954 as a safe barbiturate substitute. Experience showed, however, that its potential for addiction and the severity of withdrawal symptoms were similar to those of barbiturates.

1087. Williams' agent, Mitch Douglas, remembers discussing *The Red Devil Battery Sign* only later in the year in their talks about Williams taking up the position of writer-in-residence at the University of British Columbia with the possibility of his play being produced there.

Despite *Red Devil* having failed in three cities, Williams may have chosen to explain the lack of enthusiasm for a commercial production of the play as a conspiracy. Williams' negative and paranoid frame of mind may well have been caused by two very recent failures. On 24 January "Will Mr. Merriwether Return from Memphis?" premiered at Florida Keys Community College to mark the opening of the Tennessee Williams Fine Arts Center. The next day, in a review titled "Send Merriwether Back to Memphis," the play was judged "strange and bizarre," without a "thread of continuity" (*Key West Citizen*, 25 January 1980). On 29 January, *Clothes for a Summer Hotel* had opened at the Kennedy Center in Washington, D.C., to a very negative reception.

Painting of Robert Carroll by Williams

*Monday, 28 January 1980*

Jan. 28

Somebody named Bob Darby from Butler, Indiana, gave me this composition book, God knows when.

I am in Key West with friend Robert.[1084]

I am ravaged by insomnia, the pills don't work till daybreak.

It's like a sadly beautiful poem, the island's perfect weather.

Robert is kind to me. I think soon we will fly away from the whole gig here in the States. To where? London, Rome, then Marrakech which I've never seen.

Leave all behind. Travel under Tom Williams. Forget the world a while.


*Tuesday, 29 January 1980*

Jan. 29

The day is golden again.

The house a little clinic with two patients and no nursing or medical staff, unless the cat and Leoncia[1085] are qualified as such.

The freeze on sleep & work continues. Whatever more I make had better be soon.


*Wednesday, 30 January 1980*

Jan 30

2 hours sleep after 2 Doridens.[1086]

Got up from the penitential bed and fed the cat & had coffee, seconal with drink.

Somehow managed to write 5 pages.

Another golden day has begun as I return to bed.

Yesterday Maria called me 3 times. No word from the conspirators in New York about "Red Devil".[1087] Ah, well.

If I can survive all this, why not the flight abroad? I have nothing to lose that doesn't seem to be lost.

Self-pity or objective observation.

1088. Williams' mother, Edwina. Williams wrote in "The Man in the Overstuffed Chair": "Sometimes I wonder if I have forgiven my mother for teaching me to expect more love from the world, more softness in it, than I could ever offer?" (*CS*, p. xv).

1089. Williams' one-act play "Some Problems for the Moose Lodge," first produced at the Goodman Theatre Studio, Chicago, on 8 November 1980, would soon be expanded into a full-length play titled "A House Not Meant to Stand." (On one draft of the play, "A House Not Meant to Last Longer than the Owner" appears as a possible title.)

*On ne peut pas comprendre toujours* by Williams, 1980

Edwina Williams in Key West

*After its disappointing reception in Washington, D.C.,* Clothes for a Summer Hotel *moved to Chicago in February and then on to New York, where it opened on Williams' sixty-ninth birthday, 26 March, and again met with negative reactions from the critics. Harold Clurman sympathetically noted in the* Nation *(19 April 1980): "Habit and skill have replaced Williams's original compassion and the deep-seated need of his soul. Williams ought to allow himself a period of retirement during which he might discover a new vein."* Clothes for a Summer Hotel *closed less than two weeks later, on 6 April, and would mark Williams' last debut of a new play on Broadway.*

*On 1 June 1980 Williams learned that his mother had died. Within a week of her funeral, Williams received the Medal of Freedom from President Carter. Williams then traveled to London and Sicily with Henry Faulkner, an artist from Kentucky whom Williams had met in Key West.*

*By early July Williams had returned to Key West, where he remained for the summer. He wrote Elia Kazan (5 July 1980, HTC):*

I have just returned from a short vacation in Sicily and London. . . .

Since I have no one but "family" in my life now, I devote myself to work more and more. "Clothes" was a victim of a bad first act. . . .

I will never again make the mistake of writing about "real life legends" so that you are locked into a story that's known. My present work is very free and way out.

---

*Tuesday, 19 August 1980*

August 19 – 1980

There is a line of distinction between treachery and indifference but it is a thin line.

"She is so beautiful". Grand was, too, while dying.

Nobility of the two Roses. That is their beauty.

"If you don't appreciate the quality of — and me —"

M.[1088] was inscrutable to me then and more so now.

No matter where I go she will go with me.

"This house was not meant to last longer than me."[1089]

Of course it will. Later the old beauty and meaning of it will be valued and those who value it will maintain it.

I think Rose's house and mine should be refuges, after our time, for young writers of the South.

---

Rose Williams

*In the autumn of 1980 Williams traveled to Vancouver to take up the position of writer-in-residence at the University of British Columbia, where his play* The Red Devil Battery Sign *would be staged.*

*Williams spent the 1980 Christmas holidays in Key West and worked on expanding "Some Problems for the Moose Lodge," his play about the haunted McCorkle family, into "A House Not Meant to Stand," which was produced in Chicago on 1 April of the following year. The critic for the* Chicago Tribune *wrote (3 April 1981):*

"A House Not Meant to Stand" is a problem, a puzzle, and potentially a *play of power. At the moment, however, Williams' new drama is a work of shreds and patches of dross and substance, a drama in search of a connecting spine and, above all, in need of a properly surreal tone for its hallucinatory madness.*

*Adios Muchachos* by Williams

1090. The play "Now the Cats with Jewelled Claws" begins with two unpleasant women meeting for lunch. While they are having lunch, two young male hustlers enter to wait for their motorcycle to get repaired. One has a sexual encounter with the manager of the restaurant, a sort of grim reaper. When the young men leave, they crash their motorcycle outside, and one is gruesomely killed. The play ends with the manager leading the surviving hustler somewhere to show him his future. The play was never staged.

*Spring 1981*

Carefully (professionally) typed copies of 2-act play intended for Miami Theatre festival have mysteriously disappeared at I.C.M. Title "And Now the cats with Jewelled Claws."[1090]

Also Mitch Douglas has or had 2 copies of "The Notebook of Boris Trigorin" (Chekhov adaptation for Vancouver Play House.) – Mine has disappeared.

Under circumstances I cannot submit any more original copies of work to I.C.M. – All new work was securely bound or fastened by secure clips! Where do I from here?

*In August 1981 Williams' play* Something Cloudy, Something Clear *was performed in New York by the Jean Cocteau Repertory Company and would mark the last time during his life that Williams would have a new play performed in New York. Frank Rich wrote in the* New York Times *(11 September 1981):*

> It's no use pretending that the long dry spell in Tennessee Williams's career has ended with "Something Cloudy, Something Clear," his new play at Off-Off Broadway's Bouwerie Lane Theater. This autobiographical drama — seemingly lifted directly from the pages of his 1975 "Memoirs" — falls right into the traps that have capsized its recent predecessors. Here again are the stylized ghosts, the splintery sentimental vignettes, the watered-down appropriations from past triumphs and the baldly announced (yet undramatized) themes.

*A month later,* The Notebook of Trigorin, *Williams' adaptation of Chekhov's play* The Sea Gull, *premiered in Vancouver and was described as "an obsessive dabbling with the script which at its most obvious ranges from lachrymose to ludicrous" (*Vancouver Sun, *14 September 1981).*

*At 2:15 A.M. on 24 November 1981, after having just completed a first draft "of what may well be my last play," "The Lingering Hour," a play about a fragile unsuccessful poet who, fired from his job as a paid lover to a rich English lord and unable to support himself, plans to commit suicide, Williams typed this statement (HTC):*

> Cruelty in the reception of my work, particularly among the New York critics, did not take me by surprise nor did it inflict [a] mortal wound to my creative power.
>
> . . . When I hear them say that I have not written an artistically successful work for the theatre since "Night of the Iguana" in 1961 they are being openly, absurdly mistaken. . . .
>
> Deliberate cruelty is a thing that remains, thank God, beyond my comprehension. . . . I have been through much illness of the body: the end of my life cannot be predicted with any precision but I'm aware that it will come soon enough. I am tired.

Williams' death mask

*In April, Williams returned to Chicago where his yet-again revised play "A House Not Meant to Stand" was performed, again at the Goodman Theatre (but on the main stage). The title of the review in the* Chicago Tribune *(28 April 1982) was "Tennessee Williams's Freak House Is Doomed by a Weak Foundation," and it closed after forty-one performances. It would be the last time that Williams saw one of his plays staged.*

*On 15 May 1982 Williams ended a letter to Maria St. Just by saying that he had to do "a bit of work on a play called* The Lingering Hour — *the twilight of the world which I hope I am managing to make somewhat poetic despite its subject matter" (FOA, p. 390).*

*At the end of May, he wrote Kate Moldawer, his friend in Key West: "I don't understand my life, past or present, nor do I understand life itself. Death seems more comprehensible to me" (31 May 1982, HTC).*

*Williams spent the autumn of 1982 traveling back and forth between Key West and New York. On 11 February 1983 he traveled alone to Taormina, Sicily, and returned to the Hotel Elysée in New York after five days.*

*On the morning of 25 February 1983, Williams was found dead at the Elysée. He had choked on the small bell-shaped plastic cap of an eyedrop bottle. Asphyxia was named as the cause of death.*

The scene outside the Hotel Elysée, New York, after the announcement of Williams' death

ACKNOWLEDGMENTS

I wish to begin by expressing my gratitude to John Eastman, who entrusted me with this project and never asked how things were going, even when, perhaps, he suspected they weren't. I am most appreciative of his vision and belief.

Many people over a long period gave much of their time and energy to this book and helped transform a photocopied stack of journal pages into *Notebooks*: first and foremost, my research assistant Madeline Fergusson, whose sensitivity to detail, aesthetic judgment, and sheer acumen were invaluable. Her knowledge of the vast archives of manuscripts and letters added significantly to the depth of annotation. I would also like to thank Shannon Russell, whose research and dating of journal entries, in particular, made a great contribution.

I would like to express my gratitude to Donald Windham for his generosity and patience in answering innumerable questions over many years. His books *Tennessee Williams' Letters to Donald Windham, 1940–1965* and *Lost Friendships* provided valuable insight and information.

A number of Tennessee Williams scholars were most supportive of this book by answering questions, sharing their work, and reading the manuscript. I can never forget Allean Hale, who, when I began this project, welcomed me into her home and generously shared her encyclopedic knowledge. Others to whom I wish to express my gratitude include Robert Bray, George Crandell, Albert Devlin, Kenneth Holditch, Philip Kolin, Richard Leavitt, Lyle Leverich, Brenda Murphy, Brian Parker, and Nancy Tischler.

Williams' creative process was rarely linear, and his archives are vast, with over three thousand manuscripts (many unpublished) of plays, short stories, poems, and fragments. The curators, archivists, and staff of these collections made significant contributions. I would like to give special thanks to the following:

Rare Book and Manuscript Library, Columbia University: Jean Ashton (former director), Bernard Crystal (former curator of manuscripts), Karen Aponte-Velez, Gwynedd Cannan, Tara Craig, Claudia Funke, Jennifer Lee, Chris Lentz, Kevin O'Connor, and the staff of Columbia Libraries' Preservation Reformatting Division.

Harvard Theatre Collection, Houghton Library, Harvard University: Fredric Woodbridge Wilson (curator), Elizabeth Falsey, Annette Fern, Tom Ford, and Yuhua Li.

Pierpont Morgan Library: Robert Parks (curator of literary and historical manuscripts), Debbie Cowtavas, and Marilyn Palmieri.

Harry Ransom Humanities Research Center, University of Texas at Austin: Richard Workman (research librarian), Helen Adair, Eric Beggs, Pat Fox, Cathy Henderson (former research librarian), Linda Briscoe Myers, Pete Smith, Tara Wenger (former research librarian), and Rick Watson.

University of the South, Sewanee, Tennessee: Annie Armour and Pradip Malde.

Beinecke Rare Book and Manuscript Library, Yale University: Christopher Glover, Becca Findlay Lloyd, Anne Marie Menta, Alfred Mueller, and Naomi Saito.

Other collections that made important contributions include American Academy of Arts and Letters (Virginia Dajani); Special Collections Library, Duke University (Janie Morris); Historic New Orleans Collection (Mark Cave and Sally Stassi); New Directions (Peggy Fox and Thomas Keith); Billy Rose Theatre Collection, New York Public Library for the Performing Arts (Jeremy Megraw and Christine Karatnysky); Rare Books and Manuscript Division, New York Public Library (John Stinson); Department of Rare Books and Special Collections, Princeton University (Margaret Sherry); State Historical Society of Wisconsin, Madison (Dee Grimsrud); Poetry and Rare Books Collection, State University of New York at Buffalo (Robert Bertholf); Young Research Library, University of California at Los Angeles (Kelly Haigh and Carol Turley); Special Collections Research Center, University of Chicago (Paula Lee, Julia Gardner, and Susan Hammerman); Special Collections, Hugh H. Morris Library, University of Delaware (Rebecca Johnson Melvin and Iris Snyder); Special Collections and Archives, University of Houston (Julie Grob); Special Collections, University of Missouri–Columbia (Margaret Howell); Southern Historical Collection, Library of the University of North Carolina at Chapel Hill (Laurence Avery, Nathaniel King, and Matthew Turi); Alderman Library, University of Virginia (Christina Deane and Sharon Defibaugh); Washington Memorial Library, Macon, Georgia (Muriel Jackson and Jean Tolbert Lyndon); Department of Special Collections, Washington University Libraries, St. Louis, Missouri (Anne Posega); and Wesleyan University Cinema Archives, Middletown, Connecticut (Leith Johnson and Joan Miller).

I would also like to thank a number of Williams' friends who kindly gave of their time, insight, and material. Several stand out for their generosity and belief in this project, specifically Frances Kazan, William Jay Smith, and Andreas Brown. Others who were most helpful include Warren Beatty, Sybille Bedford, Paul Bowles, Jeanne Bultman, Jane Carter, Hume Cronyn, Mitch Douglas, Horton Foote, Charles Henri Ford, Jack Fricks, Joseph Hazan, Dorothea Forsythe Henderson, Catherine Filsinger Hoopes, Buffie Johnson, Karl Malden, Jordan Massee, Kate Moldawer, Johnny Nicholson, Harold Norse, Jim Parrott, Thomas D. Pawley III, Anne Bretzfelder Post, Dotson Rader, Richard Adams Romney, Jane Lawrence Smith, Maureen Stapleton, Peter Thompson, Esmeralda Mayes Treen, John Uecker, and Gore Vidal.

I would like to express my gratitude to the individuals who helped in the research of various locations where Williams spent significant time: in Italy, Pino Abbrescia, Contessa Simonetta Brandolini d'Adda, Virginia Attanasio Cinque, Mario Draghi, Stefano Fittipaldi, Jennifer Hanlon, Guilia Sersale, and Marchesa Anna Sersale; in Key West, Norman Aberle, Tom Hambright, and David Wolkowsky; in Spain, Guillermo de la Dehesa and Adam Lowe; and in Tangier, Joe McPhillips, Pociao, and John Hopkins.

Numerous individuals were most helpful in sharing their collections, giving permissions, and answering a broad range of queries. I would like to thank Joni Albrecht (Mary Institute, St. Louis), Peter Allmond (Bodleian Library, University of Oxford), Fred Bauman (Library of Congress), Professor Michael Bell (University of Warwick),

Alice Lotvin Birney (Library of Congress), Ethel Bloesch (University of Iowa), Michael Bloom (Cleveland Play House), Katie Bolick (*Atlantic Monthly*), Professor J. J. Boulton, Lloyd Bowers, Sheila Brynjulfson (Columbia College, Missouri), Kate Bucknell, Nancy Burris (*New Orleans Times-Picayune*), Jim Coddington (Museum of Modern Art, New York), Arnold Cooper, M.D., Gary Cox (University of Missouri–Columbia), Geiriadur Prifysgol Cymru (National Library of Wales), Barbara Thompson Davis (Estate of Katherine Anne Porter), Kate Dawson, Ronald de Leeuw (Rijks Museum, Amsterdam), Amy Draves (Cleveland Play House), Elaine Engst (Cornell University), Tom Erhardt, Clark Evans (Library of Congress), Chatham Ewing (Washington University, St. Louis), Tina Ferris, Professor Harry Finestone, John Fleischman (Estate of Josephine Johnson), Joel Gazis-Sax, Budd Gibbs (Estate of Jo Mielziner), Jon Gorman, Bill Goss, Jonathan Gray (Theatre Museum, London), Professor William Green (Queens College, CUNY), Geordie Greig, Lord Griffiths of Fforestfach, Alyce Guth (Mary Institute, St. Louis), Gloria Hammond (Time, Inc.), Jonathan Harris, Andrew Hawke, Ronald Hayman, Margaret Hedrich (New School for Social Research, New York), Carmen Hendershott (New School for Social Research, New York), Lady Henderson, Professor Kathleen Higgins (University of Texas), Leo Jansen (Rijks Museum, Amsterdam), Professor Nicholas Jenkins (Harvard University), Mara Kalnins, Professor Fred Kaplan, Jillian Kearney, Andrew Kirk (Theatre Museum, London), Helen Klaviter (*Poetry*), William Krahling, Professor Steven Kruger (Queens College, CUNY), Venita Lake (Washington University, St. Louis), Professor Melvin Landsberg (University of Kansas), Bruce Lindsay, Tom Lisanti (New York Public Library), the staff of the London Library, Professor Townsend Ludington (University of North Carolina, Chapel Hill), Jack Macauley (Estate of John C. Wilson), Professor Steven Marcus (Columbia University), Ward Marston, Anne McAlpine (Mary Institute, St. Louis), Carlos McClendon, Robert McCown (University of Iowa), Sonya McDonald (Washington University, St. Louis), Carol McKee (Cleveland Play House), Professor Edward Mendelson (Columbia University), Michael Ovitz, George Painter, R. B. Parsons (Buddhist Society, London), Professor Pam Perkins, Martin Phillips (Samuel French Ltd.), Donna Pierce, Professor Andrew Plaks (Princeton University), Carole Prietto (Washington University, St. Louis), John Randolph (Columbia College, Missouri), John Reitz, Michael Remer, Leni Riefenstahl, Laurance Roberts, Earl Rogers (University of Iowa), Jack Rogers (Stella Adler Theatre), Wade Rouse (Mary Institute, St. Louis), Terri Smith Ruckel, David Sanders, Judee Showalter (Randolph-Macon College, Ashland, Virginia), Michele Shulterbrandt, Chester Somers, Donald Spoto, Professor Steven Taubeneck (University of British Columbia), Fred Todd, Jacqueline Bograd Weld, Terry Wirtel (Washington University, St. Louis), Professor John Worthen (University of Nottingham), Iris Wright (Washington University, St. Louis), Nick Wylie (The Wylie Agency), Professor Wai-lim Yip (University of California at San Diego), and Stuart Yoak (Washington University, St. Louis).

The photographic material constitutes an important aspect of *Notebooks*. I would like to thank the individuals and institutions who provided images and photographs: Marcelle Adamson (The Illustrated London News Picture Gallery), Ellen

Adler, Lisa Aronson, Dana Atchison (Entergy New Orleans), Don Bachardy, Wendy Hurlock Baker (Smithsonian Institution), Chuck Barber (Hargrett Rare Book and Manuscript Library, University of Georgia), Amy Berman (Art Institute of Chicago), Connie Birmingham (Coe College, Cedar Rapids, Iowa), Karl Bissinger, Harriett Holland Brandt, William Britten (University of Knoxville, Tennessee), Emma Butterfield (National Portrait Gallery, London), Professor Virginia Spencer Carr, Ben Chapnick, Shirley Cochrane (Estate of Milton Lomask), Leo Cundiff, Sue Daly (Sotheby's Picture Library), DeAnn Dankowski (Minneapolis Institute of Arts), Millicent Dillon, Jennifer Dobby (Goodman Theatre, Chicago), Anita Duquette (Whitney Museum of American Art), Mary Engel (Estate of Ruth Orkin), Paul Eyre (Estate of Eyre de Lanux), Leslie Foxworth (St. Augustine Historical Society), Cynthia Franco (DeGolyer Library, Southern Methodist University, Dallas), Ed Frank (University of Memphis), Hon. Natasha Grenfell, David Houston (Ogden Museum of Southern Art), Richard Jay Hutto (Estate of Jordan Massee), Catherine Johnson, Dilcia Johnson (Corbis), Wallace Klein (University City High School, St. Louis), Matthew Kneale, Valerie Komor (Smithsonian Institution), Kristine Krueger (Academy of Motion Picture Arts and Sciences), Thomas Lanham, Claude Leavitt, Jon Lutz, George P. Lynes II (Estate of George Platt Lynes), Peter Macara (Provincetown Art Association and Museum), David McCartney (University of Iowa), Sandra Paci (DC Moore Gallery, New York), Tom Parrott, Anne Peck, Avivah Pinski (Estate of Fred Fehl), Bert Quint, Pat Rader (New York Public Library), Alastair Ramsay, Cheryl Raymond, Dinah Rogers (*New Orleans Times-Picayune*), Michael Shulman (Magnum), Tom Spain (*Charleston Post and Courier*), Danny Stockdale (Morris Library, Southern Illinois University, Carbondale), Erika Stone, Indra Tamang, Ellen Thomasson (Missouri Historical Society), Wendy Tucker, Karole Vail, Phyllis Cerf Wagner, Christopher Walling, and Lionel Wiggam.

I would also like to thank the following individuals who were involved in research, production, and the photographing of material, in particular Dolly Meieran, who brought a relentless devotion to the text and a rare inventiveness to the production of *Notebooks*, and Noreen O'Connor, for her meticulous copyediting. Others I wish to thank include Adriana Alberts, Burton Boxerman, Gerry Couch, Rebecca Ford, Elizabeth Garver, Pedro Linger Gasiglia, George Henry, Polina Khentov, Jessica Mezyk, Maria Piroli, Dwight Primiano, Lynn Roundtree, Lee Stalsworth, John Bigelow Taylor, Anne Thatcher, Peggy Volmer, Alan Wambold, Alix Weisz, Allison Whitelaw, and Donovan Wright.

I wish to express my gratitude to those, in addition to the Tennessee Williams scholars, who read *Notebooks* and offered insightful comments: Edward Albee, Ron Carlson, Walter DeMelle, Walter Isaacson, and Susan Meiselas.

Finally, I would like to thank the individuals at Yale University Press: my editor, Jonathan Brent, whose support and encouragement never wavered; Sarah Miller, assistant editor; Christina Coffin, director of production; Jessie Hunnicutt, production editor; and Brenda King, publicist.

And, never to be forgotten, my gang of four — John Randolph, Alexandra, Elliott, and Elisha — for understanding.

# CREDITS

## IMAGES

© Pino Abbrescia: 568, 638 top and bottom

Courtesy of the Academy of Motion Picture Arts and Sciences: 530 top, 663, 724 top, 728 bottom

Courtesy of Ellen Adler: 522 left, 578 top

Courtesy of Stella Adler Theatre, Los Angeles, Archives: 522 right

Courtesy of the Estate of Boris Aronson, and of Columbia University Rare Book and Manuscript Library, New York: 700

Courtesy of the Estate of Boris Aronson, and of Harry Ransom Humanities Research Center, The University of Texas at Austin: 516 inset, 530 bottom

Courtesy of Don Bachardy: 660

Courtesy of the Cecil Beaton Studio Archive, Sotheby's: 214, 488 bottom left

Photograph by Jack Beech, Collection of Kenneth Holditch: 458 bottom

© T. H. Benton and R. P. Benton Testamentary Trusts/UMB Bank Trustee/Licensed by VAGA, New York/Collection of the Whitney Museum of American Art: 494

© Bettmann/Corbis: 184, 185, 470, 502, 712

© Karl Bissinger: 183, 442, 602, 603

Jane Bowles, *Feminine Wiles* (Santa Barbara: Black Sparrow Press, 1976): 687

Courtesy of Harriett Holland Brandt: 56

Phyllis Cole Braunlich, *Haunted by Home: The Life and Letters of Lynn Riggs* (Norman: University of Oklahoma Press, 1988), Reprinted by permission of Leo Cundiff: 286, 420 left

Courtesy of Jeanne Bultman: 232, 280

Paddy Calistro and Fred E. Basten, *The Hollywood Archive* (New York: Universe, 2002): 367

Courtesy of the Estate of Josephine Johnson Cannon: 47

Courtesy of Virginia Spencer Carr: 534

Christian College, Columbia, Mo., Yearbook (1932), Reprinted by permission of Christian College: 34

Christie's, Switzerland: 574 top left

Coe College, Cedar Rapids, Iowa, *The Acorn* (1936), Reprinted by permission of Coe College: 114 bottom

© Colita/Corbis: 650

Columbia University Rare Book and Manuscript Library, New York: endpapers, 4, 41, 44 bottom, 52, 62, 76, 150, 197, 200, 213, 228, 238, 246, 258–60, 261 bottom, 262, 264, 273, 318, 322, 369 bottom, 412, 414, 415, 417 top and bottom, 426, 428, 432, 440, 448, 454, 460, 466 bottom, 476, 491, 492, 528, 548 top, 552, 562, 564, 572, 576, 582, 604 bottom, 608, 614, 616, 617, 620, 622 top, 642, 656, 667, 684 right, 696 bottom, 706, 708, 712 top, 720, 725, 729, 734 top, 737, 740, 743, 746, 749, 750, 760, 761

Photograph by Bill Wood, from Charles Criswell, *Nobody Knows What the Stork Will Bring* (New York: McDowell Obolensky, 1958): 252 left

Courtesy of DC Moore Gallery, New York, Estate of Paul Cadmus: 357 bottom

PaJaMa, *Tennessee Williams, 5 St Luke's Place, New York City, 1941*, vintage silver print, photograph by Jared French, 4⅜ x 6½ in., Collection of Christopher Walling, Courtesy of DC Moore Gallery, New York: 363

Courtesy of Guillermo de la Dehesa: 683

*Dictionary of Literary Biography: Documentary Series*, vol. 4, *Tennessee Williams*, edited by Margaret Van Antwerp and Sally Johns (Detroit: Gale Research Company, 1984): 174, 686 bottom

© Johnny Donnels: 444

Entergy New Orleans, Inc.: 458 top

Permission of the Estate of Fred Fehl, and of the Billy Rose Theatre Collection, The New York Public Library for the Performing Arts, Astor, Lenox and Tilden Foundations: 665 right

Photograph by Alexandra Feild: 560

Courtesy of Stefano Fittipaldi: 584

Courtesy of Jack Fricks: 567

Photograph by Arnold Genthe, from Arnold Genthe, *Isadora Duncan: Twenty-four Studies* (New York: Mitchell Kennerley, 1929): 337 right

Photograph by Arnold Genthe, from William Weaver, *Duse: A Biography* (San Diego: Harcourt Brace

University of Missouri at Columbia, *The Savitar* (1934), Reprinted by permission of the University of Missouri at Columbia: 97 inset

Southern Historical Collection, Library of the University of North Carolina at Chapel Hill: 314

Richard F. Leavitt Collection, University of Tennessee, Knoxville: 98, 206, 374, 510, 517, 550 right, 561, 578 bottom, 624 bottom, 644, 716

Harry Ransom Humanities Research Center, The University of Texas at Austin: 6, 7, 10, 11, 15, 21, 25, 27 right, 32, 39, 46, 48, 50, 61, 64, 66, 68, 70, 75 bottom, 79, 80, 92, 94, 100 bottom, 102, 111, 112, 114 top, 123, 126, 128, 134, 135, 138, 144 top and bottom, 146, 149, 151, 152, 156, 158, 160 bottom, 164, 168, 180, 182, 186, 202 left and right, 211, 212, 216 left and right, 218 left and right, 219 top and bottom, 222, 226, 227, 231 top and bottom, 235, 242 bottom, 244, 250, 252 right, 253 top and bottom, 255, 256, 272, 274, 275, 284 left and right, 287 top, 288, 290 top, 301, 302, 310, 311, 315, 316, 317 top and bottom, 320, 326, 328 bottom, 331, 336, 342, 344, 346, 347, 358, 365, 378, 384, 385 bottom, 386–88, 394, 396, 398, 400, 402, 404, 406, 410, 418, 422, 430, 436, 446, 452, 455, 456 top and bottom, 464 right, 474, 478, 487 top, 488 top, 490, 495, 497, 504 bottom, 513, 514, 532 bottom, 538, 548 bottom, 550 left, 574 top right, 597, 618 bottom, 622 bottom, 628 top and bottom, 636, 640, 664, 668, 670, 686 top, 699

Courtesy of Karole Vail: 526 top and bottom

Courtesy of Gore Vidal: 479

Courtesy of Phyllis Cerf Wagner: 601

Middle Georgia Archives, Washington Memorial Library, Macon: 290 bottom, 291, 292 left and right, 298, 299, 304, 307, 308

University Archives, Department of Special Archives, Washington University Libraries, St. Louis, Mo.: 27 left, 75 top

Courtesy of Lionel Wiggam: 38

Estate of Tennessee Williams: 508, 511, 654 bottom, 696 top

Courtesy of Donald Windham: 196 top, 198, 361, 434 bottom, 475, 480, 481 left and right, 487 bottom, 724 bottom

Courtesy of Donald Windham, and of Hargrett Rare Book and Manuscript Library, University of Georgia Libraries: 194, 354, 416

Yale Collection of American Literature, Beinecke Rare Book and Manuscript Library: 163, 172 top, 230, 234 bottom, 278, 313, 324 bottom, 328 top, 350, 364, 438 bottom, 482

Permission of the Estate of Bill Yoscary: 702, 738

Angel Zúñiga, *Mi Futuro es Ayer* (Barcelona: Planeta, 1983): 574 bottom

## TEXT

"Rapid Transit" and "Sun Our Father" © 1969 by James Agee, permission of The Wylie Agency.

Excerpt from a letter of Paul Bigelow reproduced with permission of the Estate of Jordan Massee.

Excerpt from a letter of Joe Hazan reproduced with permission of Joe Hazan.

Permission to reproduce Josephine Johnson poems "Trapped" and "You Who Fear Change" and excerpt from a letter courtesy of the Estate of Josephine Johnson.

Excerpts from Tennessee Williams/Elia Kazan correspondence reproduced with permission of Frances Kazan and Wesleyan University Cinema Archives.

Excerpt from previously unpublished letter by James Laughlin © 2006 by The New Directions Ownership Trust, used by permission of New Directions Publishing Corporation.

Excerpt from a letter of Frederic McConnell reproduced with permission of The Cleveland Play House.

Excerpt from a letter of Jo Mielziner reproduced with permission of the Estate of Jo Mielziner.

Excerpt from a letter of Katherine Anne Porter reproduced with permission of the Estate of Katherine Anne Porter.

Excerpt from a letter of John C. Wilson reproduced with permission of the Estate of John C. Wilson.

Excerpts from Tennessee Williams' letters to Donald Windham reproduced courtesy of Donald Windham.

*Quotations from published material by Tennessee Williams are taken from the following sources:*

*The Big Game* from *Mister Paradise and Other One-Act Plays* by Tennessee Williams, © 2005 The University of the South. Reprinted by permission of New Directions Publishing Corporation.

# INDEX

*Page numbers in italics indicate photographs and facsimiles.*

I have just fou
of The Rainbow a
-ing That you woo
end

RAIN[

EN